*Quicksilver Captain* is the story of Sir Home Popham (1762–1820), an extraordinary and under-appreciated personality of the French Revolutionary and Napoleonic Wars. Popham was a bundle of highly unusual contradictions. He achieved the rank of post-captain without a ship; he was more often employed by the War Department than by the Admiralty; and, as an expert in combined operations, he spent almost as much time serving on shore as at sea. In just over 25 years as a naval officer, Popham acted as an agent for transports, an unofficial diplomat, an intelligence officer, a Member of Parliament, an acclaimed hydrographer, a scientist and inventor, a publicist, and a government adviser, among many other roles.

Popham's career was literally as well as figuratively amphibious. So was his personality. Popham's well-known past as an illicit private trader, as well as his notorious lack of scruples, marred his reputation. People meeting him for the first time did not know what to make of him: 'He seems a pleasant man, but a dasher.' He fully understood the importance of communication and is best known for inventing a signal code that the Royal Navy used for decades. When he died, he left reams of correspondence behind him. But he also understood that words could either obfuscate or illuminate the truth, and his genius for twisting the facts to suit his own purposes made him an unreliable narrator. Many contemporaries distrusted and loathed him; after his court martial in 1807 for attacking Buenos Aires without orders (he escaped with a reprimand), many of his naval peers refused outright to serve with him again. And yet, even his greatest critics could not deny his abilities. One of his fellow naval captains wrote what could have been his epitaph: 'He is an extraordinary man, and would have been a great man, had he been honest.'

*Quicksilver Captain* paints a portrait of an ambitious man who built a career based on secrets and shadows. Popham's direct line to important patrons like William Pitt and Henry Dundas allowed him to play a role far beyond that of an ordinary post-captain. His ideas for using Britain's naval might for imperial defence and expanding British trade, as well as his knowledge of combined operations, made him the politicians' go-to expert. They wanted results, no matter what the cost, and Popham's willingness to play dirty – using bribery, threats, and experimental weaponry – appealed to them. In return, they protected him from his many foes, although in the end, they could not save him from his worst enemy – himself.

Jacqueline Reiter received her PhD from Cambridge in 2006 on the role of British national defence during the French Revolutionary and Napoleonic Wars. Her first book, *The Late Lord: the Life of John Pitt, 2nd Earl of Chatham* (Pen & Sword, 2017), illuminated the political and military career of Pitt the Younger's brother. Her articles have appeared in *History Today* and the *Journal of the Society for Army Historical Research* and she has written for the History of Parliament. She has co-written a chapter with John Bew on British war aims for the Cambridge History of the Napoleonic Wars.

# Quicksilver Captain

## The Improbable Life of Sir Home Popham

Jacqueline Reiter

Helion & Company

Helion & Company Limited
Unit 8 Amherst Business Centre
Budbrooke Road
Warwick
CV34 5WE
England
Tel. 01926 499619
Email: info@helion.co.uk
Website: www.helion.co.uk
X (formerly Twitter): @Helionbooks
Facebook: @HelionBooks
Visit our blog at helionbooks.wordpress.com

Published by Helion & Company 2024
Designed and typeset by Mach 3 Solutions (www.mach3solutions.co.uk)
Cover designed by Paul Hewitt, Battlefield Design (www.battlefield-design.co.uk)

Text © Jacqueline Reiter 2024
Maps by by Paul Hewitt, Battlefield Design (www.battlefield-design.co.uk) © Helion & Company 2024
Illustrations © as individually credited
Cover: A View of the Cape of Good Hope (Anne S.K. Brown Military Collection), Sir Home Popham (Yale Center for British Art, Paul Mellon Collection)

Every reasonable effort has been made to trace copyright holders and to obtain their permission for the use of copyright material. The author and publisher apologise for any errors or omissions in this work, and would be grateful if notified of any corrections that should be incorporated in future reprints or editions of this book.

ISBN 978-1-804514-41-2

British Library Cataloguing-in-Publication Data.
A catalogue record for this book is available from the British Library.

All rights reserved. No part of this publication may be reproduced, stored in a retrieval system, or transmitted, in any form, or by any means, electronic, mechanical, photocopying, recording or otherwise, without the express written consent of Helion & Company Limited.

For details of other military history titles published by Helion & Company Limited, contact the above address, or visit our website: http://www.helion.co.uk

We always welcome receiving book proposals from prospective authors.

# Contents

| | |
|---|---|
| Acknowledgements | vi |
| Prologue | viii |
| | |
| Preparative | 13 |
| 1 Childhood, 1762–1778 | 15 |
| 2 In the Navy, 1778–1786 | 21 |
| 3 A Change of Tack, 1786–1793 | 38 |
| | |
| Message Understood | 47 |
| 4 Flanders, 1793–1796 | 49 |
| 5 Ostend, 1796–1798 | 58 |
| 6 Russia and the Netherlands, 1799–1800 | 72 |
| 7 The Red Sea, 1801–1803 | 89 |
| | |
| Message to be Answered | 115 |
| 8 Inquiry, 1804–1805 | 117 |
| 9 'Mr Francis's Carcasses', 1804–1805 | 138 |
| 10 Domestic and Professional Life, 1803–1805 | 153 |
| 11 The Cape of Good Hope, 1805–1806 | 164 |
| 12 Buenos Aires, 1806 | 179 |
| 13 Disaster, 1806 | 195 |
| | |
| Message Not Understood | 211 |
| 14 Court-Martial, 1807 | 212 |
| 15 Copenhagen, 1807 | 231 |
| 16 Walcheren, 1809–1810 | 246 |
| 17 Northern Spain, 1810–1812 | 278 |
| | |
| Message Finished | 305 |
| 18 Frustration, 1813–1817 | 307 |
| 19 The Jamaica Station, 1817–1820 | 318 |
| Conclusion | 335 |
| | |
| Bibliography | 341 |
| Index of Royal Navy Ships | 351 |
| General Index | 352 |

# Acknowledgements

*2053: I want assistance*

This book was first suggested to me by Andrew Bamford after I gave a paper for the Society for Army Historical Research in Cambridge in November 2017, in which I briefly discussed Sir Home Popham's role in the Walcheren expedition of 1809. I initially recoiled at the prospect but, seven years on, I have absolutely no regrets. Thank you a thousand times to Andrew for suggesting Popham to me, as well as for all his support while he remained editor of the From Reason to Revolution series at Helion. I am only sorry he was not able to see the project through to the end.

The fact it has taken me seven years to write this book testifies to the fact Popham has not always been easy to research. Despite leaving unfeasible quantities of paper behind him – the man really, really, *really* liked to hear himself talk – and despite being absolutely everywhere in the historical record, no family archive survives. My telling of Popham's private life has had to be reconstructed from newspaper clippings, contemporary memoirs, and the odd reference in a letter. The exception is HCA 32/597 at The National Archives, a treasure trove of Popham's private and family letters up to the year 1793. I would never have found this box without a tip-off from Nicholas Blake, who has also been very generous with advice on all things naval, and who very kindly sent me copies of Sir Richard Keats's official correspondence at Copenhagen (1807) and Walcheren (1809). Most of my Popham obstacles, however, have been personal. The COVID-19 pandemic made it first impossible, then extremely difficult, to access libraries and archives. Just as the libraries reopened, I became seriously unwell. Once my health problems were under control, my husband and daughter also developed long-term issues. It is a small miracle Popham has seen the light of day at all, and I again owe many thanks to Andrew Bamford and to Helion for being so understanding.

Having spent so long writing, I have racked up more obligations than I can count to friends who have read over and commented on the text, answered questions about various aspects of Popham's life, passed on books and copies of manuscripts, or otherwise supported me. My greatest thanks go to Lynn Bryant, my partner in crime, who has been invested in this project from the very beginning. We have spent many happy hours talking about him, even if we *do* occasionally call him a poophead. I also owe the biggest of thank yous to Rory Muir. Rory is one of the kindest and most generous historians in the field, and his enthusiasm and willingness to spend time and effort providing feedback on my earlier drafts have made this book so much better. His support and friendship are invaluable.

Philip Ball is always a delight to talk to about Napoleonic stuff; he's passed me many manuscript references to Popham and helped me out with many an archive visit. Robert Burnham shared a document he has been working on regarding the 1806 Buenos Aires expedition. Paul Clammer generously sent me articles and manuscript material touching on Popham's last years in Jamaica. Robin Eagles answered my questions about records on Popham at the History of Parliament. Gareth Glover has shared much information with me and helped me answer several questions. Carlos Rilova Jericó, Mark Thompson, and Rob Griffith (who has also done a fabulous job editing this text) have been extremely generous in lending me books and sending material my way. Jonathan Parry and I have had many conversations about Popham's time in the Red Sea, and Tom Williams has been very stimulating to talk to about Buenos Aires. From the other side of the ocean, Paul Martinovich sent me several passages relating to Popham from the letters of Sir Pulteney Malcolm; Hailey Stewart sent me PDFs of the two existing theses on Popham; and Diana Mankowski photographed several letters for me in the Eyre Coote Papers and Melville Papers at the Clements Library in Michigan.

Other friends who deserve thanks include Rory Butcher; Graeme Callister; Jimmy Chen; Carl Christie; Marcus Cribb; Charles Esdaile; Ross Flowers; Tom Fournier; Sabrina Fröhlich; Beatrice de Graaf; John Haines; Peter Hicks; Kristine Hughes Patrone; Kate Jamieson; Bethan Jenkins; Sam Jolley; Pip Jones; Olga Kimmins; Peter Leech; Alyson Leeds; Ciarán McDonnell; Alexander Mikaberidze; Thomas Moore; Sarah Murden; Naphaphorn Nunariyasarp; Josh Provan; Pepijn Reeser; Kathryn Rix; Greg Roberts; Silvia Gregorio Sainz; Michael Schuiff; Alexander Stevenson; Geraint Thatcher; Anna Vakulenko; Jane Stemp Wickenden; Douglas Theedom; Robin Thomas; Lien Verpoest; Meaghan Walker; Zack White; Kendall Witt; and Evan Wilson. Thank you for your help and support: I couldn't have done it without you.

Writing a book is not always a lucrative exercise, and the Society of Authors allowed me to make immeasurable progress with my first draft by giving me an Authors' Foundation grant.

A final thank you goes to my husband and children, who have lived so long with Popham and endured my stories of 'You won't believe what Popham did *this* time!' – and of course to all my followers on Twitter, who have played 'Popham Bingo' with me for years. I do love seeing Popham 'pop' up in the most unexpected places.

# Prologue

'HONOURABLY ACQUITTED,' the newspapers proclaimed.[1] The news leaked out of HMS *Gladiator* in Portsmouth Harbour even before the court-martial adjourned at 3:00 p.m. At least one London paper recorded the verdict that same evening; most morning papers followed suit next day. By noon on 12 March 1807, everyone with an interest in public affairs knew that Captain Sir Home Riggs Popham RN, KM, FRS had been found not guilty of removing his naval squadron from the Cape of Good Hope and carrying it to attack the Spanish holdings on the Rio de la Plata without orders.

Over the past year, Popham had been stoking the popularity of his cause through a carefully orchestrated campaign of circulars talking up the benefits of his assault on Buenos Aires for British trade. His efforts paid off, as the extensive coverage of his trial reflected: between 12 and 14 March 1807, most newspapers reported little else. By the time Popham emerged from *Gladiator*'s state room the crowds were already waiting for him, on shore and in several boats scattered across the stretch of sea separating him from the beach. They cheered as he was rowed ashore and cheered again when he landed at Sally Port, a free man, his officer's sword back in its scabbard where it belonged.

Popham acknowledged the applause with the same good humour he had displayed throughout the three days of his trial. When his supporters unhitched the horses from his carriage to draw him to his lodgings in triumph, he tried to calm them; when this failed, he simply refused to get in. Instead, he walked through the town, followed by continued acclamations, as the church bells began to ring in his honour.

The truth was nevertheless close on the heels of the lie. The cheering crowds might have briefly deceived the newspapers, but Popham had not been 'honourably acquitted' at all. Quite the opposite: although the court-martial had only sentenced him to be 'severely reprimanded', Popham had in fact been found guilty of both charges of which he was accused. Still, as he walked through Portsmouth to the acclaim of his supporters, it looked as though he *had* been acquitted, and he took great care not to correct that impression. He returned to London a hero – all the more heroic, perhaps, for the tarnish on his laurels.

Less than a week later, Popham went to Lloyd's Coffee-House. It was an (apparently) impromptu visit, but a canny one, for the Lloyd's under-writers – and, beyond them, their clients, the merchants of the City – represented the core of Popham's support. Popham's speech was a masterpiece of spin:

---

1  *The Star*, 11 March 1807.

It is impossible for me to express what I feel on this occasion, seeing myself surrounded by the most respectable merchants of the first city in the world, marking, personally, their opinion of my exertions to promote the public welfare; and although His Majesty's Government found it expedient to arraign my conduct on my return from abroad, I trust my defence will satisfy the respectable body to whom I have now the honour to address myself, that every action of mine was directed to promote the honour and glory of my country, and that I shall ever feel myself bound to employ my humble talents for the attainment of any object conducive to its prosperity, although I feel that the wings of discretion have been materially clipped.[2]

It was one of Popham's shorter compositions – his court-martial defence had occupied the better part of four hours[3] – but it picked up on nearly every theme that ran through his controversial career. 'My exertions to promote the public welfare' was possibly founded on truth, and he may even have believed his 'every action … was directed to promote the honour and glory' of his country. Still, nearly every instance of 'promoting the public welfare' happened to coincide with an opportunity to promote Popham's welfare at the same time, whether by giving him a chance to distinguish himself before powerful patrons, by allowing him to indulge in a peacock-like display of his undeniable genius for organisation and planning, or – as in the case of the Rio de la Plata – by bringing eye-watering wealth within his grasp. As for his sly dig at the government that had 'found it expedient' to clip his wings, Popham was never behindhand in crying persecution at his enemies. Popham often protected himself from close scrutiny by portraying himself as the victim. This strategy disgusted those who saw through it, but the majority of the time it worked – at least on the intended audience.

Popham's skill in embarking and disembarking large numbers of troops under fire first brought him to the notice of the decision makers at Whitehall, but there seemed few limits to his incredible versatility. Despite remaining a captain for nearly the whole wars with Revolutionary and Napoleonic France, Popham acted as an Agent for Transports, an unofficial diplomat, an intelligence officer, a Member of Parliament, an acclaimed hydrographer, a scientist and inventor, a publicist, and a government adviser, among other roles. He served in several major campaigns across the globe and helped plan a fair few of them, from the Netherlands, Copenhagen, and Spain to India, the Cape of Good Hope, and South America. Despite this near omnipresence, he witnessed battle only three times, all before he was 20. His naval peers did not know quite what to do with him: 'I can never think of [him] … without bringing to mind the showman's description of the hippopotamus: "This 'ere is the ippopotamos or river orse, an amfiberous hanimal, wot cannot live on the land, and wot dies in the water."'[4] After his court-martial in 1807, distrust turned to loathing,

---

2 *Morning Post*, 19 March 1807.
3 *The Sun*, 10 March 1807.
4 [Fletcher] W[ilkie], 'Recollections of the British Army, in the early campaigns of the Revolutionary War, no.2', *The United Service Journal and Naval Military Magazine for 1836*, part I (London: Henry Colburn, 1836), pp.480–489.

and many refused outright to serve with him again. Yet even his greatest critics could not deny his abilities: 'He is an extraordinary man, and would have been a great man, had he been honest.'[5]

If Popham cared about this sort of opinion, he did not show it. He quickly discovered that, with the right friends, he did not need to be loved to be employed. He dragged himself out of obscurity through networking, securing an audience at the highest levels of political decision making through persistence and bloody-mindedness, but also by telling people what they wanted to hear. Popham's ideas for applying Britain's naval might to the expansion of imperial trade, as well as his practical experience of combined operations, made him the politicians' go-to expert. He managed to win the patronage of Henry Dundas and William Pitt, two of the most powerful men in Britain. Theirs was a mutually beneficial relationship. The politicians wanted results, no matter what the cost; Popham's willingness to play dirty using bribery, threats, and experimental weaponry appealed to them, as did his willingness to take on just about any task. In return, they helped him throw a veil over his questionable past.

Sir Home Popham, by Anthony Cardon after Mather Brown, 1807. (Public domain, Yale Center for British Art, Paul Mellon Collection)

Drawing Popham out of the shadows in which he moved has not been easy. Popham was not shy about his achievements: he was a skilled self-publicist who left behind a mountain of self-justificatory letters, dispatches, and articles and pamphlets. But he was also a survivor who buried the demons of his past in the same way he had done in nonchalantly accepting the cheers of the crowds outside Portsmouth on 11 March 1807: by seizing control of the circumstances in which he found himself, however unfavourable. Popham is therefore a highly unreliable narrator of his own story. His command of the English language allowed him to reshape and rebuild his career, his reputation, and his legacy. The man who helped his contemporaries communicate better across great distances, under pressure and in the heat of battle, knew very well that words could both elucidate and obfuscate, revealing facts he wanted exposed – and concealing those he did not. From the moment he stepped onto the public stage in 1793 to the moment he left it in 1820, Popham sought to shape the narrative

---

5   Paul Martinovich, *The Sea is my Element: The Eventful Life of Admiral Sir Pulteney Malcolm, 1768–1838* (Warwick: Helion, 2020), p.155.

that surrounded him – pamphleteering, bombarding correspondents with an unanswerable barrage of letters, speechifying, creating, imagining, outright lying on occasion, but often simply massaging the truth into something more palatable. He was something of a chameleon in the historical record, portrayed as 'a diplomatist afloat' ('he possessed what the Scotch call a good deal of *cleverality*');[6] a man who 'simply had a difficult job of seamanship to do, and did it supremely well';[7] 'a gambler … a fiddler, a filibuster, a raider, a buccaneer and a freebooter';[8] or simply a kind of 'Naval Quack'.[9]

Popham's ability to shape his own story, to change character and identity, was an integral part of his defence against close scrutiny: by being all these things, and none, he could not be pinned down. He remained a resourceful inventor whose usefulness covered a multitude of sins, the kind of man politicians were happy to have on their side but never fully trusted; neither demon nor saint, hero nor villain. Viewed through the deliberate communication fog of his own making, his motives remained obscure, his actions open to multiple conflicting interpretations. But, like Odysseus, Popham was too clever, too hungry for recognition. This proved his downfall: ironically for a man with so many powerful enemies, Popham was eventually defeated by the one man who was immune to the aegis of his political protectors – himself.

This, however, races to the end of an extraordinary story. For most of his life, Popham seemed indestructible. Despite several court cases, parliamentary inquiries, official investigations, and one court-martial, nothing ever seemed to stick. Popham himself came to believe he had almost superhuman qualities. '[My] Lieutenant felt so incompetent to my quicksilver Motions that he has written to resign,' he boasted on one occasion.[10] This was typical arrogance, but expressed through an unusually revealing turn of phrase. Almost by accident, Popham had discovered the perfect analogy for himself – bright, fluid, silvery fast, but also dangerous and unpredictable. Like the mercury in the thermometer, Popham's fortunes were either rocketing up or sinking down. He was, in every sense, a 'Quicksilver Captain'.

---

6 W[ilkie], 'Recollections of the British Army, no.2', p.485.
7 Hugh Popham, *A Damned Cunning Fellow: The Eventful Life of Rear Admiral Sir Home Popham KCB, KCH, KM, FRS 1762–1820* (Tywardreath: Old Ferry Press, 1991), p.190.
8 Chris Coelho, 'The Popham Code Controversy', in J.E. Pearson, S. Heuvel, and J. Rodgaard (eds), *The Trafalgar Chronicle: New Series 5* (Barnsley: Seaforth Publications, 2020), p.133.
9 The British Library [BL]: G.19449, p.xxv: Comment by Benjamin Tucker in *The Trial of Sir Home Popham*.
10 Durham University Archives (DUA): GRE/A1550b: Popham to Coote, 11 May 1798.

# Preparative

*'Preparatory to any message, a diagonal red and white flag is to be hoisted'*

# 1

# Childhood, 1762–1778

*2522: Gibraltar*

The night was so dark Captain Mark Robinson could barely see the flicker of lights on Flanders shore, three or four miles distant. All he could hear was the sea and the soft creak of wood against wood as his sailors worked the muffled oars. What should have been a half-moon was completely obscured by thick cloud; the wind blew drizzle and salt spray into his face as his launch approached the quarry. According to Robinson's compass, which he consulted periodically with the aid of a lamp covered in sacking, that quarry lay only about 100 yards away: *Etrusco*, a 1,200-ton Tuscan merchant ship on its way to Ostend.

It was July 1793, and Britain had been at war with France for five months. Robinson's frigate, HMS *Brilliant*, was cruising in the Channel on the lookout for trouble – activity in the French ports and signs of invasion, or simply privateers and hostile trade. Strictly speaking, *Etrusco* should not have fallen under any of these categories: Tuscany was part of the Holy Roman Empire and ultimately under Austrian control, which made it a British ally, and the ship had every right to be in Ostend roads. However, Robinson had reason to suspect *Etrusco* had not made directly for Ostend. On the night of 14 July, a ship matching its description had stopped off Dungeness to offload part of its cargo under cover of night, which hid it from the prying eyes of Customs officers. Catching up with *Etrusco* off Ostend – a notorious hideout for smugglers and freebooters – had persuaded Robinson of the need to intercept it before it slipped out of his reach.

That afternoon, Robinson had sent his third lieutenant, John Crispo, currently on detached service in the hired cutter *Grace*, to investigate the suspicious vessel. Crispo's report was the reason Robinson and a portion of his crew were now preparing to board this mysterious vessel. *Etrusco*, Crispo said, was 'laden with a Cargo … of Sugar, Tea, Nankeens, China Ware, Rhubarb, Sago, and other Articles'.[1] He had tried to question the captain, Balthazar Giorgi, but discovered he did not speak good enough English (or at least pretended not to). The ship's master, however, claimed to be a British subject, a former lieutenant in the Royal Navy by the unusual name of Home Riggs Popham.

Crispo assessed Popham as a dark-eyed young man with an ingratiating manner and a mobile, intelligent face. He took Crispo on a tour of the ship and explained the situation

---

1 The National Archives (TNA): HCA 42/535: *Etrusco* case on behalf of the Crown, 1798.

with disarming candour. *Etrusco*, he said, was on its way home from a trip to Canton. Crispo asked him who owned the ship and its cargo, and Popham replied without hesitation that it belonged solely to Captain Giorgi, its cargo underwritten by an Ostend-based company, Charnock & Co. This rang alarm bells, for Charnock and his colleagues were notorious for smuggling French property in East Indian ships.[2] When Crispo asked why the vessel had stopped at Dungeness, Popham told him the ship had only done so to take on a pilot.

Crispo said nothing, but he had his doubts. He had seen the ship's papers in Giorgi's name and, although they were in some disorder and all in Italian, he 'suspected them to be false'.[3] He had glimpsed several documents that appeared to mention other interested parties in the ship's rich cargo – Popham himself (who, as a British subject, was prohibited from trading in China by the East India Company monopoly), and two individuals named Jean-Baptiste Piron and Charles Samuel Constant de Rebecque. Britain and France had been at war now for five months. If *Etrusco*'s cargo belonged even in part to two Frenchmen, the ship was technically engaged in hostile trade and Popham, a self-confessed subject of His Majesty King George III, was not merely a smuggler – he was in business relations with his country's enemies. This made *Etrusco* a potential prize of war, and a prize as sumptuous as Crispo claimed this one was could not be allowed to get away. Robinson decided to risk it and take an armed party to inspect the papers himself.

Robinson's boat reached the bottom of *Etrusco*'s ladder. The crew of the merchant vessel had not been expecting to be bothered again that night; they came forward noisily as Robinson and his men reached the deck, but shrank back in silence the moment the lanterns glimmered off cutlasses and pistol butts. Robinson, his second lieutenant behind him, approached the nervous-looking man Crispo identified as Captain Giorgi. Robinson's grasp of Italian was no better than Crispo's, but his examination of the suspect papers – and a swift glance at the cargo in the hold – helped Robinson make up his mind. While Giorgi protested in broken English that his vessel was under the protection of the Imperial Court of Austria, Robinson ordered his third lieutenant to take possession of the ship and sail it to Deptford.

But someone was missing, although Robinson did not realise it until after he had issued orders that no one should be allowed to leave the prize. Eventually, Captain Giorgi admitted Home Popham was no longer on board. As soon as Crispo had left *Etrusco* earlier that evening, the so-called master had hoisted a boat and, taking as much evidence with him as possible, absconded ashore.[4]

The capture of *Etrusco* was only the beginning of a long process of litigation that stretched on until 1804, with reverberations as late as 1810. The capture of his trading vessel was a defining moment in Popham's life. Try as he might – and he did try – he never outpaced suggestions of something underhand in his dealings, that he was a liar, a freebooter, and a thief – an unprincipled smuggler.

---

2   TNA: WO 1/177: From Major General Ainslie, 30 July 1793.
3   TNA: HCA 42/535: Captain Robinson's case, 5 June 1804.
4   TNA: HCA 42/535: *Etrusco* case on behalf of the Crown, 1798.

There was something in those accusations. Piron turned out not to have much of a stake in the enterprise and Constant de Rebecque eventually proved he was actually Swiss, but partnering with Frenchmen, real or imagined, had not been Popham's greatest sin. Prior to sailing from Canton, he had drawn up a series of agreements transferring ostensible ownership of *Etrusco* to Giorgi. Outside British waters, however, it was Popham – not Giorgi – to whom the crew looked for all leadership. Because he was British and trading in the East, Popham had to pretend he was merely a member of the crew, because the East India Company had decreed all private trade by British subjects in the area to be illegal – and the agreements he had made with Giorgi showed he knew it.

But who exactly was this Popham? The Admiralty Court wanted to know, but the trouble was the man had been less than honest with his own crew. Most of those who were cross-examined knew he had a wife and growing family in Ostend, but other than that all they could say for sure was that he was not Dutch. Some described him as 'a native of Ireland' – either because he had said as much, or because he had an Irish accent. Both were possible, for Popham *was* Irish, after a sort; he just had not been born there.

Although Popham himself was not 'a native of Ireland', his parents certainly were. Joseph Popham, a well-to-do linen draper from Cork, married his cousin Mary Riggs on 1 March 1739. Despite the fact both were already in their late twenties, they had a large number of children, although the numbers apparently grew in the telling. According to one contemporary, Joseph 'had no less [sic] than forty-four children' with 'several wives'.[5] In fact, only 12 children were definitely born to Joseph, who married only twice.

Home was therefore born into a large (but not excessively so) family, well-to-do but hardly well connected. He was his father's sixth son, named in honour of his mother and most likely the 8th Earl of Home, a former Governor of Gibraltar who may have been Joseph Popham's patron. This suggests Joseph Popham may have been keen to impress his superiors: he had been appointed British consul at Tétouan, Morocco, in 1761, although his wife and children lived in the much less exotic British garrison town across the Mediterranean. 'My son Home Riggs was born 12 October 1762 on Sunday at 2 o'clock in Gibraltar,' Joseph recorded in the family bible. 'His mother departed this life about one hour after.'[6]

Popham's father remained a distant, almost alien figure in his life. They never became close, and after Joseph remarried in July 1763 – less than a year after his first wife's death, to one of her relatives, Catherine Lamb – the family grew by another six children. Joseph Popham was recalled from Tétouan in 1769 following a diplomatic fracas. After returning to Britain he lived in Chichester and Guernsey with his growing second family, but Home did not spend much time with them, although most were much closer to him in age than his full siblings.

By 1770, only three children survived from Joseph Popham's first marriage, and eight-year-old Home was very much the youngest. William, a rising star in the East India Company army, was 30, and Stephen was 25. Both took their much younger sibling under

---

5   Anon., *The Annual Biography and Obituary for the Year 1822* (London: Longman, Hurst, Rees, Orme, and Brown, 1822), vol.6, p.288.
6   Frederick W. Popham, *A West Country Family: The Pophams from 1150* (Sevenoaks: self-published, 1976), p.98.

View of Gibraltar, by Charles Dyce, ca 1849. (Public domain, Yale Center for British Art, Paul Mellon Collection)

their wing. When William first left for India in the mid-1760s, he gave Home a silver watch as a keepsake, which the young boy treasured for the rest of his life.[7] The earliest known letter from Home, written on 23 June 1770, was addressed to his eldest sibling and showed exactly how little he saw his real father, and how much he had come to view his brothers as surrogate parents:

> I am come home for my Holydays to my Brother Stephen; he tells me I shall soon see my Papa in England which I am not a little glad of as it is near three years since I saw him. I shou'd be glad to receive a letter from you and to hear you are well.[8]

Around 1767, Home had gone to live permanently with Stephen, a successful scrivener (or contract lawyer). He probably mostly stayed on his brother's estate in Ireland, which may have been where he picked up the accent that later so confused his shipmates. Otherwise, Home's childhood is an indistinct blur caught only in tantalising glimpses. He may have attended Brentford School.[9] In 1774, the year his father Joseph died, he was admitted to

---

7   E.M.E. Blyth, 'Admiral Sir Home Riggs Popham, KB, born 1762, died 1820', *Army Quarterly*, 72 (1956), p.195.
8   Blyth, 'Admiral Sir Home Riggs Popham', p.195.
9   Winifred Stokes, 'POPHAM, Sir Home Riggs (1762–1820), of Titness Park, Berks.', in R. Thorne (ed.), *The History of Parliament: the House of Commons 1790–1820*, <https://www.historyofparliamentonline.org/volume/1790-1820/member/popham-sir-home-riggs-1762-1820>, accessed 29 July 2021.

Westminster School, his brother Stephen's *alma mater*. Like Stephen, he was also admitted to Trinity College, Cambridge, on 23 January 1776.[10]

At the time he was admitted, there was no reason to suppose he would never matriculate fully. Home was bright; he had a gift for mathematics and languages, and he clearly expected to follow in his elder brother's professional footsteps. In 1775, Home was articled to Stephen for five years, with the intention of entering him eventually in one of the Inns of Court after leaving Cambridge (the same route Stephen himself had followed at the outset of his career).[11] By this time, Home depended on Stephen for everything: his father was dead, and his eldest brother William was still abroad. So long as Stephen continued to prosper, Home's own future was secure. But all was not well in Stephen's world, and Home's comfortable life was about to be turned on its head.

In 1768, while staying in Paris, Stephen impulsively married a rich heiress named Ann Yate Whiteside. She brought her bridegroom a great deal of money and land, but the marriage was not a success. Within two years the couple were living apart and Ann began an affair with a man named Hanser. Three years later Stephen, who wanted to marry again, sued for divorce. In the eighteenth century the only route to divorce was through a private act passed in the House of Lords. It was an expensive and embarrassing process, but Stephen went through with it anyway. He succeeded, but at a tremendous cost: Ann's counsel argued successfully that she should have her estates and money restored to her 'as fully and effectually as if the said Marriage between the said Stephen Popham and Ann Yate had never taken effect'.[12] Stephen lost everything, and his finances never recovered.

In 1776, the year Home was placed on Trinity College's books, Stephen moved to Dublin to escape his English debts and was elected to the Irish House of Commons for Castlebar.[13] His fortune, however, continued its relentless downward slide: 'Blest with superior talents, improved by a classical education, he fell martyr to a speculative disposition and a strong inclination for gambling.'[14] One contemporary described him as 'a famous swindler', who pretended to sell gentlemen seats in the English House of Commons over which he had no influence whatsoever.[15] It could not last and, after a year of trying to maintain his expensive

---

10  J.A. Venn, *Alumni Cantabrigienses: A Biographical List of All Known Students, Graduates and Holders of Office at the University of Cambridge, from the Earliest Times to 1900* (Cambridge: Cambridge University Press, 1953), vol.5 part 2, p.159; G.F. Russell Barker and A.H. Stenning, *The Record of Old Westminsters: A Biographical List of All Those Who Are Known to Have Been Educated at Westminster School from the Earliest Times to 1927* (London: Chiswick Press, 1928), vol.2, p.753.
11  TNA: CP 5/107/118: articles of clerkship for Home Riggs Popham, 1775.
12  'House of Lords Journal vol.34: May 1774, 11–20', in House of Lords, *Journal of the House of Lords, 1774–1776* (London, 1767–1830), vol.34, pp.178–214. Available through British History Online, <www.british-history.ac.uk/lords-jrnl/vol34/pp178-214>, accessed 29 July 2021.
13  Richard A. Waite, 'Sir Home Riggs Popham, KM, KCG, KCH. FRS, Rear Admiral of the Red Squadron: A Biography', PhD thesis, Harvard University, 1942, p.6.
14  Alfred Spencer (ed.), *Memoirs of William Hickey* (London: Hurst & Blackett, 1919), vol.2, pp.94–95.
15  G.O. Sayles, 'Contemporary sketches of the members of the Irish Parliament in 1784', in G.O. Sayles, *Scripta Diversa* (London: Bloomsbury, 1982), p.184.

lifestyle through betting and illicit deals, Stephen fled, leaving a business associate to shoulder debts of more than £10,000.[16] Stephen was declared bankrupt in September 1777 and left, precipitately, to make a new life in Bengal, where he outran his past sufficiently to become the East India Company's Advocate General at Calcutta.[17]

Home was left behind, his future in the legal profession crumbled into dust. Home never talked of how Stephen's betrayal affected him but, at nearly 16, he was old enough and clever enough to realise how much of a disaster it was. Over a decade passed before the two brothers corresponded again, and the silence was significant. Nevertheless, Stephen's absconding was the making of Home Popham. Had Stephen Popham not been a swindler – had he not gone one financial scheme too far – Home would almost certainly never have set foot on a quarterdeck in his life. As it was, Home had to hastily rethink his future. About the same time his brother Stephen arrived in India in February 1778, Home entered the Royal Navy. He joined the crew of HMS *Hyaena* as a first-class volunteer under Captain Edward Thompson.

The decision to place Home on board ship was probably not taken by Stephen himself, who had likely already fled by the time the arrangements were made. Home never explained how he came to Captain Thompson's notice, but Thompson had a habit of taking promising young men under his wing: 'Having made my Ship an Academy … my pride is to rear youth, and render them serviceable to their Country.'[18] He often visited public schools to select his midshipmen, and perhaps picked Popham out from among the lads at Westminster. Just as possibly Popham was suggested to him by a mutual friend as a likely lad with few prospects on shore. However they met, Thompson came to act 'the part of father, of instructor, and of protector' to Home and profoundly shaped his future career.[19] He was the third father-figure in Home's life, and the only one who never abandoned him. Home repaid the opportunities Thompson gave him with a fierce loyalty that endured beyond the grave.

---

16  Spencer (ed.), *Memoirs of William Hickey*, vol.3, p.248.
17  *The Gentleman's Magazine and Historical Chronicle* (1777), vol.47, p.460.
18  BL: Add MS 46120: Diary of Edward Thompson, 23 February 1785.
19  *Naval Chronicle* (1806), p.267.

2

# In the Navy, 1778–1786

*2028: I have not seen any action*

The Royal Navy was a striking change of direction for a boy destined for a less glamorous, but far less dangerous, career in the law – not that his land-lubbing past would necessarily affect the chances of promotion, as Home quickly discovered talent and catching the right eye were more important in the Navy than social connections. Popham's career depended on his ability to impress his superiors, and on those superiors' ability to bend the ears of theirs.[1] But Home was certainly at a disadvantage to many of his peers from a more naval background, not least because he was nearly 16 – 'too old to begin,' according to the future Admiral Collingwood, 'for very few take well to the sea at that age'.[2]

Still, the circumstances under which Home had become suddenly destitute may have made the Navy an attractive path for him. In 1778, Britain had been at war with its rebellious American colonies for three years, with France and Spain spoiling to join the fray. The Royal Navy was keen to recruit young gentlemen with the makings of a future officer, and there were more opportunities for distinction during war than during peace. With these patriotic thoughts in mind, Home may have pressed for the chance to join up himself. But even if the prospect of glory made his heart beat faster, there was a much more practical advantage to going to sea: it was cheap. Unlike the Army, which normally required purchasing a commission, all the Navy required by way of outlay was a trunk of warm clothes, some technical treatises, and (maybe) an annual allowance of between £20 and £30, which must have appealed to the people responsible for picking up the pieces left behind by a bankrupt running from the law.

The ship Popham was joining – HMS *Hyaena*, a 24-gun frigate with a complement of 160 men – was brand new. Over time he came to dread vessels that had not been weathered in, and even now his heart probably sank when he arrived at Salt House Dock, Liverpool, on 18 April 1778 with his clothes, his quadrant, and his crisp new copy of Robertson's *Elements of Navigation*, to find the ship's pumps working enthusiastically to get rid of the water leaking through its unseasoned timbers.[3] Once aboard, Popham might have lost his bearings in

---

1   Evan Wilson, *A Social History of British Naval Officers* (Woodbridge: Boydell and Brewer, 2017), p.110.
2   N.A.M. Rodger, *The Command of the Ocean* (London: Allan Lane, 2004), p.509.
3   TNA: ADM 51/468: log, HMS *Hyaena*, 18 April 1778.

the hubbub of a ship getting ready for sea: the boatswain's, carpenters', and gunners' stores winched on board; sailors rolling water barrels into place, along with casks of beef, bread, cheese, butter, and oatmeal; iron and stone ballast heaved out of a brig and taken down to the hold; landsmen scrubbing and scraping the decks with their holystones; and, far above, the able seamen getting the shrouds up and the masts rigged, as the enormous canvas sheets shivered and snapped in the wind with a sound like thunder.

The air of *Hyaena* had not yet become infused with the ripeness of so many unwashed men living in close proximity, but Popham may have experienced real dismay upon seeing his quarters, where he and the other midshipmen would spend all their time off-duty. On a ship of the line, midshipmen had their own dedicated space on the orlop deck; on a frigate like *Hyaena*, Popham was expected to sling a hammock and eat alongside the men on the lower deck.[4] At least he could hold onto the knowledge that frigates, and the officers who served aboard them, were the elite of the eighteenth-century Royal Navy.[5] Unlike life on a more comfortable, but less exciting, ship of the line, serving on a frigate came with plenty of opportunities to exercise independence, learn to command, and hopefully earn prize money. This was an accepted perk of naval service, and one that raised no qualms in those who expected to benefit from it.[6] Prize money would only come once the ship was ready for battle, though, and Home Popham's sea journey had not yet begun. His captain – the man responsible for his education, comfort, and future prospects – was still away recruiting inland.

Edward Thompson and his new protégé had much in common. Thompson's father had been a merchant in Hull, where Edward was born around the year 1738. He received a classical education, but his family's trade connections brought him to sea; he journeyed to Greenland in 1750 and later made several trips to India on an East India Company vessel. He claimed to have been pressed into the Royal Navy and served throughout the Seven Years War, assisting as a lieutenant at the Battle of Quiberon Bay in 1759. He made post in 1772 but, placed on half-pay, he turned to literature. He edited the *Westminster Magazine* between 1773 and 1774, contributed regularly to the *London Magazine* from 1773 to 1776, and wrote for several other papers, including the national *Morning Post*.[7] A popular poet and playwright, his combination of political and social satire, earthy humour, and accessible subject matter appealed to a broad contemporary audience, despite his muse being 'half a poet, half a tar'.[8]

---

4   S.A. Cavell, *Midshipmen and Quarterdeck Boys in the British Navy, 1771–1831* (Woodbridge: The Boydell Press, 2012), pp.11–12.
5   Rodger, *Command of the Ocean*, p.511.
6   Richard Hill, *The Prizes of War: The Naval Prize System in the Napoleonic Wars, 1793–1815* (Stroud: Sutton Publishing, for the Royal Naval Museum, 1998), p.231.
7   Anon., 'The MS Journal of Captain E. Thompson, RN, 1783 to 1785', *The Cornhill Magazine*, 17 (1868), p.619.
8   From the Prologomena to [Edward Thompson], *Sailor's Letters Written to his Select Friends in England, During his Voyages and Travels in Europe, Asia, Africa, and America from the Year 1754 to 1759* (Dublin: J. Hoey and J. Potts, 1770), vol.1, p.iv.

In terms of Admiralty clout, Thompson fell a little short of ideal. He had a significant patron in Admiral Augustus Keppel, but that gentleman, like Thompson himself, was a Whig, with absolutely no leverage over Lord North's Tory government. But Thompson was also responsible for his midshipmen's nautical education, and in this respect Popham soon discovered he had struck gold. Often midshipmen were educated aboard ship by a schoolmaster or chaplain, but Thompson had neither until 1779, when he requested a chaplain's warrant for Reverend Isham Baggs due to the 'number of young Gentleman [sic] committed to my care, whose Education I pay great attention to'.[9] Even after Baggs joined the ship, Thompson, who excelled at hydrography and navigation, oversaw the education of his 'young Gentlemen' himself.

Thompson believed there was not 'one situation in life, that requires so accomplished an education, as the sea officer', and he practised what he preached.[10] As one of Thompson's midshipmen and an officer-in-training, Popham was expected to do all the menial work of an ordinary sailor: he learned to clamber about the yardarms, furling and unfurling sails; acquired proficiency in knot-making; and served watches at all hours of the day and night. He also learned how to be a gentleman, for Thompson disliked how practical experience was often acquired at the expense of social and cerebral accomplishments. To give them authority and superiority to command, future officers had to be treated differently, and Thompson saw no reason why a naval officer's academic education should not continue aboard ship.

Having once been destined for Cambridge and Lincoln's Inn, Popham already had the preliminary qualifications of a gentleman. He had acquired 'a sufficient knowledge of [his] own language, to speak it politely, and write it correctly', and he was proficient in Latin and Greek.[11] Of the three modern languages Thompson considered vital, Popham certainly spoke French; he acquired Italian later in life when he sailed with a partly Italian crew (he never, however, knew Spanish well enough to speak or understand it).[12] Given his background, Popham was probably trained in fencing and dancing. If not, Thompson would have made certain he acquired such gentlemanly skills: 'I introduced dancing among my young Officers and my people, as too little exercize [sic] is used at sea. We mustered 12 couple[s] and I went down 6 dances.'[13]

Popham's lifelong love, however, was mathematics – a love he shared with his captain, a navigator of no small merit. Under Thompson's oversight, Popham married his mathematical prowess with more practical navigational skills. With his captain's assistance, Popham learned to follow the course of a vessel on a chart, becoming familiar with the points of the

---

9    TNA: ADM 1/2592: Thompson to Philip Stephens, 3 January 1778 [sic: 1779]. Thompson wrote that Baggs's 'character, abilities, and [personal?] life give him every plea for such a situation', but in fact Baggs was, like many other naval chaplains of the period, on the run, having been intimately involved (in every sense of the word) in the divorce of Mrs Catherine Newton, niece of the Duke of Somerset.
10  [Thompson], *Sailor's Letters*, vol.1, p.144.
11  [Thompson], *Sailor's Letters*, vol.1, p.153; John Taylor, *Records of my Life, by the Late John Taylor, esq.* (London: E. Bull, 1832), vol.2, pp.211–212.
12  BL: IOR/G/177 part 1, ff.203–204: Popham to Carlo de Rossetti, 22 April 1802 (for Italian); Popham to the governor of Montevideo, 19 September 1806, Anon., *A Full and Correct Report of the Trial of Sir Home Popham …* (London: J. and J. Richardson, 1807), Appendix Note D (for Spanish).
13  BL: Add MS 46120: diary of Edward Thompson, 20 February 1784.

compass, the direction and intensity of the wind, and the run of the current. Thompson encouraged the young officer to keep a journal, in which he sketched any coasts or headlands he passed and recorded their bearings and distances. Whenever Popham was not walking the yardarms, participating in a watch, or actively studying in the captain's cabin, he had the freedom of Thompson's extensive mobile library, which contained practical treatises on navigation as well as the works of Virgil, Ovid, and Horace; the poetry of Dryden, Pope, Milton, and Marvell; histories of Britain and France; collections of sermons; and books on natural philosophy. The remaining 40 years of Popham's life showed how completely he had become Thompson's ideal naval officer: 'a man of letters and languages, a mathematician, and an accomplished gentleman'.[14]

*Hyaena*'s first mission was to carry £50,000 to Dublin for the Irish Treasury, returning in convoy with Irish linen ships bound for Chester and Liverpool.[15] Thanks to adverse tides, however, the frigate remained at Liverpool until 24 June 1778. When it did sail, it left so unexpectedly it could not wait for its bottom to finish being properly coppered.[16] Popham never recorded his excitement at seeing the ship's crew in action or his discomfort at feeling the first rolls of the deck on the open waves, but he was at least familiar with the journey across the notoriously choppy Irish Sea. The weather turned into a full gale on 27 June, the day *Hyaena* arrived in Dublin Bay, and Popham may have started having second thoughts about his new career. Just as possibly, of course, he may have discovered a strong stomach and, once he had weathered his first storm, warmed to the idea of being at sea – even if he had not yet experienced the boundless horizons of an open ocean.

Popham's introduction to sea life was gentle, if perhaps a little boring. Having sent the Irish Treasury money ashore and spent a few days re-provisioning, watering, and completing his complement, Captain Thompson took *Hyaena* to Belfast to collect some more linen ships for the Dublin convoy. By now the journey's tedium was starting to get to some of the crew, many of whom had only been tempted on board in the first place by the promise of a £5 bounty stumped up by the principal gentlemen of Gainsborough.[17] At the beginning of July Popham witnessed his first punishment when he and the rest of the crew turned out onto the main deck to watch six men receive 12 lashes each for trying to run.[18] To keep his men away from the shore's temptations, Captain Thompson ordered *Hyaena* to cruise the Irish Sea in search of an American privateer rumoured to be in the area. Nothing came of the cruise, but Popham spent it getting used to the routine of sailing, clambering aloft to help furl and unfurl the sails, conquering his instinctive fear of heights, and learning all the parts of the ship. By mid-July *Hyaena* was back in Dublin and, after taking on more stores, it sailed with HMS *Harpy* and *Wolf* with a convoy of 11 ships. Contrary to orders, Thompson agreed to escort £900,000 worth of Irish merchandise to the Downs, 'which step,' he excused

---

14 [Thompson], *Sailor's Letters*, vol.1, p.156.
15 TNA: ADM 1/2592: Thompson to Philip Stephens, 19 June 1778.
16 TNA: ADM 1/2592: Thompson to Philip Stephens, 3 August 1778.
17 TNA: ADM 1/2592: Thompson to Philip Stephens, 16 May 1778.
18 TNA: ADM 51/468: log, HMS *Hyaena*, 4 July 1778.

himself to the Secretary of the Admiralty, 'I hope will be rather construed into assiduity and attention, than disrespect'.[19] This was the same sort of 'assiduity and attention' to orders Popham showed later in life.

Popham got his first taste of real naval experience when *Hyaena* was ordered to join the Channel Fleet. Its commander, Captain Thompson's naval patron Admiral Keppel, was keeping an eye on France, which had just allied with the rebellious Americans, splitting the Navy's attention between European and American fronts and opening the very real prospect of an invasion of British soil. These were the circumstances under which *Hyaena* joined HMS *Actaeon*, *Jupiter*, *Seaford*, and *Cygnet* to defend the Channel Islands. From the ship's mainmast, Popham could see the enemy forces gathered at Granville and St Malo, as well as the large flotilla of flat-bottomed boats assembling to carry them across the sea. The attack, however, did not materialise, and *Hyaena* spent most of its time weathering a series of storms, suffering considerable damage to its uncoppered hull. Upon its return to Spithead in November, the ship began a total refit. Over the Christmas period it was thoroughly cleaned and caulked, and restocked with iron and shingle ballast, beef, beer, and bread, along with pork, flour, raisins, pease, oatmeal, cheese, butter, oil, and vinegar. Meanwhile, its captain went to London on leave, with Home Popham in his entourage.

After nearly 10 months at sea, Popham was an integral and appreciated part of *Hyaena*'s crew. He had also become an unofficial member of Thompson's rather dysfunctional family. Captain Thompson and his 'ungrateful Wife' Mary were fully estranged.[20] Instead, he had set up house with his paramour, Mary Powell – whom he called 'Emma', perhaps to avoid confusion – and his adopted nephew, Thomas Boulden Thompson, also a midshipman aboard *Hyaena*. Thomas may have been the captain's illegitimate son – several contemporaries thought so, and Boulden Thompson himself dropped hints in that direction. But then Captain Thompson was more than happy to open heart and home to his favourite 'young gentlemen', and that included Popham. Popham responded eagerly to his captain's affection. Something in his life had been missing – his father had ignored him, his brother abandoned him – and Thompson filled the gap. He was, to Popham and Boulden Thompson alike, 'our parent', and Boulden Thompson signed himself off to Popham as 'your friend in brotherly love'.[21] Popham had finally found family he could rely on.

Through Thompson, however, Popham was also learning how politically charged service in the Royal Navy could be. In July 1778, Captain Thompson's patron, Admiral Keppel, had tried to end the invasion threat by engaging the French fleet off Ushant. He had won the battle, but not decisively, and Keppel blamed his second-in-command, Vice Admiral Sir Hugh Palliser, for failing to support him. Unfortunately for Keppel, a staunch Whig, Palliser was a Tory and a member of the Admiralty Board to boot. Incensed by Keppel's accusations, he persuaded the Admiralty to court-martial Keppel for neglect of duty and cowardice. It was a bitter, pointless affair, but one with a potentially practical impact on Popham's career:

---

19   TNA: ADM 1/2592: Thompson to Philip Stephens, 3 August 1778.
20   TNA: PROB 11/1141/170: will of Captain Edward Thompson, 13 March 1785.
21   TNA: HCA 32/597, nos.414 and 422: Boulden Thompson to Popham, 31 January, 17 February 1787.

what would happen if his captain's naval patron was cashiered? In the event Keppel was cleared of all charges, but Popham learned an important lesson: his career only partly depended on talent, and it paid to have friends in high places.

Thompson and his midshipmen were soon back aboard *Hyaena*, under orders to convoy a fleet of 41 ships and join Vice Admiral Sir John Byron in the West Indies.[22] This station was notoriously unhealthy but pivotal, given its proximity to America and the fact France and Spain both had colonies there. Serving in the West Indies thus had one very significant advantage to counterbalance the spectre of yellow fever: the richness of the area, full of sugar plantations and merchant vessels carrying spices, timber, and slaves, vastly increased the likelihood of prize money.

In fact, Popham did not have to reach the West Indies to experience the inroads contagious illness could make on men crowded together on a ship's lower decks. *Hyaena* sailed with its convoy on 7 March,

Thomas Boulden Thompson, engraved by William Ridley after George Engleheart, 1805. (Public domain, The Miriam and Ira D. Wallach Division of Art, Prints and Photographs, The New York Public Library)

carrying part of the 75th Regiment and something highly infectious. By the time it reached Gorée Bay on 10 May, over 80 men – more than half the complement – were on the sick list. The journey was highly stressful: Thompson lamented that 137 of his men had been sick, some twice, and there was virtually no medicine left on board. At the end of June, *Hyaena* limped into Carlisle Bay, Barbados, 'in a most sickly state'.[23]

Given the number of crew members affected, Popham was probably ill himself. Still, he did benefit from the epidemic, as Captain Thompson commissioned him acting lieutenant.[24] The toll sickness had taken on the ship's officer corps was probably the primary reason, but Thompson's choice testified to how much Popham had impressed his captain in his 18 months at sea. Moreover, the new Acting Lieutenant immediately assisted in his very first battle. It was not exactly a triumph. Vice Admiral Byron was in the West Indies to defend British possessions against the French under the Comte d'Estaing, whose naval force had already helped capture St Vincent and Grenada. Byron intercepted the French fleet off Grenada on 6 July, believing he had numerical superiority, but he was misinformed: d'Estaing had recently been reinforced. Byron tried to call off the fight as soon as he realised he was outnumbered, but

---

22  Popham, *A Damned Cunning Fellow*, p.9; TNA: ADM 51/468: log, HMS *Hyaena*, 7 March 1779.
23  TNA: ADM 51/468: log, HMS *Hyaena*, 7 March–26 June 1779; TNA: ADM 1/2592: Thompson to Philip Stephens, 28 June 1779.
24  TNA: HCA 32/597, no.459: commission, 25 July 1779.

this belated decision only increased the confusion on the British side. *Hyaena* was involved, although it should not have been: Thompson had been on detached orders chasing a French privateer when his frigate ran straight into Byron's battle.[25] Byron mainly used *Hyaena* to carry messages between the British ships, many of which had been separated from the main fleet and were drifting downwind. Several were badly damaged and, by the time the battle finished at dawn, it was clear the British had come off worse.

The Battle of Grenada placed d'Estaing in a commanding position, and rumours spread throughout the British West Indies that he intended to assault Barbados with 1,500 troops. At this moment of danger Captain Thompson made an odd and, as it turned out, unwise decision. A group of local planters and merchants, fearing for their livelihood, asked Thompson to provide a convoy for 20 ships back to Britain. Thompson had been worried about *Hyaena* for some time – it had not been properly coppered since being hurried out of its dockyard in Liverpool a year ago – so he was keener to agree than he should have been, given he had no orders to leave station. But Thompson did not know where Byron was and, when approached, the governor of Barbados gave Thompson permission to leave if Byron did not appear within 10 days to countermand the order.[26] Thompson, who never let a lack of specific instructions stop him doing anything (a tendency Popham inherited), took this as full authority and set sail, with a convoy of 14 merchant ships, on 11 August 1779, after borrowing some seamen belonging to HMS *Vengeance* from Barbados's naval hospital. *Hyaena* and its charges arrived safely at Spithead on 27 September. Popham was back in Britain, his pockets slightly fuller than they had been: on its way home, *Hyaena* helped capture an American schooner carrying lumber.[27] It was Popham's first taste of prize money, and it whetted an appetite that never left him.

Captain Thompson expected the thanks of the Admiralty for his initiative in convoying the valuable West Indian merchant fleet. What he actually got was a summons to a court-martial on two charges: leaving his station without orders, and stealing men belonging to HMS *Vengeance*. The trial took place on 5 November 1779 aboard HMS *Prudent* in Portsmouth. Of the two charges, Thompson was clearly guilty of the first, although for the second Thompson argued that, while he had indeed taken seven men belonging to *Vengeance*, he had left 11 men in their place.[28] The verdict reflected this: 'The court are of opinion that the charge has been proved in part; but as it appears the motives which induced Captain Thompson to leave his station … arose from a desire of doing service to his country, by securing the trade, and not from any private motives, they do only adjudge him to be reprimanded.'[29] Thompson's court-martial made a strong impression on Popham. When he himself was brought to trial in 1807, the first precedent he consulted in preparation was that of his captain and mentor.[30]

---

25  TNA: ADM 51/468: log, HMS *Hyaena*, 6 July 1779.
26  TNA: ADM 1/2592: Thompson to Philip Stephens, 29 September 1779.
27  TNA: ADM 51/468: log, HMS *Hyaena*, 11 August–27 September 1779; *London Gazette*, 26 June 1781, p.4.
28  Letter of 8 November 1779 quoted in *Caledonian Mercury*, 13 November 1779.
29  *Caledonian Mercury*, 13 November 1779.
30  TNA: ADM 1/2332: Popham to William Marsden, 4 March 1807.

The 'Moonlight Battle', engraver unknown, 1779. (Public domain, The Miriam and Ira D. Wallach Division of Art, Prints and Photographs, The New York Public Library)

His reputation cleared and his ship's hull fully coppered, Thompson, Tom, and Popham sailed on Christmas Day under Admiral George Rodney's command to re-provision Gibraltar, which had been under Spanish siege for a year. Rodney, cruising off the Spanish coast, had received intelligence of a Spanish squadron consisting of 14 sail of the line off Cape St Vincent. The weather, however, was bad, 'squally with rain', and little could be seen of the enemy. In the afternoon of 16 January 1780, HMS *Bedford* finally caught sight of a fleet to the south-east. Thompson, aboard *Hyaena*, received the signal and repeated it, but because of the heavy rain Rodney did not see it.[31] Popham, standing with Captain Thompson on *Hyaena*'s quarterdeck, could just about make out the Spanish ships looming through the mist like ghosts. Finally, Rodney caught on and made signal for his ships to form a line of battle abreast. When the enemy responded likewise, however, Rodney signalled a general chase, ordering his captains to engage the ships one by one and take the lee-gauge to prevent the enemy's retreat.[32] Following close behind the flagship, Thompson ordered *Hyaena* to repeat every signal broadcast by the admiral.

---

31  TNA: ADM 51/468: log, HMS *Hyaena*, 16–17 January 1780.
32  Lord Rodney's dispatch, 27 January 1780, in *Reading Mercury*, 6 March 1780.

As the last of the winter daylight faded to dusk, the first ships opened fire with a roar of cannons. HMS *Bedford* engaged the Spanish ship *Princessa*, alongside HMS *Edgar*, and HMS *Ajax* took on *San Domingo*. Popham, busy relaying Thompson's orders, was no doubt as startled as everyone else when a huge explosion tore through the air in a burst of heat and blinding light about 40 minutes into the action: *San Domingo* had blown up. Thompson ordered *Hyaena* to bear up for the wreck in the hope of rescuing survivors, but in vain. The ship passed another British vessel 'taking care of a large Ship, much disabled, which we judged to be Spanish', which struck its colours shortly after, demoralised by the shocking loss of *San Domingo*. Night had by now fallen completely, but the struggle continued past midnight, puncturing the darkness with bursts of blinding cannon-fire. At 2:15 a.m. on 17 January, the Spanish flagship finally struck its colours to HMS *Sandwich*. The Spanish admiral in command, Don Juan Langara, symbolically surrendered his sword to the King's son, the Duke of Clarence, then a midshipman aboard HMS *Prince George*. It was, Rodney wrote triumphantly, 'a signal victory': of Langara's 14 sail of the line, six were taken, one exploded, and two were driven ashore. Only five ships were neither taken nor destroyed.[33]

Popham was exhausted but elated. This was not his first battle, but it was his first victory, and *Hyaena* and its crew were among the day's heroes. Thompson's men had performed admirably, ensuring Rodney's orders were obeyed by relaying messages quickly and clearly. The fast-sailing frigate, no longer slowed down by substandard coppering, had come into its own. As a reward, Rodney selected Thompson to carry home duplicates of the official victory dispatch. The original was sent on 18 January in the *Childers* brig, but Thompson was keen to show off the swiftness of his vessel. *Hyaena* set sail on 9 February; it saw the lights of Portland on 27 February, and Thompson arrived at the Admiralty in London early in the morning of the 28th, two days before the captain of *Childers*. He had an audience with the First Lord of the Admiralty, Lord Sandwich, who brought him to see the King and Queen, to whom Thompson presented private letters from the Duke of Clarence.[34] Two weeks later, *Hyaena* was back on its way to re-join the fleet in the Mediterranean.

The past two years had changed Popham's life. The boy who had waited, nervously, to join *Hyaena*'s crew, his comfortable future shattered by his brother's betrayal, would not have recognised himself. He could now confidently reef and un-reef the sails with the rest of the men, without giving a thought to the distance between his feet and the deck below. He had learned a great deal about the science of navigation, more than enough to stimulate his mathematical mind. He had witnessed the importance of clear, swift, and accurate communication between ships in the heat of battle. He had started as a volunteer with no naval experience; he had already been acting lieutenant and was now rated a master's mate.[35] His captain considered him suitable to become an officer and walk the quarterdeck himself. At 18, Popham looked forward to proving Thompson right.

---

33   *Reading Mercury*, 6 March 1780.
34   *Reading Mercury*, 6 March 1780.
35   TNA: ADM 1/9548: muster, HMS *Hyaena*.

In August 1780, *Hyaena* again sailed for New York, where the war against the rebellious colonies still rumbled on.[36] Over the winter of 1780 and 1781, *Hyaena* scouted the waters between Charleston and the West Indies, picking off American, Spanish, and French merchantmen and privateers and racking up prize money.[37] In February, Admiral Rodney ordered Thompson to hoist a commodore's pendant and take command of a flying squadron of eight frigates and sloops to harass enemy merchantmen around St Kitts, which was threatened by French and Americans trading with the Dutch island of St Eustatius.[38] A month later, Thompson's duties changed again: the Dutch surrendered the colonies of Berbice, Demerara, and Essequibo (modern-day Guiana), and Thompson was appointed to oversee their organisation into British territories alongside the governor, Robert Kingston.[39] *Hyaena* took up station in the Demerara River, where two American sloops, caught unawares by the change of authority, promptly surrendered: *Hancock* and *Rake*.[40] *Rake*, a 14-gun sloop, was commissioned into British service and rechristened *Shelanagig*.[41]

The prizes taken in the Demerara River gave Thompson an excuse to look after one of his favourite midshipmen. Popham was a master's mate, not yet a lieutenant, but he had previously served as acting lieutenant and Thompson knew he was capable. *Shelanagig* was his first command. Popham's task was not difficult – he had to take the vessel from Demerara to be condemned by the Admiralty Court at Barbados – but it would bring him before the eyes of Barbados's governor and possibly lead to better things. Popham duly set sail on 24 April 1781. He fulfilled his basic mission swiftly and well, and the governor, Major General James Cunninghame, who had just heard of a victory obtained by Rear Admiral Sir Samuel Hood over the French admiral, de Grasse, ordered *Shelanagig* back to sea to carry the news to the first British ship it came upon, before joining Admiral Rodney at St Eustatius for further orders.

If Popham's enthusiasm for showing off in later life was any measure of his zeal now, he must have been delighted at this chance to distinguish himself. The first ship *Shelanagig* came across was HMS *Vaughan*, under Commander David Stow, who sent Popham to Antigua to report to Captain John Laforey, Naval Commissioner in the West Indies. Laforey loaded Popham's sloop with gunpowder for Admiral Rodney, as there was no other vessel in Antigua at the time capable of performing the service. The commanding admiral placed Popham under the orders of Rear Admiral Sir Francis Samuel Drake, who sent *Shelanagig* to Tobago with letters for the governor. Popham's supposedly short stint as commander of *Shelanagig* had now been extended three times, once by Rodney himself, and Popham must have begun to hope he might continue a little longer in command. However, when *Shelanagig* arrived in Tobago, Popham discovered Rodney had decided to purchase the ship into the Navy and commission it as a sloop of war. Popham was far too junior to take official

---

36 *Aberdeen Press and Journal*, 28 August 1780.
37 TNA: ADM 1/2593: Thompson to Philip Stephens, 13 January 1781.
38 *Hampshire Chronicle*, 23 April 1781.
39 TNA: ADM 1/2593: Thompson to Philip Stephens, 29 March 1781.
40 TNA: ADM 51/468: log, HMS *Hyaena*, 8 April 1781.
41 The name refers to ancient carvings of women displaying their vulva, possibly as protection against evil spirits.

command, so the ship was given to Commander James Keith Shepard. Popham was nevertheless allowed to remain part of the crew as acting lieutenant.[42]

*Shelanagig*'s first and only voyage as a Royal Navy sloop was an intelligence-gathering mission. At the end of May, Rodney learned that a small French squadron of two ships of the line, four frigates, and three cutters, carrying 900 troops, was on its way to invest British-held Tobago. *Shelanagig* sailed ahead of Drake's force to reinforce the island before the French could arrive, but arrived off Tobago to find a French fleet of 24 sail of the line already there. Drake – who only had six ships of the line – beat a hasty retreat. With the window for saving Tobago closing fast, Rodney reinforced Drake and *Shelanagig*, along with the *Fly* cutter and the schooner *Munster Lass*, was tasked with discovering suitable landing places for British troops in case of a French attack.[43] Unfortunately for Shepard and his men, *Shelanagig* (and *Fly*, separately) ran directly into the French fleet. Shepard gave orders to set all sails possible to escape, but the swell on the weather-beam was too strong and pushed the sloop too close to the enemy, who also took care to stay out of the way of *Shelanagig*'s lee guns.[44] The sloop was run down, boarded, and its crew taken prisoner aboard a French frigate, *La Diligente*.[45]

Popham's fortunes had been suddenly upended for the second time in his life. He was taken to Martinique, where he remained a prisoner of war for two months. On 1 August he and Captain Shepard were released on parole, but Popham's war was over until he could be exchanged for a French prisoner of equal status. Rodney therefore sent him back to *Hyaena* and Captain Thompson – not to fight, but to accompany Thompson back to England, because Popham's former captain was being sent home.

The situation in the West Indies was deteriorating, and Rodney had verbally ordered Thompson to convoy a fleet of 40 merchant vessels back to Europe. Thompson had been assured Rodney's order to take the convoy home would be sent on to him in writing, but before this happened Rodney fell ill and temporarily gave up his West Indies command to Sir Samuel Hood. Thompson knew the French fleet under de Grasse was on its way, and he needed to sail before it arrived.[46] Still, he waited in Guiana until the end of October for further instructions, then waited a further three weeks at Barbados before deciding to take the convoy home anyway. By this time, de Grasse had reached Martinique and, the day after Thompson sailed from Barbados, the island of St Eustatius surrendered to the French.[47] Thompson paused only long enough at St Kitts to propose a madcap scheme to retake it with 300 men from the local garrison – the local commander wisely demurred.[48] With the French fleet now too close for comfort, Thompson and his convoy slipped away during the night of 29 November.[49]

---

42 TNA: PRO 30/20/20/11: Popham's statement, 30 September 1784; TNA: ADM 34/732: paybook, HMS *Shelanagig*.
43 TNA: PRO 30/20/20/11: statement by Valentine Jones, September 1784; TNA: ADM 1/314: Rodney to Philip Stephens, 22 June 1781.
44 TNA: ADM 1/5319, ff.423–424: court-martial of Captain Shepard, 23 January 1782.
45 TNA: PRO 30/20/20/11: Popham's statement, 30 September 1784.
46 TNA: ADM 1/2593: Thompson to Philip Stephens, 1 September 1781.
47 TNA: ADM 51/468: log, HMS *Hyaena*, 28 October–25 November 1781.
48 Thompson to Philip Stephens, 28 November 1781, and Brigadier General Frazier to Thompson, in *St James's Chronicle*, 19–21 March 1782.
49 *Oxford Journal*, 26 January 1782.

When Sir Samuel Hood discovered Thompson had left his station without written orders, he was furious – particularly as the French re-captured Berbice, Demerara, and Essequibo, which had been under Thompson's protection, over the course of January and February 1782. The order for a court-martial was issued on 22 March, Thompson's second for disobedience in the course of three years. The trial began on 1 April 1782 aboard HMS *Warspite* in Portsmouth harbour. If Hood had expected Thompson to be cashiered, however, he was disappointed. Thompson escaped with a complete, and honourable, acquittal: the board expressed its opinion that his actions had been 'necessary, judicious and highly meritorious' due to the superiority of the enemy in the West Indies.[50] Thompson was free to serve again – not, however, aboard *Hyaena*, which had reached the end of its increasingly leaky life. In April, it was taken from Spithead to Sheerness and then to Woolwich, where it was decommissioned on 17 May.[51]

*Hyaena* may have reached the end of its professional life, but Popham's was just beginning. His parole had ended following a cartel agreed by Britain and France in 1781 and he was ready, and eager, to return to active duty.[52] Still, although he wanted to remain under Thompson's command, he could not afford to wait for the outcome of his captain's court-martial. When an opportunity presented itself to transfer to the 44-gun fifth-rate HMS *Endymion* as a Third Lieutenant on the Jamaica station in April 1782, he jumped at it. Strictly speaking he had not passed his lieutenant's examination, but the promotion was confirmed by Admiral Rodney in July, perhaps in recognition of his command of *Shelanagig*.[53] Popham and his crewmates arrived back off America in time to act as a signal ship at the Battle of the Saintes, when Admiral Rodney definitively checked a combined French and Spanish assault on British Jamaica and re-established British naval dominance in the West Indies. This was Popham's third and last naval battle, but his destiny did not lie in close fighting on the high seas.

Despite lacking opportunities to distinguish himself in the thick of a fray, Popham continued his steady climb up the promotion ladder. This involved changing ship several times. In April 1783, Popham moved from *Endymion* to HMS *Nemesis*, gaining another step to Second Lieutenant.[54] Three months later he transferred again, to HMS *Alarm*, where he served as First Lieutenant.[55] He spent hardly any time with *Alarm*, however, as the ship returned to Britain to be paid off in August 1783, leaving Popham unemployed and on half-pay.[56] It was his last official employment aboard a Royal Navy vessel until 1798. Popham did not know this, of course, but he did know his prospects of re-employment were not as

---

50  TNA: ADM 1/5319, f.555: Thompson's court-martial, 1 April 1782.
51  TNA: ADM 51/468: log, HMS *Hyaena*, 17 May 1782.
52  TNA: HCA 32/597, no.484: certificate, Commissioners for Sick and Wounded Seamen, 1 October 1781.
53  TNA: HCA 32/599: log book belonging to Popham, 1782–1783.
54  TNA: HCA 32/599: log book belonging to Popham, 1782–1783.
55  TNA: HCA 32/599: log book belonging to Popham, 1782–1783; TNA: ADM 36/10161: muster, HMS *Nemesis*; TNA: ADM 36/9639: muster, HMS *Alarm*; TNA: ADM 6/23 f.421: Popham's lieutenant commission.
56  TNA: ADM 36/9639: muster, HMS *Alarm*.

good as they might have been even a few months previously. Over the summer, the government had signed the Peace of Paris, ending the war with America, France, Spain, and the Netherlands. Popham was now one of several hundred lieutenants, most much more senior than he was, clamouring for employment in a peacetime navy.

Popham knew his best chance was to find a captain looking for a lieutenant, so he wasted no time looking up his old friend Captain Thompson. Thompson was still living with Mrs Powell and Tom Boulden Thompson, now also a lieutenant. They were delighted to see their adopted member again and 'Pop', as they called him, was soon as central a part of Thompson's extended family as he had ever been. Thompson's fortunes had languished after his court-martial but, thanks to a recent change in government, the Whigs were back in power and Thompson's political patron, Admiral Keppel, was First Lord of the Admiralty. This meant that, when Popham begged for a place on Thompson's next ship, his old captain was able to give him good news. Just before Popham appeared at Thompson's doorstep in Bedford Square, Thompson had been appointed captain of HMS *Grampus*, a 50-gun fifth-rate vessel, with a brief to investigate the area around Demerara, Berbice, and Essequibo – the South American colonies he had helped administer during the war – to locate a potential British supply station and settlement.[57] Not knowing Popham was available, Thompson had already selected his three lieutenants, but he agreed to allow Popham to accompany him as a volunteer on the understanding that he would earn his keep as a marine surveyor.[58] Thompson impressed on Popham the importance, in the uncertain world of naval employment and promotion, of having a talent as sought-after as hydrography, and Popham, always keen to stand out from the crowd, became very good at it. It was something he fell back on many times during the lean periods of his volatile career.

Despite Thompson's plans, however, Popham spent no time practising his hydrographic skills off the Americas. In December 1783, the Whigs fell unexpectedly from office. Keppel was replaced at the Admiralty by Richard, Lord Howe, who had little time for Thompson, and the new ministry under Pitt the Younger shied away from trespassing on Dutch territory in South America with the ink barely dry on the Peace of Paris. But then Thompson proposed an alternative: to investigate the other side of the ocean off Africa 'between the Latitudes of 20 and 30 [degrees] Sou[th]', specifically Cape Das Voltas, a place he had never been but where, from his research, he expected to find good harbours, fruitful soil, and a salubrious climate that would allow British Indiamen an Atlantic alternative to watering at the Dutch-held Cape of Good Hope or Portuguese Rio de Janeiro.[59]

The Pitt ministry still thought Thompson something of a rogue, but this time his ideas meshed with government priorities. The Home Secretary, Lord Sydney, was looking for a new place to send transported convicts now that North America was no longer available. A House of Commons committee had been set up to decide on the location of a new penal settlement. Botany Bay had been discussed as a possibility, but Thompson's description of Cape Das Voltas as a healthy, plentiful African Eden proved more tempting. *Grampus*

---

57   BL: Add MS 46120: diary of Edward Thompson, 13 July 1783.
58   TNA: ADM 1/2593: Thompson to Philip Stephens, 28 July 1783; Popham to the Board of Longitude, 23 July 1786, University of Cambridge Digital Library, Royal Greenwich Observatory archives, RGO 14/51 f.193, <https://cudl.lib.cam.ac.uk/view/MS-RGO-00014-00051/394>, accessed 6 December 2022.
59   BL: Add MS 46120: diary of Edward Thompson, 31 July 1783.

performed an exploratory voyage over the summer of 1784, following which Thompson met with the Prime Minister in November and with Lord Sydney in January to discuss a further, more purposeful, visit to the African coast. In mid-1785 Thompson received orders to locate a suitable harbour for a supply depot and penal colony, of which he would be governor.

Thompson's expedition had a strong scientific bent, as it was partially intended to map the western coast of Africa. As a hydrographer-in-training, Popham was officially appointed marine surveyor, for which he earned 10s 6d per diem on top of his lieutenant's pay.[60] This was an essential post on an expedition designed to chart unknown waters and, in August 1785, Popham received secret instructions directly from the hands of Lord Howe. The government wanted him to chart the coast of Africa between Cape Das Voltas and Cape Negro, surveying harbours, rivers, and bays, taking distances and soundings, and determining the nature of the soil and the produce of the country (its fruit, vegetation, and wildlife).[61] Popham also received separate instructions from the Board of Longitude to ascertain the latitudes and longitudes of the different capes off the coast. He was given a marine chronometer by its inventor, Larcum Kendall, and asked to keep a journal of his findings.[62] All this was to be for the eyes only of the Admiralty Board, the government, and the King himself. If Popham did well, there was the tantalising prospect that he would 'be rewarded by My Lords Commissioners of the Admiralty, and His Majesty's Ministers, according to your Exertions, and the Merits of your Reports'.[63]

At the end of September 1785, *Grampus*, along with *Nautilus* under Captain George Tripp, set off from Spithead.[64] The omens of success were good and the weather was pleasant. The little expedition arrived in Funchal Bay on Popham's 24th birthday, stopping at the island of Gorée to re-provision before sailing on into the unknown. Between mid-November and arriving off the slave trading station at Apollonia in mid-December, *Grampus* and *Nautilus* picked their way cautiously down the western coast of Africa, sounding and mapping as they went.

As marine surveyor, Popham ought to have spent all his time with his new chronometer, but he never shook off an urge to take on more important, unofficial, responsibilities that impinged on what he actually ought to be doing. While off Apollonia, he spent most of his time ashore, sorting out a 'palavre' regarding compensation requested by the Fante tribes for depredations committed by the local British Royal African Company settlements trading in the area since the seventeenth century. Popham discovered a taste for diplomacy, and the skills he picked up in smoothing over quarrels and acting as a go-between came in useful in later life. Despite this, his missions ashore were not especially successful. This may not have been entirely Popham's fault: the diplomatic situation between the authorities under the Royal African Company and the locals were understandably tense, as the

---

60   Jill Kinahan, 'The impenetrable shield: HMS Nautilus and the Namib coast in the late eighteenth century', *Cimbebasia*, 12 (1990), p.24; TNA: HCA 32/597, no.470: Philip Stephens to Popham, 31 October 1786.

61   TNA: HCA 32/597, no.483: instructions, 1 February 1786, issued by Captain Tripp.

62   Memorandum by Popham enclosed in his letter to the Board of Longitude, 1 June 1786, Cambridge University Digital Library, Royal Greenwich Observatory Archives, RGO 14/51, ff.195–207, <https://cudl.lib.cam.ac.uk/view/MS-RGO-00014-00051/398>, accessed 6 December 2022.

63   TNA: HCA 32/597, no.483: instructions, 1 February 1786, issued by Captain Tripp.

64   TNA: ADM 51/382: Captain's log, HMS *Grampus*, 28 September 1785.

'A new and correct map of the coast of Africa from Cape Blanco ... to the coast of Angola', by Malachy Postlethwayt, 1746. This was the territory *Grampus* explored in 1785, before sailing further south into uncharted waters. (Rare Book Division, The New York Public Library)

Company's greatest profits came from its prominent role in the slave trade. Popham spent a fortnight going up and down the coast, visiting the various forts and assessing their ability to defend themselves from attack. When he returned to the ship, he discovered his precious chronometer had not been wound properly and had stopped – a metaphor, perhaps, for the entire mission.[65]

For the expedition's good luck had begun to turn. The weather alternated from fair to stormy; the thermometer jumped to nearly 90°F (32°C), with tornadoes and heavy thunderstorms.[66] What with the heavy, humid weather, the lack of fresh water, and the unreliability of local provisions – relations were not improved when a British sailor shot and killed a native man – the crew began falling ill. 'Send us some Limes!' Captain Thompson wrote, desperately, to Popham, who was still in the midst of negotiating with the Fante chief.[67] By the end of December, 19 men were on the sick list aboard *Nautilus* alone.[68] On 14 January, at 2:00 a.m., Popham lost one of his best friends aboard *Grampus*, Midshipman John Sykes. Popham was ashore at the time, but he took a break from his work to preside over the 17-year-old boy's funeral on shore.[69] Perhaps, as six marines fired a salute across the freshly dug grave, Popham wondered where the next blow would fall. He soon found out. On 17 January, Commodore Thompson breathed his last, aged 48, and was buried at sea in Ana Chavas Bay.[70] 'Providence [has] deprived our Country by a very sudden Stroke, of an able, brave, and experienced Officer, ever Zealous in her Services,' Popham wrote.[71] He might have added that he, personally, had lost a man who had meant more to him than his own father.

Thompson's death required some shuffling, and as a gesture of goodwill to his adopted father, Thomas Boulden Thompson was offered command of *Nautilus*. Captain Tripp took over *Grampus* and, after a few more weeks of fruitless surveying, returned to Britain. Popham did not go home with them: he still had his orders to survey the coast to complete. He followed Boulden Thompson to *Nautilus*, which parted company with *Grampus* on 1 February 1786. After a lonely 52-day journey during which they did not see a single other vessel, *Grampus* arrived off Saldanha Bay, near the Cape of Good Hope, and Popham and Boulden Thompson started searching for a suitable place to found their late captain's long-planned penal colony. Thompson had told Popham of a spectacularly fertile land with grazing cattle, nomadic tribes, plentiful rivers, and precious ores; but Thompson had never actually been to the area and had relied on inaccurate journals of visiting ships and old Portuguese charts to form his opinion.[72] The land Popham and Boulden Thompson were

---

65 Memorandum by Popham, 1 June 1786, Cambridge University Digital Library, Royal Greenwich Observatory Archives, RGO 14/51, ff.195–207, <https://cudl.lib.cam.ac.uk/view/MS-RGO-00014-00051/418>, accessed 6 December 2022.
66 TNA: ADM 51/382: log, HMS *Grampus*, 22 November 1785.
67 TNA: HCA 32/597, no.78: Thompson to Popham, 3 January 1786.
68 TNA: HCA 32/597, no.91: Tripp to Thompson, 31 December 1785.
69 TNA: HCA 32/597, no.84: Alexander Kirkwood to Popham, [14 January 1786].
70 Clive Wilkinson, 'Thompson, Edward (1738?–1786)', ODNB, <https://doi.org/10.1093/ref:odnb/27260>, accessed 27 July 2021.
71 Memorandum by Popham, 1 June 1785, Cambridge University Digital Library, Royal Greenwich Observatory Archives, RGO 14/51, ff.195–207, <https://cudl.lib.cam.ac.uk/view/MS-RGO-00014-00051/398>, accessed 6 December 2022.
72 Kinahan, 'The impenetrable shield', pp.23–24.

meant to investigate was unpromising. When they found what they thought was Das Voltas Bay, Boulden Thompson sent Popham inland to investigate. Popham could not find any trace of a river, and the surrounding landscape was unremittingly barren and sandy, composed of nothing but constantly shifting dunes. Popham could not wait to get away: 'So inhospitable and so barren a Country is not to be equalled except in the Desarts [sic] of Arabia.'[73]

Popham and Boulden Thompson kept detailed diaries of their findings during their fruitless journey, full of frustration and dismay as they began to realise their mentor had given his life for nothing: 'We had sailed nearly 1,200 miles, without being able to procure a drop of Fresh Water or seeing a Tree.' In addition to the continued lack of water, which by mid-May had reached alarming proportions, the crew were beginning to fall ill again. On 17 May 1786, desperate for clean water and proper provisions, *Nautilus* abandoned its mission and made for home, 'much to the Satisfaction of every Person on Board'.[74]

---

73  Kinahan, 'The impenetrable shield', p.54.
74  Kinahan, 'The impenetrable shield', p.59.

3

# A Change of Tack, 1786–1793

*2167: Alter your course*

*Grampus* arrived back at Spithead on 23 July 1786. Having received hints that he might receive some sort of reward for his surveying, Popham's professional hopes were raised when he received a note from Lord Howe, who was away from London, telling him he would examine Popham's African charts the minute he was back at his desk.[1] But while Howe may have shown initial interest in the charts, that interest lasted only until he realised there was no chance of founding a penal settlement, or even a watering place, along the coast Popham had surveyed. Popham was about to find out first-hand how much a naval officer's career depended on connections. Howe had been no friend of Thompson's; now that Thompson was dead, he had no reason to show favour to Thompson's protégé, especially a protégé who brought bad news.

Still, Popham took a while to realise this. He moved into 39 Sackville Street, the home of a family friend, Lord Cavan, and waited to be summoned by either Lord Sydney or Lord Howe. As time ticked by and no invitation arrived, he started sending nudges to Lord Sydney's son, John Thomas Townshend, an Under-Secretary of State at the Home Office, and to Henry Martin, Commissioner at Portsmouth, an old acquaintance of Popham's brother William.[2] Nothing came of it. By September, the silence from the Admiralty had grown deafening. 'I should have expected by this [time] three or four Letters from you about Black Dick,' Thomas Boulden Thompson wrote.[3] Boulden Thompson's puzzlement soon turned to outrage as Howe's silence continued: 'I look upon him to be an *ungentlemanly fellow* … and the man who is not a *gentleman*, must be a rascal.'[4]

Popham's increasingly pointed reminders of his existence did provoke a belated response from the First Lord of the Admiralty, although it was not exactly what Popham had had in mind. Howe chided Popham for trying to jump to the top of the First Lord's to-do list and, as for the possibility of a reward for Popham's services, he did not even try to be kind:

---

1 TNA: HCA 32/597, no.477: Howe to Popham, 29 July 1786.
2 TNA: HCA 32/597, no.465: John Thomas Townshend to Popham, 30 July 1786; no.460: Henry Martin to Popham, 21 October 1786.
3 TNA: HCA 32/597, no.433: Boulden Thompson to Popham, [September 1786]. 'Black Dick' was Howe's nickname.
4 TNA: HCA 32/597, no.415: Boulden Thompson to Popham, [October 1786].

Capt[ain] Thompson might very fittingly have inferred that the Board of Admiralty would notice the merits of officers specially exemplified, [but] he is an intire [sic] stranger to the authority upon which Capt[ain] Thompson was induced to make such [a] pointed declaration in the name of His Majesty's Ministers, generally, or even on the part of the Admiralty, if meant in any other sense. He is therefore unable to render any more satisfactory assurances in reply to Lieut[enan]t Popham's letter.[5]

A good surveyor was, nevertheless, something to be cultivated – even if his services were not quite as stellar as the surveyor himself seemed to believe – and Howe decided to soften the blow by taking Popham to court and introducing him to the King. Popham was a naval officer and, therefore, a gentleman by default, but he had not been born one and was unlikely to have secured an invitation to court on his own merits.[6] Still, Popham did not recognise that Howe had temporarily elevated him above his station. He wanted more, and badgered Howe for a similar introduction to the Queen. Howe was by now mightily irritated:

Richard, Earl Howe, by Robert Dunkarton after J.S. Copley, 1794. (Public domain, Harvard Art Museums/ Fogg Museum)

> There certainly is no impropriety in every Gentleman's wishes to be presented to the Queen; an honor to which every person of that description who means to attend the Court particularly may consistently claim. But with respect to the special occasion on which you went lately to the levee, I do not conceive it to be of a nature to be made the motive for an introduction to the Queen.[7]

In other words, Popham's slender achievements did not by themselves entitle him to more royal favour.

Amazingly, Popham kept pestering the First Lord, perhaps hoping Howe would eventually do something just to get him to be quiet. 'It is here more than *currently reported* that you are going to Botany Bay as sub-Gover[no]r,' Boulden Thompson wrote towards the end of the year but, while Howe might have welcomed the opportunity to pack Popham off to the

---

5   TNA: HCA 32/597, no.468: Howe to Popham, 26 September 1786.
6   Wilson, *A Social History of British Naval Officers*, p.111.
7   TNA: HCA 32/597, no.474: Howe to Popham, 18 October 1786.

other side of the world, it was just rumour.[8] Popham's frustration turned slowly to despair. His mentor was dead and there was little chance of employment in peacetime for a man without significant connections or a great feat to back up his claims for preferment. Popham faced years of stagnation, eking out an existence on the meagre half-pay of a lieutenant. His share in the prize money from his time on *Hyaena* had hardly made him rich, and he did not manage to secure his salary as surveyor aboard *Grampus* and *Nautilus* until May 1787. Over the Christmas period, he moved from Lord Cavan's to 35 Dover Street, his brother William's house since returning from India the previous year, a rich man.

Surrounded by the luxuries his brother had bought with the money acquired through his campaigns as an officer in the East India Company's army, Popham's thoughts turned away from the Admiralty and towards the east. India had made his brother William rich; it had offered Stephen a refuge, and amnesty for past sins. Might it not also be Popham's own path to success?

Going to India, however, would mean cutting ties with the Royal Navy, perhaps for good, and Popham was not quite ready to do that. He was still willing to give the Navy first preference: on 28 December, he sent a letter to the First Lord of the Admiralty informing him the East India Company wanted a surveyor to examine the east coast of Africa between Cape False and Cape Guardafui, including the Mozambique Channel. Popham proposed this as an expedition the government might like to sponsor as it was likely to benefit British trade. 'In case you shou'd not,' Popham finished, 'I mean on your answer, with Your Lordship's permission, to request a leave of absence, from the Board of Admiralty, to go abroad.'[9] Popham, with his inflated sense of self-worth, probably expected the First Lord of the Admiralty to panic at the prospect of losing the expertise of a marine surveyor of his calibre. At first, Howe seemed to bite. He wrote agreeing to see Popham to talk over the proposal in the new year, but on 8 January 1787 Popham received a note from the First Lord that was short and to the point: 'Lord Howe presents his compliments to Lieut[enan]t Popham, and has no occasion to give him any farther trouble on the subject of the proposition lately communicated to him.'[10] Popham had given the First Lord the opportunity to retain him; Howe had snubbed him, and he no longer had any qualms about going his own way.

To proceed, Popham needed three things: a ship; the goodwill of the East India Company, which had a monopoly over British trade in India and China; and permission from the Admiralty to leave the country. The first two were not difficult. William Popham helped him source a ship, named *Madona*.[11] This ship sailed under the colours of the Holy Roman Empire, effectively addressing the second point regarding the prohibition against British citizens trading in East India Company waters, and was based in Ostend (an infamous hub for British merchants illicitly running trade in the east). Any remaining friction with the East India Company was smoothed over by William Popham, who had plenty of mercantile and political connections in Leadenhall Street, Calcutta, and Bombay.

Placating the Admiralty was not so easy. On 12 February, Popham wrote to the Secretary of the Admiralty asking for two years of leave to pursue private business in India. The Board replied they could not grant his request unless Popham obtained permission to trade

---

8   TNA: HCA 32/597, no.426: Boulden Thompson to Popham, [end of 1786].
9   TNA: HCA 32/597, no.473: Popham to Howe, 23 December 1786.
10  TNA: HCA 32/597, no.467: Howe to Popham, 8 January 1787.
11  TNA: HCA 32/597, nos.408, 422: Boulden Thompson to Popham, 31 January 1787.

from the East India Company.¹² Popham did not have 'permission' so much as an assurance the Company's directors would not interfere with him, but he told the Admiralty he had no intention of going anywhere near any East India Company settlements anyway; all he wanted to do was to go to Fredericknagore, a Danish settlement near Calcutta.¹³ The Admiralty Board saw through this transparent excuse immediately, and correspondence lapsed for a little over a month while Popham considered alternative options, such as going north to engage in the fur trade.¹⁴ In the end Popham compromised: would the Admiralty give him leave if he gave up his half-pay?¹⁵ As far as Popham was concerned, he stood to make far more money in trade than he ever would from his lieutenant's pittance. This time the Admiralty agreed and, in April, Popham went to Ostend to take possession of *Madona*. Having escaped Admiralty and East India Company oversight, Popham promptly sold the ship and, with the proceeds, purchased another, *Stadt van Weenen* (*City of Vienna*), in partnership with John McArthur, a kindred spirit who became a lifelong friend and collaborator.

From Ostend, Popham sailed to Bengal, away from Admiralty bureaucracy and towards a new life. 'I wish you luck,' Thomas Boulden Thompson wrote to his old friend 'Pop', '& [am] almost confident of your returning with (I do not say as much as will satisfy you, because I have my doubts about that sum) – a Plumb [sic]!'¹⁶

Because of the East India Company's monopoly over eastern trade, no other British subjects could legally trade in the area without Company permission. Popham did not have this, at least not overtly, but he *did* have family connections through William Popham, who used his influence as far as he was able in his brother's favour. Help also arrived from another, slightly unexpected, quarter. Stephen Popham found out his younger brother was in India, probably through William, and immediately sought to renew contact. Home was in two minds about accepting the proffered olive branch. He had cut Stephen off completely after his brother's betrayal, and even after a decade there was still a marked coldness between them. But Stephen, who had managed to ensconce himself in the East India Company establishment, was too good a contact in Calcutta not to cultivate. Home and Stephen patched up their quarrel, and Stephen introduced his brother to Sir Archibald Campbell, governor of Madras, who in turn presented him to Lord Cornwallis, Governor-General of Bengal.¹⁷ Putting his talents as a marine hydrographer to good use, Popham persuaded Cornwallis to hire him to survey part of the Hooghly River for places to construct dockyards. This ensured the Calcutta establishment came to view Popham as a useful man rather than as a nuisance bent on undermining the Company monopoly. By the end of the year, Popham was well positioned within local Indian trade and political networks. To be absolutely sure of avoiding detection, however, he changed the name of his ship again to the more exotic-sounding *Etrusco*.

---

12   TNA: HCA 32/597, no.464: Philip Stephens to Popham, 19 February 1787.
13   TNA: HCA 32/597, no.463: Philip Stephens to Popham, 22 February 1787.
14   TNA: HCA 32/597, no.408: Boulden Thompson to Popham, 31 January 1787.
15   TNA: HCA 32/597, no.458: Philip Stephens to Popham, 28 March 1787.
16   TNA: HCA 32/597, no.408: Boulden Thompson to Popham, 31 January 1787.
17   TNA: HCA 32/597, no.663: Stephen Popham to Home Popham, 29 July 1788.

Popham had reason to be grateful to Stephen. The two entered into a business partnership, which probably helped Stephen believe his actions in Home's favour had wiped the slate clean between them. But their new-found closeness was only surface-deep and the partnership nearly destroyed it. Stephen did not feel he was getting the cut of the profit he was due, and hinted Home might be cheating him by palming him off with unsaleable goods.[18] When yet another shipment in Stephen's name was deemed impossible to sell, Stephen decided he wanted out of the partnership, offering £1,000 to buy out his share of the cargo.

Professional and personal woes now became inextricably intertwined. The trouble was complicated by the fact Home had also lent money to Stephen, and suspected Stephen was trying to avoid paying him back – not an unreasonable fear, given their mutual past. Passions became heated. 'I did not expect it would come to this,' Stephen fulminated, 'but I must not be ruined in *propria persona* from y[ou]r rigidity … ag[ains]t all rules of Conscience.'[19] Stephen wrote again proposing a meeting, but he could barely contain his anger at the trap he felt Home had led him into:

> You say I am unwilling to accommodate, that I have the Ball at my Foot, that I wish to play alone – the expressions are not founded, are unjust, are indelicate – not founded as I have repeatedly proposed the fairest of all possible modes, an Arbitration by a Friend of each. You say you will have your Friend [John McArthur] only. I have agreed at Cost to that also. Who then has the Ball at his Foot?[20]

There was far more to the dispute than the matter of some unsaleable cargo, and Popham's response to Stephen's bitterness laid bare the depth of his hurt. Ten years after Stephen had left him, alone and friendless, on a Liverpool dockside, he had neither forgiven nor forgotten. Stephen, Home snarled, had made 'excellent official responses, altho' they did not tend to settle the Business; I will beg leave to decline any interview that our dispute may not amuse the Critics.'[21] Stephen was horrified at the prospect of losing his brother forever. He wrote back immediately desiring 'all matters may for ever drop' and agreeing to accept whatever Home and his solicitor McArthur decided to do.[22] This unconditional surrender prevented the dispute destroying more than just the brothers' business partnership, but only just. The two brothers continued in contact until Stephen's death in 1795, but their relationship never recovered. 'You have brought me into pretty scrapes,' Stephen complained to his brother in 1791, only partly in jest. 'You … have behaved unkindly to me.'[23] Popham was more circumspect, but he had misplaced his trust in Stephen twice, once completely, once partially. There would be no third opportunity.

Continued friendship with Stephen nevertheless brought dividends. Stephen had first introduced Home to Cornwallis, and he and William ensured their younger sibling received the protection of other high-ranking members of British Indian society, including Edward

---

18   TNA: HCA 32/597, no.658: Stephen Popham to Home Popham, 10 December 1788.
19   TNA: HCA 32/597: Stephen Popham to Home Popham, 3 February 1789.
20   TNA: HCA 32/597, no.670: Stephen Popham to Home Popham, 8 February 1789.
21   TNA: HCA 32/597, no.669: Home Popham to Stephen Popham, [8 February 1789].
22   TNA: HCA 32/597, no.668: Stephen Popham to Home Popham, 8 February 1789.
23   TNA: HCA 32/597: Stephen Popham to Home Popham, 21 February 1791.

Hay, Secretary to the Government in Bengal, and John Burgh, joint founder of the mercantile and banking firm Burgh and Barber. Burgh was an old friend of William Popham's, and Popham stayed with his family during his frequent visits to Calcutta. Burgh and his wife soon saw Popham as one of their own children. They also had a 17-year-old ward, Elizabeth Moffat Prince, the younger daughter of Captain John Prince of the *Latham* Indiaman. Captain Prince had died in 1783 and his widow had returned to Britain, but his son and two daughters remained in India. The eldest daughter, Frances, was married to James Gray, a captain in the East India Company army and natural son of Sir James Gray, which made her younger sister very well connected indeed in Calcutta society. Elizabeth was also very pretty and a talented singer.[24] Popham found her charming, and she was strongly attracted to the well-dressed, gentlemanly merchant captain. By the time Popham left Calcutta in mid-1788 to survey the Hooghly River, local gossip had the pair married off already.

Popham was abusing the trust of his host, Burgh, in flirting with a girl under his protection. Burgh was unimpressed, suspecting that Popham – whose life kept him constantly on the go between Ostend and various Indian and Chinese ports – was not entirely serious in his courtship: 'I see you heedlessly on the Brink of a Precipice, where a turn only may prove fatal to you.' He suggested Popham should break it off before it began to cause harm. 'Give yourself but time to reflect,' Burgh urged, appealing to Popham's overly well-developed ambition, 'and it is not the voice of Miss Prince, or the Claims of a Divinity alone, that shall seduce you from the Path of Honour, Fame and Fortune.'[25] Popham did not take Burgh's advice. On 19 December 1788, he and Elizabeth Prince were married. Home was 26; Elizabeth was just 18. Thankfully, Burgh came round to the match, but the couple took the precaution of naming their first child after him: Mary Burgh, born in Ostend during the autumn of 1789.[26] A second child, William Charnock, was born in 1791, also at Ostend.

Despite Burgh's fears domesticity would cramp his style, Popham's marriage was very successful. The new Mrs Popham was fully aware she would be apart from her husband for long periods, and she was more than ready to sacrifice her own comfort to guarantee his success. Possibly because of this self-effacement, Elizabeth Popham remained a shadowy presence, rarely mentioned in Popham's letters, even more rarely writing for herself, little more than a blank space at the centre of Popham's growing family. Even friends and family saw her as an extension of her husband: John Burgh referred to her as 'Little Pop', as though she had no independent existence of her own. Popham knew better. 'I have a wife that compensates me for all that is frail in friends and malignant in enemies,' he was quoted as saying and, although he typically managed to centre himself in a compliment about his own wife, the sentiment was sincere.[27] Elizabeth seems to have been a clever, resourceful woman who fully appreciated her husband's fine mind, so much that she was willing to erase her role in his success from the record.

---

24  Spencer (ed.), *Memoirs of William Hickey*, vol.3, p.291.
25  TNA: HCA 32/597, no.332: Burgh to Popham, [1788].
26  TNA: HCA 32/597, no.404: Boulden Thompson to Popham, 4 November 1789.
27  'D.' (possibly Denis O'Bryen), *Morning Post*, 18 September 1820.

The year 1791 found Popham at the peak of his happiness. He was married, with a growing family; he was making a name for himself in trade, and also beginning to make some money. It was also the year he was struck off the Navy List, as he had failed to renew his two years of leave. This was probably because he still did not have official permission from the East India Company to trade, as a result of which the Admiralty was unlikely to allow him to continue trading in eastern seas.[28] Popham did not care. Between 1789 and 1793, he traded between Ostend, India, and Canton in an ostensibly Tuscan ship under a variety of foreign flags, either as supercargo, master, or navigator, depending on whether he was sailing in British waters or coming up to a British-controlled port. The true nationality of his ship, and of the men financing and benefiting from it, was concealed through an elaborate charade of mortgages and counter-mortgages, agreements, and contracts, most undertaken through a variety of Tuscan nationals in return for a part of the proceeds. To help smooth his passages between India and Europe, Popham continued to schmooze East India Company officials. Having surveyed the Hooghly River in 1788, in 1791 he sounded the Straits of Malacca and Prince of Wales Island, discovering a channel to the south that would allow larger ships to pass through, shortening their journey and increasing their trade value. For this service he received the thanks of the governor, some silver plate, and tacit approval to do what he wanted, so long as he did it discreetly.[29]

Everything was not, however, going entirely Popham's way. Around the same time as he was writing up his survey of Prince of Wales Island, the East India Company Directors issued a resolution condemning illicit trade by British subjects in India. Popham lost his insurance as a result of this resolution, and his friends, including McArthur, warned him the Company was determined to crack down on British subjects undermining its monopoly.[30] The line Popham trod between permissibility and outright illegality was growing thin. 'Let me very strongly recommend to your attention to act with the greatest circumspection and caution, respecting your mercantile concerns, as also *to the persons* with whom you have to deal!' warned his old friend Thomas Boulden Thompson.[31] Popham knew he needed to be circumspect. He therefore purchased an American ship named *President Washington*, and renamed it *Etrusco* so as not to invalidate all his ship's papers, warrants, and permits. This allowed Popham to continue trading unnoticed, as the East India Company's officers would not be looking for him in a ship of American construction. If absolutely necessary, the ship's former owner told Popham he was ready to swear it still belonged to him.[32]

The new *Etrusco*'s first journey was to Canton and, in December 1792, Popham entered into one of his usual partnerships to fund his journey home. He agreed with Charles Samuel Constant de Rebecque, a Swiss citizen, and Jean-Baptiste Piron, a Frenchman – both former employees of the French East India Company – to sail a cargo of goods from Canton to Ostend. To ensure *Etrusco* continued to match its disguise as a Tuscan trading vessel, Popham transferred the title of captain to a Tuscan native, Balthazar Giorgi, who signed the

---

28　TNA HCA 42/535: William Popham to Popham, 5 March 1790.
29　TNA: HCA 42/535: letter of 4 November 1791.
30　TNA: HCA 42/535: Paul Maylor to Popham, 1 June 1790; McArthur to Popham, undated; William Popham to Popham, 2 June 1790.
31　TNA: HCA 32/597, no.428: Boulden Thompson to Popham, 22 September 1789.
32　TNA: HCA 42/535: Thomas Willing Francis to Popham, 18 February 1792.

insurance papers and the bill of lading for $126,596.75 worth of cargo, including 400 cases of tea marked 'R.C.' (for Robert Charnock, Popham's European partner). Popham, who only sailed as master when his ship entered British-controlled waters and ports, kept his hands clean. The extent of the subterfuge became clear when, after leaving Canton in January 1793 and stopping in Macao, Sumatra, and Java, *Etrusco* crossed paths in April with a Portuguese sloop, which revealed war had broken out on 1 February between Britain and revolutionary France. Popham and Constant de Rebecque, part-owners of the cargo, decided to rewrite the original bill of lading to leave out Jacques Baptiste Piron, a Frenchman whose goods could be taken by a British vessel as a prize.

*Etrusco* reached Crookhaven in Ireland after a six-month journey; with Giorgi masquerading as captain, everything went smoothly as the ship re-provisioned. For a while, it looked like Popham might reach Ostend unmolested. At this point, however, he overreached himself. *Etrusco* stopped off Hastings to take on a pilot for Ostend – and drop off the 400 chests of tea marked 'R.C.', where they were quietly collected by an associate of Robert Charnock.[33] This was a clear instance of smuggling, and Popham's presence off Hastings attracted the attention of Captain Mark Robinson of HMS *Brilliant*, who intercepted him before he reached the safety of Ostend Roads. By the end of the month, *Etrusco*'s cargo was before the High Court of Admiralty to be condemned as a prize; *Etrusco* itself lay captured at Deptford; and Popham, who had escaped to Ostend, began a lengthy legal process to reclaim his proceeds from a ship he swore blind had been carrying foreign-owned (but definitely not French) goods under the colours of a friendly nation. Popham's career as a merchant trader had reached a sudden, inglorious, but certainly not unpredictable, end.

Not for the first time, Popham had to rethink his whole future – and fast. When he had last had to make a significant life decision, in 1787, he had been poor, but single and unattached. Now he was married, with a growing family to feed. He had no patrons to fall back on; he had no exploits to show in his favour, other than some services rendered to the East India Company, which was unlikely to show much countenance to a man who had been undercutting their monopoly for years. Popham, however, always considered himself to be exceptional, and with good reason. He had three advantages: he had been almost constantly at sea since he was 15; he had considerable navigation and hydrographic skills; and, last but not least, he was persistent. He therefore decided to try and get himself reinstated as a lieutenant in the Royal Navy.

This was a startling decision to make, particularly as his connection with *Etrusco* began to come out very swiftly after its capture, as Popham's former crew members spilled the beans about his involvement under interrogation by the High Court of Admiralty. But Popham did have one major thing in his favour. Lord Howe had been replaced at the Admiralty by the Earl of Chatham, a politician who was more susceptible to influence than to professional imperatives, notoriously easy-going, and not exactly a stickler for detail. Armed with nothing but a few lukewarm letters from the East India Company Court of Directors and his own tremendous self-confidence, Popham engaged in a two-pronged attack. On the one side, he laid siege to Philip Stephens, the Secretary of the Admiralty, with a barrage of letters attaching copies of his African charts and his survey of Prince of Wales Island. On the other,

---

33   Evidence collected in TNA: HCA 42/535.

he tracked down his old acquaintance, Henry Martin, now Comptroller to the Navy, and pressured him to intercede personally with the First Lord.[34] Amazingly, it worked. Within a fortnight Popham took up his first professional employment of the new war, as agent for transports at Ostend.

---

34   TNA: HCA 42/535; TNA: ADM 1/3062: Popham to Philip Stephens, 21, 28 August 1793.

# Message Understood

*'The affirmative flag hoisted at the last station and repeated'*

---

# 4

# Flanders, 1793–1796

*2993: I will report your zeal*

'This appointment of Popham I find makes much Noise at Ostend,' Rear Admiral John Macbride wrote shortly after his arrival off the Flemish coast. 'The Employ he has been in has raised it.' Popham may have escaped *Etrusco* before its capture, but rumours of his involvement with the ship dogged his entire career. Like many other officers on the British staff, however, Macbride was willing to overlook Popham's background because he was 'very clever' and knew 'almost everything'.[1]

After deposing Louis XVI in 1792, France had been invaded by Austria and Prussia, which had been joined in a military alliance by Britain, the Netherlands, Spain, the Two Sicilies, Portugal, and Sardinia after Louis' execution in January 1793. Despite initial defeats, France had been unexpectedly successful in its war of self-defence: it had pushed enemy forces back into Flanders and Savoy and was expanding to reach its 'natural borders' at the Rhine, the Alps, and the Pyrenees. The British failure at Dunkirk had increased the importance of several other Flemish coastal towns, including Nieuwpoort and Ostend, where Popham's wife and growing family had lived since 1790 – the place Popham called home when not on his voyages. As Macbride's letter hinted, Popham had wormed his way to the heart of the war effort because of his familiarity with the main theatre of war.

Despite this, Popham knew his specialist knowledge was not enough to overcome past transgressions. He would have to get himself noticed, which would not be easy, as the position of transport agent was not especially glamorous and was often considered a dead-end job.[2] Transport agents liaised between Army and Navy, smoothing the embarkation and disembarkation of men, finding and preparing transports to receive troops, and coordinating them while at sea. Popham's appointment suggested that, while the Admiralty Board was happy to place him back on the list of lieutenants, it was aware of his background and not ready to place him in the way of promotion or emolument. But Popham never considered himself limited by the terms of an official remit. He did intelligence work for Rear Admiral Macbride, shuttled between London and Flanders with dispatches, and carried

---

1 TNA: WO 1/177, f.79: Macbride to Nepean, Confidential, 14 September 1793.
2 Rodger, *Command of the Ocean*, p.216; Moira Bracknall, 'Lord Spencer, Patronage and Commissioned Officers' Careers, 1794–1801', PhD Thesis, University of Exeter, January 2008, p.92.

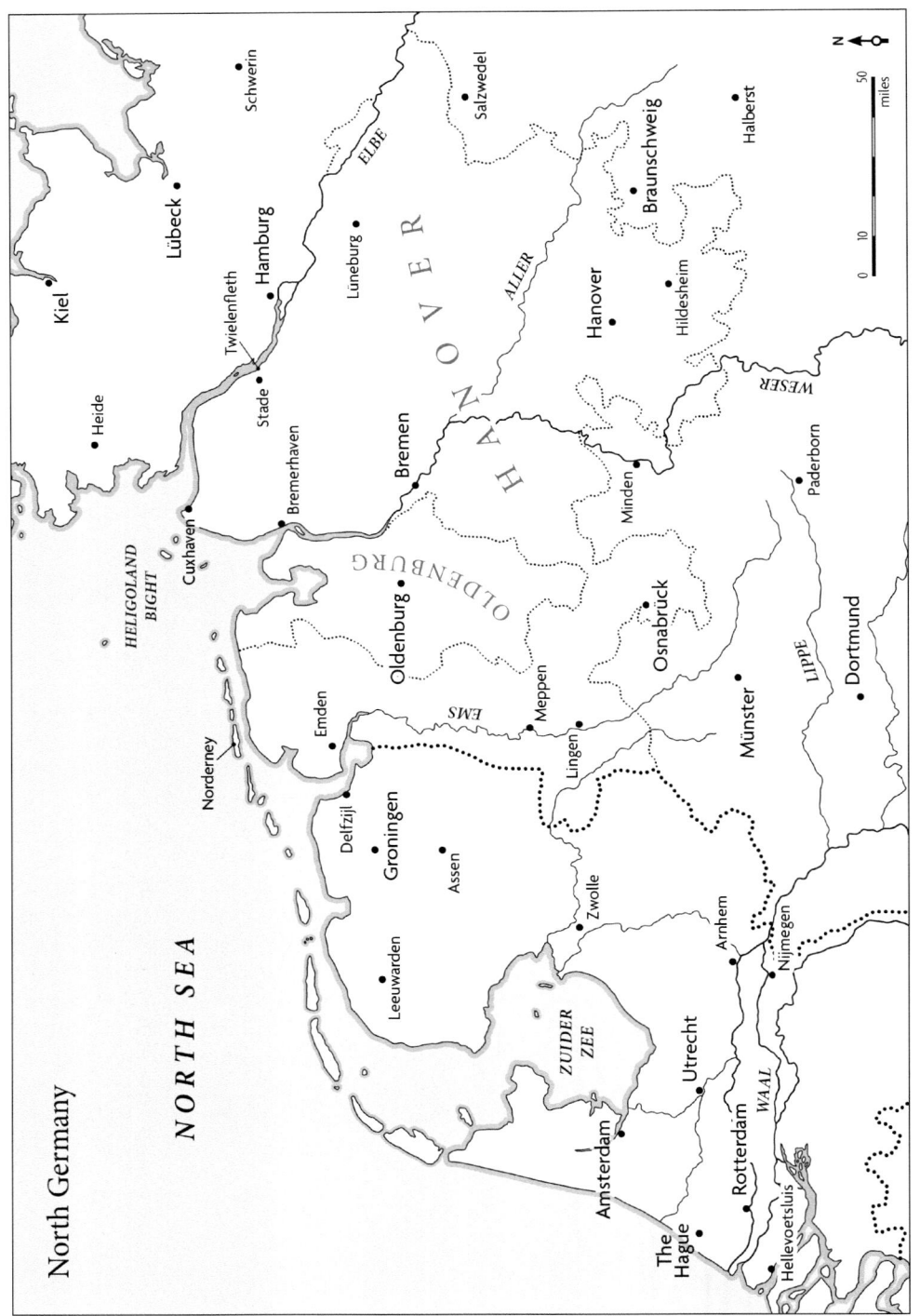

Territory of the campaign in Flanders and Germany, 1794–1796.

a verbal report to the government of the Duke of York's latest setbacks at Dunkirk.³ On his return to Flanders, he leaned upon his old network of contacts around Ostend – local fishermen, merchants, traders, smugglers – to form an auxiliary force he called 'Sea Fencibles'. These men assisted in the defence of Nieuwpoort, under siege from a force of 12,000 Frenchmen.⁴ Thanks to a timely reinforcement under Lieutenant General Sir Charles Grey, Nieuwpoort did not fall and, by November, the enemy had been temporarily driven back across the border into France.⁵ Popham also provided 100 artillerymen to man the guns in Nieuwpoort's defence, and his strenuous efforts earned Grey's trust and respect.⁶

The British war effort was falling apart, and this made it easier for Popham to work

Sir Charles Grey, by J. Collyer after Sir Thomas Lawrence. (Public domain, The Miriam and Ira D. Wallach Division of Art, Prints and Photographs, The New York Public Library)

beyond the limits of his brief. Not everyone was impressed, of course. Popham never liked sharing the limelight, nor was he a good subordinate. The Captain of the Port of Ostend, Captain Robert Bisset, nominally Popham's immediate superior, complained Popham's activities left him 'only as a looker on, with my hands in my pocket'.⁷ Although Bisset also admitted Popham was 'uncommonly clever and clear headed',⁸ others felt he was all show and no substance: 'Popham I believe talks too much and does too little.'⁹ Popham probably knew he was being talked of in such terms: he wrote, sarcastically, 'I suppose it was

---

3  *Kentish Gazette*, 13 September 1793.
4  Philip Ball, *Neither Up Nor Down: The British Army and the Flanders Campaign, 1793–1795* (Warwick: Helion & Co., 2020), p.173.
5  Steve Brown, *The Duke of York's Campaign in Flanders: Fighting the French Revolution, 1793–1795* (Barnsley: Pen & Sword, 2018), p.121.
6  Martin Robson, *A History of the Royal Navy: The Napoleonic Wars* (London: I.B. Tauris, 2014), p.8.
7  TNA: WO 1/167, f.869: Bisset to Nepean, 13 December 1793.
8  TNA: WO 1/167, f.1013: Bisset to Nepean, 27 [December] 1793.
9  BL: Add MS 46702, f.174: Captain Anstruther to Don, 1 December 1794. Many thanks to Philip Ball for this reference.

not *supposed* in my Department to think.'[10] All his 'talking too much' did, however, mean Popham's name became known in the highest circles as a man to watch. In March, the Duke of York appointed Popham to the post of Superintendent of Inland Navigation in Flanders and pressed for his promotion to master and commander.[11] The promotion was rejected, but the command meant that Popham could follow the army inland after its defeat at Tourcoing. In June, the French took Ypres; in July they finally captured Nieuwpoort, cutting the British off from coastal supply and communication. The British and their Austrian allies moved towards the Rhine, settling headquarters at Arnhem in October.[12] This retreat took them across extensive wetlands criss-crossed with rivers, channels, and dykes. Popham's role as Superintendent of Inland Navigation was more important than ever, and the Duke of York got his commissary, Sir Brook Watson, to write home to the Navy Board again recommending Popham for promotion.[13] Transport agents were not often promoted, but with the Duke's patronage behind him, for Popham it was only a matter of time.

And Popham was certainly earning that promotion. He made his value obvious at the siege of Nijmegen, a fortress on the River Waal between the Netherlands and Germany, which the Duke of York and the Austrian commander *Feldzeugmeister* Graf von Clerfait had hoped to use as a base for future operations.[14] The French, with 30,000 men, closed in on this British, Hanoverian, and Dutch-held outpost at the end of October 1794. On 27 October, Popham described the 4,000 coalition troops in the town as 'press[ed] very hard' by the enemy. Twenty thousand Austrian reinforcements were on the way, but Popham suspected the garrison would have to evacuate before they arrived. This was a problem, as Nijmegen backed directly onto the Waal, which could only be crossed by a fragile pontoon bridge of boats designed as a line of communication with the allies. In the meantime, Popham tried to keep the garrison supplied by sneaking boats laden with provisions into the town under the noses of the French pickets. Even so, he estimated the garrison only had three days of provisions left.[15]

As the Duke of York dithered about what to do, Popham suggested taking 100 British seamen to Nijmegen to ensure the pontoon bridge – the garrison's last link with the rest of the coalition army – remained in place.[16] With this reassurance, and with the knowledge that Austrians reinforcements were on their way, the Duke of York agreed to harass the French from the east in the hope that the Austrians would reach the town before it was forced to surrender. He therefore sent 15 battalions of British troops into the garrison and ordered its commander, *General der Cavallerie* Wallmoden, to hold firm.[17]

Despite a brief sortie by the coalition garrison, the French had Nijmegen completely surrounded by 7 November. One of their first concerns was to heave guns into position to fire on the pontoon bridge, which they duly did, sinking several boats. At this point

---

10   BL: Add MS 46702, f.189: Popham to Captain Beardsley, 1 January 1795.
11   Popham, *A Damned Cunning Fellow*, p.46.
12   TNA: ADM 1/3062: Popham to Nepean, 1 November 1794.
13   TNA: HCA 42/535: Sir Brook Watson to the Navy Board, 27 July 1794.
14   Brown, *The Duke of York's Flanders Campaign*, p.228.
15   TNA: ADM 1/3062: Popham to Philip Stephens, 1 November 1794.
16   Popham, *A Damned Cunning Fellow*, p.47.
17   Ball, *Neither Up Nor Down*, pp.360–361.

The Duke of York, by William Dickinson after John Hoppner, 1791. (Public domain, Anne S.K. Brown Military Collection, Brown University Library)

the British and their allies received the news that the promised Austrian reinforcements were not coming after all. Popham now advised immediate evacuation: although he could repair the damaged bridge, he could not guarantee its being able to bear cavalry or artillery under continued bombardment.[18] The evacuation took place over 7–8 November. As far as the British and Hanoverians were concerned, it was a success, even though the bridge was so damaged the men were only able to pass two abreast, knee-deep in water.[19] While the Dutch were being evacuated, however, a French marksman shot away one of the hawsers connecting the pontoon bridge to the shore, leaving the better part of a battalion stranded. According to one British account, the Dutch simply refused to cross the rickety bridge: Popham himself wrote, scornfully, that the Dutch had 'preferred surrendering to the French, to the very trifling risk of being drowned'.[20] Despite this, Popham's role in maintaining the bridge as long as possible under fire was recognised by all. Over the years, Popham's exploits at Nijmegen grew in the telling, but there was no doubt he had done well under trying circumstances: 'The garrison never would have got off, but for the exertions of Captain [sic] Popham ... whose perseverance in repeatedly repairing the bridge, under a very heavy fire of shot and shell, will ever do him honour.'[21]

Popham did not have long to wait for his reward. At the end of the month he received the news that he was now officially master and commander.[22] This promotion was almost the Duke of York's last act as commander-in-chief in Flanders, as he was recalled a few days later to Britain. His replacement Lieutenant General William Harcourt, however, had been York's second-in-command for some time and knew Popham's worth. Over Christmas 1794, Harcourt ordered Popham to establish lines of communication across the Waal. This was a much easier task than usual, because the winter had been especially hard and the Waal had frozen over almost completely. 'The Compliments of the Day to you and your Household,' Popham wrote, jauntily, to the Deputy Adjutant-General on Christmas Day. 'The River has taken but [is] not strong enough to bear [troops]; we are laying planks ... Pray for Snow as long as the Frost lasts, and Pichegru [the French commander] may amuse himself by looking at it. I wish you a merry day.'[23] By 30 December, Popham had established a strong enough passage for the artillery of the 14th, 19th, 57th, and 63rd regiments, along with nine wagons of sick men, Lord Cathcart's baggage, and 61 wagons and horses.[24]

Despite Popham's fervent prayers, the snow did not last, and Pichegru also took advantage of the ice to cross the Waal with 70,000 men on 10 January in pursuit of the coalition forces.[25] The French entered Amsterdam mid-month, cutting off a possible retreat into the

---

18  TNA: WO 1/167, f.101: Craig to Dundas, 10 November 1794.
19  Lewis T. Jones, *An Historical Journal of the British Campaign on the Continent, in the Year 1794; with the Retreat through Holland, in the Year 1795* ... (London: T. Egerton, 1797), pp.141–142; BL: Add MS 46702, f.102: De Burgh to Craig, [November 1794].
20  Brown, *The Duke of York's Flanders Campaign*, pp.229–230; Ball, *Neither Up Nor Down*, p.363; BL: Add MS 46702, f.102: De Burgh to Craig, [November 1794]; TNA: ADM 1/3062: Popham to Philip Stephens, 9 November 1794.
21  Jones, *An Historical Journal*, p.142.
22  TNA: HCA 42/535: E. Hewgill to Popham, 30 November 1794.
23  BL: Add MS 46702, f.159: Popham to Don, 'Xmas Day 1794'.
24  BL: Add MS 46702, f.168: Popham to Don, 30 December 1794.
25  Ball, *Neither Up Nor Down*, p.380; Brown, *The Duke of York's Flanders Campaign*, p.246.

View of Nijmegen, by H.J. Backer, 1836. (Public domain, Rijksmuseum, Netherlands)

Netherlands, and on the night of 16 January the British and their allies were forced to retreat towards Hanover and the North Sea coast. Popham was still with them, smoothing their path as much as possible, but there was not much he could do to ease a truly harrowing experience. The weather was bitterly cold – by some accounts as low as -20°C – and the deep snow made it difficult for many regiments to find a path, especially in the dark. Up to 6,000 soldiers may have frozen to death over the first four days of the retreat; one source claimed that, of the 34,000 men who began it, only 7,000 made it to Hanover, frittered away by French attacks, desertion, and the weather.[26] Again, Popham performed a dual role, organising the logistics of bringing the army safely across wet, boggy ground while providing auxiliary manpower through a body of seamen placed under his command. He and his seamen helped the Austrians construct batteries, but this only briefly delayed the French advance. Popham and his men had to flee across the pontoon bridge he had constructed to ease the retreat, burning it behind them to prevent the French following.[27] At least the weather now turned warmer, but this brought its own problems for Popham's department: crossing troops across swollen rivers full of ice floes was considerably more difficult than laying sanded planks down over solid ice.[28] At the same time, Popham proved himself vital in arranging the transportation of the many sick and wounded from Emden, at the mouth of the Ems river, and with hiring boats to keep lines of communication open with Britain.[29]

---

26  Carole Divall, *General Sir Ralph Abercromby and the French Revolutionary Wars 1792–1801* (Barnsley: Pen & Sword, 2018), p.63.
27  BL: Add MS 46703, f.8: Popham to Don, 16 January 1795.
28  TNA: ADM 1/2312: Popham to Nepean, 10 February 1795.
29  TNA: WO 1/172, f.195: Popham to Nepean, 23 January 1795.

The disastrous end of the campaign placed a great deal of responsibility on Popham's shoulders and this, along with the praises of the Duke of York back in London, now elevated him fully to the notice of the decision makers. Popham's duties were about to intensify, as the broader diplomatic picture shifted. The Austrians were disenchanted with their coalition experience, the Prussians were about to sign an armistice, and Spain was fighting off a French invasion of its own. The British could no longer remain on the continent without major allies. The troops would have to be brought home, and Popham, in his capacity as transport agent, was tasked with arranging it. Transports needed to be found in a hurry, and price, to an extent, was no object. Popham's trading contacts now came in helpful. In mid-February, Popham was on Norderney Island at the mouth of the Ems, pulling all the strings in his power to purchase suitable gunboats for the British to defend their embarkation – at £1,500 a pop, however, he promised to exercise some restraint.[30] 'I shall do everything in my Power, to facilitate the Navigation of this River,' he told Harcourt, signing himself off in his new role: 'Director of Navigation to the Army'.[31]

Over the next few months Popham bustled between Norderney and London, gathering as many ships as he could at Bremen Lehe, on the Weser, to carry the British troops home. Having run out of British transports, which were mainly being used to transport troops to the West Indies, Popham mined old trading contacts to provide ships and pilots familiar with the Ems and Weser river basins. He particularly exploited connections with the shipping company of Parish & Co. in Hamburg, having been friendly with the owner, John Parish, when captain of *Etrusco*. Popham's flitting visits to England paid off when, on 4 March, HMS *Daedalus* braved the bad weather and arrived off Germany with 100 transports, a cutter, and six victuallers. Once unloaded, the victuallers doubled as transports to take the wounded and sick men home.[32] Once the wounded had been sent off, Popham oversaw the embarkation of 12,000 British infantry at Bremen Lehe and foreign troops from Stade.

Popham thought he was the only man capable of overseeing the embarkation – 'much confusion may arise from my not being present' – and, although he was never one to underplay his contribution to anything, others agreed.[33] Reports that Popham might be removed to another service led to one general writing home in alarm to protest.[34] Coming so close on the heels of his actions during the British retreat across Germany, Popham's activities at the mouth of the Ems won him the recognition he needed. The Admiralty and Transport Board recognised Popham's talent for balancing the complicated logistical tasks necessary in organising transportation for such large numbers of troops and made Popham superior to the agent for transports operating in the area.[35] At the end of March, as the first shipment of troops arrived home, the Duke of York wrote to the First Lord of the Admiralty personally recommending Popham's promotion to the coveted rank of post-captain. This rank usually required the new captain to have a ship, but in this case the Admiralty made

---

30  BL: Add MS 46703, f.146: Popham to Don, 15 February 1795.
31  TNA: ADM 1/2312: Popham to Nepean, 20 February 1795.
32  BL: Add MS 46704, ff.9, 23: Popham to Don, 2, 4 March 1795.
33  BL: Add MS 46704, f.92: Popham to Don, 20 March 1795.
34  TNA: WO 1/173, f.479: David Dundas to Henry Dundas, 14 September 1795.
35  BL: Add MS 46704, f.501: Popham to Captain Sotheby, 15 March 1795.

an exception. And so, on 4 April 1795, Popham was gazetted post-captain, even though the only ship of war he had ever commanded had been the ill-fated *Shelanagig* in 1781.

Popham remained in Germany while the evacuation continued. Between 12 August and 31 October 1795, Popham hired 82 ships through Parish & Co., each covered by separate terms and conditions. He was forced into some financial haggling to sort all this out: the going price for transports in Britain at the time was 13 shillings per ton, whereas he chartered vessels at 18–19 shillings per ton, along with giving the owners 15 percent primage on the freight; 'without this last clause,' Popham said, 'no person would agree.'[36] But the situation was desperate, as Major General David Dundas, now commanding the remaining British troops, recognised: 'I am to hope … the necessary and essential aid of Money has not been with-held, without which he [Popham] can make no progress.'[37] Popham's attention to detail was certainly meticulous: he built special wharves for embarking and disembarking troops, had special rooms for the sick built in all larger ships, and arranged the provisioning of every ship himself, importing provisions where necessary.[38] He even went to Hamburg to make the arrangements, inspecting all the ships in person.[39] 'I … beg you always to consider of the difficulties I have to contend [with],' he told David Dundas, adding proudly, 'but the more they are, the more gratified I shall be in overcoming them.'[40] By this time Popham had several assistant transport agents, but Popham was not good at delegating and, by the end of October 1795, he had had enough. 'I never was so fag'd with Dogs and Devils,' he complained to Lieutenant Colonel George Don. 'I wish the Business was at an End, and if ever I have anything more to do with Transports, you may transport me to Botany Bay.'[41]

While Popham busied himself chartering yet more ships to deal with unexpected overflows of men and horses, troops began to board off Twielenfleth on 4 December 1795. The last transport did not sail until the very end of January 1796.[42] As he left the continent behind him, Popham could reflect on a job well done, and one that had brought him promotion, the patronage of the Duke of York, and the notice of Secretary of State for War Henry Dundas and Prime Minister William Pitt.[43] It was not bad for a man who, only two and a half years previously, had been forced to plead for reinstatement on the list of Navy lieutenants. Popham may have been a post-captain without a ship, but he had no expectation of remaining unemployed: indeed, less than a month after his return to London, he received notice that the Secretary of State for War wanted to offer him another job.[44]

---

36  Mary Ellen Condon, 'The Administration of the Transport Service During the War Against Revolutionary France, 1793–1802', PhD Thesis, University of London, 1968, pp.121–128, esp. p.128.
37  TNA: WO 1/173, f.585: David Dundas to Henry Dundas, 5 October 1795.
38  Condon, 'The Administration of the Transport Service', pp.128–129.
39  BL: Add MS 46705, f.128: Popham to Don, 14 October 1795.
40  TNA: WO 1/173, f.707: Popham to David Dundas, 9 October 1795.
41  BL: Add MS 46705, f.136: Popham to Don, 23 October 1795.
42  BL: Add MS 46705, ff.232, 238, 246, 275, 280: Popham to Don, 5 December 1795–29 January 1796.
43  TNA: ADM 1/798, f.385: Pitt to Dundas, 24 September [1795], showing the Prime Minister's personal interest in Popham's ability to secure 'as many more Transports as possible'.
44  TNA: ADM 1/2315: Popham's statement to the Admiralty Board, 25 January 1797.

# 5

# Ostend, 1796–1798

*2679: I can burn or destroy them, but not without a good deal of risk*

On 14 November 1796, Popham's carriage took him from his house in Sackville Street to Knightrider Street, in the shadow of St Paul's Cathedral. Here he entered Doctor's Commons and passed through the three great wooden arches to the High Court of Admiralty, where he was due to appear to give evidence in person regarding his claim to recover the proceeds of his ship *Etrusco* and its cargo.

More than three years had passed since *Etrusco*'s capture by Captain Robinson. Since then, the ship and its cargo had been condemned by the High Court of Admiralty as a lawful prize on the grounds that Popham had been 'engaged in a contraband and fraudulent Trade, prohibited by the existing Laws of this Country'. To Captain Robinson's dismay, the court also concluded that *Etrusco* 'must be considered as without a legal Owner'. This meant the ship could not be turned over to its captors, but was instead legally forfeit to the Crown.[1]

Robinson was challenging this judgement, but Popham was not especially worried. He was pleased to know Robinson would not benefit from his seizure of *Etrusco*, and hoped he might eventually be successful in his own appeal to be recognised as the ship's owner and part-owner of its valuable cargo. Challenging the Admiralty court's original judgement, however, required, if not outright lying, at least a little gentle manipulation of the truth. Still, as Popham stood before the High Court and swore not to mislead it, he probably believed he was right in principle, if not in strict fact. Nor did he merely have principle behind him: he had the protection and patronage of men high up in the government, and of the King's second son, the Duke of York. With such men to back him, and a service record to counterbalance any transgressions he had formerly committed, how could he fail?

As Popham delivered his prepared statement, the clerks of the court bent over their foolscap to take down his words. He told the court he was a former resident of Ostend but now an officer in the King's Navy, in which character he claimed to be 'the true, lawful, and sole Owner and Proprietor' of *Etrusco*, along with one-third of the goods it had been carrying. This cargo consisted of several thousand chests and bags full of sugar, 153 chests of chinaware, 44,000 canes, 95 pecouls of China root, 127 of rhubarb, 560 of sago, and 155 of benjamin, 2,400 pieces of nankeen, and 348 chests of tea. Popham did not put a figure to

---

1   TNA: HCA 42/535: case on behalf of the Crown, [1795].

all this, but his business partner Constant de Rebecque had also previously laid claim to his third of the cargo to the tune of an estimated £30,000 to £40,000.² Confident that the court would find in his favour, Popham gave no evidence, but attached a ream of unrelated affidavits from Cornwallis, the Duke of York, Lieutenant General Harcourt, and others, designed to show how high he could reach with his political protection.³

Unfortunately for Popham, the High Court of Admiralty needed more than a collection of letters signed by big names to be impressed. Six months after Popham appeared before it, the court stood by its original ruling.⁴ At least Popham could take malicious cheer in the fact that Captain Robinson's appeal to be recognised as the legal captor of *Etrusco* was also rejected, placing the man's chances of benefiting from Popham's discomfiture further out of reach. But it was small comfort, particularly as Popham's career had again hit the doldrums. Despite all his hopes for immediate re-employment, Popham had become entangled in a bureaucratic nightmare that kept him in England, bored and annoyed, for nearly two years.

Almost the minute Popham stepped off the *Mary Frances* transport in February 1796, accompanying the last shipment of troops from Bremen Lehe, he was called before the Transport Board to account for the vast expense of hiring ships from Parish & Co. The Board had been unhappy for some time at the amount of money Popham had been spending. As far back as October the previous year, Major General Dundas had been forced to intercede personally on Popham's behalf when the Transport Office threatened not to honour any further bills he ran up in Hamburg.⁵ Now the Board accused Popham of exceeding his authority in chartering the ships at all, let alone at such a cost.⁶

Popham reacted in the way he always did to any hint of blame: he recast himself as the victim. 'What I have to complain of,' he thundered, 'is, that the Commissioners of Transports have converted an enquiry … into a persecution.'⁷ This was the first, but by no means last, time Popham would claim persecution at the hands of his enemies. Frustration heightened his sense of grievance. Until the Transport Board had worked through its various reports on his expenditures, and until the Treasury solicitors had managed to come to grips with the case, Popham could not be officially employed. The Secretary of State for War, Henry Dundas, shelved his plans to send Popham on a new mission, and Popham was uncomfortably aware that the longer he remained on shore, the more likely the politicians were to forget about him.

Financial issues were a recurring theme throughout his career, and Popham grew to have a reputation. Nevertheless, Popham's trading activities in the 1780s and 1790s, although

---

2    TNA: HCA 42/535: appendix to the *Etrusco* case, [1796].
3    TNA: HCA 42/535: appendix to the *Etrusco* case, [1796].
4    TNA: HCA 42/535: case on behalf of Popham and Robert Charnock, [April 1797].
5    TNA: WO 1/173, f.781: David Dundas to Henry Dundas, 15 October 1795.
6    Condon, 'The Administration of the Transport Service', p.134.
7    Home Popham, *A Letter from Captain Home Popham, to the Lords of the Admiralty; with the Report of the Commissioners of the Transport Board, to which it is an Answer. And a Supplement and Appendix* (London: privately published, 1797), p.4.

they certainly spoke of a man unafraid to break the law in the pursuit of greater profits, could lead to over-hasty conclusions. The evacuation of British troops from the continent in 1795 was a matter of emergency. The army was stranded in territory where the French had otherwise carried all before them and dogged by the enemy at every step. Britain could not afford to abandon those men: by the start of 1795 it was becoming clear that the army sent to the West Indies was being devastated by disease. Recruitment was a constant worry for the authorities, and under these circumstances any soldiers who could be saved were precious. At the same time that the government insisted the continental troops should be returned swiftly and safely, Popham was also grappling with the problem that the Admiralty did not have enough transports available. The only solution was to hire local ones, and quickly, and the need for speed did not put Popham in a position to negotiate the most favourable terms. He relied on his contacts in Hamburg to make deals, many of them expensive, but he could (and did) argue that he had been given no choice, and probably trusted that unprecedented circumstances would stand as an excuse.

Popham often defended himself against criticism by claiming to act in an excess of zeal. This might sound specious, but in this case it was probably true, and luckily the politicians at the War Department agreed. They, not the Admiralty, had received glowing reports about Popham's activities as Agent for Transports and Superintendent of Internal Navigation; they had seen the direct consequences of Popham's work as he evacuated a whole army safely under trying conditions. There is no doubt that Popham's work in the mid-1790s struck exactly the right note in Whitehall. When the Transport Board case was finally settled in September 1797 in Popham's favour, it was probably achieved with pressure from Henry Dundas. But Popham was still afraid some of the mud from the Transport Board's investigation might stick. His ghosts were not far behind him, particularly when the *Etrusco* case began to be reported again in the newspapers. He needed to keep the attention, and favour, of his new patrons to ensure future employment and help him outrun his past.

One of Popham's most celebrated creations grew out of this desperate need to be useful. While waiting to be cleared by the Transport Board, Popham turned his thoughts to a thorny strategic problem: national defence. France had been threatening a British invasion since the beginning of the war, but the collapse of the First Coalition made the prospect much more immediate. Repeatedly defeated in its Italian territories, Austria finally made peace in 1797 at Campo Formio and, with virtually no major opponents left on the continent, France turned its attention to the British Isles. An attempted landing in Ireland at the end of 1796 only failed because of poor weather, and in February 1797 a small French force landed successfully at Fishguard, in Wales. This was swiftly rounded up by the militia, but French boots had touched British soil, and the invasion provoked a run on the banks that led to the suspension of cash payments. A thousand more French troops landed in Ireland when that country rebelled against Britain in 1798, although they were again defeated before they could do much damage and a further 3,000 men were intercepted at sea. But these episodes set a precedent, and as France built up its forces on its northern coast, British policy makers focused on the likelihood of meeting a French invasion again.

Under these circumstances, the government was open to ideas from knowledgeable members of the public, and Popham took full advantage. In January 1798, he drew up a memorandum for the First Lord of the Admiralty, Lord Spencer, which also found its way onto the desk of Secretary of State Dundas. Popham's proposals were bold: instead of waiting to defeat the enemy on land, they should be repulsed before they had even had time to recover from their journey and form up on shore. In a related report delivered to General Sir Charles Grey, Popham's acquaintance from Ostend, Popham included a survey of the French-facing coast, drawn up with a mariner's eye (and, perhaps, that of a former smuggler), noting the points where an enemy might find it easiest to introduce an attacking force.[8] To patrol the coast and assist in general defence duties, Popham proposed an entirely new auxiliary defence force of volunteer fishermen and seafaring men: the Sea Fencibles, named after the similar force he had raised in 1793 in defence of Nieuwpoort.[9]

Popham's Sea Fencibles proposal was officially adopted by the government through an Order in Council dated 14 May 1798. He suggested dividing the south and south-eastern coast of Britain into districts, each commanded by three captains and subdivided into areas under the authority of a lieutenant. The duties of the Sea Fencibles would include patrolling beaches and maintaining a fleet of armed vessels to defend Britain's commercial shipping against French privateers. They were also intended to keep watch on enemy movements and help harass an invasion flotilla. Their duties later expanded to include manning coastal fortifications and providing intelligence, informing the government of the strengths and weaknesses in defending various places around the coast.[10] Popham persuaded several authorities to endorse his plan. Sir Charles Grey, who had witnessed Popham's first Sea Fencibles corps in 1793, was particularly enthusiastic, although he sounded a note of caution about the need for steady officers to command a body that would be composed partly of smugglers.[11] This, along with the promised exemption of volunteers from the impress, turned out to be one of the strongest criticisms against the Sea Fencibles. The corps also proved expensive, rising to a cost of over £150,000 a year before being disbanded in 1810, but not before between 25,000 and 30,000 seafaring men – fishermen, pilots, elderly sailors, and bargemen – had taken advantage of the impress exemption to join.[12]

The Pitt government looked favourably on Popham's plan and sent him on a five-day journey around Hastings, Rye, Folkestone, and Dover to gauge local readiness to join the Sea Fencibles. This also doubled as an intelligence mission: Popham was specifically told to try 'the Temper of the People' regarding the government more generally, at a time when

---

8    Julian S. Corbett (ed.), *Private Papers of George, Second Earl Spencer, First Lord of the Admiralty 1794–1801* (London: Navy Records Society, vol.48, 1924), vol.2, pp.263–268, 306–311.
9    'Fencible' was short for 'defensible' and indicated a body of men raised for local defence.
10  James Davey, *In Nelson's Wake: The Navy and the Napoleonic Wars* (New Haven, London: Yale University Press, 2015), pp.167–168; Brian Lavery, *Nelson's Navy: The Ships, Men and Organisation, 1793–1815* (London: Conway Maritime Press, 1989), pp.275–277; Daniel MacCannell, *Coastal Defences of the British Empire in the Revolutionary and Napoleonic Eras* (Barnsley: Pen & Sword Military, 2021, e-book edition).
11  Corbett (ed.), *Spencer Papers*, vol.2, pp.294–295.
12  Nicholas Rogers, 'The Sea Fencibles, Loyalism and the Reach of the State', in Mark Philp (ed.), *Resisting Napoleon: The British Response to the Threat of Invasion, 1797–1815* (Ashgate: Routledge, 2006, e-book edition).

radicalism and republican feeling was feared to be high.[13] Shortly afterwards, Popham was appointed to command the Sea Fencibles between Deal and Beachy Head, the most exposed part of the southern coast, a command he held – at least nominally – until 1800.[14] This also involved advising the local military commander (Sir Charles Grey again) on repelling an invasion, something Popham, despite his usual protests that he was too lowly and unqualified to presume, greedily admitted was 'not only my Duty but very much my Inclination'.[15] However submissive he wanted to appear, humility was never his most salient characteristic.

Single-handedly organising Britain's defence was not enough for Popham, who still wanted to serve and be noticed. Thankfully, the end of the Transport Board debacle meant that, by the second quarter of 1798, he was free to take the fight to the enemy again. Popham had had nearly two years to think and he had plenty of ideas, which he revealed, informally, to Sir Charles Grey, military commander of the southern coast. One of the points Popham singled out for attack was Ostend, the biggest port on the Flemish coast, a likely port for launching an invasion and a place Popham knew well. Grey knew first-hand how adroitly Popham could exploit his local knowledge of the Dutch and Flemish coasts, and this was probably why Popham went to him first rather than to his naval superiors.

Popham's plan was to destroy the lock and sluice gates of the canal running between Bruges and Saas, to prevent troops intended for Britain being brought via that route to Ostend. This was without mentioning the damage to the enemy's inland and East Indian trade by destroying the canal, which Popham hoped would stoke bad feeling in the population towards the French government. All Popham asked for to accomplish his aims was about 2,000 infantry, a company of artillery armed with four howitzers and six fieldpieces, and about 23 ships, including bomb vessels, frigates, carronade brigs, and gunboats, along with several cutters or tenders for communicating with the shore. Popham insisted on the use of frigates with their lower gun decks cleared for troops rather than transports, which he claimed were unsuitable for such a service. 'It is supposed the Troops can be disembarked, perform the Service, and be embarked again in 8 or 10 Hours,' he concluded.[16] 'Supposed' was doing a lot of heavy lifting here, but this did not become clear to his intended audience until much later.

Over the course of April 1798, Popham fleshed out these proposals with Grey by letter and in person. The proposed commander, Major General Eyre Coote, also participated. Grey was characteristically reluctant to give the plan full-throated endorsement, but he trusted Popham: 'From my local knowledge of the country, I think the plan complicated; however, the work is trifling to the object, and Captain Popham being most sanguine in the success

---

13  TNA: ADM 1/2319: Popham to Nepean, 4 April 1799.
14  TNA: ADM 1/2319: Popham to Nepean, 4 April 1799; Anon., *Public Characters of 1806* (London: Richard Phillips, 1806), p.415.
15  William L. Clements Library, University of Michigan [WLC UM]: Coote Papers, Box 3/31: Popham to Grey, 6 April 1798.
16  WLC UM: Coote Papers, Folder 3/45: 'Secret Memorandums', no.1; Folder 3/46: memorandum, 15 April 1798, signed by Popham, Coote, and Grey.

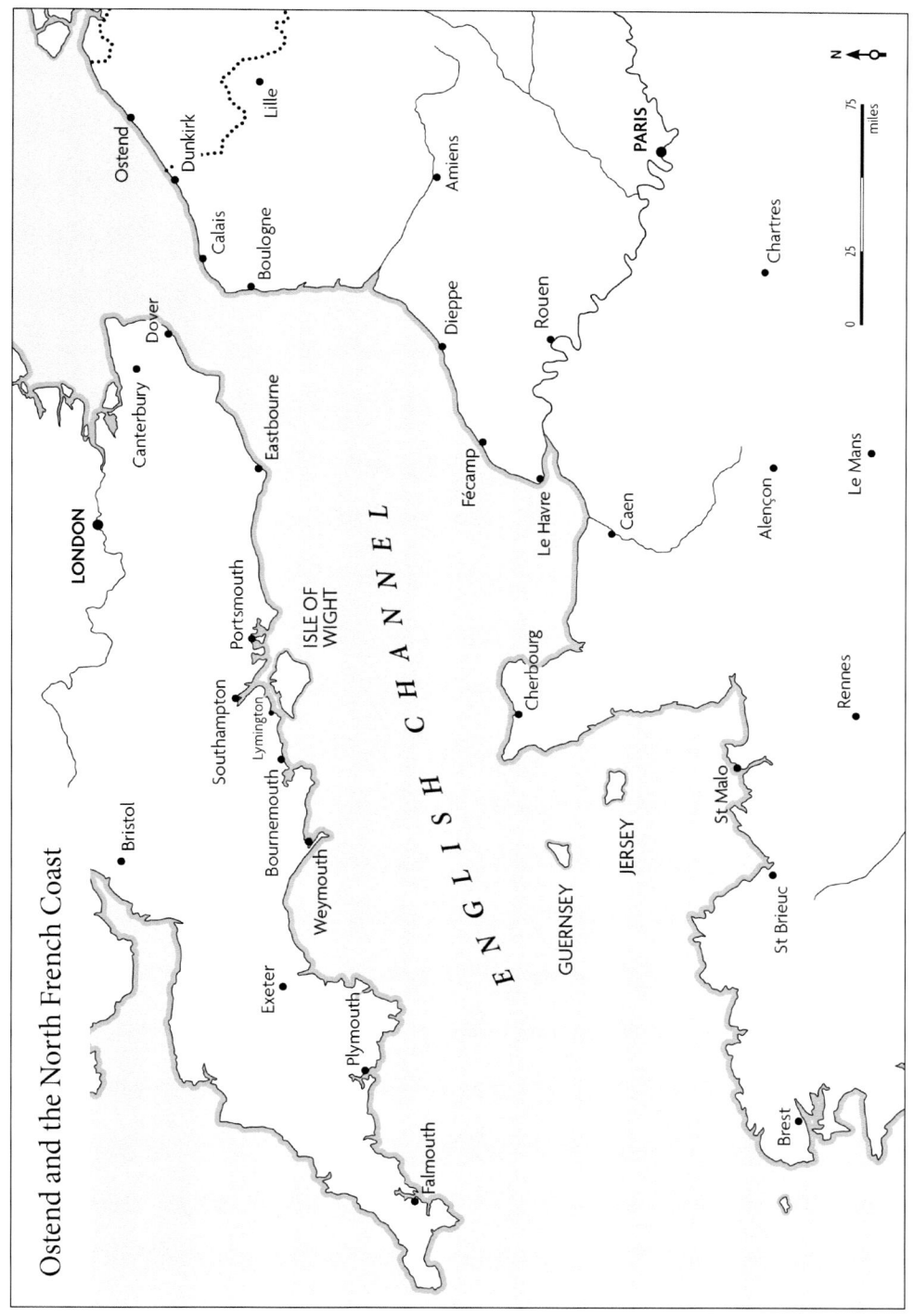

The French coast opposite southern England, 1798.

of his scheme, it may perhaps be as well to try it.'[17] With Grey's cautious support, Popham proposed an additional assault on the opposite end of the canal from Ostend, near Vlissingen (Flushing), and suggested follow-up attacks on Calais, Dieppe, Fécamp, and St-Valéry – all places where French invasion forces could be quickly concentrated, and with which Popham was familiar as a sailor.[18] He also advised an assault on the island of Ameland off the northern part of the Netherlands preparatory to an attack on the Dutch naval base at Texel, using some of the troops from Ostend once they had blown up the lock.[19] The assaults on Flushing and Ameland were added to the instructions Grey drew up for Coote.[20]

Sir Eyre Coote, by Henry Richard Cooke after Martin Archer Shee. (Public domain)

Only once Grey had agreed attacking Ostend was feasible did Popham approach his government contacts. He did so in a roundabout way, approaching Dundas's Under-Secretary of State, William Huskisson, trusting he would inform his boss of Popham's plans if he approved of them. Dundas and Huskisson were reluctant at first to credit Popham's sanguine predictions of success. Popham later recalled that Huskisson 'said if we lost no more than 150 men that it would be the cheapest expedition that ever sailed from England', while Dundas hesitated over the Flushing part of the expedition, which he thought relied too much on information from smugglers.[21] Grey talked them round, and only then did Dundas get the First Lord of the Admiralty, Lord Spencer, involved, requesting that Spencer should give Popham retrospective authority to work secretly on the Ostend plan in concert with Grey.[22]

Such a topsy-turvy chain of communication showed just how much Popham was operating outside the lines of a normal Royal Navy officer. This did not endear him to Admiralty officials and, when faced with what was effectively a *fait accompli* cobbled together by

---

17   Grey to Huskisson, 12 April 1798, Lewis Benjamin, *The Huskisson Papers* (London: Constable, 1931), pp.34–35.
18   DUA: GRE/A1428: Popham to Grey, 5 May 1798.
19   DUA: GRE/A1429: Huskisson to Grey, 5 May 1798; Corbet (ed.), *Spencer Papers*, vol.2, pp.330–331, 336–337.
20   WLC UM: Coote Papers, Folder 3/49: Grey's instructions to Coote, 8 May 1798, and additional instructions, 9 May 1798; DUA: GRE/A1375: draft plan.
21   WLC UM: Coote Papers, Folder 3/48: Dundas to Grey, 1 May 1798; Folder 3/62: Popham to Coote, 20 May 1798.
22   Corbet (ed.), *Spencer Papers*, vol.2, pp.313–314.

Popham, Grey, and Dundas behind his back, Spencer was incensed. He told Dundas flatly he did not think Popham a senior enough officer to command such an expedition and tried to appoint another officer in his place. When Popham got wind of this he got Grey to complain to Dundas, who – much to Popham's relief – chose to back him up, informing Spencer that removing the plan's projector would send the unequivocal message that Popham could not be trusted.[23]

In fact a lack of trust was precisely the problem, as Spencer's remarkable response to Dundas's letter revealed. It showed just how much work Popham still faced to overcome professional opinion that he was little more than a smuggler and a fraud:

> I have endeavoured, though not without considerable difficulty, to make such an arrangement as will allow of [Popham's appointment] … [but] Captain Popham should remember that he is a very young captain, that he never commanded a ship of war of any description (as far as I know) in his life; and I am not without apprehensions that his being placed in the command of a squadron on this occasion may give great disgust and offence to the profession, who are sufficiently irritable in these matters.

Spencer was very clear that Popham was, and always would be, a transport agent: 'Had any common transports been employed, I should for those reasons have preferred employing him as an Agent for Transports, the sort of line in which alone he has hitherto been known in the service.'[24] Spencer was making the point that appointing naval commanders was *his* turf, but he was also echoing concerns that, while a post-captain on paper, Popham's appointment had come from the Duke of York and was not backed up with practical experience. Popham knew the Admiralty remained baffled by a man with his background, and this was a large part of the reason he preferred to mine his personal contacts outside immediate naval circles to get employment. The kerfuffle over his appointment to the Ostend expedition simply confirmed to him that this instinct was correct, and it reinforced his habit of leapfrogging his nominal superiors to appeal to higher audiences he knew would be favourable.

Despite Spencer's objections, Popham was finally placed in HMS *Expedition*, a fifth-rate of 44 guns converted into a 26-gun vessel *armée en flûte* (in other words, with the lower gun decks cleared to carry troops). His small squadron consisted of three additional troop-ships (*Hebe*, *Minerva*, and *Druid*), four frigates (*Circe*, *Vestal*, *Ariadne*, and *Champion*), four sloops, two bomb ketches, and 12 gun vessels.[25] On 1 May, Dundas ordered Grey to prepare the six flank companies of the Guards, a detachment of artillery, and the 11th, 23rd, and 49th regiments of foot for the expedition (just shy of 1,800 men in total).[26] A week later Popham was aboard his new ship in the Downs, re-familiarising himself with the routine of command. He was still feeling optimistic, but keeping the expedition and its aims secret was vital to success, and the squadron was already a fortnight late in sailing. By mid-May,

---

23 Corbet (ed.), *Spencer Papers*, vol.2, pp.318–319.
24 Corbet (ed.), *Spencer Papers*, vol.2, pp.319–320.
25 Corbet (ed.), *Spencer Papers*, vol.2, pp.340n.
26 WLC UM: Coote Papers, Folder 3/48: Dundas to Grey, 1 May 1798.

Popham's tone had gone from confident to defensive, particularly as the weather turned stormy. 'Yesterday ... it blew so hard,' he reported to Spencer on 13 May. 'To-day it is squally, but I shall unmoor and go to sea in the evening if the weather appears at all settled. ... If I fail in the great object, I only wish your Lordship to enquire into every particular of my conduct before an opinion is passed.'[27] Popham did not usually speak of the possibility of defeat before he had even left harbour, but he knew he had enemies in the naval profession who would delight in his discomfiture, while his political patrons did not yet fully appreciate his talents. The ghost of *Etrusco* sailed with him always. He wanted to prepare his superiors for the worst so that, if things went wrong, they could not deny he had warned them, as a result of which they had only themselves – emphatically not him – to blame.

The gales continued until 16 May, when the wind dropped to a moderate breeze, and Popham made the signal to get underway. 'I have every reason to expect that we shall land this night,' he told Spencer, triumphantly.[28] He was wrong. The squadron arrived off Ostend the same day, but the weather continued unsettled and rainy. The expedition's secrecy had already been fatally compromised: a cutter intercepted by the squadron reported that French reinforcements were rushing to Ostend and Dunkirk.[29] Popham ordered *Harpy*, *Ariadne*, and *Expedition* to form a chain to allow Coote a line of communication from land but, while they were doing this, the wind changed and blew even harder. Popham and Coote conferred on the best course of action under the new circumstances. Both men had different priorities. Coote's official instructions spoke strongly of the need for caution; Popham needed the expedition to make an impact. Unsurprisingly, their recollections of what happened differed in several respects. According to Popham's account, Coote 'beg'd he might be landed to accomplish the great object of destroying the Canals, even if the Surf shou'd prevent his retreat'.[30] Coote, in contrast, recalled that he had been 'averse' to landing and only agreed when Popham and the rest of the naval officers assured him there was no surf.[31] Whichever party egged the other on, Popham gave orders for the troops to be landed 'as fast as possible without waiting for the regular order of debarkation'.[32] Popham and Coote then opened communications with the French commander at Ostend, as a feint to make it appear the aim of the expedition was to bombard the town.[33]

While the commanders exchanged polite insults under flags of truce, the first troops were quietly put ashore at 4:00 a.m. on 19 May. Popham, supervising from *Expedition*, noted a moderate westerly breeze but a great surf breaking against the beach. The *Asp*, *Wolverine*, and *Biter* gunboats slipped as close to the piers of Ostend as they could without being spotted;

---

27  Popham to Spencer, 13 May 1798, Corbet (ed.), *Spencer Papers*, vol.2, p.338.
28  Popham to Spencer, 16 May 1798, Corbett (ed.), *Spencer Papers*, vol.2, p.348.
29  Waite, 'Sir Home Riggs Popham', p.64.
30  TNA: ADM 1/2317: Popham's account, 20 May 1798.
31  WLC UM: Coote Papers, Folder 3/54: private memorandum by Coote.
32  TNA: ADM 1/2317: Popham's account, 20 May 1798.
33  WLC UM: Coote Papers, Folder 3/61: Coote to Dundas, 'On a Ridge of Sand Hills, Three Miles to the East of Ostend', 19 May 1798.

the *Tartarus* and *Hecla* bomb vessels also took up position. Coote was one of the first on shore to supervise the landing of the ammunition and entrenching tools for blowing up the lock. At about 4:30 a.m., someone on shore cottoned on to what was happening and the guns from Ostend rent the silence. The three gunboats by the pier returned fire immediately, joined by several of the cutters and the *Champion*, *Kite*, and *Fairy*, covering the landing of the troops as much as possible. By 5:00 a.m., almost all the troops were on shore, but not before *Wolverine*'s fore topgallant mast had been shot away. Shortly after, however, *Kite* – covered by musket fire from the decks of *Asp* and *Biter* – managed to get close enough to Ostend to start a proper bombardment. It set the town on fire and damaged several enemy ships collected in the harbour, many of which might have been used for an invasion attempt.

William Huskisson, by J. Cochran after John Graham, 1829. (Public domain, The Miriam and Ira D. Wallach Division of Art, Prints and Photographs, The New York Public Library)

Popham, who had moved to *Kite* to be closer to the action, was watching for signs that Coote was making progress. The wind was showing signs of shifting again to the north, and the tide was going out. Even if Coote was successful in blowing up the lock, Popham was beginning to wonder whether he and his men would be able to return to the ships. 'I wish you not to remain on shore much longer, unless you are certain of compleating your Object,' Popham scribbled hastily to Coote at 6:45 a.m.[34] The ships had to remain close to the shore for an evacuation to be successful, but the tide was retreating and, after an hour of firing, the *Dart* gunboat had to fall back to avoid grounding. *Asp*, *Wolverine*, and *Biter* followed suit shortly after. At 7:00 a.m., *Kite*, one of the only vessels still close enough to fire on the town, also retreated, with Popham still aboard. It was not before time: the vessel hit a sandbank, but managed to get off. Only the small bomb vessels, *Hecla* and *Tartarus*, continued firing. The rest of the squadron fell back to the eastward, searching for deeper water.

'We have been obliged to shoot off a little,' Popham warned Coote. 'We struck so hard that the Pilots were all frightened terribly. … I hope no accident will happen to you!'[35] Popham was right to be worried, but all he could do was attempt to draw the fire of the town away from the troops on land. At last, shortly before 10:30 a.m., a tremendous explosion shivered the choppy surface of the sea. Popham, back aboard *Expedition*, trained his telescope on the shore to see great columns of smoke rising from inland. Coote had been successful in his

---

34   WLC UM: Coote Papers, Folder 3/56: Popham to Coote, 'Saturday 3/4 p[ast] 6 AM'.
35   WLC UM: Coote Papers, Folder 3/55: Popham to Coote, '40 m[inutes] to 8 Sat[urda]y M[orn]ing'.

mission. Nervously, Popham kept watch for the first signs of returning troops. Sure enough, the first soldiers began to assemble on the sandhills dominating the beach. Popham immediately ordered the smaller vessels to anchor as close as possible and to stop firing to allow the men to evacuate. But just as Popham thought everything might be all right after all, a gale began to blow from the north-west. All the troops had now reached the sandhills and were making ready for embarkation, but, as the log of HMS *Expedition* put it, there was 'no possibility of landing the Boats' to rescue them.[36]

The worst had come to pass: the troops were stranded. When he realised what was happening, Coote was furious. He later complained '[the] Ships did not anchor so near the Shore as was expected and promised' and wondered why the landing boats had not waited for the troops to re-embark.[37] He nevertheless tried to get as many men as possible into some of the flat-bottomed boats drawn up on the beach, but they proved too leaky. There was nothing more to do than take the strongest possible position on the sandhills and dig some hasty entrenchments.[38] At about 6:00 p.m., as the crew of HMS *Expedition* scrambled up the swaying topgallant mast to furl the sails against the wind and the *Terrier* brig was blown out to sea, the Ostend garrison appeared, bearing down on Coote's men in three columns. Coote's men – most of whom had little ammunition, as they had been ordered to carry only bayonets – formed square in a last-ditch attempt to defend themselves against the inevitable. The *Tartarus* bomb vessel tried to cover them, but the wind blew it out of range. Then darkness fell, and Popham could see no more.

The surf was too strong to send messengers to and from shore: Popham was now as cut off from Coote as Coote was cut off from him. Tense hours ticked past as Popham waited for daylight. At 3:30 a.m., the sound of firing from the sandhills drifted across the tossing sea. Popham signalled HMS *Champion* to make one last-ditch attempt to get in closer, while *Hecla* renewed its bombardment of the town. Popham climbed back into the captain's launch and went across again to *Kite*, which he personally navigated closer to the shore. While *Kite* manoeuvred through the shallows, the sound of gunfire lapsed into ominous silence. By the time Popham managed to get ashore with the captain of *Kite* and a landing party, Coote and his men were gone, the sand streaked with blood and scattered with spent cartridges.[39]

Popham returned to *Expedition* and ordered the squadron to drop back a mile from shore. They could no longer be of any immediate use to Coote, so there was little point in remaining within range of the enemy batteries. As Popham and his officers debated what to do, he sent Captain Brown of *Kite* and Lieutenant Colonel Boone of the Guards ashore to offer an immediate exchange of prisoners. They returned an hour later with a refusal, but also with Captain Williamson, Coote's aide-de-camp, on parole. Popham listened in deepening gloom as Williamson explained what had happened. The explosion Popham had heard the previous day had completely destroyed the sluice gates of the canal but, at the last minute, Coote had been attacked by 600 men from the garrison with a cannon at their head. Coote had been shot in the thigh, although Williamson assured Popham it was nothing but

---

36  TNA: ADM 52/2994: log, HMS *Expedition*, 19–20 May 1798.
37  WLC UM: Coote Papers, Folder 3/54: private memorandum by Coote.
38  DUA: GRE/1472: Major General Burrard to Popham, 20 May 1798.
39  TNA: ADM 1/2317: Popham's dispatch, 20 May 1798; TNA: ADM 52/2994: log, HMS *Expedition*, 19–20 May 1798.

Cartoon depicting the expedition against Ostend, 1798, by James Gillray. The MP Joseph Jekyll provides two different reports on it by telegraph, using rolled-up newspapers as telescopes. (Public domain, Wellcome Collection)

a flesh-wound.[40] Williamson estimated the British had lost between 50 and 60 casualties killed and wounded, among them Coote himself and the lieutenant colonel of the 11th.[41]

It was disastrous news, although at least Coote had succeeded in destroying the canal. Popham, in his dispatch home, played this up, as well as the lightness of the casualties, although he left out the fact that Britain had effectively lost 1,100 men taken prisoner. Popham still hoped to move onto the second part of the original plan and attack Flushing, on the island of Walcheren, but this course of action was derailed by intelligence from Vice Admiral Joseph Peyton, commanding in the Downs. Flushing was much better defended than previously thought, and French reinforcements were now strung out along the entire Flemish and Dutch shore.[42] The element of surprise was well and truly gone. Not only this, but Popham knew if he began an attack elsewhere before Coote's fate had been decided, the prisoners might lose all chance of an exchange. The expedition was over.

---

40 WLC UM: Coote Papers, Folder 3/62: Popham to Coote, 20 May 1798.
41 TNA: ADM 1/2317: minutes by Captain Williamson, 20 May 1798. The number was later revised to over 160: see WLC UM: Coote Papers, Box 28/5: journal of the Ostend expedition.
42 Popham to Spencer, 20 May 1798, Corbett (ed.), *Spencer Papers*, vol.2, pp.348–349.

On 22 May the squadron returned to Margate, and Popham immediately went to London. He had hoped to get his version of events in first, but he discovered, to his horror, that Peyton had already informed the Admiralty of the disaster by telegraph.[43] Popham was relieved of his command on 4 June. The Admiralty acknowledged that he had done everything possible under the circumstances, but they clearly felt the expedition should never have been undertaken in the first place.[44] Far away in Bruges, Coote could not forgive Popham either. Although he sent him 'a 1,000 good wishes' from his sickbed in prison,[45] he felt Popham had rushed a delicate operation and doubted the extent of his local expertise.[46] Popham, aware he was in a delicate position, tried his best to pin the blame for what had happened squarely on the weather: 'I cannot contend against the elements.'[47] He praised 'poor Coote' and his gallantry to Grey, but he must have been afraid Coote would contradict his assertion that the general had pressed Popham hard, against his own inclinations, to land the troops in the first place.[48] Luckily for Popham, Coote had 'no wish … to say anything against the Navy unless they attach blame to the Army', and was in any case still a prisoner and unavailable for immediate comment.[49]

Nevertheless, Popham wanted to be sure he was not being personally blamed for what had happened. 'If before I return any person dare hint at an atom of Neglect or want of Judgement on my Part,' he told Grey, 'I beg as the Father and Patron of the Expedition that you will desire the most publick Enquiry into my Conduct, as I have done my duty in my own Conscience as becomes an Officer and I feel myself perfectly secure in your Approbation.'[50] The prospect of a new period of unemployment chilled him, and he wrote to Huskisson 'candidly' stating his wish to remain in receipt of a regular salary.[51] He knew the Admiralty would not be quick to employ him again, and he did not want his political patrons to forget about him. He need not have worried: Huskisson wrote back to his letter fishing for employment promising him that, the minute another delicate operation involving secrecy, intelligence, and seamanship came up, Popham's name would be first on the list. Dundas duly requested permission from the Lords of the Admiralty to take Popham under his authority, and on 8 May 1799, they gave it.[52]

From now on, Popham relied less on the Admiralty and more on Dundas's War Department for employment. Despite his background and his lack of success at Ostend, Popham had managed to impress the brusque, hard-nosed Secretary of State for War. Popham was intelligent, active, and willing to do virtually anything for his country; he was a man of ideas, and Dundas respected men of ideas – particularly when those ideas coincided with his. A significant part of the reason behind Popham's success was that he rapidly recognised this. Dundas had been at the War Department four years, but remained acutely

---

43 DUA: GRE/A1485: Popham to Grey, 24 May 1798.
44 TNA: ADM 1/2317: docket on Popham to Nepean, 22 May 1798.
45 DUA: GRE/A1472: Burrard to Popham.
46 WLC UM: Coote Papers, Folder 3/54: private memorandum by Coote.
47 DUA: GRE/A1476: Popham to Grey, 21 May 1798.
48 DUA: GRE/A1480: Popham to Grey, 22 May 1798.
49 WLC UM: Coote Papers, Folder 3/54: private memorandum by Coote.
50 DUA: GRE/A1476: Popham to Grey, 21 May 1798.
51 TNA: WO 1/411, ff.689–691: Popham to Huskisson, 21 November 1799.
52 TNA: ADM 1/2319: memorandum by Popham, 9 May 1799.

aware he was a civilian in charge of a war effort on a worldwide scale. With no general staff to advise him, Dundas had formed his own network of military and naval contacts, mostly men who shared his economic, imperial vision of the struggle. Popham had won Dundas's patronage and was determined to keep it; this meant broadening his horizons beyond coastal defence and the odd raid on enemy ports. With his patron's support behind him and as the European war spilled into Africa and Asia, Popham became increasingly involved in high strategy, political manoeuvring, and diplomacy, and claimed a place on an imperial, rather than narrowly European, stage.

# 6

# Russia and the Netherlands, 1799–1800

*2743: The shore is very dangerous*

By the time Popham returned from Ostend in mid-1798, the war against France had begun to shift into a new gear. Since the Treaty of Campo Formio in 1797, France had created new republics in Italy and the Netherlands and entered into a military alliance with Spain. It had also sent an army to Egypt under the command of Napoleon Bonaparte, a rising military star. Thirty thousand French troops still remained there, uncomfortably close to Britain's holdings in India, but in August 1798 the French fleet was destroyed by Nelson at the Battle of Aboukir Bay. News of this battle provoked a ripple of defiance against the French in Europe. For the first time since Popham had helped evacuate the British troops from Hanover in 1796, the British planned to send an army to the continent, and entered negotiations with Austria and Russia to forge a new military coalition.

Austria remained uncommitted, but Russian discussions were going surprisingly well. Russia had not joined the First Coalition militarily, but the new Tsar, Paul, seemed more inclined than his mother Catherine II to be friendly to Britain – particularly if Britain promised to help him eject the French from their occupation of Malta. Paul, who had been elected to head the Knights Hospitaller of Malta, took his responsibilities as Grand Master and Protector of the Order seriously. Nevertheless, Paul was famously mercurial and had spent the first two years of his reign trying to broker peace with the French. He might still change his mind about joining the coalition, and Dundas did not trust Foreign Secretary Lord Grenville's handling of the delicate situation. As the war moved away from anti-revolutionary ideology and acquired a more practical, global focus, Dundas and Grenville had begun to disagree over strategic priorities. Dundas preferred to look at the war from an economic perspective, which attracted his attention to far-flung spheres such as the West Indies, the Cape of Good Hope, and India. In contrast, Grenville thought the continental dimension was more important.[1] Dundas therefore decided to send his own envoy to Russia, even though Sir Charles Whitworth was already in St Petersburg as Britain's ambassador. Dundas claimed he could do this because he was sending a military man to help negotiate the military practicalities of a military alliance, but in fact the House of Orange had already

---

1   Piers Mackesy, *War Without Victory: The Downfall of Pitt, 1799–1802* (Oxford: Clarendon Press, 1984), p.38; Peter Jupp, *Lord Grenville* (Oxford: Clarendon Press, 1985), pp.208–210.

sent an envoy to St Petersburg for just that purpose: a Franco-Belgian general called Henri Guillaume, Baron de Stamford. Dundas, however, wanted a man on the spot who shared his priorities and was loyal only to him. He chose Popham for the task.

It seemed a strange choice. Popham had little diplomatic experience beyond what was required to negotiate transport hire from continental merchant firms. He was an extremely junior captain in the Navy with no aristocratic clout to lend him authority. There was, however, one good reason to send him out: a joint Anglo-Russian expedition to liberate the Netherlands from French domination was in contemplation, and this would require the transportation of Russian troops by sea. Popham's brief was ostensibly to work out the logistics of how this might be done, preferably using Russian ships or transports chartered in the Baltic.[2] Since the aim of the expedition was to liberate the Netherlands, it also made sense to appoint a man with local Dutch knowledge. None of this, however, would be enough to get Popham close to the Tsar, and Dundas needed him to have personal access. Paul was well known to have a fondness for men who shared his chivalric view of the world, and Dundas hoped Popham might take advantage of the Tsar's love of bold, enterprising personalities.

Popham had never been the kind of man who did anything by halves, particularly when two of the most important men in the cabinet were watching. To keep his mission secret it was announced in St Petersburg that he was coming to negotiate the importation of timber for the Navy, but he knew his mission was much more important than that and set about his unorthodox task with enthusiasm.[3] Even before he had received his official instructions, he startled and irritated the Russian ambassador, Woronzow, by pestering him repeatedly for a passport.[4] On 17 May, as soon as he had both his instructions and the required passport, Popham boarded the *Nile* lugger at Yarmouth. He spent 10 days in Hamburg hiring transports before continuing his journey on 27 May, arriving at Kronstadt outside St Petersburg on 1 June. 'You will observe,' Popham boasted to Huskisson at the War Department, 'that from the time I sailed from Yarmouth till my arrival at Cronstadt was 15 days, and … I was only 7 Days voyaging and travelling from England to Cronstadt.'[5]

Popham had moved far more swiftly than anyone expected. De Stamford had not even arrived in St Petersburg, and Sir Charles Whitworth had not prepared the Tsar for Popham's arrival. As a result, Popham had to wait until 3 June to secure the Tsar's permission to enter St Petersburg. Once in, he went straight to Whitworth, who informed him he had procured an audience for him with the Tsar. Whitworth warned Popham he would have to be very precise about the number of troops needed, where they would be sent, and what service they would perform, 'to convince [the Tsar's ministers] the subject had been well considered'.[6]

If Whitworth had known more about the man he was dealing with, he might have phrased his warning differently. Popham's instructions had focused on negotiating the transportation

---

2    WLC UM: Melville Papers, Box 14: Dundas to Popham, 10 May 1799.
3    State Library of Victoria, Melbourne, Australia (SLV): Accession no.MS 13020 (prev. M5142): Whitworth to Popham, [2 June 1799].
4    Woronzow to Grenville, 6 May 1799, Royal Commission on Historical Manuscripts, *The Manuscripts of J.B. Fortescue, esq., Preserved at Dropmore* [Dropmore MSS] (London: HMSO/Eyre and Spottiswoode, 1892–1927), vol.5, p.40.
5    TNA: WO 1/411, f.19: Popham to Huskisson, 3 June 1799.
6    TNA: WO 1/411, ff.25–36: Popham to Huskisson, 12 June 1799.

of the Russian troops; they breathed not a word on the subject of meddling in grand strategy. As Popham well knew, Dundas had only appointed him to ensure there was a man in St Petersburg capable of keeping an eye on the Foreign Office officials. But Popham was delighted at this unexpected opportunity to shape strategy more broadly. He began furiously writing memoranda for the Tsar, talking up his experience with transports and with the coast of Holland to encourage Paul to listen to him. Popham was encouraged in his scheming by de Stamford's continued absence and by Whitworth's revelation that Prussia was not likely to join the Second Coalition. Popham's role in smoothing the transportation of the Russian troops was more important than ever now no other European forces would be forthcoming. Although he told Huskisson the plan he intended to give the Tsar was 'precisely the same as I had the Honor to submit to Mr Dundas', he was not being entirely truthful.[7] The changed continental circumstances motivated him to make any alterations he wanted, which he could justify based on recent events and his local knowledge.

Tsar Paul I, by J. Mécou after Henri Benner, 1820. (Public domain, Anne S.K. Brown Military Collection, Brown University Library)

Popham's plan, which he explained to the Tsar in a memorandum dated 4 June, involved three of his favourite military objectives: to capture the island of Ameland and the Dutch fleet at Texel; to take the islands of Goree and Overflakkee, from which the coalition troops might attack the rest of the country; and to take the island of Walcheren, destroy its marine dockyard and magazines, and proceed up the Scheldt River to capture Antwerp, one of the principal naval bases in French hands. Russian troops would attack Goree, Overflakkee, and Ameland; British troops would take care of Walcheren. 'If 25,000 [men] can be spared from Russia, I have no doubt but every other arrangement will be made in England,' he finished.[8]

The first meeting between Popham and the Tsar was scheduled for the morning of 13 June and took place in the presence of the Foreign Minister, Rastopchin, and the Vice-President of the Admiralty, Admiral Kuchelev. Knowing how mercurial Paul could be, Whitworth warned Popham to take notice of the Tsar's mood before speaking, but in fact the audience

---

7 TNA: WO 1/411, ff.25–36: Popham to Huskisson, 12 June 1799.
8 TNA: WO 1/411, ff.39–50: memorandum, 4 June 1799.

went surprisingly well. Popham had only been meant to give Paul some charts of the coast of Holland, but of course Paul wanted to know more about the plan Popham had detailed in his memorandum – as Popham had known he would.[9] Paul asked questions about the government's intentions, which Popham was perfectly capable of answering, since it was his own plan he had proposed. Popham was doing what he did best: telling his audience what his audience wanted to hear. It worked. 'As soon as his doubts were removed, he [the Tsar] readily assented to furnish Seventeen Battalions for the Service in question', amounting to 18–19,000 men, to be embarked at Riga.

It was a stunning diplomatic coup, although one Whitworth was not completely sure had the backing of the authorities in Britain. All while praising Popham's 'activity, intelligence and zeal', Whitworth made sure the authorities at home knew the extent to which Popham had seized control of negotiations. 'I ... rest my defence,' Whitworth told Grenville, 'if I have any cause for apprehension, on ... the encouragement which I have received from Capt[ai]n Popham, whose constant endeavours have been to convince me that such was the importance attached to this subject, that no sacrifice would be thought too great for its attainment.'[10] Popham was also aware he was walking a tightrope. He wrote, almost plaintively, to Huskisson: 'I shall be very anxious to hear from you and to know I have acted well in your opinion.'[11] He was painfully aware that, having got Paul to promise so many troops, he had failed to fulfil the instructions he had actually been given in the first place: to ensure those Russian troops should be embarked in Russian ships. But Paul, and his foreign minister Rastopchin, both believed they had agreed that the Russian troops would be carried in British ships at British expense.[12] Popham faced the humiliation of having to write home requesting British transports instead, which he had specifically been told not to do.[13] This left him exposed if the government chose to disavow the strategic plans he had proposed to Paul. With this prospect before his eyes, Popham was forced to admit to Count Rastopchin that 'I really had no authority from England to propose plans, being sent only to devise Expedients for carrying them into Execution.'[14] His cold feet were reflected in a memorandum for the Tsar regarding his proposed attacks on Ameland and Walcheren, which concluded, significantly: 'These projects are all to be considered subject to any alterations His Majesty's Ministers may choose to make.'[15]

Popham was gambling that his success with Paul would override his failure to secure Russian transports. The problem was that the British genuinely did not have any transports to send instead, as Spencer informed Popham on 1 July.[16] Dundas, however, had a word, and by 3 July the War Department informed Popham that eight ships of war *armée en flûte* would be sent to Riga, along with sufficient tonnage for 10,000 men. At least Popham knew that, for now at least, Dundas was still ready to back him – and a fresh meeting with Paul led

---

9   TNA: FO 65/43: Whitworth to Grenville, 13 June 1799.
10  TNA: FO 65/43: Whitworth to Grenville, 23 June 1799.
11  TNA: WO 1/411, ff.105–108: Popham to Huskisson, 13 June 1799.
12  Rastopchin to Woronzow, 13 June 1799, *Dropmore MSS*, vol.5, pp.109–110.
13  TNA: WO 1/411, ff.75–87: Popham to Huskisson, 13 June 1799.
14  TNA: WO 1/411, ff.124–136: Popham to Huskisson, 20 June 1799.
15  TNA: WO 1/411, ff.139–142: memorandum, 14 June 1799.
16  Spencer to Popham, 1 July 1799, Corbett (ed.), *Spencer Papers*, vol.3, p.142.

to a promise that Russia would provide six ships of the line and four frigates to be fitted as transports under Popham's direction.[17] Britain would have to pay for it all, but the concession took a considerable amount of heat off Popham.

Popham had started out well, although his diplomatic talents did not impress everyone. De Stamford, his Dutch counterpart, described him, rather ambivalently:

> I found in M. Popham a man full of zeal, of talent, and of knowledge. He seems to me to have been born with a courage that doubts of nothing, and for whom the most difficult things appear easy; but I was immediately able to see that he joined to these qualities the kind of ambition that leads the man who is blessed with it, and who sees himself charged with some enterprise, to want to take all the glory from it for himself.[18]

Popham, for his part, dismissed de Stamford as 'a well-informed old Man, rather of insinuating manners, and more used to play[ing] the great General of Politicks in the Stadholder's House at the Hague than to consider about real military Combinations'.[19] He may have thought the Dutchman was jealous of the fact Popham's plan had been approved by the Tsar, whereas de Stamford's counter-plan – which involved taking a series of fortresses inland and partnering with Dutch rebels against French rule – had been rejected. In fact de Stamford realised Popham was acting outside his instructions, and probably knew nothing Popham had agreed with Paul regarding strategy was set in stone. His suspicions were confirmed when the official agreement was signed with Russia on 22 June. Russia pledged to provide 17,600 men, to be carried in a mix of British and Russian transports at entirely British expense. One of the articles left the whole plan open to alteration in Britain.[20]

If Popham noticed this equivocation, he did not draw attention to it. He felt he had succeeded in everything he had set out to do and wrote home, proudly: 'If your object is to get Men and Ships I have accomplished it.'[21] The first division of 7,300 men sailed from Revel on 27 July, their embarkation overseen by Popham. De Stamford was nevertheless correct that the British would not adopt Popham's Ameland-Walcheren plan. When he heard Popham was trying to commit the government to something concrete, Dundas decided – rather belatedly – to see what the military men had to say. Lieutenant General Sir Ralph Abercromby, the prospective commander of the British part of the Anglo–Russian expedition, did not even attempt to conceal his dismay. Ameland and Goree were 'too superficial' as bases for continental action. As for Walcheren, 'a strong co-operation on the part of the navy' would be required for success, and taking the island – and keeping it – would not be worth the bother, as it was of no strategic use and 'extremely unhealthy'.[22] But the

---

17  TNA: WO 1/411, ff.124–136: Popham to Huskisson, 20 June 1799.
18  De Stamford to Thomas Grenville, 29 June 1799, *Dropmore MSS*, vol.5, pp.139–141 (my translation).
19  TNA: WO 1/411, ff.349–356: Popham to Huskisson, 9 July 1799.
20  TNA: FO 65/43: Whitworth to Grenville, 15 June 1799; TNA: WO 1/411, ff.139–142: memorandum, 14 June 1799.
21  TNA: WO 1/411, ff.173–176: Popham to Huskisson, 20 June 1799.
22  Abercromby to Dundas, 21 June 1799, Corbett (ed.), *Spencer Papers*, vol.3, pp.140–141; Abercromby to Grenville, 21 July 1799, *Dropmore MSS*, vol.5, pp.165–166.

government, like the Tsar, had fallen for Popham's trick of tailoring his spiel to his audience. Encouraged by Popham's talk of an easy rebellion, the cabinet discarded Popham's Walcheren-Ameland plan, not because it was too difficult but because it was not ambitious enough.²³ Rather than just an exploratory raid on the Dutch coast, the aim was now 'to recover all the conquests made by France' in the Netherlands. Popham's success in Russia, along with the fact the government had managed to recruit a large number of militiamen into the regulars, had fed the government's marked tendency to be over-optimistic: 'an army of 50,000 men [17,000 Russians, 8,000 Swedes, and 25,000 British], acting in a country so well disposed … is a force that the feeble remains of French force in Holland and Flanders will not easily withstand', and afforded 'a reasonable prospect of success'.²⁴

Having concluded the agreement with the Tsar, Popham immediately began asking to come home. He was angling for a command in the new expedition and was afraid the Admiralty might cause trouble about his appointment, as had happened with Ostend. He asked Dundas (through Huskisson) to put in a word with Spencer for a 50 or 64-gun ship, and his success in Russia made him even more bombastic than usual:

> Have a ship ready for me that has been some time in commission and is in order, with two or three frigates, the same number of sloops of war, some bombs and gun boats, and I'll answer my existence that I put you in possession of all Holland in six weeks, and in six days in a great part of it. In this there is no speculation; and I give you my full authority to assure Mr Pitt and Mr Dundas that if I am allowed to sail with discretional power … I will give them leave to stick my Head on Temple Bar if I fail in one point.²⁵

Popham had another reason for wanting to leave St Petersburg. He always had a talent for making enemies, and his favour with the Tsar had made him several at the Russian court.²⁶ 'There are so many Intrigues in this Court that we are never safe,' he complained to Huskisson, adding, desperately, 'You cannot send for me too soon.'²⁷

But Popham was a victim of his own success. He had been talking up how indispensable he was ever since he had arrived in St Petersburg: 'If you want 10,000 more Men I dare say if *I* ask him he [the Tsar] will grant them'.²⁸ Whitworth had been picking up the refrain, if only to cover his own back: 'The character and manners of Capt[ai]n Popham seem to accord perfectly with the Emperor, by whom he is treated with uncommon civility and confidence in everything relating to this Enterprise.'²⁹ Unsurprisingly, Huskisson wrote to Popham on

---

23 TNA: WO 1/411, ff.205–215: Huskisson to Popham, 15 July 1799.
24 WLC UM: Melville Papers, Box 14: Huskisson to Popham, 3 July 1799.
25 TNA: WO 1/411, ff.229–235: Popham to Huskisson, 21 June 1799.
26 TNA: WO 1/411, ff.597–598: Popham to Huskisson, 17 August 1799.
27 TNA: WO 1/411, ff.229–235: Popham to Huskisson, 21 June 1799.
28 TNA: WO 1/411, ff.349–356: Popham to Huskisson, 9 July 1799.
29 TNA: FO 65/43: Whitworth to Grenville, 23 June 1799.

15 July to tell him to stay put, 'as I understand you are all in all with the Emperor'. Privately, Huskisson reassured him the Admiralty would not be allowed to keep him kicking his heels ashore, because Dundas and the War Department would never let it happen.[30] Even more comforting, Popham learned that the overall commander of the upcoming expedition would be the Duke of York, as the Russians had balked against Abercromby and demanded to be commanded by a prince of the blood. York had been Popham's first patron, and would surely insist on Popham's employment in the upcoming operations. Independently of this, Huskisson made the diplomatic role into which Popham had wriggled himself a little more official: Popham was instructed to continue liaising with the Tsar throughout the expedition, 'to promote harmony and good understanding between his troops and ours when they come to act together'.[31]

Back in Russia, Popham's diplomatic skills were not much in evidence outside the Peterhof Palace. 'If only Admiral Kuchelev's zeal had kept pace with his stupidity, we should have had Imperial ships for the embarkation, and all filled by next week,' he complained, 'but he is an incorrigible old sloth and hates an Englishman as much as he despises activity.'[32] There was no doubt, however, that Popham had developed a strong personal relationship with the Tsar. Paul was drawn to the keen, mercurial British officer, whose favour at the Russian court was helped by the vagueness of his brief and the informality of his position (just as Dundas had hoped). Within a week of his first meeting with Paul, Popham had started eclipsing the actual ambassador, Whitworth, who was not even invited to attend his meetings with the Tsar. Popham dined with the royal family, and Paul personally presented him to the Tsarina and the future Tsar Alexander I.[33] The Tsar even asked Popham to join the Russian navy as an admiral, which Popham refused, although he seems to have left open the possibility of doing so after the war was over.[34] Their relationship was possibly solidified by personal gratitude: much later, Popham claimed he had saved Paul's life, although he was frustratingly light on the details.[35] A few days before Popham left St Petersburg on 2 August, the Tsar requested that the *Nile* lugger that had carried Popham to Russia should be brought up to the Peterhof Palace on the seafront. Popham took Paul for a sail, which Paul enjoyed so much he brought his whole family aboard a few days later. Popham put on a show of shipboard life for them, feeding them salt beef and biscuit and allowing Paul to help set the sails. As a farewell gift, Paul gave Popham a diamond snuffbox and a ring.[36] 'I can only say the whole country was astonished at this condescension,' Popham preened.[37]

Following the *Nile* visit, Popham was taken to the Tsar's private office by Count Rastopchin. Here, the Tsar told Popham that, 'as a mark of my approbation of your zeal and conduct since your first arrival in this country', he wanted to make Popham a Commander and Chevalier of the Illustrious Order of St John of Jerusalem – a Knight of Malta. Popham

---

30 WLC UM: Melville Papers, Box 14: Huskisson to Popham, 16 July 1799.
31 TNA: WO 1/411, ff.205–215: Huskisson to Popham, 15 July 1799.
32 Popham, *A Damned Cunning Fellow*, p.70.
33 WLC UM: Melville Papers, Box 30: Popham to Lord Melville, 8 June 1814.
34 TNA: WO 1/411, ff.349–356: Popham to Huskisson, 9 July 1799; ff.679–681: Popham to Huskisson, 21 October 1799.
35 WLC UM: Melville Papers, Box 30: Popham to Melville, 8 June 1814.
36 *The Courier*, 29 August 1799.
37 TNA: WO 1/411, ff.537–548: Popham to Huskisson, 3 August 1799.

was taken by surprise, but before he could protest Paul had drawn his sword. Popham knelt; Paul repeatedly touched each shoulder with his sword, and placed the Order himself around Popham's neck. As the subject of another monarch, and as a serving military officer, Popham should not have accepted the knighthood, but he justified it at home as he had done everything else – out of necessity: 'In refusing [the Order], I risked the entire loss of the Emperor's confidence and consequently every chance of using it to promote the wishes of His Majesty's Ministers.'[38] Popham almost certainly saw it as a reward he was due for his good work – particularly as the Order, as one newspaper put it, wryly, 'has the agreeable appendage of a salary of £600 sterling a year'.[39]

The ships carrying the Russian troops departed Revel on 17 August at 4:00 a.m. with a favourable eastern breeze, Popham with them in the *Nile* lugger.[40] He accompanied the troops to Elsinore, off Denmark, where he arranged for them to be re-provisioned before disappearing ahead of them. He landed at Dover on 10 September, in the assurance that he had done his job well and with the Order of a Knight of Malta round his neck. His heart must have been singing. He had gambled on the vagueness of his brief for a stronger role in policy, and won. He knew this had probably not endeared him to the Admiralty, but he did not care. 'I am aware that I am forward in projects,' he brashly informed Lord Spencer, 'but by being modified by steadier and abler military heads they cannot be of harm, but may ultimately produce good.'[41] The protection of Dundas and the War Department had sent the shadow of *Etrusco* into temporary retreat. 'Jealousy is a damn'd thing,' Popham told Huskisson, 'and I have been so bit by it that I avoid it as I wou'd a Rattlesnake, tho' [I] have less fear at present as you have promised me an antidote for all my Poisons.'[42] His future had never looked brighter.

The expedition to Holland was already underway, as a British contingent had already sailed on 15 August – not to Walcheren or Ameland, but to the Helder peninsula in the north of the country. Den Helder was the main port of the Batavian Republic, but it had only been chosen as a target after the expedition had left, because it was considered to be the most vulnerable part of the coast and would put the British in a position to capture the Dutch fleet of 11 ships at Texel.[43] The objective was to march on Amsterdam, the capital, from which to proclaim the end of French domination and the rule of the House of Orange. As Walcheren was no longer one of the primary strategic objectives, Popham could not expect to be placed in command of a whole branch of the expedition, as he had previously thought might happen. Nevertheless, Dundas wanted him in the field. Popham had already

---

38  TNA: WO 1/411, ff.513–517: Popham to Huskisson, 29 July 1799.
39  *Oracle*, 21 September 1799.
40  TNA: WO 1/411, ff.585–587, ff.597–598: Popham to Huskisson, 17 August 1799.
41  Popham to Spencer, 12 September 1799, Corbett (ed.), *Spencer Papers*, vol.3, pp.188–190.
42  TNA: WO 1/411, f.353: Popham to Huskisson, 9 July 1799.
43  Geert van Uythoven, *The Secret Expedition: The Anglo-Russian Invasion of North Holland, 1799* (Warwick: Helion & Co, 2018), pp.116, 119; Philip Ball, *A Waste of Blood and Treasure: The 1799 Anglo-Russian Invasion of the Netherlands* (Barnsley: Pen & Sword, 2017), p.41.

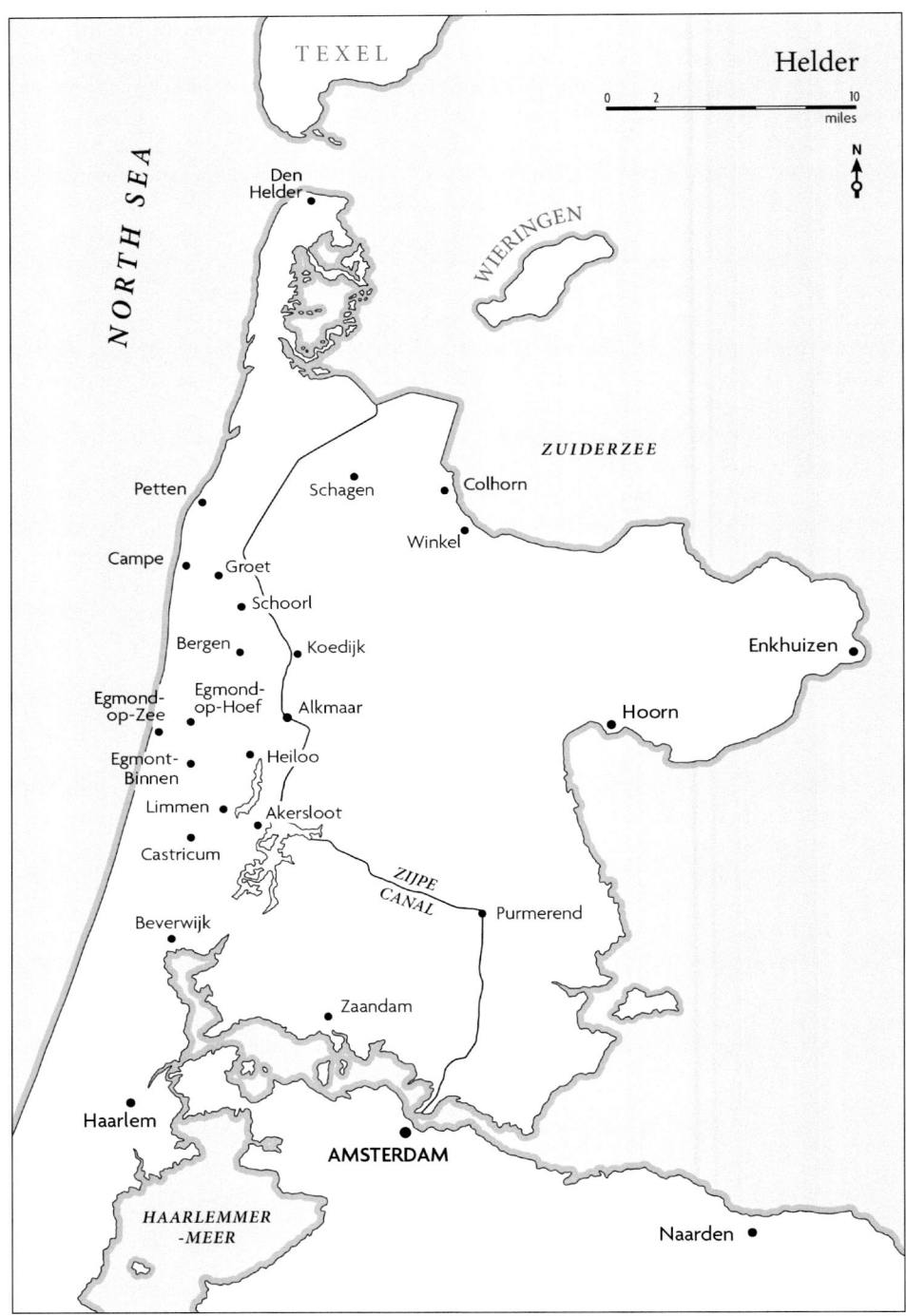

The Helder expedition, 1799.

established himself as an expert in amphibious operations in Flanders: 'He knows every inch of the country remarkably well, and, besides that, I think he may be of great use to keep all things smooth and well with the Russians.'[44] Through his talent for Russian liaison, Popham had managed to make himself indispensable.

The problem, as Popham had foreseen, was his lack of an official command through the Admiralty. A naval force had been earmarked for the Helder expedition under the command of Vice Admiral Andrew Mitchell consisting of 10 ships of the line, five sloops, and nearly 30 bomb vessels and gunships, along with over 100 transports, but without a ship Popham could not accompany them in a naval capacity.[45] When Popham cheekily asked for a commodore's pendant, which would obviously come with a ship attached, Spencer refused.[46] Other highly placed patrons, however, such as the commander of the expedition, the Duke of York, were as keen as Dundas to have Popham along. After some discussion about his exact role, the Admiralty and War Department compromised: Popham became, somewhat unofficially, the Duke of York's 'naval aide de camp', to be employed 'in such a manner as may appear most advantageous to the general good'.[47] Part of this may have been to enable him to act as liaison with the Russians, for which Popham had received instructions directly from the Tsar himself.[48] The exceedingly vague remit from the Duke of York certainly left him a great deal of latitude, much to his joy: 'I feel gratified in having so ample a field to exert myself.'[49]

Popham landed at the Helder on 14 September. Abercromby had already been in Holland with 10,000 men since 27 August, but had simply entrenched himself to wait for the rest of the allied army to join him. The enemy was the Franco-Dutch army of 20,000 men under the command of Dutch *Luitenant-generaal* Daendels and French *lieutenant général* Dumonceau, with *général de division* Brune in overall command.[50] After helping oversee the landing of the second wave of British troops, Popham set to work. He made some arrangements for inland navigation through the Commissary General's Department and began sending boats and guns by water towards Amsterdam in anticipation of the army's movement in that direction. On 15 September, his appointment as 'naval Aid de Camp at His Majesty's Pleasure' was made official in the General Orders and Popham immediately departed on 'a lone mission ... of a Special Nature'.[51] This secret mission prepared the ground for the plans Popham had been hatching for taking gunboats inland to harass the enemy, as well as scouting out the local territory to support the army's southward march.

Popham was feeling smug. The Russian troops he had hired and transported were beginning to arrive, and he was justifiably proud of his role in getting them to Holland. 'Everybody is highly pleased with their soldier-like hardy appearance,' Popham told Dundas, 'and I will be responsible to you, Sir, their appearance is the worst feature in their Character.'[52] In fact

---

44  Dundas to Grenville, 11 September 1799, *Dropmore MSS*, vol.5, pp.390–391.
45  Uythoven, *The Secret Expedition*, pp.74, 379–380.
46  Popham to Spencer, 12 September 1799, Corbett (ed.), *Spencer Papers*, vol.3, pp.188–190.
47  Popham to Spencer, 12 September 1799, Corbett (ed.), *Spencer Papers*, vol.3, pp.188–190.
48  SLV: Accession no. MS 13020 (prev. M5142): Whitworth to Popham, 22 July 1799.
49  Popham to Spencer, 17 October 1799, Corbett (ed.), *Spencer Papers*, vol.3, p.206.
50  Ball, *A Waste of Blood and Treasure*, pp.33–34.
51  TNA: WO 1/411, ff.651–654: Popham to Dundas, 14 September 1799.
52  TNA: WO 1/411, ff.651–654: Popham to Dundas, 14 September 1799.

this good opinion was not as broadly held as Popham hoped. The British were not impressed with their Russian allies, whom one observer described as 'repulsive and ferocious ... troops formed altogether for service, and not for show'.[53] More seriously, while Popham boasted of his skills in liaising between the Russian and British authorities in St Petersburg, on the ground the allies were beset by communication problems from the outset.

On 19 September, the Duke of York decided to begin the combined allied offensive. The aim was to flush the enemy out of their headquarters at Bergen and force them back on Amsterdam before the Franco-Dutch forces had time to consolidate. The attack was planned in four columns: the first under Russian Lieutenant General Ivan Hermann, attacking Bergen itself; the second, under British Lieutenant General David Dundas, to get the enemy out of the nearby villages of Walmenhuysen and Schoreldam and support Hermann's Russians; the third column, under Lieutenant General Sir James Pulteney, to secure the main road leading to the town of Alkmaar; and the fourth, under Abercromby, to cut off an enemy retreat and open the road to Amsterdam for the allies.[54] The attack began at dawn and went wrong almost immediately. General Hermann's first column started marching too soon, far earlier than any of the other columns, possibly due to a failure to synchronise watches or finalise a start time. They came upon the French before any of the supporting columns were available to assist them, with predictable results. After a fierce fight, the Russians were driven back on the town of Schoorl, with massive sandhills blocking any escape. The Russians suffered nearly 3,000 casualties and prisoners, including Hermann himself and his second-in-command, Chercekov.[55]

Popham only found out about this later, as he was not with the Russian contingent at the time. If the Tsar had intended him to stay alongside the imperial troops, Popham preferred to rely on the breadth of his British instructions to do his own thing. He was 'scampering as usual over the Country',[56] locked in amphibious contact with Lieutenant General Pulteney's division marching on Alkmaar. He and three gunboats, each armed with a 12-pounder gun, kept pace with the troops along the course of the Alkmaar Canal, while a party of seamen from Vice Admiral Andrew Mitchell's squadron accompanied General Abercromby along the seashore. Popham's gunboats were heavily engaged, and one of his captains was slightly wounded.[57] Things seemed to be going well for the British: their three columns succeeded in taking the places they were attacking, but were called back when news of the Russian debacle finally filtered through. By evening both sides were back where they had begun the day, and one British column – Abercromby's – had not even had a chance to fight.

The Anglo-Russian forces had been cooperating for less than a week, but this stalemate immediately undermined the alliance Popham had constructed. Hermann was a prisoner of war and the new Russian commander, Lieutenant General Ivan Essen, felt the British had

---

53 Edward Walsh, *A Narrative of the Expedition to Holland in the Autumn of the Year 1799* (London: Robinson, 1800), pp.47–48.
54 Uythoven, *The Secret Expedition*, pp.212–214; Ball, *A Waste of Blood and Treasure*, pp.81–82.
55 Sir Henry Bunbury, *A Narrative of the Campaign in North Holland, 1799* (London: Boone, 1849), pp.12–13; J.W. Fortescue, *A History of the British Army* (London: Macmillan, 1899–1930), vol.IV (2), pp.671–678; Walsh, *A Narrative of the Expedition to Holland*, pp.111–115.
56 SLV: Accession no. MS 13020 (prev. M5142): Whitworth to Popham, 24 September 1799.
57 Popham to Spencer, 12 October 1799, Corbett (ed.), *Spencer Papers*, vol.3, p.200.

Charge of the 18th Light Dragoons at the Battle of Alkmaar, by William Heath, 1799. (Public domain, Anne S.K. Brown Military Collection, Brown University Library)

betrayed the alliance by not coming to Hermann's aid. Popham might have been able to help repair the growing breach, but he was hindered by his lack of a personal relationship with Essen, who was writing to the Tsar to contradict everything Popham was saying about how well the alliance was going. In any case, Popham was still far too busy to devote himself to the full-time job of maintaining diplomatic relations between the British and Russian forces. He was discovering that his vague brief was as much drawback as boon: 'I never had half so much to do as I have at present. The variety of services I have to attend to cannot be described.'[58] His inland navigational skills were in demand because of the nature of the terrain, and he was also being used for liaison with the Dutch, almost certainly because of his local contacts and knowledge of the language.[59] But all his hard work did not pay off. On 2 October, the Duke of York launched a second assault on the enemy in an attempt to open the road to Amsterdam.[60] This time the fighting focused on the towns of Alkmaar and Egmont-op-Zee. Popham was exposed to what he described as 'a very heavy cannonade of ten hours', during which the seven gunboats under his command fired between 80 and 100 rounds each from four 24-pounder and three 18-pounder guns. Three gunboats sank and another of Popham's captains was injured.[61] At the end of the day, however, Alkmaar was in allied hands and the

---

58  Popham to Spencer, 12 October 1799, Corbett (ed.), *Spencer Papers*, vol.3, p.201.
59  Popham to Spencer, 4 October 1799, Corbett (ed.), *Spencer Papers*, vol.3, pp.192–193.
60  Ball, *A Waste of Blood and Treasure*, p.108.
61  Popham to Spencer, 4 and 12 October 1799, Corbett (ed.), *Spencer Papers*, vol.3, pp.193, 200.

Duke of York shifted his headquarters there. Popham, not unnaturally for someone who, only a short while previously, had pledged his head to Pitt and Dundas in return for getting the French out of Holland in six weeks, played up this success: 'I have now little doubt but this gust of fortunate wind will continue and we shall drive the French over the Meuse.'[62] But although the battle of 2 October at last allowed the allies to advance, their gains were slow and painfully acquired. Contrary to Popham's wild speculations that the Dutch were close to revolting against French rule, the locals offered no assistance. Every southward step by the allies took them further from their supply base (Vice Admiral Mitchell and his ships off the Helder). In contrast, the French were retreating on theirs: Amsterdam.

Relations with the Russian allies were also unravelling fast. Having marched brashly into trouble on 19 September, on 2 October the Russians had refused to move at all, leaving part of the British lines exposed and putting yet more strain on the alliance. Popham, of course, had not given up hope, particularly if Essen could be replaced in the Russian command. He wrote to Tsar Paul about the actions of September and early October, trying 'with as little prejudice as possible to General Essen, to convince His Imperial Majesty another officer ought to be sent to command the Army'.[63] But back in London, the Russian ambassador Woronzow was concerned when he heard of the Tsar's fury at how his army had been treated on 19 September. The only solution Woronzow could think of was to send Popham back to Russia: 'This active man, whom the Emperor loves, would immediately secure other generals to be sent in the place of those who cover the name of Russia in shame.'[64] But it was already too late for that, and things were about to get worse.

On 6 October, another battle took place in Holland. The French had retreated on the town of Beverwijk after 2 October, and the Duke of York hoped another battle would force them to move yet further south. Unfortunately, the same problem that had dogged the allies during previous battles – poor communication – struck again. Although the battle succeeded in its objective of pushing the French back, the Russian force overshot its target and got into trouble outside Castricum. 'I am sorry to say that in this affair our loss was very considerable,' Popham wrote, reluctantly, to Whitworth. Popham had been covering the left flank of the British with his gunboats at Akkersloot, so he could not positively contradict Essen's accusations that the Russians had once again been used as cannon fodder, but he tried to make light of what had happened, knowing Whitworth would show his letter to the Tsar: 'Events of the nature as described must happen in all military operations.'[65] But even Popham could not change the fact that, after five weeks, the British and Russians had barely advanced. An assault on Amsterdam was now impossible. Overnight on 7–8 October, the British and Russians retreated to their original position behind the Zijpe Canal, giving up all their territorial gains to the French, who crept slowly forwards again. The campaign was effectively over. For a while the allies considered a fighting retreat to re-embark the troops at the Helder under fire, but in the end this was not necessary. On 16 October, the Duke of York signed an armistice with the French to allow the British and Russians to evacuate unmolested.

---

62   Popham to Spencer, 4 October 1799, Corbett (ed.), *Spencer Papers*, vol.3, pp.192–193.
63   TNA: WO 1/411, f.663: Popham to Huskisson, 11 October 1799.
64   Woronzow to Grenville, 8 October 1799, *Dropmore MSS*, vol.5, p.465 (my translation).
65   TNA: WO 1/411, ff.671–673: Popham to Whitworth, 11 October 1799.

Retreat of the British and Russian troops at the Helder, by Dirk Langendyck, 1799. (Public domain, Anne S.K. Brown Military Collection, Brown University Library)

Popham blamed the weather and the state of the roads for everything. Predictably, he also blamed the last-minute change of plan that had re-routed the expedition from Walcheren or Ameland to North Holland.⁶⁶ It was the second time a campaign in which Popham had been prominently involved had failed in as many years, and he was understandably nervous that Dundas might take him up on his former offer and stick his head on Temple Bar. When the latest copy of the *London Gazette* reached Holland, Popham was aghast to discover his exploits with the gunboats had been left out. 'You as my firm Patron,' he reproached Huskisson, 'did suffer that part of [the Duke of York's] gazette letter that was flattering to me to be erased, and that to be the only part that was erased. I have felt it most grievously but never suffered this marked disaffirmance to lessen my Zeal and Exertions.'⁶⁷ Popham's pride had been hurt, but he was also worried that omitting him from the dispatches might be symptomatic of a high-level desire to disassociate from him.

As always, Popham concluded the best way to prevent this was by continuing to make himself, and his suggestions, relevant. With incredible *chutzpah*, he now suggested that the

---

66  Popham to Spencer, 12 October 1799, Corbett (ed.), *Spencer Papers*, vol.3, pp.200–201.
67  TNA: WO 1/411, ff.683–686: Popham to Huskisson, 24 October 1799.

troops evacuated from the Helder might simply sail south and pursue his original plans for taking Walcheren or Ameland.[68] But even Popham could not have believed this was a good idea, not now the French had so many troops in the Batavian Republic. In any case, Popham knew the British focus of the war was shifting away from Europe. The Second Coalition was in a process of collapse. Despite a series of victories over the French earlier in 1799, the Russians had been thrown out of Switzerland following the Battle of Zurich in September. The Austrians were also on the back foot in Italy; a few months later they were defeated by Napoleon at Marengo.[69] The British, Austrians, and Russians became locked in a destructive cycle of recriminations regarding who had been most responsible for what had happened. Meanwhile, a French army remained in Egypt, a potential threat to British Indian interests and trade.[70] With the continental picture looking increasingly gloomy, Dundas began to push the more wide-ranging aims he had been hoping to pursue in the east, and Popham, ever the chameleon, adapted to slot himself into this altered picture. Until now the war had largely been fought in Flanders, Holland, and Germany, and Popham had emphasised his European knowledge and credentials. As Dundas's vision moved east, Popham's past East India Company connections and expertise in the Indian Ocean came suddenly back into play.

For now, however, most of Popham's attention was still fixed in Europe – specifically Russia. The Tsar was furious at the campaign's failure, and the treatment of the Russian army after its close did not help. The Anglo-Russian treaty had stipulated that Britain would house the Russian troops over winter and ship them home in spring, but their commanding officer, Essen, was 'highly offended' to find they were being sent to the Channel Islands rather than being billeted in British barracks. Popham thought Essen, 'an ignorant Dog', was only causing trouble, and suggested the War Department send the Russians to Genoa to join Suvorov's forlorn forces: 'This Scheme would amuse them with a Winter's fighting instead of a Winter's plundering.'[71] Despite this irreverent attitude to Russian cooperation, for some reason the government felt Popham was still the linchpin of the faltering alliance. To make a show of favouring the Tsar's pet naval officer, therefore, George III – who had previously refused the same honour to the official ambassador, Whitworth – allowed Popham to wear his Order of the Knights of Malta in Britain and refer to himself as 'Sir', and granted him a pension of £500 a year.[72] Popham subsequently received orders to leave again for St Petersburg, ostensibly to arrange transportation for Russian troops as part of a joint Anglo-Russian assault on Minorca.[73] In reality, he was being sent to keep the Tsar in the coalition.

---

68  Popham to Spencer, 16 and 17 October 1799, Corbett (ed.), *Spencer Papers*, vol.3, pp.202–203, 204–205.
69  Alexander Mikaberidze, *The Napoleonic Wars: A Global History* (Oxford: Oxford University Press, 2020), pp.80–81.
70  Jonathan Parry, *Promised Lands: The British and the Ottoman Middle East* (New Haven, London: Yale University Press, 2022), p.46.
71  TNA: WO 1/411, ff.679–681: Popham to Huskisson, 21 October 1799.
72  *London Gazette*, 24–28 September 1799.
73  TNA: FO 65/45, ff.69–70: Grenville to Whitworth, 12 November 1799; Pitt to Grenville, 21 November 1799, *Dropmore MSS*, vol.6, pp.35–36.

The importance of the mission was clear: Popham had personal meetings with Dundas and Grenville and received his instructions from Pitt himself.[74]

Would Popham, the diplomatic ace up the government's sleeve, succeed in this last-ditch attempt at pacification? Whitworth thought not. In a ciphered letter, he wrote 'Capt[ain] P[opham]'s reception ... would not be such as to enable him to serve the Cause with equal success as when he was last here.'[75] This was not just because Popham had made enemies in St Petersburg, or because the Tsar had been seduced by the pro-French lobby at court. Whitworth, with his ambassadorial experience, had a much more realistic view of Popham's diplomatic skills than Pitt, Grenville, or Dundas. Popham's contemptuous treatment of Essen was only one symptom of a wider disease: he was too accustomed to speaking his mind.[76] Still, Whitworth could not deny Popham had some leverage with the Tsar himself. If Popham came quickly, he might succeed.

Unfortunately for all concerned, Popham took his time. 'I was three weeks pressing [him] ... to go, which he obstinately protracted,' Grenville raged.[77] Popham was still in Britain on Christmas Day, delayed by adverse winds, and bad weather continued to dog his entire journey. The previous summer, he had been so proud of racing to St Petersburg in a week; now, in winter, he travelled at walking pace. At the end of January, he abandoned his Royal Navy frigate in Norway and continued to travel alternately by cutter and by land, sometimes spending whole days struggling a handful of miles through three feet of snow. After being laid up with illness for a few weeks, he finally crawled into St Petersburg on 25 March, haggard and worse for wear. He had journeyed 1,100 miles from Stockholm at a rate of about 25 miles a day.[78]

Whitworth had been expecting Popham for nearly five months and his relief when he finally appeared was palpable.[79] But although Popham's travel difficulties were over, his diplomatic ones were only just beginning. He would have to persuade the Tsar to see him, and by the time Popham arrived Paul had stopped giving audiences to almost any foreign envoy.[80] It took Whitworth a fortnight even to get Popham the requisite passport to enter St Petersburg, where he was promptly ignored by everyone. He quickly became aware that the Order of Malta round his neck was the only mark of the Tsar's favour he had left. This put him in more than just an awkward position: he suspected he was also in physical danger. Knowing his every move was being watched, Popham asked Whitworth to pass on ciphered messages to London in invisible ink, as he himself had no safe method of communication.[81] When Popham wrote a long dispatch home on 1 April reporting that the Tsar's commitment to the cause against France was as strong as ever, Whitworth wrote an accompanying

---

74  Pitt to Grenville, 22 November 1799, *Dropmore MSS*, vol.6, p.36.
75  TNA: FO 65/45, ff.336–345: Whitworth to Grenville, 13 December 1799.
76  TNA: FO 65/45, ff.353–358: Whitworth to Grenville, 20 December 1799.
77  TNA: FO 65/45, ff.360–361: Note by Grenville, [December 1799].
78  TNA: FO 65/46, ff.93–96: Popham to Grenville, 28 January 1800; ff.99–100: Popham to Grenville, 31 January 1800; ff.265–268: Popham to Grenville, 1 April 1800; ff.187–190: Whitworth to Grenville, 6 March 1800; ff.241–242: Whitworth to Grenville, 25 March 1800.
79  TNA: FO 65/46, ff.150–151: Whitworth to Grenville, 21 February 1800.
80  Royal House Archive, The Hague (RHA): KHA A31 inv. nr 1048, letter no.11: Baron Hogguer to the Prince of Orange, 2/14 March 1800. Many thanks to Lien Verpoest for this reference.
81  TNA: FO 65/46, ff.321–322: Whitworth to Grenville, 14 April 1800.

invisible note of warning: 'If the stile or language in Sir Home Popham's dispatch to your Lordship should appear singular, ... both have been used purposely as the best adapted to the circumstances of the moment, since it is quite certain that all these dispatches will be opened and read here.'[82]

Whitworth, however, was not much safer than Popham. The two men learned the Tsar had demanded the ambassador's recall – effectively a declaration of war. 'The Emperor is literally not in his senses,' Whitworth wrote home, aghast.[83] Popham continued to press the Tsar to grant him an audience, but the closest he got was the opportunity to submit a memorial summarising his main arguments, something neither he nor Whitworth felt likely to succeed.[84] When yet another audience request on 13 April dropped into stony silence, Popham gave up and asked Whitworth for permission to go home.[85] This at last elicited a direct communication from the Tsar – a message informing Popham that, 'As I had expressed so strong a desire to return [to Britain], he cou'd not think of detaining me in this Country, and ... he therefore wish'd me a good Journey.'[86] There was no coming back from this transparent dismissal. Popham delayed his departure until 6 May in case things changed. When nothing did, he had no choice.

Regardless of whether Popham had overstated his diplomatic abilities, the problem he faced in the spring of 1800 was much bigger than one man. The Tsar would never have agreed to remain in the coalition. In December he invited Sweden, Denmark, and Prussia to join a League of Armed Neutrality aimed at preventing Britain from accessing essential naval supplies, such as hemp and timber, in the Baltic and North Sea.[87] Given what he had seen and heard in St Petersburg, Popham would not have been surprised to hear of the Tsar's murder in March 1801 by a group of disgruntled nobles – an act in which Whitworth may have been complicit.[88] After all, Popham could testify, from personal experience, that the Russian court was a dangerous place.

---

82  TNA: FO 65/46, f.280: Whitworth to Grenville, 2 April 1800. Whitworth's letters were being opened: RHA: KHA A31 inv. nr 1048, letter no.13: Hogguer to the Prince of Orange, [early May 1800]. Many thanks to Lien Verpoest for this reference.
83  James J. Kenney, 'Lord Whitworth and the Conspiracy Against Tsar Paul I: The New Evidence of the Kent Archive', *Slavic Review*, 36:2 (1977), pp.205–219, p.213.
84  TNA: FO 65/46, ff.305–310: Whitworth to Grenville, 10 April 1800.
85  TNA: FO 65/46, ff.325–328: Whitworth to Grenville, 18 April 1800.
86  TNA: FO 65/46, ff.353–354: Popham to Grenville, 29 April 1800.
87  Mikaberidze, *The Napoleonic Wars*, p.116–117.
88  Kenney, 'Lord Whitworth and the Conspiracy Against Tsar Paul I', p.219; Valentin Graf Zubow, *Zar Paul I: Mensch und Schicksal* (Stuttgart: K.F. Kochler Verlag, [1964]), p.67.

7

# The Red Sea, 1801–1803

*2231: When were you last docked?*

Popham returned to London at the end of May 1800 to find Pitt's government on the brink of crisis. With the collapse of the Second Coalition, the latent divisions within the ministry over strategy had broken open. Dundas, despairing over Britain's latest foray into continental warfare, hoped the cabinet would now turn its attention to India, which the presence of a French army in Egypt continued to threaten. He had managed to persuade his colleagues to send a force under Sir Ralph Abercromby to crush the remains of Napoleon's army, but he was feeling more and more politically alienated. The Foreign Secretary, Grenville, still hoped to keep Austria, Britain's last remaining ally, in the war. France, however – led, since November 1799, by Napoleon Bonaparte – was closing in from Italy and from Switzerland. Other factions within the cabinet wanted to sponsor a counter-revolution in France; still others felt a naval assault via Minorca or Portugal might turn the tide. Strong leadership might have shaped the chaos, but Pitt, the Prime Minister, was physically and mentally exhausted. In the background was the simmering problem of Ireland, which had rebelled in 1798. The rebellion had been suppressed but the country was still a drain on British manpower, while the politicians were distracted by the need to push through the Anglo-Irish Act of Union, which they hoped would solve all their problems in that quarter. A summer of poor harvests added to the trouble, and parts of Britain also seemed close to insurrection.[1]

With the government unable to settle on a single strategy, Popham spent the summer unemployed. He continued pushing his pet scheme of fomenting an uprising in the Batavian Republic by invading Walcheren and the surrounding islands, and met with Dundas and Spencer in June to discuss the possibility.[2] Popham was not shy about expressing his preference for Walcheren, which he described as 'a situation of more than common importance'. Establishing a British garrison there would not only deprive France of Flushing, a rich merchant hub with links to the Indies from which Popham had often sailed with *Etrusco*; it would also allow Britain to make a demonstration in favour of its allies, namely Austria, currently taking a pummelling in Italy. Possessing Walcheren might even allow the allies to

---

1    Mackesy, *War Without Victory*, pp.122, 126–127; Roger Wells, *Insurrection: The British Experience, 1795–1803* (London: Alan Sutton, 1983), pp.182–184.
2    Dundas to Spencer, 20 June 1800, Corbett (ed.), *Spencer Papers*, vol.4, p.285.

place pressure on French-held territories across the Rhine. Popham argued it would be easy to send 6,000 British troops to the island, while doing so would force the French to garrison the surrounding area with 20,000 men – 20,000 men Austria would not have to face.³

It was an attractive pitch but, after the Helder disaster, nobody in the cabinet had any intention of returning to Holland for some time. The most immediate threat now came from Russia and its Armed Neutrality, so rather than attacking Walcheren, Popham's next employment was to accompany the Baltic squadron to Copenhagen, where he was to liaise with the British envoy to Denmark – none other than Sir Charles Whitworth, his old friend from Russia, now elevated to the peerage as Lord Whitworth. For once, the appointment did not come through Dundas: it was Spencer's idea.⁴ Spencer also placed Popham in the 50-gun HMS *Romney*. For the first time since his few weeks superintending the attack on Ostend, Popham was in command of a ship.

Charles, Lord Whitworth, by H. Robinson after Sir Thomas Lawrence. (Public domain, The Miriam and Ira D. Wallach Division of Art, Prints and Photographs, The New York Public Library)

Whitworth was in Denmark because, in July 1800, a neutral Danish convoy passing through the Channel had been stopped by the British. The ship protecting the convoy, the *Freya*, had been fired on and seized, and a diplomatic crisis had ensued.⁵ The government did not want to chase the Danes into the arms of Russia's Armed Neutrality and decided to open diplomatic negotiations through Whitworth, but they also sent a Baltic squadron to drive in the point. Vice Admiral Sir Archibald Dickson was therefore dispatched with seven ships of the line, including *Romney*, with the proviso that no hostile act was to be committed unless the Danes threw the first stone.⁶

Popham, in HMS *Romney*, sailed ahead of Dickson's squadron and arrived on 16 August off Kronborg Castle at Elsinore, carefully navigating the shallow Kattegat. The Danes did not make any immediate protest at the arrival of a British man of war, but all the signs

---

3   Popham to Spencer, 11 July 1800, Corbett (ed.), *Spencer Papers*, vol.4, pp.285–290.
4   Spencer to Grenville, 1 August 1800, Corbett (ed.), *Spencer Papers*, vol.4, p.287.
5   John Ehrman, *The Younger Pitt: The Consuming Struggle* (Stanford, CA: Stanford University Press, 1996), p.394.
6   Gareth Glover, *The Two Battles of Copenhagen, 1801 and 1807: Britain and Denmark in the Napoleonic Wars* (Barnsley: Pen & Sword, 2018), p.15 and p.15n2; cabinet minute, 30 July 1800, A. Aspinall (ed.), *The Later Correspondence of George III* (Cambridge: Cambridge University Press, 1967), vol.3, no.2209.

Popham could see were for war. At Elsinore, Popham found three 74-gun Danish ships and a guardship, which he recorded in a letter for Lord Spencer's information. He also found one more 74-gun ship at Copenhagen, and learned that six others had been put into commission the previous week and were fitting out 'with all possible dispatch'. Popham also saw two regiments march into the castle and noted the Danes were mounting guns on the castle ramparts, 'that we may have the pleasure of dismounting them'.[7] Popham may have been sent to liaise with the diplomats negotiating a truce, but he was clearly gunning for a fight, and the prospect that the Danes might not take Whitworth's olive branch delighted him.

While he waited for Vice Admiral Dickson to catch up, Popham opened communications with Lord Whitworth. The ambassador had been making little diplomatic headway with the Danes, who were stringing out negotiations in the hope of military assistance from Russia. Whitworth was hamstrung by his instructions which forbade him from breaching the talks unless the Danes attacked British shipping or mercantile property in the Baltic or threw Whitworth out of the country. As none of this had happened, Whitworth could neither leave nor make an ultimatum. Popham's arrival, with news of Dickson's approach, delighted him. He hoped the British squadron, even if it did nothing, would scare the Danes into agreeing to whatever he proposed: 'Nothing will I am persuaded bring them to reason, but the fear of having the town beat about their ears.'[8] He also confirmed what Popham had hoped: the Danes were a lot weaker than they wanted to make out. The five ships at Elsinore and Copenhagen were their only force, and the six new ships in commission would not be ready for some time. Whitworth might have been hoping to avoid actual violence, but this news only whetted Popham's lust for action. Despite knowing the cabinet wished the Danes to make the first move, Popham thought Dickson's squadron should strike a pre-emptive blow: 'Every day of lost time is an advantage to the Danes.'[9]

On 17 August, therefore, when Dickson and the rest of the squadron arrived at Elsinore, Popham triumphantly announced he had a plan for just such a pre-emptive attack sorted. In his opinion, which he gave to a startled Dickson 'very freely', the squadron should position itself in a chain two miles from Kronborg Castle to cut off the main part of the Danish fleet and prepare to bombard Copenhagen. Ever the man of action, Popham felt a brief, deadly firework display would have more effect than talking round a table, allowing Whitworth to obtain all the concessions Britain wanted and more.[10] Dickson was aghast, but Popham was once again gambling that the government would not mind him going beyond the letter of his instructions. Relying on initiative, and the nebulous limits of 'discretion', was a running theme throughout his career, and he may have come to believe the main reason he continued being employed was that the government actually wanted a man whose creative interpretation of his orders might open up new strategic avenues; Dundas had, after all, backed him up when he had gone off-script in Russia. At Copenhagen, however, Popham was not under Dundas's orders but Spencer's. His reaction to the possibility Spencer might be less likely to turn a blind eye was to call the First Lord's bluff. 'I act with great pleasure and much confidence because I believe very firmly Your Lordship is satisfied of my opinions in general, and

---

7   Popham to Spencer, 16 August 1800, Corbett (ed.), *Spencer Papers*, vol.4, p.267.
8   SLV: Accession no. MS 13020 (prev. M5142): Whitworth to Popham, 19 August [1800].
9   Popham to Spencer, 17 August 1800, Corbett (ed.), *Spencer Papers*, vol.4, p.268.
10  Popham to Spencer, 17 August 1800, Corbett (ed.), *Spencer Papers*, vol.4, pp.267–270.

my steady zeal for the honour of my patrons and the credit of my country,' he wrote, almost daring him to say otherwise.[11]

Despite his clear preference for action, Popham did not interfere with the diplomatic process. In fact, he assisted in it, as *Romney* transmitted messages from Lord Whitworth on shore to Vice Admiral Dickson, using a code based on the existing naval signal book but adapted to immediate needs. *Romney* also acted as the meeting point for a parley between Vice Admiral Dickson and *Kontreadmiral* Otto Lutken on 20 August. No agreement was reached, and Whitworth subsequently presented the Danish with an ultimatum: if British demands were not met within a week, negotiations would end.[12] Whitworth did not specify what would happen next, but the presence of the British warships in Elsinore Roads was not intended to reassure. At the same time, the government in London had begun toughening its position. On 25 August, the cabinet authorised Dickson to use force if Whitworth's mission failed, and Spencer told Popham four more ships of the line were on their way.[13] The Danish government also decided to flex its muscles, and four more Danish battleships and a frigate anchored off Copenhagen on 26 August. This was particularly galling to Popham, who could not help reminding Spencer that his original plan to cut off Copenhagen from outside assistance would have prevented these reinforcements reaching the city.[14] However, after several days of sabre-rattling, on 29 August the Danes blinked first. Whitworth signed a convention with the Danish government agreeing to restore the merchant vessels that had been captured in the Channel the previous summer.[15]

This convention did not prevent the Danes from throwing their lot in with Russia's Armed Neutrality after all. In April 1801, another British squadron under Lord Nelson carried out the bombardment of Copenhagen Popham had been itching for. For now, however, Popham's job liaising with Lord Whitworth was done. On 31 August, Popham received orders to sail back to England with dispatches for the Admiralty and for Lord Grenville. Popham made Orford Ness on 4 September, and by 5 September the dispatches had reached their intended recipients.[16] Popham may not have got the action he had wanted, but at least he had done his duty.

Popham had had plenty of time during his mission to Copenhagen to assess the sailing qualities of his new ship, and he was not impressed. *Romney* was, he complained, 'the Crankest Ship I ever was in' – it carried its weight low, it leaned terribly, and sailed far too close to the waterline behind the stern.[17] The ship's state caused him major headaches the whole time he was in command, with long-term consequences for his reputation and career. But there

---

11    Popham to Spencer, 17 August 1800, Corbett (ed.), *Spencer Papers*, vol.4, pp.267–270.
12    Carl Edward Creasman, Jr., 'The naval career of Sir Home Riggs Popham from Copenhagen to Copenhagen, 1800–1807', MA Thesis, Auburn University, 1988, p.12.
13    Cabinet minute, 25 August 1800, Aspinall (ed.), *Later Correspondence of George III*, vol.3, no.2230; Spencer to Popham, 25 August 1800, Corbett (ed.), *Spencer Papers*, vol.4, p.272.
14    TNA: ADM 51/4493: log, HMS *Romney*, 26 August 1800.
15    Ehrman, *The Younger Pitt: The Consuming Struggle*, p.394n4.
16    TNA: ADM 51/4493: log, HMS *Romney*, 31 August–4 September 1800.
17    TNA: ADM 1/2321: Popham to Nepean, 3 September 1800.

was no time for a refit. The European war was effectively finished, and the government's attention was turning towards India and the Middle East. Dundas had been thinking about turfing the French out of Egypt for a long time: 'possession of Egypt will in my opinion be ... the master key to all the commerce of the world.'[18] The failure of an assault on the Spanish fleet at Cadiz under Sir Ralph Abercromby in the summer of 1800 provided Dundas with an excuse to send this 15,000-man army to Egypt instead.[19] The plan was for Abercromby to march on Alexandria; Turkey, currently Britain's ally, would attack from Syria; and a force of 5,000 East India Company men under Major General David Baird would land from the Red Sea to join with Abercromby if possible. Together, these forces should be more than strong enough to overcome the 13,000 Frenchmen Dundas estimated remained in Egypt (the number was actually closer to 24,000).[20]

Popham was ordered to take HMS *Romney*, with a small naval squadron, to carry Baird to and from the Red Sea.[21] Popham had already made a name for himself in Flanders, Germany, and the Netherlands as an expert in the amphibious movement of troops; he was a natural choice for a command that involved moving men quickly by water. As was often the case, however, Popham's mission involved more than met the eye. There were already five ships of war in the Red Sea under Rear Admiral John Blankett, who had commanded there since April 1799,[22] but Popham was explicitly not placed under Blankett's orders; nor would he be under the command of Vice Admiral Peter Rainier, who commanded in the Indian Ocean more generally. Popham had another purpose, as envisioned by Dundas in his role as President of the East India Company Board of Control. The states lining the Red Sea were nominally under the rule of the Ottoman Empire, Britain's ally, but the British government felt the Ottoman state was corrupt, unstable, and vulnerable to French influence.[23] Dundas wanted to insure against Ottoman collapse by making trade agreements with some of the larger Red Sea states, particularly Mocha, with its major trading port of Jedda, and Aden, which controlled the entrance to the Red Sea. This would at once deprive the French in Egypt of essential supplies, reduce the threat of French expansion towards India, and secure new trading partners for British goods. The mission required a delicate but firm hand to secure the required concessions, while paying due attention to local customs, culture, and religious sensibilities. Dundas, astonishingly, decided Popham could provide that delicacy.

Popham was, to put it mildly, missing the subtlety that transformed a negotiator into a diplomat. Copenhagen had betrayed his preference for the persuasiveness of a bombardment over political finesse. However, as with the Russian mission, Dundas wanted a Red Sea envoy to be under his purview and not that of the Foreign Office. Besides, Popham's Russian experience had shown Dundas that he was capable of thinking on his feet and taking the initiative in a difficult environment. Dundas did not need a career diplomat: he needed a man with an eye for detail, who was not afraid of being firm, and who, crucially, agreed with

---

18   Dundas to Spencer, [23 April] 1798, Corbett (ed.), *Spencer Papers*, vol.2, p.317.
19   Piers Mackesy, *British Victory in Egypt: The End of Napoleon's Conquest* (London: Tauris Parke Paperbacks, 2010), p.5.
20   Divall, *Sir Ralph Abercromby*, p.250; Mackesy, *British Victory in Egypt*, p.56.
21   BL: Add MS 13708, ff.9–21: Lord Wellesley to Abercromby, February 1801.
22   Parry, *Promised Lands*, p.39.
23   Parry, *Promised Lands*, p.46.

Dundas's way of thinking about the importance of commerce and of India to the broader British war effort. Popham was very much that man – or at least he persuaded Dundas that he was. As Dundas wrote to the Governor-General of India, Marquess Wellesley, 'He is so thoroughly informed upon all our wishes and views, I think there is little danger of misapprehension.'[24] So long as Dundas remained at the helm, Popham had employment opportunities queued up into the foreseeable future. Nor was he worried about the *Etrusco* case any longer, and its impact on his career. The Crown had not given up its claim on the value of the vessel and its cargo, but Popham felt bold and secure enough to address Dundas directly on the subject, and he may even have traded in his services in the Red Sea for a promise from Dundas that the *Etrusco* case would be sorted out in his favour.[25]

On 19 September 1800, Popham composed a long memorandum in the character of a man familiar with the climate and landscape of Africa and India. It included detailed suggestions regarding medical care, local practicalities, and logistical arrangements for delivering Baird's troops to their destination, while playing up the importance of Egypt to the defence of India. As befitted a man who spent much of his career facilitating clear and concise communications at sea, Popham saw his writings as a way of showcasing his ideas and thoughts, and he was singing, full-throatedly and with enthusiasm, from Dundas's strategic hymn-book, knowing his career depended on keeping the patronage of the Secretary of State for War. Typically, Popham finished by warning Dundas that, if he chose to adopt any of his suggestions, he should keep Popham's name out of it:

> I am aware that a variety of difficulties and objections will be started to everything I have suggested if it is known the Ideas come from me, but I am ready to meet them, and enter into fair discussion with any Person who may conceive he knows more of the relative Situation and Interests of the different Countries, or has more practical or Geographical knowledge of them than myself.[26]

Popham's confidence may have grown, but he still remembered the Navy did not trust him.

On 5 October, the King gave his assent to the Egyptian expedition, and official preparations began immediately.[27] Lord Wellesley was informed on 6 October of the need to send Baird and 5,000 regular and East India Company soldiers to the Red Sea.[28] Popham received Admiralty orders to rendezvous with Baird at Mocha, after calling at the Cape of Good Hope to pick up another regiment. He also received separate instructions from the East India Company's Secret Committee, copied to the Governor-General, from whom Popham would receive orders while on the spot. Popham was instructed to press for a British

---

24  Dundas to Spencer, 2 November 1800, Corbett (ed.), *Spencer Papers*, vol.4, p.238.
25  BL: Add MS 41080: Popham to Dundas, 28 November 1800.
26  National Records of Scotland (NRS): Melville MSS, GD51/1/775: Popham to Dundas, 19 September 1800.
27  Cabinet minute, 3 October 1800; the King's reply, 5 October 1800, Aspinall (ed.), *Later Correspondence of George III*, vol.3, no.2256.
28  BL: Add MS 13708, ff.9–21: Wellesley to Abercromby, February 1801.

resident at Jedda and other commercial ports in the Red Sea; to request permission to establish British factories in Mocha, with permission for residents to choose their own staff; to request that no further duties should be paid on British goods, either bought or sold; and that all merchants should be free to trade with British factories.[29]

This done, Popham settled down to getting the crank, creaky *Romney* up to spec. The ship finally got a thorough refit, but when Popham sailed at the beginning of November to the Downs, where he intended to collect the rest of his squadron, he ran straight into a storm. Popham, watching his marine barometers carefully, saw something was up and proposed a change of course towards the North Sea.[30] The wind picked up as the ship cleared the flats off Margate and came to with the best bower. As the rain began to fall and the wind got worse, Popham also deployed the small bower and the topgallant masts were brought down to ride out the storm. But the wind rapidly increased and became more westerly. Popham later described it as 'a perfect Hurricane, more resembling a Tuffoon [sic] in the China Seas than any thing I ever experienced'. The ship parted from its anchors; it was driving very quickly – Popham thought from SSE to SSW, but the visibility was so poor the compasses could barely be read. He and his men clung on, for the ship's deck heaved far too violently for them to stand unaided. The sea broke over the upper deck and washed away the bucklers;[31] the ship sprang a leak between decks; the crew was kept busy pumping hard to prevent the ship filling with water. And somewhere out to sea were the sand flats *Romney* had only just cleared.

The pilots recommended removing the masts to prevent the ship being beached. Popham hesitated, knowing *Romney* would be helpless without them, but the ship just kept leaning more and more as the waves broke over its deck, so he gave the order for the mizzen mast to be cut away. It was so beaten up that 'one blow from a small Hatchet' was enough to send it overboard. With it went one of the quartermasters appointed to oversee the steering of the ship, tangled in the rigging. Soon after the mainmast went over the side as well, along with three carronades and some 32-pounders from the main and quarterdeck to help the ship come right. For an agonising spell nothing happened, and Popham feared he had not acted in time. After what must have felt like a lifetime, the ship brought up. Popham gave orders to fire the guns to summon assistance, but the storm was too fierce for the guns to be heard. Popham finally managed to get his ship under control after rigging up jury masts at the main and mizzen. It was nevertheless, as the log book termed it, a 'disaster'. Two days later, *Romney* limped back into Sheerness harbour, shattered and subdued, firing six guns as a signal for assistance.[32]

Popham had been lucky: the only structural damage to the ship was the loss of some of the coppering on the starboard side.[33] But it had been a close call, and time was running out to meet Baird and his men at Mocha. While *Romney* was being patched up again, therefore,

---

29   BL: India Office Records (IOR)/G/177 part 1, ff.111–113: Popham's instructions, 10 November 1800.
30   According to the novel *Gentleman Jack*, Popham insisted on sailing despite protests from his pilots. It is not clear how much of the novel is fanciful, but its description of the storm matches Popham's, and that of *Romney*'s log, in most respects. Neale, *Gentleman Jack*, vol.1, pp.308–309.
31   Wooden shutters.
32   TNA: ADM 41/4493: log, HMS *Romney*, 10–12 November 1800; TNA: ADM 1/2321: Popham to Nepean, 10 November 1800.
33   TNA: ADM 1/2321: Popham to Nepean, 10 November 1800.

Popham hurried to Deal to meet with the captains of the rest of his squadron – HMS *Sensible*, troopships *Wilhelmina* and *Sheerness*, and the sloop *Victor*. *Romney* was ready by the end of November, but the stormy weather continued, and the squadron only left British waters on 5 December, sailing so swiftly to take advantage of fair winds that *Romney* left some of its water casks behind.[34]

The bad weather continued until Madeira, which *Romney* reached on 18 December, having left the slower troopships *Sheerness* and *Wilhelmina* in its wake. Popham was starting to fear he might miss the agreed rendezvous with Baird, for whom he was carrying important dispatches.[35] *Romney* and *Sensible* parted company with the slower *Wilhelmina*, *Sheerness*, and *Victor* on 27 December south of the Canary Islands and crossed the equator on 9 January. This was celebrated in the usual manner, but also – fittingly, given Popham's reputation as a martinet – with a string of punishments. Theft, contempt, and drunkenness all featured as reasons, suggesting the crew was starting to get bored.[36] Despite this, Popham felt confident he was looking after the health of his men on what was, after all, his first long-distance trip ever as a Royal Navy captain. He bragged to the Admiralty that he only had a dozen men on the sick list: 'The Provisions supplied the Romney have been of the very best Quality I ever saw, to which, with the addition of Sour Crout well washed ... the Essence of Malt made regularly into Beer with Hops, and the Lime Juice made into Punch every Evening, I materially attribute the Health of the People.'[37]

*Romney* sighted the Cape of Good Hope on 12 February and arrived in Table Bay next day.[38] While *Sensible* disembarked the troops it carried for the garrison, Popham tried to work out what his quickest route onwards might be to make up for all his lost time. He had previously planned to go east of the island of Rodrigues and carry on towards Bombay, but because he was so much behind schedule he decided to go instead through the Mozambique Channel with the aim of reaching Mocha in March – already one month later than planned.[39] Unfortunately, although the sloop *Victor* appeared at the Cape on 14 February, *Sheerness* and *Wilhelmina* did not catch up with the rest of the squadron until the end of the month. Both ships had suffered considerable sickness: 63 men, women, and children from *Sheerness* and 16 from *Wilhelmina* were buried on shore, while the ships were thoroughly fumigated, washed down with lime, and ventilated from end to end. Popham was beside himself with frustration, taking it out on anyone who was unfortunate enough to be in the vicinity, but eventually everything was ready and *Romney*, along with *Sensible* and *Victor*, the *Sea Nymph* transport, and the *Regulus* store ship, were able to leave on 1 March.[40]

The journey through the Mozambique Channel may have saved time but, after a good start, the squadron hit strong gales on 21 March.[41] 'It was not a very pleasant navigation,' Lieutenant Colonel Thomas Rudsdall, travelling in *Sensible*, told Lord Spencer with

---

34 TNA: ADM 1/2321: Popham to Nepean, 30 November, 1, 3, 4, 5 December; TNA: ADM 1/2327: Popham to William Marsden, 28 August 1804.
35 TNA: ADM 1/2321: Popham to Nepean, 22 December 1800.
36 TNA: ADM 51/4493: log, HMS *Romney*, 27 December 1800–9 January 1801.
37 TNA: ADM 1/2321: Popham to Nepean, 17 February 1801.
38 TNA: ADM 51/4493: log, HMS *Romney*, 18 January–13 February 1801.
39 TNA: ADM 1/2321: Popham to Nepean, 17 February 1801.
40 TNA: ADM 1/2323: Popham to Nepean, 17, 26 February 1801.
41 TNA: ADM 1/2323: Popham to Nepean, 22 September 1801.

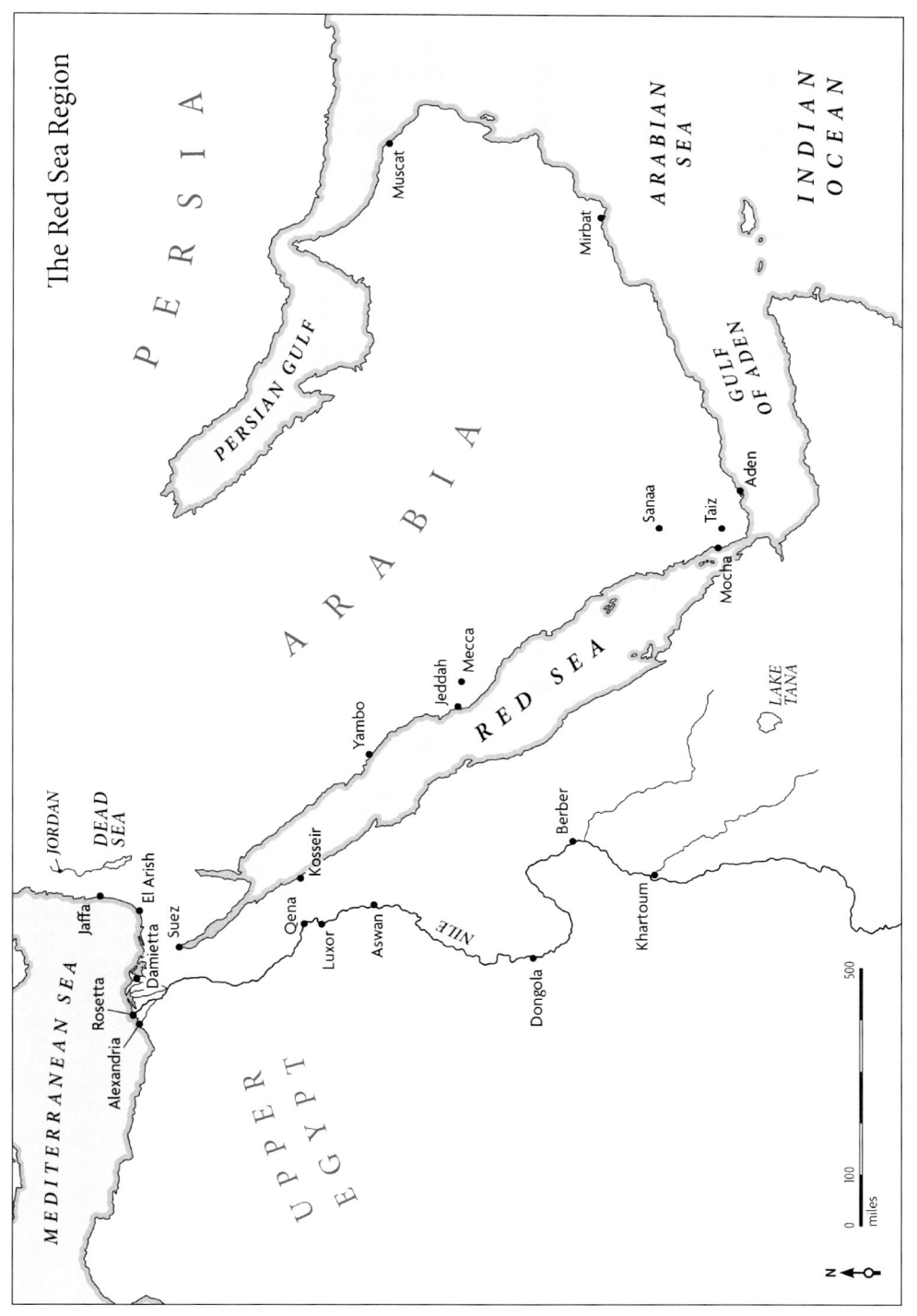

The Red Sea, 1801–1803.

remarkable understatement. '... We one night experienced a most violent squall, it came on about midnight and took us with every sail set the ship would carry, in an instant was carried away our fore and mizen top-masts, fore-yard and jib-boom, the main top sail sprung and all our sails damaged.'[42] *Romney*, thankfully, was undamaged, but *Victor* took a pummelling and *Sensible* was so crippled it had to be towed. On 3 April, the beleaguered squadron reached the Comoros Islands to take on water, where it spent several frustrating days due to 'baffling winds, anchoring and weighing and a great deal of bother'.[43] At the beginning of May, nearly three months late, the ships finally reached Aden at the mouth of the Red Sea.

Popham feared Baird might have been waiting at the rendezvous since February and went immediately ashore for news. He learned Abercromby's force had landed at Aboukir at the mouth of the Nile on 7 March and secured a significant victory

Sir David Baird, by Anthony Cardon after A.J. Oliver, 1806. (Public domain, Yale Center for British Art, Paul Mellon Collection)

two weeks later. Abercromby himself had been killed, and the rest of his army, now under the command of Lieutenant General John Hely Hutchinson, was besieging what remained of the French troops in Alexandria. Popham also discovered that, as he had feared, Baird's force of 3,000 European and 2,600 Indian troops had already arrived at Mocha, although only 12 days previously.[44] They had gone on to Jedda, so Popham left immediately to join them. Things were moving faster now, much to Popham's relief, although in his hyperactive state he still described it as only 'tolerable expedition'.[45] After inching into the shallows of Jedda Roads, sounding all the way, Popham dropped his anchor on 21 May.

Baird, a massive and athletic Scotsman about five years Popham's senior, was known for his steadiness and bravery rather than for his creativity in battle, but he and Popham hit it off almost instantly, perhaps sharing the instinct to get a job done and do it well. The two men talked about the best course of action. Baird wanted to get his force as close to Suez as possible so he could march the remaining 80 miles to join Hutchinson outside Cairo, but there was a major snag. The navigation of the Red Sea did not allow for ships to go above Kosseir, 400 miles from Cairo, between May and August, when the winds changed from a favourable southerly direction to a distinctly unfavourable northerly direction. This also

---

42  Colonel Rudsdall to Spencer, 10 May 1801, Corbett (ed.), *Spencer Papers*, vol.4, p.257.
43  Popham to Spencer, 29 March 1801, Corbett (ed.), *Spencer Papers*, vol.4, p.257.
44  BL: Add MS 13708, f.26: Lord Wellesley to Koehler, 7 March 1801.
45  TNA: ADM 1/2323: Popham to Wellesley, diary, 12 May–20 July 1801.

meant the campaign would need to conclude before the winds changed back to southerly in September, preventing Popham's squadron from dropping further down the Red Sea.[46] In other words, Popham's three-month delay was already causing problems, and the campaign was beginning at the worst possible time for naval operations. Popham therefore suggested Baird should board *Romney* and sail with him, so they could discuss how to get Baird to Cairo. Baird agreed and boarded *Romney* on 23 May.[47]

Over the next fortnight, Popham and Baird talked at great length about what would happen once he and his men were in a position to proceed inland. They also talked local policy, as Popham tried to situate himself in the midst of Red Sea politics. Popham was fulfilling his Admiralty orders, but he was mindful he was also the East India Company envoy. As he sailed, therefore, he made contact with the British envoy to Sana'a, one of the Red Sea states, sending him his credentials and asking for any local information.[48] Popham also stopped to visit Ghalib, the Sharif of Mecca, bearing presents including a pearl rosary, cotton, velvet, and satin cloth, a brace of pistols, a carriage, and an assortment of sugars and spices: cardamom, clove, and nutmeg.[49] Ghalib had significant influence as the man in whose territory lay the Muslim sacred city of Mecca. He had long shown signs of wanting independence from the Ottoman Porte, which did not make him naturally inclined to favour Britain, allied to the Ottomans. Popham presented his credentials from the East India Company and explained that he wished to open trade discussions, but he already thought he would not succeed. Popham's diplomatic limitations were showing again. He had set out believing the Sharif to be false, and that was what he found: 'I had little to expect of any intercourse with [the Sharif], especially while the French remain Masters of Egypt. … He gave such evasive Answers to all I proposed, that I was convinced he only wanted to gain time … 'till he saw the event of this Campaign.'[50]

For now, however, Popham's military duties were salient. By the time the troops landed at Kosseir on 7 June, Popham and Baird had agreed that the easiest way to get to Hutchinson in Cairo while avoiding unfavourable Red Sea winds was to brave 'the Hazards and fatigues of this dreary Desert' and march 400 miles inland.[51] It would be a nearly impossible task to get several thousand troops across a burning desert, but 'making a Bengal sepoy shake hands with a Coldstream guardsman on the banks of the Nile' was a logistical puzzle Popham could not resist.[52] The quickest route would be to march straight to Qena on the Nile and then follow the river with locally hired boats, overseen by a contingent of sailors under Popham's command. In this way, Popham estimated, it would take about 12 days to get to Qena and then between 20 and 35 days to get to Cairo, depending on winds and currents. Popham was not sure what would happen if water could not be procured en route or if the Nile overflowed, causing a detour; nor was he entirely sure how long it would take the army

---

46  BL: Add MS 13708, ff.9–21: Wellesley to Abercromby, February 1801.
47  TNA: ADM 1/2323: Popham to Wellesley, diary, 12 May–20 July 1801; TNA: ADM 51/4493: log, HMS *Romney*, 23 May 1801.
48  TNA: ADM 1/2323: Popham to John Pringle, 15 June 1801.
49  BL: IOR/G/177 part 1, f.334: questions submitted to Mahdi Ali Khan, 7 March 1801.
50  BL: IOR/G/177 part 1, f.142: Popham to Elgin, 26 June 1801; [T. Hook], *The Life of General the Right Honourable Sir David Baird, Bart.* … (London: Richard Bentley, 1832), vol.1, pp.312–313.
51  TNA: ADM 1/2323: Popham to Wellesley, diary, 12 May–20 July 1801.
52  Edward Ingram, *The British Empire as a World Power* (London: Frank Cass, 2001), p.244.

to return. But this was detail, and when Popham had an idea in his head, details did not matter. All being well, he estimated Baird would be back in Suez between September and the end of the year, when the squadron would sail up from Jedda to collect them.[53]

Popham and Baird were just getting into their stride with the planning when Rear Admiral Blankett made his first appearance on 24 June. About 60 years old, Blankett's health, and temper, had been ruined by long service in a hot climate. His reception of Popham was polite but cool. He and Rainier had been informed that Popham's superiors were not merely at the Admiralty, but also at the War Department and at India House. 'Popham's appointment precludes the necessity of my interference of affairs in the Red Sea, as he is not placed under my orders,' Vice Admiral Rainier observed, sardonically, and Blankett was just as unsure where Popham fell within the chain of command.[54] Blankett's health was bad and he had already asked to be sent home, but he also felt he was *de trop* now that Popham had appeared, and this soured his attitude.[55] When Popham told Blankett of the plans he and Baird had made to cross the desert together, Blankett refused to allow it and ordered Popham, 'at my peril',[56] to take *Romney* back to Mocha.[57] Popham was incensed: Blankett's order, he claimed, had so affected him that he had 'been obliged to begin a course of Calomel for the Liver'. Frustrated in his desire to be involved in any action, Popham went into a sulk and wrote to the Admiralty demanding to be sent home.[58] A good portion of this was pique, but some of it reflected Popham's sense that Blankett – and, beyond him, the Admiralty – was taking him for granted. At least Popham knew the Admiralty was not his only, or even his most important, employer.

Popham saw Baird and his army off on their gruelling march at the end of June and departed Kosseir on 2 July.[59] He returned to Jedda to discover Blankett's ill health had taken a turn for the worse. On 14 July, Blankett died aboard his flagship. This was good news for Popham, although it came two weeks too late for him to be able to join Baird. Still, Blankett's death meant Popham no longer had to worry about superior officers breathing down his neck. With Vice Admiral Rainier somewhere far away in the Indian Ocean, Popham now had no immediate superior other than his own initiative.

Popham's first independent act was to hand over the Red Sea command to Captain Sause of *Sensible* and go to Calcutta. This was a bizarre and startling course of action given the limitations of his Admiralty orders, and Popham could only justify it by claiming Baird had expressed the hope he would update the Governor-General on the progress made by the Indian troops.[60] *Romney* was also in desperate need of repair; the ship had received a battering before it had even left British shores, and it had not weathered the long journey to the Red Sea well. A proper refit would be possible at Calcutta, where Popham knew there were excellent dockyards. This refit, however, was only an excuse. Bombay would have been

---

53  TNA: ADM 1/2323: memorandum, 15 June 1801.
54  Creasman, 'Sir Home Riggs Popham', p.29.
55  Admiral Rainier to Spencer, 10 May 1801, Corbett (ed.), *Spencer Papers*, vol.4, pp.250–257.
56  TNA: ADM 1/2323: Popham to Nepean, 29 June 1801.
57  TNA: ADM 1/2323: Popham to Wellesley, diary, 12 May–20 July 1801.
58  TNA: ADM 1/2323: Popham to Nepean, 29 June 1801.
59  TNA: ADM 1/2323: Popham to Wellesley, diary, 12 May–20 July 1801.
60  TNA: ADM 1/2323: Popham to Nepean, 10 September 1801.

a much closer, and more logical, place to go; he would certainly never have got permission from Rear Admiral Blankett to go all the way to the other side of the subcontinent. But Blankett was dead, and what Popham really wanted was a reason to introduce himself in person to Marquess Wellesley, whose high social standing and political connections made him a man worth courting.

Popham did at least apply for permission to Vice Admiral Rainier, who politely replied that, since he had no authority over him, Popham could do whatever he wanted.[61] But Popham was only going through the motions, and he had not even waited to receive Rainier's answer. He set sail on 20 July, clearing Aden at the mouth of the Red Sea two days later. After a stormy voyage, during which *Romney* sustained still more damage, Popham dropped anchor in Kedgeree Roads, near Calcutta, on 6 August. A few days later the ship docked in Diamond Harbour on the Hooghly River, where preliminary investigations suggested it had been lucky to survive the journey at all.[62]

Richard, Marquess Wellesley, by Samuel Cousins after Sir Thomas Lawrence, 1842. (Public domain, The Miriam and Ira D. Wallach Division of Art, Prints and Photographs, The New York Public Library)

While the dockyard workers prepared *Romney* to be reconditioned at Mayapur yards, Popham turned to the real reason he had come to Calcutta and informed Lord Wellesley of his desire for a meeting. On 11 August, Lord Wellesley replied with an invitation to visit.[63] Two days later, three boats sent by Wellesley sailed through the haze of the early autumn rains to take Popham and his suite to Calcutta. Popham left for shore under a 15-gun salute.[64] As the monsoon rains set in properly, the sultry air broken with flashes of lightning and rolls of thunder, Popham and Wellesley spent several days in conversation. Popham updated Wellesley on everything he had done since his arrival in the Red Sea, naturally inflating his role in getting Baird and his men to where they needed to be, and brought him up to speed on the situation in Mocha, where he claimed the Sharif would never accept British dominance. Popham followed this up with a lengthy report on spreading the East India Company's trading monopoly to the Red Sea ports via some diplomatic magic. Militarily, Popham persuaded Wellesley to commit to sending more reinforcements to join Hutchinson and Baird at Cairo, but in early September it became clear this would be

---

61  TNA: ADM 1/2323: Rainier to Popham, 9 August 1811.
62  TNA: ADM 1/2323: repairs to HMS *Romney* in the River Hooghly.
63  TNA: ADM 1/2323: Wellesley to Popham, 11 August 1801.
64  TNA: ADM 51/4493: log, HMS *Romney*, 6–13 August 1801.

redundant: news arrived that Hutchinson had forced the French to sign articles of capitulation. The question now became whether Baird's troops could be applied elsewhere. Popham, of course, had ideas about this. Arguing that troops should never be allowed to grow bored, Popham dug into his long experience of trading in the Indian Ocean to draw up plans for attacking Mauritius (Ile de France), Manila, and Java (Batavia), and gave the Governor-General some tips on how the Portuguese territory of Macao might be defended against French encroachments.[65] He apologised for bombarding Wellesley with papers: 'I am aware, in many instances, my ideas want pruning … [My ideas] I confess are owing to the speculative formation of my brain.'[66]

As always when approaching a potential new patron, Popham was fishing to discover what kind of impression he might have made, and to decide whether to pipe down or carry on. Wellesley's response was encouraging. The Governor-General politely thanked Popham for all his advice, which had provided 'a more accurate view of the State of our Army in Egypt, as well as of the Affairs of Arabia, than I could possibly have acquired in any other mode'.[67] Wellesley did not yet know his man well enough to realise such praise would swell Popham's eagerness to show off to almost manic proportions. At the beginning of September, Wellesley left Calcutta on a visit to the province of Oudh. While he was away, he gave Popham responsibility for collecting the stores and provisions for the British army in Egypt, and placed the transports for carrying these supplies under Popham's command.[68] As often happened when offered a crumb of independence, Popham bit off a huge chunk. Instead of merely taking the transports he needed, Popham took detailed stock of the entire transport situation in the Indian Ocean and the Red Sea and advised a severe reduction in the amount of available tonnage to a total of 7,000 tonnes.[69] Popham should at the very least have secured permission for this, but he decided the authority of the Governor-General over the Egyptian army supply chain must have included responsibility for rearranging shipping in the Red Sea more generally, and sacked the majority of the transports.

What might have worked on Dundas, however, did not work on Wellesley. The Governor-General might have cast a benevolent eye on Popham's expedition proposals, since a proposal did not represent an absolute commitment, but he drew the line at actual logistical meddling. 'I dare say you will hear that Lord Wellesley has imbibed some little prejudice or jealousy, because I have acted so decidedly about the reduction of the Transports,' Popham told David Scott of the Company's Secret Committee:

> … I know confidentially he hates me and any Man who has the sense to generate Suggestions for the publick Good, and nerves to offer them with Spirit. However his publick representations and my Conduct must be the points for the Secret Committee to look at. I have done everything in my power for the Company, and if the other Points of Conduct meet a doubt, you must fight for me, as I have for you.[70]

---

65 TNA: ADM 1/2323: Popham to Wellesley, 24 September 1801.
66 Quoted in Popham, *A Damned Cunning Fellow*, p.82.
67 BL: Add MS 13708, ff.41–44: Wellesley to Popham, 1 September 1801.
68 BL: Add MS 13708, ff.44–48: Wellesley to Popham, 16 October 1801.
69 TNA: ADM 1/2323: Popham to George Barlow, 1 December 1801.
70 BL: Add MS 41080, ff.3–5: Popham to David Scott, 4 December 1801.

Popham was the more mortified as he had hoped to find a patron in the Governor-General. He could only explain away his failure to make a positive impression by casting Wellesley, whom he dismissed as 'the little marquess', as a duplicitous dilettante who did not properly appreciate Popham's genius.[71]

Wellesley's difficulties controlling Popham reflected the nebulousness of his exact role. He still wore multiple hats and reported to various government departments; because very few of his superiors had seen *all* his instructions, Popham's actions in response to one set of priorities often seemed odd when viewed from the perspective of another. Popham's military responsibilities were currently on hold following the Egyptian armistice; until he received notice that Baird was returning to Suez to re-embark his men, his appointment as the East India Company's political envoy took centre stage. In conversation with Wellesley, Popham reiterated his concerns regarding the reliability of the Sharif of Mecca and suggested he might try his luck enticing other local chiefs, for example the Sultan of Aden or the Imam of Sana'a, into an alliance. If Wellesley approved, Popham asked for official credentials elevating him from an East India Company envoy into an official ambassador invested by Wellesley in his capacity as Governor-General to act on behalf of the Crown.

Wellesley agreed that making Popham's diplomatic role official might be useful. On 16 October, therefore, he issued a secret political dispatch bringing Popham's instructions – last issued on 10 November 1800 by the Secret Committee – up to date, with a view of sending Popham to treat with the heads of state of Mecca and Sana'a.[72] As Wellesley observed, the British had not had any official contact with any of the Arab states prior to 1798, so there was very little information on what they were like – the aims of their rulers, the character of the inhabitants, and what sort of concessions an envoy might be allowed to promise in return for preferential treatment for Indian trade. Popham was thus urged to use his initiative in granting 'considerable privileges and immunities' for local merchants in Indian ports, in reducing or even cancelling duties on imports, and in arranging trade agreements regarding imports of senna in return for British supplies of broadcloth, iron, and military and naval stores, even going as far as to allow the construction of Arab ships in British Indian dockyards.

Given his experience with Popham and the transports, however, Wellesley was not about to send his man off without some practical limitations in areas that might otherwise lead to serious diplomatic disaster. Popham's instructions were tempered with repeated notes of caution. Although Popham had permission to arrange defensive treaties with the Arab states, he could only do so against the French. Wellesley absolutely forbade him from agreeing to alliances against Britain's allies the Ottomans, since a British envoy could not be seen to encourage independence from the Turks, even if doing so might make states more disposed to concessions. Wellesley also told Popham he was absolutely not to leave the coastal states. Going too far inland would just make trouble, as the states that were territorially closer to Turkey tended to be more firmly under Turkish control. While acknowledging, therefore, that a treaty might be useful with Sana'a, a state on the slopes of the Sarawat Mountains and

---

71 Quoted in Ingram, *The British Empire as a World Power*, p.247.
72 BL: Add MS 13708, ff.49–70: draft dispatch, 16 October 1801.

about 100 miles from the coast, Wellesley told Popham to get the Imam to come to him and not to go inland himself.

Even more importantly, Wellesley ordered Popham to avoid any political meddling. The fact Wellesley felt he needed to emphasise this was significant. Popham's preference for violence over solving a problem through rational discussion had been particularly evident in his interactions with the Sharif of Mecca the previous year, when Popham had first been presented at his court. After his interview, he had met with Mahdi Ali Khan, a Persian native sent by Lord Wellesley to assist Popham in the Red Sea. Khan hinted that, if Sharif Ghalib should prove recalcitrant, an uprising might be engineered on behalf of his pro-British brother Abdalla.[73] Popham immediately concluded regime change might be the solution to all Britain's problems:

> I really think if a provisional application could be made from the Porte to Lord Wellesley to remove this Usurper and place the proper Heir upon the Throne whilst we have such a Force in the Red Sea, instead of its being an unpopular Act as interfering with the Head of the Mohamedan Religion, it would give great and general satisfaction, as he is universally detested from his tyrannical and infamous Conduct.[74]

Unlike Popham, Wellesley could see regime change was not a good idea, either in Mecca or anywhere else. Mecca, therefore, was uppermost in Wellesley's mind when he told Popham to 'abstain from any mixture in such political intrigues as may be directed to the design of subverting the established Government or effecting revolutions in the state, or of affecting the life or power of any reigning Chieftain'. Local chiefs would be apprehensive that they might be next, and the Ottomans would be annoyed at any interference in states under their control. Just as practically, Wellesley reminded Popham to be sensitive to local culture: he warned him against trying to buy off the chiefs with expensive presents, and told him to pay attention to 'points of ceremony and appearance'.[75] This was good advice, and Popham, when the time came, cheerfully ignored it all.

On 27 November, Popham was invested with the office of Ambassador to the States of Arabia.[76] To allow him to make a sufficient splash, he was provided with proper letters of credence, 12 dismounted troopers from the Governor-General's bodyguard, an escort of native infantry, and a salary of 2,000 rupees per month, backdated to his arrival in the Red Sea.[77] His duties were set to begin after he had re-embarked Baird's Egyptian army, which was expected back from Alexandria following the French armistice. Before Popham could return to the Red Sea, however, the military situation changed yet again, delaying his rendezvous with Baird and sending his diplomatic responsibilities into abeyance. News arrived that Spain had invaded Britain's ally Portugal in the summer of 1801.[78] There was

---

73 BL: IOR/G/177 part 1, ff.149–150: Mahdi Ali Khan to Baird, 13 June 1801.
74 BL: IOR/G/177 part 1, ff.143–145: Popham to Elgin, 26 June 1801.
75 BL: Add MS 13708, ff.49–70: Wellesley's dispatch, 16 October 1801.
76 BL: IOR/G/177 part 1: Wellesley to Popham, 27 November 1801.
77 BL: Add MS 13708, ff.49–70: Wellesley's dispatch, 16 October 1801.
78 Mikaberidze, *The Napoleonic Wars*, pp.124–125.

now a significant chance that France might take advantage of Portugal's weakness to seize its overseas settlements, particularly those vital to British Indian trade. Macao, the route by which foreign trade entered mainland China on its way to Canton, was one such territory: although it was not directly on the Indian trade route, it had considerable East India Company trade connections. Popham knew it well; *Etrusco* had sailed from there on her last journey. Macao's commercial importance, he told Wellesley, was such that he almost prayed for France to take a swipe so Britain would have an excuse to take 'a strong position in the China Seas'.[79] Wellesley was not ready to commit British troops this far, but he and Popham were of one mind in believing the French should not be allowed to control Macao. Wellesley therefore agreed to send two Company troopships, *Asia* and *Dover Castle*, to Canton, each carrying a company of European infantry and artillery to help the Portuguese.[80]

*Romney* was fit for service again and Popham could not resist the lure of action, particularly in an area sure to be full of rich enemy trading ships. On 14 November 1801, therefore, Popham suggested to the Vice-President of the East India Company that *Romney* might accompany *Asia* and *Dover Castle* to Macao as a convoy. This was absolutely in contravention of every single order that had ever been given him – he was not even supposed to leave the Red Sea, let alone travel four and a half thousand miles to the other side of the Indian Ocean – but he glossed over his disobedience by claiming he was putting his zeal before personal comfort: 'I view the absolute necessity for a Convoy to these Ships in so strong a light that I shou'd not for one moment hesitate to sacrifice every personal consideration to the good of the public service.' He assured the Vice-President he would still be able to return to the Red Sea in time to collect Baird's troops, and reminded him there was no time to ask for permission from the Admiralty, from Leadenhall Street, or even from the Governor-General himself: 'Time is so very precious in this advanced State of the Season as to render it indispensibly [sic] necessary to direct whatever you conceive most beneficial under the Circumstances of the Case, to be carried into Execution with the utmost energy and vigor.'[81] The only possible problem was that Vice Admiral Rainier might kick up a fuss as naval commander in the Indian Ocean. As Rainier himself had already admitted, however, Popham was not under his direct command.

Still, in his letter to Rainier to warn him he was coming, Popham played up the significance of Macao and played down the situation in the Red Sea, which had been almost completely calm since the French capitulation at Alexandria. Popham also disingenuously de-emphasised his role in the plan to send *Romney* to Macao in the first place, claiming Lord Wellesley had 'left me I thought no remaining option' but to undertake the convoy. He finished by arguing that the importance of the object excused his decision to sail without orders:

> The extreme delicacy ... of undertaking any Service in these Seas without your Sanction or Command and the extensive mischief which ... I might be able to prevent by giving Convoy at least as far as the Streights of Malacca to the Armament intended for Macao from this Country, reduced me to a situation of

---
79  TNA: ADM 1/2323: Popham to Wellesley, 24 September 1801.
80  TNA: ADM 1/2323: George Barlow to Popham, 12 November 1801.
81  TNA: ADM 1/2323: Barlow to Popham, 14 November 1801.

much embarrassment and tho' I have the satisfaction to find the determination that I have made confirmed by reflection on every circumstance attending it, yet I cannot but feel great anxiety that it shou'd be honored by your approbation.[82]

Passing up an opportunity to take responsibility for a bold course of action was not something Popham often did, except when there was a prospect of failure or the likelihood of personal censure. Despite the explicit backing of the East India Company, Popham was betraying a lack of confidence that his decision to go to Macao would be well received at home. He seems to have viewed this extraordinary letter as a sort of insurance: if he was sailing into trouble, he could at least claim he had been forced by circumstances and the East India Company, whereas if all went well, the letter would no longer be of any interest to anyone. Certainly he did not intend it as a straightforward explanation of his actions, or to seek Rainier's permission. He sent the letter the day he set sail, at the very last minute. He did not even know exactly where Rainier was, but he hoped the letter would find the admiral long after Popham himself had already arrived at Macao.

Peter Rainier, engraver unknown. (Public domain, The Miriam and Ira D. Wallach Division of Art, Prints and Photographs, The New York Public Library)

*Romney* dropped down to Saugur Roads on 4 December and set sail the day after. Popham arrived at Prince of Wales Island in the Straits of Malacca on 23 December, where he found Vice Admiral Rainier's flagship, HMS *Victorious*. Despite Popham's hope that the surprise of his arrival would blunt the impact of his leaving the Red Sea without permission, Rainier was expecting him: a Company cruiser had given him notice that Popham might be coming with the troopships. On Boxing Day, Popham went on board the flagship carrying orders from the East India Company, Calcutta, and Bombay, and discovered Rainier was absolutely furious with him. The admiral had absolutely no intention of gratifying Popham, or of encouraging further disobedience, by sending him any further with the Company troops. He detached *Orpheus* from his squadron to take over the convoy and ordered Popham to hand over all but one month's worth of provisions and stores. Having effectively made sure Popham could not extend his journey even if he wanted to, Rainier pointedly reminded him of the need for 'farther prosecution of their Lordships [of the Admiralty's] Orders' and sent him back to the Red Sea, telling him he should not stop anywhere but Madras to replenish his stores.[83]

---

82   TNA: ADM 1/2323: Popham to Rainier, 5 December 1801.
83   TNA: ADM 1/171, ff.678–680: Rainier to Nepean, 27 December 1801.

Popham, who had hoped his appearing off Prince of Wales Island would give Rainier no choice but to accept his involvement in the upcoming campaign as a *fait accompli*, was taken aback. Unwisely, he tried to insist on proceeding with the transports, and Rainier lost the little patience he had left:

> I had no hesitation in replying to him that so far as bringing them on as far as Prince of Wales Island, it appeared he was perfectly justifiable ... but to have proceeded any farther with them was so evident an infringement upon their Lordships' Orders, particularly as a Commanding Officer of a Detachment of His Majesty's Ships, on a very particular Service, as could not but have incurred their manifest displeasure, who would naturally expect their Orders would find him at or near the station appointed him, of the nature which he could in no wise be a proper Judge, nor of the propriety of his remaining there.[84]

Popham was taken by surprise by the vehemence of Rainier's reaction. He dealt with Rainier's disapproval by pretending it did not exist: 'I could not exactly learn from the particular mode in which the Admiral expressed himself, whether he conceived I had acted properly.'[85] This was probably a guilty conscience talking, as Rainier's rebuke had not been delivered in especially subtle language. But he could not hide, even from himself, that his attempt to involve himself in the defence of Macao had failed. *Romney* left Rainier on 29 December and was back in Mocha Roads in the Red Sea on 12 February 1802, where Commander John Carden of HMS *Sheerness* came aboard to update Popham on local events during his seven-month absence and round trip of nearly 9,000 miles.[86]

One piece of news Carden had to bring Popham changed everything: France and Britain had concluded a preliminary peace treaty at Amiens in October. News of the definitive treaty of peace, signed on 25 March, arrived in the area on 23 April 1802. The peace marked the end of the eight-year conflict in Europe and in all the colonies and outposts where the war had also been fought. Popham must have been relieved he had not gone on to Macao after all with Rainier, but the peace led to a change in priorities. Popham had been expecting to embark immediately on his political mission as Ambassador to the States of Arabia, starting with the Sharif of Mecca, who seemed more docile since the defeat of the French in Egypt and particularly since the Turks had sent 800 troops to Jedda to re-establish control.[87] Popham had also already opened communications with the Imam of Sana'a as soon as he arrived back in the Red Sea.[88] Now, however, the unexpected peace meant Popham would be needed to help re-embark Baird's troops and carry them back to their various Indian garrisons. Instead of opening diplomatic negotiations, therefore, Popham worked slowly up towards Suez, which he reached on 18 March and where he found HMS *Wilhelmina* and a number of troop transports (*Sheerness* joined them a week later).

---

84 TNA: ADM 1/171, ff.678–680: Rainier to Nepean, 27 December 1801.
85 To Wellesley, quoted in Popham, *A Damned Cunning Fellow*, pp.91–92.
86 TNA: ADM 1/4493: log, HMS *Romney*, 29 December 1801–12 February 1802.
87 BL: IOR/G/177 part 1, ff.205–206: Popham to the Secret Committee, 4 June 1802; ff.229–231: Popham to Wellesley, 18 February 1802.
88 BL: IOR/G/177 part 1, f.206: Popham to Wellesley, 16 February 1802.

All Popham had to do was wait until Baird made contact, but he was not very good at sitting on his hands. He was burning to get started with his diplomatic mission and inactivity made him restless. Since he had sent his many memoranda to Lord Wellesley the previous year, he had been thinking about how Britain might best prevent the French establishing a position in Egypt again, even if war were to break out anew. The only solution, he thought, was to do what Wellesley had asked him to do in other Red Sea states: increase East India Company authority by establishing an official resident in Cairo. He also wondered whether it might be possible to persuade the Pasha of Egypt to overturn an old prohibition on allowing Indian goods to cross Egyptian soil on their way to Europe. Popham therefore reached out to the Pasha with a proposal for a commercial treaty. The problem was Egypt was not, technically, a Red Sea Arab state and therefore not under Popham's purview. Since turfing the French out of Egypt, the British had pursued a policy of re-establishing Ottoman control there. Attempts to deal with Egypt without involving Constantinople, particularly when there was still a large British army in the territory, was at best impolitic, at worst dangerous; the Ottomans would certainly interpret it as an attempt to negotiate with an independent state.[89] But Popham was bored and conveniently forgot all of this. He excused his actions to Wellesley by claiming news of peace in Europe had opened an opportunity to strengthen Britain's influence in Egypt, and fell back on his usual tactic of distance: it would have taken too long to check with Wellesley first, so he had gone ahead on his own.[90]

Popham was briefly delayed by news from Lord Elgin, the British ambassador to the Ottoman Porte, informing him of negotiations in Constantinople regarding the British presence in the Red Sea and instructing him to wait for the official government line before making any major agreements in the area.[91] This should have been enough to stop Popham in his tracks, and for a while he did hold back – 'I am very much at a loss how to act'[92] – but he soon decided that, so long as he made sure to negotiate only with Turkish officials, it would all be absolutely above board and could not possibly cause offence. Popham therefore opened communications with the Pasha of Egypt on 12 April and offered to visit him as soon as possible.[93] If Popham was playing fast and loose with his authority, however, the Pasha knew exactly where he stood as a dependent of the Ottoman state. He replied pointedly that Egypt was as dependent on Turkey as India was on Great Britain and that a specific treaty with Egypt would be superfluous as commercial relations already existed between Britain and the Porte.[94] Elgin's warning of higher-level negotiations had not been enough to warn Popham off the course he had chosen to take, but the Pasha's coolness should have warned him off definitively. It did not. Popham claimed an agreement providing insurance to merchants against the attacks of local chiefs in crossing the desert was necessary to give confidence to British and Indian merchants, and repeated his intention of visiting the Pasha in Cairo as soon as he could.[95]

---

89    Ingram, *The British Empire as a World Power*, p.247.
90    BL: IOR/G/177 part 1, ff.191–195: Popham to Wellesley, 23 April 1802.
91    BL: IOR/G/177 part 1, ff.216–217: Elgin to Popham, 21 October 1801.
92    BL: IOR/G/177 part 1, ff.213–218: Popham to Wellesley, 24 March 1802.
93    BL: IOR/G/177 part 1, ff.197–198: Popham to the Pasha of Egypt, 12 April 1802.
94    BL: IOR/G/177 part 1, ff.199–200: the Pasha to Popham, 17 April 1802.
95    BL: IOR/G/177 part 1, ff.201–202: Popham to the Pasha of Egypt, 22 April 1802.

Before Popham could fulfil his promise to visit the Pasha, the order to hold himself ready to embark Baird's troops arrived on 7 May.[96] With the army expected any day, Popham should have remained with his ship, awaiting further instructions. However, as he had not yet heard directly from Baird, Popham decided to leave *Romney* anyway on the 19th to go inland, accompanied by his military retinue, four of his ship's officers, a secretary and an assistant secretary, and an East India Company interpreter.[97] He was met by an officer of the Pasha's own household, accompanied by a troop of soldiers mounted on horses and dromedaries. The splendour of this welcome, however, did not presage success, and the Pasha was not going to risk his neck by agreeing to anything without authority from Constantinople. Popham might have written to Wellesley telling him he 'congratulated myself on the result' of his trip to Cairo, but in fact he returned, flattered but empty-handed, on the 29th.[98]

Predictably, and despite his assertions that he had no reason to believe the army was close, Popham discovered Baird's men had begun arriving at the Suez rendezvous shortly after he had left it, and that Baird himself had arrived on the 26th. Popham therefore put his political mission on hold while he devoted himself to the more mundane, but also more useful, task of embarking the troops onto HMS *Sheerness* and the 13 other transports earmarked to carry them. The embarkation began on 31 May. Just under 6,000 troops were embarked, along with 230 horses. *Sheerness* was sent off to convoy the troops bound to Bombay; Baird himself and his suite boarded HMS *Victor*, the captain of which was ordered to take him back to Bengal.[99] Baird did not seem to blame Popham for the fact that his lengthy march across the desert at the height of summer had all been for nothing – he and his men had arrived in Cairo shortly after the French surrender. On the contrary, he was just as impressed with Popham on his return journey as he had been coming out. When *Romney* left convoy to return Popham to the Red Sea for his ambassadorial duties, Baird wrote him a letter praising how well he had handled all the difficulties of the campaign and hoping he and Popham would meet again:

> Should it be my lot, on any future occasion to be on active Service, and where the Navy and Army, may be required to act together, I can only add, it will be to me the Source of real Satisfaction, again to co-operate with you and if not I shall but wish it may be my good fortune, to meet with an Officer, possessed of your zeal, ability and Military experience.[100]

Baird later got his wish, but for now their cooperation was at an end. Popham returned to Jedda to complete the last part of his mission: the embassy to the Arab States.

Popham arrived in Jedda on 27 June to find a letter waiting for him from Lord Wellesley. It was about as different from Baird's fulsome praise as it was possible to get. Wellesley had just received, all in one go, the dispatches Popham had been writing since February about

---

96  TNA: ADM 1/2323: Popham to Nepean, 7 May 1802.
97  BL: IOR/G/177 part 1, ff.222–226: Popham to Captain Atkinson, 14 February 1802.
98  BL: IOR/G/177 part 1, f.241: Popham to Wellesley, 26 July 1802.
99  TNA: ADM 1/2324: embarkation returns, undated; Popham to Captain Carden of HMS *Sheerness*, 29 May 1802; Popham to Captain Collier of HMS *Victor*, 3 June 1802; and Popham to Nepean, 10 June 1802.
100 TNA: ADM 1/2324: Baird to Popham, 5 June 1802.

his negotiations with the Pasha of Egypt. Wellesley's reaction can only be pieced together from the vehemence of the stinging rebuke he committed to paper in response. Unlike Rainier's muted disapproval to Popham's arrival in the Malacca Straits in December, Wellesley did not mean to be misunderstood. He was furious at Popham for going off to Cairo without securing permission, or even stopping to clarify what the political landscape looked like in the Middle East after the Treaty of Amiens. Popham had exceeded his instructions, disobeyed orders, potentially destabilised the area, and endangered British relations with the Turks:

> The Negociation which you have opened in Egypt appears to me to have exceeded the limits of your Mission to the States of Arabia, and to have proceeded upon principles inconsistent with the nature of His Majesty's engagements, and with the state of His Majesty's Negociations with the Ottoman Porte. The authority vested in you … was limited to a negociation with the Arabian States situated on the Shores of the Red Sea, for the conclusion of such engagements as those States might profess the right to contract independently of the authority of the Ottoman Porte. … [Now that Egypt was back under the sole authority of the Ottomans], your prosecution of any negociations with the Pacha of Egypt, without the express concurrence of the Porte, might occasion considerable embarrassment to the British Government both at home and in India, and might pledge the faith of this Government to engagements which could not be sanctioned by the Governor-General in Council.

Wellesley did not recall Popham or cancel his instructions, but he told Popham, firmly, that if he wanted to go back to Cairo, he needed to secure Elgin's permission first – which would take months.[101] Wellesley was not overreacting, and the ripples of Popham's unauthorised attempt to establish British supremacy in Egypt took a long time to die down. Popham's mission was still causing headaches for the Foreign Office in 1806, and Lord Elgin recalled that the 'indignation' Popham had caused at Constantinople undermined diplomatic relations with the Porte for years after.[102]

How much of an impact Wellesley's rebuke actually had on Popham is unclear, but the answer seems to have been 'not much'. In his letter to the Secret Committee on 2 August, Popham simply claimed Wellesley had conveyed to him 'his most unqualified approbation of my conduct in every respect' – an outright lie.[103] Nor did he learn anything about the need for discretion, delicacy, or respect for local politics and customs. In terms of diplomacy, Popham's strategy had not changed: it was more bull in a China shop than anything else, and closely backed by the threat of violence. British influence, he thought, could only be acquired 'by absolute conquest, or conquest in the first instance, followed up by successful political intrigue (which I contend is authorized by all usages of war)'.[104] He had a grand

---

101 BL: IOR/G/177 part 1, ff.222–227: Wellesley to Popham, 20 June 1802.
102 BL: IOR/G/177 part 1, f.382: Memorandum by Elgin, 11 August 1806.
103 BL: IOR/G/177 part 1, ff.109–110: Popham to the Secret Committee, 2 August 1802.
104 Popham to Charles Yorke, 26 November 1803, Charles William Vane, 3rd Marquess of Londonderry (ed.), *Correspondence, Despatches, and Other Papers of Viscount Castlereagh* (2nd Series) (London: W. Shoberl, 1851), vol.7, p.289.

vision for establishing East India Company influence, but not the personality, or the tools, to bring his ideas about without disruption. As a result, when he was at last able to turn his full attention to his official duties as Ambassador for the Arab States, his very first diplomatic mission ended no better than his foray into Cairo.

Popham returned to Jedda with grandiose ideas, which he had been nurturing ever since he and Wellesley had planned his diplomatic activities together on the banks of the Hooghly. His focus was on changing the mind of the antagonistic Sharif of Mecca, making a trade agreement with the Sultan of Aden (whose state partly controlled the entrance to the Red Sea), and inviting the Imam of Sana'a to visit him for a similar purpose. The Imam's inland state, now part of Yemen, was strategically placed on the land route to the Red Sea for British Indian goods. Britain had had trade agreements with Sana'a in the past, and re-opening it to British influence would be a significant coup.

Popham was conscious he had some ground to make up with Wellesley, and he was looking for success. His attempt to woo the Sharif of Mecca, however, was lacklustre. Nothing much had changed to reduce the mistrust between the Sharif and the British envoy beyond the fact the Turks had sent an occupying force and a pasha to re-establish their control over the state. Popham had hoped this might help the Sharif see the softer side of British military assistance, but Wellesley had expressly warned him not to do anything that might antagonise the Turks, and in any case Popham quickly discovered the Sharif had taken matters into his own hands by poisoning the Turkish pasha. This did not bode well for the Sharif's willingness to be reasonable. Popham nevertheless tried to talk with him, but the Sharif had no intention of submitting to an outraged tirade about the ethics of murdering official envoys, particularly from a man who had recently considered overthrowing him. Popham was informed he could visit the Sharif at Taaf, where he was 'eating Fruit', as 'it was too much trouble to come to Jedda'. Popham did not bother. Instead, he drew up a long memorandum setting down his thoughts for how East India Company trade might be increased in the Red Sea at the Sharif's expense so, as Popham put it to Lord Wellesley, 'he is the only sufferer from not meeting your Lordship's propositions in the manner it became him to do so'.[105] Once again, Popham failed to see that most of his suggestions – extending the East India Company monopoly to the Red Sea; establishing a British resident in Cairo; encouraging various smaller states to assert their independence – would anger Britain's Turkish allies. But then diplomacy was not his main aim: buttressing what he saw as the East India Company's 'vast Empire' (and impressing Wellesley, and Dundas) was.[106] He closed his letter with an apology if he had 'ill conceived our political and commercial interests', but it was false modesty: Popham was trying to show Wellesley his firm grasp of statesmanship.[107]

Popham began putting his plans for expanding British trade immediately with the Sultan of Aden, who, luckily, proved more amenable than the Pasha of Egypt or the Sharif of Mecca. Popham signed a treaty with the Sultan on 6 September.[108] He reported proudly to Wellesley: 'It goes in a few words to say, that the Port of Aden shall be open to all British Subjects and

---

105 BL: IOR/G/177 part 1, ff.227–229: Popham to Wellesley, 30 June 1802.
106 BL: IOR/G/177 part 1, f.255: Popham to Wellesley, 26 July 1802.
107 BL: IOR/G/177 part 1, f.274: Popham to Wellesley, 26 July 1802.
108 Eric Macro, 'The First British Embassy to the Yemen', *Royal Air Force College Journal*, 31:1 (1959), pp.36–38, p.38.

every person trading under the British Flag', on paying a duty of one percent over the first five years, rising to a maximum of three percent after ten.[109] Aden in fact represented the only major success of Popham's diplomatic mission in the Red Sea. Popham had spared no expense to conclude it: he had entertained the Sultan's son on *Romney* and flattered him sufficiently to get him to plead Britain's cause with his father, but, as he wrote cynically to Wellesley, 'self interest is the leading principal [sic] of every Arab, [and] I am always aware of a quid pro quo in any extraordinary instance of attention'.[110] Popham was thrilled, although he had not yet learned the difference between negotiation from a position of power and the use of military might as a threat: 'I have no doubt of giving [Aden] a decided preference as a Commercial Port, and under the Treaty at present proposed, the Company will have the Balance of Power so compleatly in their hands, that he [sic] may raise or ruin either place [Mocha or Jedda], as may best suit his Political Interests.'[111] This was of a piece with his attitude to negotiations with other local power-brokers – on one occasion he sent a present of a 32-pounder cannonball to the Dola of Mocha to make a point[112] – but it did not bode well for future success.

Fresh from his triumph at Aden, Popham turned to Sana'a. He believed the Imam, who controlled the state, might be open to talks, although he had also heard agents were at work to prejudice him against the British.[113] Popham thought he might be able to counter this by promising British protection against the local Bedouin tribes, which he had heard in some cases exacted annual contributions of 60,000 Venetian dollars to leave Sana'a unmolested.[114] But Sana'a was inland, and so Popham could only open negotiations if the Imam came to him. Lord Wellesley was by now well aware of Popham's character and had recently sent another angry letter reiterating that Popham should not leave the coastline. Popham took heed – at least initially – and sent a member of his staff, one of his lieutenants, and a local envoy to Taiz on his behalf, armed with presents, weapons, and a treaty proposal.[115] Popham's good intentions, however, did not last long. Even before his envoys had returned, Popham announced his intention to go to Taiz himself to speak to the Imam in person. This was gambling on a positive reception, but Popham probably imagined a signed commercial treaty with such a pivotal state would excuse most sins. He left *Romney* on 3 August 1802 with an entourage consisting of about 200 people: 58 sepoys and five dismounted troopers; Lieutenant Coxe, Midshipmen Shireff and Jenks, and his ship's surgeon, Mr Shoveller; Mr Robertson, Popham's secretary; Mr Hughes, his interpreter; Mahdi Ali Khan, the man who had suggested deposing the Sharif of Mecca, as liaison; and a full complement of servants. A caravan of camels carried the tents and supplies, while Popham himself travelled with Khan in a shaded carriage.[116]

---

109 BL: IOR/G/177 part 1, ff.267–268: Popham to Wellesley, 26 July 1802.
110 BL: IOR/G/177 part 1, f.265: Popham to Wellesley, 26 July 1802.
111 BL: IOR/G/177 part 1, ff.231–233: Popham to Wellesley, 25 July 1802.
112 Thomas Huskisson, *Eyewitness to Trafalgar* (London: Ellisons' Editions, 1985), p.44.
113 BL: IOR/G/177 part 1, ff.231–233: Popham to Wellesley, 25 July 1802.
114 Anon., 'Sir Home Popham's Embassy to the States of Arabia, and to the Pacha of Egypt', *The Literary Journal: A Review of Literature, Science, Manners, and Politics for the year 1803* (July to December) (London: C. and R. Baldwin, 1803), vol.2, pp.125–128, 249–253, and 443–446, p.125.
115 BL: IOR/G/177 part 1, ff.238–239: memorandum, 24 July 1802.
116 Anon., 'Sir Home Popham's Embassy to the States of Arabia', p.126.

Popham's mission betrayed his limitations as a negotiator in an unfamiliar political and cultural landscape. Prior to leaving, Popham was informed by the Dola of Mocha that the best route to take in high summer was through the mountains. Popham later accused the Dola of misleading him, and yet what doomed the expedition was not the route, but Popham's attitude to the people with whom he had to deal. He had forgotten all Wellesley's warnings about showering the local chiefs with gifts and had loaded up with trinkets, fabrics, and spices; nor had he listened to the Governor-General's advice about familiarising himself with local customs. He was not willing to look upon the native population, even those with political power, with anything more than benign condescension, and his most salient attitude towards them was contempt, as demonstrated when he told the Dola he had left *Romney* with orders to flatten Mocha if he did not return safely. Most seriously of all, his enormous entourage was a hindrance; it only drew attention.[117]

The journey began well, but the further Popham got from the familiarity of the coast the worse things got. When the party reached Dorebat, the local sheikh greeted Popham with copious presents, but then forbade him to leave his territory without paying for an armed escort. Popham had no alternative but to ransom himself by giving the sheikh 500 dollars and a tent. There were numerous disputes with locals over access to water wells, and when Popham arrived at the mountainside city of Taiz, he discovered something he should already have known: no European was allowed in. This did not stop Popham, but once he and his entourage had entered the city, the Imam delayed an audience again and again. On 12 August, Popham's surgeon was accused by the local Dola of murder after the death of a man he had tried to treat. The local mood against the foreigners turned from curious to hostile overnight. One of Popham's servants was taken hostage; other members of the party had the silver buttons pulled from their clothes. Popham realised he had outstayed his welcome and his party began the long journey back to the coast. But this meant falling back into the hands of the Sheikh of Dorebat, who immediately realised Popham's precipitate return meant he had not been well received in Taiz. One of his men twice levelled his gun at Popham himself; one of *Romney*'s officers was struck and had his sword and uniform coat, with its gold braid, torn off him.[118]

Popham returned to *Romney* on 22 August in a towering temper. He had never been delicate in dealing with the local powers, and his letter of protest to the vizier of Sana'a breathed fire: 'He would have repelled some of these insults with his bodyguard of sepoys, and probably put most of the Imam's subjects to death ... but as his character is supported by that all-powerful nation to which he belongs, he considers it beneath his dignity to command so contemptible an atonement.'[119] But Popham was not really in a position to raze any local town to the ground, as he had once threatened to do to Mocha. The East India Company would not have been happy to find him embroiling them in a war with Sana'a, Mocha, or any other Middle Eastern state, which would have caused more than just ripples of protest at Constantinople, in retaliation for a journey he should never have undertaken in the first place.

---

117 R.L. Playfair, *A History of Arabia Felix or Yemen* ... (Bombay: Education Society Press, 1859), p.124.
118 Anon., 'Sir Home Popham's Embassy to the States of Arabia', p.446; Playfair, *Arabia Felix*, pp.124–125.
119 Popham, *A Damned Cunning Fellow*, p.98.

Popham's military and political missions in the Red Sea were over, and all he wanted was to go home. He did, however, propose another detour to Calcutta to refit his ship again first. This was only an excuse; Popham knew Wellesley disapproved of many of his ambassadorial decisions, but he was still hoping to salvage a good relationship with the Governor-General and he desperately wanted a debrief to explain himself. However, Rainier objected and told Popham he should refit in Bombay instead, as it would be closer and cheaper. Popham was furious, but he was hardly in a position to protest. He spent two months in Bombay between 22 September and 27 November, and not in a good mood. His gloom deepened when he read the letter published by Wellesley following his departure. While Wellesley commended Popham for facilitating Baird's movements in the Red Sea, the Governor-General publicly dissented from Popham's diplomatic policy in Egypt, Mocha, and Sana'a.[120] The worst blow of all was that Popham learned Dundas, his patron, had been out of office since March 1801. Popham was sailing home without a government sponsor, following a performance in the Red Sea that could best be described as mixed.

Popham did not know how the new government would react to all he had done, but he was worried. 'I now … quit India after a laborious service,' Popham complained to Wellesley, 'in a country where no opportunity has presented itself by which I could gain either military Fame or Fortune; in my own profession I have rather incurred the torrent of jealousy, and I doubt if I have made a friend except the Commander-in-Chief [Baird], and the Army in Egypt.'[121] Persecution was Popham's favourite theme, and the next few years gave him plenty of scope to indulge in it.

---

120 Wellesley to the Board of Directors, 23 February 1803, in Anon., *Public Characters of 1806*, pp.424–426n.
121 Popham, *A Damned Cunning Fellow*, pp.99–100.

# Message to be Answered

*'The answer will be looked upon as the affirmative of the message being understood'*

# 8

# Inquiry, 1804–1805

*2041: I have lost an anchor*

Popham's orders from Vice Admiral Rainier instructed him to return to Britain as soon as possible. Aware that he was dealing with a man who had a growing reputation for interpreting orders creatively, Rainier pressured Popham only to deviate from his homeward route if absolutely necessary, and to give his reasons for stopping if he did.[1] Rainier had only met Popham once, but he clearly had a measure of the man – and indeed Popham could not resist taking advantage of the first opportunity that came his way to show off.

Popham arrived at St Helena on 26 January 1803 to water and re-provision. He discovered the governor, Robert Patton, in a state of anxiety. The fragile Peace of Amiens with France was less than a year old, but its longevity was in serious doubt. France, under Napoleon Bonaparte, had spent much of 1802 annexing Piedmont and Parma and dismantling the Holy Roman Empire in the German states, although this expansionist behaviour was not as worrying to Britain as a report published in the French official journal *Le Moniteur* suggesting plans for a fresh invasion of Egypt. Fearing future assaults on India, Britain broke the Treaty of Amiens by refusing to evacuate Malta, and France consolidated its hold on Switzerland and the Netherlands in retaliation.[2] As part of the Amiens settlement, the Cape of Good Hope had (controversially) been handed back to the Netherlands, which remained under French control. The handover had not yet happened at the start of 1803 and, with the peace looking increasingly precarious, the British garrison applied to St Helena for military assistance in the event that they should refuse to evacuate.[3] The problem was that a new war would threaten St Helena itself, and Patton did not want to weaken his own garrison in case of attack.

Popham's appearance off St Helena in *Romney*, therefore, was opportune, and Patton requested him to take his ship to the Cape to assist the garrison. Popham, who loved to be seen to be useful, immediately decided Rainier's instructions to return home forthwith were not worth the paper they were written on. He excused himself using what was fast becoming his favourite word: 'It is allowed that every Commanding Officer … must exercise a certain

---

1 TNA: ADM 1/2326: Captain E.O. Osborn to Popham, 19 November 1802.
2 Charles Esdaile, *Napoleon's Wars: an International History, 1803–15* (London: Allen Lane, 2007), pp.133–141.
3 TNA: ADM 1/2326: John Pringle to Patton, 13 January 1803.

discretion.⁴ Even Popham, however, could not quite bring himself to disobey direct orders to the extent of going as far out of his way as the Cape of Good Hope. Luckily, Patton had the answer: *Romney* should wait at St Helena to act as a convoy for a group of East India Company merchant ships that was expected daily, which would be vulnerable to enemy predation if war broke out before they reached Spithead. If news arrived from the Cape to suggest the situation there had escalated, Popham could reasonably justify any deviation from his orders as responding to an unexpected emergency. Popham accepted this compromise with alacrity as Patton's plan offered him the prospect of earning yet more plaudits from the East India Company. He wrote home to explain his actions, which he grandiosely elevated into a contribution to the defence of the empire: 'By delaying my return to England I certainly acquit my conscience in protecting the valuable commerce of the East India Company, whose interests I have long considered too intimately blended with [those of] the nation, to make them inseparable on general principles.'⁵

In the end, somewhat anticlimactically, the handover of the Cape to the Dutch took place as planned and without violence, so when the East India Company convoy arrived at St Helena on 16 February *Romney* set sail with them, more than three weeks after arriving in Jamestown Bay. Popham was not exactly keeping to the letter of his orders to return to Britain 'without loss of time', but he was not particularly bothered so long as the East India Company approved of his actions. He was right to rely on the Company's gratitude, and the Court of Directors presented Popham with 500 guineas as a reward.⁶ The Admiralty had less reason to be grateful, but it certainly could not say the circumstances Popham cited for breaching his orders – the looming war with France – did not exist. In fact, when Popham arrived off the Scilly Isles on 11 April, he heard there was a general armament taking place in preparation for hostilities. This was premature, as Britain did not declare war until 18 May, but the militia had been called out on 8 March and press warrants had been issued for manning the Navy.⁷ Popham's loyalty to the East India Company immediately gave way to his loyalty to the service in which he was enlisted, and he sent his lieutenants aboard the East India Company vessels he had just convoyed to press the likeliest men they could find before the ships parted company in the Downs. *Romney* went on to Chatham, where Popham took command of all the Navy ships in the anchorage as senior officer. By 26 April Popham had pressed a total of 373 men into the naval service.⁸ He may have hoped to placate the Admiralty by his industry, and it worked: the Secretary to the Admiralty docketed Popham's diary of his movements since reaching St Helena with the words 'Approve all that he has done' – including, by implication, his remaining in Jamestown Bay two weeks longer than necessary.⁹

Whatever else Popham could expect from the Admiralty remained to be seen. Normally the prospect of war (and therefore of employment) would be good news, but the political scene had changed since Popham left England in 1800. Prime minister Pitt had resigned

---

4   TNA: ADM 1/2326: Popham to Patton, 1 February 1803.
5   TNA: ADM 1/2326: Popham to Patton, 7 February 1803.
6   Popham, *A Damned Cunning Fellow*, p.102n13.
7   TNA: ADM 1/2326: Popham to Nepean, 11 April 1803.
8   TNA: ADM 1/2326: Popham to Nepean, 26 April 1803.
9   TNA: ADM 1/2326: docket, 19 April 1803, on Popham to Nepean, 18 April 1803.

in March 1801 as part of the fall-out following the Act of Union, which had tied Ireland to Great Britain politically, constitutionally, and economically. The new premier, Henry Addington, was Pitt's close friend and the change in the political landscape was less dramatic than it might have been. Popham's patron Dundas, however, was gone; so were Huskisson, Grenville, and Spencer – all the men, in fact, who had employed Popham in the past. In their places were Lord Hobart as Secretary of State for War, Lord Hawkesbury as Foreign Secretary, and Sir John Jervis, ennobled as Lord St Vincent, as First Lord of the Admiralty. The first two had no particular axe to grind with Popham, but St Vincent, despite serving in Addington's Tory government, had well-known Whig sympathies and was not a man to cross. He had turned his Admiralty tenure into a sort of crusade against the corruption, nepotism, and jobbery he felt had characterised Pitt's Navy.[10] An Act of Parliament appointing a Commission for Naval Enquiry passed in 1803 aimed at scrutinising ways to reduce expenses, achieve greater efficiency, and rid the Navy of its dependence on external contractors.[11] This did not bode well for Popham, whose back-door employments by other departments represented precisely the sort of messy, semi-official arrangements St Vincent particularly disliked.

Although news of the new government had taken time to reach the Red Sea, Popham had first learned of its existence in May 1802. Popham's first instinct was self-preservation and he knew he had ruffled feathers during his mission, so he had immediately taken up his pen to write a letter to Lord Hobart at the War Department. He passed on news of Indian and Egyptian affairs before turning, almost incidentally, to more personal matters, warning Hobart that he might hear negative things about him from Rainier and others:

> I have no doubt but you have heard how much, from pique, envy, or jealousy, I was thwarted in a variety of instances, by the professional men at the Admiralty, because I had been irregularly employed by Mr Dundas and Lord Grenville, and placed in situations of responsibility by them independently of the Navy. ... I hear from England that the impressions I complain of are stronger than ever.[12]

Popham suspected neither Hobart's War Department nor the new Admiralty would fully understand the complicated arrangements under which his employments had been shared between them in the past. He was particularly anxious about the Admiralty Board, and suspected he would not be treated with the same indulgence by St Vincent as he had been by Spencer. He nevertheless tried his best to get his feet under the table any way he could, angling with his former patron Dundas (out of office, but who, as the newly minted Lord Melville, Popham hoped still had some leverage) to put in a good word with Lord Castlereagh, President of the Indian Board of Control, for a position on the Navy Board – 'not,' Popham hastened to assure his patron, 'that I wish to relinquish a claim for more

---

10 Roger Knight, *Britain Against Napoleon: The Organization of Victory, 1793–1815* (London: Penguin, 2014), pp.103, 215.
11 Roger Morriss, 'St Vincent and Reform, 1801–1804', *Mariner's Mirror*, 69:3 (2013), pp.270, 273.
12 Popham to Hobart, 7 May 1802, in G. Douin and E.C. Fawtier-Jones, *L'Angleterre et L'Égypte: La Politique Mameluke: Tome Premier: 1801–1803* (Cairo: La Société Royale de Géographie d'Égypte, 1929), p.237. Many thanks to Jonathan Parry for this reference.

active Employment ... [for] I court difficulties ... that I may have the pleasure of trampling them under my feet'.[13]

Despite this characteristic bit of rodomontade, Popham knew his prospects of continued employment were uncertain, despite the anticipated outbreak of war on 18 May. At the beginning of that month, Popham unwisely wrote to the Secretary of the Admiralty suggesting *Romney*'s crew would not object to being re-employed under him, even though they were meant to be paid off.[14] Despite this whopping hint that he hoped for another command, *Romney* was put into commission and Popham was not appointed elsewhere. Popham found himself without a ship, without a patron, and serving a First Lord of the Admiralty he disliked. 'The Marine Lord has compleatly paralysed the British Navy and opposes every proposition from Downing Street,' Popham complained to Lord Melville. 'Thus, my Lord, the Country is served by Intrigue.'[15] There were several reasons for this outburst. Popham had suggested launching a squadron and a small military force against his favourite target, Walcheren, as a way to distract Napoleon, but St Vincent had turned him down flat. Popham was also irritated by the Admiralty's attitude to the Sea Fencibles, which St Vincent had been reluctant to call out despite the fresh threat of invasion. Most damningly of all, St Vincent did not like Popham any more than Popham liked him. With every prospect of a lengthy spell of unemployment before him, for the first time in many years, Popham was completely at a loss.

Having been laid off from *Romney*, Popham finally managed to get back to his family in London at the end of May. He was not feeling especially optimistic. 'We are all in low Spirits, and see no chance of anything active to arouse us,' he told Melville.[16] His dejection was the deeper because he had suffered a serious bereavement during his long absence. Since Popham's marriage in India in 1788, his wife Elizabeth had given birth to three boys and three girls, the youngest of whom, two-year-old Home Whitworth, Popham had not yet even met. Only a few weeks before Popham's return from the Red Sea, however, he had lost his second son, four-year-old Frederick.[17]

But Popham did not have time to grieve, and his sorrow swiftly turned to anger with the discovery that his entire career might suddenly be on the line. In July 1802, bills of exchange sent to the Navy Board by Matthew Louis, acting naval agent in Calcutta, following the refit of *Romney* and *Sensible* in 1801, finally arrived in London. The bills amounted to £80,833.5s.4d, along with an additional five percent (£3,554.18s) charged by Louis as the naval agent dealing with the relevant transactions.[18] Members of the Admiralty Board were

---

13 NRS: Melville MSS, GD51/1/68/2: Popham to Melville, 6 July 1803.
14 TNA: ADM 1/2326: Popham to Nepean, 13 April 1803.
15 NRS: Melville MSS, GD51/1/68/2: Popham to Melville, 6 July 1803.
16 NRS: Melville MSS, GD51/1/68/2: Popham to Melville, 6 July 1803.
17 *Gentleman's Magazine*, 1803, part 1, vol.73, p.291.
18 'Copy of the Report of the Navy Board, respecting the Repairs of the Romney and Sensible, and the Expenditure and Supply of Stores on board of those Ships, while under the Command of Sir H. Popham', 20 February 1804, in House of Commons, *Accounts and Papers presented to the House of Commons, respecting the Repairs &c of the Romney, and other His Majesty's Ships belonging to the*

'considerably surprised' by these enormous sums; some even experienced 'horror', to use St Vincent's more emotionally charged term.[19] As one member of the Board later recalled, the cost of maintaining Rainier's entire squadron in 1801 had been £62,056.[20] All through August and September, the Admiralty and Navy Boards fretted over whether Popham's enormous expenditure could possibly be justified. Without inspecting the ship and its logs, however, nobody could make a definitive statement either way. The Admiralty Board therefore instructed the Navy Board on 10 September 1802 to pay the bills, but to place an imprest on Louis and Popham – in other words, the Admiralty had effectively blocked Popham from getting his pay until he could account for the money he had spent.[21]

Popham was annoyed by the imprest, but he did not realise just how much trouble he was in until 18 May 1803, the day Britain declared war on France. That morning, Popham, still in Chatham, received a visit at his hired lodgings from the Dockyard Commissioner, Captain Charles Hope, and the Surveyor of the Navy, Sir William Rule. Rule informed Popham that he had a Navy Board warrant to examine *Romney* and determine what repairs had been made to it in Calcutta, as well as to question the warrant officers of the ship.[22] Popham accompanied Rule to *Romney*, along with Commissioner Hope and the Builder, Store-Keeper, and Master-Attendant of the Dockyard, who together examined every part of the ship from rigging to bilges. Popham then accompanied his warrant officers to the Commissioner's Office, where the same officials interrogated two of *Romney*'s carpenters, its caulker, and its boatswain under oath. Popham later referred to the officials, indignantly, as 'a Committee or Court', lending the whole process the flavour of a criminal investigation.[23] Most of the questions were designed to discover what state the ship had been in when it had left British shores, how it had fared on its journey to the Red Sea, and whether the repairs in Calcutta had been necessary. According to Popham, who was present throughout, the warrant officers all emphasised the effects of the damage done to the ship during the November 1800 storm 'in the most pointed manner'.[24] Rule nevertheless refused to interview Popham himself, or the lieutenants and master of the ship, as he claimed the warrant officers were in charge of the ship's stores and therefore the best

---

*Squadron lately under the Command of Captain Sir Home Popham, 1800–1805* (London: Ordered to be printed 18 and 21 February, 5, 13, 16, and 27 March, and 5 April 1805), p.2.
19  House of Commons, *Reports from the Select Committee on Papers Relating to the Repairs of His Majesty's Ships The Romney and Sensible, while under the Command of Sir Home Popham: Second Report* (London: House of Commons, ordered to be printed 24 June 1805), pp.188, 237. Many thanks to Kathryn Rix for these references.
20  House of Commons, *Second Report of the Select Committee on the Romney*, p.188.
21  Admiralty Board to the Navy Board, 10 September 1802, in House of Commons, *Accounts and Papers presented to the House of Commons*, pp.309–310.
22  Popham's version: [Sir Home Popham], *Concise Statement of Facts, relative to the Treatment experienced by Sir Home Popham since his return from the Red Sea, to which is added, the Correspondence, Naval, Military, and Commercial, to his Excellency the Most Noble the Marquis Wellesley, &c, from Sir Home Popham, during his command in the Red Sea, and his subsequent Embassy to the States of Arabia* (London: John Stockdale, 1805), pp.4–10; Sir William Rule's version: House of Commons, *Second Report of the Select Committee on the Romney*, 32–33.
23  [Popham], *Concise Statement of Facts*, p.5.
24  [Popham], *Concise Statement of Facts*, pp.5–6.

people to examine about any irregularities.²⁵ Still, Rule promised Popham a copy of any report arising from his findings.

There were echoes of the 1796 affair of the Hamburg transports in this, but this time Popham could not rely on Dundas to save him. Even so, he did not start to worry until he returned to London and tried to make an appointment to present his Red Sea charts to Lord St Vincent. By July he had not heard back from the First Lord, and the silence was beginning to make him nervous. Apart from anything else, he was hearing disturbing rumours that Rule's visit to Chatham might lead to some sort of prosecution.²⁶ A request for an interview with the First Lord to explain himself finally elicited a cool, uncommunicative reply, simply telling him the Navy Board had been ordered to report on *Romney*'s expenses and that Popham would get a copy of the report when it was issued.²⁷ Popham wrote back by return of post, saying he wanted to accelerate the investigation into his conduct and begging for permission to give evidence in person. Again, however, this letter met a wall of silence. By now, the Navy and Victualling Boards were also pressing Popham to send copies of his log books and ships' accounts from the Red Sea. Some sort of prosecution clearly *was* coming, but Popham did not yet know what shape it would take, and he was desperate to get his side of the story on record.

This was not just Popham's usual desire to over-justify himself. He was worried the Navy Board would not have all the facts about 'the circumstances under which I acted … in the Red Sea' – a very real problem, given the multiple, and complex, tasks he had undertaken in the area, military, commercial, and diplomatic.²⁸ Having run out of strings to pull in all the usual naval institutions, he leapfrogged them all and went straight to the top. He wrote a pamphlet, entitled *A Concise Statement of Facts* –actually over 200 pages long, although only about 60 pages of it was actual commentary – and circulated it among his 'friends': prominent cabinet members (the book was dedicated to the Prime Minister, Addington) and former government ministers like Lord Melville and Lord Spencer. Lord St Vincent did not rate a copy.

*A Concise Statement of Facts* was Popham's attempt to take back the initiative, and it was distinctly confrontational in tone. Popham explained his take on everything that had happened since his return to Britain, printed his entire correspondence with St Vincent and the Admiralty on the subject, and claimed he had never been provided with a copy of Rule's report on his findings at Chatham in May 1803, despite having been promised one. He flatly denied that the sum expended on repairing *Romney* and *Sensible* amounted to over £80,000, citing the figure of £9,000 instead, although he carefully omitted to explain that this was for carpentry bills on *Romney* alone.²⁹ This inflated sum, as well as the repeated refusals of the Admiralty, Navy, and Victualling Boards to allow him to defend himself in person, were,

---

25   [Benjamin Tucker], *Observations on a Pamphlet which has been privately circulated, said to be 'A Concise Statement of Facts, and the Treatment Experienced by Sir Home Popham, since his Return from the Red Sea'; to which is added, A Copy of the Report made by the Navy-Board to the Admiralty, on investigating the Account of Expenditure for the Romney and Sensible, at Calcutta, in 1801, whilst under the Orders of Sir Home Popham* (London: J. Ginger, [1805]), p.14.
26   [Popham], *Concise Statement of Facts*, pp.22–23.
27   [Popham], *Concise Statement of Facts*, pp.23–24.
28   TNA: ADM 1/2327: Popham to Marsden, 6 March 1804.
29   [Popham], *Concise Statement of Facts*, pp.11–12.

Popham asserted, evidence of a conspiracy to blacken his name: 'It appears to me that every action has been dictated by a spirit of personal prejudice.'[30]

Popham meant *Concise Statement of Facts* to put his Admiralty enemies on the defensive, and it worked. The release of the book was like lighting the fuse on a powder barrel. Members of St Vincent's Admiralty Board later claimed they had not managed to get a sight of the document until late 1804, which seems extraordinary considering Popham's industrious attempts to spread it as far as possible beyond the cabinet and among the ships in the fleet and the Sea Fencibles, even as far as the Army.[31] In November 1803, the Admiralty considered suing for libel and Popham took legal advice to prepare his possible defence, and one incident suggested Popham's pamphleteering had infuriated the Admiralty Board so much its members no longer cared about playing fair.[32] In December 1803, David Bartholomew, formerly acting master aboard *Romney* and a primary witness in the case at hand, was impressed in the Porter's Hall of the Admiralty, where he had been lured with the promise of promotion.[33] At least the *Romney* investigation suddenly began moving forward much more quickly with the publication of Popham's book, and the Admiralty Board ordered the Navy and Victualling Boards to report their findings.[34]

The Navy Board released its report on the *Romney* expenses on 20 February 1804. It was clearly intended to underline the commitment of Lord St Vincent's Admiralty and Navy Boards to the reform of abuses by making Popham into an example. The report's tone was correspondingly stiff. *Romney* had been carrying more sail than was properly allowed; its warrant officers had claimed for a twelvemonth of stores, far too much for its mission to the Red Sea; and the ship's logs had revealed a missing anchor and the repurposing of several cables, apparently to conceal evidence of their having been cut down or otherwise tampered with, suggesting the cut pieces had been sold on for profit. The report also noted the purchasing of rope and other equipment when older materials should have been recycled; highlighted the purchase of more canvas (despite the ship already having too much sail), along with extra awnings, hammocks, and other stores; and pointed to various inconsistencies between the logs and account books that had been examined. Most significantly, the report noted discrepancies between the items purchased in Calcutta and the items returned with *Romney* in Chatham in 1803, suggesting a number of things had mysteriously disappeared, with no trace of this appearing in any of the logs.[35] The report stopped short of accusing Popham explicitly of embezzlement but, taken together, this detail pointed towards one accusation: that Popham had actively encouraged Louis to sell purchased items on, before falsifying his logs and accounts to conceal the evidence.

---

30 [Popham], *Concise Statement of Facts*, p.13.
31 House of Commons, *Second Report of the Select Committee on the Romney*, p.125.
32 [Popham], *Concise Statement of Facts*, pp.ix–xi.
33 House of Commons, *Second Report of the Select Committee on the Romney*, pp.21–28; Conrad Dixon, 'To walk the quarterdeck: the naval career of David Ewen Bartholomew', *Mariner's Mirror*, 79:1 (1993), pp.58–63.
34 St Vincent to Popham, 22 October 1803, David Bonner Smith (ed.), *Letters of Admiral of the Fleet the Earl of St Vincent whilst First Lord of the Admiralty, 1801–1804* (London: Navy Records Society, 1922 and 1927), vol.2, p.226.
35 House of Commons, *Accounts and Papers presented to the House of Commons*, pp.1–8.

The first Popham heard of the February 1804 report was when William Marsden, Secretary to the Admiralty Board, informed him the imprest against him had been extended.[36] Marsden promised him the Navy and Victualling Boards would send him a copy of the report but, when Popham applied for one, the Navy Board said they had orders to send him only the accompanying papers. When Popham failed to obtain even these, the Board claimed the papers had been lost in transit between departments.[37] Over the next few months, Popham accused the Admiralty and Navy Boards outright of deliberately tampering with the evidence against him by 'surreptitiously remov[ing], or wilfully destroy[ing]' parts of it.[38] Popham often defended himself through claims of persecution; he enjoyed playing the victim, and he undoubtedly exaggerated the extent to which he was St Vincent's bogeyman in the Admiralty's crusade against naval corruption. However, despite his habit of outright lying when it suited him, Popham may have had a point. The missing documents concerned the missing anchor, the cut-up cables, and the differences between the log books – essentially the basis on which the most damning claims of the February 1804 report had been made. Their loss was a severe blow to his cause, and the Admiralty never satisfactorily explained it.

By early 1804, Popham had another reason to believe the Admiralty was singling him out. Having acted as transport agent, Army liaison, courtier, and diplomat, he had now added politician to his growing portfolio of identities. This was not an unusual step for a Royal Navy officer: many of Popham's contemporaries already sat in the Commons.[39] Popham was always keen to transmit his side of the story to the widest possible audience, whether using signal flags at sea or through public correspondence, newspapers, or pamphlets. He therefore leapt at the opportunity to make the floor of the House of Commons one more arena from which he could address his friends, and the nation beyond them.

Had Popham entered Parliament while still under the tutelage of Captain Edward Thompson, he might have followed his mentor's inclinations and voted with the Whigs. Friends who had known him before 1793 would have been surprised to see where his political allegiances had taken him. Several of Popham's earliest friends became radical journalists, such as Denis O'Bryen and John Taylor, and as a young man he had read the proscribed *Rights of Man* by Thomas Paine, which at the very least suggested he was curious about the message it contained.[40] Since those days, however, Popham's professional career had linked him inextricably with Henry Dundas, now Lord Melville. Whatever

---

36  House of Commons, *Second Report of the Select Committee on the Romney*, pp.13, 195.
37  TNA: ADM 1/2327: Popham to Marsden, 29 September 1804.
38  House of Commons, *Second Report of the Select Committee on the Romney*, p.20. See the testimony of John Rolt, pp.176–178, and Popham's speech in the Commons, 8 May 1805, in *Parliamentary Debates*, vol.4, p.640, for the contents of the lost papers.
39  One hundred naval officers served as MPs 1790–1820: *History of Parliament*, 'Members 1790–1820', <https://www.historyofparliamentonline.org/research/members/members-1790-1820>, accessed 27 February 2023.
40  TNA: HCA 32/596: this box contains a mutilated copy of the first volume among Popham's papers taken from *Etrusco*.

his radical sympathies, Popham had yoked his cart to men who had spent much of the previous decade stamping out radicalism. Still, Popham was more than happy to keep any private opinions quiet and follow his patron's lead through 'the rugged Paths of Politicks'.[41] Melville, though out of office, still had powerful contacts, foremost among them former Prime Minister Pitt the Younger. Pitt's decision to return to active politics in early 1804 gave Popham an unparalleled opportunity to attack Addington and his unfriendly Admiralty – an attack the February 1804 report may have been designed in some degree to forestall.

Following his unexpected resignation in 1801, Pitt had initially supported the new government, much to the disgust of former followers such as Lord Spencer and Lord Grenville, who both explicitly opposed Addington after the Peace of Amiens. Pitt's own doubts about his

William Pitt the Younger, by the studio of Thomas Gainsborough, 1787–1789. (Public domain, Yale Center for British Art, Paul Mellon Collection)

successor had grown steadily following Addington's first budget in 1802, which departed from some of Pitt's cherished financial maxims. Nevertheless, Pitt did not actively oppose until early 1804, when the return of George III's mental illness raised the prospect of a political crisis and Lord Grenville made a shock political coalition with the Whig party leader Charles James Fox. Grenville drew a reluctant Pitt back into the political game by suggesting he, Pitt, and Fox might make an alliance aimed at unseating Addington once and for all.

In January 1804, the likelihood of a French invasion was uppermost in the mind of most politicians. Pitt therefore decided his first assault on Addington would focus on criticising the government's national defence plans, and he needed professional advice on what angle might harm Addington the most. This was where Popham came in. Either he volunteered his services or Melville suggested him to Pitt as a likely expert, but his track record in preparing the southern coast for defence in the late 1790s, as well as his expertise regarding the coasts of France, Flanders, and Holland, qualified him to advise on defence issues. Melville and Pitt were not the only ones to recognise this; Addington's ministers had already been courting Popham on the same front, and Popham had recently given the Foreign Secretary, Lord Hawkesbury, his opinion that the massive army Napoleon was gathering at Boulogne was more likely to target Ireland, Scotland, or Wales than strike directly at London.[42] This informal contact had nevertheless failed to produce any offers of employ-

---

41  BL: Add MS 41080, ff.6–9: Popham to Melville, November 1804 [actually 1803].
42  BL: Add MS 41080, ff.6–9: Popham to Melville, November 1804 [actually 1803].

ment, and the 'persecution' Popham was experiencing from St Vincent's Admiralty Board meant he had nothing to lose and everything to gain by helping Pitt unseat the government.

Pitt wanted Popham close to him at all times, including during debates in the Commons. This meant electing Popham to Parliament, which was not easy when the existing ministry was unfavourable. Popham had in fact been trying to find a seat in the Commons on his own account since November 1803, but he had not succeeded, typically concluding St Vincent must be blocking him and complaining of 'the exertions which have been used to keep me out of Parliament'.[43] By early 1804, Popham had the big guns behind him, but even Pitt and Melville struggled to find him a suitable seat. Eventually, on 21 March, Popham was elected as one of the two MPs for Yarmouth, a close borough on the Isle of Wight with 21 voters. Such boroughs retailed for enormous sums, and Popham almost certainly did not stump up the cash himself. One of St Vincent's supporters thought Yarmouth's enormous price tag (£4,000) had been intended by Pitt and Melville as a reward for services yet to be rendered.[44] This was probably true, and Addington's government, fighting against the combined onslaught of Pitt, Grenville, and Fox, knew Popham was not simply coming into Parliament 'to maintain his ground against the Admiralty who have quarrelled with his accounts'.[45] By February 1804, therefore, when the Navy Board released its report, St Vincent's Admiralty had more than one reason to undermine Popham's reputation. The *Romney* affair had a political complexion from the very start, and circumstances ensured it only got worse.

If the February 1804 report was an attempt to muzzle or neutralise Popham at a time when he was helping Pitt drag St Vincent's reputation through the mud, it was too late. A few days after the report's release, Pitt used the occasion of a debate in the Commons on defence to complain about the state of the Navy under Addington.[46] Less than a fortnight later, he gave notice of his intention to move for a broader political inquiry.[47] The debate itself took place on 15 March 1804 and his motion failed by 201 votes to 130, but witnesses were entertained by the rare phenomenon of Pitt and Fox voting in the same lobby.[48]

Despite all the trouble taken to have him elected, Popham was unusually quiet in the House. He stuck his neck out only twice: on 28 March to defend a grant to Lord Hood for his actions at Toulon in 1793, and on 23 April to question the accuracy of the government's figures regarding the number of ships and seamen in service.[49] But he had not been elected to the Commons for his skills as an orator: he followed Pitt into the lobbies in all divisions against Addington and continued giving advice on technical matters. With Pitt and Fox

---

43 NRS: Melville MSS, GD51/1/68/1: Popham to Melville, 8 January 1803 [actually 1804].
44 BL: G.19449, p.xx: comment by Tucker in his copy of *A Full and Correct Report of the Trial of Sir Home Popham ...* (London: J. and J. Richardson, 1807).
45 Abbott to Lord Redesdale, 28 February 1804, quoted in Stokes, 'POPHAM, Sir Home Riggs'.
46 *Parliamentary Debates*, vol.1, col.1159.
47 *General Evening Post*, 8–10 March 1804.
48 *Parliamentary Debates*, vol.1, col.927–928.
49 *Morning Post*, 24 April 1804.

engaged in a joint campaign to overthrow it, the government's end was swift. On 23 April 1804, the government's majority dropped to just over 50. A few days later it was under 40. On 10 May, Addington resigned, and St Vincent went with him.[50] A few days later, Pitt returned to office. Popham's patron, Lord Melville, became First Lord of the Admiralty.

It was the best result Popham could have asked for, and he could congratulate himself on having played a small but significant role in Addington's overthrow. Nor had it come a moment too soon. Conscious that it was running out of time, and aware of Popham's role in advising Pitt, St Vincent's Admiralty had begun discussing whether to bring him to a court-martial on the strength of the findings of the February 1804 report. Its charges of embezzlement, corruption, and abuse of power were, in the words of one Navy Board member, 'amongst the most serious that could be brought against an Officer, as affecting not only his Character, but perhaps his Life', and he and his colleagues clearly hoped Popham would be cashiered.[51] The plans for a trial had not, however, advanced very far before the government fell, and they were dropped the moment the Admiralty passed into Melville's hands. At the beginning of May, the Commissioners of Naval Enquiry told the Admiralty Board they were unable to take the *Romney* affair under their remit as it was a professional, not criminal, affair. The chances of a hostile investigation dropped to near-zero.

With his patron back in office, Popham's career at last seemed to be returning to an upward trajectory. Keeping in mind the prospect of future employment, perhaps as a member of the Navy Board, Popham secured a country estate, Titness Park, near Ascot, at a yearly rate of £100 a year. Titness – described as 'a singularly large Cottage House, with rooms of large dimensions … with large gardens and hothouses', amid 100 acres adjoining Windsor Great Park – was more than grand enough for Popham to house his growing family (his wife had given birth in January to another daughter, Harriet).[52] Popham also hoped his earning the gratitude of the Prime Minister himself would finally help bring the *Etrusco* business to an end. In the summer of 1804, the High Court of Admiralty rejected an appeal by Captain Mark Robinson to secure the remaining balance of the prize money for capturing *Etrusco*.[53] At around the same time, the Procurator and Advocate General issued a report advising that Popham had not been 'aware that he was violating any Law of his Country' by his trade in India and China. As his ship had been engaged in legal business and therefore wrongly detained, their conclusion was that the Crown ought to grant Popham the balance remaining in the *Etrusco* account – about £18,000 after the deduction of Captain Robinson's legal expenses, which was all the latter got by way of compensation. A Royal Warrant, dated 24 September 1805, sealed the deal.[54]

This neat solution convinced many that Popham's windfall was part of a payoff by Pitt and Melville for his political assistance, in addition to his election to Parliament.[55] These

---

50   C.J. Fedorak, *Henry Addington: Prime Minister, 1801–1804* (Akron, OH: University of Akron Press, 2002), pp.188–201.
51   House of Commons, *Second Report of the Select Committee on the Romney*, p.15.
52   Lease, 3 June 1805, Harvard Law School Historical and Special Collections, catalogue record <https://researchworks.oclc.org/archivegrid/collection/data/236235492>, accessed 1 December 2022; *Morning Herald*, 19 June 1821.
53   TNA: HCA 42/535: judgement, 5 June 1804.
54   TNA: HCA 40/3/134: Royal Warrant, 24 September 1805.
55   BL: G.19449, p.xx: comment by Tucker in *The Trial of Sir Home Popham*.

rumours were almost certainly true: Popham had previously hinted that his patrons had intended to deal with *Etrusco* on his return from the Red Sea, and the timing of the legal recommendation to close the *Etrusco* account in Popham's favour suggests it was one of the first things the new Pitt government dealt with. Yet despite these clear marks of favour, the damage done by this blatant wheeling and dealing was more serious than even Popham himself could have predicted. He had never been popular with his naval peers, who mistrusted him as an inexperienced fraud who owed his employment to political favour. The closing of the *Etrusco* case had been a little too blatant, and in the wake of the February 1804 report Melville discovered many naval officers had completely taken against Popham. Vice Admiral John Holloway and Rear Admiral Thomas Louis, two of the officers to whom Popham had to report, disparaged him in front of the other guests at a private dinner, and Melville was forced to write testily to Popham's ultimate commander defending his chosen man:[56]

> I am well aware that Sir Home Popham is an object of envy with some, of jealousy with others, but in proportion as he is attempted to be run down, it is the duty of the Government to run him up. To the conviction of all of us he has served Government for many years in various capacities zealously and well. Anything therefore that little jealousness or captious observations may throw out with regard to Sir Home Popham individually I feel perfectly indifferent about … If any person feels the service cumbersome, there will be no doubt many others to supply their places.[57]

At least Popham now knew Pitt's government would back him up. Although he was aware his naval peers viewed him with a jaundiced eye, he told Melville, loftily, 'it has never affected me in the least, as I knew the more engines were employed against me, the higher I should ultimately rise.'[58] He could afford to be supercilious because he had a direct line to the highest levels of government. One difference in Popham's epistolary habits after 1804 was that he now felt comfortable writing directly to Lord Melville, whereas before he had often gone through an intermediary.

With the patronage of the Prime Minister and First Lord of the Admiralty behind him, Popham hoped to rise very high indeed. However, this was unlikely to happen until he had expunged the February 1804 report from his record. Melville *did* want to employ him, but when he looked into the practicalities, he discovered the rest of the Admiralty Board objected to bestowing so much favour on a man with an open censure against his name. To achieve any significant progress in his career, Popham had to meet the accusations made against him by the Admiralty and Navy Boards appointed by Lord St Vincent head-on. This was more difficult than he expected, and he did not manage to get hold of a copy of the February 1804 report until mid-September. His frustration hit record levels, and new words entered his vocabulary to describe how his character had been 'traduced by secret

---

56 Kevin D. McCranie, *Admiral Lord Keith and the Naval War Against Napoleon* (Gainesville, FL: University Press of Florida, 2006), p.137.
57 Melville to Keith, 7 October 1804, C.C. Lloyd (ed.), *The Keith Papers* (London: Navy Records Society, 1955), vol.3, p.95.
58 BL: Add MS 41080, ff.19–20: Popham to Melville, 29 July 1804.

inuendos [sic]'. And yet, certain as he was that the First Lord would support him even if he went too far, Popham's attitude towards the Admiralty Board had transformed from desperate to imperious. Once he had finally read the February 1804 report at the end of September, Popham pulled out all the stops in a long official letter to the Secretary of the Admiralty Board in which he portrayed the whole affair as a campaign orchestrated by St Vincent's Admiralty Board to blacken his name, 'blinded by their passions, and misled by their Ardent Zeal for the persecution of an Individual'. He placed his 'fullest confidence in the liberality of [Melville's] Lords Commissioners, who will divest themselves of every prejudice in forming a judgment of my case'.[59] Popham also accused the Navy Board of colluding with the dockyard officers in Chatham and Portsmouth to produce a report full of 'the most fallacious and visionary evidence'.[60] With the First Lord of the Admiralty behind him, Popham was not even trying to moderate his language.

Popham probably expected Melville to accept his protestations of innocence and sweep the February 1804 report aside as though it had never happened. But St Vincent's defunct Admiralty still had an ace up its sleeve: Benjamin Tucker, the principal author behind the February 1804 report, a former purser who had been St Vincent's private secretary. Tucker had obtained a copy of Popham's *Concise Statement of Facts* and, with St Vincent's tacit agreement,[61] decided to fight Popham with his own weapons. Published at the end of November 1804, Tucker's *Observations on a Pamphlet which has been Privately Circulated, said to be 'A Concise Statement of Facts'* ridiculed Popham, whose 'exploits', Tucker wrote wryly, '*lost nothing in the telling*'. More seriously, *Observations on a Pamphlet* included an appendix containing a complete and annotated copy of the February 1804 report.[62] The report had been confidential and Tucker's decision to publish it got him into trouble, but leaking it into the public domain publicised its contents, which until then had not been widely known. Tucker took a leaf out of Popham's book and circulated his pamphlet 'very generally, and with considerable industry' as far away as the West Indies and throughout the fleet, including the Brest squadron, where Popham was stationed at the time.[63]

Popham was predictably infuriated. This was a challenge he could not ignore, and *Observations on a Pamphlet* sparked off what Popham himself referred to as 'a paper war'.[64] Despite experiencing difficulty in finding a publisher – which he of course interpreted as further evidence that St Vincent was still trying to silence him[65] – Popham finally released *Concise Statement of Facts* to the general public in pamphlet form, with a new preface pointedly accusing Tucker of slander.[66] Popham also released an updated version of his September letter to the Admiralty Board dealing with new evidence turned up by Tucker's pamphlet. This version was even more strident than the already lurid original. 'Insinuations' became 'base insinuations'; 'the Commencement of the proceedings against me' became

---

59 TNA: ADM 1/2327: Popham to Marsden, 29 September 1804.
60 TNA: ADM 1/2329: Popham to Marsden, 25 February 1805.
61 House of Commons, *Second Report of the Select Committee on the Romney*, p.20.
62 [Tucker], *Observations on a Pamphlet*, pp.4, 45. The report is reprinted between pp.24–44.
63 House of Commons, *Second Report of the Select Committee on the Romney*, pp.20, 123, 125.
64 *Parliamentary Debates*, vol.4, col.640.
65 *Parliamentary Debates*, vol.3, col.269.
66 [Popham], *Concise Statement of Facts*, p.iv.

'the Commencement of my persecution'; 'erroneous' accusations became 'malignant and absurd'; and Bartholomew's impressment became outright 'kidnap ... after having been disgracefully dragged thro' the Streets, and put on Board a loathsome Tender'.[67] No one could beat Popham in the use of hyperbole.

The time had come to bring the *Romney* affair before the highest public authority in the country: the House of Commons. Surprisingly, it was not introduced by Popham himself, but by an oppositionist MP named Charles Kinnaird (albeit a man who had a record of holding St Vincent and his Admiralty to political account).[68] On 31 January 1805, Kinnaird gave notice in the House of Commons that he would move to produce the 20 February 1804 report with the aim of possibly opening an inquiry in future.[69] The financial dimension of the accusations against Popham made it Parliament's remit, Kinnaird argued, especially as the current Admiralty was unlikely to take up the charge.[70] Was Kinnaird speaking at Popham's behest? The *Naval Chronicle* thought the motion 'was not intended to operate in [Popham's] favour',[71] and Popham himself accused Kinnaird of deliberately picking a day to give notice when Popham had been absent on duty.[72] Nevertheless, Popham was delighted. He finally had an opportunity to defend himself publicly, and not just through the limited medium of a pamphlet. Parliamentary debates were reported in nearly every newspaper in the country, so Popham's words would echo from Land's End to John O'Groats. The minute Kinnaird sat down, Popham leapt to his feet to declare himself in favour of an inquiry. Popham had evidently come prepared: he read out some of the correspondence he had undertaken with the Admiralty Board and with St Vincent, and emphasised that the reason the Admiralty had taken so long to begin proceedings against him was that they had no case and no evidence.[73] Popham was answered by Rear Admiral Markham, MP for Portsmouth, who spoke in favour of St Vincent's Admiralty Board (of which he had been a member), but to Popham's obvious glee the issue escalated several levels when both Pitt and Fox pitched in on Popham's side.[74] With the two greatest orators in the Commons behind him, Popham proposed to go beyond Kinnaird's request to produce the Navy Board report and moved for a full investigation to clear his name.[75] Kinnaird's motion, with Popham's amendment, passed without a division.[76]

Popham had a national audience, and he rose splendidly to the occasion. He began by polishing up his popular image; there was, after all, no point in all this political pomp if the public did not even know who he was. Popham had befriended one of the editors of *The Courier*, Thomas George Street, and on 7 February the newspaper – one of the most popular

---

67 TNA: ADM 1/2327: Popham to Marsden, 20 February 1805.
68 M.J. Williams and R.G. Thorne, 'KINNAIRD, Hon. Charles (1780–1826), of Rossie Priory, Perth', from *The History of Parliament: 1790–1820*, <https://www.historyofparliamentonline.org/volume/1790-1820/member/kinnaird-hon-charles-1780-1826>, accessed 19 May 2022.
69 *London Chronicle*, 2 February 1805.
70 *Parliamentary Debates*, vol.3, cols.261–266.
71 *Naval Chronicle* (1806), vol.16, p.286.
72 *Parliamentary Debates*, vol.3, col.274.
73 *Parliamentary Debates*, vol.3, cols.266–269.
74 *Parliamentary Debates*, vol.3, cols.269–270 (Markham), cols.271–272 (Fox and Pitt).
75 *Parliamentary Debates*, vol.3, col.274.
76 *The Courier*, 6 February 1805.

London papers after *The Times* – published a long, and positive, editorial on Popham, concluding that he had 'been ungenerously treated'. Although probably not written by Popham, at least not directly, this sort of content prefigured the speeches he intended to make in Parliament. He was determined to defend himself in person and, despite having been ordered to join the Channel Fleet, he secured leave to see out a business 'of essential moment to my Character, and Interest'.[77]

On 5 March, all papers pertaining to *Romney* held by the Commissioners of Naval Enquiry were deposited before the House of Commons. Popham was able to see the evidence that had informed the February 1804 report for the first time – not that there was any doubt about the outcome of any investigation, at least not while Melville remained at the helm. The Navy Board could see the way the wind was blowing as well as anybody else. Now that the *Romney* affair was attracting parliamentary scrutiny and with the Prime Minister himself expressing an interest, the Board was anxious to distance itself from the February 1804 report. On 1 April, its members wrote to the Admiralty Board to apologise for having ever endorsed such an 'inaccurate' composition. The conclusion of the joint letter showed his former colleagues had no compunction about dropping its author, Tucker, in the mud:

> The inaccuracies and erroneous statements in the Report are imputable to the individual commissioner only who conducted the investigation; and if any censure should be considered as due to us for lending the sanction of our names to the Report, we trust that we shall stand excused before their Lordships, when they reflect that we were guided by the implicit reliance which we placed on the accuracy and industry of Mr Tucker. … It is with extreme concern we discover, from the revision of the Report, which has been occasioned by Sir Home Popham's late appeal, that our confidence has been misplaced.[78]

With the Navy Board backing away rapidly from its own report, it now seemed like Tucker, not Popham, might be the main victim of an inquiry.

And then, dramatically, everything changed – again. Popham, despite his attempts to maximise his own significance, was small fry in St Vincent's system of anti-corruption, and it now claimed a much bigger fish. In February 1805, the Commissioners of Naval Enquiry released their Tenth Report on the office of Treasurer of the Navy – an office that had been held by Lord Melville during Pitt's first administration. The Tenth Report uncovered a significant discrepancy in the Treasurer's finances. Up to £6 million in public money had been invested in private bank accounts since the beginning of the wars with France, with the interest apparently accruing to Melville as a private individual.[79] These accusations of embezzlement shook the government to its foundations: the oppositionist *Morning Chronicle* thought the Tenth Report would spell the end of Melville, and possibly of Pitt too.[80] On 8 April, following a long and dramatic debate in which Popham did not participate, although he did vote, the House of Commons censured Melville. Melville resigned

---

77  TNA: ADM 1/2329: Popham to Marsden, 13 March 1805.
78  House of Commons, *Accounts and Papers presented to the House of Commons*, pp.402–403.
79  Michael Fry, *The Dundas Despotism* (Edinburgh: University Press, 1992), p.264.
80  *Morning Chronicle*, 11 February 1805.

Caricature depicting Lord Melville attacked by the political opposition following accusations of embezzlement, by James Sayer, 1805. Popham discharges a blunderbuss, top left, labelled 'Popham's Defence'; behind him is HMS *Romney*, with a placard reading 'Wanted. Supply of naval Stores. Inquire within.' (Public domain, Wellcome Collection)

immediately, but in mid-June the Commons resolved on a full impeachment, and in July the Lords agreed.

The loss of Melville was potentially a disaster for Popham. Melville's successor at the Admiralty, Lord Barham, was not ill disposed, but Popham did not have the same rapport with him. More seriously, although Pitt's tottering government did not immediately fall over Melville's impeachment, it had been seriously weakened. There was a chance it would collapse during the next parliamentary session and that St Vincent and his friends would return. Popham needed to get any inquiry out of the way quickly before all his protectors left office but, to his dismay, he discovered everybody had lost interest. The opposition, scenting bigger game, had almost completely forgotten about him, and the beleaguered government did absolutely nothing to remind them. When Kinnaird tried to put his motion off by a fortnight, raising the possibility that it might not be addressed at all until the following year, Popham argued against. He reminded the House the whole affair had placed him and his family under a great deal of stress, but in reality the political clock was ticking.[81]

Pitt's government did not have energy for Popham's shenanigans and had absolutely no desire to expedite any inquiry. Once it became clear the issue could not be avoided, however, Pitt suggested referring it to a parliamentary committee, which would clear the schedule of the House of Commons to deal with more important things.[82] This was not Popham's preference – a committee operated away from the immediate public eye, as its proceedings were not directly reported in the newspapers – but it was the best he was going to get. The debate on 8 May, which Popham had been anticipating for weeks, was an anticlimax, with all parties agreeing to Pitt's committee proposal. Having prepared for a show-down, however, Popham could not resist grabbing the limelight on the spurious pretext that, if he did not speak, 'a silent acquiescence might be construed into a tacit acknowledgement that the motion rested on an actual charge existing against him'. He accused St Vincent's Admiralty outright of fabricating evidence before concluding, with evident relish: 'He should not deny, and it was what might happen to any officer, that he might have committed some irregularities; but he was sure, he had not been guilty of any criminal irregularities, that should call for, or warrant the criminal industry that had been employed to decry his character.'[83] Despite Popham's cockiness, the speech was not well received. The MPs sat through it in stunned disbelief before bursting into laughter at Popham's description of a letter he had written as 'short [and] pithy',[84] suggesting his reputation for prolixity was well known. Pitt had to hurry matters to a close before Popham embarrassed himself, and the government that was protecting him, even more.[85]

The select committee, with Sir John Stuart as chairman, sat for the first time on 14 May. The disgraced Tucker pointed out its failure to cross-examine any of the dockyard officers at Chatham and Portsmouth who had actually sifted through Popham's accounts, but otherwise the investigations were remarkably thorough.[86] The committee questioned nearly

---

81   *The Times*, 29 April 1805.
82   *Parliamentary Debates*, vol.4, col.626.
83   *Parliamentary Debates*, vol.4, cols.638–641.
84   *The Star*, 9 May 1805.
85   *Parliamentary Debates*, vol.4, cols.643–644.
86   BL: G.19449, pp.xxii–xxiii: comment by Tucker in *The Trial of Sir Home Popham*.

everyone from the junior clerk at the Committee of Stores all the way up to Lord St Vincent himself.[87] Most of the examinations focused on the main players in the drama: Tucker, who first gave evidence on 15 May; Charles Nixon, *Romney*'s former boatswain; and Popham himself. Popham appeared before the committee on a dozen separate occasions, more than any other witness, although there remained a gaping hole in his testimony surrounding the reason he had actually taken *Romney* to Calcutta for repairs in the first place. Being 'excessively employed on business of very great consequence' could only get him so far, particularly when other professional officers testified that Bombay would have been closer and cheaper.[88] Still, this weakness did not bother Popham in the least, and he acted like he was being given extra publicity on his own terms. He alternated between extreme eagerness to overshare and arrogant sarcasm. When one committee member asked where the anchors had been during the refit, presumably with the missing anchor in mind, Popham replied, deadpan: 'I should imagine [they were] … securing the ship.' A little later, when Popham claimed not to remember a particular discrepancy in *Romney*'s accounts, a committee member asked him if it was not part of a captain's duty to review the boatswain's expense book. Popham retorted: 'Certainly, but I hope it will appear that there is a difference between inspecting the boatswain's accounts monthly, and recollecting, after a lapse of three years, every item of expense that is in the boatswain's Expense Book.'[89]

Popham could afford to be confident. Given the Navy Board had already disavowed the report on which the entire inquiry was based, and with the government keen to hurry the business to a close, the committee was unlikely to find against him. Several important documents pertaining to the most serious charges against Popham were still missing and, although Tucker and others vehemently denied any evidence had been deliberately destroyed, the obvious absence of these papers could only work in Popham's favour. The investigation may originally have been planned to determine whether Popham had been guilty of peculation, but it swiftly morphed into an examination of who might have been responsible for framing him. Most of the witnesses understood this and bent to the prevailing wind. Many were also clearly overawed by appearing before an array of important politicians. This made it difficult for the case against Popham to come out clearly. When the committee issued its first report on 5 June, it was categorical: 'There does not appear any ground whatever to impute to Sir Home Popham any fraud, or connivance at any fraudulent or corrupt practice whatsoever.'[90] The second report, released on 24 June, provided the detail behind this finding. The committee agreed with Popham that the actual sum expended on *Romney* had been closer to £10,000 than £70,000 and noted how unusual it was to use ships' logs as evidence in an investigation, as the Portsmouth officers had been ordered to do; any discrepancies in those logs could therefore not justifiably be used as evidence of wrongdoing, as they had never been intended for this sort of purpose. The committee exonerated Tucker from the charge of deliberately destroying documents to cover his trail, but took him to

---

87  *Parliamentary Debates*, vol.5, col.8.
88  House of Commons, *Second Report of the Select Committee on the Romney*, p.95 (quotation on p.48).
89  House of Commons, *Second Report of the Select Committee on the Romney*, pp.56, 58.
90  House of Commons, *Reports from the Select Committee on Papers Relating to the Repairs of His Majesty's Ships The Romney and Sensible, while under the Command of Sir Home Popham: First Report* (London: House of Commons, ordered to be printed 5 June 1805), pp.3–5.

task for having had the confidential February 1804 report published and circulated without permission.[91] Popham had won, and his enemies – including Tucker – were disgraced.

The inquiry was a triumph for Popham. *The Courier* talked as though he had walked out scot-free from a court-martial: 'Sir Home has ... been *honourably acquitted*'.[92] That 'acquittal' came just in time for the government, as the last thing Pitt wanted was to draw attention to irregularities committed by a notorious Melville protégé at a time when Melville was himself being impeached for embezzlement. The accusations against Popham had certainly been serious, and they might have destroyed him. But Popham had benefited from the fact the men appointed to the select committee were not naval professionals and therefore did not appreciate the nitty gritty detail – what happened when anchors were lost or replaced on a foreign station; the repurposing of old cable; how many sails a ship should have in foreign seas. The loss of this granularity meant that an investigation of what Popham had done became a more general question of what he had *intended* to do. As a result, Popham stood on much firmer ground than he might otherwise have done, ostentatiously backed as he was by the government, and particularly when the missing papers and Tucker's obvious errors of judgement were balanced against the lack of any firm evidence against him.

Because of this, the *Romney* affair became much more than an inquiry into everyday naval processes. It grew into a question of corruption, a political issue mobilised across party lines – not that the accusations against Popham were evidence of a personal vendetta against him by Lord St Vincent, whatever Popham may have thought or claimed. The inquiry into Popham's expenditure in the Red Sea was merely one stitch in a bigger tapestry. Popham was unlucky in that he returned to Britain in the midst of St Vincent's drive to crack down on inefficiency, irregularity, and idiosyncrasy; after all, Popham's whole *raison d'être* involved fitting into the cracks around what was normal in the service.

Much of the sordid business sprang from the complex nature of Popham's Red Sea mission. Popham's professional role concealed other, more shadowy, tasks that elevated him far beyond his seniority and were governed by several overlapping sets of instructions, some highly secret. This meant he could defend what might seem like odd courses of action by hiding behind the impenetrable shield of 'duty', but this excuse could only be used sparingly, particularly as he often could not go into further detail about what that 'duty' actually involved. Popham hinted at this problem in a passage he added to the main text of *Concise Statement of Facts* on 2 September 1803. Popham was responding to accusations that he had 'arrogated power unbecoming my station – that I had no command – and was merely dispatched with a convoy of troops intended to cooperate with the Indian Army'.[93] The passage he added to the book described his role in the Red Sea in detail, mentioning the multiplicity of his roles – as commander of the squadron carrying the troops to Egypt; his discretionary naval role thereafter; his responsibility to the Governor-General; and his political mission as Ambassador to the States of Arabia. However, the only set of instructions he could quote in full, either in *Concise Statement of Facts* or before the *Romney* committee, were those from the Admiralty. These were very limited in scope, essentially restricted to

---

91  House of Commons, *Second Report of the Select Committee on the Romney*, pp.15–28.
92  *The Courier*, 18 July 1805.
93  [Popham], *Concise Statement of Facts*, pp.49–50.

embarking Baird and his troops, cooperating with them in Upper Egypt, and re-embarking them when they were no longer needed.[94]

At the heart of the problem was the fact Popham had served several masters – the Admiralty, the War Department, the East India Company, and Governor-General Wellesley. It meant very few people had a fully comprehensive picture of what Popham had been doing in the Red Sea. Those who did, like Melville and Spencer, were out of office and increasingly cut off from the new Addington administration. This had clear implications for the way Popham's mission was viewed, not just by St Vincent's Admiralty, but also by the naval profession in general, including men Popham had actually been working with at the time. Captain Thomas Surridge, for example, who had commanded Rear Admiral Blankett's flagship in the Red Sea, considered 'the command of the squadron [in the Red Sea] had devolved on me' following Blankett's death, as Surridge had been the senior captain – but even Surridge admitted he knew Popham had orders, which he had not seen, beyond those from the Admiralty.[95]

This still left an important question: who had been responsible for the massively high bills that had so horrified the Admiralty? The investigations of the parliamentary committee did not really come up with a definitive answer, although they did turn up one significant fact. In the absence of a ship's commanding officer, the committee established that authority for taking on stores and authorising repairs devolved on three men: the First Lieutenant, the master, and the boatswain. Along with Popham, therefore, these individuals should have been star witnesses questioned by the Navy Board in drawing up the February 1804 report. Popham had obviously not been cross-examined. Of the other three protagonists, Popham's former First Lieutenant had been away on service at the time the February 1804 report had been compiled; the acting master, Bartholomew, had been pressed and sent to another ship shortly before the writing of the report. The February 1804 report had therefore almost entirely relied on the testimony of the boatswain, Charles Nixon, who had been in hospital for most of the time the ship was in the Red Sea.[96] The committee concluded this should have made it impossible for the Navy Board to draw proper conclusions, and blamed Tucker for being negligent in collecting his evidence – but nobody noticed that Popham's absence from his ship in the first place had given rise to this confusion, as he had clearly failed to establish the correct chain of command while he was away. Popham never hid the fact he had spent hardly any time with *Romney* during the period when it was being repaired at Calcutta, and nobody on the parliamentary committee questioned the propriety of these absences. Yet the fact that there had, apparently, been nobody available to approve any expenditure in his absence was odd, and the financial irregularities the Admiralty had identified may have arisen from this power vacuum. Possibly it was all an innocent mistake arising from Popham's comparative inexperience: prior to his appointment to *Romney*, he had only ever captained one Royal Navy ship, HMS *Expedition*, and that for less than three months.

But innocence was not a trait readily associated with Popham, and another possibility was that he had known exactly what he was doing all along. Had he used his prolonged absences, and the extremely tangled chain of authority that had resulted from them, to engage in

---

94  House of Commons, *Second Report of the Select Committee on the Romney*, pp.155–156.
95  House of Commons, *Second Report of the Select Committee on the Romney*, pp.94–95, 97.
96  House of Commons, *Second Report of the Select Committee on the Romney*, p.68.

some money-making ventures he could conceal by his distance from the scene of the crime? Throughout his life, Popham faced repeated accusations of greed and subterfuge designed to bring him money. Part of this was founded on his past as a private trader in *Etrusco*, which was public knowledge thanks to the High Court of Admiralty case and the issue of the Royal Warrant settling the matter. Popham's close connection with the disgraced Melville also exposed him to accusations of corruption similar to those made against his former patron. For many, including Benjamin Tucker, the *Romney* business left too many questions unanswered. The select committee had blamed Tucker for wrongful accusation as a result of clearing Popham of all charges, and Tucker had been forced to issue a public apology for writing the 20 February 1804 report. Privately, however, Tucker stood by everything in that report: 'Every charge brought against [Popham] was fully established, in spite of the Efforts of the Navy Board to cover him and their own criminal negligence.' Like Popham, he chose to interpret his treatment as evidence of political persecution, with Pitt using the Popham affair to punish Tucker for his role in bringing Lord Melville to trial: 'Never was the effort of Party so strongly and wickedly exerted as to screen Sir Home by the Report of the Committee, from which the Service has suffered irreparable injury.'[97]

Tucker was right about the political motivation behind the government's sponsorship of the inquiry. He was also right that the reputation of the Navy had not emerged from the business unscathed, although 'irreparable injury' was an exaggeration. Tucker meant the committee's findings were tantamount to a statement that naval captains could do what they liked on station so long as they had the protection of a powerful patron, but the affair had also drawn attention to problems at the very top of the naval tree. It placed the independence of the Navy Board from the Admiralty Board in question, and suggested the one was able to dictate the actions of the other. The investigation into the February 1804 report had undermined the Navy Board's ability to look into abuses and highlighted how little scrutiny went into the composition of their official reports. Popham had not only managed to wriggle off the hook of censure: he had succeeded in making St Vincent's Admiralty and Navy Board look just as corrupt and negligent as the bodies they were investigating.

The *Romney* affair should have been a warning for everyone, but Popham did not interpret it this way. Melville's defence of Popham the previous year – that 'to the conviction of all of us he has served Government for many years in various capacities zealously and well' – still held true.[98] As long as Pitt remained in office and remembered the political services Popham had given him, Popham had nothing to fear. Rather than pointing to a need for circumspection, the inquiry had shown him the government would stand by him no matter what he did. This was the lesson Popham imbibed, and it helps explain some of his actions and decisions over the next few years.

---

97   BL: G.19449, pp.xxii–xxiii: comment by Tucker in *The Trial of Sir Home Popham*.
98   Melville to Keith, 7 October 1804, Lloyd (ed.), *The Keith Papers*, vol.3, p.95.

# 9

# 'Mr Francis's Carcasses', 1804–1805

*2907: Set fire to the vessels in the harbour*

As confident as he was that Pitt would dig him out of trouble, Popham was in professional limbo until his name was cleared by the *Romney* committee. He had languished on half-pay before, in the 1780s, but his lack of employment in 1804 was more galling. His lifestyle had become more flamboyant; he had a wife, a growing family, and an estate near Windsor. He also knew Lord Melville had employments lined up for him, and the knowledge that he was missing out on possible notoriety made his boredom worse.

Britain and France had been at war again since May 1803, and there should have been much to do for an officer like Popham whose expertise focused on the northern coast of Europe. As the British politicians struggled to construct a continental alliance, Napoleon threatened an invasion of Britain's own shores. He established a camp, headquartered at Boulogne, St Omer, and Bruges, which initially consisted of 70,000 men and grew to 140,000 over the course of 1804. The proximity of this army, which could be clearly seen through a telescope from the cliffs of Dover, caused a panic that was still being described a century later as 'the Great Terror'.[1] To carry his invasion force across the Channel, Napoleon placed a fleet of 1,000 fishing boats and specially constructed flatboats under the command of *amiral* Bruix at Calais, Ostend, Boulogne, Wimereux, Ambleteuse, and Etaples. This was a respectable force, especially when added to France's fleet of 32 ships of the line and 26 frigates. Although the Royal Navy had nearly twice as many ships of the line, these were scattered all over the world, whereas France's navy was much more concentrated in home waters.[2] The comparative strength of the Royal Navy meant many scoffed at the likelihood of a successful landing on British shores: St Vincent was (apocryphally) quoted as saying, 'I do not say the French cannot come. I only say they cannot come by water.'[3] The Royal Navy had squadrons stationed outside all the major French ports and harbours to make sure no invasion craft, let alone ships of the line, could escape. Ten ships were permanently stationed off Boulogne, Ostend, and Dunkirk, as well as the Dutch harbour of Vlissingen

---

1   H.F.B. Wheeler and A.M. Broadley, *Napoleon and the Invasion of England* (London: Bodley Head, 1908), vol.1, p.vii.
2   Tom Pocock, *The Terror Before Trafalgar: Nelson, Napoleon and the Secret War* (London: John Murray, 2002), pp.96–97.
3   Arthur Bryant, *The Years of Victory, 1802–1812* (London: Collins, 1944), p.77.

(Flushing), and a further 10 were stationed off the Dutch harbour at Texel. Twenty ships watched Brest, seven watched Rochefort, and seven were stationed outside the Spanish port of Ferrol because, even if Spain was not yet at war with Britain, it had been allied to France since the collapse of the First Coalition.[4] But the French had broken through similar blockades in the 1790s, and had even landed troops in Wales in 1797 and in Ireland in 1798. What would happen if the French again managed to get a fleet to the Irish Sea?

As the founder of the Sea Fencibles, Popham had long ago established his credentials in matters of national defence. Popham may have been under the shadow of the *Romney* inquiry, but the need to fight off a French invasion should have transcended that – or at least so Popham seems to have thought. He knew Pitt's return to office had largely been driven by attacking his predecessor's lacklustre defence policy. Addington's Admiralty, with St Vincent at the helm, had considered abandoning the existing system of opposing an enemy invasion with 'ships of the Line, Frigates, Sloops of War, and Bombs' and meeting them on their own terms in 'a conflict of Boat against Boat', but had dismissed it on the grounds that relying on gunboats would more or less hand the enemy an advantage.[5] Melville's Admiralty, however, was much more open to irregular tactics at sea, and Melville's official papers were full of (apparently seriously considered) designs for fireboats propelled by windmills, sulphur bombs to burn the invaders' lungs, and balloons to fly over the enemy ships and drop burning matches into the rigging.[6] In comparison, the expedient with which Popham was approached in the summer of 1804, and which he persuaded the government to adopt, was positively sane.

At the end of June 1804, Popham, in his capacity as a Fellow of the Royal Society (he had been appointed in 1799), sat on a secret committee of five called to look into the viability of a proposal put forward by an anonymous source known only by the name 'Robert Francis'.[7] 'Francis' was offering the government 'Nautilus', 'a Submarine Vessel 35 feet long, 10 feet wide, and 8 feet deep, capable of containing 6 persons ... [with] the property of sailing like an ordinary fishing Boat ... [and] of remaining at sea 20 days for 3 hours at a time without air'. The vessel could travel above sea-level using a set of sails, or it could plunge below by pumping water into a hollow keel, propelled by an Archimedes screw hand-cranked by one of the crew. 'Francis' proposed a fleet of 10 of these vessels, each carrying 30 'torpedoes' – or 'carcasses' – filled with gunpowder, and which could be attached to the bottom of an enemy ship via a detachable spike, or used to seal up enemy harbours and rivers.[8] 'Francis' was convinced his inventions would lead to a paradigm shift in warfare: 'As gun powder, cannon, muskets, gun locks, and even flints, all had opponents, prejudices, and established habits to encounter ... so these inventions on submarine navigation and attack may now be considered as the embryo of a total change in the military marine system, and the existing

---

4   Kent Record Office (KRO): Camden MSS, U840/O227-1: memorandum, 12 September 1804.
5   Devon Record Office (DRO): Sidmouth MSS, 152M C1804 ON/22: memorandum, 1804.
6   These documents are in the National Maritime Museum [NMM] MEL/7.
7   Along with the Royal Society's President (Sir Joseph Banks), fellow members Henry Cavendish and John Rennie, and future Royal Society Fellow William Congreve.
8   David Whittet Thomson, 'The Catamaran Expeditions', *USNI Proceedings*, 70/2/492 (1944); William Barclay Parsons, *Robert Fulton and the Submarine* (NY: Columbia University Press, 1922), pp.25–27, 33, 56–57, 73.

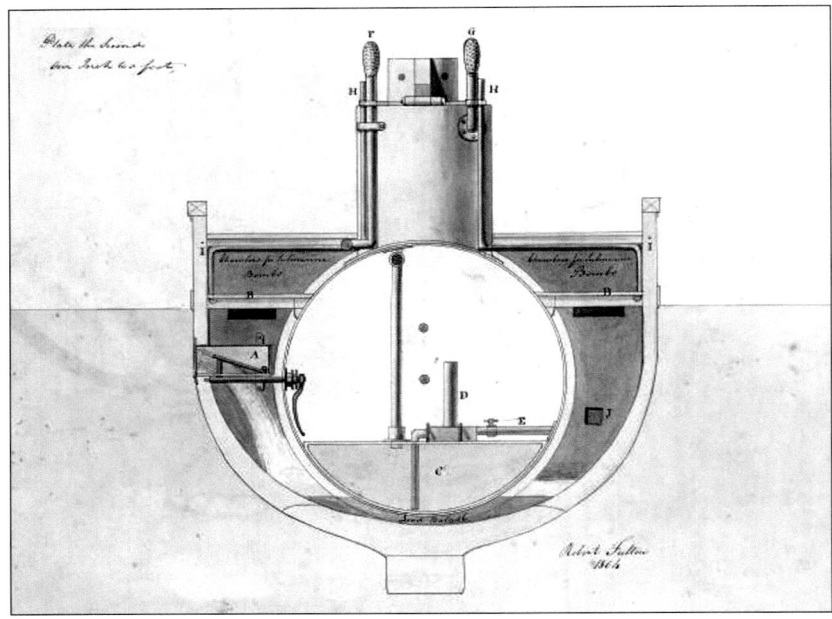

Cross-section of *Nautilus*, 1804. (Public domain, Manuscripts and Archives Division, The New York Public Library)

relative power of states.' The whopping £100,000 price tag attached to the plan reflected the inventor's confidence in its revolutionary nature.[9]

Despite, or perhaps because of, this confidence, the Royal Society committee rejected the scheme out of hand. On 30 June, however, Popham's attention was called back to 'Nautilus' and the 'carcasses' when he received a letter from 'Francis'. 'Francis' was the pseudonym of Robert Fulton, an American citizen and inventor who had come to Britain to lobby the government to take on his submarine (he tactfully did not mention that he was only in Britain because Napoleon had already passed on it). Fulton complained the committee had not given him enough time; his submarine was perfectly viable, and as proof he stated he had already spent 17 minutes underwater in one.[10] All Fulton wanted was 20 minutes of conversation with Pitt or Melville to pitch his scheme, concluding pointedly with the warning that it was better to know what kinds of experimental weapon were available in case the enemy obtained them.[11]

Fulton had found a kindred spirit in Popham. Both men were brilliant, over-confident, indiscreet, and impatient of criticism. Both were carried forward by their emotions, and expected others to be the same. More fundamentally, the two men shared a love for novelty. Popham was always on the lookout for new methods of warfare based on scientific principles, and Fulton's proposal was right up his alley. His appetite may have been whetted by the papers he had seen while he had sat on the Royal Society's secret committee; he was probably also flattered by Fulton's approach, and by the American's assumption that he

---

9   Alan Rems, 'Man of War', *Naval History Magazine*, 25:4 (2011).
10  Parsons, *Robert Fulton and the Submarine*, p.33.
11  Parsons, *Robert Fulton and the Submarine*, pp.99–100.

had personal leverage with the Prime Minister. Popham arranged to meet up with Fulton and, after a face-to-face discussion of the topic, agreed to talk to Pitt. Luckily for Fulton, Popham's pitch to Pitt could not have come at a better time. The government's first attempt to contribute to national defence – the Additional Force Act, a new defence force that would double as a recruiting pool for the regulars – had scraped through Parliament, underlining the government's precarious political position, and Fulton's project offered Pitt an opportunity to emphasise that he was doing everything he could to strengthen the country's naval defences. The Prime Minister ordered a delighted Popham to negotiate with Fulton to draw up an official contract of employment, to be signed over breakfast on 20 July.

While Pitt may have been surprisingly enthusiastic, Melville was less so. Fulton later thought the First Lord of the Admiralty had 'condemned the Nautilus without a moment's consideration', and he made an excuse not to turn up on the day appointed for the breakfast.[12] Pitt, however, met Popham and Fulton effusively. Popham and Fulton had spent the previous week drawing up a contract for Pitt to sign. Fulton pledged to sell his plans to the government for 14 years for £40,000, plus £7,000 for immediate expenses, a salary of £200 a month while he was in the government's employ, and a quarter of the value of all enemy vessels destroyed while he was on the scene. In return, if provided with 'one good Mechanecian [sic] ... an Active Sea officer [with the] ... power to choose 100 hardy seamen *out of the fleet* who are good swimmers, [and] about 40 tonnes of powder', he agreed to teach Popham everything there was to know about submarines and exploding carcasses.[13] Perhaps Popham encouraged Fulton to set his price so high; one of Fulton's biographers 'confessed that Fulton's terms were somewhat grasping'.[14] But Pitt read over the papers and signed them without comment. Pitt then asked Popham to take the contract to Melville for his signature, and the three men agreed to meet the following week to discuss the first application of Fulton's new weapon.[15]

Melville was still sceptical, but with Pitt backing the project and Popham applying his professional arguments to buttress

Robert Fulton, engraved by George Parker after Benjamin West. (Public domain, Manuscripts and Archives Division, The New York Public Library)

---

12   Cadwallader D. Colden, *The Life of Robert Fulton* (NY: Kirk & Mercein, 1817), p.56.
13   Parsons, *Robert Fulton and the Submarine*, pp.79, 81, 83–84.
14   H.W. Dickinson, *Robert Fulton, Engineer and Artist: His Life and Works* (NY: John Lane, the Bodley Head, 1913), pp.184–185.
15   Parsons, *Robert Fulton and the Submarine*, pp.100–101.

the case, he gave in. He persisted in his dislike of the submarine, though, and was more attracted by Fulton's torpedoes. Fulton proposed an 18-foot-long 'carcass', designed to float just below the surface of the water. As a contemporary described them, they resembled 'a log of mahogany', weighing about two tonnes and coated with canvas and hot pitch. They were filled with 40 barrels of gunpowder and attached to a pair of nine-foot-long planks with a bar between them for a man to sit on, half-submerged so as not to be visible to the enemy. This man could paddle the carcass through the water to the target – an enemy boat, ship, or harbour structure – and attach it securely, before setting the clockwork-regulated fuse and making his escape.[16] Melville wondered whether these explosive devices might be used to attack the enemy invasion fleet sheltering within Boulogne harbour, where British ships of the line and frigates could not reach them.

Popham and Fulton therefore cooked up a plan to destroy 'the Enemy's Fleet at Anchor under almost any circumstance'. Two ordnance vessels, two gun brigs, and a cutter would accompany twenty 12-oared boats, each manned by 12 oarsmen and five marines, and towing two explosive carcasses each into Boulogne harbour, while submarines sneaked in underwater.[17] As a result of 'the Scene of dismay which [these methods] may naturally be expected to excite', gunboats and armed vessels would try and get close enough bombard the anchored fleet and perhaps even board them.[18] Popham optimistically proposed a broad range of operations from Brest to the Helder, including Ostend, Calais, Le Havre, Rochefort, and St Malo – even Ferrol, despite the fact Britain and Spain were not yet at war. Melville nevertheless pressed for limited operations at Boulogne in the first instance, where the invasion flotilla was based. Popham agreed, taking a Boulogne assault as a test. Launching the submarines and torpedoes at the French invasion fleet would serve a triple purpose: it would destroy some of the enemy's landing craft; it would sow panic among the French forces; and it would demonstrate the efficacy of this new method of waging war.

Since Popham still could not be officially employed, this was the closest he was likely to get to active service for some time, even if he could not claim any role in an assault beyond his seniority as a Royal Navy captain. By the beginning of August he was down in Lymington under the orders of Admiral Lord Keith, the commander-in-chief of the Channel Fleet, testing out the viability of the submarine. Everything was top secret – although, as often happened, Popham may not have been able to resist giving the newspapers a tip-off that he was engaged in new and amazing work. According to the *Morning Post* for 28 August 1804, 'A number of Custom-house cutters are ordered to be put under the orders of Sir Home POPHAM, who is arrived here to inspect some new planned boats, which are building in the Dock-yard' – a report likely provided by Popham himself. Popham clearly enjoyed dashing back and forth from the coast to Woolwich, where he oversaw the construction of the torpedoes, and on to London, where he reported directly to Pitt and Melville.

---

16  Dickinson, *Robert Fulton, Engineer and Artist*, p.186; Alice Crary Sutcliffe, *Robert Fulton* (NY: Macmillan, 1915), p.114.
17  David Whittet Thomson, 'The Catamaran Expeditions', *USNI Proceedings*, 70/2/492 (February 1944); William James, *The Naval History of Great Britain* (London: Harding, Lepard and Co., 1826), vol.3, p.336.
18  BL: Add MS 41080, f.33: Popham to Melville, 17 August 1804.

Ostensibly, Popham was under Keith's command, but he took advantage of the fact he had been ordered on this mission by the Prime Minister and First Lord of the Admiralty to report directly to them. This gave Popham a direct line to Melville at the Admiralty, and he thoroughly abused it, even going as far as drawing up two different reports for Melville and Keith of his thoughts and actions.[19] But Popham also knew his nominal chief did not like his plan for using the submarines and carcasses. 'At present it seems plausable [sic],' Keith told Melville, doubtfully, 'which is all I can say.'[20] Keith's ambivalence may have encouraged Popham to approach Melville directly, and his habit of jumping over Keith's head inevitably caused friction, as Keith liked being left out of the loop even less than he liked the business Popham was engaged in. Melville himself was unhappy with the 'official Jealousies and Etiquettes' arising from Popham's behaviour, but could do little but try to persuade Popham to behave: so long as Popham was acting only in a private capacity, he did not have to observe the usual chains of command.[21]

While Popham undoubtedly benefited from the undefined nature of his role, he was, like Keith and Melville, all too aware of the dangers involved in having no official standing. 'I am quite a stranger in the fleet and merely a civilian,' he confessed to Keith.[22] This left Popham vulnerable to adverse comment, and the ongoing *Romney* affair had given his usually boundless self-confidence a severe knock. He became increasingly cagey about the submarines and torpedoes, and at one point even came close to telling Melville he had never endorsed them at all: 'I have never, my Lord, presumed to say a word on the policy of the measure, that exceeds the limit of the examination which I was directed to make.'[23] This was surprising language from the man who had lobbied Pitt to take Fulton on in the first place, but it was typical of Popham to cover his back. If something went horribly wrong, at least Popham could produce this letter as proof he had had doubts. His letters to the First Lord also suggested Popham was trying very hard to emphasise he was doing his best: 'There is not a shadow of difficulty or delay in my composition.'[24] Even though Melville was on his side, Popham knew his behaviour at Boulogne might make or break his future career. In a word, he was nervous.

The focus of Popham's business was at Lymington, opposite the Isle of Wight, where the Master Builder of the Dockyard had constructed a prototype submarine according to Fulton's specifications. Popham spent time with Fulton learning how to use the machine but soon realised that, while sound enough to carry several men underwater, the submarines depended far more on the weather and tides than was ideal for conditions in the Channel (one later report dismissed them: 'Might do in a river or very fine climate'[25]). Popham was nevertheless reluctant to write off these 'plungers or submerging Machines' completely, particularly as the government had spent so much money on them at his recommendation. Nevertheless, by mid-August he thought the submarines might be used 'as a collateral

---

19 WLC UM: Melville MSS, Box 18: Popham to Melville, 17 August 1804.
20 BL: Loan MS 57/108, no.3: Keith to Melville, 26 August 1804.
21 WLC UM: Melville MSS, Box 20: Melville to Popham, 3 November 1804.
22 Popham to Keith, 4 October 1804, *The Keith Papers*, vol.3, p.94.
23 BL: Add MS 41080, f.23: Popham to Melville, 1 August 1804.
24 BL: Loan MS 57/108, no.2: Popham to Melville, [29 August] 1804.
25 Report of Lieutenant Robinson, 20 May 1806, *The Keith Papers*, vol.3, p.129.

instrument of destruction' only.[26] He shifted his focus onto the torpedoes – the 'carcasses', or, as Popham occasionally called them, cryptically, the 'New Curiosities'.[27] But the carcasses had a tendency to leak and had to be sealed with lead, which obviously weighted them down. The clockwork mechanism, too – so vital to protect the lives of the men operating them – posed technical difficulties. The men operating them often forgot to remove the peg to start the clockwork countdown process necessary for the carcass to go off, rendering them useless.[28] Keith witnessed all this and, still less than enamoured with Popham's plan of action, began to pick holes in it. Popham, clearly afraid Keith might have the whole thing called off, protested to Melville that Keith was throwing obstacles in his path on purpose.[29] Popham's attack of insecurity meant Melville sometimes received as many as three or four letters a day updating him on tides, winds, and other logistical difficulties, as Popham was 'anxious you should know in what forwardness we are'.[30]

Popham had been trying to put all the arrangements for his attack in place by the first week of September, when the moon would be new and the night at its blackest. Popham was already nervous about the behaviour of his explosive carcasses, and he knew the chances of success would be best on a cloudy, but still, night. But for various reasons – lack of gunpowder, unfavourable winds and tides, and (as far as Popham was concerned) obstruction on the part of his superiors – nothing was ready until 8 September. Popham distracted himself by getting more information on Boulogne and planning even more future attacks, adding Amsterdam and Nieuwe Diep to the repertoire.[31] By 21 September, however, everything was ready. Two bomb vessel captains from the blockading squadron volunteered to oversee operations on the ground. Several torpedoes were loaded with 14,670 pounds of powder; 1,100 'combustible balls' – a kind of bomb that could be thrown at enemy vessels to enhance the attack – were prepared. Several 'explosion vessels', a kind of fireship designed to sail into the chaos at the most propitious moment, were also ready. Popham being Popham, he assured Melville he had all the scientific equipment, including two marine barometers, to help him identify the precise moment when sending in these weapons of war would have the best effect.[32] Popham also being Popham, he wanted his 'secret' mission to have the biggest possible splash, and he tried to persuade Pitt and Melville that what they really wanted was a midnight outing to watch Boulogne harbour burn.[33]

Towards the end of September, to his delight, Popham found the French had brought some ships out of Boulogne and into the Roads – sitting ducks for his assault.[34] For now, however, the wind was unfavourable and the moon was waxing. Popham's nerves deteriorated again as the new moon approached: if the weather did not change before it arrived, he faced the prospect of waiting another month to put all his carefully laid plans into action.

---

26  BL: Add MS 41080, f.33: Popham to Melville, 17 August 1804.
27  Popham to Keith, 15 September 1804, *The Keith Papers*, vol.3, p.88.
28  Popham to Keith, 12 August 1804, *The Keith Papers*, vol.3, p.85; NRS: Melville MSS, GD51/236: general orders, 1 October 1804.
29  BL: Loan MS 57/108, no.2: Popham to Melville, [29 August] 1804.
30  BL: Loan MS 57/108, no.7: Popham to Melville, 31 August 1804.
31  BL: Add MS 41080, f.50: Popham to Melville, 20 September 1804.
32  BL: Add MS 41080, f.53: Popham to Melville, 21 September 1804.
33  BL: Add MS 41080, f.57: Pitt to Melville, 25 September 1804.
34  BL: Add MS 41080, f.62: Popham to Melville, 27 September 1804.

The attack on Boulogne, by E.D. Lewis, 1804. (Public domain)

On 1 October, however, the wind almost miraculously shifted southerly at a moment when the tide was favourable and the night was likely to be dark. It was too good an opportunity to pass up, and Popham wrote to Keith to ask permission to proceed the following night, 2 October. Keith's exceedingly tepid reply reflected his continued ambiguities about the project: 'If you are inclined to pursue it at present I have no objection.'[35] But Popham needed nothing more. He wrote instantly to Melville to tell him the game was afoot: 'We have … only to pray for a fine Night; and your Lordship may depend on [it], something will be effected [tomorrow]'.[36]

Popham fixed himself aboard HMS *Ardent* and issued general orders for the attack. Keith allowed Popham to take three 64-gun vessels, two 50-gun ships, and a few frigates, sloops, and bomb vessels closer to the shore. The aim was now to attack whatever vessels came out of the harbour – as Popham hoped some would do, tempted by the sudden proximity

---

35  Keith to Popham, 1 October 1804, Lloyd (ed.), *The Keith Papers*, vol.3, p.89.
36  BL: Add MS 41080, f.68: Popham to Melville, [1 October] 1804.

of so many British vessels – but he had not yet abandoned hope of using the submarines. Two volunteers were ready to operate them: Lieutenant Hew Stewart, a volunteer from Keith's flagship HMS *Monarch*, and David Bartholomew, recovered from his questionable impressment and hoping to do something heroic to secure his elusive lieutenant's commission. Both would have a 'carcass' in tow, the clockwork set to 20 and 25 minutes respectively. After this opener, the main attack would consist of eight explosive casks and 'one large Carcass', timed to release in five waves between 8:00 p.m. and 10:00 p.m. Lieutenant Mainwaring of HMS *Leda* volunteered to tow the 'plungers' and their carcasses as far as he could. About three-quarters of an hour later, Captain Jackson, in command of the explosive vessel *Providence*, would set sail towards the enemy, towing yet another carcass. One hour after that, one of *Leopard*'s boats would tow out a fourth carcass, with four extra 'explosion casks' (smaller versions of the carcass) on board. At the same time, HMS *Veteran* would also send a boat with a carcass and two explosion casks, followed by a second boat carrying more casks. Finally, a boat from *Ardent* would sail carrying 'a small carcass' set to go off after 30 minutes, plus two small casks. Closing the small flotilla was the *Peggy* explosion vessel.[37] Popham reminded his men that the principal aim was not to achieve any military objective – although that would obviously be a bonus – but rather to find out if the 'carcasses' and 'plungers' were capable of being applied on a broader scale. Because this was mainly a scientific experiment, therefore, and mindful that he had no military standing in Keith's fleet, Popham gave his men strict instructions to avoid danger and retreat if too closely challenged: 'No extraordinary Risk is to be run'.[38]

At 8:00 p.m. on 2 October, with the moon concealed by clouds, Bartholomew and Stewart descended into their 'plungers' and swam off into the night. Shortly after, the boats left with muffled oars, towing their carcasses behind them. For a long while Popham could hear nothing but the whistle of the wind and the breaking of waves against HMS *Ardent*. He had hoped the boats with their carcasses might get close to the shore without being spotted, but the British ships off Boulogne had been bombarding the French for the last few days as a cover for their proximity, and the lull in their almost constant firing had not gone unnoticed. Shortly after 9:00 p.m., the silence of the night was broken by a sudden burst of musketry from the French fortifications defending the harbour. Less than an hour later, the first cannons came into play. Flashes of light rent the blackness and destroyed Popham's night vision, but he was not looking towards the coast. He was checking his watch. When 10:00 p.m. came and went with no explosion, Popham waited, tensely, for another 15 minutes, at which point the exchange between the French batteries and British ships was drowned out by a blinding column of fire followed by an almighty roar. The first carcass had gone off. All guns fell silent for a moment, as British and French alike took stock of what had just happened. When the firing continued, it was, Popham thought, considerably quieter; when the second explosion happened about seven minutes after the first it quietened even more, and almost completely stopped after the third explosion at 10:45 p.m. The night, however, was only just beginning, and Popham ordered a second wave of boats further east, where a series of five explosions went off between 2:00 a.m. and a 4:15 a.m. As Popham observed to

---

37  NRS: Melville MSS, GD51/236: general orders, 1 October 1804.
38  NRS: Melville MSS, GD51/234/1–2: general orders, 2 October 1804.

Lord Melville – present on the frigate *Aimable*, safely out of range but within sight – these boats were allowed to approach 'within a Pistol Shot without scarce any molestation'. By dawn, all boats had returned safely, with not a single man lost or wounded.[39]

Popham was jubilant: the enemy, he thought, had fought back so little because the explosions had shaken them to the core. As the British took stock the following day, however, collecting intelligence from the shore and viewing the damage through their telescopes, it soon became clear that any impact on the French had been almost entirely psychological. With the exception of 14 killed, seven wounded, and a French boat destroyed, the damage to the French lines had been superficial. Contemporaries were unimpressed. One described it as a 'costly *feu d'artifice*, which ... treated many thousand spectators, both ashore and afloat, to one of the most splendid fire-works I ever beheld'.[40] Naval historian William James pointed out the only long-term results were that the French reinforced their harbours against similar attacks in future.[41] Admiral Keith had the same opinion, and flatly told Popham he would only permit a repeat performance if 600 French vessels were to come out of Boulogne into the Roads – something that would not happen unless the French had actually decided on an invasion.[42] Even Fulton, present with Popham on HMS *Ardent*, was not satisfied with the lack of destruction, which he explained by 'a mistake, arising from the want of experience' in the operators.[43] Like Popham, Fulton was reluctant to take the blame for any shortcomings arising from the night's work.

Popham, too, was worried about how the experiment would be received by his patrons, particularly as he knew many of the government's enemies looked on the whole business as ridiculous. Despite the heavy veil of secrecy under which the operation ought to have been carried out, many had been gossiping about it, often with highly accurate details. One satirical print released towards the end of September had portrayed the upcoming attack, with one of the exploding vessels labelled 'Sir Home Popham's flagship'.[44] The *Romney* investigation was ongoing; Popham feared Pitt and Melville might decide he was too much of a liability in the wake of the Boulogne assault and drop him. His long letter to Melville of 4 October, therefore, was as much a damage limitation exercise as it was a report of what had happened. He emphasised that the aim of the experiment had not been to sow death and destruction but to frighten the enemy, and in this it had succeeded: 'I believe there was scarce an Officer who did not say, "Sir, I never saw such confusion as there evidently is this Morning, not only in Boulogne, but all along the Coast and the heights." ... I am perfectly satisfied that the Enemy will not in future consider himself so secure in Boulogne Roads as he has hitherto done.' Applying submarines and carcasses, Popham thought, would free British ships from blockade duty for active service, which would be even more important if the Spanish were to join the fray on the French side and take the fight out to sea. For all these reasons, and perhaps most importantly because the whole affair had been adopted at his

---

39  NRS: Melville MSS, GD51/236/14 (see also GD51/243/3–4): Popham to Melville, 4 October 1804.
40  Abraham Crawford, *Reminiscences of a Naval Officer, during the Late War ...* (London: Henry Colburn, 1851), vol.1, pp.146–150.
41  James, *Naval History of Great Britain*, vol.3, p.233.
42  BL: Add MS 41080, f.71: Popham to Melville, 28 October 1804.
43  Colden, *Life of Robert Fulton*, p.57.
44  Lord Buckingham to Grenville, 23 September 1804, *Dropmore MSS*, vol.7, p.234.

own urging, Popham wrote how glad he was Melville had witnessed the experiment aboard *Aimable*: 'I exceedingly rejoiced on this occasion that Your Lordship was present ... and had an opportunity of conversing with the principal Officers concerned in the application of our experiment, because Your Lordship will be able then to calculate how far you ought to appreciate my future opinions.'[45]

Popham need not have worried. Either because they were thoroughly persuaded by his arguments or because they were adept at making the most out of a bad situation, Pitt and Melville gave him the benefit of a doubt. Pitt, who tended to look on the bright side anyway, reported to a military friend that, '*as an Experiment*', the whole business had been 'highly satisfactory', admittedly more from the impression it had made on the enemy than from any long-term practical effects.[46] Pitt and Melville also worked on the King – who agreed with Keith that the Boulogne affair had been a waste of time and money – in echoing Popham's emphasis on effect rather than immediate military value. With the threat of invasion constantly hanging over everyone's head, Melville asked, 'Is it nothing either to the Spirits of this Country, or to the discomfiture of the Spirits of the Enemy, to have it established almost to a moral certainty, that this Project [of invasion] is impracticable?'[47] Popham's relief at the way his experiment had been received was clear. Perhaps slightly unwisely, he now pressed the government to support a second attack, on Calais – this time without Fulton's direct support.[48] Even more unwisely, the government agreed.

While staying at Walmer Castle, Pitt's coastal residence, Popham drew up a memorandum detailing his ideas. Instead of targeting Napoleon's invasion flotilla, he proposed to assault the fortifications of Calais themselves with the aim of shutting any enemy ships into the harbour. If the mission was a success, Popham proposed to harass the French all along the coast down to Le Havre to make them feel as vulnerable as possible. One objection to this approach was that Calais was not only a military fortification: it was also a civilian town, full of innocent bystanders. Popham, later a strong proponent of attacking an enemy town by bombardment, dismissed this objection out of hand: 'if [enemy] Vessels cannot be bombarded without injuring a Town, then it is not to be a consideration.' Popham was always keen to show how little he heeded obstacles to his plans, but in this case his eagerness to trample everything in his path – even people – may not have gone down well. Nevertheless, Pitt approved the memorandum and Popham began planning the attack.[49]

Popham devoted himself wholeheartedly to the preparations in his usual hyperactive way. On one occasion he travelled through Sandwich, Deal, Ramsgate, Sandwich again, and then Dover in his eagerness to obey the First Lord of the Admiralty's orders (his detailing the itinerary showed he was just as eager for the First Lord to know of it).[50] Despite Popham's overenthusiasm, there was one major logistical issue in the way of progress. As at Boulogne, Popham remained under political scrutiny and still could not be given a proper command.

---

45 NRS: Melville MSS, GD51/236/14: Popham to Melville, 4 October 1804.
46 NRS: Hope of Luffness MSS, GD364/1/1137/35: Pitt to Alexander Hope.
47 NRS: Melville MSS, GD51/243/1: Melville to Pitt, 14 October 1804.
48 BL: Add MS 41080, f.86: Popham to Melville, 21 November 1804.
49 BL: add MS 41080, f.76: Memorandum, 25 October 1804.
50 BL: Add MS 41080, f.71: Popham to Melville, 28 October 1805.

Popham suggested going out to Calais as a volunteer: 'I am anxious to sail … The sooner the squadron that is to be under me is named the better, for really the Moon is wasting fast.'[51] Melville, however, remembered the difficulties with Keith off Boulogne and wanted Popham on a much tighter leash: 'I think there is a great awkwardness in any person serving in a situation where he is neither the object of military command, nor entitled to give orders which others are bound to obey.'[52] For once, at least, Popham also seemed to recognise the need to do things by the book. He pressed Melville to appoint him to a ship, any ship, because until he did so, his role was neither official nor unofficial and he was completely dependent on Melville's pleasure.

In the end Melville decided the best arrangement was to borrow another ship that was already on station and give it to Popham as a temporary command. At the end of October, therefore, Popham, accompanied by his protégé Lieutenant William King, temporarily superseded Captain Bazeley in command of HMS *Antelope*.[53] Popham, despite having the command he had begged for, was not in a good mood. The weather, which had been so propitious a few days before, had changed to a blustery, rainy gale, and he was far from impressed with the quality of his new crew. While *Antelope* took on water, bread, spirits, beef, and other provisions in the Downs, Popham wrote acerbically to Melville that he was doing everything he could to get things moving despite Keith's sluggishness: 'I have no orders yet or any intimation of the extent of our future operations.'[54] This was not what Melville wanted to read when Keith was also bending his ear because Popham was, once again, ignoring the usual command chain.[55] He must have been as relieved as Popham was when, having taken on all its provisions and waited for suitable weather, *Antelope* finally got under weigh on 16 November in dense fog.[56]

The next few weeks were anticlimactic. The mist continued, and all Popham could do was peer blindly towards the French coast with the rest of the blockading Channel squadron. It was Popham's first experience of blockade and he hated every moment. The weather alternated between thick fog and squalls of blustery rain, the wind constantly swinging from east to west. Popham busied himself fine-tuning his plans. He had toned them down a little: now he wanted to focus on Fort Rouge at Calais, although he had not completely given up on an attack on Rochefort.[57] But the French were just as affected by the weather as the British and took care not to send more than a few ships out of the safety of their harbours.[58] *Antelope*'s crew were getting restless. On 23 November Popham ordered his first punishment as captain: Daniel O'Brien, seaman, received two dozen lashes for disobedience of orders.[59] Popham may well have sympathised, as he was starting to dream about disobeying orders himself. Frustrated by inaction and bored rigid, Popham eventually snapped and wrote to Melville asking him to summon him to town for a spell, 'as I do not

---

51  BL: Add MS 41080, f.71: Popham to Melville, 28 October 1804.
52  Melville to Keith, 11 October 1804, Lloyd (ed.), *The Keith Papers*, vol.3, p.97.
53  TNA: ADM 51/1491 and ADM 52/3557: captain's and master's logs, HMS *Antelope*, 31 October 1804.
54  WLC UM: Melville MSS, Box 19: Popham to Melville, 31 October (two separate letters).
55  WLC UM: Melville MSS, Box 20: Melville to Popham, 3 November 1804.
56  TNA: ADM 52/3557: master's log, HMS *Antelope*, 16–17 November 1804.
57  BL: Add MS 41080, f.86: Popham to Melville, 21 November 1804.
58  TNA: ADM 1/2327: Popham to Marsden, 19 November 1804.
59  TNA: ADM 52/3557: master's log, HMS *Antelope*, 23 November 1804.

see that my presence here, can at this moment be of the least Service'.[60] When this fell on deaf ears, he tried to persuade Melville his ship needed maintenance and would need to dock at Sheerness or Portsmouth – asking Melville to send any orders to that effect directly to *Antelope*, bypassing Keith and proving Popham had learned nothing from the 'jealousies and Etiquettes' Melville had been so keen to placate.[61] Two days later, when Popham had still heard nothing, he told Melville he would come ashore anyway, orders or no orders.[62] This, at least, jogged Melville into action and, on 26 November, Popham finally received orders through Lord Keith to proceed to Calais.[63]

This time Popham was in personal command of a small squadron of 20 ships, mostly bomb and fire vessels.[64] For the next few days *Antelope* returned to East Bay, where it took on more water and provisions in preparation for its new mission. On 1 December, it made sail in company with HMS *Aimable* and HMS *Dart*, tacking to windward and arriving off Boulogne on the 3rd.[65] The target was Fort Rouge at Calais, and Popham hoped to take advantage of the lull in the wind to attack within the next week. As the squadron sailed into position, Popham chose *Dart* as the ship from which the operation would be based, as it had been off Boulogne for a while and would be unlikely to incur suspicion. He told *Dart*'s captain, William Brownrigg, he was sending him two large carcasses made of copper and two small wooden ones. Brownrigg would remain off Calais for a few days to allow the enemy to get used to his new position. On the evening chosen for the operation, Brownrigg would fall back from the coast at sunset to allay any suspicion, then tack back in after dark, with all lights extinguished except those required to guide the boats drawing the carcasses. At around 1:00 a.m., at high tide, an explosion vessel, *Susannah*, would be sent as a bluff 'directly at the Fort' under the command of Lieutenant Stewart, a veteran of the Boulogne assault. While the French were busy fighting Stewart off (Popham hoped 'in a state of consternation'), Midshipman Bartholomew would fasten one large copper carcass to the piles of the pier. A second copper carcass, which Brownrigg volunteered to take out himself, would be sent out 10 minutes later. Popham also sent for HMS *Ardent* to join him, under Captain Winthrop. Men from *Ardent* would take the wooden carcasses as close to the entrance of the harbour as possible, attaching one to the pier head and towing the other directly into the harbour. The whole would be overseen by Captain Robert Plampin, whom Popham had been training up for months. All this, Popham concluded with satisfaction, would drive in the impression created by Boulogne that the French were not safe even in their own harbours.[66]

While he waited for *Ardent* to join, Popham continued to watch the enemy coast. The fog had set in again, making it difficult to see a great deal, but he did report some odd behaviour in Boulogne on Sunday 2 December. At noon there was a general salute: 'all the Vessels were

---

60   BL: Add MS 41080, f.88: Popham to Melville, 23 November 1804.
61   BL: Add MS 41080, f.90: Popham to Melville, 24 November 1804.
62   BL: Add MS 41080, f.92: Popham to Melville, 26 November 1804.
63   Keith to Popham, 26, 30 November 1804, Lloyd (ed.), *The Keith Papers*, vol.3, pp.102–103, 104.
64   TNA: ADM 52/3557: master's log, HMS *Antelope*, 27 November 1804.
65   TNA: ADM 52/3557: master's log, HMS *Antelope*, 1, 3 December 1804.
66   TNA: ADM 1/2328: Popham to Brownrigg and Winthrop, 2 December 1804.

dressed in the inside and in the Evening a variety of Fireworks were displayed, evidently intended as a general rejoicing day.'[67] It was in fact a celebration for Napoleon Bonaparte's coronation as emperor of the French. As soon as *Ardent* finally appeared – carrying Fulton, who had insisted on tagging along – Popham issued general orders for the assault to begin. On 8 December, *Dart* dropped back from the coast towards Dover Roads. After darkness had fallen, however, it moved back towards the shore, with the *Locust* gun brig anchored under its beam to protect the series of boats for the attack.

Popham had high hopes all would work out well, but in fact the night's activities were a damp squib. They took place in the small hours of the morning, under cover of complete darkness. Stewart went first with the *Susannah* explosion vessel and managed to make an effective distraction to the south-west of the town, knocking down some fortification breastworks. As the glow of the flames lit the sky and the sounds of alarm and gunfire reached him from land, Popham expected the rest of his scheme to go just as well. He was wrong. Bartholomew's instructions had been to paddle his carcass directly under the pier and lash it to the piles. The French, however, had not been completely distracted by the explosion vessel and spotted him immediately; Bartholomew had to retreat, taking his unexploded carcass with him. Meanwhile, the second carcass was experiencing technical difficulties. The lock kept stopping, and Fulton alarmed even Popham by unscrewing the mechanism and fixing it with only five minutes left on the clock.[68] However, when Brownrigg swam out with it, he got stuck against the piles of the pier and had to be rescued. The two wooden carcasses, which Popham had hoped to send right into the harbour, were prudently not used. At 6:00 a.m., everyone was back on board and the small flotilla retreated, tacking to the south-west before the French could launch any reprisals.

The experiment had failed, even more obviously than at Boulogne, but Popham played it up as a success. To Melville, he claimed he had proved explosion vessels could be brought right alongside French coastal fortifications. To Marsden, at the Admiralty Board, Popham emphasised that any failure ought to be attributed to the bad weather and the lateness of the season.[69] At least nobody on the British side had been hurt, but, as William James observed in his *Naval History*, 'the same good fortune attended the persons on shore.'[70] Popham still hoped he could win round the critics with a few more experiments – 'a little perseverance and management will work conviction on everybody' – but a second attempt on 12 December to get a carcass under the fort piles failed due to strong winds and the brightness of the moon, and the British discovered the French had already repaired the damage caused on the 8th.[71] The experiment simply confirmed everyone else's bad opinion of the method, and Keith swiftly and firmly shut down a proposal from another captain in his squadron to try again at Le Havre. Any optimism he might have felt about the carcasses had completely gone: 'I have but little confidence in the effect of the carcasses unless they can be placed under the object against which they are

---

67  TNA: ADM 1/2328: Popham to Marsden, 2 December 1804.
68  BL: Add MS 41080, f.98: Popham to Melville, 9 December 1804.
69  TNA: ADM 1/2328: Popham to Marsden, 10 December 1804.
70  James, *Naval History of Great Britain*, vol.3, p.341.
71  BL: Add MS 41080, f.110: Popham to Melville, 12 December 1804.

intended to be used ... but even in this way I feel they can only be used with a prospect of success on favourable occasions.'[72]

Popham was disappointed, but he had no doubt why his schemes had failed. It was certainly not his fault, as he emphasised to Lord Melville: 'You know what a strong current of prejudice I have had to contend with.'[73] But his attention was already moving on. Popham left *Antelope* on 13 December.[74] While he continued to pester Lord Melville with plans for attacking the French at Brest and Calais into the spring of 1805, his flirtation with torpedoes and submarine warfare had come to an end, particularly after he was finally cleared of all wrongdoing by the *Romney* inquiry. As for Fulton, he pressed for another carcass demonstration over the summer of 1805 (an experiment watched by Prime Minister Pitt himself), but events had already overtaken him. The British government had finally managed to put together a third continental coalition with Russia and Austria, and Napoleon's *Armée d'Angleterre* had begun disappearing from the coast to meet the coalition forces inland. The immediate threat of invasion was over – for now – and the danger receded even further in October when Vice Admiral Nelson sacrificed his life at Trafalgar to destroy the combined French and Spanish fleet. Under these circumstances, as James's *Naval History* put it, 'gun boats and catamarans' gave way 'to the operations of fleets of line-of-battle ships'.[75] Fulton returned to America, embittered and complaining he had not been paid enough for all he had done. The next time the British saw any carcasses, they were being used against them during the War of 1812.

---

72   Keith to Captain Brenton, 15 December 1804; Keith to Louis, 25 December 1804; Louis to Keith, 4 January 1805; and Keith to Louis, 6 January 1805, Lloyd (ed.), *The Keith Papers*, vol.3, pp.106–107, 107, 107–108, 108.
73   BL: Add MS 41080, f.98: Popham to Melville, 10 December 1804.
74   Creasman, 'Sir Home Riggs Popham', p.48, for the day, although there is nothing in *Antelope*'s master's log (TNA: ADM 52/3577).
75   James, *Naval History of Great Britain*, vol.3, p.341.

# 10

# Domestic and Professional Life, 1803–1805

*2814: The stranger is suspicious*

When he walked out of the *Romney* committee room in June 1805, free to serve actively again, Popham could be sure he had the full support of the most important members of the government. So long as Pitt remained in office, Popham was guaranteed employment and some degree of immunity from scrutiny, or at least a tacit promise the government would look the other way if necessary. He had enemies, but the last few months had shown they were less powerful than his protectors. He may have felt he had nothing left to fear.

And yet, despite having more than his fair share of natural self-confidence, Popham may also have experienced a degree of doubt. Although he had Pitt and Melville's blessing, that favour rested on exploits in Flanders and Germany a decade old. These had been succeeded by a series of loud and showy missions that had yielded indifferent results. Ostend, Boulogne, and Calais did not produce long-term advantages; in fact Ostend had resulted in the capture of 1,000 soldiers Britain could ill afford to lose. And even though Popham had cemented his distinction as an amphibious expert in the Red Sea, he had alienated the Governor-General of India, Marquess Wellesley. Back home, the *Romney* affair may have shown Popham could rely on his political friends, but it had also demonstrated how controversial he was in his own profession. 'He is, in general, regarded in the Service as a Naval Quack,' Benjamin Tucker wrote, acidly.[1] Tucker had a grievance, but he was not alone in distrusting Popham. Even Lord Nelson, the Royal Navy's most famous officer, had heard of Popham, and not in a good way: 'I cannot conceive how a man that is reported to have been so extravagant of [the] Government's money, to say no worse, can make a good story.'[2]

But if these thoughts crossed Popham's mind, they did not keep him awake at night. Failure did not bother him; rather, it motivated him to make himself even more indispensable. As Lord Whitworth, who knew Popham well, noted, 'I know … that you are actuated by motives which set you above … [selfish] considerations, when you can be useful.'[3] For Popham, 'being useful' was synonymous with taking centre stage. If he felt he was beginning to lose his spot in the limelight, he tried to regain it by bombarding his patrons with ideas,

---

1    BL: G.19449, p.vi: comments by Tucker in *The Trial of Sir Home Popham*.
2    Lord Nelson to Lady Hamilton, 13 January 1804, Marianne Czisnik (ed.), *Nelson's Letters to Lady Hamilton and Related Documents* (London: Routledge, for the Navy Records Society, 2020), p.420.
3    SLV: Accession no.MS 13020 (prev. M5142): Whitworth to Popham, June 1803.

from ways to source hemp and timber in India to rearranging the Channel Fleet against a possible French attack. He rarely stayed still, appearing where he felt he was most needed almost by magic: a friend laughed that he hardly knew where to find him as 'your exits and entrances are so rapid'.[4] Most crucially, Popham understood how his patrons thought, what they wanted, and what they were planning, sometimes anticipating his patrons' wishes before they even knew how to form them into words.

As Melville's thoughts turned away from European theatres of war, therefore, Popham's strategic hints and suggestions began to reflect a more global, economic, imperial remit. This was not entirely disinterested; Popham's family connections, both through his brother William in India and through his wife's relatives in eastern seas, gave him a personal stake in defending Britain's trade networks, but it did mean Popham had an ear to the ground in a way Melville's more aristocratic connections did not. This lent an undeniably pragmatic thrust to his arguments and this, along with Popham's willingness to take on all sorts of tasks, was one of the major reasons he continued being employed despite a string of damp squibs. Rather than losing faith in him, the authorities gave him an increasing variety of commissions – none of them as flashy as captaining a frigate or as lucrative as convoying a valuable trade route, but Popham did not (yet) mind this lack of professional opportunities. He had carved himself an unusual niche, and he was happy to exploit it.

Nevertheless, controversy – Popham would have called it 'jealousy' – dogged every step of his professional career. By 1805, Popham's reputation had begun to crystallise along the lines it retained for the rest of his life. This had a lot to do with recent events, but it had just as much to do with his unusual career path. Popham's professional character as a captain, and as a seaman more generally, was tainted by his comparative lack of experience. His lieutenancy may have dated back to 1781, but he had not served continuously in the Royal Navy since that time and had spent long swathes of his career ashore. By the summer of 1805 he had been a post-captain nearly 11 years but had commanded only three ships, two of them for a handful of months each. Benjamin Tucker thought Popham 'was never at sea in His Majesty's Service until he went out as Commodore to the Red Sea in 1801', which was a bit of a gloss but pointed to how irregular Popham's employment had been – and to why the Admiralty, and the Navy more generally, considered him an outsider.[5]

Despite all this, Popham was fond of broadcasting his own values as a captain, and of how assiduously he attended to the well-being of his men: 'The more you can add to the comfort of Sailors, the more you add to their health, and to the effective state of the ship.'[6] Many who sailed with Popham backed up his claim to be a considerate captain, and several officers who served under him in the Red Sea appeared before the *Romney* committee to testify to that effect.[7] Others with less reason to sing Popham's praises included Fletcher Wilkie, a military man who sailed with Popham in 1805 and 1806. Wilkie cited an occasion at Madeira when Popham used private funds to purchase fruit and London porter, the entire cargo of a merchant vessel, which he then 'served

---

4   WLC UM: Melville MSS, Box 27: Denis O'Bryen to Popham, 23 June 1811.
5   BL: G.19449, p.xiv: comment by Tucker in *The Trial of Sir Home Popham*.
6   House of Commons, *Second Report of the Select Committee on the Romney*, p.48.
7   For example Lieutenant John Hanchett, signalman on *Romney*, and Captain Carden of HMS *Sheerness*: House of Commons, *Second Report of the Select Committee on the Romney*, pp.109, 144.

without discrimination to all hands'.[8] But a healthy ship was not necessarily a happy ship, and the reality was less clear-cut. Despite asserting he had 'raised three of the best Ships' Companies that ever went to Sea', Popham's attitude to his various crews was patronising at best, downright nasty at worst.[9] Not a single ship's muster escaped his waspish tongue and critical eye. The crew of HMS *Expedition* in 1798 were 'untutor'd' and 'undisciplined'; *Romney*'s men were too landsmen-heavy and unable to control the ship in bad weather; *Antelope* was manned by 'the slightest Men I ever saw'; the men of HMS *Venerable* were 'as deficient in experience as … exuberant in vice'; and his last crew, aboard HMS *Stirling Castle*, was a 'host of dwarfs'.[10] This dismissiveness probably became a self-fulfilling prophecy: sensing their captain did not care for them, the men may have returned his contempt with disobedience, and Popham acquired a reputation as 'a taut hand, that is to say, a terrible flogger'.[11] 'I was obliged to work the Cat today,' Popham wrote more or less the first day he took on his first command in 1798, and his ships' logs attest to his being quick to dole out punishment – particularly aboard HMS *Venerable* and HMS *Stirling Castle*, his last two commands, suggesting he became stricter over the years.[12]

There was a further problem: even when appointed to a ship, Popham spent long periods ashore on other business. This went against naval regulations, which stated a captain 'was not to sleep out of the Ship from the day of his taking the command to that of his giving it up, without permission from the Admiralty or the Commanding Officer present', and his habit of doing what he liked had got him into trouble as captain of *Romney*.[13] Popham often claimed he had permission from the War Department, or the First Lord of the Admiralty himself, to be absent, but his cavalier attitude to his responsibilities did not endear him to his naval peers, or to the warrant officers who acted under him. When questioned by the *Romney* committee about where Popham had been during the 1801 repairs to the ship, Nixon the boatswain replied, with evident impatience, 'God knows where he was, [but] he was not with the ship.'[14] Popham never outgrew a tendency to go wandering off; in 1809, during the Walcheren Expedition, the commanding admiral was horrified to discover Popham had never even had his commission read aboard HMS *Venerable*, which technically meant he had never taken proper command of his own ship and was therefore not under Admiralty scrutiny.[15] This earned Popham an official rebuke and, in 1812, off the coast of Spain, he took care to check with his naval superior Lord Keith whenever he wanted to go ashore even for

---

8 [Wilkie], 'Recollections of the British Army, no.2', p.485.
9 WLC UM: Melville MSS, Box 29: Popham to the second Viscount Melville, 4 April 1813.
10 DUA: GRE/A1550b: Popham to Coote, 11 May 1798; TNA: ADM 1/2321: Popham to the Secretary of the Admiralty, 31 October 1800; WLC UM: Melville MSS, Box 19: Popham to the first Lord Melville, 31 October 1804; TNA: ADM 1/2338: Popham to the Secretary of the Admiralty, 2 February 1811; WLC UM: Melville MSS, Box 29: Popham to the 2nd Lord Melville, 4 April 1813.
11 As suggested via his fictional counterpart, Sir High Topham, in Neale, *Gentleman Jack*, vol.1, p.150.
12 DUA: GRE/A1550b: Popham to Coote, 11 May 1798.
13 Privy Council, *Regulations and Instructions Relating to His Majesty's Service at Sea established by His Majesty in Council* (London: W. Winchester and Son, 1808), p.94.
14 House of Commons, *Second Report of the Select Committee on the Romney*, p.66.
15 TNA: PRO 30/8/369, f.72: Strachan to Chatham, 2 August 1809.

a few days, forcing a frustrated Keith to inform Popham he did not need such authority in an independent command.[16]

Still, and despite this devil-may-care approach towards his ships, crews, and commands, Popham's officers seemed to approve of him, and many followed him from ship to ship. Critics suspected this fondness stemmed more from self-interest than genuine attachment: 'He took them always wherever there was a prospect of prize-money.'[17] This reflected Popham's reputation for greed, already notorious by 1805 and nourished considerably by the *Romney* affair. Money – and the lack of it – was a theme that ran through Popham's entire life. He had always been flamboyant; as a youth he had brought bolts of expensive cloth back for his own personal use from India and China and run up large bills with his tailor. His spendthrift nature made Popham enemies, including the creditor who, after Popham's departure from the Red Sea in 1803, considered seizing his furniture and having him thrown in jail.[18] At the end of Popham's life he allegedly owed his prize agent £6,000.[19] How much of this was lack of care, or simply bad luck, is unclear, but the enemies who accused Popham of recklessly chasing prizes could not overlook the inconvenient fact that he usually did not always take on the most lucrative employment opportunities. Popham had his eye on the more distant prize: courting patrons by taking on jobs nobody else wanted to do. Most of his employment took place under conditions that made it very unlikely prize money would come his way, and in fact Dundas, in persuading Lord Spencer to appoint Popham to the Red Sea in 1800, had specifically mentioned the lack of prize money opportunities as a reason for the First Lord of the Admiralty to agree.[20] This did not mean Popham ignored any freelance money-spinning opportunities that might come his way: the major example of this was of course the 1806 Buenos Aires expedition. But Popham undertook this without official permission, and it embroiled him and many of his officers in years of expensive legal wrangling. That prize money was a major reason for junior officers to follow Popham is possible, but they must have known there were surer, and less convoluted, ways to wealth in the Navy.

A more likely reason for men to seek Popham out as a captain was his deserved reputation as a scientific officer. Captain Thompson had trained him well in nautical skills, and Popham's interest in scientific innovation ran through his entire life. His proficiency in navigation and hydrography should have been an asset in his interrupted, and unusual, naval course: navigators were an 'elite' body of professionals and 'crucial players' in the imperial expansion of the eighteenth and nineteenth centuries, and Popham was proud to be such a specialist.[21] He was delighted at his election to the Royal Society in 1799 as a result of his being 'well versed in several branches of knowledge, particularly marine surveying, and that

---

16 TNA: WO 1/263, f.535: Popham to Keith, 15 October 1812; TNA: WO 1/263, ff.551–553: Keith to Popham, 20 October 1812.
17 [Wilkie], 'Recollections of the British Army, no.2', p.485.
18 Michael H. Styles, *Captain Hogan: Sailor, Merchant, Diplomat on Six Continents* (Fairfax, VA: Six Continents Horizons, 2003), p.132.
19 Coelho, 'The Popham Code Controversy', p.144.
20 Dundas to Spencer, 27 September 1800, Corbett (ed.), *Spencer Papers*, vol.4, pp.126–128.
21 Margaret E. Schotte, *Sailing School: Navigating Science and Skill, 1550–1800* (Baltimore, MD: Johns Hopkins Press, 2019), p.6.

part of practical astronomy which is subservient to the purposes of navigation',[22] and being a scientific officer was something he felt enhanced his career – although, despite becoming his greatest legacy, it did not drive it. Still, his scientific proficiency was something he often fell back on to attract attention if he thought he was being forgotten, or otherwise wanted to signal he was ready for action.

And yet, as desirable as a good navigator was in the eighteenth-century Royal Navy, Popham's hydrographic skills did not do him much good in professional circles. Lord Howe had snubbed them in the 1780s when Popham had been a young lieutenant, as a result of which he had left the service in disgruntlement. When Popham tried to re-join the Navy in 1793, his first attempt to do so on the strength of his chart of Prince of Wales Island for the East India Company had met with resounding silence from the Admiralty Board.[23] It was as though his time aboard *Etrusco* had wiped his professional slate clean: Benjamin Tucker dismissed Popham's claim to professional expertise by saying he had 'never [been] known in any other Capacity [than as an Agent for Transports]', and Lord Spencer protested against employing Popham in 1798 in very similar terms.[24] Even when he had painstakingly managed to rebuild his standing in the field, many contemporaries seemed to think his passion for hydrography was just Popham showing off. On his return from the Red Sea in 1803, Popham tried to persuade St Vincent's Admiralty to adopt a method he had devised for ascertaining the latitude of a ship according to the position of the stars. The Admiralty Board dismissed Popham's 'new' practice as 'a common one, and for which every Midshipman ought to qualify himself before he presented himself to the Navy Board to be ex[amine]d …as a Lieutenant'.[25] Others found Popham's craze for navigation amusing. In the novel *Gentleman Jack*, which mildly satirised Popham as the enterprising Captain Sir High Topham, the main character was asked during his lieutenant's exam: 'O, ho! … how long have you been star-gazing with Topham?'[26]

One thing Popham's scientific interest did do was make him more open than many of his peers to the use of new weapons. Robert Fulton's submarines and torpedoes were only the tip of the iceberg, and some schemes may have been pitched to Popham because he had acquired a notoriety for endorsing just about any suggestion. In October 1804, while working with Fulton, Popham engaged in correspondence with Irish-American engineer Michael Logan and his partner, British inventor Sealy Fourdrinier. Logan and Fourdrinier proposed an underwater ship wrecker (described as 'a sort of *chevaux* [sic] *de frise*') as 'an insurmountable Barrier [against invasion] and [as] an eternal defiance to all possible efforts of the Enemy against it … it will present to [Napoleon] and to all Europe, as clear as the Sun's light, the impossibility of attempting such an enterprise'. The two men flattered Popham by calling him 'an Officer of the first distinction in His Majesty's Service', and Popham agreed

---

22  Popham's certificate of election, 18 April 1799, Royal Society MSS, EC/179/04, <https://catalogues.royalsociety.org/CalmView/Record.aspx?src=CalmView.Catalog&id=EC%2f1799%2f04>, accessed 3 March 2023.
23  TNA: ADM 1/3062: Popham to Philip Stephens, 21 August 1793.
24  BL: G.19449, p.vi: comment by Tucker in *The Trial of Sir Home Popham*; Spencer to Dundas, 25 April 1798, Corbett (ed.), *Spencer Papers*, vol.2, pp.319–320.
25  TNA: ADM 1/2326: Popham to Nepean, 19 April 1803, and docket of the same day.
26  Neale, *Gentleman Jack*, vol.1, p.26.

to bring their plan to the attention of the Prime Minister.[27] In due course the scheme was reviewed by a panel of naval authorities and Popham proposed a trial in Yarmouth Roads, but common sense prevailed and it fell by the wayside.[28] The episode nevertheless showed two things: that Popham could not resist a gadget, and that inventors viewed him as a bit of a sap. As late as 1814 he was still being approached with crazy schemes, including one for using balloons for dropping dispatches.[29]

Popham did not merely endorse the inventions of others; he also developed his own. In 1816, a new compass and binnacle Popham had developed was officially issued to 10 ships as a trial by the Admiralty Board.[30] He was particularly fond of personalising his ships' boats. When the Navy Board attacked him in 1803 for having overspent repairing *Romney*, one of their accusations was that Popham had customised his ship's boats in a way that did not conform to Navy regulations. Popham argued back that his innovations had enabled him to use the boat in the successful rescue of a regiment stranded by the shipwreck of their transport in the Red Sea.[31] On this occasion Popham was being told off and his boasts were designed to defend himself from attack, but when his innovations were lauded for their own sake, he tended to claim more praise than he may have been due. One naval contemporary recalled fitting out an eight-oared cutter to his own specifications:

> In that boat I called one day on board the ship commanded by Sir Home Popham at Spithead. He led me aft into the stern gallery, and pointing to his boat lying under the stern, fitted exactly upon the same plan as mine, he assumed great praise to himself for having thought of such an improvement ... When Sir Home had concluded his observations, I requested him to examine my boat alongside. He did so, and expressed extreme surprise when I told him that I had adopted that plan many years before when Senior Lieutenant of a frigate, so that the contrivance did not, as he thought, originate with him.[32]

This story was at most a vague implication that Popham's unoriginal 'inventions' might owe more to the ideas of others than he was prepared to admit, but others went much further. Even during his lifetime some questioned how far his famous telegraphic signal code was actually *his* in the strictest sense of the word, and an author of a rival system came within a whisker of accusing Popham outright of plagiarism:

> The [present] author ... cannot for an instant suppose that Sir Home Popham would take merit for the invention of another; but, as thought is the prerogative of man, the thoughts of Sir Home may have run, by chance, parallel with the thoughts of the

---

27  WLC UM: Melville MSS, Box 20: Popham to Melville, 8 November 1805; the following all in Box 19: Michael Logan to Popham, 29 October 1804; Popham to Logan, 30 October 1804; and Popham to Melville, 31 October 1804.
28  WLC UM: Melville MSS, Box 20: Popham to Melville, 8 November 1805.
29  Proposal by R. Walthew, 25 April 1814, described in *Christie's* sales catalogue for 31 March 1909.
30  NMM: ADM 359/36B/101: Admiralty Board committee report, 15 November 1816.
31  [Popham], *Concise Statement of Facts*, p.27n.
32  Michael Lewis (ed.), *A Narrative of my Professional Adventures (1790–1839), by Sir William Henry Dillon, KCH, Vice-Admiral of the Red* (London: Navy Records Society, 1953), vol.1, p.415.

author. At the same time it must be observed, that had the author possessed sufficient influence to introduce *his* telegraphic signals, *previous* to the introduction of Sir Home's, Sir Home's would have remained dormant, and the author would have reaped whatever merit is attached to them.[33]

Self-confidence was not something in which Popham was in short supply; one man who had worked closely with him noted he had 'a great deal of Egotism'.[34] But, at least regarding his signals, while he borrowed liberally from the ideas of others (including his old captain, Edward Thompson), the final result was very much Popham's own, and this was recognised even by men who disliked him.

Telegraphy, indeed, was the aspect of Popham's life with which he became most closely associated. The combinatorial aspects of it appealed to his mathematical brain, and communication was a vital part of sea life: ships needed to transmit orders, information, and warnings across large distances, often under time-limited circumstances and in the heat of battle, beneath the nose of the enemy. Despite this, for much of the eighteenth century the official signal book had been severely limited in scope and involved considerable ambiguity.[35] Individual signals were often set by an admiral on station or by a commander within a squadron, reducing the extent of comprehension. In the 1790s, Lord Howe, as First Lord of the Admiralty, had attempted to unify British naval communication by making his own signal code the official Royal Navy text. The new system matched prearranged messages to numbers, using 10 numeral flags and four preparative, substitute, assent, and dissent flags.[36] The trouble, as Popham had rapidly discovered in 1800 when relaying messages to Lord Whitworth in Copenhagen, was that Howe's signals only allowed so much latitude in transmitting messages not in the signal book, and was absolutely useless when relaying messages not directly related to naval affairs – for example, information relating to a diplomatic negotiation.

Instead of making do with the existing code, therefore, Popham devised a new one based on Howe's original model that introduced a significant new element: a vocabulary of more than a thousand words with corresponding numbers, each of which could be made by hoisting three, or four, numerical flags and which could be arranged into sentences to form messages not in the signal book.[37] This was obviously more time-consuming than hoisting two or three flags to indicate a whole sentence, as in Howe's handbook, but it did mean three things: signals became much more expressive, they could apply to non-naval contexts, and whole conversations could be carried on between ships, rather than simply relaying orders.[38] Communication was a mainstay of diplomacy and naval warfare alike, and Popham's new code was versatile enough to be used for both purposes. He first published it in November

---

33 Richard Hall Gower, *A Treatise on the Theory and Practice of Seamanship, together with a System of Naval Signals* ... 3rd enlarged edition (London: Wilkie and Robinson, 1808), p.208n.
34 DUA: GRE/A1447: Coote to Grey, 10 May 1798.
35 Rodger, *Command of the Ocean*, pp.244, 254.
36 Lavery, *Nelson's Navy*, p.261.
37 W.G. Perrin, *British Flags: Their Early History, and their Development at Sea* ... (Cambridge: Cambridge University Press, 1922), pp.176–177.
38 Perrin, *British Flags*, p.177.

1800, but expanded it in 1803, 1805, and 1812, with a final edition in 1816. Each iteration vastly increased the communication possibilities. The second edition doubled the vocabulary of the first edition to 2,000 words, and added 1,000 sentences; and the 1812 edition consisted of 6,000 'primitive' words and 30,000 'real' words, 6,000 sentences, and 1,500 syllables, allowing for a total of nearly 224,000 combinations.[39]

The code was not perfect, but it became Popham's proudest achievement. This was slightly ironic because, although it arose out of the mission to Copenhagen, it otherwise had little to do with Popham's active career. The code's later editions – 1803, 1805, 1812, and 1816 – coincided with periods when he was not actively employed, and this was not accidental. Popham knew his code was a significant asset in his professional arsenal, and each new edition was a cry for attention at a time of unemployment rather than a response to a real need for change, as noted by a frustrated Secretary of the Admiralty prior to the release of the 1812 edition:

> The true question is, whether under all circumstances it is advisable, to alter, new-arrange and bring into practice, throughout so extensive and widely extended a service, the numerous Plans, and ingenious inventions, of a mind so continually at Work, for it is not to be expected that Sir Home will stop here. By next year or at least by the time that every signal man and officer becomes acquainted with the *new* proposed Code, this Gallant, and ingenious officer will be prepared with another.[40]

Any period during which Popham was not directly contributing to the war effort was almost certain to elicit a new edition of his signal code, a reflection of his own desire to run up the flags to signal his own resourcefulness and readiness for action.

His persistence paid off: in the spring of 1812 a committee of eight Navy flag officers approved Popham's new code and, in 1816, it became the official Admiralty signal book.[41] By this time, however, the wars with France were over, and Popham had to think laterally if he meant to continue using his signalling expertise to retain patronage. In the 1790s and 1800s, Britain, hot on the heels of France's system devised by Claude Chappe, had developed a network of telegraphs spanning the southern and eastern coasts, allowing the Kentish coast to communicate with London within seven minutes, and messages from Portsmouth to reach London within 15.[42] This system had been dismantled after the peace, which gave Popham an opportunity to make his mark in a related, but subtly different, field of communication. Popham therefore proposed a new telegraph system adapted to a reworked version of his signals. The code had already been used in a non-maritime context, during the Peninsular War in Portugal and Spain, when Wellington had used it to communicate across long distances. Flags were, however, less useful on land than at sea – a combination of balls and flags were used in the Peninsula, as there was less wind to allow flags to fly properly – and Popham's code had therefore been adapted to this

---

39  Perrin, *British Flags*, pp.176–177, 180.
40  NMM YOR/14/3: note, 29 May 1811, on Popham to Charles Yorke, 25 May 1811.
41  Popham, *A Damned Cunning Fellow*, p.131; Howard Mallinson, *Send it by Semaphore: The Old Telegraphs During the Wars with France* (Marlborough: Crowood Press, 2005), p.97.
42  Knight, *Britain Against Napoleon*, pp.140, 303.

new physical context.⁴³ With this experience in mind, Popham made more changes to his code and devised a specific land-based telegraph to use it, which would not require so much wind.⁴⁴ He still intended this telegraph to be used primarily for marine purposes, however, to allow merchants to communicate with the metropolis: 'Each merchant will know the exact situation of his ship, and will receive intelligence of the state of the markets at the last place she sailed from; the time she is likely to arrive at her middle port; and when she may probably be expected at her home destination.'⁴⁵

Popham's communication fixation, therefore, sprang in part from his love of talking about himself. Ironically for a man who loved to show off, many of his employments were highly secret and, although Popham was always happy to remind his patrons of his services, he was often reduced to talking around what he had accomplished, 'without tracing how he was immediately engaged'.⁴⁶ One solution was to get *other* people to talk about him instead, and this was something Popham became extremely good at. One nineteenth-century historian wrote: 'Probably no man in that generation got himself talked about so much, and did so little.'⁴⁷ This was meant to be dismissive, but it reflected Popham's character: so long as he remained in the spotlight, it did not matter if nobody knew exactly what he was doing so long as they knew he was doing *something*. Any publicity was good publicity, and Popham could control much of that publicity through his network of press contacts. He had discovered the power of newspaper connections early in life through his friend John McArthur, who had recommended in 1790 that he form a friendship with Carlo Francesco Badini, principal writer of the *Morning Herald* and former editor of the *Morning Post*.⁴⁸ Popham did not take much persuading. Whenever he found himself 'persecuted' by his enemies over the years, he took his self-justification almost immediately to a public forum. Friendships with newspaper writers and editors, such as Thomas George Street of the *Courier* and Peter Finnerty of the *Morning Chronicle*, allowed him to supplement his privately circulated self-justificatory pamphlets with material capable of reaching a much wider audience, and he was well aware of the benefits of doing so. In 1812, off the coast of Spain, Popham fretted 'from the accounts which we have seen in the Papers the publick does not imagine anything has been done' by the squadron under his command.⁴⁹ His solution was to bombard the press with articles detailing his exploits, much to the dismay of the military commander, Wellington, who wished 'Sir H[ome] Popham's exultation' had been kept quiet, as the enemy could draw a great deal of information from indiscreet newspaper publications.⁵⁰

---

43   Mallinson, *Send it by Semaphore*, pp.96–97, 137–138; Mark S. Thompson, *Wellington and the Lines of Torres Vedras* (Warwick: Helion, 2021), pp.113–115.
44   Popham, *A Damned Cunning Fellow*, p.223; Anon., *Transactions of the Society, instituted at London, for the Encouragement of Arts, Manufactures, and Commerce*, 34 (1816), pp.167–177, 175–176.
45   Anon., *Transactions of the Society* (1816), p.169.
46   [Popham], *Concise Statement of Facts*, p.27.
47   W.H. Fitchett, *How England Saved Europe: The Story of the Great War, 1793–1815* (New York: Charles Scribner's Sons, 1900), vol.3, p.107.
48   TNA: HCA 32/597, no.735: McArthur to Popham, 13 April 1790.
49   BL: Loan MS 57/108, no.41: Popham to the 2nd Lord Melville, 21 August 1812.
50   Wellington to Lord Bathurst, 12 September 1812, John Gurwood (ed.), *The Dispatches of Field Marshal the Duke of Wellington …* (London: John Murray, 1838), vol.9, pp.418–419.

Many of these articles were sent to the newspapers, and possibly even composed, by Popham's publicity team at home, chief of whom was his wife.[51] Popham's 32-year-long marriage was extremely successful, and he and Lady Popham formed a close partnership that survived the frequent turbulence of their life together. The daughter of an East India Company ship's captain, Lady Popham knew when she got married what life to a seafaring man was like, with lengthy absences, constant disruptions, and ever-present danger. Despite this, she seems to have supported Popham in his career happily enough, at least before her health began to falter between 1807 and 1812, when even Popham's official letters filled with references to his wife's rheumatism and depressed spirits. She held the fort at home while he was away, bringing up their 10 children and representing him before his political patrons and at court. Not that she was always completely satisfied with an entirely homebound role; she certainly travelled with her new husband aboard *Etrusco* in their first year of marriage, and she occasionally accompanied Popham on his naval missions, staying for example with the Parishes in Hamburg while her husband arranged the transports for the British forces. Once the children were mostly grown up, she accompanied her husband once again to Jamaica in 1817.

Popham was just as fond as a father as he was as a husband, and he showed no signs of using his profession as an excuse not to spend time with his family. Unlike his own father and eldest brother, he had no intention of being a gaping hole in the lives of his children. Many of them accompanied him aboard his various ships, the girls as much as the boys: his eldest child, Mary, even stayed with him for a while off the coast of Spain in 1812. Two of his sons followed their father's footsteps and entered the Royal Navy. The eldest boy, William, born in Ostend in 1791, served his apprenticeship at his father's side: he was a first-class volunteer aboard *Diadem* at the Cape and Buenos Aires, where his father appointed him master's mate, and accompanied Popham to Copenhagen in 1807 before striking off to follow his own career path. The other son who entered the Navy was Brunswick, in 1817, although he never served with his father. Both boys rose to become admirals. Of the other two sons who reached adulthood, one, Strachan, followed his forebears into the East India Company service; the other, Harcourt, became a lieutenant in the Royal Horse Artillery. Unfortunately, Popham's children were rarely mentioned in his surviving letters, which were mostly official and left little room for private life. 'I have a little girl who I have promised to attend to her school,' Popham wrote shortly before going to Spain in 1812, probably about Harriet, then eight, but this is only a tiny glimpse of how he, his wife, and children interacted as a family.[52]

However close Popham might have been to his wife and children, indeed, their relative absence in his correspondence is telling: they always came a long way second to his career. His personal connections were also often geared towards his own professional advancement, from his associations with newspaper editors right up to his political networks. His private political predilections remained opaque: in life he was proud to call himself a Pittite, but whether Popham's own beliefs fully tallied with those of his political masters is unclear. Still, any convictions he may have had of a different flavour were not so deeply rooted as

---

51 For example, Lord Moira to Colonel McMahon, February 1814, in A. Aspinall (ed.), *The Letters of King George IV, 1812–1830* (Cambridge: University Press, 1938), vol.1, no.405.
52 Popham, *A Damned Cunning Fellow*, p.211n14.

to survive any conflict with self-interest. This demonstrated Popham's sense of survival, but it also reflected his realism. As a man with few contacts of his own, he had to make his own way in a world run by peers and aristocrats, and this involved being both pragmatic and deferential. As far as pragmatism was concerned, Popham, in a rare display of discretion, shaped his political actions to the desires of his patrons. In terms of deference, his children's names, almost without exception, were chosen to flatter the people Popham felt were most likely to advance his career. William Charnock, born in 1791, received the names of Popham's brother and business partner, but later children reflected the higher circles in which Popham moved after 1794: Frederick, named for the Duke of York; Home Whitworth, named for the diplomat Popham had befriended in Russia and Copenhagen; Brunswick Lowther, named for the Royal Family and the Earl of Lonsdale; Strachan, named for the commanding admiral at Walcheren in 1809; and Harcourt, whose namesake had been commander-in-chief in Flanders and Germany from 1795. There was no Melville Popham, but perhaps that would have been a little too direct.

These names were expressions of respect, but they were also intended to show that Popham, and his family, had 'arrived'. His choice of children's names was as much part of his attempt to fit into genteel circles as his acquisition of Titness Park or his moving into the desirable London neighbourhoods of York Place and Portman Square. Despite all his recent disappointments, by 1805 Popham was punching far above his weight as a Navy post-captain. He moved, and corresponded directly, with the highest names in the land, including members of the Royal Family; he had a knighthood and a government pension; he was a Member of Parliament; and his wife and daughters regularly appeared at court. It was not bad for the younger son of a minor consul, whose family background was in the Irish linen trade. His professional reputation might be tarnished, but the men who mattered had not given up on him. In the summer of 1805 Popham was at last given his most important command to date. It would bring him more notoriety than anything he had done before.

# 11

# The Cape of Good Hope, 1805–1806

*2593: It is practicable*

Popham had stated more than once before the *Romney* inquiry that he had been prevented from taking up official employment because of the ongoing investigation into his conduct. Since his appointment to the Admiralty in May 1804, Melville had been hoping to send Popham on an expedition to link up with the nascent revolutionary cause in South America to disrupt the flow of riches from those colonies to Spain. With the outbreak of the long-anticipated war with Spain at the end of 1804, therefore, Popham confidently expected to be sent to South America, and in October he was making detailed plans with Melville for just such an expedition, requesting a company of artillery, a troop of cavalry, and a regiment of infantry, along with two ships, two sloops, two gun-brigs, and three cutters. He was on the lookout for a new ship, as *Antelope* was all right for coastal operations in the Channel but too flimsy for transatlantic crossings and too small to carry troops. Popham seemed aware he had some leverage here and compiled a list of requirements for Melville: 'If I were allowed to choose a Ship it should certainly be a 64' – unsuitable for line of battle, but good for convoy duty, independent operations, and troop carrying, all tasks Popham was likely to tackle during a South American mission.[1]

The ship chosen for him was the 64-gun HMS *Diadem*, which had lately been serving as a troopship. Popham later said he had been appointed to this ship 'for the express purpose of my proceeding in her … to South America', and his correspondence at the time bears this out.[2] But, although Popham did spend much of the winter of 1805 in London, the government decided to suspend the South American attack. Pitt was trying to put together a continental coalition against Napoleon and he hoped he could entice Spain to abandon its alliance with France and join it. Instead of South America, therefore, *Diadem* was ordered back out to the Channel to bulk out the blockading fleet.

Popham was not expecting this, but whether these orders were issued so suddenly that he was left ashore – as his previous biographer implies – is uncertain.[3] In fact he had secured 14

---

1 BL: Add MS 41080, ff.72–73: Popham to Melville, 11 October 1804; Robert Gardiner, *Warships of the Napoleonic Era: Design, Development and Deployment* (Barnsley: Seaforth Publishing, 2011), p.34.
2 Anon., *Full and Correct Report of the Trial of Sir Home Popham*, p.91. Melville corroborated this at Popham's court martial: Anon., *Full and Correct Report of the Trial of Sir Home Popham*, p.161.
3 Popham, *A Damned Cunning Fellow*, p.136.

days of leave to deal with the fall-out from the *Romney* inquiry in Parliament, and that leave was extended as the investigations sprawled on and on into June.⁴ This was the real reason Popham parted company with his ship in mid-March when it sailed to Spithead to join the blockading Channel Fleet, leaving it in the hands of Acting Captain James O'Bryen.⁵ Nor did he re-join the ship while it remained on blockade; Popham remained in London until the end of the *Romney* inquiry in July, and it occupied almost all his attention during that time. A couple of years later, admittedly under very particular circumstances, Popham recalled that he had spent this period 'anxiously waiting' for final orders to go to South America, but he could not have expected to go there before the parliamentary committee had reached its conclusion.⁶ Almost at the same moment as the committee cleared him, however, Popham received private intelligence about the defenceless state of the Cape of Good Hope. This news changed his priorities immediately and abruptly.

The Cape was an important strategic point, doubling as a victualling station for British ships and a well-placed troop depot for reinforcing any Indian garrisons should the French decide to launch an attack on the subcontinent. It had, however, been restored to Dutch control following the Peace of Amiens, and the Dutch were still allied to the French. Knowing there were rumours Napoleon was planning a fresh assault on British India, and knowing the government would not want France to have access to the Cape under such circumstances, Popham asked for an audience with Prime Minister Pitt via William Sturges Bourne, one of the Secretaries to the Treasury. During this audience, Popham convinced Pitt the Cape was ripe for assault, and Pitt agreed to send an expedition there. He was encouraged in this decision because there were troops on hand and a squadron ready to send, as preparations for a South American enterprise were already in train. Given Pitt still had hopes of reeling Spain into the Third Coalition, he and Popham agreed that, instead of going to South America, Popham would go to South Africa.

This decision was taken rapidly, suggesting Pitt had already been thinking about such an expedition for some time and Popham later overstated his role in bringing it about: 'The idea of an expedition to the Cape was adopted by Mr Pitt, on my suggestion'.⁷ The abrupt change of objective from South America to the Cape did, however, beg another obvious question: had Pitt totally abandoned the idea of a South American venture, or had he intended to send Popham on a double mission, to the Cape first and to Spanish America after? This was what Popham himself later insinuated, although he admitted he had never been *explicitly* ordered to take his squadron on to South America.⁸ For now, however, all the arrangements being made were for the Cape alone, and two days after Popham first spoke to Pitt, those preparations were already in full swing. The military command, at Popham's suggestion, went to his old friend Major General Sir David Baird.⁹ Popham was given command of the

---

4  TNA: ADM 1/2329: Popham to Marsden, 13 March 1805.
5  TNA: ADM 51/1743: log, HMS *Diadem*, 31 March 1805.
6  Anon., *Full and Correct Report of the Trial of Sir Home Popham*, pp.91–92.
7  Anon., *Full and Correct Report of the Trial of Sir Home Popham*, pp.91–92. Sturges Bourne testified at Popham's trial that 'I am quite sure that Mr Pitt had no such expedition in his contemplation … and I have no reason to believe that any other of the King's ministers had such an object in view', but this seems unlikely: Anon., *Full and Correct Report of the Trial of Sir Home Popham*, pp.165–166.
8  Anon., *Full and Correct Report of the Trial of Sir Home Popham*, pp.82, 90–91.
9  Anon., *Full and Correct Report of the Trial of Sir Home Popham*, p.166.

naval contingent. Coming so shortly after the end of the *Romney* inquiry, this appointment raised eyebrows. Admiral Rainier expressed amazement that Popham had been given the command over the heads of so many other senior captains, not to mention several flag officers, and thought patronage – specifically that of the Duke of York – must have been behind it.[10] Rainier was not far from the mark: Popham did have friends in high places. His appointment had nevertheless come from Pitt himself, and from Melville, who still had influence at the Admiralty despite being in disgrace.

Further information was sourced from the Army, which reported there being 3,000 enemy soldiers at the Cape, 2,000 of which were European infantry, with 1,500 reinforcements possibly on their way (two French ships had recently broken blockade from Rochefort carrying that number of troops on board). This meant the British would need a force of at least 6,000 men, although Baird thought this was not enough and unsuccessfully pressed for more.[11] Baird was given a paper total of 6,654 troops gathering at Cork for India, where Baird was instructed to send them when he was finished: the 24th, 38th, 59th, 71st, 72nd, 83rd, 89th, and 93rd Regiments, along with a detachment of the 20th Light Dragoons, 300 artillerymen, and a further 546 recruits raised under the terms of a recent parliamentary act permitting direct recruitment into the Army from the militia. Once in possession of the Cape, Baird would become lieutenant governor and reinstate the military and civil system that had existed before the territory had been handed back to the Dutch in 1801.[12]

Popham received separate orders from the Admiralty on 29 July. In addition to his own *Diadem* (64), he was instructed to take HMS *Raisonable* (64), *Belliqueux* (64), *Diomede* (50), *Narcissus* (32), and *Leda* (32) under his command, a total of four ships of the line and two frigates. He was also given the *Espoir* sloop and the *Encounter* and *Protector* gun vessels, along with five transports carrying troops, several victuallers, and a fleet of East India Company merchant ships to convoy – a sizeable force. Once the Cape had been taken, however, Popham's command would cease. He was ordered to send the troops that had originally been intended for India to the subcontinent under convoy of *Belliqueux*, while *Raisonable* would go on to St Helena to collect an East India Company convoy and take it to Spithead. Popham would be superseded by a superior officer, but his subsequent actions were never explicitly spelled out.[13] He himself seems to have believed he would return to Britain and be rewarded with a seat on the Navy Board.[14] To keep the expedition's destination secret, Popham was instructed to pretend his squadron was destined for three different locations. He himself, with *Diomede*, was to go to Gibraltar; *Narcissus* and *Leda*

---

10  National Library of Scotland (NLS): Acc. 6684/11: Rainier to Sir Pulteney Malcolm, 13 November 1805. Many thanks to Paul Martinovich for this reference.
11  Baird to Castlereagh, 21 July 1805, in George McCall Theal, *Records of the Cape Colony from February 1803 to July 1806* … (London: William Clowes and Sons for the Government of the Cape Colony, 1899), pp.227–228; Baird to Castlereagh, 18 August 1805, Theal, *Records of the Cape Colony*, pp.234–235; Baird to Castlereagh, 28 August 1805, Theal, *Records of the Cape Colony*, p.237; Baird to Castlereagh, 19 November 1805, Theal, *Records of the Cape Colony*, pp.253–254.
12  Baird's instructions, 25 July 1805, Anon., *Full and Correct Report of the Trial of Sir Home Popham*, pp.9–12.
13  Popham's Admiralty instructions, 29 July 1805, Anon., *Full and Correct Report of the Trial of Sir Home Popham*, pp.7–9.
14  NRS: Melville MSS, GD51/1/565: Popham to Melville, 13 January 1806.

were 'ostensibly for the Mediterranean'; and *Belliqueux* would be ordered to India 'without delay'. Once the captains of the squadron ships reached a certain latitude, however, they would open their *actual* orders, which were to rendezvous with Popham at Madeira. Even at Madeira, however, the ultimate destination could not immediately be revealed: the captains would simply be told to place themselves under Popham's orders.[15]

It was the largest squadron Popham had ever commanded, and the one with the most important aims. Accordingly, the Admiralty Board told Popham that, once he had taken all the ships under his command at Madeira, he could hoist the broad red pendant of a commodore.[16] A commodore (a corruption of the Spanish *comendador*) was a temporary rank adopted by the senior captain of a detachment of a fleet in the absence of the commander.[17] The *Naval Regulations* of January 1806, however, distinguished between two forms of commodore: one with an extra captain appointed to command the commodore's ship, in which case the commodore was entitled to the pay and emoluments of a junior rear admiral (later known as a 'Commodore First Class'); and the other a commodore who retained command of his own ship and did not rank as a rear admiral (later known as a 'Commodore Second Class', but known in 1805 as a 'ten-shilling commodore' after the amount of extra pay he was entitled to draw per day). This distinction had existed informally since the 1750s at least, but the *Regulations* did add that, if the commodore were 'appointed to command in Chief', he also ranked as a rear admiral.[18] The order to hoist a broad pendant did not explicitly inform Popham which kind of commodore he was to be, but he was, at least, indisputably a commodore, and he must have experienced a sense of self-satisfaction as he saw the expedition he had helped plan coming together.

At 5:00 a.m. on 28 August, after some minor delays, the squadron finally got underway, convoying 16 East India Company ships. A strong southerly wind forced the ships back into harbour almost immediately, and not until the afternoon of 31 August did a sudden change of wind allow the squadron to sail.[19] This bad luck continued, at least at first. One of the transports – *Diana*, carrying 150 men from the 59th Regiment – was blown off-course by the strong wind and, blinded by darkness, ran afoul of another, *William*, carrying 250 men from the 38th. *Diana* sprung its bowsprit and carried away *William*'s mainmast and wheel.[20] On 6 September, the wind whipped up into 'a heavy gale of wind from the westward', scattering the convoy for a day or so and carrying away the mainmast of the *Ocean*

---

15 Castlereagh to the Admiralty Board, 25 July 1805, W.G. Perrin, 'The Second Capture of the Cape of Good Hope, 1806', *The Naval Miscellany* (London: Navy Records Society, 1927), vol.3, pp.191–285, pp.205–207.
16 Order, 31 July 1805, Anon., *Full and Correct Report of the Trial of Sir Home Popham*, Appendix Note E.
17 William Falconer, *An Universal Dictionary of the Marine* ... (London: T. Cadell, 1784).
18 Privy Council, *Regulations and Instructions Relating to His Majesty's Service at Sea established by His Majesty in Council* (London: W. Winchester and Son, 1806), pp.38–39, 68.
19 Popham to the Admiralty, 28 September 1805, Perrin, 'The Second Capture of the Cape of Good Hope', pp.223–226.
20 Popham to the Admiralty, 28 September 1805, Perrin, 'The Second Capture of the Cape of Good Hope', pp.223–226; Baird to Castlereagh, 31 August 1805, Theal, *Records of the Cape Colony*, pp.238–239.

transport. After this not very auspicious beginning, things settled down, but – as Popham put it – 'we had very unsettled weather' all the way to Madeira.[21] Popham, not to mention the troops cramped aboard the pitching ships, must have been relieved to make Madeira on 27 September, anchoring in Funchal Roads the next day. Here Popham found *Raisonable*, the sloop *Espoir*, and the gun-brigs *Encounter* and *Protector*. Popham's squadron was now complete: six ships of war, 16 East India Company vessels in convoy, the sloop and the two gun-brigs, 34 transports, a hospital ship, a baggage ship, and three victuallers.[22]

Aware that the secrecy of his mission could only be preserved so long, Popham had sent *Leda* ahead with the principal Agent of Transports, Captain Butterfield, to make sure water and provisions were ready and available for the rest of the squadron.[23] The squadron re-provisioned in record time and left Madeira on 3 October, without even having completed watering and probably before the soldiers had managed to get over their seasickness. 'I deemed it right to render the destination of the armament as equivocal as possible,' Popham told William Marsden. Accordingly, although all the captains in the squadron were given the neutral port of Rio de Janeiro as a rendezvous in case of dispersal, Popham warned them 'no positive decision of touching anywhere had been made'.[24]

In accordance with Popham's Admiralty orders, the day after leaving Madeira, the sailors of HMS *Diadem* hoisted the red broad pendant of a commodore from the mainmast to an 11-gun salute from the rest of the squadron. Not so much in accordance with his orders – at least not his written ones – the pendant was that of a full commodore, equivalent to a rear admiral in rank and entitled to appoint a captain to run the everyday business of his ship. A few days later, Popham announced some changes to the squadron's command. He shifted Captain Hugh Downman of HMS *Diomede* to *Diadem* and promoted the First Lieutenant of *Diadem*, William King, to command the sloop *Espoir*.[25] Popham then issued more specific orders to his squadron that may have betrayed some clues regarding what he was really up to. He secretly ordered Captain Ross Donnelly of HMS *Narcissus*, the fastest ship in the squadron, to take his frigate ahead to re-provision at St Helena, then hoist French colours and go on to the Cape to find out if French reinforcements were on their way. Donnelly was ordered to keep a low profile and wait in Table Bay for the rest of the squadron, collecting information.[26] Meanwhile, Popham and the rest of the ships would re-provision at San Salvador, on the coast of Brazil.

---

21 Popham to the Admiralty, 28 September 1805, Perrin, 'The Second Capture of the Cape of Good Hope', pp.223–226.
22 Popham to the Admiralty, 28 September 1805, Perrin, 'The Second Capture of the Cape of Good Hope', pp.223–226.
23 Popham to the Admiralty, 28 September 1805, Perrin, 'The Second Capture of the Cape of Good Hope', pp.223–226.
24 Popham to Marsden, 18 November 1805, Perrin, 'The Second Capture of the Cape of Good Hope', pp.232–236.
25 Admiralty Board to Popham, 11 April 1806, Perrin, 'The Second Capture of the Cape of Good Hope', pp.284–285. King's promotion was not confirmed by the Admiralty.
26 Popham to Donnelly, 4 October 1805, Perrin, 'The Second Capture of the Cape of Good Hope', pp.228–230.

Popham had told Donnelly he expected the journey to take five weeks, followed by one week to re-provision and three or four weeks to make the Cape.[27] This turned out to be optimistic to quite a significant degree, although the first part of Popham's estimate (as far as Brazil) was accurate enough. On 20 October, Popham detached *Espoir* to San Salvador to prepare everything for the arrival of the squadron. A week later, he sent *Leda*, the fastest 12 Indiamen, and several transports to start the process of re-provisioning before the slower part of the squadron caught up. Knowing there were dangerous waters off the Brazilian coast, Popham gave Captain Robert Honeyman of *Leda* specific instructions, along with a number of charts and one of his own chronometers (Popham had nine). However, on the morning of 1 November, at about 3:00 a.m., two of the transports – the *King George* and the *Britannia* East Indiaman – grounded on a sandbank forming part of the Rocas Atoll, about 160 miles off the mainland Brazilian coast.[28] Both ships were lost along with everything on board, save for 12 chests of dollars fished out of *Britannia* before it went down. Remarkably, only three people died, but one of them was Brigadier General John Yorke, commanding the Royal Artillery contingent. Popham only learned of this on 2 November when he and the rest of the squadron caught up with *Leda* and Honeyman signalled to come aboard.[29] In reporting his version of the disaster, Honeyman emphasised that, according to the charts he had been given, his chronometer readings should have been accurate. Popham feared Honeyman would claim the charts he had been given were inaccurate, and argued that Honeyman had not known how to use a chronometer properly.[30] Popham's reputation as a navigator was on the line; even though he had not been present, *Leda* had been following his orders, and the only way he could avoid some blame was by accusing Honeyman of incompetence.

After 18 days at San Salvador (longer than anticipated) and a spell of bad weather, Popham called together his captains, the commanders of the Indiamen, and the masters of the transports and finally revealed their final destination: Table Bay, off the Cape of Good Hope.[31] The squadron sighted Table Mountain on 3 January 1806 and anchored to the east of Robben Island in the evening of the 4th, 'too late to do anything but take a superficial view of Blue Berg Bay'.[32] Popham had left Cork almost exactly four months ago; it was about three weeks after he had guessed he would rendezvous with HMS *Narcissus*. The journey had been long, exhausting, and difficult, but Popham's efforts to keep the men healthy had been successful: only 40 soldiers were too ill to land.[33] Because so much time had passed, Popham and Baird wanted to begin operations as soon as possible. They had not been challenged on their entry

---

27    Popham to Donnelly, 4 October 1805, Perrin, 'The Second Capture of the Cape of Good Hope', pp.228–230.
28    TNA: ADM 1/58, ff.62–64.
29    Baird to Castlereagh, 19 November 1805, Theal, *Records of the Cape Colony*, pp.253–254; Popham to Marsden, 18 November 1805, Perrin, 'The Second Capture of the Cape of Good Hope', pp.232–236.
30    Popham to Marsden, 18 November 1805, Perrin, 'The Second Capture of the Cape of Good Hope', pp.232–236.
31    Popham to Marsden, 14 January 1806, Perrin, 'The Second Capture of the Cape of Good Hope', pp.258–259.
32    Popham to Marsden, 13 January 1806, Anon., *Full and Correct Report of the Trial of Sir Home Popham*, pp.17–22.
33    Popham to Marsden, 14 January 1806, Perrin, 'The Second Capture of the Cape of Good Hope', pp.258–259.

The Cape of Good Hope, engraved by Edward Orme after W.M. Craig and J.H. Heaviside, 1806. (Public domain, Anne S.K. Brown Military Collection, Brown University Library)

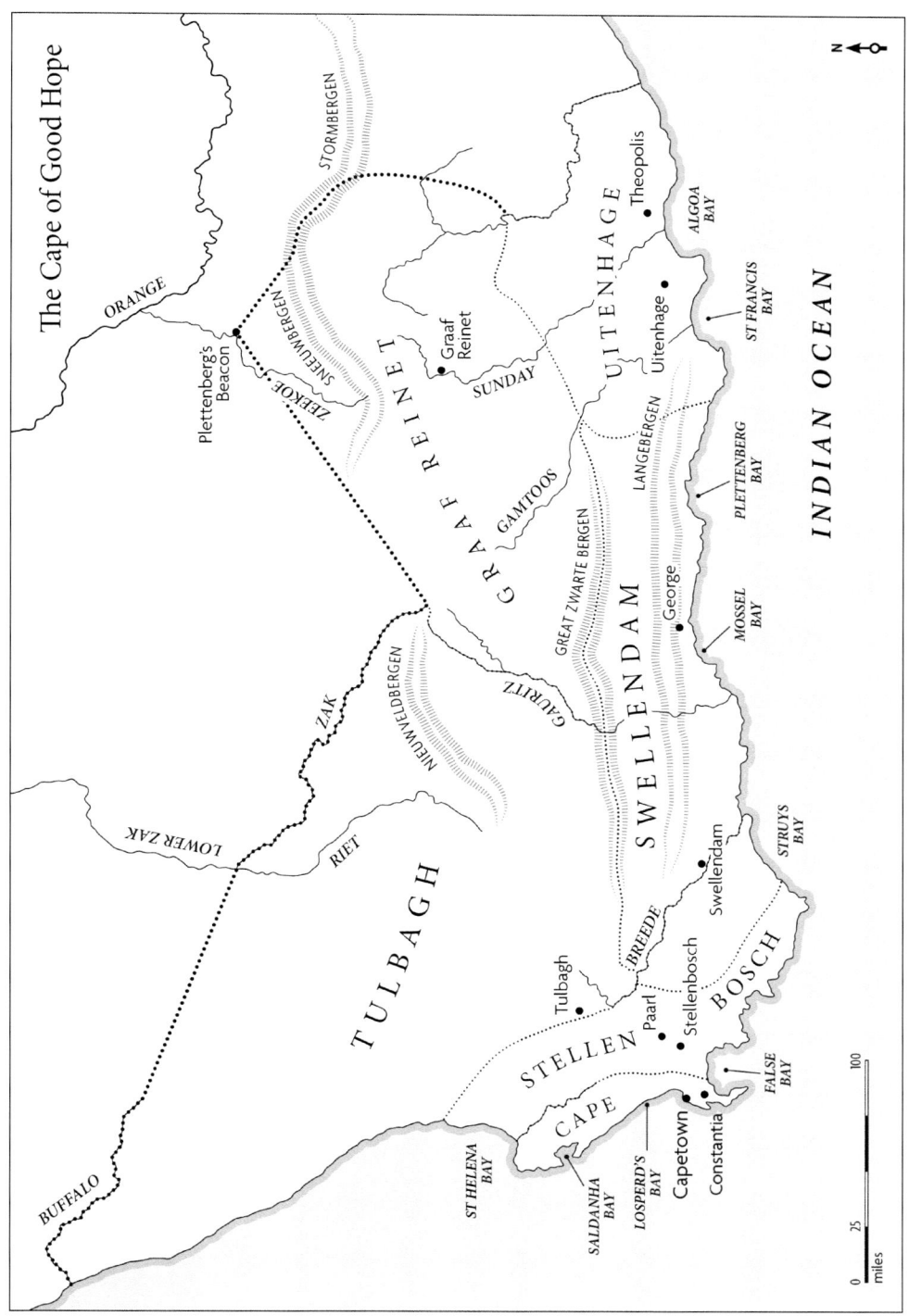

The Cape of Good Hope, 1806.

into Table Bay, which suggested they still had the element of surprise. Had they only known it, the Dutch Captain of the Port had just issued a warning to all Dutch ships in Table Bay that 'a numerous fleet [was] approaching and steering towards this Roadstead, suspected to be hostile'.[34] Popham and Baird were also acutely aware that they had not yet had any run-ins with any of the French ships known to have broken out of Rochefort. Somewhere out there, reinforcements were still at sea – and possibly heading their way.

At 3:00 a.m., after only a short rest, Popham began to oversee the disembarkation of the troops into boats, but a westerly wind had picked up and the surf was too high to attempt a landing. At daylight, therefore, Popham and Baird transferred into the *Espoir* sloop and ran up the coast from Craig's Tower to Losperd's Bay, looking for a better landing place. They plumped for Saldanha Bay, about 60 miles from Cape Town – the closest landing place Popham could safely recommend based on the weather conditions. Captain King of *Espoir* was therefore ordered to go ahead with Captain Smyth of the engineers to reconnoitre a specific landing spot, while *Diomede* accompanied the transports carrying the 38th Regiment and 20th Light Dragoons under Brigadier General William Carr Beresford.[35] Overnight, however, the wind dropped, and the officers examining the beach reported the surf had also gone down significantly. Another reconnaissance under Brigadier General Ronald Ferguson, the military third in command, confirmed a landing might be possible at Losperd's Bay, 20 miles from Cape Town. This was obviously preferable, and at 12:30 p.m. *Diadem*, *Leda*, and *Encounter* took positions offshore, along with the gunboat *Protector*, to cover the landings. Meanwhile, the remainder of the army, along with six light fieldpieces and two howitzers, clambered into the boats of *Diadem*, *Raisonable*, and *Belliqueux*.

The route to the shore, as Baird later wrote, was through 'a confined and intricate channel', and although the surf was much less violent than it had been, the landings were still rough.[36] The Highland Brigade (71st, 72nd, and 93rd Regiments) were first ashore and encountered the most difficulties. One of the landing boats, in Popham's words 'under an anxiety probably to be first on shore', overshot the safe landing site; the boat overturned, and 36 men of the 93rd were drowned.[37] Popham, as always, was very keen to assure the Admiralty this was not his fault: 'I trust my country will acquit me of having applied every expedient that could be devised, to prevent the occurrence of an accident which I so sincerely deplore'.[38] On this occasion, he may have had a point: a landing had only been undertaken at all because of the urgency of the case. Nor did conditions improve. By 8:00 p.m., the surf had increased so much Popham ordered the landings to stop. The rest of the troops earmarked for the assault (the 24th, 59th, and 83rd Regiments) landed next morning, along with Captain Downman of *Diadem* and a detachment of marines and two fieldpieces. Popham himself transferred to *Leda* and sailed to the head of the bay, along with *Encounter* and *Protector*, to find an appropriate place to land the battering train.[39]

---

34 Theal, *Records of the Cape Colony*, p.259.
35 Popham to Marsden, 13 January 1806, Anon., *Full and Correct Report of the Trial of Sir Home Popham*, pp.17–22.
36 Baird to Castlereagh, 12 January 1806, Theal, *Records of the Cape Colony*, pp.270–275.
37 Official returns, 6 January 1806, Theal, *Records of the Cape Colony*, p.260.
38 Popham to Marsden, 13 January 1806, Anon., *Full and Correct Report of the Trial of Sir Home Popham*, pp.17–22.
39 Popham to Marsden, 13 January 1806, Anon., *Full and Correct Report of the Trial of Sir Home Popham*, pp.17–22.

This duty completed, Popham watched the troops through his glass as they advanced 'with an unparalleled rapidity' through the sandy, scrubby terrain and up into the rocky mountains beyond. The first clash between Baird and the Dutch defenders occurred the next day, on 8 January. The Dutch were almost completely unprepared for the attack and the fighting was over very quickly. Baird led his men across the Blaauwberg mountain range separating the troops from their objective, where they discovered enemy light troops waiting for them and, beyond, the main army drawn up in two lines to defend the city. After a hot fight an attempt by the enemy to turn Baird's right flank failed, and the Dutch retreated through the Hottentots Holland pass, leaving the road to the city open. On the morning of 9 January, the British continued their march on Cape Town, taking up a position on the Salt River to allow further communication with the squadron. Under these circumstances, Cape Town surrendered immediately. At 6:00 p.m., the squadron fired a royal salute as the Dutch colours were replaced with British ones on the ramparts of the Castle of Good Hope. Official returns of the killed and wounded noted a total of about 15 killed and just under 200 wounded for the British. In contrast, the Dutch defenders were reputed to have lost 700 men killed and wounded.[40]

Baird later reported in his official dispatch his 'warmest acknowledgements and commendation' of the naval cooperation. Popham's ships had 'constantly coasted the Enemy's shore' throughout the attack on Cape Town, 'throwing Shot among [the enemy's] Troops and People'.[41] To Popham's dismay, however, this activity – along with providing a marine battalion under the command of Captain Byng – formed the sum total of his contribution: 'No brilliant service fell to the lot of the squadron I have the honour to command.' He nevertheless felt, due to the logistical difficulties involved in landing the troops, it had been 'the most laborious duty I ever experienced'. The surf had heightened again, and it took Popham until the evening of 9 January to manage to get ashore after the end of the military action; even so, his boat was swamped and King of *Espoir* only narrowly escaped drowning.[42] Once ashore, Popham was nettled to discover Brigadier General Ferguson had already negotiated and signed the capitulation with the Dutch commandant, 'I thought rather precipitately'. Perhaps partly out of pique, Popham claimed the terms ignored a number of naval concerns and refused to endorse them. With Baird backing him up, Popham forced the Dutch to sign revised terms the following day. Ever the diplomat, Popham explained to the indignant commandant 'that he was the supplicant and therefore he must have the patience to discuss every point'.[43] In their final form, the terms stated that the British would take possession of the city, allowing the garrison to march out with full honours of war, following which all French and Dutch citizens present in the garrison would be shipped straight home. The agreement guaranteed private property, confirmed rights as previously held under British rule prior to

---

40  Popham to Marsden, 13 January 1806, Anon., *Full and Correct Report of the Trial of Sir Home Popham*, pp.17–22; official returns, 6 January 1806, Theal, *Records of the Cape Colony*, p.260; Baird to Castlereagh, 12 January 1806, Theal, *Records of the Cape Colony*, pp.270–275.
41  Baird to Castlereagh, 12 January 1806, Theal, *Records of the Cape Colony*, pp.270–275.
42  Popham to Marsden, 13 January 1806, Perrin, 'The Second Capture of the Cape of Good Hope', pp.250–251.
43  Popham to Marsden, 13 January 1806, Perrin, 'The Second Capture of the Cape of Good Hope', pp.250–251.

1802, but required two French ships that had been sunk in Table Bay to be floated, following which they – and the 68-gun *Bato*, which the Dutch had tried to burn – would be repaired. Popham sent Captain Downman of *Diadem* home with dispatches in *Espoir* and promoted his protégé, William King, to command *Diadem* in Downman's absence.[44]

'I know no instance where a stronger degree of confidence and unanimity has been exemplified between the two professions, than on the present occasion,' Popham gloated to the Admiralty.[45] He was feeling very pleased with himself. Six months after he had first suggested attacking the Cape, the place was in British hands again. Quite apart from the fact his plans had worked out (for once), Popham had finally caught up with Captain Donnelly of HMS *Narcissus*, who had been gathering intelligence in Table Bay over the previous two months. Donnelly's cruise had been fruitful. In October, on his way south, he had destroyed several French privateers and liberated a captured British ship, the *Horatio Nelson*. He had also captured a brig, *Le Prudent*, of 12 guns and 70 men. On Christmas Eve, he had fallen in with a French ship of war near Table Bay, on its way to give succour to the Dutch garrison (and probably carrying intelligence of the coming British attack). Other ships had also been taken, including a Dutch sloop carrying naval stores. All in all, Donnelly had done well, particularly from the point of view of prize money – in which Popham, as commodore holding a rank equivalent to that of a flag officer, hoped to take a significant share.[46]

The main fighting over, Popham still expected to be superseded at the Cape by a superior officer. As he wrote to the Secretary of the Admiralty, 'However fortunate I may consider myself by the result of the Expedition … I cannot presume to imagine that I may be thought competent to remain any length of time on a station of such importance as that of the Cape of Good Hope'.[47] He did not, however, expect to remain long unemployed. As soon as the dust had settled following the capture of the Cape, Popham wrote privately to Lord Melville, still out of office but whose influence and patronage still counted for much in a government headed by William Pitt. 'I am satisfied both as a publick Person and private Friend that nothing can more highly gratify Your Lordship than receiving a Letter from this place; in the first Instance as to its political Importance, and the next as to the successful Issue of my Exertions,' Popham wrote. 'I have written to go home at the fall of the year, and I hope by that time my exertions here and the regulations I make will induce Mr Pitt to think I am eligible at least to some Situation at the Navy Board.'[48] So sure was Popham that this would come to pass that he actually surrendered his seat in Parliament by taking the Manor of East Hundred in Berkshire.[49]

---

44 Popham to Marsden, 13 January 1806, Perrin, 'The Second Capture of the Cape of Good Hope', pp.250–251.
45 Popham to Marsden, 13 January 1806, Anon., *Full and Correct Report of the Trial of Sir Home Popham*, pp.17–22.
46 Donnelly to Popham, 13 January 1806, Perrin, 'The Second Capture of the Cape of Good Hope', pp.254–257.
47 Popham to Marsden, 28 January 1806, Perrin, 'The Second Capture of the Cape of Good Hope', pp.261–262.
48 NRS: Melville MSS, GD51/1/565: Popham to Melville.
49 Waite, 'Sir Home Riggs Popham', p.141; Anon., *Members of Parliament* (1878), part 2, p.22. He was re-elected for Shaftesbury on 31 October 1806, while still abroad: Anon., *Members of Parliament* (1878), part 2, p.232.

If Popham had one eye on the future, his other was fixed firmly on the present. There was unfinished business at the Cape. *Luitenant-generaal* Jan Willem Janssens, the military commander at Cape Town, had retreated after the battle of 9 January into the surrounding districts with about 1,200 men. He had good supply lines, and Popham and Baird were worried he might raise some opposition among the local farmers and try a second attempt at resistance from inland. In contrast, British supplies were in trouble. The Cape had recently suffered a series of bad harvests, and a preliminary investigation of the city stores had revealed only about two days of grain remaining.[50] Unable to rely on supplies from the surrounding countryside until it had been completely pacified, Popham agreed with Baird to send *Leda* to St Helena and another ship to Rio to get flour. The two men also considered Bengal and Madagascar as sources of rice, and Popham mused about the possibility of sending one or two ships of war from England with biscuit.[51] But the most immediate solution was obviously to neutralise Janssens, who currently controlled supplies from the interior. Baird therefore sent Beresford to take the village of Stellenbosch with the 59th and 72nd Regiments and force Janssens to capitulate.[52] Popham later sent the 83rd, with *Raisonable* and *Belliqueux* as convoy, to False Bay to help cut off Janssen's retreat should he choose to move further inland.[53] But although Janssens initially issued a proclamation urging the locals to maintain their resistance to the British, he knew he could not hold out indefinitely. He signed terms with Beresford on 18 January, according to which 'the whole of the settlement of the Cape of Good Hope, with all its dependencies, and the rights and privileges held and exercised by the Batavian Government, will be considered as surrendered by the governor, Lieutenant General Janssens, to his Britannic Majesty'. This was ratified by Baird and Popham at Cape Town on the 19th.[54]

Popham was not entirely happy with terms he considered to be 'more liberal than the nature of the case required', but recognised the treaty was preferable to 'the horrors of a long, predatory war'.[55] One reason for this was that the French ships from Rochefort were still unaccounted for. The news of the Battle of Trafalgar of 21 October 1805, which effectively neutralised the possibility of a French naval attempt to relieve the Cape, had not yet arrived in the southern hemisphere, and Popham feared all his good work might be undone if an enemy squadron turned up after all. Intelligence received at the end of January 1806 suggested *contre amiral* Linois had left the Cape the previous November with the French ships *Marengo* and *Belle-Poule* and run north 'to commit as many depredations as possible'. Popham imagined he was by now running low on water and stores, and suspected Linois and his two ships would call in soon at the Cape to re-provision. Popham therefore set sail

---

50 Baird to Castlereagh, 13 January 1806, Theal, *Records of the Cape Colony*, pp.276–280.
51 Baird to Castlereagh, 13 January 1806, Theal, *Records of the Cape Colony*, pp.276–280; Popham to Marsden, 13 January 1806, Perrin, 'The Second Capture of the Cape of Good Hope', pp.257–258.
52 Baird to Castlereagh, 13 January 1806, Theal, *Records of the Cape Colony*, pp.276–280.
53 Popham to Marsden, 28 January 1806, Anon., *Full and Correct Report of the Trial of Sir Home Popham*, pp.22–23.
54 Popham to Marsden, 22 January 1806, Anon., *Full and Correct Report of the Trial of Sir Home Popham*, pp.23–27.
55 Popham to Marsden, 22 January 1806, Anon., *Full and Correct Report of the Trial of Sir Home Popham*, pp.22–23.

on 29 January in HMS *Diadem*, accompanied by *Diomede*, *Narcissus*, and *Raisonable*, to cut Linois off before his arrival.[56]

In fact Linois never got as far as the Cape – he was defeated by Vice Admiral Duckworth off St Domingo on 6 February – but Popham had no way of knowing this for several months. Popham's cruise did allow him to send off HMS *Belliqueux*, with 15 transports of troops and the East India convoy, en route to India (as per Popham's original orders of July 1805). Popham returned to Table Bay in mid-February to see off the transports carrying the prisoners back to Holland according to the capitulations of 10 and 19 January, but he then set sail again immediately. He was still expecting Linois to make an appearance around the first week of March.[57] On 21 February, however, Popham made another capture: *Rolla*, a French letter of marque sent to Cape Town for re-provisioning. *Rolla* was captured by a British crew dressed in French disguise, so the ship's commander did not realise he was being duped until the last minute and had no opportunity to destroy his dispatches. His correspondence included letters from Linois to Janssens and to the Minister of Marine in Paris. Although they were 'rather too equivocal' in their phrasing to allow any accurate estimate of what Linois' current location might be, Linois stated he was in 'extreme distress' regarding water and provisions and would certainly be calling in at the Cape for more. As some Indiamen were expected to arrive at the Cape at the beginning of April, Popham proposed to sail out to meet them and bring them in safely. He also wrote to the Admiralty requesting permission to keep HMS *Raisonable* with him, despite having been ordered to send the ship to St Helena following the fall of the Cape.[58]

These were the first signs that Popham was veering from the course of action prescribed in his July 1805 orders. These orders had admittedly not been very specific regarding his actions after the Cape was taken, but their basic purport – send reinforcements to India, then return home for further orders – were clear. Still, more than six months had passed since those orders had been issued. Popham could defend his decision to retain *Raisonable* and stay at the Cape because there was a real concern the French might appear on the horizon at any moment. Popham had also never received orders issued in mid-September 1805, which had been captured at sea by the French, reiterating his previous instructions to transport two regiments to India as soon as possible.[59] The circumstances at the Cape were, moreover, still in flux, and immediately after Popham wrote home to retain *Raisonable* they changed again. The day after capturing *Rolla*, a neutral Danish ship bound for Batavia arrived in Table Bay carrying news from India suggesting British reinforcements were not so urgently needed there. Popham also heard for the first time of the Battle of Trafalgar, and of the French victory over the Austrians at Ulm the previous October.[60] Another source of

---

56 Popham to Marsden, 28 January 1806, Perrin, 'The Second Capture of the Cape of Good Hope', pp.260–261.
57 Popham to Marsden, 21 February 1806, Perrin, 'The Second Capture of the Cape of Good Hope', pp.262–263.
58 Popham to Marsden, 22 February 1806, Anon., *Full and Correct Report of the Trial of Sir Home Popham*, pp.27–28; testimony of Captain King, Anon., *Full and Correct Report of the Trial of Sir Home Popham*, p.192.
59 Anon., *Full and Correct Report of the Trial of Sir Home Popham*, pp.13, 15–16.
60 Popham to Marsden, 22 February 1806, Anon., *Full and Correct Report of the Trial of Sir Home Popham*, p.27; Popham's defence, p.94.

intelligence arrived soon after. The morning after *Diadem*, *Leda*, and *Diomede* had returned from their cruise in search of the ever-elusive Linois, 'a ship was discovered coming from the southward under a press of sail'. Although it had not yet declared its allegiance, Popham was pretty sure it had to be French; he therefore ordered his ships to hoist Dutch colours and waited for the French to take the bait. The suspected French ship soon hoisted French colours in response and stood towards *Diadem*. When they got within hailing distance, Popham ordered the Dutch colours hauled down and hoisted British ones instead, calling across to the enemy vessel to surrender. The ship turned out to be a 46-gun frigate, *La Volontaire*, detached from the squadron under the command of *contre amiral* Willaumez to go ahead to the Cape and arrange water and provisions. *La Volontaire* carried 217 British troops from the 2nd and 54th Regiments whose transports had been captured in the Bay of Biscay, as well as news of France's victory over Russia at Austerlitz on 2 December. With Austria and Russia both out of the war, the Third Continental Coalition – which Pitt had hoped Spain might eventually join – was over.[61]

Popham was starting to realise the circumstances under which he had left Britain, which had prevented him going to South America and circumscribed his activities in South Africa, no longer applied. In immediate terms, however, the picture he was forming was not necessarily positive. The French had the whip-hand over Europe, and not one but two French squadrons were now known to be at sea. At least Linois, whom Popham had previously been expecting, was no longer a threat: information from *La Volontaire* suggested he was going north towards the Brazils. But the second division under Willaumez, which Popham had not known about until now, was more alarming. It reportedly consisted of eight ships of war, one of which was said to be commanded by Jerome Bonaparte, Napoleon's brother. If Willaumez and Linois joined forces –unlikely, but not impossible – Popham could expect 12 sail of the line, four frigates, and a corvette. He once more used this news as an excuse to rip up his July 1805 orders, urging the Admiralty again to allow him to retain *Raisonable* and mooring this ship, along with *Diadem* and *Diomede*, as close to the Cape as possible to protect it. *Narcissus* and *Leda* he placed in defensive positions to the southeast.[62] Having previously written to Melville of his intention to go home, Popham now asked the Admiralty for permission to remain at the Cape: 'All the means which I can command shall be held ready to apply in such a manner as may be deemed most advantageous to the public service.'[63]

Over the next few weeks, Popham waited anxiously for a sail – or, in the worst-case scenario, 12 sail – to appear. He remained heavily dependent on information gleaned from the odd whaler and merchantman coming into harbour: a Hamburg brig reported having been boarded by Willaumez, accompanied by seven ships, three weeks before at a latitude of 33° south and a longitude of 6° east. This was uncomfortably close to the Cape, although Popham could not learn whether Willaumez was continuing south or whether he might

---

61 Popham to Marsden, 4 March 1806, Anon., *Full and Correct Report of the Trial of Sir Home Popham*, pp.28–29, p.94 (Popham's defence), pp.193, 208 (trial testimony).
62 TNA: ADM 1/2331: Popham to Marsden, 8 March 1806.
63 Popham to Marsden, 7 March 1806, Anon., *Full and Correct Report of the Trial of Sir Home Popham*, pp.144–148.

actually have been on his way north to the West Indies.[64] Faced with this uncertainty, Popham continued on high alert, although the longer it took the French to arrive, the more likely it was they had gone north. Popham was reacting to immediate circumstances, as specific instructions from Britain would take months to arrive and the picture at the Cape was changing on a daily, perhaps even hourly, basis. But *La Volontaire* had more secrets aboard, and these heralded Popham's most dramatic, and craziest, departure from his official orders yet.

---

64 Popham to Marsden, 20 March 1806, Anon., *Full and Correct Report of the Trial of Sir Home Popham*, pp.31–33.

# 12

# Buenos Aires, 1806

*2601: The prize is on shore*

In a remarkable coincidence, one of *La Volontaire*'s crew had been an old acquaintance of Popham's: Wilhelm Steetz, a Hamburg merchant who had been pressed into the French navy and was now an *enseigne de vaisseau* (a rank somewhere between a midshipman and a lieutenant). Steetz and Popham had first met during Popham's stint as transport agent in northern Germany and bonded over a shared love of hydrography, but fell out of touch after Steetz entered the French navy.[1] The moment he heard Popham was in command of the British naval forces at the Cape, however, Steetz made himself known to his former friend and said he had information to provide. What the German had to say changed the course of Popham's career completely.

Steetz suggested to Popham that Willaumez was not likely to try and retake the Cape, as he almost certainly still did not know the Cape was in British hands. Instead, Willaumez was most likely to go north, away from South Africa and towards Brazil.[2] Popham later suggested Steetz's information was critical in forming the decisions he was about to take. Why Steetz's information was more credible to Popham than any of the evidence coming in from brigs and whalers that Willaumez was still close at hand is not clear; it probably depended on what Steetz's relationship with Popham had been in the past, and whether Steetz gave up any other information Popham thought more prudent to suppress in his official letter to the Admiralty. Nevertheless, and despite the fact his official dispatches continued to transmit reports regarding Willaumez and Linois until the end of March, Popham now decided the French squadrons were no longer an immediate threat.

This turned out to be accurate: at the end of March, an American trading vessel, *Elizabeth*, arrived at the Cape and confirmed all Steetz had said. But Popham now made a further, mind-boggling, mental leap, putting together all the information that had been trickling in from various sources for weeks. If the French were no longer a danger, and Trafalgar and the collapse of the Third Coalition meant Spain was no longer a potential British ally, Spain's colonies were fair game again. Rather than preparing to go home in accordance with his July

---

1 Anon., *État Général de la Légion d'Honneur depuis son Origine* … (Paris: Testu and Co., 1814), vol.2, p.40; Arrêté, 2e Jour Complentaire, An 11 (19 September 1801), H. Plon & J. Dumaine (eds), *Correspondance de Napoléon Ier*, (Paris: Imprimerie Impériale, 1861), vol.7, pp.329–330.
2 Popham to Marsden, 20 March 1806, Anon., *Full and Correct Report of the Trial of Sir Home Popham*, pp.148–149.

1805 orders, therefore, Popham decided that, in the absence of any other immediate threat, he might use the force under his command for the purpose of the long-projected project of attacking Spanish South America.

On 24 March, Sir David Baird, busy establishing his military-civilian governorship over the Cape, wrote home that Popham had asked for a regiment of 500 men to attack the Spanish settlement of Buenos Aires on the Rio de la Plata. Baird wanted to hear from home first about the military and diplomatic situation on the continent, but he was inclined to agree: 'If nothing occurs, and ... the colony remains in the same [state of] tranquillity that it is [in] at present, I may then perhaps spare him the regiment.'[3] On 28 March, Popham enlisted the help of *Elizabeth*'s master, a merchant named Thomas Waine, to convince Baird that Buenos Aires was ripe for the picking. Waine wrote to Popham that he had been three times to the Spanish city; it had access to plenty of grain, something the Cape did not have; the inhabitants strongly disliked their authoritarian government; and it was poorly defended. 'From my knowledge of the minds and dispositions of the inhabitants,' Waine told Popham, 'I can assure you that His Majesty's squadron under your command with a small military assistance would with ease take possession', either of Buenos Aires or of its more military neighbour, the fortress of Montevideo. The inhabitants would welcome the invaders with open arms, and the Plata River basin, which included several silver mines – *plata* meant 'silver' in Spanish – would 'be a mine of wealth'.[4]

While Baird was mulling Popham's proposition over, Popham had already started implementing his plans. On 3 April, he ordered Captain Honeyman of the *Leda* to cruise for intelligence off Maldonado, Montevideo, and Buenos Aires in preparation for 'either a predatory expedition in that river or one of regular debarkation'.[5] On 9 April Popham wrote to the Secretary of the Admiralty suggesting that, since Willaumez's arrival was now 'very improbable', the squadron might go to South America to cut off any supply routes between Willaumez and French-held Mauritius. This at least had some bearing on British India, as Mauritius remained a threat to British holdings on the subcontinent, but it was the first sign the Admiralty might have had that Popham was going rogue. Popham himself seemed to realise his proposals stretched his instructions somewhat and couched them with excuses: employing his squadron was always better than 'remaining idle', and a short cruise off South America might lead to 'advantages', although he did not yet specify what those were.[6] To back up his decision to leave his station and go west rather than east, Popham claimed he had 'received some intelligence respecting the weak state of defence which Montevideo and Buenos Aires were in'. This sounded very grand, but the testimony was rather weaker than Popham made it out to be: it came from an able seaman in the squadron named Fisher, who had previously spent eight years in Buenos Aires.[7] Popham was already scouring his own squadron for evidence to back up his own inclinations.

---

3     Baird to Colonel J.W. Gordon, 24 March 1806, John D. Grainger, *The Royal Navy in the River Plate, 1806–1807* (London: Navy Records Society, 1996), p.16.
4     TNA: ADM 1/5378: Waine to Popham, 28 March 1806.
5     Popham to Honeyman, 3 April 1806, Grainger, *The Royal Navy in the River Plate*, p.18.
6     Popham to Marsden, 9 April 1806, Grainger, *The Royal Navy in the River Plate*, pp.34–35.
7     Popham to Marsden, 13 April 1806, Anon., *Full and Correct Report of the Trial of Sir Home Popham*, p.35 (the original is in TNA: ADM 1/5378); evidence of Captain William King, Anon., *Full and Correct Report of the Trial of Sir Home Popham*, p.208.

Popham was determined to get his way and went ashore a second time to press Baird for a regiment 'with every argument in my power'. Baird's biographers have been reluctant to admit he may have been complicit in Popham's plans: one wrote 'Baird was not convinced' by Popham's arguments, while another noted that Baird had 'been over-persuaded' by the 'sophistry of Sir Home Popham'.[8] None of Baird's apologists, however, could get over the crucial fact that Baird did agree to send Brigadier General Beresford and the 71st. There were at least sound strategic reasons for the expedition from the Cape's point of view, particularly in terms of securing a source of grain – even if Popham's later contention that the Cape and South America were 'considered as a part of [the same] station' slightly strained the truth at the seams.[9]

From this point things moved so swiftly Popham must have been prepared for the decision in advance. On the 12th, HMS *Diadem* spent the day embarking troops and taking on provisions. Within 24 hours everything was ready. 'The whole of [the 71st] ... are embarked, and we only wait a breeze to sail,' Popham reported to the Secretary of the Admiralty.[10] That breeze came the next day, and the squadron – *Diadem, Raisonable, Narcissus, Diomede,* and *Encounter,* along with five transports full of troops – set sail on 14 April.[11] Only a few weeks previously, Popham had been expecting an enemy attack on the Cape at any minute.

Expressions at the Admiralty must have been a picture when Popham's 13 April 1806 letter was opened and read, but Popham almost certainly did not expect the Pitt government to be much surprised. After all, the assault on South America had a long pedigree. Melville had been thinking about it since the original rupture between Britain and Spain in the 1790s, and for many years Popham had expected to be chosen to put his plans into action. In August 1801, Popham, then in the Red Sea, had written 'that Mr Dundas proposed sending me to South America when the Red Sea service was finished' and that his mission in the east had mainly been designed to give him 'a greater field to recommend myself'.[12] Peace and the fall of the Pitt government had put an end to those plans, but the Addington government had picked them up again after the renewal of war with France, when a war with Spain had also seemed imminent.[13]

Around the same time, in the summer of 1803, Popham first met with Francisco de Miranda, a Spanish American separatist from Trinidad who was plotting to make his homeland the base for a general uprising against the Spanish overlords. Once a fervent revolutionary who had served as a general in the French army, Miranda had been imprisoned during the Terror and eventually forced to seek asylum in Britain. He had since been trying to interest the British government in his attempts to foment independence in South

---

8   Arthur H. Haley, *Our Davy: General Sir David Baird (1757–1829)* (Liverpool: Bullfinch Publications, [1989]), p.130; [Hook], *The Life of Sir David Baird*, vol.2, pp.136–137, 141.
9   Anon., *Full and Correct Report of the Trial of Sir Home Popham*, p.102.
10  Popham to Marsden, 13 April 1806, Grainger, *The Royal Navy in the River Plate*, p.35.
11  TNA: ADM 51/1615: log, HMS *Diadem*, 13, 14 April 1806.
12  Quoted in Popham, *A Damned Cunning Fellow*, p.92.
13  Anon., *Full and Correct Report of the Trial of Sir Home Popham*, p.90.

America. Miranda and Popham were introduced on 1 August 1803 by Alexander Davison, a government contractor and agent who had been imprisoned for electoral fraud and had been under parliamentary investigation for peculation. This background of persecution and political subterfuge gave Popham and Davison the basis for a lasting friendship. Davison's circle of friends included Popham's solicitor Germaine Lavie, his old business partner John McArthur, and (most significantly of all) Lord Melville himself, and it may be that Popham was put into contact with Miranda with the aim of putting together a specific plan.[14] Popham and Miranda hit it off instantly. Popham quickly realised that Miranda's plans, even though they touched on the delicate political question of fomenting colonial rebellion, might bring plentiful advantages for British trade, which was struggling in war-torn Europe and relying increasingly on its colonies for a reliable outlet. Miranda saw in Popham's keenness an opportunity to get his ideas heard, and Popham did not discourage Miranda from believing he had considerable political leverage.

South America was entirely new to Popham, who was much more knowledgeable about western Europe and India, but he saw this unfamiliarity as a challenge. In November 1803, having met frequently with Miranda and conducted his own extensive research, Popham sent Addington's Home Secretary, Charles Yorke, a long memorandum on the subject of South America. Popham claimed Spain derived 50 million dollars a year from its South American colonies, and that depriving it and its overseas territories of this wealth (and of timber for its navy) would strike a strong enough blow to warrant an expedition even before thinking about the value of South American trade for Britain. 'If Spain is once confined to its European navigation and commerce,' Popham concluded, 'she will not be long considered a maritime power.' Miranda proposed to use his own connections to raise a local army of 15–20,000 men; Britain needed to provide no more than two companies of artillery and two squadrons of dismounted cavalry, along with a small naval force – three frigates, an armed Indiaman, and two smaller vessels – pledged by Alexander Davison in his capacity as a naval contractor.[15] Popham proposed to attack Chile, Peru, and Mexico, as well as Caracas (Miranda's native soil), opening a communication with Indian commerce through the West Indies. The Rio de la Plata was not one of Popham's primary targets, but he did note it might be considered a viable secondary target. Popham proposed to oversee this expedition and claimed Miranda had personally requested his participation. In case there were any objections, Popham reminded Yorke the affair was unlikely to lead to great renown: 'It is an Enterprise more of political arrangement and particular management, than Military Exploit.'[16] He said nothing about the prospect of prize money.

Popham later claimed 'some steps were taken for carrying this projected expedition into effect',[17] but nothing practical came of it. In September 1804, however, with Pitt and Melville in power again, Popham reminded Melville of Miranda's plans for South America.[18] Information from Trinidad suggested the Spanish colony teetered on the brink

---

14 Martyn Downer, *Nelson's Purse: The Mystery of Lord Nelson's Lost Treasures* (London: Corgi, 2005), pp.345, 390.
15 Popham to York, 26 November 1803, Londonderry (ed.), *Castlereagh Correspondence*, vol.7, p.292.
16 BL: Add MS 45041, f.1: Popham to Yorke, 'Thursday' [early 1804].
17 Anon., *Full and Correct Report of the Trial of Sir Home Popham*, p.90.
18 BL: Add MS 41080: Popham to Melville, 18 September 1804.

of revolution. If Britain could provide Miranda with weapons and troops, Popham told Melville proudly, 'Trinidad will be one of the finest possessions under the [British] Crown, and ... the most liberal export channel for all our manufactures that I am acquainted with'. Intrigued, Melville invited Popham to dine with him and Pitt at Wimbledon to fine-tune a plan. Popham told them Miranda needed two ships of the line, two sloops, two gun-brigs, and three cutters, along with one regiment, a company of artillery, and a troop of cavalry.[19] Melville promised Popham a suitable ship for the command of such an expedition, and Pitt asked Popham and Miranda to draw up a more in-depth memorandum to be laid before the cabinet.[20] With the aid of a force of 3,000 regulars and 4,000 sepoys from India, Popham pledged to deprive Spain (and its ally, France) of South American revenue, channel those profits seamlessly into British pockets, secure trade routes to the Cape of Good Hope and to India, increase British wealth and morale, and – not incidentally, given Pitt's political problems – secure 'the popularity and stability ... [of the] Government that undertook' such an expedition.[21] As tempted as Pitt may have been by these proposals, they were shelved while there was a prospect of Spain joining the Third Coalition. Still, Popham claimed 'the object was not lost sight of ... I sailed from England [for the Cape] under the strongest conviction that I should at some future period ... receive orders to strike a blow at South America.'[22]

The problem was that none of this formed a specific remit to assault South America after the fall of the Cape of Good Hope. Popham's later claims that attacking Spanish America was the logical sequel to taking the Cape were weak: the last time he had spoken of South America to the government, he had been told to wait for more propitious continental circumstances. Even if he could claim those circumstances existed after the collapse of the Third Coalition and the victory at Trafalgar, his orders from the Admiralty breathed not a word about crossing the Atlantic. But he managed to convince himself that his South American schemes had already been tacitly approved in principle by the government. Doing something – anything – was 'far preferable to the alternative of allowing the squadron I have the honour to command to moulder away its native energy ... in a state of cold defensive inactivity'.[23] Popham's sudden decision to go to South America in March 1806 fed into his pathological need to be of use, and (just as crucially) to be witnessed by his patrons doing something useful. The intangible benefits of a South American expedition – the influence, the renown – were high if he succeeded. It was a huge gamble, but a calculated one, based on opportunity, (relative) proximity, and the conviction that the government would back him unquestioningly, once it had got over its surprise at finding him 4,000 miles away from where it expected to find him. The *Romney* inquiry had demonstrated the likelihood of this loud and clear. And then, of course, there was prize money. The millions of dollars Spanish America brought to Spain and France, which Popham had talked up so much to Addington and Pitt, might also bring him great wealth. Whatever Popham later claimed about his

---

19   BL: Add MS 41080, ff.70–71, 73–74: Popham to Melville, 11 October 1804.
20   Anon., *Full and Correct Report of the Trial of Sir Home Popham*, p.91.
21   TNA: ADM 1/58, ff.273–282: memorandum, 14 October 1804.
22   Anon., *Full and Correct Report of the Trial of Sir Home Popham*, p.94.
23   Popham to Marsden, 13 April 1806, Anon., *Full and Correct Report of the Trial of Sir Home Popham*, pp.36–38.

devotion to his country, his motives were no more selfless than they had been the day he had chartered *Etrusco* and sailed it under foreign colours to East India Company seas.

Less than a week after leaving the Cape, one of the troop transports – *Ocean*, carrying 200 men – was dismasted and separated from the rest of the squadron during a storm. Popham had lost nearly a fifth of his force at a stroke.[24] He thought the transport might attempt to re-join the squadron at St Helena, and calling there was also an excellent opportunity to pick up more troops to bulk out his force. Popham knew his old friend the governor, Robert Patton, had been ordered by the East India Company to give any assistance in his power to Baird and Popham's forces 'in any operation in which you may be required by them to assist'.[25] Popham sent HMS *Narcissus* ahead to warn Patton the squadron was on its way, along with a letter explaining his motives for attacking South America and requesting as many troops as Patton could spare to help open this new avenue for British and Indian commerce.[26] The squadron arrived at St Helena on 28 April and Popham found he had been right to hope for Patton's generosity. The governor provided him with 150 infantry under the command of the lieutenant governor of the island, Lieutenant Colonel William Lane, along with 100 artillerymen and two howitzers.[27]

Popham's visit to St Helena also allowed him to catch up on the latest news from home, and what he heard shook the very foundations of his little expedition. A vital part of Popham's plan had been his certainty that Pitt would back him to the hilt, no matter what the circumstances, but the biggest news coming out of Britain was that Pitt was no longer Prime Minister. He had died, aged 46, on 23 January 1806, and the government had passed into the hands of the Whigs, Popham's political enemies.

For Popham, the news could not have been worse. It was, he told Melville in horrified disbelief, 'the greatest national calamity that ever befel [sic] our Country'. He added, as well he might, 'to my personal feelings it has been such a shock that I shall not easily recover.' All his dispatches home, which he had tailored to a knowing and favourable political audience, had been arriving on the desks of people who had hated him for years. He did not yet know who had the Admiralty, as the latest newspapers available at St Helena did not contain the full arrangements of the new government, but there was a significant possibility that Lord St Vincent might have been restored to the helm. The prospect was enough to make Popham break out into a sweat. 'I am now toiling under such speculative promise of approbation, either from different policy, or different Sentiment, that I proceed with little pleasure,' he confessed.[28] But it was too late to back out. Having talked Baird round and secured extra troops from Patton, Popham was committed. It was Buenos Aires or bust.

---

24 *Ocean* only re-joined the squadron in mid-June, off South America.
25 Anon., *Full and Correct Report of the Trial of Sir Home Popham*, Appendix Note F.
26 Popham to Patton, 23 April 1806, Grainger, *The Royal Navy in the River Plate*, p.24.
27 TNA: ADM 1/5378: Popham to Marsden, 30 April 1806; Patton to Popham, 1 May 1806, Anon., *Full and Correct Report of the Trial of Sir Home Popham*, p.52.
28 NRS: Melville MSS, GD51/1/94: Popham to Melville, 30 April 1806.

Aware that he had some serious damage limitation to do, Popham wrote another long letter to the Admiralty explaining his motives for leaving the Cape – this time in the full knowledge that the men reading his dispatches might be unfriendly. Popham was at pains to persuade the as yet unknown members of the Admiralty Board that his expedition had 'not arisen from any sudden impulse or the immediate desire of gratifying an adventurous spirit'. Aware that the new men at the Admiralty had probably not seen it before, he included a copy of his 1804 memorandum on a cooperation with Miranda and reiterated his persuasion that the Rio de la Plata would provide a much-needed source of grain for the Cape. This, however, was 'the least important consideration': the most important was the opportunity South America held out for British trade. The rest of his dispatch read like a manifesto. He listed the produce of the area from which Britain might benefit: 'gold, silver, precious stones, cocoa, indigo, cochineal, copper, wool, hemp, hair, wheat, gums, drugs, horn ... hides and tallow'. But his expedition was emphatically not one of conquest: 'There can be no idea of moving a man into the country; the object will be to gain ... by negotiation ... the offer of a liberal trade'.[29] This emphasis on trade was partly self-preservation, and Popham hoped his expedition 'would be a popular one, even if it should not exactly meet the policy of the present Minister'.[30] This was Popham's insurance against official disapproval. If he could win over the government's financial backers, the government itself could hardly attack him, even if they wanted to.

Having picked up their reinforcements, Popham and Beresford boarded *Diadem* and set sail from St Helena on 2 May. Over the next few days Captain King of *Diadem* kept his men busy exercising small arms and pikes, firing blank cartridges at an imaginary enemy, and furnishing the ship's boats with carronades. The ship's forge was constantly at work making ammunition.[31] Popham wanted the men in his squadron to be ready for close-quarters fighting. This was because Popham wanted to bulk up Beresford's infantry with a body of 2,000 sailors under the command of King; the squadron's tailors were busily at work making up red jackets from fabric bought at St Helena to help this 'Royal Marine Battalion', or 'Marine Blues', blend in with the rest of the army.[32] As the squadron approached the coast of South America, Popham ordered his men to exercise the great guns as well as their small arms.

On 28 May, Popham reeled his commodore's pendant down from *Diadem* and hoisted it aboard *Narcissus* instead. *Diadem*, the heavier troopship, stayed with the rest of the convoy the squadron had been escorting since St Helena, while *Narcissus*, the faster frigate, went ahead to scout out potential landing sites.[33] On 8 June *Narcissus* arrived at Isla de Flores at the head of the Rio de la Plata and within sight of the fortress of Montevideo. It was Popham's first sight of one of the expedition's main military targets. Through his telescope, he could make out the Cerro, rising 500 feet above sea-level, its steep slopes running down

---

29   TNA: ADM 1/5378: Popham to Marsden, 30 April 1806.
30   NRS: Melville MSS, GD51/1/94: Popham to Melville, 30 April 1806.
31   TNA: ADM 51/1615: log, HMS *Diadem*.
32   Journal of Lieutenant Robert F[ernyhough], *Military Memoirs of Four Brothers ... engaged in the service of their country ...* (London: William Sams, 1829), pp.82–83; C. Northcote Parkinson, *Samuel Walters, Lieutenant, R.N.* (Liverpool: University Press, 1949), p.42.
33   Grainger, *The Royal Navy in the River Plate*, p.29.

Buenos Aires and the Río de la Plata, 1806.

to the water's edge and a long fortified wall surrounding the town. He could make out the masts of several ships in the harbour, also well protected by the embrasures of the strong fortress beyond it.

*Narcissus* picked its way cautiously along the coast, hoisting American colours to avoid attracting too much attention. Two days after arriving, it boarded a Portuguese brig bound for Rio Grande and carrying the governor of the Chilean settlement of Valdivia. Also on board was an old Scots pilot named Russel, a lucky stroke as Popham was able to get some intelligence out of a former fellow countryman. Apart from giving tips about how to navigate the shallow, sandy-bottomed river, Russel planted another seed in Popham's mind by telling him a large sum of silver destined for Spain had just arrived in Buenos Aires.[34] Russel thought the city was only protected by a handful of militia and about 100 regulars, the rest of whom had been ordered to garrison Montevideo.[35] Russel's testimony confirmed a decision Popham had begun making ever since he had laid eyes on the mighty walls of Montevideo: Buenos Aires, the softer – and much richer – target, would be the first object of a British attack. Popham knew his activities in South America needed to make a big enough splash to win round the new government. Sending home a massive fortune in captured silver would, he calculated, do much more than capturing a single military fortress. The prospect of more prize money, obviously, also helped – even if it was not the most important factor in his decision.

First, though, Popham had to convince his army counterpart, and that meant waiting for HMS *Diadem* to arrive with Brigadier General Beresford. As soon as the squadron was reunited at Isla de Flores on 13 June, therefore, Popham immediately summoned a council of war. Beresford was not at all pleased with Popham's change of plan. He wanted to attack Montevideo first: although it was the stronger fortress, the enemy had not yet noticed the British ships in the river, and it made little sense, militarily speaking, to attack Buenos Aires when the Spanish could rely on a steady stream of reinforcements from Montevideo. In contrast, Popham argued that taking Buenos Aires – the capital of the viceroyalty – would strike a blow at the enemy's morale from which they might not recover. He further pressed that Buenos Aires had better supplies, which, after several weeks at sea, was no small consideration.[36] Neither man mentioned the silver – at least not officially – or the prospect of prize money, but Popham won the argument. The larger ships in the squadron would remain at the mouth of the Rio de la Plata to blockade Montevideo, while the smaller ships and troop transports would advance up the river to bring the attack to Buenos Aires.

The squadron split up on 15 June to put this plan into action. Popham shifted his flag again to *Narcissus*, this time accompanied by Beresford. The seamen who had been trained as infantry were divided up between *Narcissus*, *Encounter*, the transports with the shallowest drafts, and *Justina*, an East India Company vessel Popham had hired at St Helena.[37] *Diadem* remained behind to distract Montevideo, while *Raisonable* and *Diomede* cruised

---

34 Alexander Gillespie, *Gleanings and Remarks Collected during Many Months' Residence at Buenos Ayres* ... (Leeds: R. Dewhirst, 1819), p.41.
35 Popham to Marsden, 8 July 1806, Grainger, *The Royal Navy in the River Plate*, pp.40–42.
36 Ben Hughes, *The British Invasion of the River Plate, 1806–1807* (Barnsley: Pen & Sword Military, 2013), p.29; TNA: ADM 1/58, f.290; Popham to Marsden, 8 July 1806.
37 TNA: ADM 51/1615: log, HMS *Diadem*, 16 June 1806.

off the town of Maldonado – the next most significant military point on the coast – as a diversion.[38] It was not an easy journey: *Narcissus*, possibly one of the largest ships of war that had ever ventured so far up the river, struck ground almost immediately.[39] A few days later *Narcissus* struck again, in under three fathoms. This was Chico Bank, which was liberally covered in the remains of previous wrecks as a reminder of how difficult Buenos Aires was to attack from the river. At times the depth of the water alongside the ship was only 13 feet, and *Narcissus* only managed to get off the bank by offloading its guns into *Encounter*. All Popham's experience as a navigator in difficult, shallow waters was brought to bear. One witness remembered him as a hive of activity, with almost superhuman patience: 'Those trying occasions evinced a great equanimity of temper, and an unruffled genius, which uniformly marked and directed both his words, and his actions.' He transferred from *Narcissus* to *Encounter* every day to help his ships pick their way through the difficult conditions, directing operations personally.[40]

Only once did Popham betray his nerves. On 24 June, as the little squadron approached its target, Beresford issued general orders in which he announced that he had the authority of Sir David Baird to call himself a major general. Popham's own position in the order of naval seniority could be questioned, but until now he had been pretty sure of one thing: that he was equivalent in rank to Beresford, who had been a brigadier general during the campaign at the Cape. However, there had been a general brevet since the expedition had left Britain in July 1805, and Baird had decided to give Beresford the local rank of major general, trusting that he was only anticipating a promotion that had already occurred.[41] Through this promotion, Beresford overtook Popham in the joint Army-Navy hierarchy, automatically entitling him to a larger share of any prize money. This was almost certainly why Beresford waited two and a half months to announce his status to Popham, who exploded. 'If this proceeding is allowed to be established as a precedent,' Popham fulminated to the Secretary of the Admiralty, naval officers 'may be superseded in their relative rank by the whim or caprice of any general officer, not meaning, however' – he added, in a hilarious back-pedal – 'to apply this term to the present occasion.'[42] But he could do nothing to overturn this *fait accompli* and had to continue being civil to his military counterpart, although the atmosphere between the two men must have been somewhat strained.

By 25 June, the little force reached Buenos Aires. At this point the river was about 20 miles wide – about as wide as the narrowest part of the English Channel – and the flatness of the countryside meant the low, squat buildings of the city could only be made out through a good telescope. The river remained extremely shallow, and *Narcissus* could not get close enough to the shore to disembark troops. Popham took *Encounter*, a much smaller vessel, and the commandeered merchant vessel *Justina* in as close as he dared in the hope that they would at least be able to cover the disembarkation of the troops. By this time, the Spanish

---

38  TNA: ADM 1/58, f.290: Popham to Marsden, 8 July 1806. HMS *Leda* was still reconnoitring the Spanish American coast.
39  Richard Thompson, quoted in Grainger, *The Royal Navy in the River Plate*, p.34.
40  Gillespie, *Gleanings and Remarks*, p.42.
41  Baird to Colonel Gordon, 14 April 1806, quoted in [Hook], *The Life of Sir David Baird*, vol.2, p.140. In fact Beresford did not actually become a major general until April 1808.
42  Popham to Marsden, 24 June 1806, Grainger, *The Royal Navy in the River Plate*, pp.33–34.

Attack upon Buenos Aires by General Beresford, engraver unknown, 1806. (Public domain, Anne S.K. Brown Military Collection, Brown University Library)

had worked out something was going on: a fleet of shallow vessels came out to pester the British ships, and Popham saw a body of troops drawn up on the heights. The point Popham selected for disembarkation was Quilmes, about 10 miles from the city itself. Because even the transports could not get close enough to the strand, the troops had to wade through half a mile of waist-high muddy water, but after months of inaction, the prospect of finally doing something meant they were willing to face the discomfort. 'The poor fellows went on shore in the highest spirits imaginable,' one eyewitness recalled.[43] The men were landed unopposed during the evening of the 25th, as the winter light drew in and the night began to grow chilly.

The enemy now retreated about two miles along the beach to the village of Reduccion. In the falling darkness, Popham, scrutinising the shore from the deck of *Justina*, thought there was 'a fine plain between the two armies', which might be a good place for a pitched battle to secure a swift advance to the city. Daylight the next morning, however, revealed the 'plain' to be nothing more than 'a morass in a high state of verdure' – in other words, a swamp. At least the enemy did not attack, perhaps convinced that the swamp would prevent the British from going any further inland.[44] It did not. Beresford and his troops moved carefully towards the city, watched – but still not attacked – by Spanish forces. Only belatedly did they launch a brief assault before retreating across the River Chuelo, burning the

---

43 Quoted in Grainger, *The Royal Navy in the River Plate*, p.34.
44 Popham to Marsden, 8 July 1806, Grainger, *The Royal Navy in the River Plate*, p.38.

bridge behind them to slow the British down. But it was too late. The viceroy, the Marquis de Sobremonte, had already left Buenos Aires, retreating inland with as much treasure as he could lay his hands on, leaving the city in the hands of an aide-de-camp and a handful of soldiers and militia. On 27 June, once the British had crossed the Chuelo and taken position outside the city, Beresford summoned the viceroy's representative to surrender. Following a short negotiation, redcoats hoisted the British flag over the city walls on 28 June. The battery fired a royal salute, which was promptly returned by Popham's ships, lying in the river basin beyond.[45]

Popham had been watching everything from *Justina*, but rushed ashore the moment the smoke from the gunfire had cleared. Once he had congratulated Beresford and checked the surrender terms, he set to work. Where was the viceroy and, more importantly, the treasure? Intelligence from the stunned inhabitants suggested Sobremonte was about 60 miles away, 'certainly very much within the power of an active detachment'.[46] After a swift discussion with Popham, Beresford agreed to send Captain Robert Arbuthnot and six dragoons, along with 20 men from the 71st on horseback. Popham, who was seeing all his long-laid plans come to fruition at last, was very pleased. 'We have succeeded in taking the capital,' he wrote to Baird. 'The object of this country is much greater than my most sanguine expectations led me to conceive … This country is the greatest acquisition Great Britain has ever had, and I may say far exceeding all the extensive territory in the upper parts of India which the great [Lord] Wellesley acquired with so much loss of blood and treasure.'[47] The harbour, he reported, contained ships with cargoes amounting to 1.5 million Spanish dollars, which he had returned to their owners as 'an early record to the country of the great liberality of His Majesty's government'.[48] Popham's joy was considerably increased when a messenger from Captain Arbuthnot arrived on 8 July to report the viceroy's treasure had been found in the village of Lucan. It amounted to about half a million Spanish dollars in silver, which bulked out the treasure taken in Buenos Aires to a total of $1.3 million in public money (about £600,000).[49] Of this money alone, Baird, as military commander-in-chief, eventually took £16,500 in prize money; Popham and Beresford each expected to receive £12,600.[50]

The reality of the prize money he had been dreaming about for so long was enough to make Popham giddy. 'I think you will be fifty thousand pounds richer than the last time you shook me by the hand,' he gloated to Baird, 'and double that sum if we take Monte Video, which I am sure we could do immediately but that we have not troops to garrison both places.'[51] Still, behind Popham's delight, his awareness that the British lacked manpower was significant. Although things appeared tranquil, Popham and Beresford knew they faced the sullenness of shock rather than calm acceptance of the new status quo. This did not prevent Popham trying

---

45 Popham to Marsden, 8 July 1806, Grainger, *The Royal Navy in the River Plate*, pp.40–42; Marcus de la Poer Beresford, *Marshal William Carr Beresford* (Dublin: Irish Academic Press, 2018), pp.11–12.
46 Popham to Marsden, 8 July 1806, Grainger, *The Royal Navy in the River Plate*, pp.40–42
47 Popham to Baird, 6 July 1806, Grainger, *The Royal Navy in the River Plate*, p.36.
48 Popham to Marsden, 8 July 1806, Grainger, *The Royal Navy in the River Plate*, pp.37–39.
49 Popham to Marsden, 8 July 1806, Grainger, *The Royal Navy in the River Plate*, pp.40–42; Chris Coelho, *Pirates in Uniform: The Conspiracy to Invade Buenos Aires that Triggered a War* (privately published, 2019, e-book edition), n535.
50 *Northampton Mercury*, 27 September 1806.
51 Popham to Baird, 6 July 1806, Grainger, *The Royal Navy in the River Plate*, p.36.

to convince the Admiralty Board all was well. 'The natives of the [surrounding] villages … [are] perfectly satisfied,' he assured the Secretary of the Admiralty.[52] Popham later came to believe his own lies, but at this point he still felt success was precarious and made preparations for what might happen if the Spanish tried to retake Buenos Aires. Amid the barrage of letters he wrote to the Admiralty on 8 July was one defending the decision he had forced on Beresford to give up the attack on Montevideo, showing Popham still feared the British might be attacked in the rear by the fortress he had persuaded Beresford not to take.[53] Beresford had already asked the War Department for one regiment of dragoons and two regiments of infantry, and Popham now pressed the Admiralty Board to send him four frigates, three or four sloops, and 10 'of the largest gun brigs', including two or three large enough to carry mortars.[54] Popham had abandoned the fiction that his expedition simply aimed at diverting supplies of silver and other trade resources away from the enemy and into British markets. He was now trying to entrench Britain in the war of conquest he had so explicitly disclaimed.

But in the weeks that followed the British capture of Buenos Aires Popham only had a small amount of energy to devote to worrying. He alternated between visits ashore to confer with his military counterparts and indulging in a mammoth public relations exercise, writing letters to everyone he knew at home – newspaper editors, merchants, bankers, politicians, aristocrats, even the Prince of Wales.[55] 'I apprehend there are few instances to be had, none indeed that come within my knowledge, where such a conquest was obtained with so little loss and no expense,' Popham wrote proudly to Melville. As always, he laid emphasis on the value of the country to trade. The Rio de la Plata was 'within 60 or 70 days' sail of all the principal commercial countries on the face of the globe', placing Britain at a stroke at the centre of networks for tallow, copper, lead, tobacco, indigo, wool, and tanned hides. In return, South America would 'consume nearly two millions annually of our manufactures, and in a few words all the trade of this rich province will be turned from the channel of the enemy to our own country.'[56]

Most importantly, Popham wrote a circular addressed to the mayors and corporations of Britain's largest commercial cities, which his journalist contacts had published in the newspapers. It was pure propaganda: 'Hitherto the trade of this country has been cramped beyond belief, and the manufactures of Great Britain could only find their way to this rich province by means of neutral bottoms and contraband intrigues – but from this moment its trade will be thrown open.'[57] Popham was banking on his circular promoting interest among British merchants, which would in turn drive government policy. Many merchants received more personalised messages, particularly merchants from Popham's circle of friends and family, whom he encouraged to take full advantage of the new prospects on offer. One, Mr Holloway (allegedly Popham's brother-in-law), was given £100,000 by Alexander Davison

---

52 Popham to Marsden, 8 July 1806, Grainger, *The Royal Navy in the River Plate*, pp.40–42.
53 Popham to Marsden, 8 July 1806, Grainger, *The Royal Navy in the River Plate*, pp.39–40.
54 Popham to Marsden, 8 July 1806, Grainger, *The Royal Navy in the River Plate*, pp.40–42.
55 Royal Archives: GEO/Main/40624–40628: Popham to the Prince of Wales, 7 July 1806. Georgian Papers Online, <http://gpp.rct.uk>, accessed 28 September 2022.
56 Popham to Melville, 12 July 1806, Grainger, *The Royal Navy in the River Plate*, pp.45–46.
57 Popham to the Master of Lloyd's Coffee-House, 8 July 1806, *British Mercury or Wednesday Evening Post*, 24 September 1806.

– the man who had first introduced Popham to Miranda – to establish a business centre in Buenos Aires, trading partly in cotton.[58] Nor did Popham merely look after the business prospects of others. Advancing his country's well-being was always intimately tied with his own private interests, and his mercantile background meant he was well placed to know how best to exploit the new markets. 'An instance of the money-getting spirit of S[ir] Home came to my knowledge lately,' Lady Holland (whose Whig sympathies did not predispose her towards Popham) wrote in her diary. 'He wrote to the merchants of Manchester advising the exportation of certain goods, but to his own agent he bid him send him, upon speculation, a large quantity of silk stockings, with a hint that this order should not transpire.'[59]

Popham was aware he could rely on men like Baird who, on getting news of Popham's success, immediately prepared a ship of the line (HMS *Lancaster*) and a frigate (HMS *Medusa*) carrying two detachments of dragoons, ammunition, medical stores, and 2,000 men from the 38th and 47th Regiments of Foot under the command of Lieutenant Colonel Thomas Backhouse.[60] But Popham also knew his enemies at home were still at work, and that he could probably count the government among them. He had gambled his whole career on success at Buenos Aires – more so, indeed, than he had realised when he had set out in April in the belief that a friendly government was still at the helm. To emphasise the points he was making in his letters, therefore, Popham designed a grand display of the wealth of the country he had just invaded. He hesitated about whether to return home himself,[61] but eventually sent his voluminous dispatches and private letters home aboard HMS *Narcissus*. The ship was also stuffed to the gills with captured silver – $1,086,208 of the total $1,291,323 taken, some of which was kept back as a military treasury.[62] Popham gave Captain Donnelly strict instructions about how he wanted his victory to be portrayed before the British public. *Narcissus* arrived at Spithead on 15 September and Donnelly received a rapturous welcome. The treasure was carried from Spithead in eight wagons drawn by a cavalcade of 50 beribboned horses. Thirty sailors from the 'Royal Marine Battalion' rode alongside, flying captured Spanish colours and towing a captured cannon. On the outskirts of London they were met by Alexander Davison at the head of his volunteer corps, the Loyal Britons. They, and the Clapham Volunteers, gave the silver an honour guard through the city as onlookers lined the streets and crowded the windows. Davison's wife draped the wagons with two blue silk colours embroidered with the words '*Buenos Ayres – Popham – Beresford – Victory*' before the parade passed along the Strand to the Bank of England, 'followed by a great concourse of people, and accompanied by the exhilarating shouts of the multitude'.[63] Here the silver was weighed, and the crowd cheered when the Bank official announced that it amounted to 27 tons, 17 hundredweight, and four pounds.[64]

---

58  Herbert Compton (ed.), *A Master Mariner. Being the Life and Adventures of Captain Robert William Eastwick* (London: T. Fisher Unwin, 1891), p.220.
59  Earl of Ilchester (ed.), *The Journal of Elizabeth, Lady Holland* (London: Longmans, Green, and Co., 1908), vol.2, p.195.
60  Baird to Popham, 14 August 1806, Grainger, *The Royal Navy in the River Plate*, p.79; Baird to Beresford, 24 August 1806, Grainger, *The Royal Navy in the River Plate*, p.79; Hughes, *The British Invasion of the River Plate*, p.96.
61  Popham to Marsden, 20 July 1806, Grainger, *The Royal Navy in the River Plate*, p.50.
62  *Morning Post*, 15 September 1806.
63  *Morning Advertiser*, 22 September 1806; *Royal Cornwall Gazette*, 27 September 1806.
64  *Morning Herald*, 22 September 1806.

This attempt to woo the mercantile interest paid off: 10 days later, the City of London voted to bestow a ceremonial jewelled sword on Popham in thanks for his lucrative expedition.[65]

The Admiralty's response to all this pageantry was probably more mixed. Popham's old enemy St Vincent was not on the new Board, but a number of his supporters were, including Benjamin Tucker as Second Secretary and Rear Admiral Markham as one of the professional Lords of the Admiralty. Popham's April dispatches from St Helena declaring his intention to attack Buenos Aires – which arrived in London at the end of June – had hit the Admiralty Board like a ton of bricks. The First Lord sputtered to the Speaker of the House of Commons that Popham 'had left the Cape without a single ship of war'.[66] It took a month for the Admiralty Board to recover enough to order Popham home 'forthwith'.[67] To replace him, they sent out Rear Admiral Charles Stirling, without troops – at least not at first – but with supplies for the squadron and troops already *in situ*. He also carried a successor for Baird at the Cape, whose involvement in the South American scheme had not gone unnoticed.

Despite its initial horror, however, the government hedged its bets. It was not prepared to endorse what Popham had done directly, but the clear benefits of exploiting South America were too tempting. The government was feeling vulnerable and in need of the kind of boost a popular conquest might offer. The death of Charles James Fox, the Foreign Secretary and one of the most talented members of the ministry, threw his colleagues into chaos and disrupted peace negotiations that had been going on with France since July. When the first rumour of Buenos Aires' surrender arrived by telegraph on 12 September, therefore, the Prime Minister, Lord Grenville, wondered whether Buenos Aires might become a bargaining chip at the peace table in exchange for restoring the Kingdom of Naples.[68] Grenville's government was certainly fully on board with Popham's vision of the economic benefits of the new South American conquest. The Privy Council issued an order on 17 September announcing that British subjects and merchants from Buenos Aires could engage in trade on the same terms as in the West Indies, and planned to send out customs officers to collect duties.[69]

The government also, reluctantly at first but with gradually greater enthusiasm, began to plan further British expansion in South America. Another expedition was planned for Chile consisting of 3,000 men under Brigadier General Robert Craufurd; a second force under Major General Arthur Wellesley (the future Duke of Wellington) was intended to capture Manila, land at Mexico, and join with Craufurd in Panama before marching south.[70] Rear Admiral Stirling, who had been detained since July, finally sailed in mid-October with

---

65 *The Times*, 4 December 1807.
66 Charles, Lord Colchester (ed.), *The Diary and Correspondence of Charles Abbot, Lord Colchester …*, (London: John Murray, 1861), vol.2, p.73.
67 Admiralty Board to Popham, 28 July 1806, Grainger, *The Royal Navy in the River Plate*, p.112.
68 Grenville to Lord Lauderdale, 14 September 1806, *Dropmore MSS*, vol.8, p.333; Grenville to Lord Lauderdale, 22 September 1806, *Dropmore MSS*, vol.8, p.352; Grenville to Howick, 29 September 1806, *Dropmore MSS*, vol.8, pp.366–368.
69 Anon., *Full and Correct Report of the Trial of Sir Home Popham*, Appendix Note H; Lord Auckland to Grenville, 29 November 1806, *Dropmore MSS*, vol.8, p.449.
70 Grainger, *The Royal Navy in the River Plate*, pp.112–113.

3,000 men from the 40th and 87th Regiments of Foot, the 95th Rifles, and the 17th Light Dragoons as reinforcements for Beresford.[71] This was exactly what Popham had hoped would happen, and in fact to do anything else would have been out of step with the reaction of the country. As Grenville himself admitted, 'The capture of Buenos Ayres, trumpeted up as it has been by Popham and his agents, has already produced such an impression here as will make the surrender of that conquest most extremely difficult.'[72] While the government was not about to crown Popham the hero of the hour, the nation's joyful response to the fall of Buenos Aires muted its reaction to what he had done. Although the Admiralty Board therefore disapproved 'a measure of such importance being undertaken without the sanction of His Majesty's Government', its members were 'nevertheless pleased to express their entire approbation of [Popham's] judicious, able, and spirited conduct'.[73]

The fall of Buenos Aires was certainly wonderful news at a time when reports from the continent were nearly all grim. Manchester was one of many cities that passed a resolution thanking Popham for his exertions, noting that 'the Commercial advantages [of his conquest were] ... extensive beyond calculation'.[74] Merchants immediately began putting together private fleets to exploit the new market Popham had promised them. The newspapers were full of advertisements calling for ships, passengers, or crew. 'Direct for Buenos Ayes, the fast-sailing ship *Eleanor* ... has excellent Accommodations for Passengers. Three-fourths of her Cargo positively engaged';[75] the *Lancaster, Ellen, William Heathcote, Jane, Lady Frances, Lady Carleton*, and *Crisis*, all sailing from Manchester, all advertised for passengers, goods, and freight at the same time;[76] and the *Morning Herald* helpfully provided a list of items most in demand on the new market: 'light western woollen cloths, printed linens ... hardware, rings of small value, and buttons ... plated Sheffield goods ... flowered cotton and Manchester velvets ... the muslins, calicoes, cottons'.[77] Even auction houses wanted in. One newspaper advertised the necklaces, gold seals, keychains, pencil cases, oyster forks, and other miscellaneous plate and necklaces confiscated from a bankrupt jeweller as being 'well calculated for the market of Buenos Ayres'.[78] Over 100 merchant vessels set sail for South America after the publication of Popham's circular.[79] One contemporary recalled it 'set every broken-down clerk and supercargo on the *qui vive*, emptied all the stores in Manchester and Liverpool, and sent us out as much long cloths, printed calicoes, and sheetings, as would have reached across the Pampas to St Jago'. However, they 'all arrived a day after the fair'.[80] By the time news of Buenos Aires had reached Britain, and long before the first merchant ships had even thought of setting sail, the 'fair' was already over.

---

71  Hughes, *The British Invasion of the River Plate*, Appendix I, p.226.
72  Grenville to Lord Lauderdale, 22 September 1806, *Dropmore MSS*, vol.8, p.352.
73  Anon., *Full and Correct Report of the Trial of Sir Home Popham*, pp.79–80.
74  Grainger, *The Royal Navy in the River Plate*, p.125.
75  *Public Ledger and Daily Advertiser*, 7 October 1806.
76  *Manchester Mercury*, 30 September 1806.
77  *Morning Herald*, 18 September 1806.
78  *Morning Advertiser*, 28 October 1806.
79  Hughes, *The British Invasion of the River Plate*, p.85.
80  W[ilkie], 'Recollections of the British Army, no.2', p.198.

## 13

## Disaster, 1806

*2259: The enemy is coming out*

Back in Buenos Aires, the British forces were not nearly as secure as Popham had tried to make out in his dispatches. For one thing, his sailors were freezing from the lack of proper slops, since apparently nobody had pointed out to Popham that it was the middle of winter in July.[1] The lack of provisions was a continuing problem. Now that Buenos Aires was in British hands, it was cut off from the provinces, and no meat was being brought to market any more. Popham had found a source of salt beef from a British merchant in the city, but even this was two years old and Popham urged more to be sent from the West Indies, India, the Mediterranean, even the Cape, which – according to Popham's original reasons for invading South America – should have been benefiting from Buenos Aires' rich provisions rather than the other way round. There was also little wheat and wine had to be purchased from Paraguay.[2] Even water had to be brought in from outside the city.[3] Popham was already going on the defensive in his dispatches home, warning the Admiralty there was a 'spirit of enterprise being excited by French intrigue' in Buenos Aires.[4] He was not wrong about the coming resistance, although he was mistaken about it being French in origin: Spanish forces were being secretly raised in the localities. Convinced any major challenge would come from Montevideo, however, Popham returned to *Diadem*, still blockading the fortress town with *Raisonable*, *Diomede*, and *Leda*. Aware that Buenos Aires was still not safe, he sent the transport *Walker* to reconnoitre the north channel of the river and the gun brig *Encounter* to watch the passes between the northern and southern shore at Conchas.[5] HMS *Leda* anchored 12 miles off Buenos Aires to watch the city, and Popham sent *Raisonable* to Rio de Janeiro for provisions and naval stores, anchors, and cables.[6]

On 31 July Beresford asked Popham to keep an eye on a miscellaneous local force under the command of a Franco-Spanish nobleman, Santiago de Liniers, who had been mustering troops in the vicinity of Montevideo. Meanwhile, Beresford himself went

---

1  Popham to Marsden, 8 July 1806, Grainger, *The Royal Navy in the River Plate*, p.42.
2  Popham to Marsden, 9 July 1806, Grainger, *The Royal Navy in the River Plate*, pp.43–44.
3  Popham to Marsden, 19 July 1806, Grainger, *The Royal Navy in the River Plate*, pp.49–50.
4  Popham to Marsden, 20 July 1806, Grainger, *The Royal Navy in the River Plate*, p.50.
5  Popham to Marsden, 19 July 1806, Grainger, *The Royal Navy in the River Plate*, pp.49–50.
6  Popham to Captain Rowley, 27 July 1806, Grainger, *The Royal Navy in the River Plate*, pp.51–52.

View of Buenos Aires from the Plaza de Toros, by Emeric Essex Vidal, 1820. (Public domain, Rare Book Division, The New York Public Library)

to meet another force of 1,500 rebels being raised at Pedriel by a local dignitary, Juan Martin de Pueyrredon, and defeated it easily on 1 August.[7] This was, however, only a distraction for the main event. A huge storm hit on 3 August – 'a dreadful hurricane', in the words of one witness – dispersing the British ships in the river.[8] Popham immediately understood this might give any Spanish forces wanting to approach Buenos Aires from Montevideo an opportunity to do so unmolested. While *Diadem* struck its topgallant masts in an effort to ride out the storm, Popham transferred to *Encounter* and tried to bring it as close to the shore as possible, but the easterly wind was too strong. Visibility was also terrible, obscuring Popham's view of whatever might be going on ashore. Now thoroughly worried, Popham sent King out with 150 men from *Diadem* in a galivat (a small two-masted ship) with the intention of manning some gunboats, but the weather blew them back too. The storm continued throughout 4 August, until finally the wind dropped sufficiently on the 5th to allow Popham to reach HMS *Leda*. Here, to his horror, he discovered Liniers had taken advantage of the storm to escape Montevideo with his men, braving the weather to cross the river at Colonia under the nose of the British schooner watching the ford.[9] Three thousand men were on their way to attack Beresford at Buenos Aires.

Popham immediately began organising for battle, sending all the Marine Blues under King ashore to take command of the gun vessels at Buenos Aires. The wind, however,

---

7   Popham to Marsden, 25 August 1806, Grainger, *The Royal Navy in the River Plate*, pp.59–65.
8   Ensign Gavin of the marines, quoted in Grainger, *The Royal Navy in the River Plate*, p.52.
9   Popham to Marsden, 25 August 1806, Grainger, *The Royal Navy in the River Plate*, pp.59–65.

picked up again into a proper hurricane. The *Walker* transport lost its rudder; five of the six gunboats were washed ashore; *Diadem*'s launch and barge sank, as did *Leda*'s launch and another small vessel. As King wrote to Popham, this was 'a loss not to be repaired at this present time'.[10] Popham, still aboard HMS *Leda*, could do little to help; *Leda* was itself in great danger, clinging on in as little as four fathoms with two anchors and its yard and top-masts struck.[11] On 8 August, the storm turned into heavy rain, which still prevented Popham from being able to see anything on shore. Totally blind and cut off, Popham could only speculate about what was going on. He consoled himself with the knowledge that the rain made the roads 'totally impracticable for anything but cavalry' – although this also meant Beresford could not leave Buenos Aires, even if he needed to.[12]

Popham remained in this tense state of limbo for several days. He heard that King had taken advantage of a slight lull in the storm to gather all the small craft and schooners he could find and make his way to San Isidro point, still about four miles from the town but 'the best possible situation to interrupt the army if they attempted to approach the town at low water'. Here King found the enemy flotilla of six gunboats, three armed schooners, and two launches, but could not get close enough to inflict any damage.[13] King could just about make out the enemy forces still camped inland, but two days later they disappeared overnight and he sent an emergency message to Beresford to warn him something was up. Beresford ordered King to send *Walker* to Colonia to watch the roads, but shortly after sent a further message that the enemy was entering the city and he was under attack. King immediately set out in *Encounter* with two armed schooners and worked painstakingly back along the shore against the wind, but darkness fell before he could make sufficient progress and he was forced to anchor for the night in two and three-quarter fathoms.[14]

Popham was still aboard *Leda*, pacing up and down the quarterdeck. He knew something was happening on shore – the wind carried across the sound of crackling muskets and the deep rumble of cannon-fire – but, cut off by the weather and the shallowness of the river, he was infuriatingly powerless. On the morning of 11 August, King sent a message saying Spanish colours had been hoisted on the walls of the city. Popham immediately had a boat winched onto the river and went ashore, while the other ships in the squadron started firing on the Spanish outposts. Here, with the sound of cannons uncomfortably close, King filled his commander in on the details. It was worse than Popham could have imagined. On 10 August, Liniers had entered Buenos Aires and fought the British back to Plaza de Toros. The citizens threw their lot enthusiastically in with the liberators. For Popham, who had somehow managed to convince himself that the inhabitants had simply been comparatively restrained in expressing full-throated support for the British invaders, this was the ultimate treachery. 'The inhabitants were all armed and sheltered on the tops of the houses and churches with the design of carrying on a war of ambush,' he fulminated to Marsden. The enemy's aim had been 'to avoid by every means a general action and to place his men in such a situation that they could fire at our troops,

---

10  King to Popham, 12 August 1806, Grainger, *The Royal Navy in the River Plate*, p.54.
11  Popham to Marsden, 25 August 1806, Grainger, *The Royal Navy in the River Plate*, pp.59–65.
12  Popham to Marsden, 25 August 1806, Grainger, *The Royal Navy in the River Plate*, pp.59–65.
13  King to Popham, 9 August 1806, Grainger, *The Royal Navy in the River Plate*, p.54.
14  King to Popham, 12 August 1806, Grainger, *The Royal Navy in the River Plate*, pp.54–55.

while they remained in perfect security themselves.'[15] Beresford had tried signalling to Popham to send boats to evacuate the British forces at Ensenada, but the poor weather had obscured everything, and none of the British ships could have moved anyway. Beresford and his men had retreated to the castle, the last stronghold of the city, and as far as King knew, they were still there waiting to be rescued.

It was the worst possible outcome for the campaign, particularly as Popham had spent the last weeks feeding home triumphant reports of success. But he did not have time to think about the long-term consequences of what had happened. His priority was to get the British out of Buenos Aires if it was still possible to do so. However, the weather continued to conspire against him. King reported that he had already tried to move *Encounter* closer to the shore to harass the enemy, but the wind had increased again and 'nothing could be done'. All King had been able to do was send some schooners ahead to collect any sick and wounded British soldiers that might have escaped the city. Even as Popham laid plans to embark the wounded and cross the Riachuelo towards Ensenada, the weather worsened still more and the ships spent another uneasy night: one of them, the commandeered merchant vessel *Justina*, was 'nearly on her beam ends, and very little water under her'.[16]

At 8:00 a.m. on 12 August, the wind dropped sufficiently for Popham to order *Encounter* closer to the shore, ready to engage if the water should rise high enough. King spent the next two hours getting the schooners and the gunboats that had not been wrecked over the last few days in place, and at 10:00 a.m. the ships began bombarding the city harbour. It was too little, too late. Around the time King had been manoeuvring his boats, the Spanish had begun a last push on the British in the castle, wheeling down three pieces of artillery. Lieutenant Colonel Denis Pack and the 71st succeeded in disabling the guns, but the citizens sheltered themselves again on the roofs of the houses and the enemy brought another gun onto the roof of one of the local churches. At 1:00 p.m. King saw a flag of truce hoisted on the castle walls, and shortly afterwards he received a message from Beresford ordering him to stop firing. The gunboats immediately made weigh and any British boats remaining in the harbour began to work their way out while there was still time for them to escape. But the citizens of Buenos Aires, who had spent the past three or four weeks under the British yoke, did not respect the truce. Popham later heard that 10,000 men entered the castle square and continued shooting at the British, forcing Beresford to threaten to return fire if they did not stop. The same thing was happening as the British gunboats tried to get away: the Spanish brought a cannon down to the strand and began firing on them as they retreated. The schooner *Belem* ran aground and had to be abandoned; the merchantman *Justina* could not get out of the harbour in time; and a gunboat and a smaller vessel were also left behind. At least the marines inside the city managed to get away and were embarked by *Encounter* at Ensenada, after spiking two fieldpieces and throwing them into the river.[17]

Popham must have been having flashbacks to Ostend in 1798, when he had watched fruitlessly as Major General Coote and nearly every single one of his men had been swept up by the enemy. The casualties at Buenos Aires were worse. A total of 164 men had been

---

15   Popham to Marsden, 25 August 1806, Grainger, *The Royal Navy in the River Plate*, pp.59–65.
16   King to Popham, 12 August 1806, Grainger, *The Royal Navy in the River Plate*, pp.54–55.
17   King to Popham, 12 August 1806, Grainger, *The Royal Navy in the River Plate*, pp.54–55; Popham to Marsden, 25 August 1806, Grainger, *The Royal Navy in the River Plate*, pp.59–65.

killed and a further 115 wounded: nearly every single man had been captured, including a significant number of Marine Blues from the squadron. As at Ostend, Popham could not believe the enemy had anything in mind other than an exchange of prisoners. He therefore immediately set sail with his flotilla for Montevideo, where he hoped a show of force, in addition to the blockade that had been in place for some weeks, would encourage the Spanish military commander there to intercede with his counterpart at Buenos Aires on Beresford's behalf. Believing he had the upper hand, Popham imperiously reminded Montevideo's governor, in a thinly veiled threat, that he still had about 100 Spanish prisoners aboard the squadron.[18] This set the tone for a lengthy, and futile, correspondence over the next few weeks. At first, Popham thought he was making headway: he received a letter from Beresford requesting him to send transports to Buenos Aires to collect the troops. Popham duly sent the *Triton*, *Willingdon*, *Walker*, and *Ocean* transports to St Iago, near Ensenada. However, every day the enemy gave new reasons not to embark the prisoners, until at the end of the month Popham received a letter from the Spanish telling him a local *felucca* had been chased and fired on by British ships, as a result of which the Spanish had no choice but to renew hostilities.[19] This, Popham fulminated to the commander of Montevideo, was 'a low, vicious, contemptible falsehood, a mere fabrication, to serve a purpose unworthy the character of any nation whatever'.[20] But he had no choice but to call the transports away, empty.

Had Popham only known it, the whole business was already pointless: Beresford and his men were no longer in Buenos Aires. The locals, encouraged by their victory over the British, had decided it was time to rebel against Spain. An emergency *cabildo* (gathering of notables) voted to refuse viceroy Sobremonte's re-entry into the city and elected Liniers to leadership instead. Aware there would be reprisals for the attack on Beresford, Liniers and the *cabildo* started putting together a much larger army – by October, 8,500 men had been raised – and the British prisoners of war were progressively moved inland.[21] Between the beginning of September and the beginning of October, the men were marched out of Buenos Aires in small groups and moved several hundred miles away.[22] This was a clear violation of the treaty of surrender, but Popham had himself helped seal the fate of Beresford's men. His so-called 'diplomacy' had been on full display throughout, and in the wake of the incident with the *felucca* he indulged in an orgy of name-calling. The Spanish refusal to release Beresford was 'a real piece of knavery'; Liniers was an 'assassin'; 'murders' had been committed; Spanish behaviour was 'immoral' and 'irreligious'. In the end Popham abandoned all pretence at subtlety and simply threatened to blow the Spanish and their city to kingdom come, since '[acts of violence were] sometimes considered necessary … under the confidence of its ultimately becoming an act of humanity, from saving many by the

---

18    Popham to the Governor of Montevideo, 15 August 1806, Grainger, *The Royal Navy in the River Plate*, p.58.
19    Juan Gutierrez de la Concha to Popham, 29 August 1806, Grainger, *The Royal Navy in the River Plate*, p.67.
20    Popham to the governor of Montevideo, 4 September 1806, Grainger, *The Royal Navy in the River Plate*, pp.68–70.
21    Hughes, *The British Invasion of the River Plate*, pp.88–95.
22    John D. Grainger, *British Campaigns in the South Atlantic, 1805–1807* (Barnsley: Pen & Sword, 2015), p.119.

sacrifice of a few'.[23] As Popham's successor noted when he looked over the correspondence, it 'was of such a nature as [to] put all idea of conciliation out of the question'.[24]

Inevitably, Popham's thoughts were already turning away from Beresford's plight and towards the problem of how the news of Buenos Aires' re-capture might be received at home. He still did not know the full details of the Whig ministry that had been formed in February, and he had not heard from home once since leaving Britain the previous July. A few weeks after Beresford's capture, however, Popham finally found out who his new boss was at the Admiralty: Lord Howick (although Popham did not realise his information was already out of date, as Howick had been replaced in September 1806 by Thomas Grenville, the Prime Minister's brother). Howick was the son of General Sir Charles Grey, Popham's military patron since 1793, but he was also one of the most virulent anti-Pittites in the Foxite camp, and Popham's heart must have sunk on learning the identity of the First Lord. His letter to Howick of 29 August had a double purpose of testing the political waters and talking up his own merits. It was a remarkable piece of political wriggling. He began with an apology for his own politics: 'I must ever acknowledge with extreme gratitude the signal marks which I have invariably received of Mr Pitt's confidence and personal attachment.' Despite this, Popham hastened to assure Howick this personal attachment did not mean he could not perform well under a different political master. He finished with his usual dash of professional patriotism, hoping Howick would be 'satisfied my humble talents and professional acquirements have been in every instance most zealously and actively debated to advance in totality the public service'.[25]

Having done his best to win round the First Lord, Popham also needed to write to the Admiralty Board. This was by far the harder task, and it showed. He wrote with the air of a man making his last speech at the foot of the gallows: 'When the events of war cease to be favourable to any armament, I consider it the duty of commanding officers to state all the circumstances under their knowledge or information with clearness and perspicacity, which either progressively or suddenly led to a reversal of fortune.' While Popham took full credit for taking Buenos Aires, he was at pains to stress that losing it had not been his fault. It had only happened because of 'deliberate acts of treachery and perfidy … how little dependence there is to be placed in the most sacred treaty made with a Spaniard'! Instead of gratitude for their liberators, the locals had all along been secretly plotting rebellion. Presciently, Popham predicted Spain would regret everything that had happened, as the 'mob' that had turned against their British overlords would just as soon turn on the colonial authority. He waxed lyrical in depicting Beresford's 'last efforts to induce the enemy to a general engagement in the great square, his gallant little army falling fast by shots from invisible persons, and the only alternative which could present itself to save the useless effusion of so much valuable blood was a flag of truce', clearly hoping the pathos would transform the Admiralty

---

23 Popham to the governor of Montevideo, 19 September 1806, Anon., *Full and Correct Report of the Trial of Sir Home Popham*, Appendix Note D.
24 Rear Admiral Stirling, quoted in Grainger, *The Royal Navy in the River Plate*, p.181.
25 DUA: GRE/B49/1: Popham to Lord Howick, 29 August 1806.

Board's anger into admiration.²⁶ Even so, Popham waited until 3 September to send his dispatches by HMS *Diomede*, allegedly because he had to wait for some of his squadron to come back with water but mainly because he was reluctant to send home bad news.²⁷

Popham still expected the government to fight for Buenos Aires – if only because, as a result of his July circular, a fleet of merchant ships was surely on its way. The only question was how long his squadron could hold out before reinforcements arrived. Provisions were a real problem now Buenos Aires was overtly hostile, and Popham's men were beginning to show signs of scurvy.²⁸ Completely blind to reality, Popham informed Howick that the British might reclaim the initiative in South America if they captured Montevideo and announced their intention to help Buenos Aires free itself of Spanish shackles. Fomenting colonial rebellion was absolutely not British government policy, but Popham refused to admit his mission might have been a foolish waste of time, money, and men. He still insisted Britain would emerge from the mess a winner in the long-term strategic game: 'This country is at present lost to Spain and [its] trade [is] likely to be annihilated for a considerable time.'²⁹

Charles, 2nd Earl Grey, by Samuel Cousins after Thomas Lawrence, 1828. (Public domain)

Popham was the more desperate to win Howick's support because he had finally received dispatches from the Admiralty. What they contained chilled him: the Admiralty Board had expressed its 'unqualified disapprobation … of every part' of his conduct. Popham was uncharacteristically anxious; he knew he was in real trouble. In a desperate attempt to pre-empt further disapproval, Popham began writing directly to Lord Howick with semi-regularity – his usual trick when caught in a pinch was to bypass the chain of command and go straight to the top. He desperately reeled off a list of transparent excuses: everything he had done had been for the good of the country; his former services had always been stellar; Lord Nelson himself had approved his signalling system; and he had formerly enjoyed the 'protection … with which I was long honoured' by Howick's father Lord Grey – bare-faced cheek, but Popham's last trump in a losing game. Desperate, he fell back on his old theme

---

26  Popham to Marsden, 25 August 1806, Grainger, *The Royal Navy in the River Plate*, pp.59–65.
27  Popham to Marsden, 3 September 1806, Grainger, *The Royal Navy in the River Plate*, p.68.
28  Popham to Marsden, 3 October 1806, Grainger, *The Royal Navy in the River Plate*, p.87.
29  Popham to Howick, 9 September 1806, Grainger, *The Royal Navy in the River Plate*, pp.75–77.

of persecution and warned Howick not to listen to rumours spread by men jealous of his success: 'I know, my lord, I have many enemies'.[30]

Popham told the First Lord he intended to stay in the Rio de la Plata as long as necessary. He made a show of reluctance about not coming home, but in fact he did not want to leave. His only hope was that a sufficiently stunning success might offset everything that had happened; with his 'many enemies' looking forward to gobbling him up whole the moment he stepped back on home shores, he had to make sure he stuck in their gullet. He was, however, in no position to make any move against the Spanish without help. Luckily, the 2,000 men Baird had sent from the Cape of Good Hope started to arrive at the beginning of October. It was not enough for a full attempt to re-capture Buenos Aires, but Popham had already decided his best bet was to take Montevideo. Two and a half months after he had talked Beresford out of just such an attack, Popham was tacitly admitting his military counterpart may have had a point about the need for a fortified stronghold on the coast from which the British could launch future assaults.

Popham knew his career hung on the success of the operation and was ready to take risks. Lieutenant Colonel Thomas Backhouse, however, who commanded the reinforcements, was – not unreasonably, given recent shenanigans – much more cautious than Popham liked, and the two men quickly clashed. Popham wanted to use his squadron to blockade the town as a distraction while the troops landed further away and marched along the coast. Backhouse, mindful of how well that strategy had gone down at Buenos Aires, preferred to land his troops as close as possible to Montevideo while the squadron covered the landing with a bombardment.[31] Popham, however, doubted his ships could get close enough to the fortress to make much impact. He interpreted Backhouse's refusal to follow his instructions to the letter as 'natural torpitude' and complained to Howick that he had 'little confidence' in the man.[32] This did not bode well either for cooperation or for success, but the two of them managed to thrash out a compromise. Backhouse would land at Montevideo; *Leda* and *Medusa*, with the *Triton*, *Charlotte*, and *Hero* transports, would bombard the town in line, protected by the *Encounter* and *Protector* gunboats. *Lancaster* and *Diomede*, both larger ships, would add to the bombardment from further out.[33] Popham was not entirely happy with the arrangement, but in any case heavy winds prevented anything being done at all until 28 October, when the wind swung to a more favourable easterly direction. At 10:00 a.m. Popham made the signal to bombard the north gate of the fortress, but because of the wind and the shallowness of the river the larger ships could not get close enough to assist the smaller gunboats; *Leda* touched bottom and had to retreat further out to avoid getting beached.[34]

As his ships clearly could do little damage to the fortress walls, Popham now 'proposed to Colonel Backhouse, indeed pressed it on him' to take the town of Maldonado' (Backhouse later claimed taking Maldonado had been his idea, but whether this was because Popham had

---

30   Popham to Howick, 29 September 1806, Grainger, *The Royal Navy in the River Plate*, pp.85–86.
31   Popham to Baird, 17 November 1806, Grainger, *The Royal Navy in the River Plate*, p.102.
32   Popham to Howick, 4 November 1806, Grainger, *The Royal Navy in the River Plate*, p.99.
33   Popham to Marsden, 9 October 1806, Grainger, *The Royal Navy in the River Plate*, p.89.
34   Grainger, *The Royal Navy in the River Plate*, p.84.

Plan of the town and harbour of Montevideo, 1807. (Public domain)

planted the suggestion in his head or was simply inflating his own importance is unclear).[35] Maldonado was a peninsula guarding the northern entrance to the Rio de la Plata, about 80 miles from Montevideo. This was hardly next door, but the town was easily defensible from the island of Goritti and would probably suit the British as a fortress in which to hunker down and await reinforcements, and in any case Popham was more worried about immediate impact than long-term effects.[36] On 29 October, the men of the 38th Regiment were shuffled onto *Leda* and *Medusa* and Popham, in *Diadem*, accompanied them to Maldonado. The little squadron arrived at 5:00 p.m. The elements were, for once, in Popham's favour: the wind was not too strong, the beach seemed smooth, and the embarkation began immediately, with the troops bulked out with marines from *Medusa* and the remaining Marine Blues. The British advance faced little resistance, and by 8:00 p.m. the force of 400 men had captured the town with only two killed and four wounded. The island of Goritti surrendered shortly after, and its batteries now protected the British ships in the roadstead.[37]

The capture of Maldonado was a crumb of good news to offset the Buenos Aires disaster. Even at his most optimistic, however, Popham knew the British position was desperate. Although his intelligence sources suggested Montevideo was only defended by 700 militiamen, a band of 3,000 'rabble' from the countryside, and some European privateers under the command of a Frenchman named Mordelle (nicknamed 'Maincourt' as he only had one arm), Popham was not going to make the same mistake he had at Buenos Aires of underestimating the strength of local resistance.[38] He held well back from a fresh assault on Montevideo; instead, he positioned his squadron to ensure a swift re-embarkation from Maldonado in case of emergency. HMS *Raisonable* and three armed transports moved in close to the shore to defend the squadron's source of water and cover any retreat; a battery of 18-pounder guns was constructed in the sandhills overlooking the fortress.[39] In this uneasy position, Popham and his men waited for more men, and ships, to rescue them, knowing the Spanish would not wait long before attacking.

If Popham had learned something from the Buenos Aires debacle, however, he had not learned enough. When Buenos Aires was first re-captured he had told Lord Howick that any 'trifling errors' he might have committed had been totally offset by his 'excess of zeal for the public service'.[40] Now, in mid-November, riding in HMS *Diadem* off Maldonado, Popham was just as sure any attempt to blame him for what had happened was wholly attributable to a desire for 'political revenge'. 'If I had not been a partisan of Lord Melville's or Mr Pitt's,' he told Baird, 'we should have had long e'er this dispatches, generals, reinforcements, and everything necessary in a service on a most extended scale.'[41] And yet he knew political fortunes were transient, and he was naturally optimistic. He hoped for a speedy restoration

---

35 Popham to Marsden, 28 October 1806, Grainger, *The Royal Navy in the River Plate*, pp.89–91; Backhouse to Windham, 31 October 1806, Grainger, *The Royal Navy in the River Plate*, p.97.
36 Popham to Marsden, 28 October 1806, Grainger, *The Royal Navy in the River Plate*, pp.89–91.
37 Popham to Marsden, 30 October 1806, Grainger, *The Royal Navy in the River Plate*, pp.94–95; Backhouse to Windham, 31 October 1806, Grainger, *The Royal Navy in the River Plate*, pp.97–98.
38 Popham to Admiral Stirling, 6 December 1806, Grainger, *The Royal Navy in the River Plate*, pp.183–84.
39 Memorandum, 9 November 1806, Grainger, *The Royal Navy in the River Plate*, p.100.
40 Popham to Howick, 29 September 1806, Grainger, *The Royal Navy in the River Plate*, p.85.
41 Popham to Baird, 17 November 1806, Grainger, *The Royal Navy in the River Plate*, p.102.

of the Pittites, who would forgive any trespasses he might have committed: 'The time ...may come when all will be right again, and it may be our watch upon deck.'[42]

At the end of November, Popham finally received a letter from Rear Admiral Charles Stirling announcing his approach with reinforcements and supplies. Both troops and provisions were desperately needed, but Stirling was a much more senior officer, which meant Popham would be forced to strike his flag as commodore. The rest of the campaign would be under Stirling's direction, not his. Still, playing second fiddle was much better than being sent home to face a hostile Admiralty, and it never crossed Popham's mind that he might not simply be taken under Stirling's command.[43] When Stirling arrived at the beginning of December in HMS *Sampson*, therefore, having rushed ahead of his own squadron after receiving news of the fall of Buenos Aires, Popham welcomed him warmly. Stirling and Popham had already met once, in 1784, when Popham had still been under the tutelage of Captain Thompson. Stirling later admitted he had never liked Popham's 'professional, or public character much', but initially everything between them was civil enough.[44] The two men had several conferences to discuss strategy, and Popham updated Stirling on the situation facing the British in Maldonado. This professionalism, however, lasted only up until the moment Stirling dropped his bombshell. During one strategy meeting, when Popham kept talking about 'we' and outlining his plans for his personal involvement in future operations, Stirling handed Popham the Admiralty orders of 28 July ordering him home 'forthwith' and told him he had ordered HMS *Sampson* to take him home with a convoy in tow, calling in at the Cape and St Helena on the way.

Going home was the last thing Popham wanted to do, since he knew what would be waiting for him on his return – at best, unemployment; at worst, disgrace and the possibility of being cashiered (had he been aware that a government official had said 'If Popham is not shot, we deserve to be conquered everywhere, both at sea and on land, and in negotiation', he might have added the prospect of losing his life).[45] For a short while he appears to have been speechless. Eventually he managed to observe that the Cape and St Helena were 'a long way about', but was too shocked to say anything else. He did ask if he might go home in HMS *Diomede* rather than HMS *Sampson*, as he thought *Diomede* might go directly to St Helena while *Sampson* took the slower route with the convoy to the Cape, but Stirling said he did not have the option to lose two ships at the same time.[46]

Stirling thought there was nothing more to say, but, as he himself confessed, he did not really know Popham. Popham, who had moved to HMS *Raisonable* to give way for Stirling aboard *Diadem,* began to plan the best way to avoid going home. His first expedient was to play up his usefulness in a river with such difficult navigation. In response to any objection regarding the fact that he had been ordered home by the Admiralty, he resorted to a familiar scheme when he did not have direct orders to be somewhere but wanted to be in on

---

42    Popham to Baird, 17 November 1806, Grainger, *The Royal Navy in the River Plate*, p.102.
43    Popham to Edward Gorman, 30 November 1806, *The Royal Navy in the River Plate*, p.106.
44    NMM: MRK/102/7/8: Stirling to Admiral Markham, 27 December 1806.
45    Henry Brougham to Lord Rosslyn, 3 October 1806, in Henry Brougham, *The Life and Times of Henry, Lord Brougham, written by himself* (Edinburgh: William Blackwood and Sons, 1871), vol.1, pp.357–358.
46    Stirling to Marsden, 12 December 1806, *The Royal Navy in the River Plate*, pp.193–194.

the action anyway – he offered to be Stirling's unofficial aide-de-camp. When this approach did not work, Popham deployed the sarcasm. He reminded Stirling that the Admiralty order for his recall used the word 'forthwith': 'certainly according to the explanation of the first writers on the English language, the word "forthwith" particularly used on this occasion means *quickly*', which was incompatible with being sent home with a slow-moving convoy due to stop at the Cape and St Helena. And yet, in the same breath as Popham asked to be allowed to sail home more quickly, he also begged for permission to wait – for news, for a quicker ship, for his business accounts on shore and at Rio to be cleared.[47]

Under these circumstances Stirling, who thought he had issued Popham with an order and that was that, began to lose patience. But it was Popham, not Stirling, who put the first foot wrong. He again asked to go home directly rather than with *Sampson* and the convoy, but urged Stirling to allow it because slowing his journey would deprive him of his constitutional right to defend himself swiftly – which showed his awareness of a likely prosecution waiting for him at home.[48] When Stirling called Popham's bluff, saying he would happily detain *Sampson* for 24 hours to allow Popham to sort out his affairs, Popham made a serious tactical mistake: he lost his temper.[49] In stunningly insubordinate language, he flatly denied Stirling had the legal power to compel him to go via the Cape and St Helena and threatened to open legal proceedings against him if he tried to force the issue.[50] When Stirling continued to ignore him, Popham asked if Stirling meant to use force to compel him to board *Sampson*. A horrified Stirling replied it was a startlingly ungentlemanly thing to suppose he might use force on 'an officer of your rank and consequence to the state'. Nevertheless, this time it was Stirling who had made a mistake: his words meant he could *order* Popham to leave, but not enforce it. Popham immediately announced he intended to leave aboard HMS *Rolla*, an American merchantman bought into the Royal Navy. Stirling was so relieved Popham was leaving at all that he was inclined to overlook the fact Popham was ostentatiously planning to do so in any ship but the one Stirling had earmarked for him.[51] 'Farewell!' Stirling wrote to Popham, with palpable relief. 'I heartily wish you a good passage; and that you may long enjoy domestic felicity.'[52]

Officially, Stirling excused Popham's temporising to the Admiralty Board as a hope that future 'active operations' might give him an opportunity to redeem himself, and that was almost certainly part of the story.[53] Privately, however, Stirling guessed Popham was waiting for news from the merchantmen galvanised by his trade circular, which were only just beginning to arrive in South America. Stirling also suspected Popham had some 'business ashore' to attend to, which – and while Stirling was very reluctant to name this outright, his meaning was very clear – involved covering the traces of illicit dealings with local merchants, such as purchasing unneeded stores at outrageous prices before selling them

---

47   Popham to Stirling, 7 December 1806, Grainger, *The Royal Navy in the River Plate*, pp.185–186.
48   Popham to Stirling, 8 December 1806, Grainger, *The Royal Navy in the River Plate*, p.188.
49   Stirling to Popham, 8 December 1806, Grainger, *The Royal Navy in the River Plate*, p.189.
50   Popham to Stirling, 8 December 1806, Grainger, *The Royal Navy in the River Plate*, pp.189–190.
51   Stirling to Popham, 9 December 1806, Grainger, *The Royal Navy in the River Plate*, p.191.
52   Stirling to Popham, 9 December 1806, Anon., *Full and Correct Report of the Trial of Sir Home Popham*, Appendix Note L.
53   Stirling to Marsden, 12 December 1806, Grainger, *The Royal Navy in the River Plate*, pp.193–194.

on (just as had been implied during the *Romney* affair a few years previously).[54] Stirling candidly admitted he did not fully understand Popham's motives: he would, however, have known of the *Romney* affair and of Popham's reputation, and may simply have jumped to the conclusion that similar things had been going on at Buenos Aires. Still, it was equally likely that Popham's 'business ashore' had less to do with embezzlement and more to do with private trade. Lady Holland's story about Popham's silk stocking speculation was pure gossip, but it was not unlikely to be true. Popham's instinct for profit had been honed by his six years as a merchant trader aboard *Etrusco*. One of his business contacts was a man reputed to be Popham's brother-in-law, Mr Holloway, whose ship, *Anna*, was on its way to South America from Britain.[55] Holloway's ship was packed to the gills with merchandise, and Stirling thought, almost certainly accurately, that Popham had a stake in it – possibly even that he was the ship's real owner.[56]

To Stirling and others, at the time and since, chasing personal gain seemed the only possible explanation for the many crazy decisions Popham had made since taking the Cape of Good Hope. Many historians have accused Popham of planning the whole expedition to the Rio de la Plata to line his own pockets. Some have gone further: Richard Waite, in a 1940s PhD thesis, directly accused Popham of stealing $51,990 from the silver taken at Buenos Aires, an accusation echoed most recently by Chris Coelho.[57] The story arose from a discrepancy in the amount of silver handed over by the Spanish and the amount of silver actually embarked on HMS *Narcissus* and subsequently received at the Bank of England. John Grainger, however, points out that the sums recorded on several occasions varied because they were approximations based on the weight of the bullion rather than a countable sum. Grainger could not prove Popham had taken anything, although 'one would not be at all surprised if his fingers were sticky'.[58] This is reasonable. Popham's motives in attacking the Rio de la Plata were certainly not selfless, but if Stirling was right and he had private speculations in the area, illicit or otherwise, Popham was more likely to benefit from the *éclat* of the full amount of silver being publicly weighed at the Bank of England. Secure in the knowledge that he would eventually see a significant proportion of it as prize money (or so he thought), Popham used the silver as a way of publicising the success of his mission in the City, thereby increasing mercantile interest in South American trade – a trade in which Popham, and his contacts, had a hefty stake.

Stirling was probably right that Popham refused to leave the Rio de la Plata because he wanted to find out whether his investment, safely packed away in Holloway's hold, had crossed the ocean safely, but there may have been another motive. Holloway was also a business partner of Alexander Davison, the man who had first introduced Popham to Francisco de Miranda and who had encouraged Popham's schemes at the government level. Davison and Popham had a common point of contact: Lord Melville, the disgraced former First Lord of the Admiralty. Popham had been sending regular letters home to Melville and other

---

54  NMM: MRK/102/7/8: Stirling to Admiral Markham, 27 December 1806.
55  NMM: MRK/102/7/8: Stirling to Admiral Markham, 27 December 1806. Stirling thought Holloway was Lady Popham's brother.
56  NMM: MRK/102/7/8: Stirling to Admiral Markham, 27 December 1806.
57  Waite, 'Sir Home Riggs Popham', pp.153–154; Coelho, *Pirates in Uniform*.
58  Grainger, *British Campaigns in the South Atlantic*, p.89.

Pittites using Davison as an intermediary. He now expected Holloway's ship to bring him replies from the great men who represented his only chance of salvation. As Popham had written to Baird, 'Lord Melville shall judge of my case, and with his decision I shall rest satisfied.'[59] Popham wanted to know if Melville would stand by him no matter what. There was no point even thinking of going home otherwise.

Popham therefore needed to wait until *Anna* arrived, and to read the letters it carried. If it carried none, he was as good as cashiered; if it carried good news, it did not matter what he did to remain in the river. Popham knew his future depended on political favour, not on his commanding admiral's goodwill. He was already beginning to recast the hapless Stirling as an instrument of political persecution: 'There are in the letters of Admiral Stirling some very marked features of the disposition which Ministers felt [towards me]'.[60] His quarrel with Stirling had an unpleasant personal dimension; Stirling thought Popham put the captains in the squadron up to talking him down among the men, a proceeding he thought was very close to fomenting mutiny.[61] But Stirling, thanks to his delivery of the Admiralty instructions ordering Popham home, had also become a way Popham could show how he was being hounded by the Whig government even halfway round the globe. 'I cannot, sir,' Popham wrote to Stirling, 'quietly surrender my liberty, protected as it is by the 29th chapter of Magna Charta [sic], and other proud acts in the British constitution; nor can I agree to be made a precedent that might arm a minister with the power of exercising political revenge against any officer, however high his rank and situation.'[62] It was an odd, almost unhinged, letter to send to a superior officer, but Popham had his eyes on a higher audience, and he later had the letter published to drive in the full extent of his 'persecution'. Stirling later tried his best to sort out what had happened in a letter to the Secretary of the Admiralty. He was genuinely afraid he had made Popham angry – 'I often make mistakes when speaking too frankly' – but he remained convinced 'some purpose not evident to my senses' lay behind Popham's bad behaviour. All Stirling could guess at this stage was that Popham either simply wanted 'to quarrel with me … or to induce me to do some overt act'.[63] He never seems to have realised the role he played in Popham's pantomime.

By mid-December, in any case, the two men were ignoring each other, giving the whole affair the appearance of a playground dispute following which both parties had retreated to opposite corners to sulk. Popham only broke the silence on 13 December to report rumours that neutral American merchants in Buenos Aires planned to re-capture one of the commandeered merchant brigs and return it to America – and even then he wrote only to 'avoid the imputation of sullenness or obstinacy' (the Popham equivalent of blowing a raspberry).[64] Otherwise, Popham strung out his preparations to leave for two weeks, slowly preparing the brig *Rolla* for his passage and waiting for news from Britain that would determine his actions and his future.

---

59   Popham to Baird, 16 December 1806, Grainger, *The Royal Navy in the River Plate*, pp.196–197.
60   Anon., *Full and Correct Report of the Trial of Sir Home Popham*, Appendix Note L.
61   NMM: MRK/102/7/8: Stirling to Admiral Markham, 27 December 1806.
62   Popham to Stirling, 10 December 1806, Anon., *Full and Correct Report of the Trial of Sir Home Popham*, Appendix Note L.
63   Stirling to Marsden, 10 December 1806, Grainger, *The Royal Navy in the River Plate*, pp.193–194.
64   Popham to Stirling, 13 December 1806, Grainger, *The Royal Navy in the River Plate*, p.195.

Finally, on 26 December, Captain Eastwick of *Anna* arrived in the river with Mr Holloway's precious cargo. The merchant vessel *Pheasant* arrived the same day, carrying Holloway himself, who had been sent on ahead of the convoy by HMS *Narcissus*. Stirling later thought Holloway's arrival must have been hastened because he carried important news for Popham, and he may not have been wide of the mark.[65] Eastwick quickly discovered Popham was on board *Raisonable* and climbed aboard to pay him a visit to pass on some private letters. What those letters contained is a mystery, but if Popham had been hoping for letters and verbal instructions suggesting his adventures would be defended by his patrons at home, he clearly got them. He and a band of close supporters, including King, boarded *Rolla* that same evening and left at 2:00 a.m., quietly, under cover of darkness.[66] Stirling only discovered he had gone the next day.

Stirling may have been uncomfortably aware Popham had stolen a march on him, but one thing made him feel better: Popham was going home, following a failed expedition he had planned and executed, to a government and Admiralty that were far from favourable to him at the best of times. Whoever Popham's backers in London were, they were not in power. His future in the Royal Navy seemed bleak. Popham's own thoughts as he sailed home in *Rolla* were not recorded, but he and his companions – all of whom were, metaphorically as well as literally, in the same boat – almost certainly spent the journey planning their next move.

---

[65] NMM: MRK/102/7/8: Stirling to Admiral Markham, 27 December 1806.
[66] Parkinson, *Samuel Walters*, p.54; NMM: MRK/102/7/8: Stirling to Admiral Markham, 27 December 1806.

# Message Not Understood

*'The affirmative flag, with a white pendant under it'*

# 14

# Court-Martial, 1807

*2632: Question him strictly*

Popham landed at Weymouth on 16 February 1807 after a remarkably quick journey of 53 days and reached London the next day. His first priority was to visit the Admiralty, a matter of form, and his second was to feed the London newspapers appropriate reports, a matter of self-justification. Popham had been addressing a broad national audience for the past eight months: even as he stood in the Admiralty's chequered entrance hallway, he was trying to predict the reaction of the country – an audience he hoped would be more favourable than their Lordships of the Admiralty, who after all held only his professional career in their hands.

Popham's abilities as a self-publicist had never come in so handy. Although the Admiralty officials remained tight-lipped about their intentions, Popham knew he was likely to be arrested and court-martialled and he was already preparing for what would come. Accordingly, the morning papers on 18 February were full of his return and the unusual circumstances under which he had left South America. The *Oracle* expressed horror that Popham had been forced to return in 'a Prize Brig [*Rolla*], *without a single Gun on board*, which rendered the passage very hazardous'.[1] Popham also wanted the newspaper reports to convey the message that the situation he had left behind him in the Rio de la Plata was far from lost. The *Oracle* continued: 'There appears to be very little doubt entertained by Sir Home respecting the re-capture of [Buenos Aires], at pleasure, and without much difficulty.' The Pittite *Morning Post* carried more detail the next day. The paper summarised Popham's *quiproquo* with Stirling and asserted Popham had urged an attack on Montevideo as the first step in re-capturing Buenos Aires, which he expected to be 'an easy conquest'. The article talked up the capture of Maldonado as essential to the army and navy and quoted a private letter written by Popham to an unnamed friend, which, if it actually existed, clearly stated his much broader intended audience: 'I lament the loss of any part of the good opinion of the Merchants, who (as well as my Country), I have faithfully served, and whose interests were always nearest my heart. I am, nevertheless, still perfectly satisfied, *that only a temporary suspension of commercial intercourse*

---

1   *Oracle and Daily Advertiser*, 18 February 1807.

The Admiralty. (Public domain)

has taken place by the re-capture of Buenos Ayres.'² All this information can only have come from one source.

Having launched the first salvo in his paper war, Popham set about gathering information about the political situation. For all he claimed to be in control, he knew he was in trouble and he wanted to gauge his chances. He quickly discovered the situation was mixed. A lot had happened in the seven weeks it had taken him to travel home. The most important thing – not good – was that news of the Spanish re-capture of Buenos Aires had arrived in London on 2 January. Popham's own carefully constructed account did not arrive for another three weeks, ruining his hopes of getting his version of the story in first.³ More positively, and as Popham had anticipated, the capture of Buenos Aires had been very popular with the mercantile classes, whose support the beleaguered ministry desperately needed. There was already talk of more troops being sent to re-capture the city under a senior general – exactly what Popham had been hoping for all along. These rumours became reality in March, when the Secretary of State for War, William Windham, sent out 10,000 men to the Rio de la Plata under the command of Lieutenant General John Whitelocke.

One other thing in Popham's favour was that the Grenville government was not strong. Only the fact the Pittite opposition was itself divided had allowed it to weather a lacklustre year of military operations, the collapse of military and political alliances on the continent,

---

2   *Morning Post*, 19 February 1807. *The Times*, the government organ, only announced his return on 19 February, suggesting the government took a couple of days to realise what Popham was doing.
3   Grainger, *The Royal Navy in the River Plate*, pp.114, 153; Colchester, *Diary and Correspondence of Charles Abbot*, vol.2, p.90.

and, most disastrously of all, the failure of peace talks with Napoleon. But the government's weakness cut both ways. Popham knew ministers would be looking for a scapegoat for everything that had gone wrong at Buenos Aires, and he was an obvious target. Popham therefore began preparing for legal proceedings, writing to the Board of Admiralty for copies of papers, correspondence, and precedents, including the court-martial of his mentor Captain Edward Thompson for disobeying orders in the West Indies. All this suggested Popham had spent the last few weeks on board ship planning his defence, guessing the government would want to make an example of him.[4]

The Admiralty did not leave him long in suspense. On 18 February, the Marshal of the Court of Admiralty, John Crickitt, knocked on Popham's Wimpole Street door and informed him he was under arrest. Two days later the First Lord of the Admiralty, Thomas Grenville, informed the House of Commons that Popham (still an MP) was in custody pending a court-martial. This was a formality: as a gentleman, Popham's parole was sufficient to allow him his liberty, although he could neither attend the Commons nor wear his officer's sword, which would remain in the Marshal's care until the court-martial had handed down its verdict. The sense of unreality surrounding the whole affair was increased by Popham's acting as though nothing had happened. The Irish socialite Mrs Calvert met him shortly after his return to London. Despite his being under arrest, she thought 'he seem[ed] most perfectly at ease' and that he talked about his upcoming trial 'with the greatest unconcern'. Her assessment of him was eloquent in its pithiness: 'He seems a pleasant man, but a *dasher*.'[5]

The Admiralty agreed Popham was not to be trusted. The same day Popham was placed under arrest, the Board sent him a copy of the charge under which he would be tried. This simply stated that he had been sent out on 29 July 1805 in HMS *Diadem* to assist Baird in taking the Cape of Good Hope, but that his proceeding to the Rio de la Plata had been done with 'no direction or authority whatever'. On the contrary, he had withdrawn 'from the Cape the whole of the naval force which had been placed under his command for the sole purpose of protecting it … notwithstanding he had received previous information of detachments of the enemy's ships being at sea, and in the neighbourhood of the Cape, and notwithstanding he had been apprized that a French squadron was expected at the Mauritius'. The charge concluded, ominously: 'So flagrant a breach of public duty should not pass unpunished.'[6]

But the truth was the government did not really know how to frame the accusations against Popham. With the South American campaign still ongoing, the ministers hesitated to make Popham into too much of an example lest a happy ending in South America turned him into a martyr. At the same time, they could not pass up the unparalleled opportunity to get rid of an annoying enemy. Thomas Grenville, the First Lord of the Admiralty, wrote to his brother Lord Buckingham that he had considered going further with the charge but had preferred to

---

4   Popham's return may have occurred after Beresford's capture, but it occurred well before Whitelocke's disastrous failure to re-capture Buenos Aires in July 1807, which led to the complete withdrawal of troops from that quarter. Whitelocke himself was cashiered – a fate that might have given Popham pause had it occurred before his own trial.
5   Mrs Warrenne Blake (ed.), *An Irish Beauty of the Regency: … the Unpublished Journals of the Hon. Mrs. Calvert, 1789–1822* (London: John Lane the Bodley Head, 1911), p.71.
6   Anon., *Full and Correct Report of the Trial of Sir Home Popham*, pp.69–70n.

confine it 'to the one simple and undeniable proposition, viz. that being ordered to carry out a force to the Cape and for India, he had no justification for going a-buccaneering to South America'. Grenville had met Popham before and was keen to avoid allowing him to 'run loose upon private conversations of which no traces can be found', but thought that, if the case got 'fair play ... there can be but one result more or less of condemnation'.[7] The problem was that, by confining the charge to the basic facts, Grenville had made a rod for his own back. Popham absolutely *was* going to claim he had received unofficial orders to proceed to Buenos Aires. He had already begun feeding reports to that effect to the press, first through London papers like the *Morning Post* and the *Morning Advertiser*, and then further afield in the provincial newssheets. As early as 2 March, provincial papers like the *Gloucester Journal* and the *Hampshire Chronicle* claimed Popham must have had verbal orders and 'unlimited instructions' to attack Buenos Aires from Pitt and Melville themselves.[8]

Now he was certain the court-martial would actually take place, Popham began to plan for it with a vengeance. This was his chance to lay his side of the story before a truly national audience. Popham had always enjoyed justifying himself to as many people as he possibly could, but this would be the biggest audience he had ever had – bigger certainly than he could reach through privately circulated pamphlets, and the reportage was likely to be more trustworthy than the piecemeal and often badly reported parliamentary debates published in the newspapers. If he could get the publicity that was already swirling around the whole affair just right, if he could get the right stenographers and newspaper editors on his side, there was no telling how many people he could reach through a targeted, well-argued defence through the national press.

On 2 March 1807, the Admiralty issued an order to form a court-martial in Portsmouth on HMS *Gladiator* consisting of 13 officers. The list of members was startlingly top-heavy: including the president, William Young, eight members of the court were admirals – one Admiral of the Blue, four vice admirals, and three rear admirals. As the *Morning Advertiser* noted, this was unusual for trying a man who, after all, only ranked in the Navy as a post-captain.[9] Considering the Admiralty had reprimanded Popham for elevating himself to the rank of commodore with a captain under him, this suggested some degree of cognitive dissonance at the top levels regarding what rank Popham had actually held at the Cape and Buenos Aires. Either way, choosing so many high-ranking officers caused problems from the outset. Although the Admiralty had issued its order to convene the court-martial at

---

7   Thomas Grenville to Lord Buckingham, 6 March 1807, Duke of Buckingham and Chandos (ed.), *Memoirs of the Court and Cabinets of George the Third* ... (London: Hurst and Blackett, 1855), vol.4, pp.130–131.
8   *Gloucester Journal*, *Hampshire Chronicle*, *Morning Advertiser*, 2 March 1807. See also *Hereford Journal*, 4 March; *Caledonian Mercury*, 9 March; and *Morning Post*, 14 March.
9   *Morning Advertiser*, 2 March 1807. The official court martial list was: president, William Young, Admiral of the Blue; Vice Admirals Sir Erasmus Gower, John Holloway, Bartholomew Samuel Rowley, and Henry Edwin Stanhope; Rear Admirals James Vashon, Sir Isaac Coffin, and Sir Richard John Strachan; and Captains Thomas Graves, Matthew Henry Scott, John Irwin, and the Hon. Courtenay Boyle (TNA: ADM 1/5378).

the beginning of March, many of the officers composing it – some of whom had to come from as far away as Scotland – did not reach Portsmouth until the 6th. Although Popham welcomed the opportunity to spend more time preparing, he made a great show of being more ready to begin than his accusers. He left London on the afternoon of 3 March, accompanied by the Marshal of the Court of Admiralty, his barrister William Harrison, and his solicitor Germain Lavie. With him was also John McArthur, his old friend and former business partner, who was also a legal expert on naval courts-martial. The party arrived in Portsmouth at about 1:00 p.m. on the 4th, where they were met by the Deputy Judge Advocate of the Fleet with a copy of the final charge, a request for a full list of witnesses, and the news that the trial would not be held until all the board had arrived.

This gave Popham a day or two more to work on his side of the story. It also gave him time to cause trouble. He presented the Deputy Judge Advocate with a list of witnesses that read like a political who's who: William Huskisson, William Sturges Bourne, Lord Whitworth (who did not in the end appear), and William Marsden were all on the list, with Lord Melville's name being most prominent. At this point, however, Popham stopped playing along. He protested that one look at the final charge had been enough to tell him it had been expanded. The original version, which he had seen when Crickitt had arrested him, had been supported by three official documents, whereas the new version contained 18. None of these documents changed the material content of the charge, but Popham was understandably angry that he had not been given time to digest it all or possibly summon more witnesses. 'It will be impossible for me under the circumstances of this late communication to say, whether it will be practicable for me to be ready tomorrow,' he threatened, but in the end Sir Richard Strachan – the last missing member of the court-martial – did not arrive until then anyway, which meant the trial could not begin until 6 March.[10]

The morning of 6 March dawned with clear skies and a heavy frost. As soon as the sun had risen completely in the sky, a gun fired aboard HMS *Gladiator* as the signal for a court-martial. Half an hour later, another gun went off to summon the court aboard. Visitors braved the chilly weather and crowded the boats from the shore, clambering uncertainly up the ladder to the gangway running round the waist of the ship. The admirals composing the court were received with a salute and a roll of drums from the marine guard, and the court-martial began to assemble beneath the low ceiling of the great cabin. Witnesses and members of the court cosied up with journalists and stenographers, naval and military officers, seamen, ordinary citizens, and the cream of polite society. Popham's plight (and his assiduous public relations campaign) had stirred up considerable interest: he was going to get the vast audience he wanted, even before taking the broader national reportage into consideration. The journalist of one newspaper spotted Popham's old friend Lord Cavan, several other generals, a clutch of admirals, 'all the Captains of the ships lying at this port', 'a great number of other military and civil officers', and even 'several distinguished ladies' in the audience.[11] Secretary of the Admiralty William Marsden had never seen 'so many fine Laced Coats collected in one place.'[12]

---

10  TNA: ADM 1/2332: Popham to Marsden, 4 April 1807; *Morning Advertiser*, 6 March 1807.
11  *Belfast Commercial Chronicle*, 14 March 1807; *The Sun*, 10 March 1807.
12  NMM: MRK/104/2/22: Marsden to Admiral Markham, [6 March 1807].

Popham's own barge soon arrived in the shadow of the hulk, the sailors raising their oars straight up as it came alongside. There was a hum of interest as Popham entered the great cabin in his full dress uniform, gold lace sparkling in the crisp winter sunshine. He 'appeared in perfect spirits,' reported the *Morning Advertiser*, walking on deck 'with his usual steady and undaunted air' – although the marine guards only carried, rather than presented, their arms as the prisoner passed.[13] The sun's rays picked out the ostentatiously empty sword scabbard at his waist. The 13 members of the court and all the presiding officers, as well as Popham, took their oaths. Crickitt took Popham to the left of the board table. He was offered a seat and refused, remaining standing and uncovered next to his counsel Harrison, his solicitor Lavie, and his friend McArthur. On the right side of the table stood the Deputy Judge Advocate, Moses Greetham, acting for the prosecution. Behind him, somewhat unusually – as Popham repeatedly pointed out, they took the place of the Admiralty solicitor, who more usually attended courts-martial but remained in London – were Counsel to the Admiralty Thomas Jervis and his assistant Mr Bicknell. Jervis's presence at the trial may have been intended as a reminder that Popham could not expect any mercy from these men, who represented an Admiralty filled with personal enemies: Jervis was, after all, Lord St Vincent's second cousin.

The *Morning Advertiser*, which had been carrying Popham's official line for some weeks, breezily dismissed the prosecution case and belligerently suggested Popham would put up a fight: 'The case for the prosecution will not occupy many hours; but it is expected the defence will take some time.'[14] Still, the first day did not provide any real opportunity for fireworks. The court sat for a total of four hours, two of which were spent reading through the evidence relating to the charge. The other two consisted of everyday business, mostly revolving around the need to keep the deliberations of the court as confidential as possible until everything was over. Admiral Young, as president, asked the (many) newspaper reporters who were present to stand on the right-hand side of the room, where he made them promise 'upon their honour, not to publish a single tittle of the proceedings, until the trial was terminated', and forbade them to take away their notes until the trial was complete. The one reporter who refused to agree was expelled from the ship.[15] Young's order was standard procedure, but he may have given it partly in the knowledge that Popham might use carefully chosen plants from among the reporters to condition the way the trial reports were circulated around the country.

Jervis began proceedings by reading out the 18 pieces of evidence the Admiralty had produced against Popham as part of the charge. These included Popham's instructions to go to the Cape in 1805; various items of correspondence from the Admiralty Board instructing him to send reinforcements onto India; Popham's letters to the Admiralty Board reporting the capture of the Cape and the putative movements of Willaumez and Linois' squadrons; and Popham's letters of 13 and 30 April 1806 reporting his snap decision to go to Buenos Aires. There were also some letters from Baird to the War Department, written after Popham had left, reporting that the lack of a squadron had allowed a French frigate, *La Cannonière*,

---

13 *Morning Advertiser*, 9 March 1807.
14 *Morning Advertiser*, 6 March 1807.
15 *The Times*, 9 March 1807.

to escape from Table Bay.[16] Popham listened to everything being read out in silence, then immediately went on the offensive. He began by protesting about the new evidence accompanying the charge, and added for good measure that there were mistakes in the transcriptions Jervis had just read out. As an example, he cited a letter from Baird of 14 April, in which Jervis had included a line stating that Willaumez had gone 'to the West', whereas in fact Willaumez had gone to 'the West *Indies*'.[17] Admiralty Counsel Jervis was not impressed. Possibly he had been warned about Popham's tendency to go off on lengthy tangents, and requested the defendant to stay on topic. Jervis's response, however, played into Popham's hands, handing him an opportunity to take the moral high ground by claiming 'he wished that any document laid the Court should be correct' – at once identifying flaws in the prosecution's case right at the start of proceedings, and also implying the Admiralty's evidence could not be trusted.[18]

The prosecution closed its proceedings, at which point Popham should have begun presenting his defence. Despite the fact the trial was already delayed, however, Popham spoke only to ask for more time. The Admiralty counsel, he claimed, had introduced evidence 'which he had never before seen or heard of'.[19] With one eye on the reporters, he observed that, as the trial was likely to be well publicised, he wanted to be ready and he wanted to be accurate. He therefore asked for three more days to prepare.[20] His request flabbergasted the court, which had been hoping to get the business over with as quickly as possible. One witness, William Marsden, thought the Admiralty had botched its case from the outset, handing Popham an ace he was unlikely not to use.[21] Jervis, as a compromise, agreed to hand over copies of the letters used in evidence to Popham's solicitor, Lavie, and the court agreed to adjourn until 11:00 a.m. the next morning. There was only a slim likelihood of the trial being able to progress, however, as Popham still declared outright he would not be ready, adding, with typical bombast, that 'he would willingly stay up all night for the purpose, if that would enable him to comply with the wishes of the court'.[22]

It was all play-acting: Popham was playing for time, whetting the appetite of the politically conversant part of the nation. 'From the discussions which had taken place in the House of Commons and from ... animadversions which had appeared in the public prints, upon his conduct,' one newspaper reported him telling Admiral Young, 'he wished that his defence should not only be laid before the Court, but before the public in general.'[23] From the very beginning, Popham was clear that he did not care much about the verdict of the 13 men sitting around the table in *Gladiator*'s great cabin; they were not the jury he was hoping to convince. He was playing a game with the Admiralty, and he had unquestionably won the first round: the prosecution had managed to cast a cloud over the quality of its own evidence and hand control of the timetable to the defendant. When the court

---

16  TNA: ADM 1/5378: evidence listed; evidence reproduced at length in Anon., *Full and Correct Report of the Trial of Sir Home Popham*, pp.1–2.
17  *The Sun*, 10 March 1807; *Morning Post*, 11 March 1807.
18  Anon., *Full and Correct Report of the Trial of Sir Home Popham*, p.61.
19  Anon., *Full and Correct Report of the Trial of Sir Home Popham*, p.64.
20  Anon., *Full and Correct Report of the Trial of Sir Home Popham*, pp.64–65.
21  NMM: MRK/104/2/22: Marsden to Admiral Markham, [6 March 1807].
22  Anon., *Full and Correct Report of the Trial of Sir Home Popham*, p.66.
23  *British Press*, 11 March 1807.

again assembled on *Gladiator* at 11:00 a.m. on Saturday 7 March and when President Young asked Popham whether he was ready to enter into his defence, nobody was surprised when he again pressed for an adjournment until 9:00 a.m. on Monday. When Jervis complained Popham's request was extraordinary, Popham sarcastically replied that Jervis's presence as prosecutor instead of the Admiralty Solicitor was not exactly ordinary either. After some toing and froing between the two men the court cleared for an hour to deliberate, but by this stage there was clearly no time for Popham to begin his defence even if he had wanted to. The Judge Advocate told Popham the court had agreed to adjourn, but only if it were placed on record that there was 'no *material* difference' between the current charge and the one that had been served to Popham a fortnight previously.[24] The trial broke up early again, having achieved nothing for the second day running.

If Popham was feeling stressed about the likely outcome of his trial, he betrayed no sign of it. The newspaper reporters described him as 'in perfect spirits', his manner of speaking as 'eloquent, animated, and happily pointed'.[25] With his calmness and self-possession, he did not seem like a man fighting for his career – perhaps even his life. He seemed almost to be enjoying himself. He had shown an uncanny ability to shape the proceedings, a sharp wit for which Jervis was clearly no match, and a knowledge of the law that surprised nobody who knew of the months he had spent as his brother Stephen's clerk at Lincoln's Inn. Popham liked to portray himself as a rugged, uneducated seaman who 'could not be supposed to have any knowledge of the technical terms or professional calling of the bar', but he was playing a part.[26] He was using all the tricks in the lawyer's book – playing for time, delaying, distracting, obfuscating. There was no moment during the trial when he was not in control, either of himself or of his arguments, and he was ruthless in exploiting the errors of his opponents to his advantage.

Popham finally deigned to give the court his defence on 9 March, the third day of his court-martial. The great cabin of *Gladiator* was packed again, 'even more crowded than on the first day, there being several distinguished ladies present'.[27] Popham was aware of the size of his audience, and his performance, aimed more at the stenographers scribbling away than at the court itself, was epic. Never one for concision, Popham spoke over the course of four hours; after standing for three of them, he had to sit down for the last hour. He spoke largely from notes, but extemporising more and more as he warmed to his themes. He set himself up as the plucky underdog, persecuted as ever by the powerful and mighty Admiralty, and brashly denied he had done anything wrong: 'I am brought to trial by that superior authority to which every officer in His Majesty's naval service looks up for reward and protection, for having zealously, and to the best of my judgement and abilities, employed within the limits of my station, the means placed at my disposal in making a successful attack on a possession belonging to the enemy, instead of suffering the squadron I commanded to remain inactive.'[28] Not only had he been falsely accused, but the very wording of the charge preferred against him was unprecedented: in stating that 'so flagrant a breach of public duty

---

24 Anon., *Full and Correct Report of the Trial of Sir Home Popham*, pp.67–75.
25 *Morning Advertiser*, 9 March 1807; *Morning Post*, 9 March 1807; *Dublin Evening Post*, 17 March 1807.
26 Anon., *Full and Correct Report of the Trial of Sir Home Popham*, p.170.
27 *The Sun*, 10 March 1807.
28 Anon., *Full and Correct Report of the Trial of Sir Home Popham*, pp.76–77.

should not pass unpunished', the Admiralty was sending him 'to receive at your hands not justice but punishment'. To put it simply, 'My conduct is prejudged': Popham was arraigning the Admiralty for perverting the purpose of a court-martial, transforming it into a tool to persecute an individual.[29]

Persecution was a common theme for Popham, but in this case a clever one. By focusing attention on the *way* the charge had been formulated rather than its contents, Popham neatly avoided having to place too much emphasis on rebutting the allegations against him (which he could not effectively do), reframing the whole exercise as a personal, political attack rather than an accusation made in good faith. He was picking his own ground for the upcoming battle and explicitly addressing his defence, not to the court (which had already had its verdict dictated to it) or to the Admiralty (which had already 'prejudged' him), but to the country at large. Popham was well aware the court-martial was as much a 'public inquiry' as a trial, and he had already been feeding his intended audience elements of his defence over the past year, through newspaper reports talking up the value of Buenos Aires for British trade and stressing how Popham's invasion had slotted into the government's longer-term global strategic planning. Popham's four-hour defence was merely the next step in that campaign. He was confident because he was pretty sure he carried the country with him, no matter what the trial's outcome.

This confidence was just as well, because the actual contents of his defence were necessarily vague. Popham, as Thomas Grenville had feared, emphasised the conversations he had had with Pitt and Melville – conversations he could prove happened, but which had not been recorded. He candidly admitted he had 'no positive directions or express authority' to go to Buenos Aires from the Cape, but denied his deciding to go anyway translated into direct disobedience. His defence primarily turned on the use of discretion, which he contended was a prime principle of the Navy on the most distant stations. In one of many examples of outright cheek, he cited numerous instances of naval officers using their discretion to depart from the precise letter of their orders, including Lord St Vincent's unauthorised attack on Tenerife –Popham lingered, with clear enjoyment, on the failure of this expedition.[30] But Popham was not merely trying to reveal his enemies as hypocrites for attacking him for something they would not punish their own for doing. His definition of 'discretion' was very specific: he claimed it gave commanders licence to pick their own target if they had no other immediate object of attack, and if they had 'knowledge of the sentiments of the Government' – in other words, if they knew the government had plans beyond what was explicitly stated in their written orders. The conclusion was inescapable. As attacking South America had been 'a favourite project of Mr Pitt', Popham could not have committed a crime by going from the Cape to South America without waiting for explicit orders to do so. If anything, he could only be punished for 'an excess of zeal' in anticipating orders that would have come eventually, had Pitt not died when he did.[31]

This was slightly specious as Popham could not prove Pitt had ever even intended to send him to Buenos Aires at all, but he skated over that, throwing in a profusion of detail about tides, winds, and weather at the Cape to demonstrate he had not left it completely

---

29 Anon., *Full and Correct Report of the Trial of Sir Home Popham*, pp.77–78.
30 Anon., *Full and Correct Report of the Trial of Sir Home Popham*, pp.81–84.
31 Anon., *Full and Correct Report of the Trial of Sir Home Popham*, pp.89–91, 124.

defenceless.³² Following this professional interlude, Popham returned to his favourite theme of persecution: the Admiralty had known all this, which was why they had only added *parts* of his dispatches of 9 and 30 April 1806 to the charge, deliberately omitting the sections where Popham had informed them the French squadron under Willaumez was sailing away from – not towards – the Cape to make it look as though he had abandoned his post at a time when a French attack was still hourly expected. Popham also complained that the Admiralty had never acknowledged the role of his squadron in the Cape's capture. He contrasted the Board's silence with that of the War Department's warm congratulations to Baird, once again drawing attention to the intended audience for his defence: 'Whence this difference? I leave it, gentlemen, to your reflections – I leave it to the reflections of my country!'³³

Popham made no attempt to disclaim his role in suggesting the attack on Buenos Aires, arrogating complete responsibility to himself: it was a scheme 'which I had the honour of submitting' to the Pitt government. But Popham knew the government had not yet abandoned the Rio de la Plata, and this gave him some ammunition. He warned that, if anything went wrong in South America from now on, it could only be because the government had failed to follow up on the opening he had made for them. Even more pertinently, the reinforcements that had been sent were implicit approval of all Popham had done. Because they could not attack him for the expedition to South America without looking like hypocrites, Popham claimed the government was simply trying to silence him in any way possible. Popham also complained the government had done nothing to counter rumours the whole expedition had only been designed for the purpose of prize money and personal gain. Popham pulled the cloak of morality and national pride around his shoulders, stating, again more for the benefit of the newspaper hacks: 'The good of my country was my sole object.'³⁴

Having accused the government of framing him for political reasons, Popham wrapped up his defence by representing himself as a victim standing for every captain in the Royal Navy. If the court found him guilty, they would create a dangerous precedent. If an officer's scope for action was limited to the wording of his instructions and subsequent correspondence from a distant Admiralty Board, 'the result will be, I venture to foretell, ruin to the British Navy'. An officer could not be expected to refrain from responding to immediate circumstances, particularly if his actions might underpin the grand strategy he knew his employers had at heart. Popham's last words were addressed over the heads of the board to the scribbling journalists in the audience, and their readers beyond them – 'the nation at large': 'On your decision in this instance depends the future conduct and enterprise of the Navy of Great Britain. ... I stand before you, not for having failed in the fulfilment of orders, but for having done more than my strict duty against the common enemy.' On that basis, he finished by hoping to receive at the hands of his judges 'an HONOURABLE ACQUITTAL'.³⁵

It was a bravura performance full of claims of persecution and perversion of justice. Popham had accused the Admiralty counsel of abusing his position, personally insulted Lord St Vincent and most of the Admiralty Board, flatly stated the government had cherry-picked evidence to score political points against him as a Pittite appointee, and accused his enemies

---

32  Anon., *Full and Correct Report of the Trial of Sir Home Popham*, pp.106–108.
33  Anon., *Full and Correct Report of the Trial of Sir Home Popham*, pp.111, 116, 118, 123.
34  Anon., *Full and Correct Report of the Trial of Sir Home Popham*, pp.125–130, 134, 137.
35  Anon., *Full and Correct Report of the Trial of Sir Home Popham*, pp.140–143.

of undermining the fundamental principles on which the whole Royal Navy existed. Popham had not shied away from the notoriety he had acquired from his actions or tried to minimise his own role. He made absolutely no attempt to disentangle himself from the Buenos Aires expedition; confident that it would eventually succeed in the long term – and that, if it did not, he could make it look like the failure was entirely due to the government's lack of follow-up – he had bound himself intimately with all that had happened. The morning's high drama surely could not be surpassed – and then Popham called his first witness: Lord Melville.

There were murmurings around *Gladiator*'s state room as Pitt's former First Lord of the Admiralty walked calmly to the end of the table and swore the oath as witness. The fact Popham had subpoenaed him had been reported in the newspapers for weeks, but many had doubted he would actually turn up. In fact Melville's testimony was somewhat anticlimactic. He began by

*Henry Dundas, Viscount Melville*, by R. Freeman after Henry Raeburn. (Public domain, The Miriam and Ira D. Wallach Division of Art, Prints and Photographs, The New York Public Library)

categorically refusing to reveal any state secrets, effectively hamstringing any attempt by Popham to uncover anything Melville and Pitt had been unwilling to set down on paper – and Melville swiftly confirmed there was nothing on paper that could support Popham's cause.[36] Melville agreed Popham had suggested attacks on South America several times since 1803, but refused to be drawn on the extent to which his schemes had shaped official strategy and experienced convenient memory failure when asked outright if he had ever thought of sending Popham to Buenos Aires. However, when Melville's words were parsed to get beyond the politician-like evasions with which they were couched, he did admit Popham had been appointed to *Diadem* to cooperate with Miranda in South America. Moreover, when asked by Jervis if Popham had been appointed to 'any command authorizing him to attack any part of South America', he replied 'Certainly not', but immediately added a qualifier: 'In the proper sense of those words.' Melville's answers nevertheless reminded the audience in *Gladiator*'s state room that Popham's defence relied heavily on conversations that had not been transcribed. On the one hand, this meant Popham could (and did) claim his cause seemed weaker than it actually was because he could not use evidence that revealed

---

36  Anon., *Full and Correct Report of the Trial of Sir Home Popham*, p.163.

government secrets – exactly what Thomas Grenville had already suspected Popham would do.³⁷ But Popham also suffered under a severe handicap because his most critical witness – Pitt, the one man who had been present at every conversation Popham cited – was dead.

Popham could not get Pitt on the witness stand, but he did try to get as close to the late Prime Minister as possible. Melville's testimony was a serious coup, even if Melville had not been as explicit as Popham might have liked. Melville had been one of Pitt's closest political colleagues; he had made a favourable impression simply by appearing in Popham's support, and it did not really matter that he had not actually said anything new. Melville was followed in the witness box by Pitt's former Secretary of the Treasury, William Sturges Bourne, who confirmed the attack on the Cape of Good Hope had arisen out of intelligence Popham had conveyed to Pitt (although he could not recall if South America had also been specifically mentioned).³⁸ Sturges Bourne was followed by William Huskisson, whose keenness to help his friend Popham was visible in his pallor and the fact his arm was in a sling: he had broken it only a few days previously and was still feverish.³⁹ Like Melville, Huskisson's appearance caused a stir.⁴⁰ Unlike Sturges Bourne, he did remember Popham and Pitt talking about Buenos Aires, and added that 'certain steps' had been taken at the Admiralty after Popham's departure for the Cape with the aim of loosening Spain's hold on South American trade – although, tantalisingly, he gave no further details.⁴¹

Popham now asked the obvious question: had Huskisson known 'of any political objection existing at the time I sailed to the Cape … to prevent my having received some instructions, direct or provisional, on the subject of Mr Pitt's views towards South America?'⁴² This was too much for Jervis, who tried to have this question dismissed as irrelevant. It was not the first time he had intervened during the witness cross-examination; most of those interruptions had been rejected by Admiral Young, who clearly sympathised with Popham's frustration at Jervis's 'quibbling'. Once again Young sided with Popham, and Huskisson was permitted to answer, agreeing that the collapse of the Third Coalition had removed any political objection to an assault on South America – although Jervis scored a point by getting Huskisson to admit Pitt would not have ordered an assault on Buenos Aires in 1805 because he had still been hoping to detach Spain from France.⁴³ But Popham quickly regained the upper hand. When Jervis asked Huskisson whether Pitt had ever given Popham 'a positive or a provisional order to attack Buenos Aires after his attack of the Cape', Popham objected: 'I never asserted or insinuated any such thing.' He argued Jervis was leading the witness to deny something Popham had never claimed happened in the first place. When Admiral Young allowed the question to be put, Huskisson simply denied Pitt had ever given Popham 'positive or provisional instructions', which – given Popham had just said the same thing – only made Jervis look ridiculous.⁴⁴

---

37   Anon., *Full and Correct Report of the Trial of Sir Home Popham*, p.171n.
38   Anon., *Full and Correct Report of the Trial of Sir Home Popham*, pp.164–166.
39   *Belfast Commercial Chronicle*, 16 March 1807.
40   *The Sun*, 10 March 1807.
41   Anon., *Full and Correct Report of the Trial of Sir Home Popham*, p.174.
42   Anon., *Full and Correct Report of the Trial of Sir Home Popham*, p.169.
43   Anon., *Full and Correct Report of the Trial of Sir Home Popham*, pp.170–171.
44   Anon., *Full and Correct Report of the Trial of Sir Home Popham*, pp.172–173.

Huskisson's testimony was the last of the day. Popham's lengthy defence meant the first witnesses were not summoned until early afternoon, when there were only a few hours of winter light left. Not that Popham had any interest in continuing: by the time Huskisson left the witness box, his case was looking better than many had expected. Still, he was far from safe. Popham had tried to use his witnesses to prove *implicit* authorisation from the Pitt government to go to Buenos Aires, although he himself admitted he had never been *explicitly* ordered to do so, and he had not really succeeded. Melville had wriggled out of committing his government to anything compromising, Sturges Bourne's evidence had been completely useless, and Huskisson had not been able to second-guess Pitt's intentions for Popham's actions after taking the Cape. The paper evidence still suggested the plan had been for Popham to return to Britain, and for the troops not needed at the Cape to go on to India. Despite this, Popham had successfully demonstrated that plans to attack South America had been at an advanced stage before the target switched to the Cape. Melville, Sturges Bourne, and Huskisson, prominent Pittites all, had boosted his cause simply by appearing on his behalf. If the government had wanted to score points by bringing Popham to trial, he had shown he could play their game just as well – perhaps better.

The court sat for the fourth time on Thursday 10 March. The day began at 9:00 a.m. to take full advantage of the daylight hours available, particularly as Popham had amply demonstrated he was not averse to spinning out time. In fact the president, Admiral Young, opened proceedings by reminding Popham he was not here to get free publicity: 'You will, during the remainder of this trial, endeavour to avoid embarrassing our consideration, or protracting the course of our proceeding … [by confining] yourself to the points necessary for your defence against the charge now under our consideration.'[45] The court went on to hear some of the remaining witnesses. First up was former Secretary of the Admiralty William Marsden. Popham began by ignoring Admiral Young's warning to avoid tangents completely, asking Marsden whether it was usual to word a charge using loaded terms like 'flagrant breach of public duty'. All Admiral Young's hopes of hastening the pace of the trial died instantly as the court became embroiled in a long discussion about whether Popham was allowed to take issue with the wording of the charge itself. Popham made a short speech reiterating that the charges against him showed 'a degree of severity and harshness … which was quite unusual towards officers in similar situations'. This trod over ground that was becoming wearingly familiar to his listeners, but this time he went further, claiming the Admiralty had trumped up its exaggerated charges as a way of committing judicial murder: since the accusations against him were 'of the highest nature', the court might be open to sentence him to death.[46] The name of Admiral Byng, executed in 1756 for failing to do his duty at Minorca, hung ominously, but unspoken, in the air. Admiral Young managed to get Popham back on topic by waiving the question, and Marsden performed a remarkable impression of a piece of bureaucratic wood in the witness box, remembering exactly as much detail about naval arrangements for the Cape and Buenos Aires as had been placed on the official record and nothing else.

The next three witnesses almost certainly fell under Admiral Young's definition of a waste of court time, although they did at least speak somewhat to the charge. First came Thomas

---

45  Anon., *Full and Correct Report of the Trial of Sir Home Popham*, pp.174–175.
46  Anon., *Full and Correct Report of the Trial of Sir Home Popham*, p.177.

Wilson, a London merchant with South American business connections, who remembered giving Popham information about the defenceless state of Buenos Aires in the summer of 1805 before attention switched to the Cape of Good Hope.[47] After him came Thomas Browne, Master-Attendant at the Cape after the British captured it. He thought the Cape well defended from the landside, and testified that having a squadron present would not have improved that defence because of tides and prevailing winds (using the capture of the French frigate *La Cannonière* with the assistance of land artillery as an example).[48] The final witness of the day was Captain William King, the man Popham had promoted captain of *Diadem*. King was well known to have benefited from Popham's patronage; his promotion to captain had not yet been confirmed, and his future career rested on Popham's ability to speak for him. Jervis was particularly suspicious of King's veracity. He seemed convinced Popham's designs to go to Buenos Aires from the Cape had been of long standing, and that King knew this. When King said he had first learned of Popham's plans to attack Buenos Aires in late March 1806, Jervis repeatedly pressed him to admit he and Popham had spoken about a putative expedition prior to 21 March. This choice of a very specific date suggested he had some evidence, but if he did, it was not of a nature that could be publicly produced. The court eventually had to intervene to get Jervis off King's back.[49]

The Admiralty counsel nevertheless got his revenge. A little later, while King was talking about taking *La Volontaire* in February 1806, Jervis spotted an inconsistency with Thomas Browne's claim that Royal Navy ships could not have defended the Cape against a French attack. Jervis tricked King into admitting that *Diadem*'s capture of *La Volontaire* showed it *had* been possible for a ship of the line to make a difference – which negated nearly all Browne's previous evidence. Aware he had lost some of his advantage, King stayed silent when Jervis pressed him to admit Popham should have ensured at least one ship remained to cruise off the Cape. King's lame attempt to deflect the question by suggesting it was not really applicable to the Cape of Good Hope – 'It would be advantageous at all times to have ships cruising in every possible situation that enemies' ships may be found in; but with respect to the particular advantage to the Cape, I do not see any' – sounded weaker than if he had simply agreed with Jervis outright.[50] Jervis had definitely won this round for the prosecution.

At this point it was 4:30 p.m., darkness was drawing in, and even Popham was growing tired. He rose to ask permission to withdraw his final four witnesses, as he felt their testimony would simply duplicate what Wilson, Browne, and King had already said. This suggested the trial was at last drawing to a close and that the next day was likely to be the last. But Popham had not forgiven King's humiliation at the hands of the Admiralty counsel, and the last half-hour of the day's proceedings were enlivened, and lengthened, by his sarcastic Jervis-baiting. When Jervis agreed with the rest of the court that Popham's remaining witnesses were likely to produce inadmissible evidence, Popham again passed sarcastic comment about Jervis's superiority in matters of law. Even as he reminded his opponent he was but a simple post-captain, however, Popham cheekily urged Jervis to check

---

47   Anon., *Full and Correct Report of the Trial of Sir Home Popham*, p.180.
48   Anon., *Full and Correct Report of the Trial of Sir Home Popham*, pp.181–182, 183–188.
49   Anon., *Full and Correct Report of the Trial of Sir Home Popham*, p.201.
50   Anon., *Full and Correct Report of the Trial of Sir Home Popham*, pp.202–203.

out Tytler's *Law of Evidence*, which suggested he remembered more from his days as his brother's clerk at Lincoln's Inn than he was letting on. Jervis, incensed, rose to the bait, protesting that Tytler was 'not authority', whereupon Popham sneered: 'Then I suppose no authority is to be acknowledged but yours, sir.'[51]

The court assembled again at 9:30 a.m. for what everyone knew was likely to be the final session. Would Popham spend it basking in the limelight? Of course he would. When the president asked Popham if he had any further witnesses to call, the defendant rose and began a speech. As Admiral Young listened incredulously, Popham complained that much of the evidence he had brought over the last few days had been attacked by Jervis as irrelevant, and asked to submit 27 more pieces of correspondence to the court, again undermining his self-characterisation as a humble professional sailor by citing the well-known legal authority William Blackstone's *Commentaries*: 'The best evidence the nature of the case will admit of, shall always be required if possible to be had; but if not possible, then … the best evidence that can be had, shall be allowed.'[52] Introducing so much new material at this late stage of proceedings was startlingly insolent, even for Popham, and when President Young objected, Popham turned again to the journalists in the room:

> My motive for the production of these papers is to acquit my character, and to remove every injurious impression which the reflections propagated against it, particularly in my absence from the country [i.e. in Parliament], are calculated and evidently designed to produce. To defeat such slanderous views, I feel that it will be sufficient to make my case fully known.[53]

Young testily reminded Popham 'that any reflection which may have been made in the House of Commons, or elsewhere, upon your conduct, can have no influence upon our minds', but he was not Popham's intended audience. Popham continued in his role of injured patriot, mugging shamelessly for the galleries: 'My private feelings have been very seriously wounded, and both my private and public character grossly misrepresented' by his 'enemies' (never identified, but presumably well understood by the people who mattered), who wanted nothing more than to allow the charges preferred against him 'to afford some countenance to the unworthy imputations attempted to be affixed to my motives of action'.[54] In other words, if the court considered the official charges against him true, the nation would also judge him guilty of all the slanderous things that had been said about him in *The Times*, on the floor of the House of Commons, and in coffee houses around the country.

The reaction of the court to Popham's speechifying suggested they, too, realised the case would not be decided by 13 men around *Gladiator*'s state room table. They allowed the letters to be read, giving Popham even more of a last word than would otherwise have been the case. The new evidence mostly consisted of letters touching on the government's recent reinforcements to South America, but also included correspondence relating to the defence of the Cape after Popham's departure and Popham's attempts to release Beresford and his

---

51  Anon., *Full and Correct Report of the Trial of Sir Home Popham*, p.211.
52  Anon., *Full and Correct Report of the Trial of Sir Home Popham*, p.216.
53  Anon., *Full and Correct Report of the Trial of Sir Home Popham*, p.221.
54  Anon., *Full and Correct Report of the Trial of Sir Home Popham*, p.222.

men after their capture. Popham continued to speak after the letters had been read, one eye firmly on the audience outside *Gladiator*, as it had been all along:

> I here close my defence, and I throw myself upon the wisdom and justice of this honourable Court. My feelings and my character have suffered severely; but I trust to your judgement to relieve the one and rescue the other. If I have, in the exercise of my zeal, exceeded the strictest bounds of discretion, I hope it will be evident that I have been actuated solely by a desire to advance the honour, the glory, and the interest of my country.[55]

It was a bravado performance to close five days of bravado performances. But would it have the intended effect? At 10:30 a.m., the court cleared to deliberate on the verdict. Popham spent the next four and a half hours pacing the quarterdeck, much as he did on a daily basis as a ship's captain, only this time with the Admiralty Marshal a few paces behind. He chatted with witnesses and appeared at ease, but he, like everyone else, must have been wondering what was happening in the great cabin. Time ticked on; noon came and went, then one, then two. At last, at 3:00 p.m., a messenger summoned all strangers back to the courtroom.

Popham was called up to the table, where he stood, hat in hand, the late afternoon light playing on the weather-beaten lines around his eyes. The members of the court sat arrayed with wooden expressions as Jervis rose to read out the sentence: 'The Court having maturely considered the nature of the charges, heard all the evidence and having fully deliberated upon the whole of this case, are of opinion, that the charges have been proved.' The room broke into murmurs, which got louder as Jervis explained how the court had expressed its opinion that Popham's conduct in withdrawing the squadron from the Cape and taking it to Buenos Aires was 'highly censurable'. And then, just as everyone thought Popham's career was over, came the astonishing final words: 'But, in consideration of circumstances, the Court doth adjudge him [Popham] to be only SEVERELY REPRIMANDED, and he is accordingly hereby severely reprimanded.'[56]

Against an incredulous hum, Popham stepped forward, bowed to the table, and accepted his sword back from Marshal Cricket. One newspaper said that 'the manly dignity of his deportment [did not] abate for a moment' as the sentence was read, but Popham, like the rest of the audience aboard *Gladiator*, must have been wondering what would happen next.[57] If he had been found guilty of the charges against him, what did this mean in practice? The reprimand delivered and his sword returned, he was now a free man, but could he be employed again with such a stain against his name? What, most importantly of all, did 'in consideration of circumstances' mean? But nothing more was said, and the trial broke up. Popham returned to his barge and sailed back to Sally Port, where he walked to his lodgings, followed by curious crowds and cheering supporters.

---

55  Anon., *Full and Correct Report of the Trial of Sir Home Popham*, p.223.
56  Anon., *Full and Correct Report of the Trial of Sir Home Popham*, p.224.
57  *Dublin Evening Post*, 17 March 1807.

Popham did have a great many supporters, possibly more than at the beginning of the trial, because the embargo on news reporting had only whetted the appetite of the public for news. Popham had gleefully capitalised on this, and he and his defence team had been communicating feeding journalists correspondence and exclusive tip-offs throughout the trial.[58] His notoriety increased with the astonishing verdict, at once a conviction and an acquittal. Many thought someone had had a word with the court-martial panel, and some outside influence may well have been brought to bear, although if so it was done so subtly no evidence of it has survived. But even Popham probably did not know why the court had held back from the killing blow. Possibly Popham's parade of high-profile Pittites, like Melville and Huskisson, had had its intended impact; perhaps the government's implicit endorsement of the Buenos Aires adventure by sending reinforcements would have made it embarrassing to reach any other finding. Perhaps the board was simply convinced by Popham's appeal to discretion. Something had stayed their hand, and Popham's almost miraculous survival only added to his glamour. The Pittite *Morning Post* thought that the surprisingly lenient sentence showed Popham had convinced the court he had had the blessing of the Pitt government for his actions, particularly as the prosecution had failed to prove otherwise:

> How is it likely to be known that Sir Home Popham acted without orders? How was it to be known that the secret verbal communications he had had with the Chief Minister at the time, were not a sufficient warrants [sic] for the expedition against Buenos Ayres? Even as it was, these verbal communications have had so much weight with the tribunal … as to mitigate very much their sentence: for it cannot be supposed that the mitigation arose from the success of the enterprize.[59]

The *Newcastle Courant* abandoned all nuance in reaching its conclusion that Popham had, effectively, been completely exonerated: 'The statements of Sir Home, as to the views of Mr Pitt's ministry on South America, and of his being confidentially employed by them, were proved in evidence by Lord Melville, Mr Sturges Bourne … [and] Mr Huskisson'.[60] The *Leeds Intelligencer* went further. It agreed Popham had been politically persecuted and called for revenge: 'There are *others* who deserve to be more severely reprimanded than Sir Home.'[61]

Popham had been found guilty of the charges against him and his professional future remained in the balance, but he had resoundingly won the publicity battle. He had always known of the power of communication, and his experience with the press during his trial had only confirmed him in this conviction. For days the newspapers reported little other domestic news: the whole transcript of the trial appeared all over the country once the embargo on reportage had been lifted, and transcribed volumes began appearing in the bookshops almost immediately. As early as 14 March, the *British Press* advertised *The Trial at Large of Sir Home Popham*, to be published by Longman, Hare, Reese, and Orme of Paternoster Row and by Motley of Portsmouth (a second edition appeared by 20 March

---

58 The *Morning Post* and *Morning Advertiser* (both pro-Popham) printed almost identical accounts of how Popham was likely to conduct his defence in advance of the trial, on 6 March 1807.
59 *Morning Post*, 14 March 1807.
60 *Newcastle Courant*, 14 March 1807.
61 *Leeds Intelligencer*, 23 March 1807.

containing 'a true Copy of the Defence, corrected by — Lavie, Esq., the Friend of Sir Home').[62] The *British Neptune* released what it called 'the most complete and most perfect History of the Proceedings' of the trial, and *The Sun* advertised that a compressed version would be given in *Steel's List of the Royal Navy* in April.[63] The authorised report of the Popham team, possibly edited by John McArthur and certainly released with Popham's blessing, was not long behind these other versions. It began with a cheeky dedication 'to the Navy of England', before apologising for taking so long to be published: it had been 'impeded by causes somewhat similar to those which led to the persecution of Sir Home Popham'.[64]

Popham had become notorious, and he undeniably enjoyed his transformation into a Robin Hood-like transgressive figure. His return to London on the evening of 13 March was noted in the *Morning Post*, as was his first visit to the Admiralty after his trial on the 20th.[65] The *Morning Advertiser* noted that rumours of Popham's intention to return to Parliament 'excited a good deal of expectation'.[66] Would Popham speak as scathingly of the government as he had done of Jervis in the state room of *Gladiator*? In fact Popham kept quiet in the Commons, but *The Times* could not resist putting a speech into Popham's mouth that played on all the usual tropes and his well-known love of publicity:

> It is impossible for me, under the circumstances in which I appear before you, to pass over the honours I lately received in the great cabin of the *Gladiator*. I say honours, because I am willing to suppose, and I trust that you will assent to the reasonableness of my supposition, that when disgrace falls short of general expectation, it may certainly be considered in the light of a negative degree of honour; as the culprit at a criminal bar who expects to be hanged, thinks whipping almost tantamount to a reprieve. I therefore, Gentlemen, cannot but look upon a severe reprimand, under the apprehensions which afflicted me, as a comparative state of fame and reputation. But wherefore do I talk of fame and reputation?[67]

But *The Times* had misjudged the mood. The *Morning Post* thought Popham had won the war for its readers' hearts: 'Sir Home Popham lives in the affections of his Country, where Ministerial animosity cannot reach him.'[68]

Not that Popham had to worry about 'Ministerial animosity' much longer. His notorious luck held in spectacular fashion and, within a fortnight of the end of his trial, the Grenville government was no more. This had nothing to do with Popham's trial or Buenos Aires: it had committed political suicide by trying to force the King to allow Catholic officers to serve in all ranks in the Army and Navy. The King, who considered Catholic concessions to be against his coronation oath, replaced Grenville with a new ministry under the Duke of Portland. The Pittites, Popham's patrons, were back in power; 'our watch' was 'upon deck'

---

62 *British Press*, 14 and 20 March 1807.
63 *Morning Advertiser*, 21 March 1807; *The Sun*, 26 March 1807.
64 Anon., *Full and Correct Report of the Trial of Sir Home Popham*, Dedication, p.iii.
65 *Morning Post*, 14 March 1807; *St James's Chronicle*, 21 March 1807.
66 *Morning Advertiser*, 16 March 1807.
67 *The Times*, 19 March 1807.
68 *Morning Post*, 20 March 1807.

again.[69] After all his attempts to associate his actions with Pitt's grand strategy, Popham had good reason to believe a Pittite government would overlook the stain of the court-martial verdict on his reputation.

As lucky as Popham had been, however, his court-martial acted as a slow poison that gradually killed his career drop by drop. He had not lost political favour, but he had lost Pitt and Melville, who were willing to push him forward and protect him because they knew what he could do for them. The new Portland government was politically weak, and the 1807 General Election came close to producing a hung parliament. The new ministers had every reason to keep a man as infamous as Popham at arm's length, despite his obvious attempts to associate himself with Pitt's memory during his trial. This realisation, however, took time to sink into Popham's consciousness. And yet in the late spring of 1807, Popham had some reason to be optimistic. In May Popham

George Canning, by Charles Etienne Pierre Motte after Henri Grévedon, 1827. (Public domain, The Miriam and Ira D. Wallach Division of Art, Prints and Photographs, The New York Public Library)

was elected to Parliament for Ipswich, a clear sign he had not lost political approval.[70] His old acquaintance Huskisson was still in office, as was Huskisson's friend, the new Foreign Secretary George Canning, and Popham had previously worked well with Portland's Secretary of State for War, Lord Castlereagh. But while Huskisson was an influential advocate, Canning and Castlereagh still needed convincing as patrons, and he had little contact with the First Lord of the Admiralty, Lord Mulgrave (although he could place some pressure on him through their mutual friend William Lowther, Earl of Lonsdale, whom Popham had known since 1804).

Still, although his patronage networks were shaky, someone had saved Popham's career. Now he needed to show how useful he could be to prove it had been saved for good reason. He needed a mission, and the circumstances of 1807 were in his favour. The government also needed a strong signal to show they were different from the Grenville government – better, stronger, more proactive. The best way to do this was by involving Britain once more in the continental war against Napoleon. Popham's priorities and those of the new government therefore meshed perfectly, even if Popham was not the conduit the ministry would have preferred to make its point.

---

69  Popham to Baird, 17 November 1806, Grainger, *The Royal Navy in the River Plate*, p.102.
70  Anon., *Members of Parliament*, Part 2 (1878), p.249.

## 15

# Copenhagen, 1807

*2874: Set fire to the town*

After the death of the Third Coalition on the fields of Ulm and Austerlitz, the Grenville government had held aloof from any more continental alliances. This helped in their attempt to make a clean break with their interventionist predecessors, but alienated potential allies like Russia and Prussia while failing to make any impact against Napoleon. Prussia had eventually been forced to make a humiliating peace after military defeat at Jena and Friedland, and Russia had actually allied with Napoleon after a meeting between Tsar Alexander and the French emperor at Tilsit. Meanwhile Napoleon began turning his thoughts to old projects of a British invasion. First, he tried to close Europe to British imports by imposing the Continental Blockade, aware that Britain's strength was rooted in its pockets. Second, he began rebuilding the naval force that had been destroyed at Trafalgar. This project was helped by France's increased influence in the Baltic after Tilsit, which gave Napoleon control over the pine forests of the north (and cut Britain off from the same source). Building a sufficient number of new ships would take time, but British decision makers were terrified Napoleon would make up for his lack of immediate naval clout by borrowing the fleet of another country, as he had done with Spain in 1805. The Netherlands was high up on the list of unfriendly countries with a significant naval presence: in 1806, Napoleon had installed a puppet monarchy there under his brother Louis. France's new ally, Russia, might also lend its ships, and even if it did not, it might put pressure on the other naval powers in the Baltic to join the alliance.

The neutral kingdom of Denmark was a particular worry, although its fleet – reported at the end of July 1807 to amount to 18 sail of the line, 11 frigates, 10 sloops, four floating batteries, and several small gunboats, with three 74-gun ships still on the stocks – was far from ready for sea and there was no sign it was fitting out.[1] This did not reassure the British government, which remembered what had happened when Russia had thrown its lot in with France at the tail-end of the previous war. Denmark's active participation in Russia's Armed Neutrality, designed to keep Britain out of the Baltic, had ended with Nelson's destruction of the Danish fleet at Copenhagen in 1801. Certain members of the cabinet, including the Foreign Secretary George Canning, now thought a pre-emptive assault on Denmark might prevent another Armed Neutrality, preserve Britain's supply of naval stores from the Baltic,

---

1  TNA: ADM 1/5: Report from Captain Francis Beauman, 25 July 1807.

and prevent a Napoleonic invasion by allowing Britain control over the Danish fleet. Ostensibly, such an expedition would simply make a display of force to keep the Danes in line; after all the government already had an ambassador, Brook Taylor, on the spot, and sent a further envoy, Francis Jackson, to negotiate a treaty of alliance between Britain and Denmark at the beginning of July. In reality, however, neither diplomat was encouraged to make any concessions. Instead, Canning persuaded the cabinet to send a force of about 25,000 men under Lieutenant General Lord Cathcart, accompanied by a fleet of over 120 vessels under Admiral James Gambier, including 25 ships of the line, 14 frigates, and between 30 and 40 sloops, along with a large number of gunboats and bomb vessels.² Part of Cathcart and Gambier's orders involved 'persuading' the Danes to allow Britain to 'borrow' their fleet for safe-keeping. This was supposedly to protect it from French depredations, but if diplomatic negotiations failed, as was expected, the British forces in the Baltic were ordered to capture the fleet by any means necessary.³

William, Lord Cathcart, by Henry Meyer after John Hoppner, 1807. (Public domain, The Miriam and Ira D. Wallach Division of Art, Prints and Photographs, The New York Public Library)

In planning the expedition to Copenhagen, Canning needed professional advice, and Popham's guilty verdict did not prevent him being one of the men to whom he turned for it. 'I believe *you* know he planned this Expedition,' Lady Popham wrote, proudly, to Lord Melville, and Popham himself added, 'I trust from all you know of the origin … of this Expedition, that you will more than ever be satisfied I have not possessed your good opinion without deserving it.'⁴ Popham may have been painting out the role of other advisers to make his own role stand out more, but he was the obvious man to turn to for help on planning a large amphibious expedition. Even if the Baltic was not his usual sphere of operations, Popham had gained some knowledge of the waters around Copenhagen in 1800. For a government eager to distance itself from its predecessors, moreover, employing Popham – who had complained so loudly at his court-martial that he was being politically persecuted as a Pittite favourite – had added value. Canning therefore persuaded Mulgrave, the First

---

2    Glover, *The Two Battles of Copenhagen*, pp.109–110, 226–228; TNA: ADM 1/5: Gambier's breakdown of the ships under his command, 7 September 1807.
3    TNA: WO 6/14, ff.7–8: Castlereagh to the Admiralty Board, 18 July 1807.
4    WLC UM: Melville MSS, Box 23: Lady Popham to Melville, 18 September 1807; Popham to Melville, 11 September 1807.

Lord of the Admiralty, to appoint Popham to the expedition as Captain of the Fleet, effectively aide-de-camp to Gambier as commanding admiral. Unlike the ambiguity of Popham's appointment to commodore in Buenos Aires, this was explicitly equivalent in rank to a flag officer and automatically elevated him above the other captains serving in the fleet.

But if the government had hoped to push this appointment through quickly, quietly, and uncontroversially, it was swiftly disabused. Popham had never been popular in the Navy, where he was viewed as a charlatan who had got lucky with the Army. The *Romney* affair had done serious damage to his reputation among his peers, and Buenos Aires and the court-martial killed off any lingering traces of good feeling. While Popham had been almost continuously employed as an adviser by various governments, his professional service record was very thin: he had spent only a handful of years as captain of a vessel, and he had not seen battle since the early 1780s. Several captains with a more glorious history were forced to make way for this upstart Captain of the Fleet, among them Captain Thomas Byam Martin of HMS *Prince of Wales*, Gambier's flagship, who found himself unceremoniously sent ashore for the duration of the campaign. Even Gambier himself was at pains to emphasise Popham's appointment had not been 'a voluntary act of mine'.[5] Many thought there must have been a mistake, or that the Admiralty had bowed to outside pressure from the Duke of York, Popham's former patron.[6] Most, however, were simply outraged that a man court-martialled for disobeying orders should be rewarded with such an important naval command. Mulgrave's Admiralty had, in the words of former Secretary of State for War William Windham in the Commons, 'to the encouragement of all insubordination, and the subversion of all discipline, to the scandal and indignation of the British Navy, … taken him [Popham ] fresh from the strong censure of the court-martial, and elevated him over the heads of so many valiant and deserving officers, his seniors in command'.[7]

Away from Parliament, three senior captains attached to the Danish expedition – Sir Samuel Hood, Richard Keats, and Robert Stopford – issued an official protest to Gambier to express their 'extreme sorrow and concern' at Popham's appointment:

> The principles under which we have been brought up induce us to make any sacrifice that the service of our country may require. We are ready to proceed to any immediate service, but we rely that as early measures will be taken without injury to the service as can be effected to relieve us from the humiliating situation in which the appointment of Sir Home Popham as Captain of the Fleet we feel ourselves placed.[8]

This did not go down well at the Admiralty, which castigated the three officers for presuming to interfere with the ordinary course of naval appointments.[9] Popham interpreted this

---

5   Gambier to Thomas Byam Martin, 17 July 1807, in R.V. Hamilton (ed.), *Letters and Papers of Admiral of the Fleet Sir Thomas Byam Martin* (London: Navy Records Society, 1898), vol.1, pp.326–327.
6   Admiral Sir Charles Pole to Thomas Byam Martin, August 1807, quoted in Hamilton, *Letters and Papers of Sir Thomas Byam Martin*, vol.1, pp.333–334.
7   *The Times*, 1 August 1807.
8   Protest by Hood, Keats, and Stopford, printed in Hamilton, *Letters and Papers of Sir Thomas Byam Martin*, vol.1, pp.330–331.
9   *Naval Chronicle* (1808), vol.19, p.68.

dressing-down as meaning he had the government's full support, and unwisely took aim at the three officers who had attacked him, condemning what he called a sort of 'mutiny' and comparing their remonstrance to 'that sort of combination which the law punishes in journeymen mechanics' – in other words, an illegal strike.[10] Hood, Keats, and Stopford responded by taking a leaf out of Popham's own playbook. They hired a journalist to work up a pamphlet, which printed their protest in full and compared their service record with Popham's, to his detriment:

> The services of the remonstrating captains, when called upon to cede their rank to Sir Home Popham, were from *seventeen to nineteen years post*, during which time they were almost constantly employed; whilst the actual services of Sir Home Popham little exceeded *four years*. He had *never* served as captain under any admiral – had never been in a line of battle – nor had ever commanded a ship in action.[11]

This was unfair, given Popham's employment record had involved long periods of service off, not on, the quarterdeck, but this negative publicity had its intended effect: it caused the ministry to regret the risk they had taken in appointing such a controversial man as Captain of the Fleet. The government feared the political repercussions of their choice, particularly if Popham did something stupid, which he had a track record of doing. Mulgrave, and others, may have cautioned Popham to keep his head down as much as possible. When Popham's appointment was attacked in the Commons at the end of July, the Treasurer of the Navy assured his listeners that Popham would have no opportunity to disobey orders again: 'He was now under the command of a superior officer, and no such error was likely to be repeated.'[12] Popham heeded the warnings. Despite his privileged position as Captain of the Fleet, his activities throughout the expedition were uncharacteristically modest. He refrained from sticking his neck out and, as a result, remained largely anonymous in the official dispatches home.

HMS *Prince of Wales*, with Gambier and Popham aboard, arrived on 27 July off Copenhagen after a smooth voyage hastened by favourable winds. Gambier immediately detached Keats with a squadron to blockade the entry to the Great Belt, the principal naval approach to Copenhagen, and stop any non-British vessels going in or out – itself a declaration of war, although as yet the peace talks still nominally continued.[13] Over the course of the following week, Popham used his navigational skills to guide the fleet closer to the Danish capital. He sent officers on shore to procure provisions and collect intelligence, and the Danes made no attempt to stop them. A contemporary witness recorded how nobody could believe Britain

---

10  Anon., *Full and Correct Report of the Trial of Sir Home Popham*, p.xxx.
11  Anon., *A Discourse upon the True Character of our Late Proceedings in the Baltic* ... (London: W. McDowall for Maxwell and Wilson, 1808), p.116.
12  *The Times*, 1 August 1807.
13  TNA: ADM 1/5: Gambier to Keats, 27 July 1807.

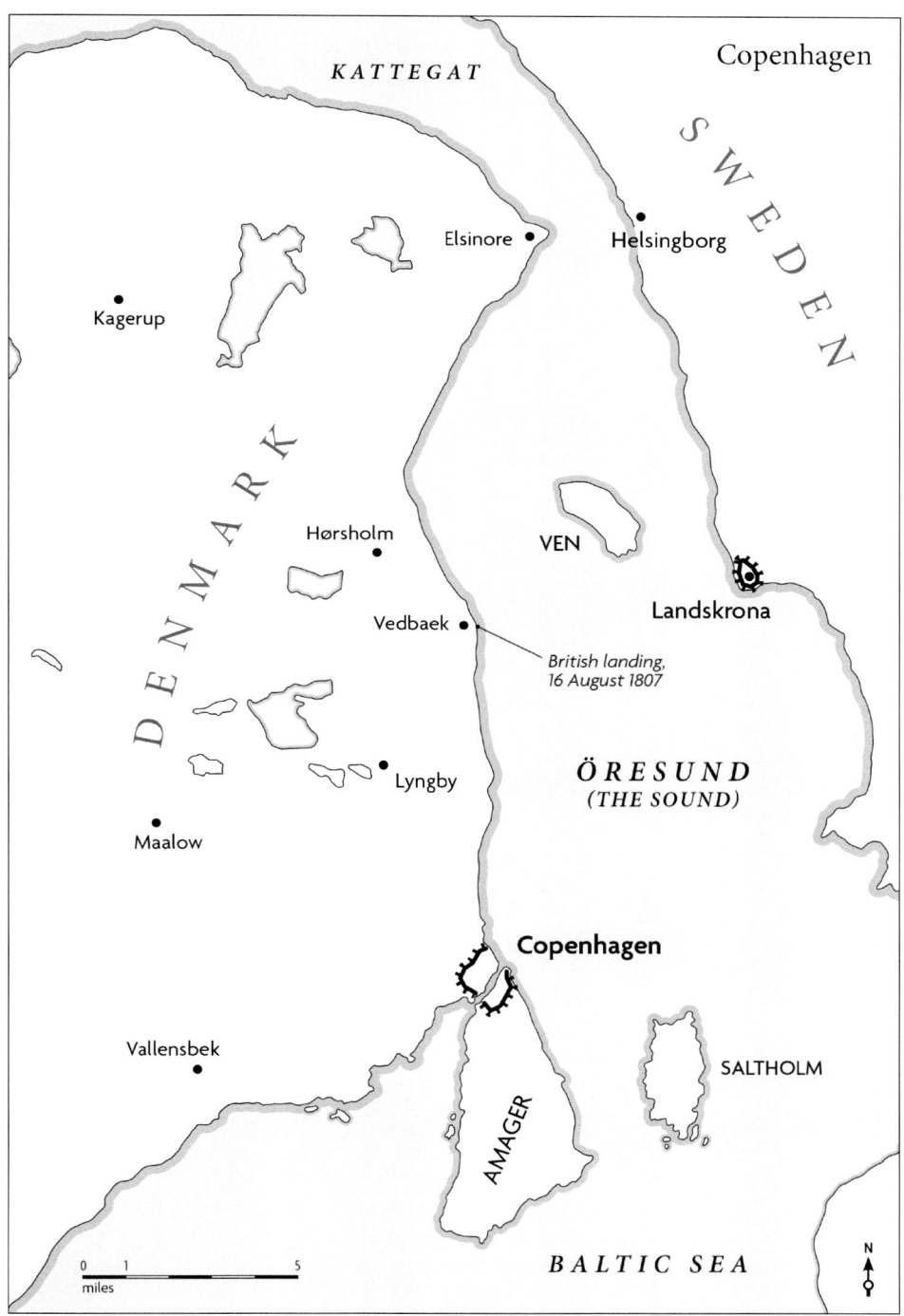

Copenhagen and surroundings, 1807.

might attack 'the only Kingdom, that was … attached … by the strongest of all ties, *self Interest* and I may add self Existance [sic]'.[14]

The British government, however, knew the dispute was unlikely to end diplomatically. Castlereagh sent Lord Cathcart secret instructions informing him the British diplomats in Copenhagen had been ordered to pass on information about Denmark's military defences, and that Cathcart should lose no time in preparing for military operations.[15] Sending a large army and fleet to the Danish capital had not been calculated to make any friends in the Baltic state, but then diplomacy was no longer the point. Capturing the Danish fleet, not frightening Denmark into staying neutral, was now the primary aim of the expedition. Despite the original plan being that any captured Danish ships would be kept in trust and returned at the war's end, Castlereagh now hinted they might permanently pass into the Royal

James Gambier, by George Clint after William Beechey, 1808. (Public domain, The Miriam and Ira D. Wallach Division of Art, Prints and Photographs, The New York Public Library)

Navy: 'It is certainly of great Importance that an unfettered discretion should remain to His Majesty to restore the Fleet or not to Denmark, at the conclusion of the War, according as the Politics of that Court *at that time* may appear in prudence to justify it.'[16] Gambier, for his part, received instructions to destroy the harbour, arsenal, docks, and defences of Copenhagen, and even to occupy the island of Zealand as a semi-permanent British garrison in the Baltic. Although this would only happen if things reached 'such an Extremity with Denmark as to leave us no hope for the future', the government clearly hoped and expected such an 'extremity' would come to pass.[17] The expedition had become an outright act of hostility and annexation.

Still, the looming war with Denmark seemed likely to be very one-sided. As HMS *Prince of Wales* approached Elsinore Castle in 'a heavy squall, with a great deal of Lightning and Rain', Popham transferred into the smaller frigates and sloops in the fleet to investigate Danish defences and take soundings in the shallower waters.[18] The intelligence he collected while carrying out this activity confirmed that Denmark's fleet was lying in ordinary, without

---

14  Claudia Schnurmann (ed.), *John Parish's Journal at Copenhagen* (Berlin: Lit Verlag, 2022), p.52.
15  TNA: WO 6/14, ff.23–31: Castlereagh to Cathcart, 27 July 1807.
16  TNA: WO 6/14, ff.34–37: Castlereagh to Cathcart, 3 August 1807.
17  TNA: WO 6/14, ff.38–41: Castlereagh to Gambier, 3 August 1807.
18  Schnurmann (ed.), *John Parish's Journal*, p.56; TNA: ADM 51/1673: log, HMS *Prince of Wales*, 8 August 1807.

even enough manpower to sail out of harbour. While there were nearly 16,000 British troops lying off Copenhagen, there were only about 5,000 Danish regulars on the island of Zealand, where Copenhagen was located (although there were also 18,000 militiamen).[19] The Danes did have other troops on the mainland in Holstein, but these did not seem in a hurry to reinforce the capital, and Commodore Keats's squadron would almost certainly stop them doing so.

This imbalance between defenders and attackers might have encouraged the British to tighten the diplomatic thumbscrews, but the British envoys on land made little effort to maintain diplomatic language. On 7 August, Francis Jackson – having agreed a course of action with Gambier – gave the Danes an ultimatum: if they did not agree to every British demand by 14 August, there would be consequences. He did not need to explain what those consequences would be, as Copenhagen's fate was already sealed whatever the Danes decided. In passages that were prudently omitted from the *London Gazette*, Gambier told Castlereagh that, if the deadline of 14 August passed without a complete Danish climb-down, he and Cathcart would evacuate the diplomats, land the army, and attack the city. Gambier was not a fan of a pre-emptive attack, but, possibly urged on by Popham, he could see it was necessary to finish the campaign before the weather turned cold for winter.[20]

Popham was certainly pressing Gambier for hotter action, just as he had done in 1800 when he had urged a demonstration of British power to back up Whitworth's diplomatic negotiations. In addition to his hydrographic duties, he spent time ashore reconnoitring the best places for landing large bodies of troops and liaising with provision suppliers. This gave him an opportunity to look up old friends, including the merchant John Parish, who had settled in Copenhagen after escaping the Napoleonic encroachment on Hamburg. Popham had not seen Parish since his time as Agent for Transports in the 1790s and invited him aboard *Prince of Wales*, where the two men had a genuinely warm reunion. But knowing he had a friend in the beleaguered Danish capital encouraged the normally secretive Popham to hint at the near-certainty of a military assault. 'As a friend,' Popham whispered to Parish that he should 'get off from Copenhagen as soon as possible as in all probability it would soon become a scene of action'.[21]

On 12 August, Cathcart and Gambier conferred aboard *Prince of Wales* on the best course of action to take, with Popham in attendance as Captain of the Fleet. Neither naval nor military commander had much heart for what they were by now expected to do, but they agreed with Popham that the whole business should be concluded as quickly as possible. Popham's intelligence suggested the Danes were at last, rather belatedly, preparing for a fight. Brook Taylor, the British ambassador, reported the Prince Royal of Denmark had arrived and that the language of the Danish Foreign Minister suggested 'no terms would be listened to'. With the ultimatum deadline of 14 August approaching, the British diplomats began leaving Copenhagen before they were trapped and forced to undergo the British assault from the side of the defenders. Jackson and the British consul left on the 13th, and Taylor boarded HMS *Cambrian* on the 14th.[22]

---

19  TNA: WO 1/187, f.9: Brook Taylor to Gambier, 2 August 1807.
20  TNA: WO 1/187, ff.21–23: Gambier to Castlereagh, 8 August 1807.
21  Schnurmann (ed.), *John Parish's Journal*, p.57.
22  TNA: WO 1/188, ff.91–93: Cathcart to Castlereagh, 13 August 1807.

As Gambier welcomed the British diplomats aboard, Popham oversaw the assembly of British troops by brigade. This was what he was best at, and he was being given an unparalleled opportunity to show himself worthy of his controversial appointment as Captain of the Fleet. Contrary winds delayed landing the troops until the 15th, when the fleet and transports weighed anchor and plied to windward to the south. At 5:00 p.m., *Prince of Wales* followed the transports into Vedbaek (Wybeck) Bay, about halfway between Elsinore and Copenhagen. Gambier watched as the troops were set on shore under cover of *Surveillante*. Popham oversaw the disembarkation of the army reserve, along with the first shipment of ordnance. The landing went smoothly and a second portion of the army under the command of Major General Brent Spencer was also successfully landed further up the Sound as a diversion.[23] Meanwhile, Gambier and Cathcart, acting on information that the British landing had provoked rioting in Copenhagen, issued a proclamation to fire the locals up further against their rulers: 'We come … to your shores, Inhabitants of Zealand! not as Enemies, but in self-defence, to prevent those who have so long disturbed the peace of Europe, from compelling the force of your Navy, to be turned against us.'[24] This had the expected impact. On 16 August, *Generalmajor* Ernst Peymann, commanding in Copenhagen – the Prince Royal, who had briefly shown his face to raise morale, had prudently absconded – declared all British property under sequestration. War between Britain and Denmark broke out officially next day.[25]

The British force marched inland in three columns to invest the capital from the land side and, as Popham continued overseeing the disembarkation of the cavalry and artillery park, the Danes made their first attempts to fight back. On 17 August, the Crown Battery in Copenhagen roared into life and a squadron of Danish gunboats left the harbour, worked up the coast, and began cannonading the British left with grape and round-shot, setting one of the troop transports on fire. As the British troops fought back as best they could, Popham dispatched a force of gunboats and bomb vessels as close to the harbour as possible – although, because of the shallows, this was still 'at a considerable distance'. The counter-attack was nevertheless successful and the enemy retired back into the harbour.[26] Popham spent the following night getting the gun-brigs to swap their carronades for heavier but more impactful 18-pounder guns, but they were not able to get in close enough to stop the Danish boats bombarding the soldiers digging the British siege lines on shore.[27] Although good progress was being made, Popham decided not to land any more troops on Amack Island as it was too difficult to cover them in the shallows there. The remaining troops eventually landed in the north of Koge Bay on 21 August, along with the battering train for a siege.[28]

As the British troops continued marching inland, Brigadier General Frederick Decken of the King's German Legion took a Danish outpost and captured 850 men and 180 wagons

---

23 TNA: WO 1/188, ff.103–113: journal of the Army, 14–22 August 1807; TNA: WO 1/187, ff.25–6: Gambier to Castlereagh, 16 August 1807.
24 TNA: WO 1/187, ff.29–35: proclamation, 16 August 1807.
25 TNA: WO 1/187, f.45: response by Peymann, 16 August 1807.
26 TNA: WO 1/188, ff.103–113: journal of the Army, 14–22 August 1807; TNA: ADM 51/1673: log, HMS *Prince of Wales*, 17 August 1807.
27 TNA: WO 1/188, ff.103–113: journal of the Army, 14–22 August 1807.
28 TNA: WO 1/188, ff.103–114: journal of the Army, 14–22 August 1807.

of gunpowder on the 19th. The ease with which he did this suggested Popham's intelligence about Denmark's weak defences had been well founded. In a passage redacted out of the *London Gazette*, however, Decken reported he had been 'attacked in almost all Villages by Peasants armed with forks' and that the local countryside was full of hostile locals 'exasperated against the British' – not surprisingly under the circumstances.[29] Despite this local defiance, the Danes made little attempt to launch an outright defence of Copenhagen, possibly because they were so thoroughly outnumbered. By the 21st, the official British casualty returns were only 13 killed and wounded, mostly from Decken's affair of the 20th.[30] The British lines moved forward on the 24th beyond the suburbs of Fredericksberg, when the garrison made a brief sortie. This was driven back and the British settled down to build their final landside batteries 800 yards from the city walls.[31] Popham was back and forth on land to help, organising the lending of ships' guns, consulting with the engineers on their requirements, and overseeing the positioning of the gunboats and blockships.[32]

Until now, the British had advanced rapidly, but things slowed down so much Gambier sent Popham to Cathcart on 24 August to find out what was going on.[33] Despite Popham's attempt to chivvy Cathcart into further action, the next fortnight brought little progress. Cathcart, who had never been entirely on board with this pre-emptive campaign, was hesitating. Everything he saw suggested the Danes were hopelessly unequal to the full might of the British invading forces. This was brought home by a battle fought by the reserve under Major General Sir Arthur Wellesley at Koge on 29 August. Wellesley successfully headed off a body of Danish reinforcements destined for Copenhagen from the southern islands, capturing 1,500 men and a large amount of ordnance, but although Cathcart described the battle as a 'useful' and 'brilliant' victory, most of the enemy had been untrained militia.[34] Diplomat Francis Jackson, sheltering aboard *Prince of Wales*, described the captives from the battle as 'miserable wretches … fit for nothing but following the plough', dressed in coarse woollen coats and wooden clogs: 'The *battle* was not a very glorious one, but this you will keep for yourself.'[35] Nor were the locals more reconciled to the British invasion, and Wellesley's reserve was now tied down suppressing insurgents inland. Cathcart and Gambier were growing remarkably ambivalent about how to complete their mission. On 29 August, the two commanders went against their instructions and approached Peymann with a fresh ultimatum: if the Danes would allow Britain to 'borrow' their fleet until the end of the war, all hostilities would be suspended.[36] Peymann refused.

---

29   TNA: WO 1/188, ff.149–154: report, Brigadier General Decken, 19 August 1807.
30   TNA: WO 1/188, ff.103–113: journal of the Army, 14–22 August 1807.
31   TNA: WO 1/188, ff.131–141: journal of the Army, 22 August–1 September 1807.
32   Cathcart to Gambier, 26 August 1807, in Georgiana, Lady Chatterton (ed.), *Memorials, Personal and Historical of Admiral Lord Gambier, GCB* … (London: Hurst and Blackett, 1861), vol.2, p.31.
33   TNA: WO 1/188, ff.103–113: journal of the Army, 14–22 August 1807; John D. Grainger, *The British Navy in the Baltic* (Woodbridge: The Boydell Press, 2014), p.170.
34   TNA: WO 1/188, ff.173–178: Cathcart to Castlereagh, 2 September 1807.
35   Francis Jackson to his mother, 1 September 1807, in Lady Jackson (ed.), *The Diaries and Letters of Sir George Jackson* … (London: Richard Bentley, 1872), vol.2, pp.207–208.
36   TNA: WO 6/14, ff.56–57: Cathcart and Gambier to Peymann, 29 August 1807; TNA: WO 1/188, ff.119–128: Cathcart to Castlereagh, 31 August 1807.

Cathcart still hoped for a regular siege, following the textbook method of investing the town, building defences, and digging trenches, shifting them closer and closer to the city until its defences could be breached and a capitulation negotiated – a process that might take weeks or months.[37] Cathcart doubted the capability of the naval blockade to keep enemy ships from Copenhagen, as 'bad weather and dark nights' might allow reinforcements to slip through. He also suspected the enemy were likely to destroy their fleet rather than let it fall into British hands.[38] The alternative was bombardment: attempting to force the city to surrender using a combination of powerful artillery and incendiary tactics, a much quicker solution – but one that would endanger the lives of civilians caught in the town and potentially leave Copenhagen uninhabitable.[39] Gambier nevertheless favoured bombardment, as he was worried about the prospect of winter ice beginning to form in the Belt, blocking the British ships in. Popham joined his admiral in urging a swift and decisive end to the campaign. His temper had been pricked by the foggy calm that had set in at the end of August, and he was getting restless. His mood was not improved when a British vessel – a transport converted into a gunboat and manned with seamen from HMS *Valiant* – was blown up by enemy shells during a sortie on 31 August. Most of the men managed to jump overboard and were saved, but about 20 men were wounded, some of whom later died, and two were killed outright.[40] British blood was being shed for no obvious purpose. It was time to finish the campaign.

On 1 September, therefore, in heavy rain and a lightning storm, Cathcart and Gambier summoned Copenhagen one last time, giving Peymann the option to surrender the Danish fleet or submit to a bombardment.[41] Peymann requested permission to speak to the King of Denmark for further instructions, as he did not have the authority to surrender the royal fleet.[42] The British commanders interpreted this as a refusal and ordered the bombardment to begin. Popham sent an officer from *Prince of Wales* with 50 seamen to help man the mortar batteries on land. These consisted of 48 mortars and howitzers, along with twenty 24-pounder guns, all of which opened at 7:30 p.m. on 2 September. The batteries were supported by the bomb ships, which had been manoeuvring into position for days. Within two hours the city was on fire in two different places.[43] The assault continued all night long, the enemy's response 'very slack', although the British gunboats took the brunt of 'a heavy and incessant cannonade' from their Danish counterparts and the land batteries.[44] The firing went on throughout the 3rd and 4th, when Gambier and Popham, watching from the deck of *Prince of Wales*, noticed 'a very large fire' in the city – one of the larger churches collapsed, its steeple toppling out of the sky.[45] On 5 September, with the city fires raging 'with great

---

37 Gavin Daly, *Storm and Sack: British Sieges, Violence and the Laws of War in the Napoleonic Era, 1799–1815* (Cambridge: Cambridge University Press, 2022), p.19.
38 TNA: WO 1/188, ff.119–128: Cathcart to Castlereagh, 31 August 1807.
39 Daly, *Siege and Sack*, p.20.
40 TNA: ADM 1/5: Captain Young of HMS *Valiant* to Gambier, 31 August 1807.
41 TNA: WO 1/187, ff.77–79: summons of 1 September 1807.
42 TNA: WO 1/187, ff.81–82: Peymann's response, 1 September 1807.
43 TNA: ADM 1/5: Gambier to the Admiralty, 7 September 1807; TNA: ADM 51/1673: log, HMS *Prince of Wales*, 2 September 1807, for the officer and 50 men.
44 TNA: WO 1/188, ff.187–188: Cathcart to Castlereagh, 3 September 1807; TNA: ADM 1/5: Gambier to the Admiralty, 7 September 1807.
45 TNA: ADM 51/1673: log, HMS *Prince of Wales*, 4 and 5 September 1807.

The bombardment of Copenhagen, by Johan Lorenz Rugendas II, 1820. (Public domain, Anne S.K. Brown Military Collection, Brown University Library)

The bombardment of Copenhagen by the British forces, 2–5 September 1807, by Henry Martens, 1845. (Public domain, Anne S.K. Brown Military Collection, Brown University Library)

violence',[46] Cathcart called a ceasefire to find out if the Danes were ready to treat. Peymann requested 24 hours to prepare a capitulation agreement, but this was denied.[47] At noon on the 6th the enemy finally agreed to all British demands on the condition that the firing stopped immediately. More than 300 houses and a church had been completely destroyed, and thousands more damaged. A conservatively estimated 450 civilians had been killed, 900 wounded. 'Many houses were still smouldering,' one eyewitness recalled, bitterly. '... Mothers were bewailing the melancholy fate of their slaughtered children, and there was not one but deplored the loss of some fondly beloved relative or dearly valued friend.'[48]

Gambier's dispatch reporting the surrender commended Popham's behaviour during the short campaign: 'I feel it my duty to make a particular acknowledgment of the aid I have derived from Sir Home Popham, Captain of the Fleet, whose prompt resources, and complete knowledge of his profession, especially of that branch which is connected with the operations of an Army, qualify him in a peculiar manner for the arduous and various duties with which he has been charged.'[49] It was the first time the admiral had mentioned his Captain of the Fleet in his formal correspondence, and in many ways it was a routine commendation of the sort that was expected and required in an official dispatch. Very unusually, Popham had spent the campaign keeping a low profile, helping oversee the landing of the troops, securing provisions, sounding out the coastline, and procuring intelligence. Mindful that the government considered him to be on a sort of probation following his court-martial, he was on his best behaviour, which apparently involved restricting himself to his duties and making himself easy for Gambier to find. Being a good boy for the commanding admiral must have been hard for Popham after so many years of being his own man, but it paid off. Cathcart had selected the Deputy Quarter-Master General, Lieutenant Colonel George Murray, and Major General Sir Arthur Wellesley to negotiate the capitulation on the Army's behalf, and Gambier chose Popham to represent the Navy.

Popham and his two fellow negotiators moved quickly, mindful that the Danes might still change their mind. They landed late in the evening on the 6th, signed the capitulation on the 7th, and ratified it at noon on the 8th. The Danes agreed to surrender the citadel and dockyard with immediate effect, as well as to hand over the fleet and naval stores to a British representative. Despite the British government's flirtation with the idea of using Zealand as a Baltic military base, the British pledged in return to evacuate the island within six weeks.[50] Popham, still deputising for Gambier, officially took possession of the ships and stores captured from the defeated enemy, and assisted Vice Admiral Sir Henry Stanhope (Gambier's second-in-command) in assessing the state of the captured fleet. The prize for which Britain had pre-emptively gone to war and destroyed a whole city turned out to consist of 18 ships of the line, seven frigates, eight sloops, seven brigs, 21 gunboats, and four schooners.[51] Stanhope and Popham noted that 'few of the Ships are in any considerable progress of equipment' – something the British had suspected for some time, but which

---

46   TNA: WO 1/187, ff.93–94: Cathcart to Castlereagh, 5 September 1807.
47   TNA: ADM 1/5: Gambier to the Admiralty, 7 September 1807.
48   Glover, *The Two Battles of Copenhagen*, pp.158–159, 258
49   TNA: ADM 1/5: Gambier to the Admiralty, 7 September 1807.
50   TNA: WO 1/187. ff.101–106: capitulation, 8 September 1807.
51   TNA: ADM 1/5: list of Danish ships, 7 September 1807.

was nevertheless left out of the *Gazette* as it undermined the urgency of the need to attack Denmark in the first place.[52] Four of the ships had to be immediately destroyed as they were in no fit condition to sail to Britain. One 64-gun ship was cut to pieces in the dock; the other three were sailed out onto the shoals near Copenhagen and wrecked.

The Danish fleet was nevertheless physical proof that the expedition had fulfilled its objectives, and Popham probably hoped his involvement in bringing the trophies home would paper over any remaining uncertainty about him among the men he hoped to win over as long-term political patrons. His international notoriety following the Buenos Aires expedition, however, did not play in his favour. The French press gleefully reported a dispute between Popham and the Danish commandant over missing ordnance, suggesting any stolen cannons were most likely to be found in the possession of Sir Home Popham himself.[53] The official *Moniteur* published a lengthy screed decrying Popham as 'the shame of the navy' and concluded that employing such a pirate as Captain of the Fleet was typical of the British, whose attack on a neutral power had already shown a startling level of villainy.[54] The *Moniteur* was hardly a trustworthy reflection of French public opinion, but the fact Popham's name was being used to bring the British down did not go unnoticed in London, where the significance of what had just happened for the international political and military situation was only just beginning to break on the men who had Popham's career prospects in their hands.

Popham was not yet worried about the impact of his role in a highly controversial campaign. He was in excellent spirits: a campaign he had helped plan and execute had, for once, been a complete success. Popham wrote privately to Melville, claiming he had personally dictated the third and fourth articles of the capitulation – the meat of the agreement – regarding transferring the Danish fleet and naval stores into British care. The letter was extraordinarily boastful even by his usual standards. 'I wish you could hear Admiral Gambier's opinion of me now,' he gloated. 'I think and I am vain enough to think, he would astonish you.' Popham believed Copenhagen would wipe his slate clean of all transgressions, leaving only his achievements, and Popham was never in the mood to play those down: 'Has any man in the Kingdom done so much[?] is there an Instance on record of an Individual having done so much in such distant quarters[?]' He fully expected to be rewarded for everything he had done, both at Copenhagen and elsewhere, and finished his letter to Melville hungrily: 'All I ask of the present Administration and of my Country is to give me a patent Place not less than a thousand a Year.' With either false modesty or a genuine twinge of uncertainty, however, he added: 'I am so unlucky a dog that I never expect anything to succeed for myself.'[55]

Popham was right to doubt, and Gambier's gratitude for Popham's services did not stretch to choosing him to carry the dispatches announcing the campaign's success. This was a much sought-after responsibility, which came with a reward of £500 and, in the case of important campaigns, a knighthood or even a baronetcy. Instead of Popham, however, the honour went to Captain Collier of *Surveillante*. As Captain of the Fleet, Popham felt

---

52  TNA: ADM 1/5: Gambier to the Admiralty, 7 September 1807.
53  *Journal de l'Empire*, 25 November 1807.
54  *Gazette Nationale ou le Moniteur Universel*, 26 December 1807.
55  WLC UM: Melville MSS, Box 23: Popham to Melville, 11 September 1807.

carrying the dispatches was his 'birthright'; when Gambier explained his expertise was required to help Vice Admiral Stanhope fit out the Danish ships for the sea and re-embark the army, Popham was only partly mollified. He had expected to underline his success by representing it personally to the government, perhaps mindful that Gambier had not been especially effusive about him throughout the campaign: 'When all is finished, these Services [I have rendered] may be forgot in London.'[56]

But Popham was too distracted by his responsibilities to worry much about what he could expect when he got home. The British wanted to get away from Copenhagen as quickly as possible, despite the fact the government in London was still hoping to use Zealand as a base to bar the French from the Baltic.[57] Popham had always responded well to pressure, and his exertions in getting the Danish fleet ready to sail delighted and surprised Gambier: 'We have proceeded with wonderfull expedition by the help of the Army in equipping the Danish ships and embarking the stores from the Arsenal, which has exceeded my most sanguine expectations.'[58] By the end of September, 14 Danish ships had moved out of harbour, loaded with timber and stores.[59] Three Danish ships set sail for the Nore on 3 October, and five more ships of the line and one brig sailed under convoy on the 14th, their crews topped up with volunteers the Admiralty had recruited from Britain's merchant seamen with the promise of a bounty and indemnity from the press.[60] Once the troops were all re-embarked, *Prince of Wales* led the fleet home at 7:00 a.m. on 21 October, carrying over 330 officers and men of the Coldstream Guards.[61]

Popham left Copenhagen still full of hope for the future. Not being chosen to take the dispatches home had shaken him a little, but it had not dented his confidence much. He knew he had done a good job as Captain of the Fleet, particularly in getting the Danish prizes ready to sail home. His expectations were all the greater because he was aware the Prime Minister himself had offered Gambier a peerage, and that Gambier had requested further rewards for his second-in-command and Captain of the Fleet:

> Lord Gambier sent for me on the closing a dispatch, and said 'Now, Popham, the Baronetcy or the Red Ribbon?' My answer was, 'Sir, you know I have very little value for the former because I have no fortune to leave my Son.' However this was an argument he combated so forcibly that I really thought he had some very confidential authority to propose the two, but to persuade me to take the Baronetcy.[62]

Unfortunately for Popham, the timing of Gambier's request was catastrophic. In mid-September, news had arrived in London of the definitive failure of Popham's South American experiment. Lieutenant General Whitelocke had been sent with a new army in March to

---

56  WLC UM: Melville MSS, Box 23: Popham to Melville, 11 September 1807.
57  TNA: WO 6/14, ff.51–52: Castlereagh to Cathcart, 5 September 1807.
58  TNA: WO 1/187, ff.157–158: Gambier to Castlereagh, 27 September 1807.
59  TNA: ADM 1/5: Gambier to Admiralty, 19 September 1807.
60  TNA: ADM 1/5: Gambier to William Wellesley Pole, 14 October 1807; TNA: ADM 51/1673: log, HMS *Prince of Wales*, 14 October 1807.
61  TNA: ADM 51/1673: log, HMS *Prince of Wales*, 20 and 21 October 1807.
62  BL: Loan MS 57/108, no.8: Popham to Melville, 23 November 1807.

re-capture Buenos Aires, but his attempt to do so had ended in complete disaster. Some of the responsibility could be, and was, deflected onto the Grenville government that had sent Whitelocke out, but the outcome of the second Buenos Aires expedition did not make Portland's cabinet more likely to trust any ideas Popham might come up with.

When the rewards for Copenhagen were handed out at St James's Palace, therefore, Popham was not one of the men kissing the King's hand. Popham was disgusted; he was also beginning to be afraid. He complained to Melville of

> this unprecedented neglect, nay I may go further, I may call it marked disapprobation, and contempt, as strong as could have been shewn if the expedition had failed in toto, and the causes of its failure had been solely ascribable to my want of energy Judgement and professional Knowledge ... I certainly did expect some mark of His Majesty's favor; I proudly felt that there were fifty thousand Witnesses to my exertions and it was impossible for words to mark more strongly the appreciation of my Services, than they did in the despatches of Admiral and General. ... There is no instance on record where an Admiral has been made a Peer that something has not been done for the Captain of the Fleet.[63]

The fact Popham had chosen Melville's ear to bend on this subject was not coincidental. Popham was beginning to realise his only hope might be for Melville to return to office, either in the cabinet or, better still, as Prime Minister. Beyond his complaints, therefore, Popham was trying to persuade his former patron to return to London, as 'many would flock' to his standard. Popham felt he could speak frankly to Melville, and that their shared experience of political persecution allowed him to approach his patron on a more equal footing. But deep down, even Popham knew Melville's impeachment had cast a long shadow, just as Buenos Aires was a huge millstone round Popham's own neck. As the rollercoaster year of 1807 drew to a close, things were not looking especially bright. 'There is a damn'd deal of ingratitude in the World,' Popham complained to his greatest political patron, including himself in that statement as much as Melville.[64]

---

63   BL: Loan MS 57/108, no.8: Popham to Melville, 23 November 1807.
64   BL: Loan MS 57/108, no.8: Popham to Melville, 23 November 1807.

# 16

# Walcheren, 1809–1810

*2483: How many men have you lost?*

To Popham's mounting concern, the 'damn'd deal of ingratitude' continued to afflict his career into 1808. For much of the second half of 1807 and the first half of 1808, Popham was hardly out of the newspapers, and not in a good way. Much of this publicity involved the division of prize money from the Cape of Good Hope and Buenos Aires campaigns. The parading of the Buenos Aires silver through the streets of London had caught the public imagination, but the practicalities of dividing the spoils had caused a great deal of bad feeling between the protagonists in the campaign – particularly when Beresford, who had escaped from South America and returned to Britain, heard about the dispute surrounding Popham's rank as commodore.

Had Popham been entitled to call himself a commodore at Buenos Aires with the right to appoint a captain under him, he would have been entitled to a full eighth of the prize money arising from the expedition. Popham had entered into an agreement on that basis with Sir David Baird, who claimed a share of the prize money as overall military commander, even though he had not been present at Buenos Aires. According to this agreement, the flag officer's eighth would be divided into fifths, of which Beresford would receive one-fifth and Baird and Popham two-fifths each.[1] But if Popham had not been a 'full' commodore – if he had only been a 'ten-shilling commodore' – the flag officer's eighth would have to be divided between Baird and Beresford alone, with Popham dividing two-eighths of the prize money with his fellow squadron captains and the other equivalent officers in the Army. The distribution of the Buenos Aires prize money, therefore, swiftly transformed into an unpleasant legal free-for-all. Both Baird and Beresford petitioned the Privy Council to issue a warrant barring Popham from the booty, and Popham was challenged by the former captain of HMS *Narcissus*, Ross Donnelly, in the Court of Common Pleas. Popham, Donnelly's lawyers argued, had 'assumed the Rank of a Flag Officer without the slightest Authority' and deprived 'the General Officers of a considerable Part of their Prize Money and his Brother Captains of One-Third of Theirs'. The court found in favour of Donnelly, and Popham was ordered to pay his former subordinate £2,004 17s 2d in damages.[2]

---

1 *The Times*, 21 July 1807.
2 Anon., *A Correct Account of the Trial at Large between Ross Donnelly, esq, a Post-Captain in His Majesty's Navy, Plaintiff, and Sir Home Popham, Knt, Defendant, before Sir James Mansfield, Chief*

Popham had higher hopes of success in defeating Baird and Beresford's petitions before the Privy Council, which was controlled by the Pittite government. Whatever they thought about him and his South American antics personally, publicly Popham expected ministers to stand by him as Pitt's chosen man. The Admiralty initially refused to confirm that he had ever had a right to the rank of flag officer, but when Popham's name came up for Captain of the Fleet at Copenhagen a few months later, it miraculously changed its mind.³ The King's Advocate mused that, even if Popham legally had no right to claim a flag share, the division of booty was the King's prerogative and the King could therefore ultimately divide the booty in any way he saw fit.⁴ But the government dropped this sort of language completely after Copenhagen, as the prize money debate reminded them just how little they wanted to court more adverse commentary by giving so controversial a man as Popham yet more of a reward. When the warrant for distributing the Buenos Aires booty was issued in July 1808, therefore, it divided the 'flag share' eighth between Baird and Beresford and cut Popham out of the equation entirely, 'there being no Flag Officer, or Person entitled to be esteemed as a Flag Officer, employed upon the said conjunct Expedition.'⁵ Popham was not exactly out of pocket: he received just under £6,000 in prize money. Beresford, however, received about £12,000, and Baird nearly £24,000.⁶

Despite the government's best efforts to contain it, the dispute over the Buenos Aires booty quickly spilled out into the political domain. Captain Ross Donnelly, fresh from his victory in the Court of Common Pleas and still angry about what he felt was Popham's duplicity, had failed in a petition to the Privy Council to get Popham blocked completely from sharing in *any* part of the prize money. Convinced Popham had somehow bribed the Privy Council to take his side, Donnelly approached Popham's political enemies, offering to dish the dirt on Popham's misdeeds at the Cape and Buenos Aires. With the assistance of Sir Richard Keats, one of the three officers who had countersigned the protest against Popham's appointment at Copenhagen, Donnelly drew up a memorandum making several serious accusations, many of which were enhanced by specific examples countersigned by Donnelly himself in the margin:

> Although Sir Home Popham unblushingly asserts that he has taken two Capitals of Two Quarters of the Globe ... yet he never put himself within common Shot, nor was one fired at him during these Expeditions, but he basely ran away from [Buenos Aires] at the moment Gen[eral] Beresford was overwhelmed with Multitudes, without sending even a Flag of Truce to enquire the Fate of those whom he got into this Scrape ... Had this part of his Conduct come under the Revisal of his Court Martial, it would not probably have fared so well with him.

---

*Justice of His Majesty's Court of Common Pleas, and a Special Jury, on Saturday, the 27th of June, 1807, at Westminster Hall* ... (London: T. Cadell and W. Davies, 1807), pp.101–108.

3   Marsden to Popham, 15 April 1807, Anon., *Trial Between Donnelly and Popham*, p.128; TNA: PC 1/3823: opinion signed by Lord Mulgrave, Sir James Gambier, and Sir Richard Bickerton, 25 June 1807.
4   TNA: PC 1/3823: John Nicholls to Sir William Fawkener, 3 October 1807.
5   House of Commons, *Papers Relating to Property Captured at Buenos Aires* ... (London: Ordered by the House of Commons to be printed, 27 April and 1 May 1812), pp.10–11; quotation from Captain Edmonds' petition of 10 July 1808, p.11; details of flag share on p.12.
6   Hughes, *The British Invasion of the River Plate*, p.57.

Donnelly clearly had his eyes on a potential inquiry, offering his testimony at the bar of the Commons and suggesting other captains might also be willing to testify.[7]

Donnelly could do Popham little harm by himself, but he had contacts. On 4 December 1807, radical City of London alderman Robert Waithman told the Court of Common Council – the heart of the City of London's economic and political power, and a body the government was always eager to keep on-side – that it ought to expunge a vote of thanks it had passed in 1806 recognising Popham's capture of Buenos Aires. To buttress his argument, Waithman brought in a number of details he could only have got from Donnelly's memorandum, or from Donnelly himself. He parroted, almost word for word, Donnelly's criticisms of Popham's thin service record: 'He did not mean to dispute Sir Home Popham's capacity as a navigator; he might be a very wise and brave officer; but he did not recollect any great exploit he had ever done for his country. He did not think Sir Home ever saw a line of battle formed, nor did he ever hear of his being in any engagement.'[8] The Court of Common Council rejected Waithman's motion, but less than two months later Popham was challenged again, this time in the House of Commons by the MP for Yarmouth, Stephen Lushington. Donnelly's memorandum had accused Popham of receiving the £18,000 Privy Council grant for *Etrusco* as a sweetener following his election to Parliament in 1804. Lushington repeated this claim, inflating the sum to £25,000 paid by the government as compensation for what he described, flatly, as a smuggling venture: '[Popham] carried a cargo to Canton in China; having taken in a fresh cargo there, of which a French supercargo at Canton had a share, he sailed … to Dungeness, where he landed goods, or, in plain English, smuggled them'.[9]

Aware that Pittite probity was bound up in the murkiness of Popham's past, the government tried to head off the attack by noting that, if Popham had breached any laws, the East India Company had clearly chosen to turn a blind eye.[10] Lushington backed off and appeared to drop the matter, but on 31 May he returned to the fray with a motion censuring Popham directly. Lushington had used the intervening months to do his research. He repeated all the old claims: that Popham had broken the terms of his leave; that he had engaged in subterfuge to conceal the true ownership of *Etrusco*; that he had illegally landed goods on English soil. Two aspects of Lushington's charge, however, were entirely new. The first was an accusation that Popham had offered Captain Robinson of *Brilliant* £40,000 to release *Etrusco* when it had first been captured (Popham loudly denied this from across the floor of the House). The second was even more serious. Lushington claimed to have seen a bill of lading for *Etrusco* that included 40 cast iron guns and some small arms, 'but it nowhere appears how they were disposed of; and it has been said they were sold to the native powers [in India], some of whom were at that period engaged in hostility with us'. This was an outright charge that Popham had sold weapons to Mysore, which had been at war, on and off, with British India until Tipu Sultan's final defeat at Seringapatam in 1799. Lushington held back, however, from landing the killing blow: 'I have no proof of this.'[11]

Lushington was not the only one who had done his homework. Popham's defence filled nearly 20 columns in the *Parliamentary Debates* and he clearly enjoyed giving it. He began

---

7   BL: Add MS 37887, ff.198–206; BL: Add MS 37284, ff.152–159.
8   *The Times*, 4 December 1807.
9   *Parliamentary Debates*, vol.10, cols.452–453.
10  *Parliamentary Debates*, vol.10, col.456.
11  *Parliamentary Debates*, vol.11, cols.721–734.

by dismissing the motion as yet another attempt 'to traduce me, and to render me odious to the country'. Having identified Lushington's attack as little more than another example of groundless political persecution, Popham let himself go:

> No pains have been spared, no means scrupled at, to lower and vilify my character: the poisoned arrows of mine enemies have been aimed at me both as a public man and a private individual; they have raked into every part of my life to find out some personal weakness, in order to use it as a calumny against me: the follies of my youth, and any attendant foibles, have been held out to the public as the most enormous crimes: all the private transactions of my life have been gone into, and such an effect has it had, that unless I yield in all cases to what I consider an imposition, a threat of impeachment is held out against me, and this by the house entertaining discussions on private transactions.

Popham had a flair for drama, and he was determined to make this performance – and it *was* a performance – memorable:

> Good God, sir! Is it possible that one of [the members of the House of Commons] … could have been guilty of carrying arms and ammunition to the enemies of his country? Such a person surely ought to be tied to a stake in Palace-yard. With the house, however, it will rest to say, what ought to be the fate of any man who falsely and flagitiously brings such a charge against one of its members.

The rest of his speech went over all the accusations and rebutted them with more bravado than evidence. Popham concluded by correcting a point of detail. Lushington had cited £25,000 as the sum Popham received from the government for *Etrusco*; in fact he had received only £16,000, plus expenses. With this cheeky attempt to underline Lushington's shaky grasp of the facts, Popham retired from the House to allow his fellow MPs to vote on the motion of censure. It was comfortably rejected by 126 votes to 57.[12]

Popham had always been the flamboyant hero in his personal narrative, and it was not surprising that he characterised Lushington's attack on him as part of a broader political assault that had been going on for years. During his speech in the House of Commons, Popham read excerpts of letters from colleagues who had been happy to hear of his appointment as Captain of the Fleet at Copenhagen and challenged Lushington to find three officers (a veiled reference to Keats, Stopford, and Hood's official protest) who thought he had done a bad job in his command. This was more for the benefit of his patrons than for Lushington, who must have wondered why Popham had devoted so much time on Copenhagen during a debate about *Etrusco*. But Popham knew very well that his court-martial, and its verdict, made him a bigger target for his enemies, who wanted to destroy him once and for all. What he does not seem to have realised was that it was working.

---

12   *Parliamentary Debates*, vol.11, cols.734–752.

Fresh from success at Copenhagen, Popham expected his schemes to continue meeting with high-level approval, and that he would be the one sent out to execute them. In the autumn of 1807, he wrote a long memorandum on naval warfare for First Lord of the Admiralty Mulgrave, copying in the Foreign Secretary, George Canning (whom he did not know, but who, as a close friend of William Huskisson, Popham hoped would act as his champion in the cabinet). The memorandum offered a fascinating insight into Popham's own priorities, as well as what he thought those of the government were – or ought to be. Having abandoned his plans of invading English shores from Boulogne, Popham thought Napoleon was most likely to attack Britain either through Ireland or via India, and this should be matched by a change in Britain's own strategic drive. Instead of blockading the enemy's fleet in its ports, which he thought 'ruinous', Popham suggested posting 20 ships of the line permanently off the coast of Ireland and headquartering the Channel Fleet at Beerhaven. To protect the route to India, Popham suggested capturing Tenerife and making it into a naval station. Moving Britain's main Atlantic watering station away from Madeira would make it easier to assault Spain's South American holdings, Popham's favourite project, and he was probably aware the government was still toying with sending another military force to the Rio de la Plata.[13] With this in mind, Popham suggested sending 16,000 infantry and four regiments of dismounted dragoons to South America. To avoid a debacle on the scale of 1806, Popham urged that the British should openly support South American independence, offering a commercial alliance with the new state.[14]

To Popham's consternation, the government ignored him. This was partly because the international context changed significantly in 1808 when Napoleon tried to place Spain under the kingship of his brother Joseph and ignited a rebellion against his rule. Britain formed an alliance with Spain and sent an army to the Peninsula to help liberate it. With Spain now on Britain's side, Popham's Spanish American obsession became embarrassing. A campaign against Trinidad or the Rio de la Plata was clearly not going to happen, but to Popham's rising alarm there was no sign of employment anywhere else either. In May 1808 his hopes were raised when he was appointed captain of HMS *Venerable*, but although he spent the spring in Cork harbour in the expectation of being sent on service, nothing came of it, and he does not seem to have taken proper command of the ship.[15] Since Copenhagen, his only official employment had been to chair a committee examining existing British charts, a body he had lobbied the Admiralty to form. In September 1808, therefore, Popham made another play for employment. The Rio de la Plata was out of the question – 'I will not venture a word on the Subject of South America' – but Popham reminded his audience that India was still a likely French target. To defend it, Popham proposed sending an amphibious force to capture Mauritius, which would have the dual effect of protecting British India and neutralising French-sponsored piracy in the Indian Ocean. While Popham proposed Vice Admiral Sir Albemarle Bertie for the overall command, he strongly hinted that he himself would like to go out with HMS *Venerable* to lead the attack, while Bertie would remain at

---

13 'Memorandum for Cabinet Measures suggested respecting South America', 21 December 1807, Londonderry (ed.), *Castlereagh Correspondence*, vol.8, pp.97–100.
14 BL: Loan MS 57/108, no.12: memorandum, December 1807; see BL: Add MS 89143/2/29/8 for a slightly different copy (dated 6 November 1807).
15 BL: Egerton MS 2137, f.202: Popham to J. Lambert, 24 April 1808.

the Cape of Good Hope to direct operations from afar: 'If the *Venerable* may be considered a proper Ship to conduct the Blockade under the orders of Admiral Bertie, she might sail immediately for the Brazils and the Cape and orders from thence forwarded to India.'[16]

When the First Lord 'appeared to give a fostering smile to the [Mauritius] proposition', Popham believed he would soon be setting sail.[17] The only trouble, he was told, was that he had requested 7,000 infantry for the job, whereas most of Britain's disposable force was currently in the Peninsula under Lieutenant General Sir John Moore. Popham, who considered the war in Spain a distraction from Britain's real concerns, railed to Lord Harrowby – one of his few remaining government contacts – about this 'hobby-horsical' obstruction: 'surely the golden object of India ought to have some paramount consideration?'[18] But there were political as well as strategic obstacles to his plans. The Mauritius plan was not put into action for another year and, when it was, Popham himself was not involved. He continued to hold out hope, however, all the way into December, when he received a letter from Mulgrave that made him physically ill. 'Mulgrave deserves to be kicked,' he scrawled, almost illegibly, to his friend Denis O'Bryen from his sickbed. Rather than sending Popham to Mauritius in *Venerable*, Mulgrave proposed to take him out of his current ship and put him on half-pay for six or seven months until HMS *San Domingo* could be made ready for him. Mulgrave then proposed to send Popham, not to Mauritius, but to the West Indies, a lucrative but notoriously unhealthy station. Popham was sick and tired of being given substandard commands – as he put it, being 'kick[ed] … from one end of the World to the other' – and he desperately wanted a plum post, if only to put paid to the growing rumours that he was out of favour with the government.[19] Popham, with his inflated sense of self-worth and conveniently forgetting how controversial he had become, thought he deserved better than this. But although he was convinced he was being fobbed off, he did not seem to realise why.

Henry Phipps, 1st Earl of Mulgrave, by William Skelton after William Beechey, 1808. (Public domain, Yale Center for British Art, Paul Mellon Collection)

---

16   BL: Loan MS 57/108. no.9, 10a: Popham to Melville, 10 September 1808.
17   BL: Loan MS 57/108, no.12: Popham to Melville, 14 October 1808.
18   BL: Loan MS 57/108, no.10a: Popham to Lord Harrowby, 23 September 1808.
19   BL: Add MS 45498, f.39: Popham to Denis O'Bryen, [5 December 1808].

Popham's frustration was increased by family difficulties. In September 1808 Lady Popham gave birth prematurely to a sickly baby who only survived 13 months.[20] Under these circumstances, being beached could be interpreted a blessing, and as Popham wrote to Robert Dundas – heir to Lord Melville and a cabinet member as President of the Board of Control – he had 'rather liberally' availed himself of the Admiralty's permission to spend some time ashore with his family.[21] But this was putting a brave face on an unpalatable situation, and Popham was getting increasingly irritated. He knew he could not rely on 'that Scoundrel Mulgrave' for employment.[22] In January 1809, however, Popham had the opportunity to renew old friendships when the Duke of York was attacked in Parliament for selling military commissions through his mistress, Mary Anne Clarke. The investigation into York's activities caused a sensation, and York was forced to resign as Commander-in-Chief of the Army. The government was hamstrung by political weakness, but elements of Pitt's former following mobilised in York's favour. Lady Hester Stanhope, Pitt's niece, was at the hub of this network. She remembered Popham from 1804 when he had been preparing to attack the French flotilla at Boulogne. Mindful that he would want to defend the Duke of York, and that he had plentiful press connections, she engaged him in the Duke's political defence.

Popham did indeed have good reason to support the man who had given him his first professional opportunity to shine, and initially threw himself enthusiastically into York's cause. He got his newspaper and pamphleteering contacts to publish pro-York accounts and drummed up as much support as he could from all shades of the political spectrum.[23] Popham himself wrote 'a paper upon the *licentiousness of the Press*', which Lady Hester Stanhope was in two minds about – 'it is very extraordinary and very bold' – but which she ultimately thought would '*do good*'.[24] But Popham was not the kind of man to remain aboard a sinking ship. Public opinion was against the Duke of York, and no amount of pamphleteering, no matter how 'extraordinary' or 'bold', was going to save him. As soon as this became clear, Popham used ill health as an excuse to stay away from the final divisions in the House of Commons. This allowed him to distance himself from the Duke, but destroyed his credit with Lady Hester: 'I have never had common patience with [Popham], since he behaved so shabbily in not coming down to the house to vote for the Duke ... Illness was no excuse, he s[houl]d have come down in his bed gown and night cap'.[25]

Popham's behaviour did not win him much favour with the government, either. The Portland ministry simply did not have the energy for trimming troublemakers. Still reeling from the York affair, the Portland ministry was also beset by the apparent failure of their first attempt to get involved in the Iberian Peninsula. Although Sir Arthur Wellesley had been victorious over the French at Vimeiro, his superior officer, Sir Hew Dalrymple, had apparently thrown away every advantage he had gained by signing the Convention of Cintra. This had led to a military inquiry at Chelsea and a great deal of political discussion over the

---

20   BL: Loan MS 57/108, no.10: Popham to Robert Dundas, 23 September 1808.
21   BL: Loan MS 57/108, no.10: Popham to Robert Dundas, 23 September 1808.
22   BL: Add MS 45498, f.37: Popham to Denis O'Bryen, [4 December 1808].
23   Denis O'Bryen, *A Narrative, by ... D. O'Bryen, in consequence of the attack made upon him ... in the House of Commons ... Part the Second* (London, 1820), p.25.
24   BL: Add MS 70959, f.86: Lady Hester Stanhope to General Grenville, 'Saturday night' [1809].
25   BL: Add MS 70959, f.73: Lady Hester Stanhope to General Grenville, 6 July [1809].

government's ability to plan and execute war strategy. Matters were not improved when the army under Sir John Moore had been outflanked by the French and suffered a horrendous winter march to the Spanish coast. Moore fought a last-ditch battle at Corunna in January 1809 to cover the evacuation of his men, losing his life in the process. Moore's victory could not obscure the fact he had been retreating in defeat, and the return to British shores of his bedraggled army, 'naked and worn down [in] appearance',[26] was a horrifying reminder to the public of the reality of the struggle against Napoleon.

Popham was aware the government was the weakest it had been for some time. Instead of offering his support, however, he interpreted this vulnerability as an opportunity to push out a set of men who were unfavourable to him and seriously toyed with joining the political opposition in Parliament.[27] But this would have brought him into contact with men who actually hated him – members of the former Addington government; Lord St Vincent; Lord Grey – and helping them to power would be like cutting off his nose to spite his face. Popham thus decided things were unlikely to change unless he could persuade Lord Melville to come back to power. Melville had stood trial in 1806 before the House of Lords and been acquitted of embezzlement; he was technically free to return to active politics. Encouraged by Popham and others, therefore, Melville came to London to offer his services, perhaps as First Lord of the Admiralty, to prop up the tottering government.[28]

Popham suspected Melville's return to office would be followed by an offer of employment, and he therefore pulled every political string on his patron's behalf. His activities, however, quickly became embarrassing. Popham approached an old patron from Flanders, Lord Moira, a close associate of the Prince of Wales, to persuade him to meet with Melville to discuss a political alliance. Moira, however, had no interest in overthrowing the government before it imploded by itself. He dismissed Popham's plotting as 'in truth nugatory' and told him off for acting in a manner that was bound to set tongues wagging, doing 'just enough … to give an undefined supposition of engagement, which is embarrassing without any tendency to be useful'.[29] Melville, too, was reluctant to be drawn into the web Popham was trying to weave. He claimed he had no desire to return to office, not because he was not wanted in government – 'If I had any such desire I daresay I should not find much difficulty in accomplishing it' – but because he knew the only way to return was to replace the government wholesale. If the King ordered him to form a government, Melville told Popham, he would not hesitate, but 'no such desire or command has ever been intimated to me'.[30] Popham reluctantly obeyed Melville's command to desist, but the prospect that his old patron and protector might one day return to power remained at the back of his mind.

Beyond this political scheming, continental circumstances were changing. Following the apparent collapse of their strategy in the Iberian Peninsula, the Portland government

---

26  NRS: Hope of Luffness MSS, GD364/1/1182, f.38: Brownrigg to Alexander Hope, 28 January 1809.
27  BL: Add MS 70959, f.73: Lady Hester Stanhope to General Grenville, 6 July [1809].
28  Fry, *The Dundas Despotism*, p.299.
29  WLC UM: Melville Papers, Box 25: Moira to Popham, 27 February 1809.
30  NRS: Melville MSS, GD51/1/138: Melville to Popham, 4 March 1809.

changed tack in choosing their next big push against France. This time, Popham would be closely involved. He had to be, because the government's new plan adopted a part of his oldest, and dearest, scheme – an assault on the Dutch island of Walcheren.

The Netherlands had long been a maritime power, and the nation's shipping capabilities had been in French hands for some years, as were all the Dutch harbours, well placed to launch an invasion of British shores. The importance of the country to British interests had only grown since Napoleon had installed his brother Louis as King of Holland. Walcheren, one of the islands governing the entrance to the Scheldt river basin, was a particularly significant strategic point. The island's main harbour, Vlissingen (Flushing in English), was an important trading hub for the Dutch East Indies and a strong fortification, as well as a prominent shipbuilding harbour guarding the approach to Antwerp, one of Napoleon's biggest shipbuilding ports and home to a considerable naval arsenal. The French navy might have suffered a severe blow at Trafalgar, but Napoleon had made it clear he would rebuild, and Antwerp and its dockyards were a key part of that regeneration.

Popham had first drawn up a detailed plan to assault Walcheren in 1798 as a sequel to his attack on Ostend.[31] This had not taken place due to the partial failure of the Ostend expedition, but the government had kept Popham's plan on file, and Popham had fleshed it out further in 1799 when he had proposed Walcheren as a potential destination during the planning stages of the Helder campaign.[32] The inglorious end of the Second Coalition and the Russian exit from the war had put paid to any further plans in that direction, but Popham used the occasion to point out that a British assault on Walcheren might be a profitable way to involve British troops on the continent while keeping potential allies interested – particularly Austria, long supposed to have a hereditary stake in what had once been known as the Austrian Netherlands.[33] This made Walcheren a tempting target for a government on the lookout for continental confederates. Until now, however, an attack on Walcheren had never reached the serious planning stage. This was partly because the difficulties involved in sending any expedition to the area. The terrain of the Scheldt river basin – shallow, convoluted, and studded with islands of various sizes – meant any expedition would have to involve Army and Navy working in close cooperation. Moreover, Walcheren was close enough to French soil that the defenders could rush reinforcements quickly to the area if required, or cut the dykes and flood the boggy landscape to impede an invader's advance. And of course the area was known to be unhealthy.

In 1809, however, the stars finally aligned to make a Walcheren expedition not only possible, but desirable. Sensing an opportunity to open a new front against Napoleon while he was distracted by the revolt in Spain, Austrian diplomats opened negotiations with Britain for a new military alliance. In return for a down payment of £2 million and monthly stipends of £200,000, Austria pledged to fight Napoleon in the east while Britain provided a military diversion. Austria had hoped Britain would do so in Germany, but success there depended on the unlikely possibility that Prussia would join the coalition as well. Mindful of what Popham had once said about an assault on Walcheren making Austria a happy ally, and mindful too of the danger of a French invasion from Dutch shores

---

31  Memorandum, 27 May 1798, Corbett (ed.), *Spencer Papers*, vol.2, pp.355–356.
32  Thomas Grenville to Grenville, 12 July 1799, *Dropmore MSS*, vol.5, p.135.
33  Popham to Spencer, 11 July 1799, Corbett (ed.), *Spencer Papers*, vol.4, pp.286–290.

in Dutch ships, Castlereagh, the Secretary of State for War, dug out the old plans for an assault on the Scheldt. Knowing, however, that the Austrians would want something impactful, Castlereagh added an ulterior aim to Popham's plan: a march on Antwerp to destroy the arsenal and dockyards, as well as any ships that might be found there. Popham had originally proposed taking Walcheren with no more than 12,000 men. Castlereagh, despite continuing to describe the expedition as 'a *Coup de Main*', more than tripled that number to 40,000, with more than 600 ships to be provided by the Admiralty.

Ironically, the Scheldt had not featured prominently in Popham's thinking for some time: for most of the past few years, he had been more focused on South America and Mauritius than Europe. Nor was Popham at first more than superficially connected to the 1809 expedition. Although Castlereagh

Robert Stewart, Viscount Castlereagh, by W. Evans after Thomas Lawrence, 1814. (Public domain, Library of Congress)

had already been planning the expedition for some weeks, Popham only became involved in June, when he was called into the Admiralty by the First Lord. 'That scoundrel Mulgrave' had not mellowed towards Popham in the least, but Popham was one of the foremost authorities on Flanders and the Netherlands and the government needed information, as well as reassurance that an attack on Walcheren and Antwerp was feasible. There was no promise of employment. All Mulgrave wanted was for Popham to flesh out his thoughts about a potential expedition, which he duly did: he guaranteed the Navy could disembark a sizeable force near Antwerp on the left bank of the Scheldt, testified the French could not protect their ships from attack above the city defences, and echoed his more detailed plan from 1798, which he claimed it would not be necessary to alter much despite the addition of Antwerp as an objective.[34] As usual, Popham had much more to do with the Secretary of State for War, with whom he met several times. Through Castlereagh, Popham became more closely involved in the planning process, and his importance was reflected in the fact that, a week after the meetings with Mulgrave, Castlereagh introduced Popham to the Earl of Chatham, Master-General of the Ordnance and the expedition's military commander (and also, significantly for Popham, Pitt's elder brother).[35]

---

34 Anon., *Minutes of Evidence taken before the Committee of the whole House appointed to consider the policy and conduct of the late Expedition to the Scheldt* (London: [no publisher], 1810), pp.89–95; Sir Home Popham and Robert Plampin, 'Opinion Respecting the Practicability of effecting a Landing between Sandfleet [sic] and Fort Lillo', 19 June 1809, printed for the House of Commons, 1 March 1810. The information about the French inability to retreat upriver was not set down on paper, and Popham's precise words later became the subject of controversy.

35 Anon., *Minutes of Evidence*, p.61.

Popham's enemies later portrayed him as the evil genius behind the whole expedition, which was not surprising given his notorious connection with the area: 'The contriver of this scheme was said to be – as indeed it turned out to be – Sir Home Popham; who, by his insinuating and plausible address, had prevailed on [the Secretary of State for War, Lord Castlereagh] ... to undertake it.'[36] At the other extreme Popham's modern biographer, mindful of the fate of the expedition, downgraded Popham's role to that of amphibious expert: 'He simply had a difficult job of seamanship to do, and did it supremely well.'[37] Popham himself later claimed that, although 'accessary' to the decision making process, he had given the government no advice beyond 'the opinion of a Naval Officer upon a military question'.[38] He was able to get away with this because the plan, as adopted, was much more ambitious than his 1798 proposal. But Popham was more than just an expert the government occasionally called on for advice.

John Pitt, 2nd Earl of Chatham, studio of John Hoppner. (Courtesy of the Commando Forces Officers' Mess, Royal Marines Barracks, Plymouth)

Although he later tried to distance himself from the expedition, his language before it sailed was very different. Walcheren was Popham's first official employment in two years. It was also Britain's biggest amphibious expedition of the war. It was his chance to shine, to show how integral he – and his ideas – could be to the British war effort, and he was unwilling to talk down his role in what the military commander Lord Chatham described as a mission 'of great splendour and importance'.[39] Walcheren might well become the turning point of the war, the moment Napoleon realised how vulnerable he was to a British attack on his own soil. If it succeeded, Popham's future would be guaranteed and his past slate wiped clean. His will, which he updated before setting out in July, stated that he was 'about to proceed on a particular Service of which my Memory has been sound enough to have the Plan and make the Arrangements'.[40] He wanted to be remembered as 'the Atlas of the whole operation'.[41] The

---

36  Sir John Barrow, *An Auto-Biographical Memoir of Sir John Barrow, Bart., Late of the Admiralty ...* (London: John Murray, 1847), p.304.
37  Popham, *A Damned Cunning Fellow*, p.190.
38  Anon., *Minutes of Evidence*, pp.59, 65.
39  Chatham to Castlereagh, 23 June 1809, Londonderry (ed.), *Castlereagh Correspondence*, vol.6, p.282.
40  TNA: PROB 11/1634/323: will of Sir Home Popham.
41  Francis Culling Carr-Gomm (ed.), *Letters and Journals of Field-Marshal Sir William Maynard Gomm, GCB ...* (London: John Murray, 1881), p.131.

final plan may have been altered and scaled up, but it was still 'his', and Popham wanted to ensure the authorities recalled him as one of the expedition's acknowledged authors.

As preparations for 'his' expedition advanced in earnest, however, Popham began to realise not everything was going according to plan. The size of the 'Grand Expedition' reflected the importance of the object, but it made everything cumbersome and hampered quick movement. 'I see the season advancing fast,' Popham told Castlereagh, 'and, if we are imperceptibly led on till the midsummer fine weather is past, we shall have the most dreadful of difficulties, the elements, to encounter.' Popham remembered the troubles of helping the Duke of York's army traverse the boggy ground of north Germany and Holland in 1794–1795, as well as the washed-out expedition to the Helder in 1799. To save time, he persuaded Castlereagh to adapt some of the ships of the line to carry troops instead of using transports, which were 'the greatest clog to every sort of expedition, particularly those in which promptness and celerity are so essential to success'.[42] Having bound up his reputation with the expedition and its outcome, Popham's perfectionism was on full display, although he did not seem to understand that attending to every detail would further compromise speed:

> In general, Expeditions are so hurried off at the last, and with such little previous arrangement and attention to equipments, that it is the occupation of a long Voyage to get all the appointments perfect; but here, every thing must be perfect before it moves, every man must know his Duty, and every implement its place, for it is more than possible that the whole armament may be in action, before it has time to sleep after quitting the Shores of England.[43]

Popham had another reason to be nervous. One thing was becoming increasingly clear: the expedition might have sprung from his idea, he might have 'had the Plan' of it and 'made the Arrangements', but the Admiralty still had no intention of employing him. Lady Hester Stanhope, who had not forgiven Popham for abandoning the Duke of York, was exultant about this. Although she admitted Popham had 'been used like a dog', he had, she crowed, 'expected to have a grand naval command, in which I am delighted to say he is *disappointed*'.[44] Part of the problem may have been that one of the three men who had protested against Popham's appointment as Captain of the Fleet at Copenhagen, Rear Admiral Sir Richard Keats, was to be naval second-in-command, and there were whispers he had refused to serve with Popham.[45] Official correspondence, however, suggests Keats did not let personal dislike obstruct his professionalism, and Popham must have realised any reluctance to employ him came from much higher up. The government had burned itself before by appointing Popham Captain of the Fleet at Copenhagen, and it had no intention of repeating that mistake again. Castlereagh might have pushed harder on Popham's behalf, but he was blissfully unaware

---

42   Popham to Castlereagh, 13 June 1809, Londonderry (ed.), *Castlereagh Correspondence*, vol.6, p.274.
43   TNA: PRO 30/8/368, f.166: Popham to Chatham, 18 June 1809.
44   BL: Add MS 70959, f.73: Lady Hester Stanhope to General Grenville, 6 July [1809].
45   *The Anti-Jacobin Review and Magazine* (1810), vol.35, pp.421–422.

that he himself was one of the main reasons his colleagues were keen to avoid stirring up trouble. George Canning had been intriguing to have Castlereagh sacked since the disaster at Corunna, and had persuaded Prime Minister Portland to go through with it after the end of the Walcheren expedition.

Popham first realised he would not have a specific command towards the end of June, when he had already been advising Castlereagh for two weeks. Since he was one of the Navy's foremost amphibious experts and had helped plan the expedition in the first place, Popham had fully expected to be Captain of the Fleet, and he could not believe he would not be appointed to the expedition in some prominent capacity. As he had done to the Duke of York at the Helder in 1799 under similar circumstances, Popham begged Lord Chatham, 'as the strongest mark of gratitude and respect in my power to manifest for Your Lordship and Family', to 'accept my Services as your naval Aid de Camp'.[46] But Chatham demurred, and by July Popham was getting really anxious. Someone, somewhere, had to be intriguing against him: he was being passed over because of 'the pretended unpopularity that is presumed to attach to me ... fostered by the hand of Influence'. He was persuaded Chatham, with whom he seems to have felt his loyalty to Pitt the Younger gave him some sort of personal rapport, could protect him.[47] Popham may have overestimated Chatham's desire to rock the boat in his favour – Chatham was not a boat-rocker, and he was also canny enough to know when he was being buttered up for an ulterior purpose. Still, Popham knew he could not be kept away from the expedition without this appearing odd. The Admiralty Board was reluctantly coming to the same conclusion, but maintained its refusal to appoint Popham in any other capacity than as an ordinary post-captain. On 4 July, it very deliberately reappointed him captain of HMS *Venerable*, a ship he had only nominally been commanding for the past year.[48]

Popham was horrified, especially when he heard the naval commander-in-chief would be Rear Admiral Sir Richard Strachan, whose patron was Lord St Vincent and who knew Popham only from serving on his court-martial board. Popham did not believe Strachan was his enemy, but he had plenty of reasons to think he might not be favourable. 'In point of policy this is wrong,' Popham fulminated to Chatham. This was already *his* expedition, and he did not want Strachan to appoint someone else as Captain of the Fleet who would 'reverse all his arrangements'. He could best be employed in a position of responsibility where he could maintain contact with Strachan and Chatham, oversee the embarkation and disembarkation of troops and horses, and advise on the complex navigation of the Scheldt. He could do none of this as captain of HMS *Venerable*, where he would be immediately responsible to a divisional commander and have no contact whatsoever with the commanders-in-chief.[49]

Desperate, Popham appealed to both Chatham and Strachan, who luckily both realised Popham was integral to a plan that hinged so strongly on his proposals and personal knowledge. Chatham later claimed he had never insisted on Popham's being Captain of the

---

46   TNA: PRO 30/8/368, f.170: Popham to Chatham, 20 June 1809.
47   TNA: PRO 30/8/368, f.173: Popham to Chatham, 3 July 1809.
48   TNA: ADM 1/2334: Admiralty Board note, 4 July 1809. The ship's muster recorded him as being absent on Admiralty business: TNA: ADM 53/1236, muster, HMS *Venerable*.
49   TNA: PRO 30/8/368, f.176: Popham to Chatham, 5 July 1809.

Fleet, but Strachan certainly did, informing the Admiralty Board that he would not otherwise accept the naval command.[50] This suggested Strachan was not as poorly disposed as Popham had feared, but the Admiralty Board was unimpressed. The only reason Strachan had been picked for the command was because he had already been in command of the British squadron posted off the Scheldt; he was hardly indispensable, and the Board therefore tried to call his bluff. However, the only other naval commander they could find at such short notice was Sir Samuel Hood, who had also countersigned the protest against Popham in 1807 along with Keats and refused to have anything to do with an expedition in which he was so closely involved.[51] With time pressing more and more, the Board agreed to an unofficial compromise. Strachan agreed to sail, but without a Captain of the Fleet – although he would shift his flag from HMS *San Domingo* to HMS *Venerable*, in which Chatham and his suite would also travel.[52] This effectively made Popham Captain of the Fleet in all but name.

As Lady Hester Stanhope put it, gleefully, this compromise meant he accompanied the expedition 'only as a sort of hanger on to the Commander-in-Chief, as he says, to *prevent the Army being Cut to Pieces*'.[53] This was a slight exaggeration, but Popham had no official authority beyond his capacity as a rather junior post-captain. Still, he had to be satisfied with the arrangement, which at least proved he was much more than what he appeared, ostensibly, to be: merely 'captain of the [HMS] *Venerable*'.[54] But Popham could hardly promote himself and appoint another captain for HMS *Venerable* under him, freeing him up to act as Strachan and Chatham's special adviser; the last time he had tried that trick, at Buenos Aires, he had got into a great deal of trouble. Popham nevertheless had no intention of acting as a 'proper' captain of HMS *Venerable*, and the fact he had never officially taken command of the ship gave him a handy loophole. He had been on shore the entire time he had been *Venerable*'s captain so far, with Captain Andrew King serving temporarily in his place. So long as Popham continued to avoid completing the process of taking full command, he could easily be detached on other services, leaving *Venerable* and its day-to-day business in King's hands as 'unofficial' flag captain. This underhand arrangement, however, left Popham vulnerable: so long as he did not actively take command of *Venerable*, he was not technically its captain. If anyone realised this, they could get him sent home as an unattached civilian who had no business being on the Walcheren expedition at all.[55]

Perhaps partly to legitimise his position, Popham invited a startling number of civilians on campaign with him. Some of these men were looking for a safe passage to the continent on business, such as the merchant David Irving; others were keen to play a military role, like Lord Yarmouth, who brought his private yacht to boost the strength of the enormous fleet. Still others were there because they had never had an opportunity to see Antwerp before and were anxious not to miss '*the Fun*'.[56] They all had one thing in common: Popham

---

50  TNA: PRO 30/8/369: memorandum, 10 February 1810.
51  NRS: Melville MSS, GD51/1/141/2: Lord Lonsdale to Melville, 15 July 1809.
52  Strachan to William Wellesley Pole, 4 August 1809, Anon., *A Collection of Papers Relating to the Expedition to the Scheldt* (London: A. Strahan, 1811), pp.407–408.
53  BL: Add MS 70959, f.73: Lady Hester Stanhope to General Grenville, 6 July [1809].
54  *Parliamentary Debates*, vol.15, col.clxxxii.
55  TNA: PRO 30/8/369, f.72: Strachan to Chatham, 2 August 1809.
56  Cumbria Archive Centre (CAC): DLONS/L1/2/70: Lowther to Lord Lonsdale, [July 1809], original emphasis.

had invited them because they were influential and belonged to strong political and social networks. Irving was a protégé of the Duke of Rutland; Yarmouth's mother was the Prince of Wales's current mistress; and Lowther was the son of Popham's patron the Earl of Lonsdale. Popham had two reasons to invite these men along. The first was to play up his connection with the powers that be, not necessarily defined as members of the current cabinet but based on a sort of obligation to a Pittite ideal. Popham's second reason for inviting so many civilian observers was to make sure he had enough highly placed witnesses to testify to the results of his brilliant strategising.

For much the same reason, Popham also invited a large number of journalists to accompany the expedition. This seems extraordinary given how secret the expedition was meant to be, but to Popham, who always appreciated the value of publicity, it made sense. Among his more respectable connections was his long-standing friendship with Thomas George Street of the *Courier*, who had already worked with Popham during the invasion of Buenos Aires, and his newspaper now took instructions from Popham on how to present Walcheren to the public. Popham also invited the *Morning Chronicle* journalist Peter Finnerty as a semi-official war correspondent. The *Chronicle* was an opposition paper, and Popham probably thought Finnerty – whom he had first befriended at his court-martial – might put a favourable spin on the expedition in a quarter that was not likely to support a government-sponsored venture. But Finnerty was an Irish radical who had previously been convicted of sedition, and bringing him to Walcheren was just another example of how detached Popham had allowed himself to become from reality.[57]

According to the plan for the expedition, the military force of 40,000 men would be split across four different, but interdependent, objectives. The first was to land 2,000 men at Cadzand, off the mainland, to disable the enemy batteries there. Without this, the British fleet would find it difficult to access the West Scheldt, which was more easily navigable than the shallow East Scheldt for ships of war. The second force, consisting of 8,000 men, would capture the island of South Beveland and await further orders. The third force (12,000 men) would land on Walcheren and besiege Flushing, while the British ships in the West Scheldt sealed the town off from the river. Simultaneously, the Navy would carry the remaining 18,000 men up the West Scheldt and land them at Sandvliet. This force would disable the largest forts straddling the river, Lillo and Liefkenshoek, allowing Strachan's ships to follow them. If everything happened at the right time, the British might reach Antwerp within two weeks – although this depended on favourable winds, weather, and navigation, not to mention good luck.

But luck appeared in particularly short supply. Popham had pressed Castlereagh to send the expedition out by 27 June at the latest to take advantage of the longest days of the year and a full moon.[58] However, various difficulties unavoidably connected with getting nearly 40,000 men and more than 600 ships and vessels ready meant the troops did not even begin to gather in

---

57 Ivon Asquith, 'James Perry and the *Morning Chronicle*, 1790–1821' (PhD thesis, University of London, 1973), p.241n3; Elias Duran de Porras, 'Peter Finnerty, An Ancestor of Modern War Correspondents', *Textual and Visual Media*, 7 (2014), pp.46, 53.
58 Anon., *Minutes of Evidence*, p.59.

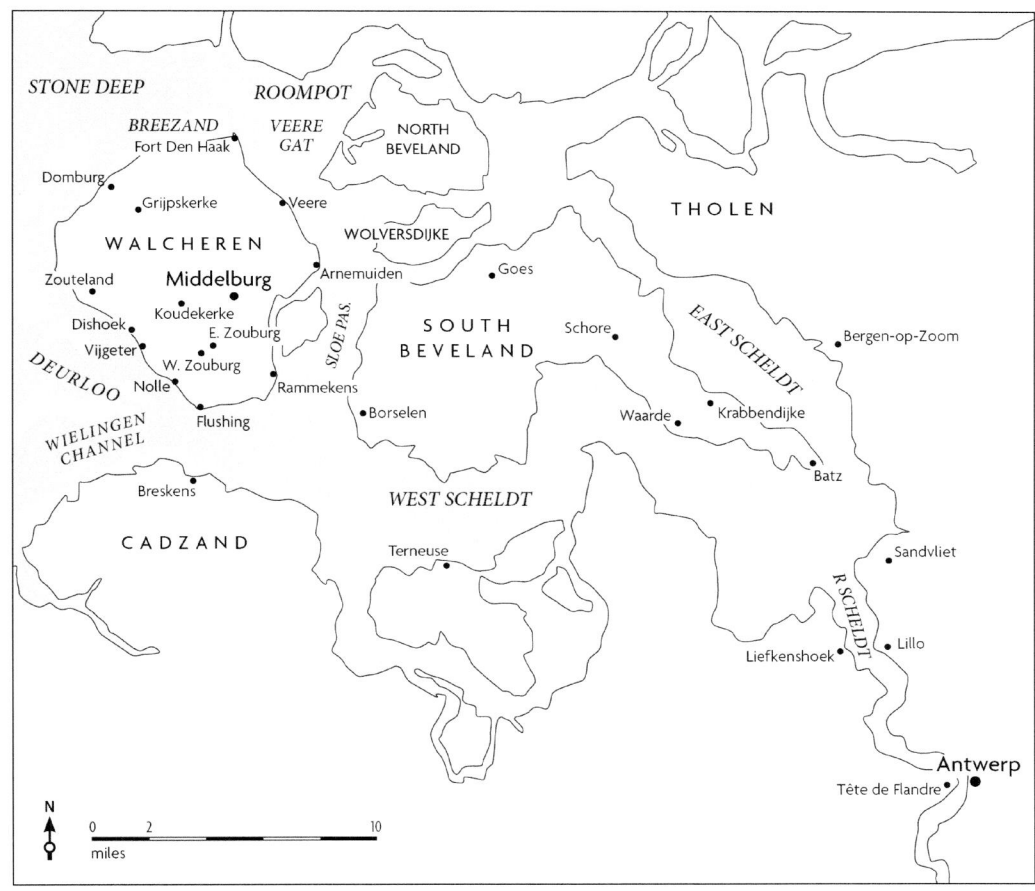

Walcheren, 1809.

the Downs and at Portsmouth until that time. Embarkation began in mid-July, and Chatham himself – a leisurely man not known for rapidity of movement – did not embark aboard HMS *Venerable* at Deal until the 26th, a month after Popham had wanted to be off. The chances of maintaining secrecy were by now extremely slim. Evidence from the French newspapers suggested the enemy was well aware of the aims of the expedition, and news also arrived that the Austrians – Britain's only continental allies – had been heavily defeated at the battle of Wagram. One of the main reasons for sending the expedition to Walcheren in the first place had been to act as a diversion, but there was now a strong possibility that Austria might sue for peace, freeing up significant French troops to send to Antwerp. Remembering, however, the advice Popham had given Lord Spencer in 1799 that a successful assault on Walcheren might keep Austria fighting, Castlereagh and Chatham decided to go ahead with the campaign.[59]

---

59  Jacqueline Reiter, *The Late Lord: The Life of the 2nd Earl of Chatham* (Barnsley: Pen & Sword, 2017), pp.109–110.

As the troops were still embarking, news arrived in Deal that something unexpected had happened: 11 enemy ships of the line, along with several frigates, had come down the Scheldt from Antwerp and were currently at Flushing, sitting ducks for a British attack. Strachan, who was much better at open sea fighting than amphibious operations, was delighted. Rear Admiral Lord Gardner was watching the enemy ships carefully with six sail of the line, and Strachan wanted to send a flotilla of four more, including *Venerable*, to capture or sink them. There was a real prospect that one of the aims of the expedition – to destroy France's fleet in the Scheldt – might be achievable without landing a single soldier. Destroying the arsenals and fortifications of Antwerp would not, however, and sinking the French fleet would be the quickest way to attract Napoleon's attention to the area. With the army still embarking and the Portsmouth division yet to join the rest of the expedition, Chatham refused Strachan permission to sail, particularly *Venerable*, which would have deprived him of quick access to Popham. It was the first sign of dissension between the military and naval commanders. Popham's illusions about the extent of his personal influence over the two commanders were being stripped away. If he had hoped to trade on his former connection with Pitt, Chatham's brother, he was slowly realising this meant nothing unless he could persuade Strachan and Chatham to read from the same strategic page.

The first two of the expedition's three divisions – one under Keats' command with the troops for South Beveland under Lieutenant General John Hope, the other under Strachan with the troops for Antwerp – sailed early in the morning of 28 July and anchored in the evening in the Stone Diep off Walcheren. However, by the time the third division commanded by Rear Admiral William Otway arrived next morning, Popham's fear that 'the elements' would interrupt the campaign had come to pass: a storm was blowing hard from the southwest. As Commodore Edward Owen detached a squadron of ships carrying Lieutenant General Lord Huntly and 2,000 men to silence the French batteries at Cadzand, Popham transferred from *Venerable* into the sloop *Sabrina* with orders from Strachan to guide Keats' division through the narrow channel of the Veere Gat into a sheltered anchorage known as the Roompot. This would allow Keats access to the East Scheldt to land Hope's troops on the northern shore of South Beveland, but both men quickly realised the anchorage might provide a safe haven for the entire fleet, which was so much buffeted by the gale that several ships had already run aground in the shallows of the Scheldt estuary. This was a significant change of plan – only half the fleet should have entered the East Scheldt, while the other half should have carried the troops for Antwerp straight down the West Scheldt – but Popham knew that bringing all the ships through the Veere Gat might be the only safe option under current conditions. He also knew there was a good beach for landing troops on Walcheren's northern shore at Bree Zand. Popham therefore told Chatham he would 'pawn my reputation that I will get all of our Troops on shore by [Fort] Den Haak'.[60]

Popham was as good as his word. He returned to *Venerable* to guide the remaining ships of war through the Veere Gat. This was his opportunity to shine, and he took full advantage. Within an hour and a half, the ships had come safely through the narrow, dangerous passage to their new anchorage. Popham was the man of the hour: Chatham used his first official dispatch home to express 'in the strongest Terms, my Admiration of the distinguished

---

60  TNA: PRO 30/8/368, f.179: Popham to Chatham, 29 July 1809.

The British landing on Walcheren, by A. Lutz, 1809. (Public domain, Rijksmuseum, Netherlands)

Abilities with which the Fleet was conducted through the Passage into the Vere Gat'.[61] Even Keats admitted Popham had acted 'with great judgement'.[62] It did look like Popham had single-handedly saved the expedition from disaster, but nobody had yet stopped to think about how these new circumstances might affect future operations. The original plan had been to land at Domburg, on the north-western side of the island, which would have placed the fleet within easy access of the West Scheldt and a dash to Antwerp once Cadzand's batteries were silenced and Flushing's guns masked. It would also have allowed landing troops, guns, and equipment closer to Flushing. Sailing the main part of the fleet into the Roompot made it much more difficult to enter the West Scheldt, and the East Scheldt was too narrow for larger ships of war. Popham may have saved the troops and ships, but he had, very possibly, doomed the chances of a swift advance on Antwerp. Lieutenant General Robert Brownrigg, Chatham's Chief of Staff, did not mince his words: 'I consider the unfortunate necessity which obliged the whole armament to have been assembled in the Roompot, as fatal to the ulterior objects of the Expedition.'[63]

For now, everything was action. The troops landed near Fort den Haak, as Popham had promised, and the enemy made very little attempt to stop them. Having temporarily taken

---

61  Chatham to Castlereagh, 2 August 1804, Anon., *A Collection of Papers*, p.72.
62  Keats to Strachan, 30 July 1809, Anon., *A Collection of Papers*, pp.417–418.
63  *Parliamentary Debates*, vol.15, col.5xc.

command of *Venerable*, Popham relinquished it again and landed with Chatham, either because Strachan had ordered him to (as Popham later claimed) or because Chatham had personally requested his assistance (as Strachan suggested).[64] Popham was certainly benefiting from the ambiguity of his role: he landed with the military commander-in-chief and spent the next few days moving about the island, appearing where any action was taking place to lend his assistance: 'He would not leave us when there was nothing to do in his own sphere, until it was out of character for him to go further.'[65] Popham remained with Chatham long enough to make sure the commander-in-chief and his staff were secure, which was not a foregone conclusion. After landing, a detachment of troops under Lieutenant Colonel Denis Pack had captured a small enemy battery and chased some of the retreating enemy to the nearby town of Veere. Here they foolishly got too close to the town walls and lost seven dead and 27 wounded, plus prisoners, to enemy fire. When he heard of this, Popham feared the enemy might attempt a larger counterattack and urged Chatham, who had set up headquarters at Fort den Haak, to re-join the troops being landed at Bree Zand. Pack subsequently sent a message that everything had gone quiet, but Popham was not satisfied with leaving an enemy town so close to the British landing place. With Chatham's tacit permission, Popham took a squadron of gunboats to Veere, where he assisted Lieutenant General Alexander Mackenzie Fraser in erecting a small battery and bombarding the town into submission.

Veere surrendered on 1 August, but not without a fight. Two gunboats were sunk during the course of the bombardment. These vessels had only been present because Popham had ordered them there, and this got him – and Chatham – into trouble. When Strachan, who had not given permission for the gunboats to cooperate with Fraser, heard what had happened, he was incandescent. 'I cannot approve of the manner in which the Naval Force has been applied this morning to the great waste of Ammunition and Stores without effecting one good purpose,' he raged at Chatham. 'I shall be most happy at all times, my Lord, to meet your wishes and to forward by every means in my power the Operations of the Army … but I hope whenever your Lordship wishes to have the Navy employed in a particular way, that you would be pleased to signify your wishes to me.'[66] Part of Strachan's anger arose from the fact he felt he had no control over a member of his own fleet, and Chatham was probably not happy to be dragged into the controversy either. Popham, currently with Chatham at Middelburg – the capital of Walcheren, which Chatham had selected as his headquarters – had managed to annoy both commanders at a stroke. He had also destroyed the advantage of his nebulous position, as he now discovered Strachan had the power to rein him in. On 4 August, after spending several days searching for him (including not finding him aboard his own ship), Strachan forced Popham to read his commission aboard HMS *Venerable*, completing the process of taking command of his ship and effectively reducing him to the status of an ordinary ship's captain. Now that he was officially chained to his vessel, Popham could no longer use the excuse of 'detached commands' to do whatever he wanted.

---

64  TNA: ADM 1/2336: Popham to Barrow, 9 March 1810; Strachan to Pole, 4 August 1809, Anon., *A Collection of Papers*, p.409.
65  Carr-Gomm (ed.), *Letters and Journals of Field-Marshal Sir William Maynard Gomm*, p.131.
66  TNA: PRO 30/8/369, f.66: Strachan to Chatham, 31 July 1809.

The British attack on Veere, by F. Dietrich, 1809. (Public domain, Rijksmuseum, Netherlands)

This was the more frustrating for Popham as the expedition, which had begun so swiftly and well, had begun to stall. By 3 August, the British had invested Flushing and taken Veere and Rammekens. This secured access to the Sloe Passage between Walcheren and South Beveland, which until Cadzand fell and Flushing's guns were silenced was the only way the British could get significant numbers of troops and equipment into the West Scheldt. This was good news, but the Sloe, like the East Scheldt, was very narrow and shallow. To make swifter progress the British needed to secure the Deurloo Passage between Flushing and Cadzand, but on 4 August news arrived that Lord Huntly had called off his attack on Cadzand due to a shortage of landing craft. Meanwhile, a contrary wind kept Strachan from bringing enough ships round from the Roompot to complete the investment of Flushing from the river. While the engineers struggled to get guns down Walcheren's boggy roads, the French took advantage of the incapacitated British ships to sail reinforcements into Flushing.[67] Half a dozen boats passed across the channel every day, and many of the British troops destined for Antwerp had to be landed on Walcheren to make up for the now unknown number of defenders. There were also disturbing rumours that the French were rushing 25,000 troops to Antwerp under the command of *maréchal* Lefebvre or *maréchal* Bessières (some even said Napoleon himself was on his way).[68] The tension not only frayed relations between Chatham and Strachan, as Chatham simply could not understand why

---

67 Jacqueline Reiter (ed.), 'Day after Day Adds to our Miseries: The Private Diary of a Staff Officer on the Walcheren Expedition, 1809, Part 1', *Journal of the Society for Army Historical Research*, 96:386 (2018), pp.131–151, p.148.
68 National Army Museum (NAM): 1968-07-261: diary of Captain Frederick Trench, 10 August 1809.

Strachan had not yet moved any ships into the West Scheldt, but also between Chatham and Popham. Chatham had been angered by the fall-out from Popham's actions at Veere, and he now remembered, all too well, Popham's assurances of how easily the Navy could transport large numbers of British soldiers to Antwerp.

Popham had ground to make up with both commanders and he knew it. He devoted most of his time to trying to get them to meet and discuss future strategy, hoping proximity would remind them of how resourceful he could be. He was also aware that face-to-face discussions were essential for the military and naval forces to continue working together in relative harmony under unfavourable conditions. He was not especially successful in his efforts, however, partly because he could never track the hyperactive Strachan down and partly because the lethargic Chatham was far too easy to find as he never left headquarters. Popham therefore chose to focus his efforts on wooing back Chatham's trust. On 5 August, Popham drew up a memorandum for the military commander proposing a new plan of action now that Cadzand remained in French hands. What if it was actually not necessary to get to Antwerp at all? What if Flushing was in fact the only objective the British needed to worry about? Popham pointed out that, if the British possessed both Walcheren and South Beveland, Antwerp would simply not matter because the British would be able to blockade the mouth of the Scheldt like a cork in a bottle: 'If Flushing is captured, whether the [enemy] Fleet is captured or not, it cannot well get out of the Scheld [sic]; in short, Flushing is the Key of the Scheld … [and] the Enemy's Fleet must rot at Antwerp.' Possession of Walcheren would also permit future raids along the Dutch or Flemish coast, for example at Hellevoetsluis.[69] But with the Navy still unable to enter the West Scheldt, Popham's suggestion of other targets such as Hellevoetsluis did not amuse Chatham. The military commander made no response to the plan, and Popham grew more and more disillusioned.

On 7 August the wind finally changed, allowing Strachan to shut off the communication between Flushing and Cadzand. Now the West Scheldt was finally accessible, Strachan ordered Popham to take a flotilla of gunboats down to Fort Batz, at the southernmost point of South Beveland. Here he would cooperate with Rear Admiral Keats, who had worked his squadron painstakingly down the East Scheldt after disembarking Hope's troops at the beginning of August. Popham's instructions also included the need to hasten the movement of troops through the Sloe Passage. Popham might have told Chatham Flushing was the most important military target, but Strachan had only ever seen the town as a distraction from the destruction of the French fleet and dockyards at Antwerp. He now intended to focus on what he had always considered the expedition's 'main object'.[70] Strachan also ordered Popham to sound the river and place buoys to guide the line of battle ships when they finally arrived.[71] This was all part of his plan to take a dozen sail of the line up river as far as he could go to attack the French fleet, emulating the success of the Battle of Basque Roads, when Lord Cochrane had trapped a French squadron up a narrow river and destroyed it.[72] Popham may have been flattered that Strachan wanted him to be an integral part of this ambitious scheme, but it may also

---

69  TNA: PRO 30/8/368, f.183: memorandum, 5 August 1809.
70  TNA: PRO 30/8/369, f.103: Strachan to Chatham, 8 August 1809.
71  Strachan to Pole, 13 August 1809, Anon., *A Collection of Papers*, p.429.
72  CAC: DLONS L1/2/70, f.10: Lowther to Lord Lonsdale, 11 August 1809.

have crossed his mind that Strachan wanted to get him further away from headquarters, tethered to specific instructions to keep him out of trouble.

Popham left Walcheren on 7 August, expecting to rendezvous at Batz with Keats in the East Scheldt and with a squadron of frigates in the West Scheldt, which Strachan hoped to force through the Deurloo Channel on the 9th.[73] The weather, as it had been since the arrival of the British at the end of July, was wet and stormy, but for Popham it was all go. He arrived at Batz to find Keats in the middle of a scuffle: the French had sent two frigates, 30 brigs, eight schooners, and 14 gunboats downriver to dislodge the British and cause havoc.[74] Keats sent 30 flatboats armed with carronades to meet Popham, who turned up just in time to help hound the French retreat to Fort Lillo. Keats and Popham may have hated each other, but they managed to work well together in a pinch. A short time after Popham joined Keats' force, six enemy gunboats had been driven ashore: five were burned, and the sixth captured.[75] A French advance vessel of six guns was cut off by Popham's flotilla 'and handsomely burnt'. Popham chased the remaining ships two miles below Forts Lillo and Liefkenshoek, but the enemy escaped behind the safety of the fort guns. Popham reported to Strachan, with self-satisfaction, that he had counted three sail of the line, three frigates, and about 70 gun-brigs and luggers, 'besides a great Number of armed Vessels of every Description', near Lillo, in addition to the other ships of the line already known to be at Antwerp: 'and yet the Enemy has suffered us to obtain this Anchorage with so little Trouble, and scarce any Loss'.[76] What he omitted to mention, but what he must have known, was that the enemy did not see the point in attacking further because they knew they were safe from the British behind a chain boom constructed between Lillo and Liefkenshoek. More ominously, the French had managed to withdraw their ships all the way upriver beyond Antwerp's defences – something Popham had assured the British government would be impossible.[77]

For the next few days, Keats and Popham watched the enemy tensely. Until Strachan came down the river with his ships of the line, Keats, with his nine frigates, 18 sloops and gun-brigs, and four divisions of gunboats, was vulnerable to an enemy attack.[78] The enemy did not come, however, safe behind their boom. Popham spent his time sounding out the mouth of the river in accordance with his orders and reconnoitring the East Scheldt to see whether the 44-gun vessels the enemy was rumoured to have between Bergen op Zoom and Tholen could be attacked.[79] On 13 August, Popham heard the sounds of distant bombardment: the British batteries had finally opened on Flushing, joined on the 14th by 12 ships of the line Strachan had managed to force through the Deurloo. The town surrendered at 2:00 a.m. on the 15th. Popham, still taking soundings aboard HMS *Skylark* three miles below Lillo, must have been annoyed to miss the action. He would only have been partially mollified to learn

---

73  In fact, this did not happen until the 11th.
74  Strachan to Pole, 11 August 1809, Anon., *A Collection of Papers*, pp.423–424.
75  Keats to Strachan, 12 August 1809, Anon., *A Collection of Papers*, pp.430–431.
76  Popham to Strachan, 13 August 1809, Anon., *A Collection of Papers*, pp.469–470.
77  Popham later refused to say whether this had been official advice, which suggests it almost certainly was: Anon., *Minutes of Evidence*, p.65.
78  Keats to Strachan, 15 August 1809, Anon., *A Collection of Papers*, pp.450–451.
79  Keats to Strachan, 14 August 1809, Anon., *A Collection of Papers*, pp.450–451.

A view of Flushing during the British bombardment, by Henry Aston Barker, 1810. (Public domain, Anne S.K. Brown Military Collection, Brown University Library)

Strachan had mentioned him and his services in the West Scheldt in his official dispatch: 'I have much Pleasure in bearing the most ample Testimony to the Exertions of Sir Home Popham with the advanced Flotilla in the upper Part of the West Scheldt, which has been of the most essential Service.'[80] Otherwise, the most exciting occurrence was a sighting of Napoleon's brother Louis, King of Holland, who came with his suite to examine the British squadron at Batz. Popham ordered one of his gunboats to open fire and had the satisfaction of seeing King Louis' cavalcade scatter in all directions.[81]

All of Walcheren and South Beveland were now in British hands, and there was still a very slim chance the British might still be able to attack Antwerp if they moved quickly. Yet the same old sluggishness persisted; if anything, it got worse. The troops and siege equipment for Antwerp were still partially stuck in the East Scheldt, and Chatham did not leave Walcheren until 21 August, after which he spent a mind-numbing three days crossing South Beveland to reach Batz. This was partly because Chatham knew his troops would not arrive before he did (he was correct: the last transports only arrived at Batz on 25 August), but it was also a recognition on Chatham's part that the ulterior aims of the expedition were too difficult to achieve. There were now 35,000 French between Bergen op Zoom and Antwerp, and the enemy had cut the dykes to flood the land between Bergen and Lillo.[82] Worse, when Strachan finally arrived at Batz on 21 August, he confirmed what Popham had already suspected: all but three French ships of the line and two frigates had been taken beyond the defences of Antwerp and were entirely out of reach.[83]

---

80  Strachan to Pole, 17 August 1809, Anon., *A Collection of Papers*, p.436.
81  Jacqueline Reiter (ed.), 'Day after Day Adds to our Miseries: The Private Diary of a Staff Officer on the Walcheren Expedition, Part 2', *Journal of the Society for Army Historical Research*, 96:387 (2019), p.249.
82  Jacqueline Reiter (ed.), 'Day after Day Adds to our Miseries: The Private Diary of a Staff Officer on the Walcheren Expedition, Part 3', *Journal of the Society for Army Historical Research*, 97:388 (2019), p.27.
83  Strachan to Pole, 22 August 1809, Anon., *A Collection of Papers*, pp.454–455.

Even Popham had to admit the campaign was limping to a close. Strachan, however, was absolutely incensed at the idea that he might have to go home without having achieved a single naval objective. He could not believe that, even with the six sail of the line that had accompanied him to Batz and the 26 frigates and 120 gunboats and sloops under his command, he could not do any more. He was furious with Chatham, whose slowness and incompetence he thought had cost him the chance to fulfil his instructions. Strachan therefore ordered Keats to prepare to land a large number of troops near Sandvliet, even though he knew there were 15,000 French troops waiting in the immediate area, and told Popham to get the fireships ready to assault the dockyards.[84] Strachan also gave Keats instructions to cooperate with Lieutenant General Lord Rosslyn to advance on Antwerp, effectively going behind Chatham's back. Keats wisely refused to do anything without Rosslyn's cooperation, and Rosslyn passed the details of the whole business to Chatham. Relations between the military and naval commanders had been strained; now they ceased completely.

Strachan, remembering Popham had considered himself to be close to Chatham and possibly assured by Popham that Chatham would listen to him, decided to send him to military headquarters to see if he could talk Chatham round. In his desperation to keep the campaign on track, the admiral was restoring Popham to the private liaison role he had tried so hard to circumscribe earlier that month. Strachan told Chatham Popham was authorised to give orders directly in Strachan's name, to accelerate any forward movement and to reassure Chatham that whatever he wanted done would be carried out instantly.[85] But, whatever he had said to Strachan, Popham was by now one of the last people Chatham would want to see. The commanding general was disgusted with the naval part of the expedition and increasingly persuaded that any delays in the army's advance were entirely due to Strachan's inability to get the troop transports and equipment through the Sloe, or his ships down the West Scheldt. Stewing in bitterness, Chatham was unlikely to respond well to the one man who had been a constant throughout the expedition since the very beginning – the man whose smooth talking had persuaded the government, and Chatham himself, to go ahead with it. 'I shall be happy to obey any Commands which your Lordship may think proper to convey to me,' Popham wrote to Chatham, hopefully, but Chatham had nothing to say.[86] He sent Popham back to Strachan on 20 August without a reply.[87]

Part of the reason Chatham had stopped communicating with Strachan was pique, but there was another reason – one Popham was not aware of. The troops on Walcheren and South Beveland had begun to fall ill. The prevalence of marsh fevers on the boggy islands of Walcheren and South Beveland was well known, but nobody had expected illness to be so abrupt in its appearance, or to spread so quickly. By the time Chatham reached Batz on 25 August, 2,702 men out of a total of 37,727 men were ill and 14 had already died.[88] With disease tearing through the army at a terrifying rate, the campaign was effectively over. But it was Popham who, reluctantly, provided the final nail for the coffin of the Walcheren expedition. On 25 August, he accompanied Chief of Staff Brownrigg and several other officers

---

84  Strachan to pole, 22 August 1809, Anon., *A Collection of Papers*, pp.454–455.
85  TNA: PRO 30/8/369, f.118: Strachan to Chatham, 19 August 1809.
86  TNA: PRO 30/8/368, f.185: Popham to Chatham, 18 August 1809.
87  Strachan to Pole, 22 August 1809, Anon., *A Collection of Papers*, p.455.
88  TNA: WO 190: proceedings of the Army, 25 August 1809.

to Sandvliet to reconnoitre the landing place he had proposed for the British troops in June. The reconnoitring party did not linger as their presence immediately attracted an alarming number of French soldiers, but they were there long enough to note that the sand there was too hard for cavalry, while a long dyke running along the beach would expose landing troops to enemy fire.[89]

The day after this discovery, Chatham called a meeting between Strachan, Keats, Popham, and the senior military officers. Ostensibly, this was to discuss how to get to Antwerp; in reality it was to decide whether to continue the campaign at all. Brownrigg, fresh from his visit to Sandvliet, drew up a memorandum for the attendees summarising the bleak situation. The British had 30,000 effective soldiers – a number that was shrinking every day – and 8,000 of those would have to remain behind to garrison Walcheren and South Beveland. A further 8,000 would have to guard the provision depots, which left only 14,000 men to reduce Forts Lillo and Liefkenshoek to allow the Navy access to the river, before jointly assaulting Antwerp. The latest reports of the enemy's strength suggested the French could easily muster 35,000 men and more were on the way. The countryside between Antwerp and Liefkenshoek was completely under water.[90] Once everyone had read and digested the memorandum, Chatham put two questions before Strachan and his subordinate officers: could the siege of Antwerp be attempted? If the answer was no, what else might be attempted towards carrying out the expedition's ultimate object?

The discussions over Chatham's questions spilled over into the following day, not because the generals disagreed on the main points – they were more or less unanimous in their opinion that nothing further could be done – but because Strachan desperately wanted to attempt to fulfil his naval instructions. While he admitted Antwerp was out of reach for a *coup de main*, he felt it was necessary to try and burn the French fleet and bombard the dockyards, or at least to sink some ships in the river to block the egress of any more vessels. The problem was the army would have to disable Forts Lillo and Liefkenshoek to allow Strachan to get his ships far enough upriver. Even Keats thought this no longer possible, and Strachan eventually had to give up the point. He and Keats, and Popham, left before the Army men had finished deciding, but they already knew what the determination would be. Strachan, whose temper was never steady at the best of times, went back to his billet and wrote an angry letter to the Secretary of the Admiralty he would later regret: 'I found them [the generals] decidedly of Opinion that no Operation could be undertaken against Antwerp, with any Prospect of Success … I had already, in the most unqualified Manner, offered every Naval Assistance to reduce these Fortresses, and also in Aid of every other Operation of the Army.'[91]

Popham, who had hoped to apply his special skills in advancing the army and navy jointly towards Antwerp, now had to help organise a retreat back to Walcheren. This began on 29 August and took four chaotic days. Popham's warning to Castlereagh at the beginning of the campaign that 'transports are the greatest clog to every sort of expedition', and his recommendation to substitute them for ships of war *armée en flûte*, may have made sense

---

89  TNA: WO 190: proceedings of the Army, 25 August 1809.
90  BL: Add MS 49505, f.45: memorandum by Brownrigg, 26 August 1809.
91  Strachan to Pole, *London Gazette*, 2 September 1809.

at the time, but the resulting lack of transports now came back to bite.[92] Because there was little or no communication between army and navy, the sick were arriving on Walcheren with no wagons ready to carry them. The weather, which had been so wet, now turned blazing hot, and sick men had to lie in the heat for several hours with no cover. The hospital equipment had, through some oversight, been shipped with the Quarter-Master General's equipment and was somewhere in transit; there was not enough bark (quinine, used to treat malarial fevers) to give them. And even when the men were transported away from where they had been landed, there was nowhere to put them. Very few houses in Flushing were sound enough to house the sick, Middelburg was full, and the church at Veere, which was also pressed into service, could house only 350 men.[93] And the men continued to fall ill: by the end of August there were 5,000 sick on South Beveland alone.[94]

Popham might have applied his celebrated organisational powers to help, but he was too busy trying to bridge the widening gap between the two commanders-in-chief. As his campaign fell apart in spectacular fashion, any pretence that he was merely captain of HMS *Venerable* was completely abandoned, and he was being used almost exactly in the same manner as a Captain of the Fleet. He alternated between Strachan, who raged at the Army's incompetence, and Chatham, who was equally persuaded the Navy's poor cooperation had let him down. Popham knew he was in an exposed position as one of the expedition's originators, with few political friends left. He therefore tried his best to mollify both commanders, persuading Strachan to offer to withdraw some of his more pointed letters and assuring Chatham of his own continued devotion:

> Your Lordship must be aware that not only my disposition, but every sentiment of Justice, and policy, commands my feeble Efforts to be applied to prevent even a shadow of difference between you and Sir Richard Strachan. I have been placed, as everybody must allow, in a situation of extreme delicacy, not to say difficulty and my object has been so to direct my energies to the totality of the publick Service, that each Commander-in-Chief, I hope I may still continue to say Friend, shou'd be prompted by a fair and an impartial view of my Conduct, to cover any act of erroneous Judgement, or indiscretion if it existed, by the marked Zeal which I trust I have shewn on every occasion to accomplish whatever objects they had in contemplation to effect.[95]

Popham could see the breach between Chatham and Strachan was unbridgeable, and he knew he would have to pick a side eventually. In the end he decided to stick with Strachan. He and Strachan had never been particularly close before the campaign; Strachan had always been, as Popham called him, 'the child of Lord St Vincent',[96] and Strachan's treat-

---

92  Popham to Castlereagh, 13 June 1809, Londonderry (ed.), *Castlereagh Correspondence*, vol.6, p.274.
93  Reiter (ed), 'Day after Day Adds to our Miseries, Part 3', pp.33–34; Coote to Castlereagh, 14 September 1809, Anon., *A Collection of Papers*, pp.135–136; *Parliamentary Debates*, vol.15, cols. ccccxix, 5xci; and R.W. Jeffery (ed.), *Dyott's Diary, 1781–1845* (London, 1907), vol.1, p.285.
94  TNA: WO 190: proceedings of the Army, 30 August 1809.
95  TNA: PRO 30/8/368, f.193: Popham to Chatham, 1 September 1809.
96  BL: Loan MS 57/108, no.11: Popham to Robert Dundas, 13 October 1809.

ment of Popham during the early stages of the expedition suggested he recognised the need to keep the wayward captain on a tight rein. But Chatham, like the other Army generals, remembered whose idea Walcheren had originally been. Chatham had also discovered the journalists Popham had invited to join the campaign from the major London newspapers were still enthusiastically sending reports home, fanning the flames of the disaster.[97] And yet if Chatham was cutting ties with Popham, Popham could also see Chatham himself was finished, politically and militarily. Even if Chatham had remained favourable, Popham would probably have tried to distance himself. He did not need any more millstones around his own neck at a time when the expedition with which he had taken so many pains to associate himself, which should have allowed him to rise, phoenix-like, from the ashes of his court-martial, had become a total and unmitigated debacle.

By 4 September, the troops had completely retreated back to Walcheren. Within days the French had again taken possession of South Beveland. Meanwhile, the sickness among the British forces had reached cataclysmic proportions. By 7 September, 10,948 men were sick, 'nearly one-third of the entire strength'.[98] Many of the senior generals were falling ill. Fraser died; Thomas Graham went home half-dead; many others, including Rosslyn, also left, pleading ill health. Dispatches had also finally arrived from London after a worryingly long silence. It was bad news. Chatham was being recalled in disgrace; that much was expected, but the weak government had not been able to withstand the campaign's failure. Castlereagh had finally discovered Canning's machinations against him, and the two men fought a highly publicised duel. The Duke of Portland had a stroke and the whole government collapsed like a pack of cards. The new Prime Minister was Spencer Perceval, whom Popham was uncomfortably aware had never liked him much. Most seriously of all for Army–Navy relations, Strachan's letter to the Admiralty of 27 August, complaining that the military men had decided not to proceed to Antwerp in the face of the Navy's insistence that more could and should be done, had been published. If there had ever been a chance of mending Chatham's relations with Strachan, it was gone now, and Popham too was *persona non grata*, as many thought he had prompted Strachan to write the letter. Brownrigg thought it had been 'a trick, calculated to preserve [Strachan's] popularity, and to make out a Case for Popham, that all that related to the Navy was plain sailing'.[99]

Chatham left for home on 14 September, leaving Walcheren in the reluctant hands of his second-in-command, Sir Eyre Coote. As he had come out, he went home in Popham's ship, HMS *Venerable*. Popham, however, was not with him, which probably came as a relief to both men. Popham had spent virtually no time during the campaign aboard his own ship. Continuing in his role as unofficial Captain of the Fleet, he remained with the commanding admiral until Strachan himself was ordered home by the Admiralty at the end of September.

---

97 BL: Add MS 49505, f.39: Brownrigg to J.W. Gordon, 28 August 1809.
98 Reiter (ed.), 'Day after Day Adds to our Miseries, Part 3', pp.38–39.
99 BL: Add MS 49505, f.69: Brownrigg to J.W. Gordon, 7 September 1809. For suspicions that Popham wrote the letter, see Anon., *Brief Remarks Upon the Public Letter of Sir Richard Strachan and the Narrative of the Earl of Chatham* (London, 1810), pp.12, 16, 19.

Popham may have intended to remain longer, but he seems to have been suffering from a slight touch of 'Walcheren fever' himself.[100] He arrived with Strachan at Deal on 1 October, and the two men went straight to report to the Admiralty.[101] Popham was determined to help Strachan make a case for the naval side of the campaign, as Chatham's most likely strategy to save his own skin would be to pile blame onto the failure of the naval cooperation. For once in his life, Popham threw himself wholeheartedly into the defence of his chosen profession. He settled in Blake's Hotel in Jermyn Street, where Strachan was also based, and the two men discussed their plan of action. They became so close that when his tenth child was born on 24 November, Popham baptised him Strachan.

With the government in flux, it was not yet clear who would become First Lord of the Admiralty. Popham suspected it would probably still be Mulgrave, but there was a possibility Lord Melville might finally return to office on the back of the chaos. The omens seemed excellent when Melville's son Robert was given the position of Irish Chief Secretary and later offered the position of Secretary of State for War, and Popham resumed his intriguing on Melville's behalf with enthusiasm.[102] Unfortunately for Popham, he was not *au fait* with internal Dundas family politics. Melville was perfectly amenable to returning to office, but not in a lesser position than his son, and Robert's being offered the War Department rankled.[103] Melville's greed kept him out of Perceval's government until his death two years later. Popham – and Strachan – were still friendless in the new government.

Despite, or perhaps because, of this, the government seemed reluctant to deal the finishing blow regarding Walcheren. Chatham had left the island in mid-September, but 16,000 increasingly sickly troops remained on Walcheren, and the beleaguered government had little energy to decide what to do with them. Chatham even remained in the cabinet as Master-General of the Ordnance – perhaps the best possible evidence the government was so weak it could not even purge so embarrassing a member. There was still a possibility that holding onto Walcheren – the only tangible benefit acquired by the expedition – might salvage some credit for the government, providing Britain with a strategic foothold on the edge of Napoleon's empire and allowing the Navy to blockade the French fleet in the Scheldt. Popham had spotted this advantage to keeping the island in early August, but by the end of autumn it was clear that maintaining a garrison on Walcheren was far too costly. On 9 December, the troops and stores were embarked aboard the British ships; on the 11th, the defences of Flushing were destroyed; and the last soldiers left on the 27th. Within two days, Walcheren had been annexed to France.[104] Napoleon was not taking any more chances.

Popham was under no illusions: now the campaign was over, the government would be looking for a scapegoat for what had gone wrong. Some sort of political reckoning was

---

100 *British Press*, 19 September 1809; *The Pilot*, 9 October 1809.
101 *The Sun*, 2 October 1809.
102 Fry, *The Dundas Despotism*, pp.299, 301.
103 Fry, *The Dundas Despotism*, pp.301–302.
104 Martin R. Howard, *Walcheren 1809: The Scandalous Destruction of a British Army* (Barnsley: Pen & Sword, 2011), pp.195–197.

The Walcheren inquiry into the misconduct of the Army Medical Board, attributed to Thomas Rowlandson, 1810. (Public domain, Wellcome Collection)

coming, with a weak government and military hospitals all over the country overflowing with Walcheren sick. Sure enough, as soon as Parliament had reassembled after the end of its recess, the opposition MP Lord Porchester moved in the House of Commons on 26 January 1810 for a committee of inquiry into Walcheren. Popham was familiar with political inquiries, having been investigated by one after his return from the Red Sea. This, however, would not be a select committee, the findings of which might depend very much on who composed it. The Walcheren committee would be composed of every member of the Commons, all of whom would be allowed to ask questions, and the proceedings would form a part of the publicly printed parliamentary debates. This had both pros and cons for Popham. As an MP, he would be able to ask questions and perhaps help shape the course of proceedings. Whatever he said would be publicised immediately, and he well knew the value of that. But he would not be able influence the other members of the committee, many of whom would not be friendly to him, and it meant the course of the inquiry would be unpredictable. On the other hand, as the government was as much in the dock as any other member of the expedition, the inquiry might bring down the ministry. Given Popham had no more allies in government, that might well be good for him.

Popham knew his best chance of survival was to meet any inquiry head-on. After Porchester had introduced his motion, therefore, Popham rose to support it, claiming he also spoke for Strachan and immediately associating himself with the Navy, for which he also claimed to speak by extension.[105] The inquiry began on 2 February, and Popham appeared before it on the 10th. He had already decided what his course of action would be: to play down his role in the planning, and to play up the fact he had merely participated in the expedition as a ship's captain. All his angst from the summer about being overlooked as the author of the expedition, not to mention about the failure to appoint him Captain of the Fleet, were gone; humility – and self-effacement – were the new orders of the day. When asked how much he had been involved in the planning process, Popham did not deny he had been consulted as an acknowledged expert in amphibious operations, but claimed his advice had 'merely [been] matter of opinion' and passed the buck by saying most of the issues on which he had been consulted had been military rather than naval questions. Other responses were also designed to turn aside the course of questioning. When asked whether it would have been possible to take British ships up to Antwerp at all despite the enemy's boom, he pointed out that nine ships of the line had got as far as Fort Batz, three and a half miles away from Fort Lillo – an answer that managed to avoid addressing the real question while playing up his own role in getting the British forces as close to Antwerp as they ever did. The only question Popham outright refused to answer, without any attempt to evade or reframe it, was whether he had ever officially advised that the French fleet could not possibly get above the Antwerp defences. Popham admitted he had always thought the area above Antwerp too shallow for ships of the line, but he simply refused to answer when asked if he had said as much to any government minister.[106]

Given how much publicity Popham had sought for his role in the expedition up to the moment of its failure, the questions he had to answer were remarkably tame. This was partly

---

105 *Parliamentary Debates*, vol.15, col.201.
106 Anon., *Minutes of Evidence*, pp.59–67.

because Popham carefully avoided committing himself to any absolutes, but it was also because Parliament's interest was shifting to the bigger fish. Strachan was examined on 15 February. Popham, a part-time politician who had been before a committee before (not to mention a court-martial), had stayed cool under cross-examination; Strachan was not so accustomed to this sort of engagement. One witness recalled that, 'when his name was called, his face was as white as a sheet. He was agitated, and his friends immediately sent for a glass of wine for him.'[107] Popham, sitting in his place as MP for Ipswich, could do little to intervene as Strachan tripped over himself again and again, admitting he had not been well acquainted with the navigation of the Scheldt, that he had never had adequate plans of Antwerp, Lillo, or Liefkenshoek, and that British ships would never have been able to cover the army's retreat from Antwerp without a favourable change of wind, as well as getting hopelessly muddled with his dates.[108] Altogether, it was not a heartening performance, and Popham may have suspected more trouble was coming his way as Strachan frequently mentioned him as the only person on the expedition with any significant knowledge of the river's navigation.[109] But then the whole inquiry took a sudden, very different turn.

Popham had been expecting some sort of self-justificatory attack from Chatham ever since the general had come home from Walcheren in mid-September. Chatham's gambit was characteristically slow in coming, but on 16 February, the day after Strachan's cross-examination, Lieutenant General William Loftus, Chatham's personal friend, laid a new piece of evidence before the House of Commons: a narrative written by Chatham for the King, telling his version of what had happened at Walcheren. The contents of the paper were exactly what Popham had been expecting. Chatham placed full responsibility for the campaign's failure at the Navy's door: 'Why the Army was not brought up sooner to the destination from whence its ulterior Operations were to commence, is purely a Naval Consideration, and ... the delay did in no shape rest with me, or depend upon any Arrangements in which the Army was concerned.' Chatham stressed his army had achieved most of its military aims by 3 August, while Strachan had failed to blockade Flushing before 7 August and had not managed to get any ships of the line past Flushing until the 11th. The paper then detailed Strachan's slowness in getting the supplies and transports through the Sloe Passage between 18 and 25 August, by which time any further advance was impossible. 'Notwithstanding every Effort on my part with the Admiral,' Chatham concluded, 'the Armament was not assembled at the point of its destination 'til the 25th and of course ... the means of commencing Operations sooner, against Antwerp, were never in my Power.'[110]

The narrative was a gift to Chatham's enemies, and to Popham and Strachan in particular. For one thing, Chatham had taken advantage of his role as a Privy Councillor to approach the King directly, rather than laying his narrative before the Secretary of State for War as the military commander of the expedition. Chatham had also botched his timing badly. He had composed his narrative in October, but only laid it before the King and the cabinet in February. This raised the possibility that either the King had had the document for four

---

107 James McGrigor, *The Autobiography and Services of Sir James McGrigor, Bart.* (London: Longman, Green, Longman, and Roberts, 1861), p.248.
108 *Parliamentary Debates*, vol.15, cols.ccxlviii–cclxi.
109 *Parliamentary Debates*, vol.15, col.ccxlviii.
110 TNA: PRO 30/8/260, f.20: Chatham's Narrative, 15 October 1809.

months before Chatham had passed it on to his cabinet colleagues, or that the document had gone through several iterations and only the latest had found its way to a wider audience.[111] The political opposition, which had been looking for a way to attack the government through Walcheren, could not believe its luck; Chatham was still a cabinet minister, and the way he had submitted his narrative by taking advantage of the royal prerogative was potentially unconstitutional. Popham, too, quickly saw the advantages offered by Chatham's narrative. Chatham, by targeting Strachan and the Navy, had played right into Popham's hands, allowing him to paint Strachan as the injured party and blotting out any lingering negative impressions from his disastrous testimony. Equally usefully, the furore over the narrative distracted the Commons committee from seeking to identify who might have been responsible for the Walcheren disaster, taking more heat off Popham. In the end the narrative's only victim was its author; within a fortnight Chatham had resigned as Master-General of the Ordnance.

Chatham's disgrace suggested the inquiry was approaching its end. On 31 March, after a few days summing up all the relevant points and arguments, the opposition wrapped the business up with a motion censuring the government for the Walcheren expedition and its aftermath. The MPs balked at voting for something that would almost certainly lead to the government's collapse and the censure on the government was rejected by 275 votes to 227. Even the retention of Walcheren until December was approved by 253 votes to 232.[112] Popham had survived the inquiry, against all odds. He had been lucky. Had the committee focused more strongly on investigating his role in the expedition, the government would neither have been able, nor willing, to protect him. Chatham's narrative had been a welcome distraction, without which he might have struggled to maintain control of proceedings.

Having survived Walcheren, Popham seems to have been confident of returning to his former prominence in decision making circles. The omens of success, however, were not good. With Canning's departure from office (and Huskisson's), Popham had even fewer friends in high places than before. The Portland government had taken British forces into three major continental embroilments, and Popham had been a major influence behind two of them. He had seen Copenhagen and Walcheren as an opportunity to show the world he had recovered from his court-martial and that he still enjoyed political support. The problem was that he associated himself so closely with the two expeditions that his fate hung on their outcome. Copenhagen had not failed, but the furore over Popham's appointment as Captain of the Fleet had damaged him. As for Walcheren, it had been an unmitigated disaster from which he was never completely able to disentangle himself. What should have been opportunities, therefore, became nails in his professional coffin. Although the war against Napoleon continued for another four years, Popham was actively employed for only about eight months of it. Like a cat, Popham usually managed to land on his feet, but Walcheren was his ninth life. It had done what Buenos Aires and the court-martial had failed to do: it had killed his career. Although Popham never quite believed it, there was no coming back.

---

111 Reiter, *The Late Lord*, pp.146–150.
112 Howard, *Walcheren 1809*, p.210; Reiter, *The Late Lord*, p.164.

# 17

# Northern Spain, 1810–1812

*2251: I am certain I can beat the enemy*

> Pray what did Sir Home Popham do?
> He's kill'd, they say, a man or two!
> Did Sir Home Popham do no more?
> Yes, he's wounded three or four!
> Now, is this all you say he's done?
> No, he besides has spik'd a gun;
> And this is all? Indeed, 'tis true,
> But is not half he said he'd do.[1]

Popham was delighted to learn Mulgrave was leaving the Admiralty as part of the reshuffle caused by Chatham's resigning the Ordnance. Less positively, he was replaced by Charles Yorke, who had served in Addington's government and remembered all too well how Popham had helped destroy it. Popham's future therefore depended on a man who had every reason to hate and distrust him. And yet, despite Yorke's deeply rooted dislike, the new First Lord realised Popham was better employed than left to stew in his own bitterness. At the beginning of August 1810, he was instructed by the Admiralty to join his ship, HMS *Venerable*, 'forthwith' at Spithead.[2] Popham complied, and requested to join the squadron blockading the French port of Cherbourg. This made sense, given Popham's background and local knowledge, and the Admiralty's agreement reflects how important his familiarity with the local waters was considered to be despite recent controversies and disasters. But these controversies were catching up with him, and at least one junior captain serving off Cherbourg, Charles Paget, refused to serve under him.[3] The Admiralty had to look for something else for Popham to do, and this led to his first major employment in over a year.

Now that Walcheren had finished so disastrously, the focus of the war had shifted to the main sphere in which Britain still had active troops: the Iberian Peninsula. The French had been here since 1807, and the British, under Sir Arthur Wellesley, had been assisting the

---
1 Anon., *The Spirit of the Public Journals for 1812* (London: James Ridgway, 1813), vol.16, p.296.
2 TNA: ADM 1/2336: note, 6 August 1810.
3 NLS: Acc. 6684/1: Captain Pulteney Malcolm to his wife, 9, 17 August 1810. Many thanks to Paul Martinovich for these references.

Spanish in repelling the invasion. Wellesley had fought a much-needed victory against the French at Talavera, for which he had been made Lord Wellington. Now, however, the French, who were much more numerous than the British, were pushing Wellington back on Lisbon in retreat. Britain's Spanish allies nevertheless still had a mixture of regular and *guerrilla* forces operating on the northern coast of Spain under the command of *Mariscal de Campo* Francisco Mariano Renovales. The British had a small naval squadron in the area of five frigates and a sloop under Captain Robert Mends of HMS *Arethusa*, liaising with the main supply depot at Corunna and attacking French supply lines.[4] Mends had spent the summer of 1810 cooperating with the local *guerrillas* in attacking French garrisons along the coast and creating diversions for the Spanish troops further inland.[5] Renovales had written to Mends suggesting further joint operations and claiming the town of Santoña, in Cantabria, would make an excellent logistical base for supplies and communication.[6] Mends, who was keen to improve relations with the *guerrillas*, passed this information on to the Admiralty and pressed for a larger naval force.

The Admiralty was intrigued, and Popham – with his lengthy experience of coordinating amphibious operations – was an obvious choice to send with naval reinforcements. Cantabria was far enough away from Britain that he would be no trouble; Popham might have protested he could be of better use off the Flanders and north French coast, which he knew so well, but perhaps his lack of local knowledge would make him less likely to go off half-cocked. His instructions, issued on 20 August, were to liaise with the Spanish *junta* (or local government) in Galicia to carry out 'a desultory and distracting kind of warfare' against the French in northern Spain and 'if practicable, to drive them out of those provinces altogether'. It was also a fact-finding exercise: Popham was instructed to get information about what the Spanish wanted, how many men they had, and the best ports to act as logistical hubs.[7] It was emphatically not a command, although Popham expected it to turn into one.

After a six-day journey battling strong southerly winds, *Venerable* reached Corunna on the evening of 5 September 1810. Here Popham found HMS *Arethusa*, along with HMS *Narcissus*, *Dryad*, and *Semiramis*, and a brig, *Goldfinch*. The next day Renovales came aboard Popham's ship to introduce him to three members of the *junta*. Popham also caught up with Captain Mends, who reiterated that Santoña was the best possible base on the Cantabrian coast for sheltering British ships and allowing the Spanish army a depot on which to retreat or resupply. Mends also said he had promised Renovales all the assistance he could give, and outlined an idea about landing guns from HMS *Medusa* and *Narcissus* to help land operations. Popham decided his best option was to go ashore and find out as much as he could about the status quo before returning immediately to Britain to report. He still, however, fully expected to be sent out again within the month to lead the cooperation himself: 'I am satisfied the *Venerable* will be able to return here from England long before General Renovales can be ready.'[8]

---

4 Christopher D. Hall, *Wellington's Navy: Sea Power and the Peninsular War, 1807–1814* (London: Chatham Publishing, 2004), p.192.
5 Hall, *Wellington's Navy*, p.193.
6 TNA: ADM 1/2337: Renovales to Mends, 18 August 1810.
7 Popham, *A Damned Cunning Fellow*, p.194.
8 TNA: ADM 1/2337: Popham to Gambier, 8 September 1810.

On 7 September, Popham met the remaining members of the *junta*. Renovales passed on some letters that had been captured from three French generals (Drouet, Barthelemy, and Bonnet), which suggested the enemy had no money with which to pay their men, found it hard to find supplies, and were falling sick in large numbers. Popham heard that the Spanish had about 23,300 troops in northern Spain, and that Bayonne was France's most essential depot for arms, ammunition, provisions, and stores, with Bilbao and San Sebastián coming second and third. Crucially, the French depended on their supplies being carried about by water, which meant British naval cooperation with the Spanish could be very useful indeed. Renovales pressed his pet plan of making Santoña a supply base, but Popham was not entirely sure of the wisdom of this, especially as the French had been busily reinforcing the other northern coastal towns since Mends and Renovales' joint attacks earlier in the summer. Popham also noted how shocked Renovales was when shown evidence the enemy had 10,000 men in the area, 4,000 of whom could be brought to Santoña within three or four days. Popham did not have a very high opinion of either Renovales or the *guerrillas* with whom he would be cooperating, and whom he referred to as 'brigands' throughout his report, to the dismay of the clerk who filed it.[9]

Despite this, Popham was reluctant to speak against joint operations, particularly as he knew this might turn into long-term employment. 'Upon the whole,' he concluded, cooperation with Renovales 'opens a great field for enterprise, much greater indeed than I ever apprehended would have been offered from that country.' The British would, however, need a safe harbour where their ships could shelter from the enemy and from the weather. The Spanish had hitherto been rather jumpy about a British presence on their territory. Gibraltar had never been forgotten; more pertinently, neither had Popham's recent history in South America. Popham therefore had to ask, '*in the most delicate manner*', whether a British garrison on the northern Spanish coast would be possible. His idea was that two or three regiments, 'a few Artillery Men, some Guns, and two Engineers' might be spared to put Santoña in a state of defence and open a communication with 'the Brigands'. Renovales would also need arms, ammunition, biscuit, and other provisions from the British depot at Corunna. If this could be provided, Popham finished, with his accustomed brashness, 'I will pledge myself, if not completely to cut off, most materially to check all Supplies going from Bayonne to Spain except by land'.[10]

As soon as he had got everything out of Renovales and the *junta* that he needed, Popham returned to his ship and left as soon as he received a favourable wind on 9 September. He clearly felt this was not adieu, but *au revoir*. Once home, he wrote to Yorke at the Admiralty to recommend sending either a regiment of troops or a body of artillery to north Spain, and concluded pointedly: 'I have certainly pressed the business, and probably prematurely [?], but whoever may be the officer sent to conduct this Enterprise, I am satisfied he will have no occasion to report that I have asked for a single thing not essential to the success of the Expedition.'[11] Whatever Popham may have hoped and expected, he was not going to be that officer: Yorke informed him

---

9   'Why brigands?' appears scribbled in pencil after the term has been used about a dozen times.
10  TNA: ADM 1/2336: Popham to Gambier, 9 September 1810.
11  NMM: YOR/14/3: Popham to Charles Yorke, 25 September 1810.

Guerrillas, 1812, by Alphonse Charles Masson, ca 1910. (Public domain, General Research Division, The New York Public Library)

by return of post that he was to join Lord Gambier, now commander-in-chief of the Channel Fleet, to relieve HMS *Valiant* in Basque Roads. Popham made no attempt to conceal his disappointment. He had believed the mission to Cantabria meant his previous transgressions had been forgiven and knew it would look bad if he was not sent back out. He somewhat pathetically threw himself on Yorke's 'Candor and consideration': 'I know how strongly this change of destination, will operate to my prejudice, and that my friends who have assured me by precise Words how strongly prejudices do exist against me, will be apprehensive that I have neither the power, talent or exertion to remove them.'[12] Popham could not stand the thought that the Admiralty's decision not to employ him might be interpreted as a sign he had fallen out of favour. His mood was not improved when he joined the Channel Fleet and found 'a general kind of buz [sic]'

---

12   NMM: YOR/14/3: Popham to Charles Yorke, 26 September 1810.

prevailing to that effect.[13] His paranoia forced Yorke, referring to repeated passages in Popham's letters regarding the existence of a conspiracy against him, to tell him in no uncertain terms to drop it.[14]

Yorke, in his slightly nettled response to Popham's pleading, did not give a reason for not sending him back to Spain; he simply passed the buck to Gambier, whom he claimed had simply decided not 'to supersede Captain Mends in the Command of the North Coast of Spain, where he has been acting for a great length of time with so much advantage to the Common Cause'.[15] Perhaps the government simply had not been convinced by Popham's report; the War Department was also hearing pessimistic opinions about the likelihood of cooperation with the *guerrillas* from other sources.[16] This probably was not the only reason, though, as Captain Mends continued to work with Renovales off northern Spain. At first, things went well. The joint Spanish-British force took Gijón, but Santoña was quickly retaken by the French and Mends's squadron was beaten back to the less well-sheltered harbour of Vivero, where a gale in November caused serious damage to HMS *Narcissus*. Retreat to Corunna did not help, and HMS *Arethusa* and *Surveillante* were badly damaged in another storm in December.[17] Mends blamed the weather for his failure, but Popham, still smarting from losing the Spanish command, was less generous. 'Capt[ain] Mends … had failed,' he told Robert Plumer Ward, a Lord of the Admiralty, adding firmly that if he had been there instead, 'he would *not* have failed.'[18]

Popham was especially bitter because he was bored rigid with reporting French movements on the coast between Ushant and Belle-Ile. As he often did when bored, he began making adjustments to his signalling system, and one of the first things Popham did when he returned to Britain in the new year was to solicit permission from the Admiralty Board to draw up a new edition of his signal book.[19] This was also very obviously a way of attracting the notice of his superiors, as he wanted to get off the Cherbourg station as quickly as possible. But Popham soon discovered he had been right in suspecting the Admiralty had reasons for not sending him back to Spain. Popham had secured six weeks' leave to attend Parliament. He made no speeches, but assisted in as many parliamentary sessions as he could in the hope of finding one of the Secretaries of the Admiralty there and bending their ear. He was not subtle: Robert Plumer Ward recalled Popham bearing down on him to complain 'of being not only ill-treated, but insulted, by the Admiralty'. Whereas Popham expected to be heard with some sympathy, however, some of his troubles had finally come home to roost. Peter Finnerty, one of the journalists who had accompanied the Walcheren expedition and a notorious Irish radical, had just been sent to prison for lambasting the former Secretary of State for War, Castlereagh, in the *Morning Chronicle*. During the course of his trial, Finnerty had brought up Popham's name and produced evidence that Popham

---

13   NMM: YOR/14/3: Popham to Charles Yorke, 7 October 1810.
14   NMM: YOR/14/3: Charles Yorke to Popham, 10 May 1811.
15   NMM: YOR/14/3: Charles Yorke to Popham, 28 September 1810.
16   TNA: WO 1/261, ff.41, 47–50: Brigadier General Walker to Lord Bathurst, 10 September 1810.
17   Hall, *Wellington's Navy*, pp.194–195.
18   Edmund Phipps (ed.), *Memoirs of the Political and Literary Life of Robert Plumer Ward …* (London: John Murray, 1850), vol.1, p.396.
19   TNA: ADM 1/2338: notes, 6 May 1811.

had invited him to join the expedition to Walcheren.[20] To Popham's horror, Ward cited this as the reason the Admiralty had been ignoring him:

> I said to him [Popham], much more in earnest than in jest, 'Sir Home, I won't hear you, I will never speak to you again; I will have nothing to do with a man who allies himself with a pilloried rebel, such a scoundrel as Finnerty.' He seemed disconcerted, and asked why not? I said ... that for a man that pretended to any sense, talents, or loyalty, to invite the blackest incendiary in the kingdom to accompany the troops on any expedition, but especially to Walcheren, was what nobody would have believed! ... I told Popham, seriously ... that he would find my impressions upon the whole matter not at all singular, for all his friends thought of it in the same way. He looked vexed, and said with some bitterness, he wondered how it should have that effect.[21]

Finnerty was probably an excuse for keeping Popham unemployed, but Popham's inability to recognise this was typical – as was his instinctive refusal to see how anybody could interpret what he had done as anything but 'an excess of zeal'. Even at this stage, he did not fully understand why his actions had been so controversial.

Things got worse for Popham when his only real remaining political patron, Lord Melville, died suddenly in May 1811. As Popham's old friend Denis O'Bryen wrote, 'Wrapt in the eternal shade, your departed friend can never more be of the slightest use to you and yours.'[22] Popham knew it all too well. In September, *Venerable* was ordered back to Cherbourg to relieve HMS *Egmont* and serve under Sir Pulteney Malcolm, although Malcolm thought Popham would find a way to get out of it if he could. Malcolm also noted Popham had the mumps, which presumably meant he was in a huff rather than physically unwell.[23] Popham was certainly annoyed. He was still paranoid – 'very jealous of the animadversion of others'[24] – and he was no fonder of blockade duty than he had ever been, as it 'not only destroys all our Ships and wears out our Naval resources, but [also] harasses the Men, vitiates their Animal Spirits, and may ultimately have the most unpleasant not to say most fatal results'.[25] Still bored and desperate for attention, Popham spent the winter at sea focusing on perfecting a new edition of his signals and, as Malcolm had predicted, pulling every string in his reach to be sent elsewhere. Popham also spent time on his political duties. In March 1812 he made his last recorded speech in Parliament on the subject of a proposed breakwater for Plymouth.[26] His disillusionment with the Admiralty again convinced him to flirt with the political opposition, just as he had done in 1809. He made sure to send Lord Grey, the

---

20 Jacqueline Reiter, '"A Melville Expedition": Sir Home Popham's Political Networks and the Walcheren Expedition of 1809', in Zack White (ed.), *The Sword and the Spirit: Proceedings of the First 'War and Peace in the Age of Napoleon' Conference* (Warwick: Helion & Co., 2021), p.59.
21 Phipps (ed.), *Memoirs of Robert Plumer Ward*, vol.1, pp.396–398.
22 BL: Loan MS 57/108, no.14: Denis O'Bryen to Popham, 23 June 1811.
23 NLS: Acc. 6684/2: Pulteney Malcolm to his wife, 15 September and [December 1811]. I am grateful to Paul Martinovich for this reference.
24 NMM: YOR/14/3: Popham to Charles Yorke, 27 April 1811.
25 BL: Loan MS 57/108, no.18 : 'Copy of a Paper delivered to Lord Melville ... May 1812'.
26 *Parliamentary Debates*, 17 March 1812, vol.22, cols.18–23.

former First Lord of the Admiralty and leader of the opposition, a copy of his updated signal code, and offered political support in return for Grey and other opposition MPs supporting his cause in the Buenos Aires prize money controversy.[27]

In late spring, however, a massive change took place in Popham's fortunes when a government reshuffle replaced Yorke at the Admiralty with the second Viscount Melville. Popham's connection with this man was weaker than it had been with his father, but he did find that the new Lord Melville, whatever his family history, considered patronising Popham to be a hereditary obligation. Popham was sure this appointment would lead to immediate employment and he was not disappointed. Towards the end of April 1812, Popham learned he would go back to the northern coast of Spain after all, to put into practice the 'desultory and distracting kind of warfare' he had first suggested in September 1810. Under his command in HMS *Venerable* would be HMS *Magnificent*, HMS *Diadem* (his old troopship, carrying a battalion of 700 marines), five frigates – HMS *Medusa*, *Surveillante*, *Hotspur*, *Rhin*, and *Iris* – and two sloops, *Rover* and *Lyra*.[28] Popham was to join Sir George Collier, currently senior captain off northern Spain in *Surveillante*, who had taken over from Captain Mends in cooperating with Renovales. Considering Popham's previous record of going above and beyond orders, he was also warned to take 'the utmost caution in undertaking or pursuing any particular measure' and 'absolute[ly] prohibit[ed] to endanger the safety of His Majesty's Ships, or that of the Marine Battalion for any Object which shall not be in magnitude and probable consequences worthy of so great a risk'.[29] Popham was placed under the command of his old acquaintance Lord Keith, which was probably not much of a pleasure for either of them, although as Pulteney Malcolm observed, Popham 'will find various plausible reasons for communicating direct with the Admiralty'.[30] Malcolm knew Popham well, for this was exactly what happened.

Lord Keith, engraver unknown after John Hoppner. (Public domain, The Miriam and Ira D. Wallach Division of Art, Prints and Photographs, The New York Public Library)

27 DUA: B49/1/6–7: Popham to Lord Grey, 3 and 7 April 1812.
28 Silvia Gregorio Sainz, 'Sir Home Popham's Mission in 1812: Santander, A British Logistics Centre?', in Zack White (ed.), *The Sword and the Spirit: Proceedings of the First 'War and Peace in the Age of Napoleon' Conference* (Warwick: Helion & Co., 2021), p.65.
29 TNA: WO 1/262, f.443: Croker to Keith, 19 May 1812.
30 NLS: Acc. 6684/2: Pulteney Malcolm to his wife, 29 July 1812. Many thanks to Paul Martinovich for this reference.

Popham's appointment had been contentious, as every one of his commands had been since his court-martial.³¹ This did not matter much to Popham, but he was also beginning to realise the second Lord Melville was not his father. Melville was his only patron; as Popham told him candidly, 'I have neither a claim on, or an attachment to, any member of [the government] but Your Lordship.'³² His future prospects depended on Melville's goodwill, and this, despite their mutual hereditary obligation, still had to be earned. This made Popham more than usually unctuous, and also uncharacteristically nervous about underperforming. When the Prime Minister, Spencer Perceval, was murdered in May 1812, Popham panicked at rumours Melville might leave the Admiralty for the Ordnance. His efforts to prove to Melville that he was 'a zealous Officer who in this description of [amphibious] War has had much practise [sic]'³³ were balanced by an awareness that he was on his last warning: 'If any accident happens to the Squadron, or the Troops, I shall be torn to pieces.'³⁴

Popham's mission was delayed by private difficulties. His wife, now in her early forties, was expecting their twelfth baby. Her pregnancies had become increasingly difficult with age, and on 17 May 1812 she went into premature labour. The child was another boy, named Harcourt after Popham's friend Lord Harcourt, but Lady Popham developed a fever after the birth and remained extremely unwell for some months.³⁵ This meant Popham was not able to join the *Venerable* until nearly June, and also that he spent his time off the Spanish coast distracted by the prospect of bad news from home. This domestic situation may have been partly why Popham made the bizarre decision to take his eldest daughter Mary with him to the Spanish coast. Presumably she was not meant to be in harm's way, and he may have hoped she would catch the eye of an officer.³⁶

*Venerable* set sail from Plymouth on 2 June and arrived off Corunna on the evening of the 9th. Popham immediately summoned aboard Lieutenant Colonel Sir Howard Douglas, a British officer serving as a liaison between the British and the local Spanish forces, and *Capitán General del Ejército* Francisco Castaños, the local Spanish military leader. Douglas and Castaños filled Popham in on the current situation, which had changed considerably since Popham had last been on the Spanish coast. In 1810, Lord Wellington had been retreating back to Portugal and the French had 350,000 men on Spanish soil.³⁷ Now, in 1812, nearly 100,000 of that invading army had been called away to other theatres of war.³⁸ This, along with the French meeting a setback in the shape of Wellington's defensive lines along the heights of Torres Vedras, had allowed the British to seize the initiative again. As

---

31  Hall, *Wellington's Navy*, p.200.
32  BL: Loan MS 57/108, no.29: Popham to Melville, 19 July 1812.
33  BL: Loan MS 57/108, no.23: Popham to Melville, 14 July 1812.
34  WLC UM: Melville Papers, Box 28: Popham to Melville, 3 November 1812.
35  BL: Loan MS 57/108, no.75: Popham to Melville, 27 October 1812.
36  The *Kentish Gazette*, 22 September 1812; NMM JOD/43: Lieutenant Robert Deans' diary, June 1812 ('Miss Popham …a very pleasant girl'); NLS: Acc. 6684/2: Pulteney Malcolm to his wife, [17 August? 1812] (many thanks to Paul Martinovich for this reference).
37  Mikaberidze, *The Napoleonic Wars*, p.274.
38  Charles J. Esdaile, *The Peninsular War: A New History* (London: Penguin, 2003), p.502.

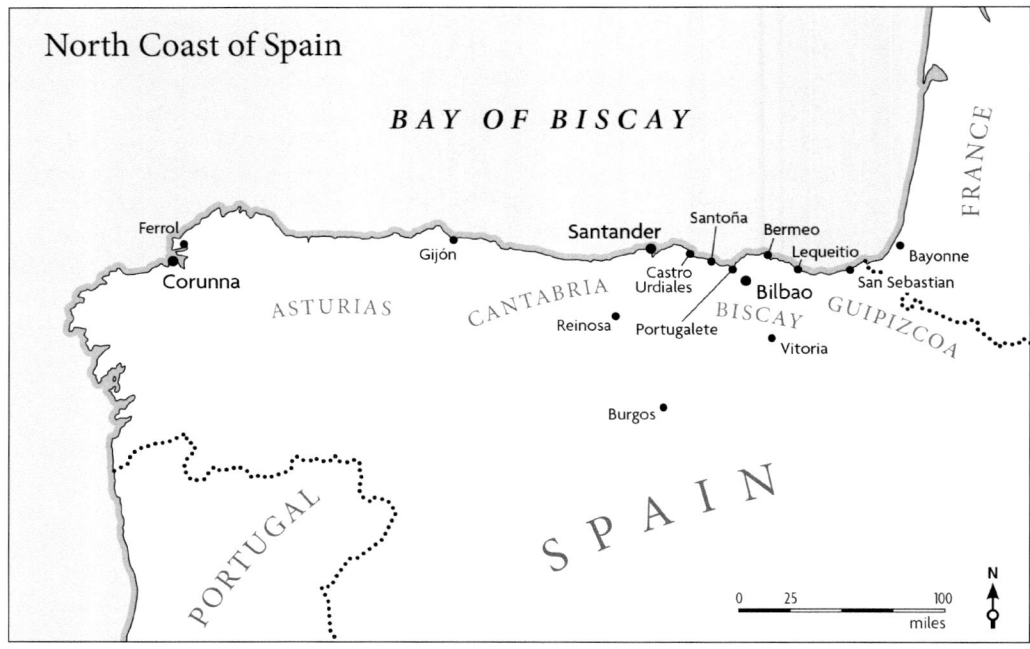

The northern coast of Spain, 1812.

Wellington moved his army of nearly 80,000 men further into Spain to bring *maréchal* Marmont's army to decisive battle, Popham would have three main roles on the coast. The first was to establish and maintain communications with the Spanish allies. The second was to establish a depot on the coast to supply the Spanish in northern Spain and act as a logistics and communication hub for Wellington. The third was to act as a diversion for the French army in the north under *général de division* Caffarelli, who would try to join with Marmont the moment his superior was threatened. At Castaños' disposal in northern Spain was the Seventh Army under *Teniente General* Gabriel Mendizábal, under whom were *Brigadier* Juan Diaz Porlier, *Coronel* Francisco de Longa, *Mariscal de Campo* Renovales, and *Brigadier* Francisco Epoz y Mina.[39] In addition, there were thousands of *guerrillas* under the leadership of men like Don Gaspar Jauregui.

Popham decided to begin operations at Bermeo, near Bilbao and close to the French border, which was relatively undefended and seemed a soft target. Popham was joined by Sir Howard Douglas and *Brigadier* William Parker Carrol, an Irishman who had joined the Spanish army as a liaison officer and who now 'very handsomely offered his Services as a Volunteer'. They sailed on 18 June, while *Surveillante*, *Medusa*, *Rhin*, and *Lyra* stood inshore to examine the coast. Popham was right that Bermeo was an easy place to start: the enemy evacuated the town without a shot being fired. Don Gaspar of the *guerrillas*

---

39  Sainz, 'Sir Home Popham's Mission in 1812', pp.66–67 and n17; Charles Oman, *A History of the Peninsular War, 1 September 1812–5 August 1813* (Oxford: Clarendon Press, 1922), vol.6, pp.254–255.

then proposed a joint follow-up attack on the nearby coastal town of Lequeitio. Popham doubted Gaspar would be able to gather enough men but, on the agreed night (19 June), he found the local hills 'crowned with *Guerrillas*'. Lequeitio, however, was a tougher nut to crack than Bermeo. The enemy retreated into a hill fort overlooking the town and 'a fortified Convent' in the town itself. On 20 June Popham tried to land the marines, but HMS *Diadem* could not get close enough to shore because of a sudden storm. News now arrived that the enemy was rushing in more troops to relieve Lequeitio. There was no time to lose in pressing the garrison to surrender, even though the *guerrillas* were not yet fully entrenched against a counterattack. 'I felt extremely uneasy ... for to have compromised [the *guerrillas*] in the smallest degree in the first combined operation with His Majesty's squadron might ultimately have been attended with the serious consequences,' Popham recalled, again betraying an untypical timorousness in his command, but having begun the operation he felt he had no choice but to see it through.

At dawn *Venerable* opened fire on the hill fort, but the ship was too far away and made no impact. At 10:00 a.m., Popham and Douglas decided to send some men ashore from *Surveillante* to erect a battery on Isla San Nicolas, a steep, rocky island in the mouth of the harbour, which the French had presumed inaccessible and left undefended. The sea was still very choppy and Popham doubted they would be able to land a single man, let alone a gun, but somehow the men succeeded in levering a 24-pounder cannon up the cliff, assisted by 100 seamen, 400 *guerrillas*, and 36 pairs of bullocks. At 4:00 p.m. the gun fired its first shot, and by sunset it had breached the fort's wall. The first party of *guerrillas* who attempted to storm it were repulsed, but the second managed to take the fort, and the enemy survivors escaped to join their colleagues in the convent.

Night was now falling, but at dawn on 21 June Popham landed another 24-pounder gun near the fortified convent, the last refuge of the enemy. The convent was now covered from three sides: Isla San Nicolas, the shore, and the ships in the harbour, and the French commander decided it was time to surrender himself and his 300 men. Popham distributed the town's military stores to the *guerrillas* while Sir Howard Douglas oversaw the destruction of the fortifications. Popham was not sure whether this was a good idea – he had been wondering whether Lequeitio might turn out to be the supply depot he was searching for – but the *guerrillas* recommended its destruction, so he acquiesced to keep good relations. It was not a moment too soon, and Popham heard that 1,100 enemy reinforcements bound for Lequeitio had turned back when they heard the Spanish and British were in possession of the town.[40]

It was a very good start to Popham's cooperation with local troops.[41] Among the letters captured in the fort was evidence that the French were worried about the appearance of Popham's squadron off the north coast, which showed the mission was already having its intended effect.[42] Renovales now pressed Popham to join in an attack on Bilbao, so the squadron went to Portugalete at the mouth of the Bilbao estuary.[43] Popham, however, was

---

40  TNA: WO 1/263, ff.5–13: Popham to Keith, 21 June 1812; S.W. Fullom, *The Life of General Sir Howard Douglas* ... (London: John Murray, 1863), pp.166–169.
41  TNA: WO 1/262, f.530: Douglas to Lord Liverpool, 21 June 1812.
42  Fullom, *The Life of Sir Howard Douglas*, p.169.
43  TNA: WO 1/263, ff.17–25: Popham to Keith, 25 June 1812.

nervous. The first operation might have gone well, but it had not gone completely smoothly. He was incensed at the failure of *Diadem* to land the marines and repeatedly pestered Lord Melville to send a replacement troopship, as 'really the *Diadem* is a very inconvenient Vessel for this Service'.[44] Melville was thoroughly baffled at Popham's condemnation of his old ship – 'your account of the *Diadem* has surprized [sic] us, as she was always supposed to be …well adapted to the species of service on which she is employed' – but he agreed to send HMS *Fox* and *Latona* instead.[45] Still, Melville did not fully understand the reason for Popham's vituperation. Popham was feeling insecure, and as always when he felt this way, he was on the lookout for someone, anything, to carry the blame.

While Captain Malcolm of *Rhin* was sent to destroy the works at Plencia, Popham landed, with Douglas and Carrol, to reconnoitre the area around Bilbao. Although they were forced back on board *Venerable* immediately by news of advancing reinforcements, they destroyed the castle of Algorta and several batteries before leaving to sow more destruction at Portugalete. Popham smugly reported the enemy commander's 'outrageous' reaction when he found his batteries all destroyed.[46] All in all, it had been a very satisfying few days, and Popham was soon planning his next series of raids, this time on the French-held town of Santoña. Popham, remembering his conversations from 1810 with Mends and Renovales, still wondered whether this town might prove the elusive logistics base from which to supply the British and Spanish armies and protect his squadron. He busied himself sourcing ammunition, muskets, and engineering supplies, while watching the French in Guetaria, which they had reinforced to a garrison of 3,000 men. The hope was that, in cooperation with the *guerrillas*, Popham could help cut this garrison off from its supply base. Still coasting from his June successes, Popham was warming to his task and even beginning to feel cheerful, although he was still conscious he had to prove himself worthy of his command to his superiors: 'I hope you [Lord Keith] will be satisfied that the Enemy has not a moment's rest, or shall he as long as my conduct appears to meet Your Lordship's approbation.'[47]

At this point, however, and despite his acute awareness of the need to tread carefully, Popham made a serious mistake of judgement. Because operations had moved so far along the coast from Corunna, and because he was receiving so many applications for weapons and supplies from the Spanish, Popham decided it would be better for them – and, also, for him – if the main arms depot were to be moved nearly 400 miles from Corunna to Machichaco. Popham was right that this would almost certainly save his squadron time and effort, but he typically forgot other parties also depended on Corunna as a depot, for whom going all the way to Machichaco would be a major detour – Wellington, for example. As so often happened when he was trying his hardest to be useful, Popham was starting to hinder more than help. When the Admiralty Board heard what Popham was proposing to do, its members were horrified. Croker, Secretary to the Admiralty, wrote to Popham reprimanding him for even thinking of such a logistical alteration. Even Melville wrote, more mildly but still firmly, to stop Popham making a serious mistake.

---

44   BL: Loan MS 57/108, no.21: Popham to Melville, 30 June 1812.
45   BL: Loan MS 57/108, no.22: Melville to Popham, 13 July 1812.
46   TNA: WO 1/263, ff.17–25: Popham to Keith, 25 June 1812.
47   TNA: WO 1/263, ff.33–39: Popham to Keith, 29 June 1812.

Croker's letter reached Popham first, in mid-July, after he had destroyed all the batteries in the Bilbao River, assisted in the capture of Castro Urdiales, and seen 10,000 Spaniards flock to enlist. He was forming a good working relationship with many of the Spanish military leaders, particularly with Longa and Mina, and his swagger had begun to return: 'Such is the confidence of all the Spaniards in me that from the General to the Soldier they all ask for my Orders – when they hear the operation is planned by me they are certain it will succeed.'[48] Croker's letter was like taking a cold shower. It fully re-activated Popham's lingering insecurity and led to a massive, and slightly insubordinate, overreaction. Popham let rip to Lord Melville, whom he (perhaps erroneously) considered a sympathetic ear: 'When I was arrested to be tried by a Court Martial on going to South America I did not feel half so much as I did when I read [Croker's] letter.' But beyond the indignation was a kernel of real fear: 'We have lost Five Weeks in the delivery of Arms, we have lost the Services of Ten Thousand Men by not having Arms, and above all I have lost *that on which I had a pride, the conceit that I possessed the confidence of Government.*'[49] The possibility that Croker's slap-down might reflect a growing loss of approval among Croker's superiors worried Popham. Several months later Croker's letter still made him uneasy; Popham promised Melville, somewhat fractiously, that he would not 'repeat the Errors of my early Service on this Coast, by invading the Forms of Office in asking in an irregular Manner for that which I consider necessary'.[50]

Having taken Castro Urdiales with little trouble, Popham's fortunes now took a turn for the worse. Popham and Mina, along with Gaspar's *guerrillas*, mounted an attack in mid-July on the port of Guetaria. Popham landed troops at two points to reconnoitre for batteries, but a gale blew up and he only just managed to re-embark his people.[51] The next day Popham tried again but, although he managed to arrange his ships' guns into a battery within range of the fort, he was still in the process of subduing it when *général de brigade* Aussenac appeared with 3,000 reinforcements. For the first time, Popham had to engage in an emergency evacuation. Thirty men and two guns were left behind.[52] At least Popham could console himself with the discovery that these reinforcements had been re-routed to Guetaria instead of joining with Marmont.

The importance of this was demonstrated to the full on 22 July, when Wellington, who had been keeping pace with Marmont's army for days, spotted a vulnerability in his enemy's overextended line and attacked just outside Salamanca. The result was a significant victory, described by Rory Muir as 'Wellington's finest'.[53] The battle 'transformed the military situation in Spain.'[54] The French were forced to abandon Andalusia in the south and lift the siege of Cadiz. Wellington's tactics and strategy were immediately responsible, but Popham, in drawing Caffarelli towards the northern coast of Spain, had also played his part. Caffarelli

---

48  BL: Loan MS 57/108, no.24: Popham to Melville, 14 July 1812.
49  BL: Loan MS 57/108, no.29: Popham to Melville, 19 July 1812 (italics mine).
50  BL: Loan MS 57/108, no.65: Popham to Melville, 15 October 1812.
51  BL: Loan MS 57/108, no.23: Popham to Melville, 14 July 1812.
52  TNA: WO 1/263, ff.403–409: Popham to Keith, 25 September 1812; Popham, *A Damned Cunning Fellow*, pp.200–201.
53  Rory Muir, *Salamanca 1812* (New Haven, CT: Yale University Press, 2001), p.x.
54  Huw J. Davies, *Wellington's Wars* (New Haven, CT, Yale UP, 2012), p.153.

The Battle of Salamanca, 22 July 1812, by John Augustus Atkinson, 1813. (Public domain, Anne S.K. Brown Military Collection, Brown University Library)

had committed to giving Marmont reinforcements of 8,000 men and 22 artillery pieces, but sent only a fraction of what he had promised.[55] Salamanca was Wellington's vindication, but it was also Popham's, as the British general himself admitted: 'I beg leave you congratulate you upon the success of your operations. They have been of great use to me, as I know that Caffarelli was prevented from detailing more than Cavalry to Marmont's assistance, and that he had even recalled a division of Troops that had marched for that purpose. I trust therefore, that you will not discontinue them.'[56]

This, however, was not Popham's decision to make. With Marmont's army neutralised, one of the main reasons for him to remain on the north coast of Spain was gone. The First Lord of the Admiralty was also keenly aware of the passage of time. Melville had not forgotten the struggles of Popham's predecessor, Mends, against the elements, and began to hint to Popham that he might need to start thinking of coming home.[57] Melville's attempt to put pressure on Popham to wrap up his business was especially untimely because Popham

---

55  Richard Herzog, 'The Royal Marine and Insurgent Operations in the Salamanca Campaign, 1812', in Gordon C. Bond and J.W. Rooney, Jr. (eds), *The Consortium on Revolutionary Europe, 1750–1850: Proceedings, 1992* (Tallahassee, FL: Institute on Napoleon and the French Revolution, Florida State University, 1993), pp.67–68.
56  BL: Loan MS 57/108, no.42a: Wellington to Popham, 4 August 1812.
57  BL: Loan, MS 57/108, no.31: Melville to Popham, 4 August 1812.

had finally found his long-sought-after logistics base: the port of Santander.⁵⁸ Wellington, having marched into Madrid, had decided to besiege the fortified town of Burgos, and Santander (less than 100 miles away) would be a very convenient depot, assuming its harbour was as safe for the British squadron as Popham suspected it would be. Spanish generals Porlier and Longa, with 4,000 men, were already investing the town. Because they had no siege artillery, however, Popham landed a battery on Isla de Mouro. He and Porlier agreed the battery would bombard the castle, while Popham would land his marines in Sardinero Bay to the north and Spanish troops attacked the town.

At 2:00 p.m. on 27 July, Popham transferred to the *Surveillante* and led *Medusa* and *Rhin* into the harbour, with *Lyra* and *Insolent* running ahead to sound. Together, the three frigates bombarded the castle as the battery on Isla de Mouro opened fire, but the attack was unsuccessful: 27 British were killed and 31 wounded, among them Captain Sir George Collier of HMS *Surveillante* and Captain Thomas Willoughby Lake of HMS *Magnificent*. For the first, but not last, time Popham blamed the reverse on a lack of Spanish cooperation:

Don Juan Díaz Porlier, by H. Creace, 1815. (Public domain, Anne S.K. Brown Military Collection, Brown University Library)

> I certainly did expect that [Spanish general] Porlier according to his sacred Promise would have been in the Town before I entered the Harbor. But when I saw Capt[ain] Lake [who had gone ashore with the marines] formed in the Hills, I had nothing left but to dash pass [sic] the Castle … or subject him to a most disastrous embarkation in which we must have lost two hundred Men.

Popham signalled from *Surveillante* for his squadron to turn their guns onto the castle defending the harbour, which eventually evacuated under fire, saving Lake and his men.⁵⁹ Popham tried to play down the failure by emphasising the French could not hold out much longer, and he was right: after the arrival of Spanish reinforcements, the French evacuated Santander over the night of 2–3 August, spiking 18 guns.⁶⁰

Popham went ashore on 3 August and confirmed the safety of the harbour's anchorage. There were rumours the town's inhabitants were pro-French, so Popham issued a proclamation

---

58  TNA: WO 1/263, ff.61–62: Popham to Keith, 26 July 1812.
59  BL: Loan MS 57/108, no.46: Popham to Melville, 30 August 1812.
60  Sainz, 'Sir Home Popham's Mission in 1812', p.66; Popham, *A Damned Cunning Fellow*, p.202.

recommending the inhabitants keep calm and quiet as the occupiers meant no ill. He also called for supplies – bread, wine, and meat – which the town provided.[61] The next few days were spent making the necessary preparations to transform the town into a communications hub, as well as allowing the squadron to replenish its provisions. The wounded Sir George Collier and Captain Lake both had to be sent home with HMS *Magnificent*. Popham was unhappy to lose them, but even more so to lose *Magnificent*, 'for we have yet a great deal to do'.[62] With one of his ships going home, Popham had to look for future assistance to the chief of the recently arrived Spanish reinforcements: *Teniente General* Gabriel Mendizábal, overall commander of the Spanish Seventh Army.

So far Popham had enjoyed remarkably good relations with the Spanish, despite his propensity to refer to them as 'brigands'. He probably hoped to strike the same rapport with Mendizábal, but the limits of Popham's liaison skills were about to be stripped bare. Relations between Popham and Mendizábal were not likely to be harmonious: Mendizábal was one of many Spanish officers who disliked Popham on principle 'consequent to some old misunderstanding at Buenos Ayres'.[63] Beyond this, however, Mendizábal and Popham had wildly different priorities. This became amply clear from their first meeting on 8 August. Popham still hoped to dislodge the French from the major ports of Guetaria and Santoña, which were, along with San Sebastián, virtually the only coastal fortifications left in French hands. Mendizábal, in contrast, was concerned with protecting Bilbao, the capital of the province, which the French were trying to re-capture. Mendizábal wanted to protect his army's flank; Popham, with no flank to protect, simply wanted to justify his continued presence on the coast.

For now, however, Popham and Mendizábal agreed Renovales would go to Deba, Longa would cover Bilbao, and Porlier would march to assist Wellington at Burgos. Mina would watch the French garrison at Vitoria, the main stronghold on the French border. Mendizábal, meanwhile, would assist Popham in a new assault on Guetaria.[64] Not everyone was convinced of the wisdom of attacking Guetaria: Mina, for example, warned Popham the enemy had 7,000 or 8,000 men there.[65] But Popham was keen to capitalise on his previous successes, sugaring the pill for his reluctant Spanish ally: 'I think Buonaparte will be highly incensed to see the Victorious Colours of Mina hoisted on the Walls of one of his Frontier Towns.'[66] Popham was also showing off for Wellington, to whom he provided a copy of his signal code to use as a communications cipher.[67] Wellington did not think a cipher was strictly necessary, and he probably regretted giving into Popham's wheedling, as Popham was not shy of correcting Wellington whenever he got the code wrong.[68]

While Wellington and his army entered Madrid in triumph, Popham went up to Bilbao, where Mendizábal had his headquarters, to discuss the attack on Guetaria. But

---

61 Sainz, 'Sir Home Popham's Mission in 1812', pp.69–70.
62 BL: Loan MS 57/108, no.32: Popham to Melville, 6 August 1812.
63 Keith to Melville, 5 September 1812, Lloyd (ed.), *The Keith Papers*, vol.3, p.284.
64 TNA: WO 1/263, ff.77–79: Popham to Keith, 8 August 1812.
65 TNA: WO 1/263, ff.153–155: Mina to Popham, 9 August 1812.
66 TNA: WO 1/263, ff.91–92: Popham to Mina, 8 August 1812.
67 BL: Loan MS 57/108, no.35a: Wellington to Popham, 11 August 1812.
68 BL: Add MS 41084, f.4: Popham's corrections on Wellington to Popham, 27 September 1812.

circumstances for the Spanish had changed. Mendizábal's attention was distracted by French reinforcements, which had arrived on the north coast in the wake of Salamanca with clear intentions of attacking Bilbao. Longa had already fought French *général de brigade* Soulier in two minor actions, while Renovales and Porlier came under attack from *général de brigade* Rouget at Durango. On 15 August, the French tried again, attacking Renovales outside Bilbao. On this occasion HMS *Rhin* was able to assist the Spanish and Renovales destroyed a French garrison by himself. These French assaults were nevertheless obviously the prelude to something more concerted, and Mendizábal called Longa up to Bilbao to join with Renovales in expectation of a larger assault.[69]

At this point, Popham arrived at Mendizábal's headquarters in a highly patronising mood. Aware of the Spanish difficulties but unable to appreciate their full extent, he began by delivering what he himself referred to as 'a severe Lecture … on the Subject of military precaution'.[70] Mendizábal, he emphasised, had to keep up the offensive if he wanted to keep the French away from Bilbao, and Guetaria, the nearest French supply depot to the main enemy garrison at Vitoria, was still the best target.[71] Popham launched into a detailed plan involving Mina's regulars and Gaspar's *guerrillas* working together while the Spanish marched part of their army out of Bilbao to catch the French in a pincer movement, and pledged to establish some batteries to fire on the town if the Spanish commander would agree to cover the building of the works.[72] According to Popham, Mendizábal agreed in full to everything – but most probably Popham simply took the Spanish commander's assent to this extraordinary attempt to tell him how to do his own job as read: 'There was so much reason in the project of Guetaria, that Mendizábal could not but agree to it.'[73] He was so confident Mendizábal would cooperate he had already sent HMS *Medusa* off Deba to embark Spanish troops for the assault, and he now began collecting 3,000 feet of planking to build gun platforms to convert his ships' guns for land use. His intention was to build 10 batteries of two guns each, with the aim of opening a bombardment on 20 August.[74]

On 17 August, Popham was back in Santander, fully expecting Mendizábal to march that very day for Guetaria. Here he heard from Carrol, who warned Popham the French were amassing forces in the vicinity of Bilbao.[75] This should have been a warning to Popham to liaise more closely with Mendizábal, but instead he sailed from Santander on 19 August to Santoña, where he found HMS *Rover*. A messenger arrived from HMS *Rhin* to say Mendizábal's troops had marched on 17 August as expected, but this turned out to be incorrect: Mendizábal had in fact been called away to Zamoza by enemy movements.[76] The French were launching their anticipated attack to re-capture Bilbao: troops had left Vitoria,

---

69  TNA: WO 1/263: correspondence covering 12–15 August 1812: ff.118–120: Popham to Keith, 16 August; ff.121–123: Popham to Keith, 16 August; f.255: Longa to Popham, 15 August; ff.347–354: Carrol to Wellington, 24 August.
70  BL: Loan MS 57/108, no.36: Popham to Melville, 16 August 1812.
71  BL: Loan MS 57/108, no.36a: Popham to Mendizábal, 16 August 1812; TNA: WO 1/263. ff.121–123: Popham to Keith, 16 August 1812.
72  TNA: WO 1/263, ff.125–128: Popham's plan, 16 August 1812.
73  TNA: WO 1/263, ff.121–123: Popham to Keith, 16 August 1812.
74  TNA: WO 1/263, f.259: Popham to Longa, 16 August 1812.
75  TNA: WO 1/263, ff.137–138: Carrol to Popham, 18 August 1812.
76  TNA: WO 1/263, f.141: Carrol to Popham, 19 August 1812.

and the garrison at Durango was reinforced by 1,300 men, with a further 6,000 infantry and 300 cavalry waiting nearby. On 20 August, Mendizábal fell back to take a defensive position between Durango and Bilbao. He did send orders to Mina and Gaspar to march to Guetaria if they could, but he did not know where they were and assumed they were probably otherwise engaged.[77]

None of this was unexpected; the news Popham had been receiving for days should have prepared him for it. Yet he heard of what had happened with 'astonishment'.[78] He bombarded Mendizábal with irritated letters, reminding him of the course of action agreed on the 16th and showing a complete lack of appreciation of Mendizábal's problems.[79] Even as Popham was furiously writing these letters, Mendizábal was under attack at Bilbao. He managed to repel one assault of about 6,000 men at Bolueta, and at daybreak the next day launched a successful counterattack against 3,000 enemy and 300 cavalry in a bloody, five-hour-long action.[80] But Popham was not thinking of the Spanish context: he was thinking of himself, with one eye on the reaction of his superiors back in Britain: 'If I go from here I never can return again until I am ordered by my Government from England, because England will be disappointed, and Lord Wellington may be disappointed.'[81] This was not just rhetoric. Popham was desperately worried failure at Guetaria would overshadow all his good work in the run-up to Salamanca.

Popham immediately began detailing everything that had gone wrong with the abortive assault on Guetaria, placing the blame squarely with Mendizábal. He heavily implied Mendizábal had never intended to attack Guetaria at all, despite agreeing to Popham's plan of 16 August, and that he had acted in bad faith throughout. This was not very generous to the Spanish general, who had his own difficulties in the face of rapidly changing circumstances. Carrol, who had much more experience of dealing with the Spanish and was actually on the spot in Bilbao, pointed out that, had Mendizábal moved towards Guetaria, the enemy would have slid 20,000 men behind him and cut off his communications and supplies.[82] Popham did not care. Military realities meant nothing to him if he could draw no reflected glory from the situation. 'Some theoretick Nonsense about the Art of War got into [Mendizábal's] head,' he complained to Melville, 'and he thought it was wrong to leave Bilbao uncovered' – a startlingly short-sighted thing to say as Mendizábal was beaten back at the end of the month, allowing the French to reoccupy the provincial capital.[83]

Popham was not just feeling frustrated 'in consequence of his [Mendizábal's] ridiculous manoeuvres'.[84] He had now been off the north Spanish coast three months and, since Salamanca, he had achieved very little. He was powerfully aware of the need to make a splash, particularly as he had promised Melville great things: 'all that Men can do shall be done.'[85] In retaking Bilbao, the French had shown they were far too capable of re-capturing

---

77  TNA: WO 1/263, ff.271–272: Mendizábal to Popham, 20 August 1812.
78  TNA: WO 1/263, ff.275–282: Popham's report on Guetaria.
79  TNA: WO 1/263, ff.150–151: Popham to Mendizábal, 21 August 1812.
80  TNA: WO 1/263, ff.103–105: Carrol to Lord Liverpool, 24 August 1812.
81  TNA: WO 1/263, ff.331–333: Popham to Mendizábal, 21 August 1812.
82  TNA: WO 1/263, ff.347–354: Carrol to Lord Bathurst, 24 August 1812.
83  BL: Loan MS 57/108, no.43: Popham to Melville, 28 August 1812.
84  BL: Loan MS 57/108, no.46: Popham to Melville, 30 August 1812.
85  BL: Loan MS 57/108, no.36: Popham to Melville, 16 August 1812.

towns taken by the Spanish and British. The weather would soon become too bad to justify keeping a large squadron close to the coast, and even Santander's protected harbour would become a danger if the enemy re-captured the town and the wind prevented the ships from escaping.[86] As though to underline the point, the beginning of October was particularly stormy. Gales dispersed troopships carrying reinforcements to Corunna, buffeted Lord Keith's squadron in the Bay of Biscay, and kept Popham's squadron pegged in Santander harbour for two weeks.[87] Popham was running out of time.

His best hope was that Wellington would insist on his remaining off the coast as long as possible. Wellington's siege of Burgos gave Popham's role potentially fresh importance: the more he could distract the enemy, the less likely it was that Wellington's siege would be interrupted. Popham therefore wrote to Wellington on 16 September to warn him the squadron might be recalled at any moment.[88] In fact Lord Keith had already recognised how important Popham might be and had already issued him with fresh orders to remain on station if Wellington needed his help. But this was only a temporary reprieve: Keith emphasised that Popham should return to Britain the moment Wellington no longer needed him.[89] Bad news was also coming in from the front line. Popham's First Lieutenant returned from a mission to Burgos on 15 September with reports that the town fortifications were stronger than expected, which meant a potentially protracted siege.[90] Wellington might have to turn south before he was surrounded by *maréchal* Soult, *maréchal* Suchet, and King Joseph, who had combined to bring a force of 60,000 men into the field, and a British retreat inland would leave Popham and his squadron isolated and exposed.

While he waited for more news from Burgos, Popham looked for a way of making his indispensability more obvious. Guetaria was still at the top of Popham's list of priorities, and he 'fairly dragooned' Mendizábal into attacking it again mid-September, although without any serious expectation of success.[91] He was right to doubt: Mendizábal, still reluctant to expose his men for the sake of Popham's whims, showed absolutely no signs of wanting to cooperate.[92] He told Popham he did not feel comfortable attacking Guetaria without reinforcement from Mina, who was eight days' march away, effectively killing any attempt to take the town.[93] Popham was incensed, and he made no attempt to hide his disgust: 'So favourable an opportunity never existed or ever will again be presented.'[94] In fact Mendizábal was not as cowardly as Popham assumed. The enemy was on the march, and 14,000 men were on their way to Guetaria.[95] Popham's thoughts therefore turned to another fortified coastal town: Santoña, a vital point of communication between the French forces and their frontier base at Vitoria, and a threat to the British squadron at Santander so long as it remained in French

---

86   TNA: WO 1/263, ff.551–553: Keith to Popham, 20 October 1812.
87   TNA: WO 1/263, ff.495–497: Lieutenant Colonel Bourke to Lord Bathurst, 11 October 1812.
88   Sainz, 'Sir Home Popham's Mission in 1812', p.73.
89   BL: Loan MS 57/108, no.59f: Keith to Popham, 12 September 1812.
90   Carole Divall, *Wellington's Worst Scrape: The Burgos Campaign, 1812* (Barnsley: Pen & Sword, 2012), p.38.
91   BL: Loan MS 57/108, no.50: Popham to Melville, 15 September 1812.
92   TNA: WO 1/263, ff.411–418: Bouverie to Popham, 23 September 1812; TNA: WO 1/263, ff.403–409: Popham to Keith, 25 September 1812.
93   TNA: WO 1/263, ff.451–454: Mendizábal to Popham, 18 September 1812.
94   TNA: WO 1/263, ff.427–433: Popham to Mendizábal, 22 September 1812.
95   TNA: WO 1/263, ff.403–409: Popham to Keith, 25 September 1812.

hands. The only problem was that it was hardly the easiest of pickings along the northern coast, and would require impeccable cooperation between British and Spanish – something that had been singularly lacking recently.

At least Popham's warning to Wellington that the squadron might be recalled had not fallen on deaf ears. Partly in a bid to keep the squadron on station, the military commander ostentatiously called on Popham for supplies throughout the siege of Burgos, beginning with a request for 40 90lb barrels of gunpowder from Popham's ships.[96] Popham was delighted at this opportunity to show off how useful he could be, particularly as he knew Wellington was writing to the cabinet about it. 'You may rely on it that I shall do everything that can be done for Lord Wellington,' he told Lord Melville. '… I have long anticipated that necessity would force him to have recourse to this place in preference to any other; common sense points out the wonderful superiority of convenience.'[97] Popham's keenness to make his mark, however, inspired another rash brainwave in the vein of his suggestion to move the arms depot from Corunna to Machichaco. When writing for more gunpowder, Wellington had hinted at his lack of proper siege guns: 'It is unfortunate that you should have plenty of Cannon and ammunition but that you want good Soldiers; and I no want of the latter but very little of the former.'[98] Popham took note of this and wondered whether he could fix the shortage by placing 'a chain of Ships' Guns before Burgos'.[99] An idea had begun to germinate in Popham's mind, although he did not yet act on it.

Success at Santoña might have a positive impact with Wellington and with the Admiralty, so Popham continued preparing for a siege, collaborating with local authorities in the Santoña area to provide wood and iron for gun carriages and establishing a foundry for casting guns and shot.[100] But Popham was still not sure he could trust Mendizábal. Even as he was making ready to attack Santoña he was preparing the ground for failure, sending one of his captains to Wellington and then on to Britain to complain about his cooperation woes.[101] He even asked Wellington if 6,000 or 7,000 Spanish troops could be sent to Santoña under another general, preferably Porlier or Longa, with whom Popham had more of a rapport.[102] The failure of Popham's liaison role – a major reason he had been sent to Spain in the first place – was complete, much of it in public dispatches addressed to British cabinet ministers. Popham, who blithely copied Lord Melville into every dispute he had with Mendizábal, did not seem to realise how much he was hurting his own cause with his only remaining political patron. Melville was already getting annoyed with his protégé constantly asking for more – more marines; more troopships; more ammunition; more regulars.[103] If Popham could not do anything useful with those resources, like take Santoña, he would soon have outstayed his welcome on the Spanish coast.

---

96  TNA: WO 1/263, ff.483–484: Wellington Popham, 26 September 1812; BL: Loan MS 57/108, f.59a: Wellington to Popham, 2 October 1812.
97  BL: Loan MS 47/108, no.55: Popham to Melville, 30 September 1812.
98  TNA: WO 1/263, ff.483–484: Wellington Popham, 26 September 1812; BL: Loan MS 57/108, f.59a: Wellington to Popham, 2 October 1812.
99  BL: Loan MS 47/108, no.55: Popham to Melville, 30 September 1812.
100  TNA: WO 1/263, ff.543–546: Popham to Wellington, 9 October 1812.
101  BL: Loan MS 57/108, no.59: Popham to Melville, 6 October 1812.
102  TNA: WO 1/263, ff.539–540: Popham to Wellington, 10 October 1812.
103  BL: Loan MS 57/108, no.74: Popham to Melville, 26 October 1812.

Arthur Wellesley, Duke of Wellington, by William Heath, 1814. (Public domain, Anne S.K. Brown Military Collection, Brown University Library)

Popham may have cared less about such impressions because he thought he had finally received an endorsement from Wellington. On 12 October, Wellington had responded to fresh alerts from Popham that he might imminently be recalled: 'If you were not known to be in that Ship [HMS *Venerable*], ... the Enemy as well as [the] Spaniards will be convinced that nothing is intended to be done ... and I apprehend that I shall have upon my hands in Castille more of Enemy than I can well manage.'[104] Popham was jubilant as he imagined Wellington's gratitude would help persuade the Admiralty to keep him on station, but his delight soon cooled as he took stock of what the general had actually written. Wellington's praise had not exactly been fulsome – Wellington stated, for example, that removing the squadron would not matter in broader strategic terms – and, worse, the letter had been a secret, ciphered one sent to Popham alone. A private pat on the head could not be printed in the papers, and Popham was as obsessed with shaping his reputation at home as ever. Within days his elation had transformed into outright disgruntlement, and he complained he was 'ruining my constitution and fortune for the Honor of being flattered by Lord Wellington'.[105]

Popham's disappointment only increased his desire to show Wellington how useful he and his squadron could be. Inevitably, this over-eagerness to please led him to undo all the good work he had done in winning Wellington's support at a stroke. Popham decided to put his long-meditated plans into action for supplying Wellington with siege guns for Burgos. Wellington had already hinted this would be inconvenient, but Popham seemed to think Wellington's emphasis on the distance between Santander and Burgos had been a challenge rather than an attempt to stop any unauthorised activities on his part. Without waiting

---

104  BL: Loan MS 57/108, no.64a: Wellington to Popham, 12 October 1812.
105  BL: Loan MS 57/108, no.71: Popham to Melville, 19 October 1812.

for Wellington's permission, therefore, he landed two 24-pounder guns from *Venerable* and sent them to Reinosa, about halfway between Burgos and Santander, where he hoped Wellington would send an escort to collect them:

> I trust to Your Lordship's kindness and liberality to excuse me for trying this Experiment as far as Reynosa; I have nothing to do, and turning everything in my mind it occurred to me that Your Lordship would like that the practicability of transporting heavy Guns should be ascertained. The Guns will be at Reynosa at daylight on Sunday morning, as I have ascertained that it is possible to get them there in thirty-six hours. If Your Lordship approves of the thing and will do me the honor to send to me, I will engage to have as many as you please at Reynosa in forty-eight hours. ... If Your Lordship wants Ten [more] you shall have them immediately.[106]

Popham was sure Wellington could only appreciate this stroke of genius. 'We are to hope that some more obstacles will be presented to us to overcome,' he crowed to Melville: 'nothing will give me more pleasure.'[107] But Popham had overplayed his hand, as he so often did. Wellington was about to raise the siege of Burgos and begin one of the most gruelling retreats of the war. When the unsolicited guns appeared, Wellington simply sent them back with a polite, but cool, note: as he was preparing to raise the siege and withdraw, 'I shall not therefore want the guns which you were so kind as to send'.[108]

With Wellington turning against him and Melville's letters becoming fewer and further between, Popham's negativity returned with a vengeance. He was uncharacteristically tired; his letters home reeked of pessimism regarding 'the horrors of this coast', the lateness of the season, and the improbability of successful coordination with Spanish troops.[109] Feeling aggrieved at the lack of public acclaim for his exploits, Popham's thoughts revolved more than ever around home and Lady Popham, who was still unwell after the birth of her last child.[110] Nor could he bring himself to begin besieging Santoña, although he must have known it was his last chance to prove his worth. In October he received news that Wellington had finally left Burgos and was moving away from the coast. Based on his most recent orders from Keith and Melville, this should have been the end of the mission, but Popham did not want to end on such an anticlimax. He told Melville he was now responsible for keeping the Army of the North from crossing the Ebro and harrying Wellington's retreat.[111] But with communications lines increasingly stretched, Popham had to piece together Wellington's distant movements from scraps and hearsay. As always, he was inclined to believe the best of the reports he received, passing on rumours of a British and Spanish victory over Soult outside Burgos at the end of October. There was no such victory; in fact, at that point the French were reoccupying Madrid, and Popham probably knew, deep down, that things were not

---

106 BL: Loan MS 57/108, no.72a: Popham to Wellington, 16 October 1812.
107 BL: Loan MS 57/108, no.72: Popham to Melville, 21 October 1812.
108 BL: Loan MS 57/108, no.73c: Wellington to Popham, 21 October 1812.
109 BL: Loan MS 57/108, no.77: Popham to Melville, 31 October 1812.
110 BL: Loan MS 57/108, no.75: Popham to Melville, 27 October 1812.
111 BL: Loan MS 57/108, no.73: Popham to Melville, 23 October 1812.

William Congreve, by James Lonsdale, 1807. Popham supported the use of Congreve rockets at Copenhagen (shown here), at Walcheren, and off the north coast of Spain. (Public domain, Anne S.K. Brown Military Collection, Brown University Library)

going well.[112] Rather than make arrangements to evacuate his squadron, however, he continued to pester the government for more troops, asking for Congreve's rockets and two regiments of infantry for an attack on Santoña that had started sounding more like a play for time than an actual plan of action.[113]

Popham's plans for Santoña also exposed more of his dispute with his Spanish allies – what Popham described as Spanish incompetence, and what Mendizábal saw as a complete lack of perspective and priority on Popham's part. On 16 November, Popham wrote to Mendizábal, asking for the Spanish general's help in attacking Santoña. He reminded Mendizábal of the town's importance but, in so doing, let slip one of his underlying concerns for taking the place, and it was not that the French would strengthen their position in the north of Spain by possessing it: 'It is a painful task to be obliged to trouble Your Excellency so frequently on this subject, but I feel confident that you'll pardon me when you consider the particular situation in which I am placed; Lord Wellington presses me on one hand, and His Majesty's Ministers equally, if not more anxious[ly], on the other.'[114] As usual, Popham had one eye on the immediate military situation and one on the more distant prospect of how his actions would be viewed at home. Mendizábal was thoroughly unimpressed. Although he did allow Popham one last meeting on 5 December, this did nothing but make Popham 'indignant'.[115] Mendizábal was no fool, and must have realised that Popham's position was less secure than he wanted to make out – and that he need only wait for his Popham-shaped problem to disappear.

---

112 TNA: WO 1/263, ff.579–581: Lieutenant Colonel Bourke to Lord Bathurst, 8 November 1812.
113 BL: Loan MS 57/108, no.74: Popham to Melville, 26 October 1812.
114 WLC UM: Melville Papers, Box 28: Popham to Mendizábal, 16 November 1812.
115 BL: Loan MS 57/108, no.85: Popham to Melville, 30 December 1812.

In fact the game was up whether Popham took Santoña or not. Whatever Popham wanted Melville to think, his squadron could no longer be an effective diversion: Caffarelli had left the coast to chase Wellington, and only 20,000 French remained on the north coast.[116] Without Mendizábal or Gaspar, without more marines and seamen to man the guns, and without spades, shovels, or gunpowder, nothing useful could be done, especially as Popham was now hearing Wellington was beyond Salamanca – in other words, that he had lost every single piece of ground gained in the north since the summer.[117] For the first time, Popham began talking seriously of going home, at least for the winter. 'It will be better for us to give up the pursuit all together [sic],' Popham told Melville, 'and return to England with the large Ships and the Marines, till a more favorable opportunity offers for our exertions.'[118] He nevertheless confidently expected to be sent out again in the spring, when the weather improved.

Unfortunately for Popham, news of his ostentatious failure to win over his Spanish allies had found its way home by a variety of channels. Lieutenant Colonel Bourke, at Corunna, noted that, although Popham had managed to befriend Mina, 'I was sorry to find he was not on such a good footing with Longa or General Mendizábal as it might be advantageous to the Service he should be.'[119] Popham's own correspondence proved this friction was affecting his ability to carry out his instructions, and the message was getting through to the highest levels. He had always been an odd choice of commander for the Admiralty to send as a Spanish liaison officer, as many of the military men he would be dealing with had neither forgotten nor forgiven Buenos Aires. For his part, Popham viewed the Spanish with a healthy pinch of xenophobia. 'The Spaniards are a description of people to whom too much liberality ought not to be shewn,' he wrote not long after the capture of Beresford in 1806, and his behaviour off the Spanish coast suggested he had not changed his mind in six years.[120] On 4 December, the Admiralty issued orders to Lord Keith 'to recall Capt. Sir Home Popham in the *Venerable* with the troop ships and marines and direct them to proceed to Portsmouth for further orders and no longer to consider them as under his command' – Popham would not be returning.[121] Melville also wrote privately to Popham, telling him he had informed Lady Popham of her husband's recall.[122] He was clearly anticipating another protest from Popham, another insistence on stretching out the deadline for his return; but, for a man who had so often claimed concern about his wife's health, there could be no appeal once he knew Lady Popham was anticipating his imminent arrival.

Popham's recent correspondence about 'giving up the pursuit all together' allowed Melville to claim he was only following Popham's own desires in closing the campaign. But leaving Spain with Santoña still in enemy hands was not what Popham had envisioned. The French kept a foothold on the coast, which would allow them to retake a number of fortresses and undo everything Popham had achieved over the summer. Popham expected to be kept on station long enough to complete his unfinished business and, although he

---

116  Popham, *A Damned Cunning Fellow*, p.209.
117  BL: Loan MS 57/108, no.79: Popham to Melville, 27 November 1812.
118  WLC UM: Melville Papers, Box 28: Popham to Melville, 21 November 1812.
119  TNA: WO 1/263, ff.619–620: Lieutenant Colonel Bourke to Colonel Bunbury, 26 December 1812.
120  DUA: B49/1/2: Popham to Howick, 9 September 1806.
121  TNA: ADM 1/2343: note, 4 December 1812.
122  BL: Loan MS 57/108, no.83: Melville to Popham, 4 December 1812.

hoped 'some more active employment' would be found for him in future, he did not intend that to happen until after 'the History of Santoña [was] decided'.[123] Santoña was still his last chance to redeem himself for the disappointment of the autumn months. As Popham told Keith, 'The Service on which I am employed is so very various and complicated in all its bearings, and in many parts of a nature so extremely novel, that I have long hesitated to hope that I shall get through it without some blame.'[124] When he wrote this, he did not know he had already run out of time. He only found out on 13 December, when HMS *Fairy* arrived in Santander carrying the orders for his recall.[125]

Retrospectively, Popham's record off the Spanish coast was viewed positively, and historians have been full of praise. Rory Muir called Popham's activities 'probably the best example of naval cooperation of the whole war in the Peninsula'.[126] Charles Esdaile thought Caffarelli's Army of the North was 'run ragged' by Popham's antics.[127] Charles Oman put it most simply: as a diversion, Popham was 'brilliantly successful'.[128] At the time, however, contemporaries were less impressed with what was, effectively, a bit of a flop. Popham may have helped distract Caffarelli and prevented him meeting up with Marmont prior to Salamanca; he may have helped delay the end of the Burgos campaign by continuing his diversions into October. After Wellington had left Burgos, however, Popham's remaining off the coast became a problem, and he was very lucky he did not suffer the same fate as Captain Mends. All he managed to do was draw attention to how badly he got on with his Spanish allies. He may not have called them 'brigands', but he treated them as little better. He also managed to irritate everyone he worked with – not just Mendizábal, but also Wellington, Keith, and ultimately his patron, Melville, who eventually had enough of ironing out the ructions Popham created wherever he went.

Wellington, in particular, although he claimed to have hoped Popham would remain at Santander for the whole winter, was remarkably limp in his praise.[129] Wellington, like Melville, had got fed up of Popham's repeated complaints about the Spanish and his persistent jumping ahead of orders – the sending of *Venerable*'s guns to Reinosa, for example, at a time when they could only embarrass Wellington's need for a swift retreat. The closest thing Popham got to an official endorsement in Wellington's public dispatches was Wellington's letter of 26 December to Lord Bathurst, in which he admitted Popham's activities had been 'of essential service to the army' – but even this was prefaced by the caveat that the squadron's operations had been independently carried out and not directly connected with the army's movements.[130] Privately, Wellington wrote waspishly to Lord Liverpool:

> Sir H[ome] Popham is a gentleman who piques himself on overcoming all difficulties. He knows the time it took to find transport even for about 100 barrels of

---

123 BL: Loan MS 57/108, no.84: Popham to Melville, 7 December 1812.
124 NMM: KEI/37/2: Popham to Keith, 5 December 1812.
125 Sainz, 'Sir Home Popham's Mission in 1812', p.78; Waite, 'Sir Home Riggs Popham', p.209.
126 Rory Muir, *Britain and the Defeat of Napoleon, 1807–1815* (New Haven, CT: Yale UP, 1996), p.207.
127 Esdaile, *The Peninsular War*, p.391.
128 Charles Oman, *A History of the Peninsular War, October 1811–31 August 1812* (Oxford: Clarendon Press, 1914), vol.5, p.558.
129 Wellington to Melville, 26 December 1812, Gurwood (ed.), *Wellington Dispatches*, vol.6, p.222.
130 Wellington to Bathurst, 26 December 1812, Gurwood (ed.), *Wellington Dispatches*, vol.6, p.222.

powder and a few hundred rounds of musket ammunition that he sent me. As for the two guns that he endeavoured to send me, I was obliged to send my own cattle to draw them, and felt great inconvenience from the want of those cattle in subsequent movements of the Army.[131]

This letter, addressed to the Prime Minister himself, may have had more weight in cabinet circles than any of Wellington's lukewarm commendations. And although Wellington was rarely lavish with his compliments, his criticism was backed up by others. One of Popham's squadron, HMS *Rhin*, had gone home in October to refit. Captain Charles Malcolm's report to Lord Melville emphasised the bad weather conditions facing the squadron, and this clearly influenced Melville in his decision to recall Popham, but Malcolm's opinion of Popham as a commander – which, according to Malcolm's elder brother, Pulteney, was not good – probably also had a bearing.[132]

Once he had ensured Mendizábal was able to fortify Santander, Popham set sail for home on 21 December in squally weather.[133] Popham was still jumpy about possible reasons for his recall, and his sense of self-preservation was at its most acute. The moment he arrived off the Isle of Wight on 30 December, he began penning a long explanatory letter to Lord Melville. To justify his lack of broader success off the coast, Popham delivered a strongly pessimistic analysis of the war in the Peninsula:

> You may probably be astonished at the following very concise opinion about the war in Spain, but as it is … meant merely for yourself, and to enable you to decide by subsequent merits how far I have any judgment, I shall come at once to the point.
> If the war continues, unless you can find a force, either by subsidising Sweden, or Russia, to land in the North of Spain, the French never can be conquered in that country. If Lord Wellington has the same opportunity and meets with similar success against Soult this year, as he did against Marmont last year, they will collect again and prevent his crossing the Ebro; their means of reinforcement are so very much at hand, that it is hardly to be conceived what they will do. … In short, my lord, if you cannot send Twenty Thousand Troops (foreign or British) to the North, I am most decidedly apprehensive that the French will never be conquered in Spain.[134]

Given events in the Peninsula over the next few months, Popham's letter seems extraordinary, but it was a letter he had no choice but to write. He had gone out boasting to do all that was humanly possible, and he had to rationalise his failure by claiming his challenge had turned out to be superhuman. His best hope was that Melville would agree that

---

131 Wellington to Liverpool, 23 November 1812, Gurwood (ed.), *Wellington Dispatches*, vol.9, p.574.
132 NLS: Acc. 6684/1: Pulteney Malcolm to his wife, 23 August 1812. Many thanks to Paul Martinovich for this reference.
133 TNA: ADM 51/2957: log, HMS *Venerable*, 21 December 1812.
134 BL: Loan MS 57/108, no.85: Popham to Melville, 30 December 1812.

responsibility for what had happened lay with Mendizábal and the Spanish, and not with the squadron or its commander.

Popham still did not realise how much his continued complaints about his allies had undermined his cause, but he was soon disabused. On 5 January, less than a week after he had sent his letter to Lord Melville, he learned *Venerable* would not be going back to the Spanish coast and that Collier, in *Surveillante*, would take over the command once more. An old patron, Lord Moira, the newly appointed Governor-General of India, had asked for Popham to convey him to his new station, and Lord Melville had acquiesced. This could be interpreted as an honour – Moira had, after all, specifically requested his services – but Popham, who so desperately wanted to prove how active and useful he could be, did not see it that way. He was horrified. This was no 'situation of activity and advantage'; there would be no chance of prize money or of distinguishing himself. It was a purely ceremonial trip, carrying a man who was known to be heavily in debt and addicted to the pleasures and comforts of high aristocratic life, which Popham would be expected to provide at his own cost. Further, Melville told Popham he was being taken away from *Venerable* and given *Stirling Castle* instead.

This made some sense, as *Stirling Castle* was a new ship suited to carrying a colonial governor while *Venerable* had been on active service for years. Still, the unwanted transfer convinced Popham he was being chastised. He wrote immediately to Melville begging to see him in person 'before I am practically superseded in the *Venerable*'. His letter confirmed his awareness that he had failed in his Spanish mission: 'I am aware from a variety of circumstances that the Service on which I have been employed, has not fully gratified the unnatural expectation which has been established about its Issue.' Popham feared he was losing, or had lost, the goodwill of the only man in government he could rely on: 'The Truth is, that to you, and only you, have I ever looked either for approbation, or favor, and in each I have been gratified.' It was no more than he had said before, but his tone now was more panicked than mournful. He could not understand what might have turned Melville against him; the only thing he could think of was that he had shown too little, not too much, zeal. If so, he begged Melville to reconsider, to have pity, and above all, to keep him actively employed: 'I am induced to speak candidly, and to say, if another little Squadron is in agitation for the Southward, consisting of one line of Battle Ship and two Frigates, the nomination of the *Venerable* [with Popham remaining as captain] wou'd be a distinction, which wou'd silence the suspicions of many, that I have not pleased my Superiors.'[135] Popham's entire career had been built on proving how useful he could be, and he had always relied on protectors to shield him against his enemies. What would happen if he lost that protection? What would his enemies do when they realised he had lost Melville's approval?

Popham's appeal cut no ice. On 21 January 1813, the Admiralty confirmed his appointment to *Stirling Castle*.[136] 'I tried very hard to continue in the *Venerable*,' he despaired to Keith, 'but I was overpowered.'[137] Popham had spent the last six months trying to prove to the world that he was still relevant, employable, and favoured. This was the result. It was not exactly a punishment, but it was not at all what Popham had wanted, and over the next 18 months things got significantly worse, because Popham made very little attempt to hide or control his bitterness.

---

135 WLC UM: Melville Papers, Box 28: Popham to Melville, 5 January 1813.
136 TNA: ADM 1/2343: note, 21 January 1813.
137 NMM: KEI/37/2: Popham to Keith, 23 January 1813.

# Message Finished

*'A diagonal blue and yellow flag, which may be hoisted or not according to circumstances, or the telegraph flag hauled down'*

## 18

# Frustration, 1813–1817

*2824: I have not succeeded*

Popham had to accept the inevitable, but his reluctance to take up his new command was obvious. Although he had agreed to join *Stirling Castle* as soon as possible on 23 January, he had still not done so by 8 February, when the Admiralty Board issued him with an order to proceed to his new ship 'without loss of time'.[1] Popham took possession of the vessel on 10 February and immediately asked for leave.[2] The request did not go down well, and a few days later he wrote to Melville to explain he had only had seven days of leave since returning from Spain and had business to transact: 'When I have the Honor of seeing Your Lordship I pledge myself to satisfy you that my Conduct has been most correct, never swerving from any rule of Service.'[3] He seemed certain Melville would grant him an interview, and that when it took place he could change Melville's mind about sending him to India.

But by the end of February, Popham was about to leave London for Portsmouth and had not yet had his expected audience with the First Lord. It did not occur to him that Melville may have been avoiding him deliberately, and he hoped Melville would make a visit to Portsmouth to visit the dockyard, during which he would also find time to have a word with the new captain of HMS *Stirling Castle*. Only at the beginning of April did it dawn on him that Melville was not going to come and his spirits dropped again. As often happened, he took out his frustrations on his new crew – a 'wretched' bunch, against whom his predecessor had already warned him 'in stronger Terms than I ever heard from any Man'. Apparently Popham had been out with a ruler and a tally chart, as he reported, stiffly, to Melville that 137 of the men were only between 4'11" and 5'4" in height and physically incapable of manning the large 32-pounder guns.'[4]

Popham's attitude towards the journey he was being sent on was the closest he ever came to outright insubordination. Creative interpretation of instructions was one

---

1   TNA: ADM 1/2344: Popham to Croker, 23 January 1813; Admiralty Board to Popham, 8 February 1813.
2   TNA: ADM 51/2819: log, HMS *Stirling Castle*, 10 February 1813; WLC UM: Melville Papers, Box 28: Popham to Melville, 17 February 1813.
3   WLC UM: Melville Papers, Box 28: Popham to Melville, 17 February 1813.
4   WLC UM: Melville MSS, Box 29: Popham to Melville, 4 April 1813.

thing; point-blank refusal of the task the First Lord of the Admiralty had ordered him to undertake was quite another. There was a rumour Popham had asked for permission to bring his wife and children with him to sea as company for Lady Moira, but that Lady Moira had refused him.[5] Certainly his temper was exceedingly sour, and it was rubbing off on all that surrounded him, including his patron Melville. Luckily for Popham, he seems to have realised he was on the brink of doing something stupid and pulled himself back in time. 'I am now myself again', he reassured Melville in April. He had received his orders to sail with HMS *Indefatigable* and a convoy of Indiamen, and clearly realised he was never going to get out of the commitment. He nevertheless made it very clear he wanted to be re-employed as quickly as possible following the conclusion of this unwanted mission: 'I need I trust no Security that I shall use every Exertion to return to Europe.'[6]

Lord Moira and his suite boarded *Stirling Castle* on 14 April, and Popham set sail on the 20th.[7] Popham's acceptance of his duties did not translate into his being gracious about it, and it was not a happy journey. By the time the ship put into Funchal in mid-May, Popham's crew, which perhaps bore the brunt of his bad temper, was showing signs of mutiny. When Popham discovered 'some evil disposed person or persons' had cast off the fore topsail overnight, the punishments began. Altogether 16 men were tied to the grate and lashed with the cat: 36 lashes for disobedience, 24 for 'uncleanliness', and between seven and 18 for 'neglect of duty', while the men found responsible for loosening the fore topsail received 60 and 36 lashes respectively. More punishments followed the next day – again for uncleanliness, for seamen falling asleep on duty, for theft – and yet more, on a dozen seamen and marines, on 4 May.[8] The consequences of this regime were not long in coming. At 9:00 a.m. on 8 May, the First Lieutenant told Popham the men were 'assembling on the Forecastle and mak[in]g a great noise'. The mate of the watch had ordered them to disperse and allow the marines to pass through to the head, but one of the seamen, Thomas Connolly, had assaulted a marine and started a violent free-for-all. Popham immediately ordered Connolly to be put in irons and receive 72 lashes. Upon stripping off his shirt, however, Connolly hesitated, 'upon which the Captain directed a file of marines to present and shoot him if he did not strip in one minute'. Mindful that this order might actually spark insurrection, Popham also ordered the rest of the marines to be 'ready to act upon the Ship's Company if they attempted a rescue'.[9]

After that the ship's company settled into a sullen state of truce, and Madeira was sighted on 11 May. On the 13th, *Stirling Castle* moored off Funchal and Lord Moira and his family went ashore while the ship replenished its stores of water, beef, vegetables, and wine for the honoured guests. On 20 May the ship set off once more, only stopping at Tenerife to take on yet more wine. The ship's company stayed quiet and the journey remained uneventful, but Popham was still in a towering bad mood. Foolishly, and despite the opportunities the journey

---

5   *London Chronicle*, 27 July 1813.
6   WLC UM: Melville MSS, Box 29: Popham to Melville, 13 April 1813.
7   TNA: ADM 51/2819: log, HMS *Stirling Castle*, 14 and 20 April 1813.
8   TNA: ADM 51/2819: log, HMS *Stirling Castle*, 28–30 April, 4 May 1813.
9   TNA: ADM 51/2819: log, HMS *Stirling Castle*, 8 May 1813.

offered to cosy up to the new Governor-General of India, he even unleashed his temper on Moira. *The Times* gleefully passed on stories of Popham's pettiness: 'He does not allow any of Lord Moira's staff to dine with him, nor any of his servants … to have anything but the ship's provisions; [and] went to sea from hence [Madeira] without waiting for the furniture that his Lordship had on shore coming on board.'[10] Lady Popham placed a robust rebuttal of these 'base and scandalous fabrications' in the *London Chronicle* of 28 July, but the ship's log showed that a boat did have to be sent out on 20 May to collect Moira's luggage and servants that had somehow remained ashore when the ship sailed. Moira himself ascribed the attack in *The Times* to Henry Veitch, the East India Company's outgoing consul to Madeira, whom Popham had deeply and deliberately insulted. Still, he confirmed Popham had refused to pay for the servants' board and had provided only 'very indifferent provision for us', criticising the 'saddest frothing stuff' Popham passed off as fine wine and condescendingly dismissing it as the result of 'the pecuniary difficulties under which we knew him to labor'. Some of this may have been unfair criticism from an aristocrat used to fine living, but Moira's defence of Popham suggested the captain had been getting on his nerves:

The Earl of Moira, by George Parker after Martin Archer Shee. (Public domain, The Miriam and Ira D. Wallach Division of Art, Prints and Photographs, The New York Public Library)

> His character is so freakish and his temper so little under command, that there were two or three occasions on which it was necessary to bring him quietly to recollection. This, however, was done steadily and without anything like altercation. When he had once acknowledged himself in the wrong all remembrance of the circumstance was banished from our minds. … I should grieve to have Sir Home placed in an unfavorable light, because, with all those injudicious tricks by which he has entailed a host of enemies on himself, there is essential good in him.[11]

Popham himself seemed to realise his future depended on pleasing Lord Moira, and he reined himself in. But for many, it was too late. Moira's correspondent dismissed the

---

10  Reprinted in *London Chronicle*, 28 July 1813.
11  Moira to Colonel McMahon, 26 February 1814, in A. Aspinall (ed.), *The Letters of King George IV, 1812–1830* (Cambridge: Cambridge University Press, 1938), vol.1, pp.397–398.

Governor-General's 'much too favorable' assessment: '[Popham] has unquestionably some resource but his acquirements are superficial and his judgement is far from solid – he is much more likely to mislead those who w[oul]d trust to him, by his plausibility, than to aid their views by any correct or useful information.'[12] Popham never recognised that the number of people who agreed with Moira's opinion of him had shrunk since Walcheren, and was shrinking more every day.

On 29 September, *Stirling Castle* finally arrived in Saugur Roads, where Moira and his suite boarded the *Hastings* pilot schooner for Calcutta.[13] Popham accompanied him, expecting to leave India in mid-November after some repairs to his ship. On his return to Saugur on 17 October, however, he discovered everything had gone wrong. In Popham's absence, his semi-mutinous crew had developed a contagious disease that brought them out in serious ulcers. The ship's surgeon reported that the worst cases had 'part of the Shinbone exposed, in others the bones of the Toes are bare, and in [a] few cases the Toes have fallen off' completely.[14] Popham was unable to sail until 21 November, when his sick had returned from Calcutta hospital. He then set sail directly into a storm, followed by three days of complete calm, after which *Stirling Castle* limped into Covelong for provisions. More storms then chased the ship into Pondicherry, where Popham left 87 of his sickest men ashore. The log showed men dying every day: even Popham was referring to this as 'a very serious calamity', and trying desperate expedients to preserve his remaining men's health – stoves 'constantly burning in the Well and Wing, Fire Balls of prepared Gunpowder and Vinegar, and Benzoin burnt two or three times a day particularly after the Hammocks were down and unlashed that the Bedding might be well saturated with that wholesome Resin'.[15] It was not a very merry Christmas, with many of the healthier men being punished again for mutinous conduct and Popham waiting, 'in a most anxious state of expectation', for a large sum of bullion to arrive from Calcutta before he and his increasingly sick crew could go home.[16]

Popham had always prided himself on maintaining the health of his men, and he knew none of what had happened since leaving Britain would reflect well on him. 'I most sincerely regret, that such a train of circumstances have [sic] so immediately followed each other,' he wrote to the local commanding officer, Vice Admiral Sir Samuel Hood, on 1 January 1814.[17] He hoped active employment would help reconcile the Admiralty to what had happened, but when he returned to Spithead at the end of March 1814 he discovered international circumstances had changed dramatically in the 13 months he had been at sea. Following the battle of Leipzig the previous October, Napoleon had retreated to Paris, where the allied forces had followed him – including the British under Wellington, who had invaded France across the Pyrenees and driven the French out of Spain exactly as Popham had argued he would never be able to do. Napoleon surrendered in April and the Treaty of Paris had ended the decade-long war. Allied diplomats were gathering at Vienna to discuss the terms of the

---

12  Aspinall, *Letters of King George IV*, vol.1, p.505.
13  NMM: MKH/171: Popham to Sir Samuel Hood, 1 January 1814.
14  NMM: MKH/171: Surgeon Graham to Popham, 13 October 1813.
15  NMM: MKH/171: Popham to Sir Samuel Hood, 1 January 1814.
16  NMM: MKH/171: Popham to Sir Samuel Hood, 1 January 1814; TNA: ADM 1/2819: log, HMS *Stirling Castle*, for the last fortnight of December 1813.
17  NMM: MKH/171: Popham to Sir Samuel Hood, 1 January 1814.

peace, Napoleon had been exiled to the island of Elba, and all Popham's hopes for one last wartime command, one final chance to prove his usefulness, had evaporated.

This was even more disastrous as Popham quickly became embroiled in a serious controversy. He was about to regret having insulted the consul at Madeira, Henry Veitch. Shortly before leaving Madeira the previous May, Popham, possibly distracted by the difficulties of the journey out, had allowed four East India ships to leave his convoy and hurry on to Brazil unprotected. This left those ships vulnerable to enemy privateers, and Veitch had written home accusing Popham of disobeying orders by allowing the four ships to proceed to Brazil without him.[18] The Admiralty Board was aghast, although its horror was tempered by the knowledge that the Indiamen had arrived safely at the Cape of Good Hope on their return journey in April 1814.[19] As for Popham, his fragile temper finally snapped. He wrote a long explanation of his conduct, in which he angrily took out the stress of the last year on the Admiralty Board for having sent him on a piddly convoy duty when he could have been consolidating all his greatest achievements (listing these in full):

> My whole life, Sir, has been devoted to my Country, and I will not allow that my Zeal has ever been behind anyone in the Service of the Navy. The many important Stations and Duties which have from time to time been allotted to me, not amongst the least of which are the Command of the Expeditions to the Cape of Good Hope and Buenos Ayres … my being afterwards employed as Captain of the Fleet at Copenhagen where I had the honor of receiving their Lordships' particular approbation and the Thanks of both Houses of Parliament and since in various situations, and the last while on the Coast of Spain co-operating with Lord Wellington, whose liberal and most flattering appreciation of my Zeal and Exertions have been transmitted to their Lordships and publicly recorded in the Dispatches of His Excellency: Blended with these, the benefit I have rendered in advancing and improving our Signal System at the Expence of my own unwearied and never ending application; until brought, I venture to assert, to a State of Character to distinctness simplicity and powers of Comprehension unrivalled in Europe if not thro' the World.

Having given 'so many practical demonstrations of my zeal and unwearied attentions to the Public Service', Popham railed, 'I did hope that their Lordships would have given me full credit for accelerating the Voyage in which I was thus last engaged: a Service as it was of most inferior nature as far as it related to the Common place duty of protecting a Convoy, compared with those to which I have alluded.'[20]

The Admiralty Board received this screed without batting an eyelid. Completely ignoring Popham's self-justification, it informed him his defence was 'very far from being satisfactory'. An irate Popham received notification of 'their [Lordships'] mark'd dissatisfaction of proceedings which … exposed the trade of His Majesty's Subjects to unnecessary risk'.[21] It

---

18   TNA: ADM 1/2346: Popham to Croker, 8 June 1814.
19   BL: IOR/G/9/7, ff.278–281: Pringle to Ramsay.
20   TNA: ADM 1/2346: Popham to Croker, 8 June 1814.
21   TNA: ADM 1/2346: docket, 14 June 1814, to Popham to Croker, 8 June 1814.

was a quiet reminder that Popham could not always rely on Lord Melville to get him out of trouble. Popham did not take that warning to heart, but he seemed to realise he was in danger of losing the First Lord's favour – and that chilled him.

⚓

On 4 June 1814, Popham was promoted to the rank of Rear Admiral of the White.[22] Although most post-captains blessed with a long enough life eventually became admirals, Popham's career had not exactly run a normal course. As a man who had always courted controversy and who had only recently had his wrist slapped by the Admiralty for neglect of duty, Popham should have taken the promotion and kept his head down. Less than a week after reaching flag rank, however, he was hinting to Lord Melville about how he might be employed. The crowned heads of Europe were in Britain to celebrate the peace: a military review was planned in London for mid-June, and a naval review in Portsmouth a few days later. Knowing Tsar Alexander of Russia would be one of the guests, Popham not-so-subtly suggested he might play a role in the ceremonies, hoping to catch the eye of an old acquaintance. Eliding out the role of Tsar Paul, Popham claimed Alexander had been responsible for giving him the Star of Malta and that he would be delighted to show it off on the big day.[23] Since 1810, however, Popham's paranoia had been in overdrive. He claimed one of the Lords of the Admiralty, Sir Joseph Yorke, would block any attempt to employ him because 'I am *a damn'd* cunning fellow, and that I shall monopolize all the Credit to myself if anything is well done',[24] but this defiance could not conceal a streak of real fear: he could not simply turn up to the review unemployed, for if he did Tsar Alexander would certainly realise 'that I am in disgrace'.[25]

The review took place at Portsmouth on 20 June. Popham, however, was not one of the 60 pendants present, as Melville had ignored his massive hint. Instead, Popham received orders to remain in command of *Stirling Castle*, as his amphibious expertise was needed one final time: he was tasked with embarking a body of Russian troops and convoying them to Cherbourg, where he would transfer them aboard another squadron that would escort them the rest of the way back to Russia.[26] As with the previous year's voyage to India, Popham's enthusiasm in obeying his orders was distinctly lacking. He complained to George Grey, the commissioner of Portsmouth dockyard, that his masts were rotten and he had several essential repairs to make, but he would set sail despite these considerable defects.[27] *Stirling Castle* sailed in the afternoon of 12 June in company with the *San Domingo, Impregnable, Chatham, Montagu, Merope, Bedford, Magnificent, Leyden*, and *Bucephalus*, escorting a Russian troopship. Popham remained moored in Cherbourg Roads for about a week,

---

22   *Naval Chronicle*, vol.31, p.509.
23   WLC UM: Melville Papers, Box 30: Popham to Melville, 8 June 1814.
24   Royal Archives: GEO/MAIN/21446–21447: Popham to Colonel McMahon, 10 June 1814. Georgian Papers Online, <http://gpp.rct.uk>, accessed 27 June 2023.
25   WLC UM: Melville Papers, Box 30: Popham to Melville, 8 June 1814.
26   *Chester Courant*, 21 June 1814. It is not clear where the troops had come from: they are simply described as 'part of the army lately employed on the Continent'.
27   TNA: ADM 1/2346: Popham to George Grey, 11 June 1814.

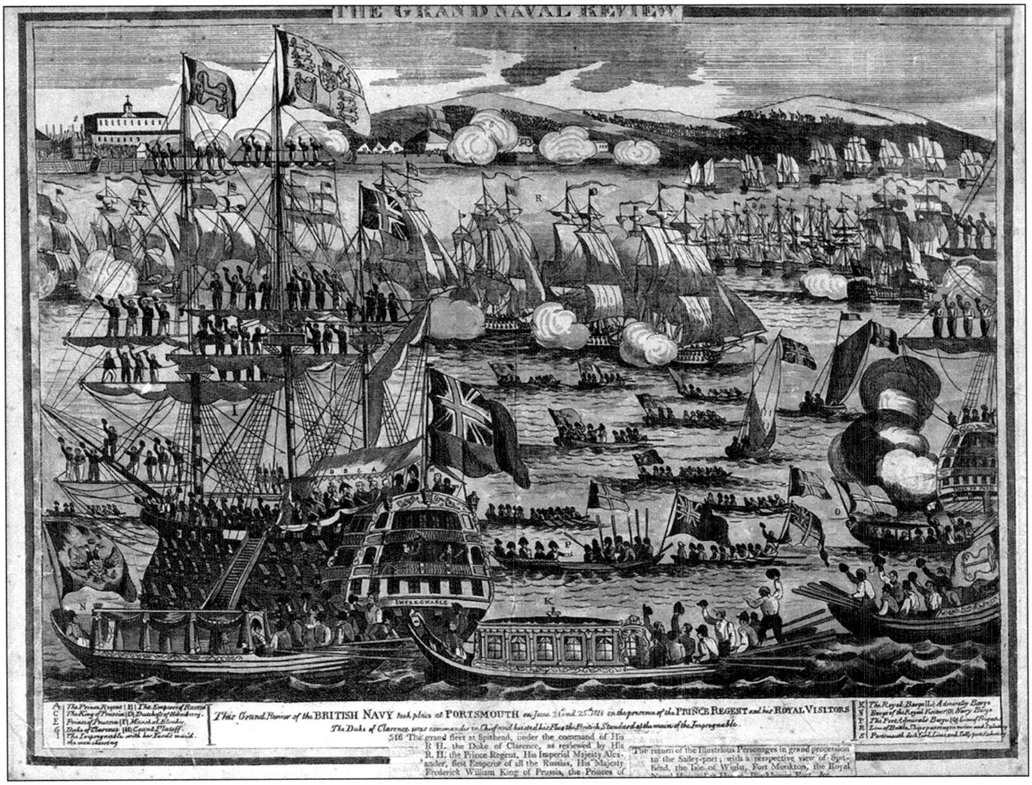

The Grand Naval Review, 24–25 June 1814. (Public domain)

continuing his repairs, before returning to Spithead on 20 June and leaving the ship the next day.[28] *Stirling Castle* was his last ship, but he had no cause to remember it fondly – and the future was as uncertain as ever.

⚓

For the second time in his life, Popham found himself beached, in peacetime, with an Admiralty that seemed unwilling to listen to him. His disappointment eased a little in January 1815 when he was one of the many military and naval officers created Knight Commander of the Bath, at last a home-grown British order to pin to his chest alongside the Maltese Cross, but he remained unemployed. His 20 years of service and connections with the family of the First Lord seemed to have alarmingly little weight. When he had been snubbed by Lord Howe in 1786, Popham had left the Navy and branched off independently; *Etrusco*, and the associated adventures, had been the result of that decision. Now, in 1814,

---

28  TNA: ADM 51/2819: log, HMS *Stirling Castle*.

Popham was again at a loss. While he may have seen this as an opportunity to spend more time with his family, domestic life had never really been his scene. How long could Popham remain tamely on shore?

Just as Popham was beginning to despair, the political and military backdrop changed in the most unexpected way. In February 1815, Napoleon escaped from Elba and made it to Paris, where he re-declared himself emperor with the support of the French military. The possibility of another lengthy and bloody European struggle left the politicians aghast, but Popham was delighted. It was, he told Melville excitedly, 'a moment so critical to the Interests of Europe in general'. Popham's optimism about the likelihood, even probability, of a wartime employment was increased by the knowledge that the theatre of war was likely to focus around Flanders and northern France, 'the Country ... over which I have so often travelled'. He bombarded Melville with plans, reports, and random thoughts, urging him to persuade King Louis XVIII (who had fled Paris for Lille) to move his court to Dunkirk, which should be made into a port of communication from which a squadron should be appointed to harass the French coast. Popham was not shy about recommending an admiral for that command: 'I venture to hope that if any Service is to be performed on the Coast of Flanders or in the Scheldt, where I have so long served, that I shall have the Honor to receive Your Lordship's Commands to hoist my Flag at Deal that I may be ready to proceed to the opposite Coasts whenever the moment of avowed War shall arrive.'[29]

Popham was certain he would be employed, and his disappointment must have been crushing when, instead of participating in the Waterloo campaign, he was instead ordered to raise his flag in HMS *Iris*, a receiving ship at Deptford in the Thames.[30] Rather than chasing glory off the Flanders coast, Popham found himself overseeing the impress and acting against smugglers. Despite his new rank, it was as if he had regressed in his career progression to the 1790s. It was not exactly the glorious part in the ultimate defeat of Napoleon he had envisioned. The closest he got to Napoleon's defeat at Waterloo in June 1815 was reading about it in the newspapers. But he had not yet completely despaired about being put on the shelf, and convinced himself that, having passed him over several times in a row, Lord Melville would now feel he was in need of a reward. When the vanquished Napoleon was exiled to the Atlantic island of St Helena, therefore, Popham angled for that command. It was a startlingly bold and outlandish request, as the St Helena command would guarantee him face-to-face contact with the former emperor of France. Even more startlingly, Popham not only requested the posting: he actually advertised in the papers that he had got it.[31] This may have been an attempt to shame Melville into finally giving him what he wanted, or he may have been genuinely persuaded he would get his way. Napoleon himself was sure he would come out, and grilled his doctor, O'Meara, on Popham's background and career in advance of his arrival.[32] If Popham felt any embarrassment when the command actually went to Rear Admiral Sir Pulteney Malcolm, he kept it hidden.

---

29   WLC UM: Melville Papers, Box 30: Popham to Melville, 25 March 1815.
30   Waite, 'Sir Home Riggs Popham', p.210.
31   NLS: Acc. 6990: Pulteney Malcolm to his wife, 15 February 1816. Many thanks to Paul Martinovich for this reference.
32   Private collection: O'Meara's notebook, 22 [May] 1816. Many thanks to Peter Hicks for this reference.

Deptford, by William Bernard Cooke, ca 1812. (Public domain, Yale Center for British Art, Paul Mellon Collection)

Popham was sure his run of bad luck had to end soon, but instead of being sent somewhere better, he lost the employment he actually had. Popham's role in the Thames was not especially exciting or lucrative, but politicians had long memories. In March 1816, opposition MP George Tierney brought up the matter in the Commons: why had Popham been appointed to Deptford, when the wartime naval stations should be wound up now there was peace? The Secretary of the Admiralty blandly replied that a Flag officer was required to oversee the process of reducing the stations to a peace establishment, as paying off the vessels and crews 'was done in a more economical manner' in this way.[33] Given Popham's well-known controversies regarding naval economy, Tierney probably rolled his eyes at this official explanation, and several radical newspapers picked up on the needless expense of keeping a flag officer in office with nothing to do. 'This establishment must cost many thousands in the year, and is quite unnecessary,' thundered the *Public Cause*. 'We remember that during the hottest part of the war there was no Admiral at Deptford. ... Surely then there can be no necessity for one now!'[34] The *Morning Herald*, meanwhile, complained Popham had spent £5,000 fitting up his state cabin in HMS *Iris*.[35] Regardless of whether the Admiralty had intended to wind up Popham's appointment so soon, the command's days were numbered. At the end of April, the position of Port Admiral at the Deptford station was abolished, and Popham struck his flag.[36]

---

33   *Morning Post*, 16 March 1816.
34   *Public Cause*, 3 April 1816.
35   *Morning Herald*, 24 April 1816.
36   *Evening Mail*, 29 April 1816.

Popham was again at a loose end, although this time at least not all the publicity swirling around him was negative. His signal code had finally been officially adopted by the Admiralty, and Popham seized the opportunity to attract a little more limelight by recommending that the widows of artificers who had lost their lives during the Napoleonic Wars should be employed making new flags for every ship.[37] At the end of May, Popham attended the annual meeting of the Society of Arts in Freemason's Hall, where his signal code earned him a gold medal.[38] Popham was also spotted as part of the entourage of the Duke of Gloucester, whose marriage in July was celebrated with a series of dinners, balls, and court levees. Popham had been appointed to Gloucester's household in January 1806, presumably as a preliminary step in the Pitt government's attempt to bring him to the Navy Board, but he had never before had time for a largely ceremonial role. It was only one sign of many that Popham was waiting, increasingly impatiently, for his fortunes to change.

In mid-September, Popham began making plans to go to Paris, which had been occupied by British troops since the end of the Napoleonic Wars. Given the post-war circumstances – Bonapartist conspiracies were rife – this may not simply have been a holiday, although he did take the opportunity to visit his daughter Mary and her husband, Lieutenant Colonel John Parker, at their house in France.[39] Popham came and went across the Channel several times over the next year, suggesting he returned frequently to London, perhaps to report on French affairs. His desperate desire to be useful risked irritating a government that was no more well disposed towards him than it had been a year previously, but in fact at some point in summer 1817 he received a letter from Lord Melville.[40] The good news was that Melville had finally decided on the best way to employ his wayward rear admiral, and this time it would be a proper command. The bad news was that Popham was being sent to the West Indies, to replace Rear Admiral John Douglas as Commander-in-Chief of the Jamaica Station – a notorious graveyard for the naval, military, and civilian men who were unlucky enough to be sent there. During the British campaigns in the West Indies in the 1790s, 50,000 soldiers had died over the space of five years. Twenty years on, mortality on Jamaica among troops averaged about 13 percent per year.[41]

But a gift-horse was a gift-horse, even if it was haunted by the spectre of yellow fever. To sweeten the pill, Popham also received (*in absentia*) the honour of Knight Companion of the Guelphic Order in 1818 – a Hanoverian order, but considered by many to be George IV's own personal preserve as ruler of Hanover.[42] This mark of favour may have decided him. Jamaica was in any case a respectable posting, with the use of a grace-and-favour house – the Admiral's Pen – and a salary of £2,190 a year.[43] Newspaper reports about the appointment,

---

37  *Taunton Courier*, 2 May 1816.
38  *Evening Mail*, 3 June 1816; *Hereford Journal*, 5 June 1816.
39  *The Sun*, 28 October 1816.
40  DUA: B49/1/8: Popham to Lord Grey, 23 September 1817.
41  David Geggus, 'Yellow Fever in the 1790s: The British Army in Occupied Saint Domingue', *Medical History*, 23 (1979), pp.38, 40, 58.
42  Andrew Hanham, 'Regency Knights: The Royal Guelphic Order, 1815–1837', *The Coat of Arms* (3rd ser.), 4:2 (2008), pp.115–117. Popham was one of only two British KCHs in 1818, and only the 15th Briton to receive that class of the Order since its inception in 1815: William A. Shaw, *The Knights of England* (London: 1906), vol.1, p.454.
43  TNA: ADM 1/270: Josiah Rowley to John Wilson Croker, 25 August 1820.

possibly written by Popham himself, placed a defiant spin on the appointment. *The Sun* declared 'His nomination has given general satisfaction in the naval circles, as the urbanity of manners and ready attention displayed on all occasions by this Gentleman have proved him every way worthy of the appointment, and of the confidence that must be reposed in him.'[44] This probably came as a surprise to the 'naval circles' in question, who saw Popham as a square peg in a round hole at best. Still, if Popham had qualms about his new appointment, he kept them to himself, and planned for his wife and children to come with him. This seemed an odd decision, although it was less so when compared to Popham's decision to take Mary to the Peninsula in 1812. Mary herself, and her sister Caroline, were both married and did not come out to Jamaica. Popham's two youngest daughters, however – 21-year-old Honora and 13-year-old Harriet – did, as did 15-year-old Home Whitworth, seven-year-old Strachan, and five-year-old Harcourt. Brunswick, aged 12, was swiftly found a place as a first-class volunteer aboard HMS *Andromache*.

On 23 November 1817, Popham raised his flag aboard HMS *Sybille*, and he and his family left British shores on 21 December. Given his notoriously unhealthy destination, Popham's thoughts may have echoed those of another passenger bound for Jamaica: 'It was a melancholy reflection, to think … how few [of us] might … ever see their native country more.'[45]

---

44   *The Sun*, 1 October 1817.
45   Sheila Scott (ed.), *My Dear Cath…: The Story of an Army Doctor's Wife in 1818–1819, letters of Anne (née Cairns), the wife of Andrew Anderson, surgeon in the 92nd Regiment (Gordons) in Ireland and Jamaica* (Privately Published, 1976), from the Wellcome Collection, RAMC/1227, p.19.

# 19

# The Jamaica Station, 1817–1820

*2157: It is the commanding officer's order*

Popham's posting to Jamaica may have been a poisoned chalice, but it was still an honourable appointment. Jamaica had been British since the mid-seventeenth century, when it had been captured from Spain. A slim, fertile, mountainous island about 145 miles long and 50 miles wide at its broadest point, it covered an area of 4,450 square miles. Sugarcane flourished, and by the end of the eighteenth century Jamaica had 769 sugar plantations producing over 150,000 hogsheads of sugar and 686 coffee plantations, producing 30 million pounds of coffee and with an annual produce of over £8 million.[1] The island acted as a mercantile hub: traders went home carrying South American indigo, cochineal, cocoa, mahogany, cattle, and horses, along with sugar and North American cotton, and returned laden with British haberdashery, furniture, glass, soap, and cotton manufactures.[2] But repeated French incursions during the Napoleonic Wars and natural disasters such as hurricanes, earthquakes, and fires had severely dented Jamaican trade. South America had also erupted in a series of rebellions against Spain: Buenos Aires had led the way in 1810, declaring its independence as the state of Argentina, and many Spanish colonies in modern-day Peru, Chile, Venezuela, and Bolivia had swiftly followed suit. Spain had been a British ally since 1808, an alliance reaffirmed by the 1814 Treaty of Paris, so this left British merchants open to depredations from pirates, privateers, and freebooters operating on both sides of the struggle.[3] Political changes in Britain, too, had an impact. Jamaica's economy was almost entirely driven by slave labour, and the island's value and productivity had declined since the abolition of the slave trade in 1807. However, as slavery itself had not been abolished, there were over 345,000 slaves in Jamaica in 1817, against a white population of about 20,000.[4]

---

1 W.J. Gardner, *A History of Jamaica from its Discovery by Christopher Columbus to the year 1872 …* (London: T. Fisher Unwin, 1909), pp.320–321.
2 Gardner, *A History of Jamaica*, p.323; Roger Knight, *Convoys: The British Struggle against Napoleonic Europe and America* (New Haven, CT: Yale University Press, 2023), pp.185–186, 198.
3 Matthew McCarthy, *Privateering, Piracy and British Policy in Spanish America, 1810–1830* (London: Boydell Press, 2013), pp.47, 49, 57.
4 H.P. Jacobs, *Sixty Years of Change, 1806–1866* (Jamaica: Institute of Jamaica, 1973), Cultural Heritage Series vol.2, p.39; Gardner, *A History of Jamaica*, p.254.

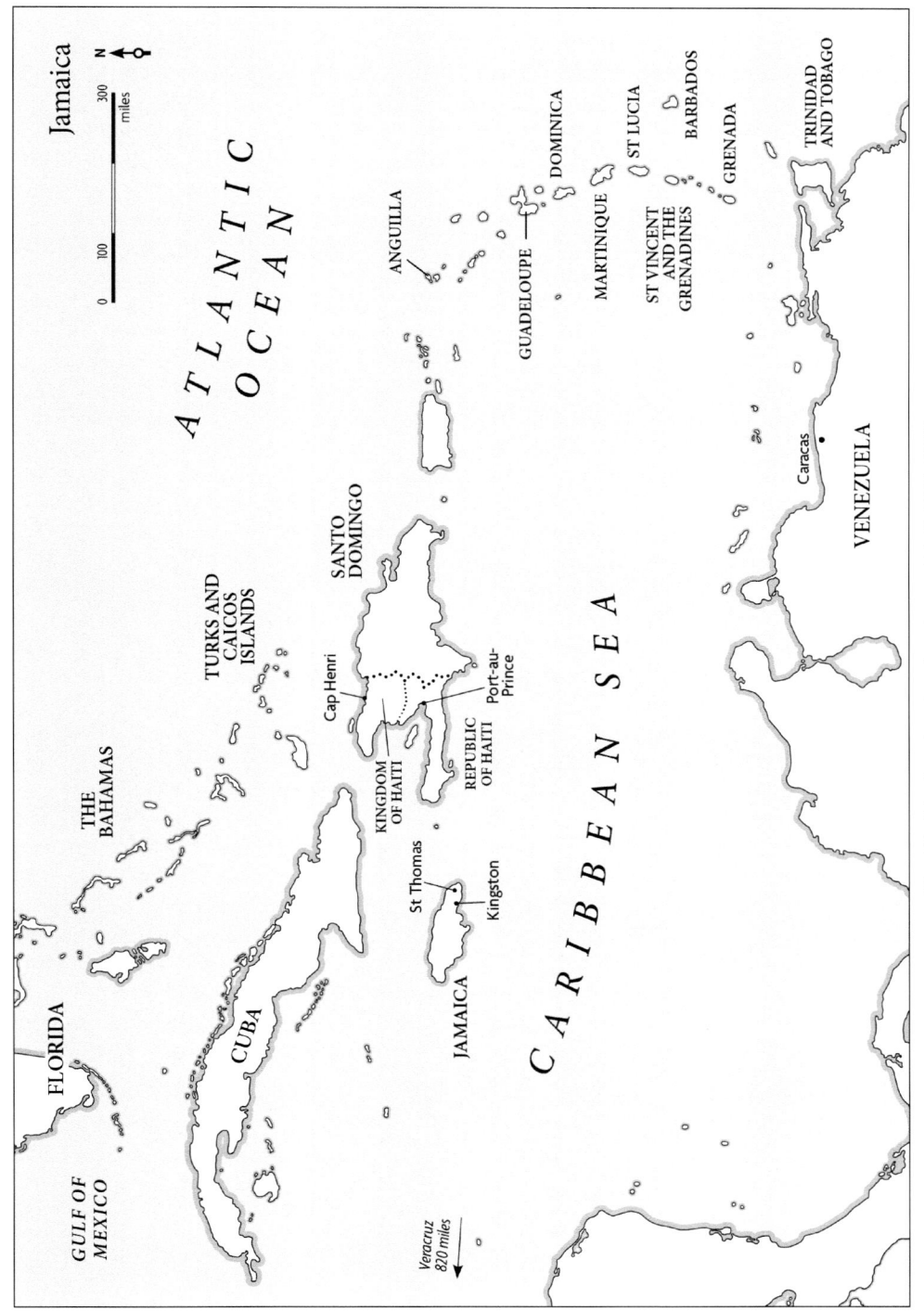

The West Indies, showing Jamaica and Haiti, 1818–1820.

This demographic anomaly strongly shaped the two years of Popham's command. When Popham arrived in the West Indies in January 1818, he discovered the white population lived in constant fear that the black slave population would rise up against them. This was not groundless: more than 25 years previously, in 1791, the slave population of the French colony St Domingue had done just that. Over the course of 13 blood-drenched years, the white planters on the island had either been killed or escaped, many seeking asylum in Jamaica. The former French colony, now rechristened Haiti, had eventually settled uneasily into a black republic in the south under the presidency of the mulatto Alexandre Pétion, and a black monarchy in the north ruled by King Henri I – the former slave Henri Christophe (the other half of the island, Santo Domingo, remained Spanish). The two islands were so close that ash from the burning coffee fields of Haiti had blown across the ocean to Jamaica, and the Jamaican white population worried the wind might carry more than ash.[5]

Prior to the abolition of the slave trade, 5,000 slaves had arrived in Jamaica each year, manacled together in the belly of the slave ships before being dragged out and sold in the slave market at Kingston for about £60 a head. They were then set to the back-breaking work of planting, harvesting, and milling the sugarcane, the stronger adults grinding the crop in the mills, the elderly and sick weeding the fields, the children doing lighter work in the gardens and animal pens. All along they were whipped and beaten by specially employed drivers.[6] Conditions had marginally improved since the abolition of the slave trade, as there was no influx of fresh slaves to replace the maimed and the dead, but not by much, and the white population was uncomfortably aware Haiti held out a tempting example for a population that was predominantly enslaved. A Maroon (runaway slave) revolt in 1795 was rumoured to have been started by French Republican agents; four years later a further conspiracy had been uncovered, leading to the deportation of over 1,000 Haitian slaves. Thereafter conspiracies, plots, and attempted rebellions occurred regularly, culminating in a mutiny in 1808 at Fort Augusta among 50 African soldiers in the West India Regiment, which resulted in the death of two officers. In 1819, 2,555 slaves were reported to be 'Maroon' in the Jamaican mountains, and who were feared to be forming 'dangerous confederacies'.[7]

Popham sailed into these complicated conditions at the end of January 1818, hoisting his flag as naval commander-in-chief of the Jamaica station on 26 January 1818. He was not in a good mood: he was ill, having picked up a slight bowel complaint during the journey, and when he and his family finally came ashore after five weeks aboard ship, he discovered his official residence at the Admiral's Pen – 'a very comfortable country-house, standing in some fifty acres of grass land, exhibiting a very park-like appearance'[8] – was in 'a state of dilapidation'.[9] The cesspool needed emptying, livestock were escaping through broken fences, the chimneys kept catching fire, and the kitchen was so bad Popham and his family had to send to a tavern for their meals.[10] Popham could get away with staying aboard the

---

5   Clinton V. Black, *The Story of Jamaica, from Prehistory to the Present* (London: Collins, 1965), p.118.
6   Black, *The Story of Jamaica*, pp.95–99.
7   Richard Hart, *Slaves who Abolished Slavery: Blacks in Rebellion* (Mona: University of the West Indies, 2002), pp.13, 225, 227.
8   Capt. Sir H.V. Huntley, *Peregrine Scramble* (Paris: A. and W. Galignani and Co., 1849), pp.50–51.
9   TNA: ADM 80/156, f.18: Popham to William Hewitt, Clerk of the Board of Works, 1 February 1818.
10  TNA: ADM 80/156, ff.57–61: Popham to the Duke of Manchester, 26 February 1818.

Alexandre Pétion, unknown engraver, ca 1807–1818. (Public domain, John Carter Brown Library)

various ships in his squadron – he wrote his letter of complaint from *Sybille* – but his wife and five children could not be expected to stay with him, and anyway, he had to work.

Popham wanted to make his mark and show the First Lord of the Admiralty he was worthy of the trust invested in him. In the past, this ambition had often translated into unsound decisions, but if Melville had sent Popham to the Caribbean to keep him away from madcap schemes, he had underestimated his man's ability to act as a chaos magnet. Given Popham's history in Buenos Aires, sending him to a station likely to have plenty of correspondence with Spanish colonial governors in South America might not have been the best idea. Popham used his introductory letters to the various local governors – Don Augustin Figueras in Havana, Don Juan Ruiz de Apodaca in Mexico, and Don Montalba in Cartagena – to take them to task about piracy and privateering, perhaps a way of emphasising that, whatever his predecessor's policy had been, his would be different. To Apodaca in particular, he was initially all smiles, and he even offered him the loan of a British frigate when he heard some Spanish vessels had been damaged in a storm.[11] But Apodaca did not respond in kind, and within a few months Popham was writing to Lord Melville describing the Spaniard as 'a most bitter Enemy', who 'would rather the Insurgents should be all-powerful than give a shade of advantage to the English in any point of view'.[12] Since an important part of Popham's mission involved cultivating smooth relations with his Spanish counterparts, this attitude must have worried Melville. The Admiralty took neutrality with the former Spanish colonies extremely seriously: when the Board heard one of Popham's captains had possibly compromised that neutrality by offering a British convoy for a Spanish merchant fleet, that captain was recalled instantly to Britain and his ship paid off.[13]

Another important diplomatic aspect of Popham's role involved engaging with the British merchants in Jamaica, whose wealth and interests were closely married to those of their country. In this respect, he got off to a good start. Popham, whose mercantile background was solid enough, thoroughly sympathised with the merchants who were being threatened by Spanish and South American privateering and made their cause a priority. He had had his five-week journey to Jamaica to familiarise himself with the background, and he thought he knew how to help: establish a solid and regular convoy system on a pattern borrowed from the wartime convoy duties he had undertaken, providing the merchants with confidence that their ships would be protected by Royal Navy vessels to their destination. Virtually the first official letters he wrote were to prominent Kingston merchant firms: 'I shall be happy on all occasions to receive from you, or any other Merchants in Jamaica any suggestions which may occur to them as likely to promote the Commercial Interests of this Island.'[14] As soon as he had established himself in post, Popham put his promise into action and issued an invitation to the island's most prominent merchants to meet with him, 'either collectively or by a Committee of five', to reach 'some regular and salutary arrangement' for the protection of their trade.[15]

---

11  TNA: ADM 80/156, ff.65–66: Popham to Apodaca, 27 February 1818; f.71: 8 March 1818.
12  NMM: MEL/104/18: Popham to Melville, 26 December 1818.
13  TNA: ADM 1/269: Barrow to Popham, 27 June 1818.
14  TNA: ADM 80/156, ff.62–63: Popham to Buchanans and Co., 27 February 1818.
15  TNA: ADM 80/156, ff.50–52: Popham to George Kinghorn, 18 February 1818.

Harbour Street, Kingston, Jamaica, by James Hakewill, 1824. (Public domain, Anne S.K. Brown Military Collection, Brown University Library)

The meeting took place on 14 March. Popham had previously submitted his proposals to the president of the Jamaican Assembly, and was delighted to discover that the Assembly had passed his plan unanimously and deputed a committee of merchants to inform him.[16] The plan suggested appointing a regular system of convoys departing at fixed periods, by which merchants could be sure of having protection for their trade whenever they had merchandise to transport.[17] The delighted merchants accepted Popham's family into Jamaican society and Popham did his best to blend in, even purchasing two slaves to look after his family.[18] But Popham's good relations with the local powers lasted only so long as he adopted the island's cultural norms, which – given the tensions between the white minority and the black slave majority – involved not giving any countenance whatever to people of colour, particularly any who might come from Haiti, doubly tainted by race and by revolution. Under these circumstances, Popham's decision to wade into one of the biggest controversies in the immediate Jamaican vicinity – the continuing, and growing, tension between the republic and monarchy of Haiti – could only end badly.

Popham had never had a poor opinion of his own diplomatic skills, and he may genuinely have believed his magic touch would heal all political, social, and historical divisions

---

16  *British Neptune*, 3 May 1818.
17  TNA: ADM 80/156, f.108: Popham to the governor of Honduras, 2 April 1818.
18  TNA: T71/81, f.24: 'A Return of Slaves in the Parish of Kingston …' 28 June 1820, via <Ancestry.com>. Many thanks to Sarah Murden for this reference.

in Jamaica's troubled island neighbour. The island's divisions left British trade vulnerable: privateers from each half were likely to prey on the British trade vessels engaged in business with the other half and, although the island had reached an uneasy *status quo*, there was always a chance one of the halves would attack the other (or, indeed, that France would launch a campaign to re-capture its divided former colony). If Popham could resolve the Haitian problem, it would be a real diplomatic coup. But he was treading on delicate ground. Neither the republic nor the monarchy of Haiti had been officially recognised by Great Britain. Although there had been trade relations with both since the beginning of the nineteenth century, Britain had secretly agreed at the Congress of Vienna not to prevent a French attempt to invade their former colony and reintegrate it into their overseas empire.[19] Any attempt to get involved in the internal troubles of the island might complicate ongoing diplomatic discussions at home. Popham must have known Haiti was still a playing card in the diplomatic deck of the Congress system, just as he was well aware of the tensions in Jamaica whenever the subject of Haiti came up. Haiti was an issue that needed careful handling, and Popham's predecessors had largely kept their distance, protecting British trade with the island but otherwise not getting involved. Not that this fazed Popham in the least. As he breezily told one British merchant based in Haiti, 'I feel myself competent to decide upon all the important points in question.'[20]

All Popham needed was an opening and, shortly after his arrival in Jamaica, he got what he wanted when a political bombshell burst on Haiti. The president of the Haitian republic, Alexandre Pétion, died suddenly on 29 March 1818.[21] This was, on the one hand, a dangerous situation: stability was not a word many would have used to describe post-revolutionary Haiti, and the island's frequent power struggles had usually been accompanied by political turmoil and bloodthirsty reprisals. Conscious that there was considerable British trade with the island to the tune of about £1.5 million, Popham sent HMS *Primrose* immediately to Port-au-Prince, the republican capital, to liaise with the British merchants based there.[22] Captain Phillott returned to report that the island was calm, and that both the new president of Haiti, Jean-Pierre Boyer, and the ruler of the northern kingdom, Henri Christophe, continued well-disposed to Britain and had no intention of disrupting a lucrative trade that might eventually lead to official recognition of their country.

To Popham, therefore, the danger immediately transformed into an opportunity. One reason British trade with Haiti was so interrupted was because privateers from one part of the island might attack trade going to the other: but what if Popham could broker a deal between the two halves of the island? No agreement could have been reached between Pétion and King Henri, who had been mortal enemies, but Boyer was more of a blank page, and early reports from Phillott suggested he was not ill disposed.[23] Popham was

---

19  Julia Garfield, 'Haiti and Jamaica in the Remaking of the Early Nineteenth-Century Atlantic World', *William and Mary Quarterly*, 69:3 (2012), p.613.
20  TNA: ADM 80/156, ff.169–170: Popham to Robert Sutherland, 21 May 1818.
21  Paul Clammer, *Black Crown: Henry Christophe, the Haitian Revolution and the Caribbean's Forgotten Kingdom* (London: Hurst & Co, 2023), p.261.
22  *Military Register*, 1 July 1818; TNA: ADM 80/156, ff.125–226: Popham to Messrs Miller & McLeod, 17 April 1818.
23  TNA: ADM 1/269: Phillott to Popham, 10 May 1818.

further encouraged when Boyer made the first move. A Haitian brig, the encouragingly named *Le Philanthrope*, arrived in Port Royal on 22 April, carrying Boyer's aide-de-camp, *colonel* Délice Lerebours, and *sous-lieutenant* Lechat. The governor of Jamaica, the Duke of Manchester, was at his country residence, but Popham took it upon himself to greet the envoys, inviting them to dinner at the Pen and treating them as guests of honour.[24] This was good policy – the British merchants in Port-au-Prince would not have thanked Popham had he done anything differently – but it did not make him any friends among the Kingston merchants. All the good work Popham had done by putting his convoy system in place was swept away the instant he recognised Boyer's men as his social equals:

> Yet he received them! He invited them to dinner! they dined with him and his family! He placed his wife between two of these black men! Nay, he sent his own carriage, with white servants, to convey them from the landing-place to his house ... Did Sir H. Popham receive these people in his public capacity? If he did, how could he presume to act in direct opposition to the known policy of the British Government, which disclaims any intercourse with the people of St Domingo, and the recognition of their functionaries, and any public knowledge of their existence?[25]

These stories found their way to the British newspapers. Some tried to defend him – the London-based *New Times* claimed the story had let forth 'such a torrent of abuse ... as if the worthy Admiral had actually established civil and religious liberty in the very centre of human slavery'[26] – but others were horrified at the idea that a British official could acknowledge ambassadors who were not only republican, but Black.[27]

Popham should have been used to abuse in the papers by now, but his pride and reputation were still stung. Perhaps he had thought himself beyond such attacks, now he was an admiral in faraway Jamaica. 'If the detail of my conduct furnishes the discontented with pretexts to sow dissentions in the country, and raise a turmoil against me,' he wrote, striving to sound lofty, 'I hope they will be more amused, than I shall be ultimately injured, by the false notion which they choose to entertain of my conduct.'[28] Popham, however, was feeling unusually low, and not just because of the attacks in the papers. His son Home, now 17, had developed 'a pulmonary affection', probably tuberculosis. His health was not improved by the heat, so in late autumn his concerned parents sent him to Vera Cruz in HMS *Sybille* in the hopes that a change of air might slow or even halt his decline. In December, however, Popham learned his son had died on 30 November: 'His death was unexpected and almost sudden. Scarcely had he placed himself on a sofa, when he spoke a short sentence, spit some blood, and expired without a struggle.'[29] Popham was crushed by the death of his namesake, born in 1801 when his career was still fresh and the world was before him. He tried

---

24 Thomas Madiou, *Histoire d'Haiti, 1811–1818* (Paris: Editions Fardin, 1818), vol.5, p.491.
25 *World and Fashionable Sunday Chronicle*, 13 July 1818.
26 *New Times*, 13 August 1818.
27 *Champion*, 17 August 1818.
28 TNA: ADM 80/156, ff.169–170: Popham to Robert Sutherland, 21 May 1818.
29 *Imperial Weekly Gazette*, 27 March 1819.

to distract himself from his pain with his work and, in search of a knotty problem to keep his thoughts occupied, he decided the time had come to broker a deal between the two halves of French Haiti. On 4 May 1819, therefore, he announced his decision to visit King Henri I of the northern, monarchical part of the island.[30]

Popham probably focused on the monarchy first because he thought it was more open to persuasion. The king, former slave Henri Christophe, had connections with abolitionists in Britain and considered himself something of an Anglophile; he even called himself an Englishman, having grown up in the British colony of Granada before coming to St Domingue as a child. Perhaps, too, Popham felt a monarchy would be more tractable than a republic. He nevertheless had a poor opinion of Christophe himself, whom he had previously described to Melville as 'an

Henri Christophe (King Henri I of Haiti), by Blasius Höfel, 1815. (Public domain, Anne S.K. Brown Military Collection, Brown University Library)

arbitrary savage, aiming at absolute Monarchy, cruel in the extreme, universally hated'.[31] Popham had never been inclined to give people of colour the benefit of a doubt, but his prejudices evaporated the moment he set foot in Cap Henry on 16 May 1819. He and his party were met by a guard of honour, which conveyed him to a house in the centre of town boasting a library, an army of servants, and a guardhouse (it was never made clear whether this was to protect Popham or to stop him exploring too much on his own). The King deputed his secretary, Baron Dupuy, as liaison – Dupuy had lived in the United States for a few years and spoke fluent English – who took Popham to the Duc de Marmelade, the governor of the city, for a splendid breakfast: 'soup, fish, and all the other component parts of a splendid dinner … together with wine of every description; in short, the greatest *gourmand* would have smiled at the succession of courses and the good things that constituted them'. Over the six days of his visit, Popham and his entourage toured the battle sites of the recent revolution, witnessed a review of some of King Henri's 35,000 soldiers, visited some hospitals, and sat in on some lessons at the local schools, which the King was running on a British model overseen by British teachers. Every night a ball was held in Popham's honour, with sets 'in the Creole style' interspersed with more traditional English country dances.[32]

As naval commander-in-chief of the Jamaica station, Popham was in Haiti as a representative of the British nation, as the Haitian authorities were well aware. At a dinner held by the

---

30   *Edinburgh Magazine and Literary Miscellany* (1819), vol.84, p.369.
31   Popham, *A Damned Cunning Fellow*, p.230.
32   [G. W. Courtenay], 'Iphigenia, Port Royal, June 6, 1819 (on board of which the writer was a Lieutenant)', *Blackwood's Magazine* (1821), vol.IV, pp.546–552.

Duc de Marmelade, following a toast to the health of George III, Popham responded with a speech and a toast to the 'health of the Good King Henry'. One witness wrote: 'The Haytians appeared to devour every word he uttered, and *received the toast with more enthusiasm than I ever witnessed*' – perhaps because Popham had just become the first British official to call the man usually referred to as 'General Christophe' by his royal title.[33] The next day, Popham secured an audience with the King. He was impressed with the palace, its artificially air conditioned rooms staffed by a *Garde-du-Corps* wearing dark green coats with red facings and a profusion of gold lace; he was even more impressed with the King himself, wearing a plain green coat, white satin breeches, and red leather boots, 'his hair … perfectly gray [sic], his countenance very intelligent, and his whole person well proportioned; his manners are particularly pleasing, without the slightest appearance of affectation or arrogance'. Popham was already disposed to think well of anyone who flattered his pride and self-worth so much, but Henri, a good judge of character, made sure to compliment Popham 'on his well-known abilities, and … the Popham code of signals now used in the navy'. Popham took the opportunity to discuss the British merchants trading with southern Haiti, and tackled the subject of what Haiti might do with runaway Jamaican slaves. The King, for his part, hoped he might impress Popham enough to get him to suggest his government should officially recognise this new kingdom. Although he did not invite Popham to visit the Citadelle, the gargantuan mountaintop fortress that was the first thing all visitors to Cap Henry observed from the sea, he dropped enough hints that the British party knew the place contained 360 pieces of artillery and 400 tonnes of gunpowder. When Popham asked Henri when he intended to restore the parts of the capital that still bore charred signs of the fire that had ravaged it during the revolution – a fire allegedly started by Henri's own hand – the King replied, meaningfully, that he intended to restore it only when Haiti's independence had been acknowledged by France and guaranteed by Britain.[34]

Popham left Cap Henry on 23 May. The visit had been fruitful for both sides. King Henri had done his best to show his nascent kingdom in a positive light: when Popham returned to his ship, he found aboard presents of wine, livestock, and fruit, along with His Majesty's best compliments.[35] If Henri had hoped to use Popham's visit as a way of publicising the success of his attempt to raise his part of the island out of the ashes of civil war, he had succeeded. A few weeks after his visit, Popham wrote Melville a detailed memorandum on Haiti. He explicitly referred to the ruler of monarchical Haiti as 'king' and suggested a trade agreement between Britain and Cap Henry with the express purpose of undercutting growing Danish trade in the Caribbean.[36] His memorandum described what he had been able to gather together from conversations with Baron Dupuy and others regarding the population, economy, and military preparedness of monarchical Haiti, as well as its political structure. He acknowledged that his six-day visit had not been enough to form a comprehensive view, and that a lot of information had been concealed from him, probably deliberately. Nevertheless, he was optimistic. He noted the workers were cheerful and well taken care of; the production of the country seemed to be growing; and the King's civilising

---

33 [Courtenay], 'Iphigenia, Port Royal, June 6 1819', p.550.
34 [Courtenay], 'Iphigenia, Port Royal, June 6 1819', pp.547, 549.
35 [Courtenay], 'Iphigenia, Port Royal, June 6 1819', pp.551–552.
36 Clammer, *Black Crown*, pp.281–282.

mission was going well. King Henri was an Anglophile, who was bringing the children of the country up to speak English as well as French. As for the King himself, Popham had completely changed his mind:

> The Character formerly entertained of Christophe in the Island of Jamaica, and even up to the last Year, was that he was arbitrary, cruel, and oppressive. That he is arbitrary to a certain degree even now there can be no question, but the merchants who reside at Cape Henry are unanimous in their opinion that he is considerably less arbitrary than he was formerly, less oppressive, especially to strangers, and that no particular act of cruelty has [recently] occurred.

Popham did not suggest Britain give Haiti official recognition via trade treaty, but he strongly hinted that King Henri would be amenable to one.[37] Popham was probably hoping any further attempts at official recognition might be made through him, since he already had a personal rapport with King Henri.

What Popham's visit did not do was improve his relations with the planters in Jamaica. To them, the idea of recognising Haiti in any way was tantamount to encouraging Jamaica's own sizeable slave population to revolt and establish their own independent form of government. But Popham's hopes that his visit to Cap Henry might turn into something concrete did not come to pass. Britain was too concerned with constructing new alliances with France and Spain to wade too deeply into a political quagmire in the Caribbean. In Jamaica, apart from annoying the planters, his efforts merely incurred the amusement of his military colleagues, many of whom viewed the whole episode as a reflection of Popham's eccentric character. 'His Majesty played his part admirably, they say, and the Admiral is no bad actor himself,' wrote the military commander-in-chief, Major General Henry Conran. 'I should have enjoyed a peep.'[38] Popham was nevertheless very pleased. He had identified, in Haiti, an opportunity to bring himself forward again before the First Lord of the Admiralty. He had been so well received by King Henri he seems to have forgotten Boyer's comparative coolness in the republic. Perhaps he imagined his silver tongue would overcome all obstacles. Either way, he felt there was nothing he could not achieve. 'I am persuaded, my Lord,' he wrote to Melville, 'that if there is anything in reason which you wish to be accomplished at Hayti, I can at this moment get it done.'[39]

Popham's cockiness was quickly tempered by much less pleasant circumstances, and within weeks a much more immediate crisis had reared its head. From the summer of 1819 onwards, Jamaica suffered one of the worst outbreaks of yellow fever in recent memory, and the pace of death continued relentlessly into 1820. 'The mortality here has been awful,' a local doctor wrote in August 1819. 'One week I believe out of 300 men who were well on Sunday 53 were buried before the next.'[40] Surrounded on all sides by horrifying levels of death and disease, Popham worried for his family, who were still in Jamaica. They, in turn,

---

37 Bodleian Library (BoL): W.Ind.s.7–8, f.321: Popham to Melville, 29 July 1819. Many thanks to Paul Clammer for this reference.
38 TNA: CO 137/149, f.182: Conran to Henry Goulburn, 13 June 1819.
39 BoL: W.Ind.s.7–8, f.321: Popham to Melville, 29 July 1819.
40 Scott, *My Dear Cath*, pp.20–21.

View of Port Royal and Kingston harbours, Jamaica, by P. Mazell, 1774. (Public domain, Wellcome Collection)

were worried about him, and with good reason. In March, Popham suffered a mild stroke. He recovered reasonably quickly, but it caused something of a stir: rumours quickly spread that his life was in danger, even that he had already died.[41] Popham was not dead, but he was as shaken as anyone else by what he correctly interpreted as a warning to slow down, and his family and physicians persuaded him he needed to take a holiday. HMS *Sybille*, captained by his son William, carried him round to Port Morant, on the eastern point of the island, from where he travelled to the mineral baths at St Thomas to try the waters.

A few days after Popham's return to Port Royal, on 27 March, his daughter Honora complained of a headache while accompanying her parents on a tour of the harbour. She was taken aboard HMS *Sybille* to rest, but she did not leave the ship again alive. Within three days she was dead of yellow fever, in the same cabin where her brother Home had died a year previously.[42] 'I think she will never recover [from] the severity of the shock,' an acquaintance reported of Lady Popham, whose hysterics on the loss of her daughter made friends fear for her sanity.[43]

'At 6 the Admiral left the Ship,' the log of HMS *Sybille* recorded for 31 March.[44] The short entry gave nothing away, but Popham came ashore a shattered man. His health, which had already suffered a significant blow, never recovered from the shock of losing a second child to the Jamaican climate. His immediate reaction to the loss was typical: he threw himself back into his work with renewed enthusiasm, trusting that the St Thomas waters would have done everything for him that medicine could not. For the second time in as many years he turned to the Haitian problem to chase away the shadows of grief. Recent developments suggested the time might be ripe for a new attempt to broker a deal between Haiti's republic and monarchy. The southern, republican part of the island had been under attack for some time from Jean-Baptiste Perrier, known as 'Goman', an independent rebel supported by King Henri in the north (the King had created Goman 'Comte de Jérémie' in recognition of his efforts to destabilise the southern state). In February 1820, however, President Boyer decisively defeated Goman and his insurgents, meaning that for the first time since its creation the republic was united and at peace.[45] Boyer's newly strengthened position was bad news for King Henri, who appealed to Popham in April for diplomatic assistance. The Haitian King wanted to pre-empt any attempt from the south to attack his kingdom by extending an olive branch to Boyer, proposing an alliance based on recognition of his monarchy as an independent state. He asked Popham to act as intermediary between him and Boyer, and Popham – who still felt flattered by the rapturous welcome Henri had given him the previous year – accepted.

Strictly speaking Popham should have kept his distance, given Britain traded with both parts of French Haiti and had as yet recognised neither as an official state. Both Boyer and King Henri had a strong interest in getting Popham to endorse their position, and Henri must have felt Popham's agreement to take his side boded well.[46] Popham's rashness in

---

41  See, for example, the *Morning Herald*, 8 May 1820.
42  *British Press*, 30 May 1820.
43  *New Times*, 30 May 1820.
44  TNA: ADM 51/2030: log, HMS *Sybille*, 31 March 1820.
45  Clammer, *Black Crown*, p.275.
46  Clammer, *Black Crown*, p.279.

wading once again into troubled diplomatic waters reflected his need for distraction, and he must have realised brokering a peace between the two warring Haitian states would guarantee him a place in the history books. He began with a visit to Port-au-Prince, arriving in heavy rain on 27 April.[47] He was taken by carriage to the president's private lodgings at the Palais National and quickly made contact with his old acquaintance, *colonel* Lerebours, whose reception in Jamaica had got Popham into so much trouble. After a tour of the republican capital and watching a review of Haitian troops (where he was overheard telling one of his entourage that King Henri's troops were 'much superior to those of the republic in their dress and their discipline'), Popham was given an official dinner before being taken by Boyer to his country house at Thor Le Volant. Here, in private, Popham – possibly betraying a state secret in doing so – revealed to Boyer that France had designs to invade Haiti and make it a French colony again. He then made the proposal he and King Henri had already decided between them: to ensure Haiti could defend itself against French attack, the republic and monarchy should mutually recognise and support each other. Popham assured Boyer that Britain, as a nation that had abolished the slave trade and had no reason to distrust a state run by former slaves, would stand as guarantor for the treaty against any French protest.[48]

Jean-Pierre Boyer, president of the Republic of Haiti, by Antoine Maurin, 1830. (Public domain, Anne S.K. Brown Military Collection, Brown University Library)

Boyer's response was 'bullish'.[49] He knew that, since Goman's defeat, he had the upper hand over King Henri and it was only a matter of time before the monarchy collapsed anyway. He reportedly told Popham the King's 'reign of terror' would not last out the year.[50] He knew, too, Popham had no authority to make any promises on Britain's behalf, and that his best chance of recognition from Britain would be to approach the country directly once he was the president of an already united country. Boyer therefore thanked Popham for his concern, but refused, in no uncertain terms, his efforts at mediation:

---

47  TNA: ADM 51/2030: log, HMS *Sybille*, 27 April 1820.
48  Madiou, *Histoire d'Haiti*, vol.6, pp.85–89; *Anti-Gallican Monitor*, 17 December 1820.
49  Clammer, *Black Crown*, pp.283–284.
50  Popham, *A Damned Cunning Fellow*, pp.236–237.

The moment in which you propose to me an approximation between the Government of the north and that of this part, is not the suitable time for opening up the past … The union which you desire for the happiness of the Haytian people, might soon be affected [sic], if the Chief of the North, yielding to the interest of the people in general, would only abandon the unfortunate idea that he is a better Haytian than the other Haytians, and that in him alone resides the primitive faculty of finding the means to govern the country in a suitable manner.

If King Henri could not recognise the republic and its constitution, Boyer wrote, 'it is not my fault'.[51] Time, Boyer knew, was on his side, and not on that of King Henri – perhaps not on Popham's side either, as Boyer must have been aware of how ill Popham had been.

Popham left Port-au-Prince on 1 May and arrived four days later at Cap Henry. A series of entertainments were put on for him, although Popham could not attend most of them as he was in deep mourning for George III and for his daughter, who had not yet been dead six weeks.[52] He nevertheless attended a military review by the young Prince Royal, Victor-Henry, before being taken to the King's mountain palace of Sans Souci and dining, at the King's right hand, from tables covered with damask and rich plate. Popham's spirits must have been lifted by this display of wealth and privilege, designed to reflect the importance with which he and his mission were viewed at the Haitian court. He left Haiti on the evening of 14 May and sat down immediately to write to Boyer. The King, he wrote, was

sincerely disposed to enter into an arrangement of the most perfect amity with his friends in the West and the South … you may rely on him to fulfil all his engagements with exactitude. Consider this object [a treaty between the two parts of Haiti] very seriously; it is the cause of humanity, and it depends only on you to give me all assistance to accomplish it. … Write to me clearly and frankly on this subject, that I may try to level the difficulties.

This willingness to prove himself the friend of all Haiti was slightly marred by a not-very-veiled threat of what might happen if Boyer rejected his advances and attacked the north instead: 'Never think of making war; do not attempt to move beyond your frontiers because, if you do, I will consider you as an aggressor and you will be held responsible in the eyes of the whole world for the consequences of a civil war.'[53] Popham still considered violence to be one of the most important tools of diplomacy. Boyer's wooden response merely reiterated his letter of 1 May: 'You may be perfectly comfortable, *Monsieur l'Amiral*, in all that concerns me; my efforts are constant to avoid deserving such well-founded reproaches.'[54]

On 19 May, Popham left HMS *Sybille* at Port Royal. Within a few days he had received Boyer's dismissive responses to all his overtures. His last-ditch mission to establish a strong and united Haiti that would guarantee British mercantile interests in the region had failed.

---

51 Quoted in *The Anti-Gallican Monitor*, 17 December 1820.
52 *Morning Herald*, 2 August 1820, quoting the *Royal Gazette* of Haiti, 30 May 1820.
53 Clammer, *Black Crown*, pp.283–284; the letter is quoted in Madiou, *Histoire d'Haiti*, vol.6, pp.87–88 (my translation).
54 Madiou, *Histoire d'Haiti*, vol.6, pp.88–90 (my translation).

Popham had spent his whole life looking for some sort of legacy. The closest he ever came was his signal code, but perhaps he had truly believed his magic touch might bring peace to one of the most war-torn, blood-soaked corners of the Caribbean. If so, his illusions were shattered. The disappointment, along with the strain of all the voyaging, was all too much; sometime towards the end of the month, Popham suffered another stroke, much more severe than his first. This time his physicians would brook no argument. If Popham tried to work through his illness again, he would kill himself. They recommended that he resign his post as commander of the Jamaica station and return immediately to Britain.[55] In an indication of how ill Popham must have been feeling, he agreed.

Popham knew he would not be coming back: his tour of duty had only been meant to last three years anyway, and his time was almost up. This knowledge may have helped ease the decision to bow to the physicians' advice. He would not miss Jamaica, where he had buried two of his children; nor would he miss many of the people with whom he had had to deal for the last few years. 'I have been so seriously indisposed, that the Physicians who have attended me have announced it as their Opinion, that the extreme state of debility to which I am reduced makes a change of Climate necessary to prevent a return of the Malady with which I have been attacked,' he wrote to Commissioner Woodriffe, one of the people he would miss the least.[56]

Popham left Jamaica on 15 June, boarding HMS *Sybille*. His next five weeks would be spent resting as much as possible in the great cabin, the place his son Home and daughter Honora had both breathed their last, while his eldest boy William sailed him home. The ship weighed and left Port Royal at 5:00 p.m. on 16 June. Fort Charles saluted the admiral's flag with 17 guns, and at 7:00 p.m. the ship made all sail for England.[57] First, however, Popham had one last role to play as the naval commander-in-chief in Jamaican waters. On 20 June, *Sybille* put into Cap Henry. Ostensibly this was to allow the Deputy Secretary to Jamaica's General Post Office to arrange for a regular mailbag between Cap Henry and England for the convenience of Jamaica's merchants, but this should not have needed Popham to go ashore – and yet he did, while *Sybille* replenished its water and took on beef, bullocks, and fresh vegetables.[58] What did Popham do in Cap Henry? Did he make one last visit to King Henri, to inform him of the failure of his mission to Boyer? Did he, as several sources later claimed, go beyond his remit once more and propose a treaty between Britain and the Kingdom of Haiti, by which 40,000 Africans rescued by the Royal Navy from slavers would be sent to Cap Henry to form a military force with which to combat Boyer's inevitable attack, whenever it came?[59] Whatever the truth, Popham's visit was short and *Sybille* sailed away from Cap Henry on the afternoon of 25 June. Any treaty Popham might have had to propose on his return home was soon rendered void. Within weeks King Henri, like Popham, had suffered a stroke, which precipitated a military coup. Boyer took advantage of the chaos to invade with 20,000 men; King Henri, sick and abandoned, shot himself; and by the end of October,

---

55  TNA: ADM 1/270: certificate of J. Macnamara, E.N. Bannoff, and Charles Clinton, 2 June 1820.
56  TNA: ADM 80/157: Popham to Woodriffe, 30 May 1820.
57  TNA: ADM 51/2030: log, HMS *Sybille*, 15, 16 June 1820.
58  *British Neptune*, 31 July 1820.
59  Madiou, *Histoire d'Haiti*, vol.6, p.249.

the miracle Popham had tried to achieve by diplomacy had happened by force: former French Haiti was united under the republic.[60]

But Popham never learned the fate of the Haitian King. HMS *Sybille* ran through the Needles and arrived at Spithead in the evening of 26 July.[61] Next morning, Popham ran down his flag and went ashore, with his wife and remaining children. The newspapers recorded him being 'in a low debilitated state of health'; he nevertheless went straight to London, where he made his final report as commander-in-chief to the Admiralty Board.[62] In mid-August Popham and his wife went together to Cheltenham, where they hoped the waters would help bring him back to health. But they did not have the power to reverse years of Popham driving himself at a punishing pace, or to neutralise serious existing physical problems. 'I have been troubled with my pains in the head these last three days, and pulsation has been affected from 73 to 59,' Popham wrote to a friend.[63] He had always lived on borrowed time; now it was running out. On 11 September 1820, Popham suffered a third, fatal, stroke. He was a month from his 58th birthday.

Popham died as he had lived – unexpectedly. 'A bolt from heaven could not be more sudden or shocking ... than was the sight of Sir Home's name in an obituary,' a friend recalled.[64] Six years later, his widow had not yet recovered from the suddenness of her loss: 'If Limbs had been torn from me, I could not have been more lacerated.'[65] Popham had always been a fluid figure, shaping the narrative surrounding him to suit his interests. Fittingly, most of his obituaries now got most of the facts of his life completely wrong, with the majority asserting him to have been born in Ireland. They paid lip service to a man who had been more controversial than successful. His record was rarely detailed, perhaps for fear of stirring up adverse comment: 'His public employments and services ... as matter of history, are generally known.'[66] One article, however, written by a man who claimed to have been Popham's friend for 45 years, stood out from the rest. It was full of regret for a life engaged in a race against itself, a race that never quite reached the finish line:

> The briskness of his body was alone equalled by the activity of his mind; and the general charge against him was that he did, not *too little*, but *too much*. ... The rapidity of Sir Home Popham's movements was the true type of his creative understanding. Never, perhaps, had a man a more resourceful mind – more clear of the rhetoric; more pregnant with the practical. ... Wherever a British interest could be served, or a life saved, there was Sir Home Popham found ... It was to this indefatigable vigilance he fell – an untimely sacrifice.[67]

As the flags ran down the signal post for the last time, Popham could not have written himself a better epitaph.

---

60  E.L. Griggs and C.H. Prator (eds), *Henry Christophe and Thomas Clarkson: A Correspondence* (Berkeley and Los Angeles, CA: University of California Press, 1952), p.76.
61  TNA: ADM 51/2030: log, HMS *Sybille*.
62  *British Neptune*, 31 July 1820.
63  'D', possibly Denis O'Bryen, *Morning Post*, 18 September 1820.
64  'D', possibly Denis O'Bryen, *Morning Post*, 18 September 1820.
65  BL: MSS EUR D742/9, f.44: Lady Popham to Lady Raffles, 14 August 1826.
66  *The Sun*, 15 September 1820.
67  'D', possibly Denis O'Bryen, *Morning Post*, 18 September 1820.

# Conclusion

*2824: I have not succeeded*

Popham's death caught his contemporaries by surprise. He had genuine charisma and, like his first captain, Edward Thompson, formed lifelong attachments among those who sailed with him. Thomas Huskisson, a midshipman with Popham in the Red Sea, recalled his 'peculiarly gentlemanly manner of attaching everyone to him'.[1] People had often remarked on his omnipresence, his constant bustle, his need to remain useful and relevant: 'He is what they [his naval peers] call too meddling, by which they mean to imply (without being aware of it) that he makes himself very useful upon all occasions and in all ways; he is so used to be[ing] actively employed, and is besides naturally so bustling, that what is evidently an exertion with most men is reduced to a habit with him.'[2] His passing left an eerie stillness where once there had been so much hyperactivity.

Inevitably, however, controversy kept pace with the compliments. 'To paint the minute lights and shades of Sir Home Popham's character I leave to his historian,' wrote one obituary:

> The life of a saint, if very minutely scanned, will be found sullied by many of the blemishes incident to human nature. Sir Home Popham had his share of them, probably a large one ... His abilities were superior, and he appeared as if conscious they were so, which gave offence to many ... He has gone through a life chequered with many vicissitudes more freely than many of his colleagues, and when his personal failings are buried under the ocean of oblivion, his public talents and services will place him high on the list of those who have 'deserv'd well of their country'.[3]

Another obituary thought Popham's life, though 'as brilliant as it was serviceable', would always be overshadowed by three things – *Etrusco*, the *Romney* affair, and Buenos Aires.[4] His previous misconduct coloured every perspective of his career and shaped every assessment of his character.

---

1   Huskisson, *Eyewitness to Trafalgar*, p.55.
2   Carr-Gomm (ed.), *Letters and Journals of Field-Marshal Sir William Maynard Gomm*, pp.131–132.
3   'Oceana', 'Particulars of the Life of Rear Admiral Sir Home Popham', *The New Bon Ton Magazine, or, Telescope of the Times* (London: J. Johnston, 1820), vol.V, p.371.
4   Anon., *The Annual Biography and Obituary for the Year 1822*, vol.6, p.307.

Popham's monument at Sunninghill, Windsor. (Author's photo)

One side of Popham's monument, dedicated to the bombardment of Copenhagen in 1807 and showing Popham's signal book. (Author's photo)

Another side of Popham's monument, dedicated to the Cape of Good Hope in 1806 and showing instruments of navigation. (Author's photo)

This complicated legacy reflected the mixed nature of Popham's own life. He had not been a typical sailor; most of his peers had neither trusted him nor understood the part he had often played. It did not help that several campaigns on which he was employed, some of which had been his idea, failed, often spectacularly. The loud and far-reaching disasters at Ostend, Buenos Aires, or Walcheren outweighed his more subtle successes in Flanders, Russia, or Copenhagen. He had an unquestionable talent for putting noses out of joint – 'I know … I have many Enemies'[5] – and 200 years after his death, Popham still polarises opinion. Some historians consider him almost a fraud, one of those 'showy egotists' who 'made fools of themselves'.[6] Even the more positive characterisations balance the good with the bad – 'remarkable and controversial', in the words of Martin Robson.[7] And yet, even as his star began to wane, Popham was seldom without employment of some sort. He managed to convert sensible men, like Melville and Pitt, to his schemes. How did he do it? Was it simply his excess of *'cleverality'*,[8] or his ability to spin a good yarn?

Popham's success stemmed principally from the fact that he was, as the quotation at the beginning of this chapter put it, 'very useful upon all occasions and in all ways'. His country needed a versatile man who was not afraid of getting his hands dirty. Early nineteenth-century Britain was something most other nations at war with France were not (with a few exceptions, like the Netherlands or Spain): it was a predominantly maritime power, with a nascent empire. This gave Britain trade networks, and military concerns, all over the world, and much of British strategy revolved around protecting its colonies and securing strategic naval stations – as well as destroying, or more preferably capturing, those of the enemy. The foremost proponent of this 'blue-water' strategy during the wars was Popham's main patron, Henry Dundas, Lord Melville:

> From our insular situation, from our limited population not admitting of extensive continental operations, and from our importance depending on so material a degree upon the extent of our commerce and navigation, it is obvious, that, be the causes of the war what they may, the primary object of attention ought to be, by what means we can most effectually increase those resources on which depend our naval superiority, and at the same time diminish or appropriate to ourselves those which might otherwise enable the enemy to contend with us in this respect. Navigation and commerce are inseparably connected, and that nation must be the most powerful maritime state which possesses the most extensive commerce. … It is therefore as much the duty of those entrusted with the conduct of a British war to cut off the colonial resources of the enemy, as it would be that of the general of a great army to destroy or intercept the magazines of his opponent. … Exertions of that nature ought to admit of no limitation.[9]

---

5   DUA: B49/1/1/3: Popham to Lord Howick, 29 September 1806.
6   Roger Knight, 'After Trafalgar', in Quentin Colville and James Davey (eds), *Nelson, Navy and Nation* (London: National Maritime Museum, 2013), p.225.
7   Robson, *A History of the Royal Navy*, p.96.
8   W[ilkie], 'Recollections of the British Army, no.2', p.485.
9   25 March 1801, as reported in William Cobbett, *Parliamentary History of England … to 1803 …* (London, 1819), vol.35, cols.1072–1073.

Popham was well placed to benefit from Melville's 'unlimited' view of how the war should be fought. With no centralised decision making apparatus beyond the cabinet, Melville and his fellow ministers looked for unofficial strategic advice from a small group of specialists, and this gave enterprising men with ideas an opportunity they might not otherwise have had to get their ideas heard. Popham, fuelled by the ambition and supreme self-confidence he never lost, grabbed the modest notoriety he acquired in the field of amphibious operations with both hands and ran with it. He never looked back.

At first glance, Popham might seem a surprising choice for Melville to take under his wing. He was an outsider, with no significant contacts either Navy or society. His background in illicit trade did not help, and he had more than a lack of patrons to overcome on re-joining the Navy in 1793. But he had plenty to offer, and the fact he was markedly different from many of his naval peers worked in his favour. His time aboard *Etrusco*, and his family networks in the East India Company, provided him with experience in Indian and Asian seas more broadly. He could focus on immediate national defence if required, but he also saw the bigger, 'blue-water' picture, recognising the need to marry Britain's imperial imperatives with more immediate continental objectives. Most importantly of all, he learned, very quickly, what the authorities wanted to hear from him – and he gave it to them.

Popham's resourcefulness and quick thinking allowed him to thrive at a time when communication networks were slow and unreliable and news could take four to six months to travel from one side of the world to the other. As Popham himself pointed out at his court-martial, discretion, and the ability to make important decisions based on changing circumstances, was an essential part of a naval captain's arsenal. Discretion was not just a word Popham used to excuse his actions; it was a valued quality in an early nineteenth-century war fought on a global scale. Popham may have taken the definition of discretion a little further than most, but his political sponsors continued employing him, which suggests they felt his tendency to go off-script was a risk worth taking. Trusting Popham was a gamble that sometimes went wrong, as at Buenos Aires; but often it also went right, as in Flanders or Russia. He was constantly suggesting brand new schemes, and he never let the failure of a previous one deter him. This also appealed to his political masters, including Melville, for whom effect was often just as important as success:

> I am as much satisfied as I ever was of any proposition in my life, that we cannot so effectually annoy the enemy … as by constant unremitting offensive operations … It is not a matter of any moment whether on each occasion substantial mischief is done. The teasing the enemy and keeping them constantly alarmed on the coast … is of itself real good done to the feelings of the country and real mischief done to the government of France.[10]

Popham's raids – Ostend, Boulogne, Calais – may not have achieved their objectives, but they had allowed the British to show the French what they were made of. It did not matter whether Popham succeeded, so long as he continued inventing ways to make the *impression* that Britain was capable of fighting back against the French. But Popham's ability to adopt

---

10   Dundas to Spencer, 27 May 1798, Corbett (ed.), *Spencer Papers*, vol.2, pp.351–352.

a global perspective of Britain's wartime needs had been shaped to Melville's particular predilections and preferences, and the loss of his main political patron coincided with, and compounded, some of Popham's most highly publicised failures. The next generation of politicians who replaced Pitt and Melville did not know Popham well, and their governments were comparatively weak, which made them less likely to turn to a man who laughed in the face of controversy. That did not mean they did not like what Popham had to tell them. It did, however, mean Popham had to take more care – and being careful was not in his nature.

Popham's rollercoaster career showed how one man could help shape an unfocused, but dynamic, British strategy. It also demonstrated how wrong things could go without an established central planning process to coordinate, and check, independent initiatives. Ultimately, victory over France came from continental diplomacy and the forging of continental coalitions in Europe, not from independent imperial venture. Extending Britain's economic and colonial power nevertheless did enable its post-war economic recovery and industrial growth, and gave it more clout at the peace table. Because of this, men like Sir Home Popham were able to make their contribution towards defeating Napoleon, however small.

# Bibliography

## Manuscripts

*The Bodleian Library, Oxford (BoL)*
W.Ind.s.7–8: R.S. Dundas MSS

*The British Library (BL)*
Add MS 13708: Wellesley MSS
Add MS 37284, ff.152–159: Memorandum on Sir Home Popham with commentary by Ross Donnelly and Sir Richard Goodwin Keats (copy in Add MS 37887, ff.198–206)
Add MS 41080, 41084: Correspondence between Popham and the Viscounts Melville
Add MS 45402: Hardwicke MSS
Add MS 45498: Correspondence of Popham and Denis O'Bryen
Add MS 46120: Diary of Edward Thompson
Add MS 46702–46705: Correspondence between Popham and George Don
Add MS 49505: J.W. Gordon MSS
Add MS 70959: Correspondence of Lady Hester Stanhope and General Richard Grenville
Add MS 89143: Correspondence between Popham and George Canning
Egerton MS 2137
G.19449: Annotations by Benjamin Tucker to his copy of *A Full and Correct Report of the Trial of Sir Home Popham* (London: J. and J. Richardson, 1807)
India Office Records (IOR) G/9, G/177 part 1
Loan MS 57/108: Correspondence between Popham and the Viscounts Melville
MSS EUR D742: Correspondence between Lady Popham and Lady Stamford Raffles

*Cumbria Archive Centre (CAC)*
DLONS: Lonsdale MSS

*Devon Record Office*
152M C1804 ON/22: Sidmouth MSS: Undated memorandum [1804]

*Durham University Archives (DUA)*
GRE, B49: Grey MSS

*Kent Record Office*
U840/O227-1: Camden MSS: Memorandum on the naval force, 12 September 1804

*The National Archives (TNA)*
ADM 1/5: Admiral's Correspondence, Copenhagen, 1807
ADM 1/58–59: Commodore's Correspondence, Cape of Good Hope and Buenos Aires, 1806–1807
ADM 1/171: Admiral's Correspondence, East Indies, 1801–1803
ADM 1/269, 270: Admiral's Correspondence, Jamaica, 1818–1820

ADM 1/314: Commander-in-Chief West Indies Correspondence, 1782
ADM 1/798: Transport Board Correspondence, 1794–1795
ADM 1/2312–2313, 2315, 2317, 2319, 2321, 2323–2324, 2326–2329, 2331–2346, 2592–2594: Captain's In-Letters
ADM 1/3062: Lieutenant's In-Letters
ADM 1/5319: Court-Martial Papers
ADM 1/5378: Court-Martial of Sir Home Popham, 1807
ADM 1/9548: Muster, HMS *Hyaena*
ADM 6/23, f.421: Popham's Lieutenant's Commission
ADM 25/105–111: Half-Pay List, 1783–1786
ADM 32/2994: Log, HMS *Expedition*, 1798
ADM 34/732: Paybook, HMS *Shelanagig*
ADM 36/9639: Muster, HMS *Alarm*
ADM 36/10161: Muster, HMS *Nemesis*
ADM 36/10336: Muster, HMS *Grampus*, 1783–1786
ADM 36/10702: Muster, HMS *Nautilus*, 1786
ADM 51/382: Log, HMS *Grampus*
ADM 51/468: Log, HMS *Hyaena*
ADM 51/1491: Log, HMS *Antelope*, 1804–1805
ADM 51/1615: Log, HMS *Diadem*, 1805–1806
ADM 51/1673: Log, HMS *Prince of Wales*, 1807
ADM 51/1743: Log, HMS *Diadem*, 1804–1805
TNA ADM 51/2030: Log, HMS *Sybille*, 1817–1820
ADM 51/2819: Log, HMS *Stirling Castle*, 1813–1814
ADM 51/2957: Log, HMS *Venerable*, 1808–1813
ADM 51/4493: Log, HMS *Romney*
ADM 52/3557: Master's Log, HMS *Antelope*, 1804–1805
ADM 53/1236: Muster, HMS *Venerable*
ADM 80/156–157: Correspondence Relating to Jamaica, 1818–1820
CO 137/149: Jamaica Correspondence, 1819
FO 65/43–46: Correspondence Regarding Russia, 1799–1800
HCA 32/594–599: Materials Seized Aboard *Etrusco*
HCA 40/3/134: Royal Warrant Regarding *L'Etrusco*, 24 September 1805
HCA 42/535: Proceedings Regarding *Etrusco*
PC 1/3823: Cape of Good Hope and Buenos Aires Prize Papers, 1806–1812
PRO 30/8/260, 368–369: Chatham MSS
PRO 30/20/20/11: Statement by Home Riggs Popham, 30 September 1784
WO 1/167–173, 177: Flanders Campaign, 1793–1795
WO 1/187–188: Copenhagen, 1807
WO 1/411: Popham's Mission to Russia, 1799
WO 1/261–263: Peninsular War, 1810–1812
WO 6/14: Out-Letters, Copenhagen, 1807
WO 190: Proceedings of the Army, Walcheren Expedition
PROB 11/1141/170: Will of Captain Edward Thompson, 13 March 1785
PROB 11/1634/323: Will of Sir Home Popham

*National Army Museum (NAM)*
1968-07-261: Diary of Captain Frederick Trench

*National Library of Scotland (NLS)*
Acc. 6684, 6990: Pulteney Malcolm MSS

*National Maritime Museum (NMM), Greenwich*
JOD/43: Diary of Robert Deans, 1812
KEI/37: Keith MSS

MEL/7, 104: Melville MSS
MKH/171: Hood MSS
MRK/102, 104: Markham MSS
YOR 14/3: Yorke MSS

*National Records of Scotland (NRS)*
GD51: Melville MSS
GD364: Hope of Luffness MSS

*Public Record Office of Northern Ireland (PRONI)*
D3030: Castlereagh MSS

*Royal House Archive, The Hague*
KHA A31 inv. nr 1048: Correspondence of Baron Hogguer with the Prince of Orange

*State Library of Victoria, Melbourne, Australia (SLV)*
Accession No. MS 13020 (prev. M5142): Correspondence between Charles, Lord Whitworth and Sir Home Popham

*William L. Clements Library, University of Michigan (WLC UM)*
Coote MSS
Melville MSS

## Online manuscript repositories

*Georgian Papers Online*
Royal Archives: GEO/MAIN/21446–21447: Popham to Colonel McMahon, 10 June 1814 <http://gpp.rct.uk>, accessed 27 June 2023
Royal Archives: GEO/Main/40624–40628: Popham to the Prince of Wales, 7 July 1806, <http://gpp.rct.uk>, accessed 28 September 2022

*Harvard Law School Historical and Special Collections Catalogue*
Catalogue record for the Lease of Titness Park, 3 June 1805, <https://researchworks.oclc.org/archivegrid/collection/data/236235492>, accessed 1 December 2022

*Royal Society MSS*
Popham's certificate of election as a fellow of the Royal Society, 18 April 1799, EC/179/04, <https://catalogues.royalsociety.org/CalmView/Record.aspx?src=CalmView.Catalog&id=EC%2f1799%2f04>, accessed 3 March 2023

*University of Cambridge Digital Library*
Popham to the Board of Longitude, 1 June 1786, Royal Greenwich Observatory Archives, RGO 14/51, ff.195–207, <https://cudl.lib.cam.ac.uk/view/MS-RGO-00014-00051/398>, accessed 6 December 2022
Popham to the Board of Longitude, 23 July 1786, Royal Greenwich Observatory Archives, RGO 14/51, f.193, <https://cudl.lib.cam.ac.uk/view/MS-RGO-00014-00051/394>, accessed 6 December 2022

## Newspapers and periodicals[1]

Aberdeen Press and Journal
Anti-Gallican Monitor
The Anti-Jacobin Review and Magazine
Belfast Commercial Chronicle
British Press
British Mercury or Wednesday Evening Post
British Neptune
British Press
Caledonian Mercury
Champion
Cobbett's Political Register
The Courier
Derby Mercury
Dublin Evening Post
Edinburgh Magazine and Literary Miscellany
Evening Mail
Exeter Flying Post
Gazette Nationale ou le Moniteur Universel
General Evening Post
Gentleman's Magazine and Historical Chronicle
Gloucester Journal
Hampshire Chronicle
Hereford Journal
Imperial Weekly Gazette
Ipswich Journal
Journal de l'Empire
Kentish Gazette
Lancaster Gazette
Leeds Intelligencer
Le Moniteur
London Chronicle
London Gazette
Madras Courier
Manchester Mercury
Military Register
Morning Advertiser
Morning Chronicle
Morning Herald
Morning Post
Naval Chronicle
New Times
Newcastle Courant
Newcastle Journal
Northampton Mercury
Oracle and Daily Advertiser
Oxford Journal
The Pilot
Public Cause
Public Ledger and Daily Advertiser
Reading Mercury
Royal Cornwall Gazette
St James's Chronicle
The Star
The Sun
Taunton Courier
The Times
The World and Fashionable Sunday Chronicle

## Primary Material

### Articles

Anon., 'Sir Home Riggs Popham', *The Annual Biography and Obituary, for the Year* 1822 (London: Longman, Hurst, Rees, Orme, and Brown, 1822), vol.6, pp.288–307

Anon., 'Sir Home Popham's Embassy to the States of Arabia, and to the Pacha of Egypt', *The Literary Journal: A Review of Literature, Science, Manners, and Politics for the year 1803* (July to December) (London: C. and R. Baldwin, 1803), vol.2, pp.125–128, 249–253, and 443–446

Anon., *Transactions of the Society, instituted at London, for the Encouragement of Arts, Manufactures, and Commerce*, 34 (1816), pp.167–177

[Courtenay, G.W.], 'Iphigenia, Port Royal, June 6, 1819 (on board of which the writer was a Lieutenant)', *Blackwood's Magazine* (1821), vol.IV, pp.546–552

'Oceana', 'Particulars of the Life of Rear Admiral Sir Home Popham', *The New Bon Ton Magazine, or, Telescope of the Times* (London: J. Johnston, 1820), vol.V, pp.366–372

[Wilkie, Fletcher], 'Recollections of the British Army, in the early campaigns of the Revolutionary War, No. 2', *The United Service Journal and Naval Military Magazine for 1836*, part I (London: Henry Colburn, 1836), pp.480–489

---

1   Principally accessed via the British Newspaper Archive, British Nineteenth Century Newspapers, and the Times Digital Archive.

## Books

Anon., *A Collection of Papers Relating to the Expedition to the Scheldt* (London: A. Strahan, 1811)
Anon., *A Correct Account of the Trial at Large between Ross Donnelly, esq, a Post-Captain in His Majesty's Navy, Plaintiff, and Sir Home Popham, Knt, Defendant, before Sir James Mansfield, Chief Justice of His Majesty's Court of Common Pleas, and a Special Jury, on Saturday, the 27th of June, 1807, at Westminster Hall* ... (London: T. Cadell and W. Davies, 1807)
Anon., *A Discourse upon the True Character of our Late Proceedings in the Baltic* ... (London: W. McDowall for Maxwell and Wilson, 1808)
Anon., *A Full and Correct Report of the Trial of Sir Home Popham* ... (London: J. and J. Richardson, 1807)
Anon., *Brief Remarks Upon the Public Letter of Sir Richard Strachan and the Narrative of the Earl of Chatham* (London, 1810)
Anon., *État Général de la Légion d'Honneur depuis son Origine* ... (Paris: Testu and Co., 1814), vol.2
Anon., *Members of Parliament*, Part 2 (1878)
Anon., *Minutes of Evidence taken before the Committee of the whole House appointed to consider the policy and conduct of the late Expedition to the Scheldt* (London: [no publisher], 1810)
Anon., *Public Characters of 1806* (London: Richard Phillips, 1806)
Anon., *The Spirit of the Public Journals for 1812* (London: James Ridgway, 1813), vol.16
Aspinall, A. (ed.), *The Later Correspondence of George III* (Cambridge: Cambridge University Press, 1967), vol.3
Aspinall, A. (ed.), *The Letters of King George IV, 1812–1830* (Cambridge: Cambridge University Press, 1938), vol.1
Barrow, John, *An Auto-Biographical Memoir of Sir John Barrow, Bart., Late of the Admiralty* ... (London: John Murray, 1847)
Blake, Mrs Warrenne (ed.), *An Irish Beauty of the Regency: ... the Unpublished Journals of the Hon. Mrs. Calvert, 1789–1822* (London: John Lane the Bodley Head, 1911)
Bonner Smith, David (ed.) *Letters of Admiral of the Fleet the Earl of St Vincent whilst First Lord of the Admiralty, 1801–1804* (London: Navy Records Society, 1922 and 1927), 2 vols
Buckingham and Chandos, Duke of (ed.), *Memoirs of the Court and Cabinets of George the Third* ... (London: Hurst and Blackett, 1855), 4 vols
Brougham, Henry, Viscount, *The Life and Times of Henry, Lord Brougham, written by himself* (Edinburgh: William Blackwood and Sons, 1871), 3 vols
Bunbury, Sir Henry, *A Narrative of the Campaign in North Holland, 1799* (London, 1849)
Carr-Gomm, Francis Culling (ed.), *Letters and Journals of Field-Marshal Sir William Maynard Gomm, GCB* ... (London: John Murray, 1881)
Chatterton, Georgiana, Lady (ed.), *Memorials, Personal and Historical of Admiral Lord Gambier, GCB* ... (London: Hurst and Blackett, 1861), 2 vols
Cobbett, William, *Parliamentary History of England ... to 1803* ... (London, 1819),
Cobbett, William (ed.), *Cobbett's Parliamentary Debates* ... (London: R. Bagshaw, 1804–1812), vols 1–20
Colchester, Charles, Lord (ed.), *The Diary and Correspondence of Charles Abbot, Lord Colchester* ... (London: John Murray, 1861), 3 vols
Compton, Herbert (ed.), *A Master Mariner. Being the Life and Adventures of Captain Robert William Eastwick* (London: T. Fisher Unwin, 1891)
Corbett, Julian S. (ed.), *Private Papers of George, Second Earl Spencer, First Lord of the Admiralty 1794–1801* [*Spencer Papers*] (London: Navy Records Society, vol 48, 1924), vol.2
Crawford, Abraham, *Reminiscences of a Naval Officer, during the Late War* ... (London: Henry Colburn, 1851)
Czisnik, Marianne (ed.), *Nelson's Letters to Lady Hamilton and Related Documents* (London: Routledge, for the Navy Records Society, 2020)
Douin, G., and Fawtier-Jones, E.C., *L'Angleterre et L'Égypte: La Politique Mameluke: Tome Premier: 1801–1803* (Cairo: La Société Royale de Géographie d'Égypte, 1929)
Falconer, William, *An Universal Dictionary of the Marine* ... (London: T. Cadell, 1784)
F[ernyhough], Lieutenant Robert et al., *Military Memoirs of Four Brothers ... engaged in the service of their country* ... (London: William Sams, 1829)
Gillespie, Alexander, *Gleanings and Remarks Collected during Many Months' Residence at Buenos Ayres* ... (Leeds: R. Dewhirst, 1819)

Gower, Richard Hall, *A Treatise on the Theory and Practice of Seamanship, together with a System of Naval Signals* ... (London: Wilkie and Robinson, 1808)

Grainger, John D., *The Royal Navy in the River Plate, 1806–1807* (London: Navy Records Society, 1996)

Gurwood, John (ed.), *The Dispatches of Field Marshal the Duke of Wellington* ... (London: John Murray, 1838), vols 6, 9

Hamilton, R.V. (ed.), *Letters and Papers of Admiral of the Fleet Sir Thomas Byam Martin* (London: Navy Records Society, 1898), 3 vols

House of Commons, *Accounts and Papers presented to the House of Commons, respecting the Repairs &c of the Romney, and other His Majesty's Ships belonging to the Squadron lately under the Command of Captain Sir Home Popham, 1800–1805* (London: House of Commons, ordered to be printed 18 and 21 February, 5, 13, 16, and 27 March, and 5 April 1805)

House of Commons, *Papers Relating to Property Captured at Buenos Aires* ... (London: Ordered by the House of Commons to be printed, 27 April and 1 May 1812)

House of Commons, *Reports from the Select Committee on Papers relating to the Repairs of His Majesty's Ships The Romney and Sensible, while under the Command of Sir Home Popham: First Report* (London: House of Commons, ordered to be printed 5 June 1805)

House of Commons, *Reports from the Select Committee on Papers relating to the Repairs of His Majesty's Ships The Romney and Sensible, while under the Command of Sir Home Popham: Second Report* (London: House of Commons, ordered to be printed 24 June 1805)

House of Lords, *Journal of the House of Lords* 1774–1776 (London, 1767–1830), vol.34

Huntley, Capt. Sir H.V., *Peregrine Scramble* (Paris: A. and W. Galignani and Co., 1849)

Huskisson, Thomas, *Eyewitness to Trafalgar* (London: Ellisons' Editions, 1985)

Jones, Lewis T., *An Historical Journal of the British Campaign on the Continent, in the Year 1794; with the Retreat through Holland, in the Year 1795* ... (London: T. Egerton, 1797)

Ilchester, Earl of (ed.), *The Journal of Elizabeth, Lady Holland* (London: Longmans, Green, and Co., 1908), vol.2

Jackson, Lady (ed.), *The Diaries and Letters of Sir George Jackson* ... (London: Richard Bentley, 1872)

Lewis, Michael (ed.), A Narrative of *my Professional Adventures (1790–1839), by Sir William Henry Dillon, KCH, Vice-Admiral of the Red* (London: Navy Records Society, 1953, 1956), 2 vols

Lloyd, C.C. (ed.), *The Keith Papers* (London: Navy Records Society, 1955), 3 vols

Londonderry, Charles William Vane, 3rd Marquess (ed.), *Correspondence, Despatches, and Other Papers of Viscount Castlereagh* (2nd Series) (London: W. Shoberl, 1851)

McGrigor, James, *The Autobiography and Services of Sir James McGrigor, Bart.* (London: Longman, Green, Longman, and Roberts, 1861)

O'Bryen, Denis, *A Narrative, by ... D. O'Bryen, in consequence of the attack made upon him ... in the House of Commons ... Part the Second* (London, 1820)

Parkinson, C. Northcote, *Samuel Walters, Lieutenant, R.N.* (Liverpool: University Press, 1949)

Phipps, Edmund (ed.), *Memoirs of the Political and Literary Life of Robert Plumer Ward* ... (London: John Murray, 1850)

Plon, H., and Dumaine, J., eds, *Correspondance de Napoléon Ier* (Paris: Imprimerie Impériale, 1861), vol.7

Popham, Home, *A Letter from Captain Home Popham, to the Lords of the Admiralty; with the Report of the Commissioners of the Transport Board, to which it is an Answer. And a Supplement and Appendix* (London: privately published, 1797)

[Popham, Sir Home], *Concise Statement of Facts, relative to the Treatment experienced by Sir Home Popham since his return from the Red Sea, to which is added, the Correspondence, Naval, Military, and Commercial, to his Excellency the Most Noble the Marquis Wellesley, &c, from Sir Home Popham, during his command in the Red Sea, and his subsequent Embassy to the States of Arabia* (London: John Stockdale, 1805)

Popham, Sir Home, and Plampin, Robert, 'Opinion Respecting the Practicability of effecting a Landing between Sandfleet [sic] and Fort Lillo', 19 June 1809, printed for the House of Commons, 1 March 1810

Popham, Sir Home, *Telegraphic Signals; or Marine Vocabulary* ... (London: T. Egerton, 1803)

Privy Council, *Regulations and Instructions Relating to His Majesty's Service at Sea established by His Majesty in Council* (London: W. Winchester and Son, 1806)

Privy Council, *Regulations and Instructions Relating to His Majesty's Service at Sea established by His Majesty in Council* (London: W. Winchester and Son, 1808)

Royal Commission on Historical Manuscripts, *The Manuscripts of J.B. Fortescue, esq., Preserved at Dropmore* [Dropmore MSS] (London: HMSO/Eyre and Spottiswoode, 1892–1927), vols 1–10

Schnurmann, Claudia (ed.), *John Parish's Journal at Copenhagen* (Berlin: Lit Verlag, 2022)

Taylor, John, *Records of my Life, by the Late John Taylor, esq.* (London: E. Bull, 1832)
Theal, George McCall, *Records of the Cape Colony from February 1803 to July 1806 ...* (London: William Clowes and Sons for the Government of the Cape Colony, 1899)
[Thompson, Edward], *Sailor's Letters Written to his Select Friends in England, During his Voyages and Travels in Europe, Asia, Africa, and America from the Year 1754 to 1759* (Dublin: J. Hoey and J. Potts, 1770)
[Tucker, Benjamin], *Observations on a Pamphlet which has been privately circulated, said to be 'A Concise Statement of Facts, and the Treatment Experienced by Sir Home Popham, since his Return from the Red Sea'; to which is added, A Copy of the Report made by the Navy-Board to the Admiralty, on investigating the Account of Expenditure for the Romney and Sensible, at Calcutta, in 1801, whilst under the Orders of Sir Home Popham* (London: J. Ginger, [1805])
Walsh, Edward, *A Narrative of the Expedition to Holland in the Autumn of the Year 1799* (London, 1800)

## Secondary Material

### Articles

Anon., 'The MS Journal of Captain E. Thompson,' *The Cornhill Magazine*, 17 (1868), pp.610–40Blyth, E.M.E., 'Admiral Sir Home Riggs Popham, KB, born 1762, died 1820', *Army Quarterly*, 72 (1956), pp.195–200
Coelho, Chris, 'The Popham Code Controversy', in J.E. Pearson, S. Heuvel, and J. Rodgaard (eds), *The Trafalgar Chronicle: New Series 5* (Barnsley: Seaforth Publications, 2020), pp.133–147
de Porras, Elias Duran, 'Peter Finnerty, An Ancestor of Modern War Correspondents', *Textual and Visual Media*, 7 (2014), pp.41–62
Dixon, Conrad, 'To Walk the Quarterdeck: The Naval Career of David Ewen Bartholomew', *The Mariner's Mirror*, 79:1 (1993), pp.58–63
Garfield, Julia, 'Haiti and Jamaica in the Remaking of the Early Nineteenth-Century Atlantic World', *William and Mary Quarterly*, 69:3 (2012), pp.583–614
Geggus, David, 'Yellow Fever in the 1790s: The British Army in Occupied Saint Domingue', *Medical History*, 23 (1979), pp.38–58
Hanham, Andrew, 'Regency Knights: The Royal Guelphic Order, 1815–1837', *The Coat of Arms* (3rd ser.), 4:2 (2008), pp.101–124
Herzog, Richard, 'The Royal Marine and Insurgent Operations in the Salamanca Campaign, 1812', in Gordon C. Bond and J.W. Rooney, Jr. (eds), *The Consortium on Revolutionary Europe, 1750–1850: Proceedings, 1992* (Tallahassee, FL: Institute on Napoleon and the French Revolution, Florida State University, 1993), pp.62–69
History of Parliament, 'Members 1790–1820', <https://www.historyofparliamentonline.org/research/members/members-1790-1820>, accessed 27 February 2023
Kenney, James J., 'Lord Whitworth and the Conspiracy Against Tsar Paul I: The New Evidence of the Kent Archive', *Slavic Review*, 36:2 (1977), pp.205–219
Kinahan, Jill, 'The impenetrable shield: HMS Nautilus and the Namib coast in the late eighteenth century', *Cimbebasia*, 12 (1990), pp.23–61
Knight, Roger, 'After Trafalgar', in Quentin Colville and James Davey (eds), *Nelson, Navy and Nation* (London: National Maritime Museum, 2013)
Macro, Eric, 'The First British Embassy to the Yemen', *Royal Air Force College Journal*, 31:1 (1959), pp.36–38
Morriss, Roger, 'St Vincent and Reform, 1801–1804', *Mariner's Mirror*, 69:3 (2013), pp.269–290.
Perrin, W.G., 'The Second Capture of the Cape of Good Hope, 1806', *The Naval Miscellany* (London: Navy Records Society, 1927), vol.3, pp.191–285
Reiter, Jacqueline (ed.), 'Day after Day Adds to our Miseries: The Private Diary of a Staff Officer on the Walcheren Expedition, 1809, Part 1', *Journal of the Society for Army Historical Research*, 96:386 (2018), pp.131–151,
Reiter, Jacqueline (ed.), 'Day after Day Adds to our Miseries: The Private Diary of a Staff Officer on the Walcheren Expedition, Part 2', *Journal of the Society for Army Historical Research*, 96:387 (2019), pp. 231–250
Reiter, Jacqueline (ed.), 'Day after Day Adds to our Miseries: The Private Diary of a Staff Officer on the Walcheren Expedition, Part 3', *Journal of the Society for Army Historical Research*, 97:387 (2019), pp.26–44

Reiter, Jacqueline, '"A Melville Expedition": Sir Home Popham's Political Networks and the Walcheren Expedition of 1809', in Zack White (ed.), *The Sword and the Spirit: Proceedings of the First 'War and Peace in the Age of Napoleon' Conference* (Warwick: Helion & Co., 2021), pp.44–62

Rems, Alan, 'Man of War', *Naval History Magazine*, 25:4 (2011)

Rogers, Nicholas, 'The Sea Fencibles, Loyalism and the Reach of the State', in Mark Philp (ed.), *Resisting Napoleon: The British Response to the Threat of Invasion, 1797–1815* (Ashgate: Routledge, 2006, e-book edition)

Sainz, Silvia Gregorio, 'Sir Home Popham's Mission in 1812: Santander, A British Logistics Centre?', in Zack White (ed.), *The Sword and the Spirit: Proceedings of the First "War and Peace in the Age of Napoleon" Conference* (Warwick: Helion & Co., 2021), pp.63–80

Stokes, Winifred, 'POPHAM, Sir Home Riggs (1762–1820), of Titness Park, Berks.', in R. Thorne (ed.), *The History of Parliament: the House of Commons 1790–1820* <https://www.historyofparliamentonline.org/volume/1790-1820/member/popham-sir-home-riggs-1762-1820>, accessed 29 July 2021

Thomson, David Whittet, 'The Catamaran Expeditions', *USNI Proceedings*, 70/2/492 (1944)

Wilkinson, Clive, 'Thompson, Edward (1738?–1786)', *ODNB*, <https://doi.org/10.1093/ref:odnb/27260>, accessed 27 July 2021

Williams, M.J., and Thorne, R.G., 'KINNAIRD, Hon. Charles (1780–1826), of Rossie Priory, Perth', *The History of Parliament: 1790–1820*, <https://www.historyofparliamentonline.org/volume/1790-1820/member/kinnaird-hon-charles-1780-1826>, accessed 19 May 2022

## Books

Asquith, Ivon, 'James Perry and the *Morning Chronicle*, 1790–1821' (PhD thesis, University of London, 1973)

Ball, Philip, *A Waste of Blood and Treasure: The 1799 Anglo–Russian Invasion of the Netherlands* (Barnsley: Pen & Sword, 2017)

Ball, Philip, *Neither Up Nor Down: The British Army and the Flanders Campaign, 1793–1795* (Warwick: Helion & Co., 2020)

Benjamin, Lewis, *The Huskisson Papers* (London: Constable, 1931)

Beresford, Marcus de la Poer, *Marshal William Carr Beresford* (Dublin: Irish Academic Press, 2018)

Black, C.V., *The Story of Jamaica, from Prehistory to the Present* (London: Collins, 1965)

Bracknall, Moira, 'Lord Spencer, patronage and commissioned officers' careers, 1794–1801', PhD Thesis, University of Exeter, January 2008

Brown, Steve, *The Duke of York's Campaign in Flanders: Fighting the French Revolution, 1793–1795* (Barnsley: Pen & Sword, 2018)

Bryant, Arthur, *The Years of Victory, 1802–1812* (London: Collins, 1944)

Cavell, S.A., *Midshipmen and Quarterdeck Boys in the British Navy, 1771–1831* (Woodbridge: The Boydell Press, 2012)

Clammer, Paul, *Black Crown: Henry Christophe, the Haitian Revolution and the Caribbean's Forgotten Kingdom* (London: Hurst & Co, 2023)

Coelho, Chris, *Pirates in Uniform: The Conspiracy to Invade Buenos Aires that Triggered a War* (self-published, 2019)

Colden, Cadwallader D., *The Life of Robert Fulton* (NY: Kirk & Mercein, 1817)

Condon, Mary Ellen, 'The administration of the Transport Service during the war against Revolutionary France, 1793–1802', PhD Thesis, University of London, 1968

Creasman, Carl Edward, Jr., 'The naval career of Sir Home Riggs Popham from Copenhagen to Copenhagen, 1800–1807', MA Thesis, Auburn University, 1988

Daly, Gavin, *Storm and Sack: British Sieges, Violence and the Laws of War in the Napoleonic Era, 1799–1815* (Cambridge: Cambridge University Press, 2022)

Davey, James, *In Nelson's Wake: The Navy and the Napoleonic Wars* (New Haven, London: Yale University Press, 2015)

Davies, Huw J., *Wellington's Wars* (New Haven, CT, Yale UP, 2012)

Dickinson, H.W., *Robert Fulton, Engineer and Artist: His Life and Works* (NY: John Lane, the Bodley Head, 1913)

Divall, Carole, *Wellington's Worst Scrape: The Burgos Campaign, 1812* (Barnsley: Pen & Sword, 2012)

Divall, Carole, *General Sir Ralph Abercromby and the French Revolutionary Wars 1792–1801* (Barnsley: Pen & Sword, 2018)

Downer, Martin, *Nelson's Purse: The Mystery of Lord Nelson's Lost Treasures* (London: Corgi, 2005)

Ehrman, John, *The Younger Pitt: The Consuming Struggle* (Stanford, CA: Stanford University Press, 1996)
Esdaile, Charles J., *The Peninsular War: A New History* (London: Penguin, 2003)
Esdaile, Charles, *Napoleon's Wars: An International History, 1803–15* (London: Allen Lane, 2007)
Fedorak, C.J., *Henry Addington: Prime Minister, 1801–1804* (Akron, OH: University of Akron Press, 2002)
Fitchett, W.H., *How England Saved Europe: The Story of the Great War, 1793–1815* (New York: Charles Scribner's Sons, 1900), vol.3
Fortescue, J.W., *A History of the British Army* (London, 1899–1930), 13 vols
Fry, Michael, *The Dundas Despotism* (Edinburgh: University Press, 1992)
Fullom, S.W., *The Life of General Sir Howard Douglas* ... (London: John Murray, 1863)
Gardner, W.J., *A History of Jamaica from its Discovery by Christopher Columbus to the year 1872* ... (London: T. Fisher Unwin, 1909)
Gardiner, Robert, *Warships of the Napoleonic Era: Design, Development and Deployment* (Barnsley: Seaforth Publishing, 2011)
Glover, Gareth, *The Two Battles of Copenhagen 1801 and 1807: Britain and Denmark in the Napoleonic Wars* (Barnsley: Pen & Sword, 2018)
Grainger, John D., *The British Navy in the Baltic* (Woodbridge: The Boydell Press, 2014)
Grainger, John D., *British Campaigns in the South Atlantic, 1805–1807* (Barnsley: Pen & Sword, 2015)
Griggs, E.L. and Prator, C.H. (eds), *Henry Christophe and Thomas Clarkson: A Correspondence* (Berkeley and Los Angeles, CA: University of California Press, 1952)
Haley, Arthur H., *Our Davy: General Sir David Baird (1757–1829)* (Liverpool: Bullfinch Publications, [1989])
Hall, Christopher D., *Wellington's Navy: Sea Power and the Peninsular War, 1807–1814* (London: Chatham Publishing, 2004)
Hart, Richard, *Slaves who Abolished Slavery: Blacks in Rebellion* (Mona: University of the West Indies, 2002)
Hill, Richard, *The Prizes of War: The Naval Prize System in the Napoleonic Wars, 1793–1815* (Stroud: Sutton Publishing, for the Royal Naval Museum, 1998)
[Hook, T.], *The Life of General the Right Honourable Sir David Baird, Bart.* ... (London: Richard Bentley, 1832)
Howard, Martin R., *Walcheren 1809: The Scandalous Destruction of a British Army* (Barnsley: Pen & Sword, 2011)
Hughes, Ben, *The British Invasion of the River Plate, 1806–1807* (Barnsley: Pen & Sword Military, 2013)
Jacobs, H.P., *Sixty Years of Change, 1806–1866* (Jamaica: Institute of Jamaica, 1973), Cultural Heritage Series vol.2
James, William, *The Naval History of Great Britain* (London: Harding, Lepard and Co., 1826), 5 vols
Jupp, Peter, *Lord Grenville* (Oxford: Clarendon Press, 1985)
Knight, Roger, *Britain Against Napoleon: The Organization of Victory, 1793–1815* (London: Penguin, 2014)
Knight, Roger, *Convoys: The British Struggle against Napoleonic Europe and America* (New Haven, CT: Yale University Press, 2023)
Ingram, Edward, *The British Empire as a World Power* (London: Frank Cass, 2001)
Lavery, Brian, *Nelson's Navy: The Ships, Men and Organisation, 1793–1815* (London: Conway Maritime Press, 1989)
MacCannell, Daniel, *Coastal Defences of the British Empire in the Revolutionary and Napoleonic Eras* (Barnsley: Pen & Sword Military, 2021, e-book edition)
Mackesy, Piers, *War Without Victory: The Downfall of Pitt, 1799–1802* (Oxford: Clarendon Press, 1984)
Mackesy, Piers, *British Victory in Egypt: The End of Napoleon's Conquest* (London: Tauris Parke Paperbacks, 2010)
Madiou, Thomas, *Histoire d'Haiti, 1811–1818* (Paris: Editions Fardin, 1818), vols 5–6
Mallinson, Howard, *Send it by Semaphore: The Old Telegraphs During the Wars with France* (Marlborough: Crowood Press, 2005)
Martinovich, Paul, *The Sea is my Element: The Eventful Life of Admiral Sir Pulteney Malcolm, 1768–1838* (Warwick: Helion, 2020)
McCarthy, Matthew, *Privateering, Piracy and British Policy in Spanish America, 1810–1830* (London: Boydell Press, 2013)
McCranie, Kevin D., *Admiral Lord Keith and the Naval War Against Napoleon* (Gainesville, FL: University Press of Florida, 2006)
Mikaberidze, Alexander, *The Napoleonic Wars: A Global History* (Oxford: Oxford University Press, 2020)
Muir, Rory, *Britain and the Defeat of Napoleon, 1807–1815* (New Haven, CT: Yale UP, 1996)
Muir, Rory, *Salamanca 1812* (New Haven, CT: Yale University Press, 2001)
Muir, Rory, *Wellington: The Path to Victory, 1769–1814* (New Haven, CT: Yale University Press, 2014)
Neale, W. Johnson, *Gentleman Jack: A Naval Story* (London: Henry Colburn, 1837), 2 vols
Oman, Charles, *A History of the Peninsular War, October 1811–31 August 1812* (Oxford: Clarendon Press, 1914), vol.5

Oman, Charles, *A History of the Peninsular War, 1 September 1812–5 August 1813* (Oxford: Clarendon Press, 1922), vol.6
Parry, Jonathan, *Promised Lands: The British and the Ottoman Middle East* (Princeton, NJ: Princeton University Press, 2022)
Parsons, William Barclay, *Robert Fulton and the Submarine* (NY: Columbia University Press, 1922)
Perrin, W.G., *British Flags: Their Early History, and their Development at Sea …* (Cambridge: Cambridge University Press, 1922)
Playfair, R.L., *A History of Arabia Felix or Yemen …* (Bombay: Education Society Press, 1859)
Pocock, Tom, *The Terror Before Trafalgar: Nelson, Napoleon and the Secret War* (London: John Murray, 2002)
Popham, Frederick W., *A West Country Family: The Pophams from 1150* (Sevenoaks: Self-published, 1976)
Popham, Hugh, *A Damned Cunning Fellow: The Eventful Life of Rear-Admiral Sir Home Popham KCB, KCH, KM, FRS 1762–1820* (Tywardreath: Old Ferry Press, 1991)
Reiter, Jacqueline, *The Late Lord: The Life of John Pitt, 2nd Earl of Chatham* (Barnsley: Pen & Sword, 2017)
Robson, Martin, *A History of the Royal Navy: The Napoleonic Wars* (London: I.B. Tauris, 2014)
Rodger, N.A.M., *The Wooden World: An Anatomy of the Georgian Navy* (London: Fortuna Press, 1988)
Rodger, N.A.M., *The Command of the Ocean* (London: Allan Lane, 2004)
Russell Barker, G.F., and Stenning, A.H., *The Record of Old Westminsters: A Biographical List of All Those Who Are Known to Have Been Educated at Westminster School from the Earliest Times to 1927* (London: Chiswick Press, 1928), vol.2
Sayles, G.O., 'Contemporary sketches of the members of the Irish Parliament in 1784', in G.O. Sayles, *Scripta Diversa* (London: Bloomsbury, 1982)
Schotte, Margaret E., *Sailing School: Navigating Science and Skill, 1550–1800* (Baltimore, MD: Johns Hopkins Press, 2019)
Scott, Sheila (ed.), *My Dear Cath…: The Story of an Army Doctor's Wife in 1818–1819, Letters of Anne (née Cairns), the Wife of Andrew Anderson, Surgeon in the 92nd Regiment (Gordons) in Ireland and Jamaica* (Privately Published, 1976), from the Wellcome Collection, RAMC/1227
Shaw, William A., *The Knights of England* (London: 1906)
Spencer, Alfred (ed.), *Memoirs of William Hickey* (London: Hurst & Blackett, 1919), vol.2
Styles, Michael H., *Captain Hogan: Sailor, Merchant, Diplomat on Six Continents* (Fairfax, VA: Six Continents Horizons, 2003)
Sutcliffe, Alice Crary, *Robert Fulton* (NY: Macmillan, 1915)
Thompson, Mark, *Wellington and the Lines of Torres Vedras* (Warwick: Helion, 2021)
Venn, J.A., *Alumni Cantabrigienses: A Biographical List of All Known Students, Graduates and Holders of Office at the University of Cambridge, from the Earliest Times to 1900* (Cambridge: Cambridge University Press, 1953), vol.5 pt. 2
Uythoven, Geert van, *The Secret Expedition: The Anglo-Russian Invasion of North Holland, 1799* (Warwick: Helion & Co., 2018)
Waite, Richard A., 'Sir Home Riggs Popham, KM, KCG, KCH. FRS, Rear Admiral of the Red Squadron: A biography', PhD thesis, Harvard University, 1942
Wells, Roger, *Insurrection: The British Experience, 1795–1803* (London: Alan Sutton, 1983)
Wheeler, H.F.B., and Broadley, A.M. *Napoleon and the Invasion of England* (London: Bodley Head, 1908), 2 vols
Wilson, Evan, *A Social History of British Naval Officers* (Woodbridge: Boydell and Brewer, 2017)
Zubow, Graf Valentin, *Zar Paul I: Mensch und Schicksal* (Stuttgart: K.F. Kochler Verlag, [1964])

# Index of Royal Navy Ships

*Aimable* 147–148, 150
*Antelope* 149–150, 152, 155, 164
*Ardent* 129, 145–147, 150–151
*Arethusa* 279, 282
*Ariadne* 65–66

*Bedford* 28–29, 312
*Belliqueux* 166–167, 172, 175–176
*Brilliant* 15, 45, 248

*Champion* 65, 67–68

*Dart* 150–151
*Diadem* 162, 164, 166, 168, 172, 174, 176–177, 181, 185, 187, 195–197, 204–205, 214, 222, 225, 284, 287–288
*Diomede* 166, 168, 172, 176–177, 181, 187, 195, 201–202, 205

*Encounter* 166, 168, 172, 181, 187–188, 195–198, 202
*Espoir* 166, 168–169, 172–174
*Expedition* 66–68

*Gladiator* viii, 215–216, 218–219, 222, 226–227, 229
*Grampus* 33–34, 36, 40

*Harpy* 24, 66
*Hecla* 67–68
*Hyaena* 20–22, 24–32, 40

*Iris* 284, 314–315

*Kite* 67–68

*Lancaster* 192, 194, 202
*Leda* 146, 166, 168–169, 172, 175, 177, 180, 195–197, 202, 204
*Lyra* 284, 286, 291

*Magnificent* 284, 291–292, 312
*Medusa* 192, 202, 204, 279, 284, 286, 291, 293

*Narcissus* 166, 168–169, 174, 176–177, 181, 184–185, 187–188, 192, 207, 209, 246, 279, 282
*Nautilus* 34, 36–37, 40, 139–141

*Prince of Wales* 233–234, 236–239, 244
*Protector* 166, 168, 172, 202

*Raisonable* 166, 168, 172, 175–177, 181, 187, 195, 204–205, 209
*Rhin* 284, 286, 288, 291, 293, 302
*Rolla* 176, 206, 208–209, 212
*Romney* 90, 92–93, 95–96, 98–101, 105–107, 109, 112–113, 117–118, 120–123, 126–127, 130–131, 134–139, 143, 147, 152–156, 158, 164–166, 183, 207, 233, 335
*Rover* 284, 293

*Sampson* 205–206
*San Domingo* 29, 251, 259, 312
*Sensible* 96, 98, 100, 120, 122
*Sheerness* 107, 109
*Shelanagig* 30–32, 57
*Stirling Castle* 155, 303, 307–308, 310, 312–313
*Surveillante* 238, 243, 282, 284, 286–287, 291, 303
*Sybille* 317, 322, 325, 330, 332–334

*Tartarus* 67–68

*Valiant* 233, 240, 281
*Venerable* 155, 250–251, 258–259, 261–262, 264, 271–272, 278–279, 283–285, 287–288, 297–298, 300–301, 303
*Victor* 96, 98, 109

*Wilhelmina* 96, 107

# General Index

Abercromby, Lieutenant General Sir Ralph 76, 78, 81–82, 89, 93, 98
Addington, Henry 119, 122, 125–127, 136, 139, 181–183, 253, 278
Aden 93, 98, 101, 103, 111–112
Alkmaar 82–83
Ameland 64, 74–77, 79, 85–86
Amsterdam 54, 79, 81–84, 144
Antwerp 74, 254–255, 259–263, 265–270, 272, 275–276

Backhouse, Lieutenant Colonel Thomas 192, 202
Baird, Lieutenant General Sir David 93–96, 98–105, 107–109, 114, 136, 165–166, 169, 172–173, 175, 180–181, 184, 188, 190, 192–193, 202, 204, 208, 214, 217–218, 221, 246–247
Barbados 26–27, 30–31
Bengal 20, 41, 43, 99, 109, 175
Berbice 30, 32–33
Beresford, Major General William Carr 172, 175, 181, 185, 187–192, 194–200, 202, 226, 246–247, 300
Bergen 82, 267–268
Bertie, Vice Admiral Sir Albemarle 250–251
Bilbao 280, 286–289, 292–294
Blankett, Rear Admiral John 93, 100–101, 136
Boulden Thompson, Thomas 25, 33, 36–39, 41, 44
Boulogne 125, 138, 142–144, 146–151, 153, 250, 252
Boyer, Jean-Pierre 324–325, 328, 330–333
Brest 129, 139, 142, 152
British Army, cavalry regiments of: 20th Light Dragoons 166, 172
British Army, infantry regiments of: 38th 166–167, 172, 192, 204; 59th 166–167, 172, 175; 71st 166, 172, 181, 190, 198; 72nd 166, 172, 175; 83rd 166, 172, 175; 93rd 166, 172
Brownrigg, Lieutenant General Robert 263, 269–270, 272

Brownrigg, Commander William 150–151
Bruges 62, 70, 138
Buenos Aires viii, 156, 162, 180, 184, 187–188, 190–202, 204–205, 207–208, 212–215, 217, 220–225, 227–229, 233, 243, 245–248, 259–260, 277, 284, 300, 318, 322, 335, 338
Burgos 291–292, 295–298, 301
Byron, Vice Admiral Sir John 26–27

Cadiz 93, 289
Caffarelli, *général de division* Louis-Marie-Joseph-Maximilien de 286, 289–290, 300–301
Calais 64, 138, 142, 148–150, 152–153
Calcutta 20, 40–41, 43, 100–102, 106, 114, 120–121, 123, 134, 136, 310
Canning, George 230–232, 250, 258, 272, 277
Canton 16–17, 44–45, 105, 248
Cap Henry 326–328, 332–333
Cape Das Voltas 33–34
Cape of Good Hope, the viii–ix, 33, 36, 72, 94, 96, 117–118, 162, 165, 168–169, 174–181, 183–185, 188, 193, 195, 202, 205–207, 214–215, 217, 220–221, 223–227, 246–247, 251, 311
Cape Town 172–173, 175–176
Carrol, *Brigadier* William Parker 286, 288, 293–294
Castaños, *Capitán General del Ejército* Francisco Castaños 285–286
Castlereagh, Robert Stewart, Viscount 119, 230, 236–237, 255–258, 260–261, 270, 272, 282
Cathcart, Lieutenant General William, Lord 54, 232, 236–240, 242
Charnock, Robert 16, 43, 45, 163
Chatham, 118, 121–123, 129, 133
Chatham, John Pitt, 2nd Earl of 45, 255–256, 258–259, 261–266, 268–273, 276–278
Collier, Captain Sir George 243, 284, 291–292, 303
Constant de Rebecque, Charles Samuel 16–17, 44–45, 59

352

Coote, Major General Eyre 62, 64, 66–70, 198, 272
Copenhagen ix, 90–93, 159–160, 162–163, 231–232, 234, 236–240, 243–245, 247, 249–250, 257, 277, 311, 338
Cork 17, 166, 169, 250
Cornwallis, General Charles, 1st Marquess 41–42, 59
Corunna 253, 258, 279–280, 282, 285, 288, 295–296, 300
Crispo, Lieutenant John 15–16

d'Estaing, *vice amiral* Comte Charles-Henri 26–27
de Grasse, *lieutenant général des armées navales* François-Joseph Paul de 30–31
de Stamford, Henri Guillaume, Baron 73–74, 76
Decken, Brigadier General Frederick 238–239
Demerara 30, 32–33
Deptford 16, 45, 314–315
Dickson, Vice Admiral Sir Archibald 90–92
Donnelly, Captain Ross 168–169, 174, 192, 246–248
Douglas, Lieutenant Colonel Sir Howard 285–288
Downman, Captain Hugh 168, 172, 174
Drake, Rear Admiral Sir Francis Samuel 30–31
Dublin 19, 24
Dundas, Major General David 57, 59, 82
Dundas, Henry *see* Melville
Dundas, Robert *see* Melville
Dungeness 15–16, 248
Dunkirk 49, 51, 66, 138, 314

East India Company, the 16–17, 20, 22, 40–41, 43–45, 86, 93–94, 99, 101, 103, 105–106, 108–109, 111, 113, 118, 136, 157, 162, 166–168, 184, 187, 248, 309
Egypt 72, 86, 89, 93–94, 99, 102, 107–108, 110–111, 114, 117, 135–136
Essen, Lieutenant General Ivan 82–84, 86–87
Essequibo 30, 32–33
*Etrusco* 15–17, 41, 44–45, 49, 56, 58–60, 66, 79, 89, 94, 105, 127–128, 137, 157, 162, 184, 207, 248–249, 313, 335

Ferguson, Brigadier General Ronald 172–173
Ferrol 139, 142
Flanders, 15, 49, 51–52, 54, 77, 81, 86, 93, 125, 153, 163, 253, 255, 279, 314, 338
Flushing 64, 69, 89, 139, 254, 260, 262–263, 265–267, 271, 273, 276

Fraser, Lieutenant General Alexander Mackenzie 264, 272
Fulton, Robert 139–143, 147–148, 151–152, 157

Gambier, Admiral James 232–234, 236–240, 242–244, 281–282
Ghalib, Sharif of Mecca, 99, 103–104, 107, 111–112
Gibraltar 17, 28, 166, 280
Giorgi, Balthazar 15–17, 44–45
Gorée 26, 34,
Goree (Dutch island) 74, 76
Grenada 26–27
Grenville, Thomas 200, 214, 220, 223
Grenville, William Wyndham Grenville, 1st Baron 72, 75, 87, 89, 92, 119, 125–126, 193–194, 213, 215, 220, 229–231, 245
Grey, General Charles, 1st Earl 51, 61–62, 64–65, 70
Grey, Charles, 2nd Earl 200–202, 204, 253, 283–284
Guetaria 288–289, 292–295

Haiti 320, 323–324, 326–328, 330–334
Hamburg 56–57, 59–60, 73, 122, 162, 177, 179, 237
Hanover 55, 72, 316
Harcourt, Lieutenant General William 54, 56, 59, 162–163, 285, 317
Hawkesbury, Robert Jenkinson, Lord 119, 125
Helder, Den 79, 81, 84, 86, 90, 142, 254, 257–258
Henri I, King of Haiti 320, 324, 326–328, 330–333
Hermann, Lieutenant General Ivan 82–83
Honeyman, Captain Robert 169, 180
Hood, Rear Admiral Sir Samuel 30–32, 218, 233–234, 249, 259, 310
Howe, Admiral Richard, Earl 33–34, 38–40, 45, 157, 159, 313
Howick, Lord *see Grey, Charles, 2nd Earl*
Huntly, Lieutenant General Lord 262, 265
Huskisson, William 64, 70, 73–75, 77–79, 85, 119, 216, 223–224, 228, 230, 250, 277, 335
Hutchinson, Lieutenant General John Hely 98–99, 101–102

Jackson, Francis 232, 237, 239
Jamaica 32, 162, 316–318, 320, 322, 324–326, 328, 331, 333
Jedda 93, 95, 98, 100, 107, 109, 111–112

Keats, Rear Admiral Sir Richard 233–234, 237, 247, 249, 257, 259, 262–263, 266–267, 269–270
Keith, Admiral George Elphinstone, 1st Viscount 142–151, 155–156, 284, 288, 295, 298, 300–301, 303
Keppel, Admiral Augustus 23, 25–26, 33
King, Captain William 149, 168, 172–174, 185, 196–198, 209, 225
Kingston 30, 320, 322, 325
Kosseir 98–100

Le Havre 142, 148, 151
Liniers, Santiago de 195–197, 199
Linois, *contre amiral* Charles Alexandre Léon Durand de 175–177, 179, 217
Liverpool 21, 24, 27, 42, 194
Longa, *Coronel* Francisco de 286, 289, 291–293, 296, 300

Macao 45, 102, 105–107
Machichaco 288, 296
Madeira 96, 154, 167–168, 250, 308–309, 311
Malacca, Straits of 44, 106
Malcolm, Rear Admiral Sir Pulteney 283–284, 314
Maldonado 180, 188, 202, 204–205, 212
Marmont, *maréchal* Auguste de 286, 289–290, 301–302
Martin, Henry 38, 46
Mauritius 102, 180, 214, 250–251, 255
Melville, Henry Dundas, 1st Viscount x, 57, 59-61, 64–65, 70–79, 81, 84–87, 89–91, 93, 94, 102, 111, 114,, 119–120, 122, 124–129, 131, 133, 135–145, 147–154, 156, 164, 166, 174, 177, 181–184, 191, 204, 207–208, 215–216, 220, 222–224, 228, 230, 232, 243, 245, 252–253, 273, 283, 338–340
Melville, Robert Dundas, 2nd Viscount 252, 273, 284–285, 288–290, 294, 296, 298, 300–303, 307–308, 312, 314, 316, 322, 326–328
Mendizábal, *Teniente General* Gabriel 286, 292–296, 299–303
Mends, Captain Robert 279–280, 282, 284, 288, 290, 301
Mexico 182, 193, 322
Mina, *Brigadier* Francisco Epoz y 286, 289, 292–295, 300
Miranda, Francisco de 181–183, 185, 192, 207, 222
Mitchell, Vice Admiral Andrew 81–82, 84
Mocha 93–96, 98, 100–101, 107, 112–114

Moira, Francis Rawdon-Hastings, the Earl of 253, 303, 308–310
Montevideo 180, 185, 187, 191, 195–196, 199, 201–202, 204, 212
Moore, Lieutenant General Sir John 251, 253
Mulgrave, Henry Phipps, 1st Earl of 230, 232–234, 250–252, 255, 273, 278

Nelson, Vice Admiral Horatio Nelson, 1st Viscount 72, 92, 152–153, 201, 231
Nieuwpoort 49, 51–52, 61
Nijmegen 52, 54

Ostend 15–17, 40–41, 43–46, 49, 51, 58, 61–62, 64–68, 70, 72, 77, 90, 138, 142, 153, 162, 198–199, 254, 338

Pack, Lieutenant Colonel Denis 39, 198, 264, 272
Paul I, Tsar of Russia 58, 72–76, 78–79, 84, 87, 312
Perceval, Spencer 272, 285
Pétion, Alexandre 320, 324
Peymann, *Generalmajor* Ernst 238–240, 242
Peyton, Vice Admiral Joseph 69–70
Piron, Jean-Baptiste 16–17, 44–45
Pitt, William x, 33, 57, 61, 77, 84, 87, 89, 118–119, 125–128, 130–131, 133, 135, 137–144, 147–148, 152–153, 164–166, 174, 177, 181–184, 200, 204, 215, 220–224, 228, 230, 247, 252, 255, 258, 262, 316, 338
Popham, Brunswick Lowther 162-163, 317
Popham, Caroline 317
Popham, Harcourt 162–163, 285, 317
Popham, Lady Elizabeth 43, 120, 162, 179–180, 232, 252, 285, 298, 300, 309, 330
Popham, Frederick 120, 163
Popham, Harcourt 162–163, 285, 317
Popham, Harriet 127, 162, 317
Popham, Home Whitworth 120, 163, 317, 325, 330, 333
Popham, Honora 317, 330, 333
Popham, Mary 43, 162, 285, 316–317
Popham, Stephen 17–20, 40–42
Popham, Strachan 162–163, 273, 317
Popham, William 17–18, 38, 40–41, 43
Porlier, *Brigadier* Juan Diaz 286, 291–293, 296
Port Royal 325, 330, 332–333
Portland, William Cavendish-Bentinck, 3rd Duke of 229–230, 245, 252–253, 258, 272, 277
Portsmouth viii, x, 27, 32, 38, 129–130, 133–134, 150, 160, 215–216, 228, 261–262, 300, 307, 312

Prince of Wales Island 44–45, 106–107, 157

Rainier, Vice Admiral Peter 93, 100–101, 105–107, 110, 114, 117, 119, 121, 166
Renovales, *Mariscal de Campo* Francisco Mariano 279–280, 282, 284, 286–288, 292–293
Rio de Janeiro 33, 168, 195
Robinson, Captain Mark 15–16, 45, 58–59, 127, 248
Rochefort 139, 142, 149, 166, 172, 175
Rodney, Admiral George 28–32

St Eustatius 30–31
St Helena 117–118, 166, 168, 175–176, 184–185, 187, 193, 205–206, 314
St Kitts 30–31
St Malo 25, 142
St Petersburg 72–74, 77–78, 82, 86–88
St Vincent, Admiral John Jervis, 1st Earl of 119–124, 126–131, 133–139, 157, 184, 193, 217, 220–221, 253, 258, 271
San Sebastián 280, 292
Sana'a 99, 103, 107, 111–114
Santander 291, 293, 295, 297–298, 301–302
Santoña 279–280, 282, 288, 292–293, 295–296, 298–301
Scheldt, the 74, 254–255, 258–260, 262–263, 265–269, 273, 276, 314
Sea Fencibles, the 51, 61–62, 120, 123, 139
Signal code, Popham's 158–160, 284, 292, 316, 333
Spencer, George, 2nd Earl 61, 64–66, 75, 77, 79, 81, 89–92, 96, 119, 122, 125, 136, 156–157, 261
Spithead 25, 27, 32, 34, 38, 118, 158, 165–166, 192, 278, 310, 313, 334
Stanhope, Lady Hester 252, 257, 259
Stanhope, Vice Admiral Sir Henry 242, 244
Stirling, Rear Admiral Charles 155, 193, 205–209, 212, 303, 307–308, 310, 312–313
Stopford, Captain Robert 233–234, 249

Strachan, Rear Admiral Sir Richard 163, 216, 258–260, 262, 264–273, 275–277
Suez 98, 100, 103, 107, 109
Sydney, Thomas Townshend, 1st Viscount 33–34, 38

Taylor, Brook 232, 237
Texel 64, 74, 79, 139
Thompson, Commodore Edward 124, 156, 159, 205, 214, 335
Tobago 30–31
Trafalgar, Battle of 152, 175–176, 179, 183, 231, 254
Transport Board, the 56, 59–60, 62
Tripp, Captain George 34, 36
Tucker, Benjamin 129, 131, 133–137, 153–154, 157, 193

Veere 262, 264–266, 271

Walcheren 69, 74–77, 79, 85–86, 89–90, 120, 155, 163, 254–256, 258–262, 264–273, 275–278, 282–283, 310, 338
Wellesley, Richard, 1st Marquess 94, 101–105, 108–114, 136, 153, 190,
Wellington, Field Marshal Sir Arthur, 1st Duke of 160–161, 193, 239, 242, 252, 278–279, 285–286, 288–292, 294–302, 310–311
West Indies, the 26–27, 30–32, 56, 60, 72, 129, 178, 182, 193, 195, 214, 218, 251, 316, 320
Whitelocke, Lieutenant General John 213, 244–245
Whitworth, Sir Charles 72–75, 77–78, 84, 86–88, 90–92, 153, 159, 216, 237, 317
Willaumez, *contre amiral* Jean-Baptiste Philibert 177, 179–180, 217–218, 221
Windham, William 213, 233

York, HRH Frederick, Duke of 30, 51–52, 54, 56–59, 65, 78, 81–85, 163, 166, 233, 252, 257–258

# From Reason to Revolution – Warfare 1721-1815

http://www.helion.co.uk/series/from-reason-to-revolution-1721-1815.php

The 'From Reason to Revolution' series covers the period of military history 1721–1815, an era in which fortress-based strategy and linear battles gave way to the nation-in-arms and the beginnings of total war.

This era saw the evolution and growth of light troops of all arms, and of increasingly flexible command systems to cope with the growing armies fielded by nations able to mobilise far greater proportions of their manpower than ever before. Many of these developments were fired by the great political upheavals of the era, with revolutions in America and France bringing about social change which in turn fed back into the military sphere as whole nations readied themselves for war. Only in the closing years of the period, as the reactionary powers began to regain the upper hand, did a military synthesis of the best of the old and the new become possible.

The series examines the military and naval history of the period in a greater degree of detail than has hitherto been attempted, and has a very wide brief, with the intention of covering all aspects from the battles, campaigns, logistics, and tactics, to the personalities, armies, uniforms, and equipment.

## Submissions

The publishers would be pleased to receive submissions for this series. Please email reasontorevolution@helion.co.uk, or write to Helion & Company Limited, Unit 8 Amherst Business Centre, Budbrooke Road, Warwick, CV34 5WE

## You may also be interested in:

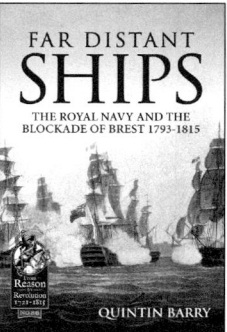
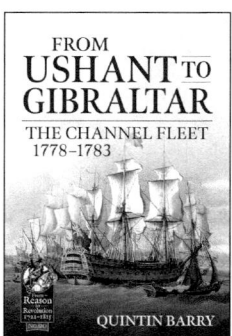
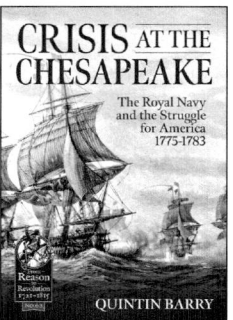
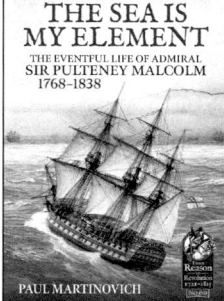
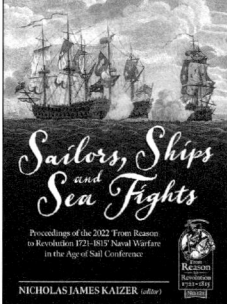
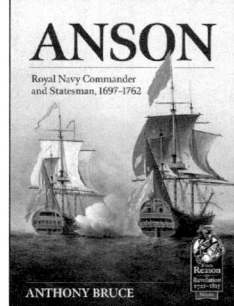